AMERICAN LAW YEARBOOK 2013

A GUIDE TO THE YEAR'S MAJOR LEGAL CASES AND DEVELOPMENTS

ISSN 1521-0901

AMERICAN LAW YEARBOOK 2013

A GUIDE TO THE YEAR'S MAJOR LEGAL CASES AND DEVELOPMENTS

GALE
CENGAGE Learning

Detroit • New York • San Francisco • New Haven, Conn • Waterville, Maine • London

American Law Yearbook 2013

Project Editor: Lisa Kumar

Product Manager: Stephen Wasserstein

Editorial Support Services: Andrea Lopeman

Rights Acquisition and Management: Robyn Young

Composition: Evi Abou-El-Seoud

Manufacturing: Rita Wimberley

Imaging: John Watkins

Product Design: Pam Galbreath

For product information and technology assistance, contact us at
Gale Customer Support, 1-800-877-4253.

For permission to use material from this text or product,
submit all requests online at **www.cengage.com/permissions.**
Further permissions questions can be emailed to
permissionrequest@cengage.com

Gale
27500 Drake Rd.
Farmington Hills, MI, 48331-3535

ISBN-13: 978-1-57302-221-7
ISBN-10: 1-57302-221-7
ISSN: 1521-0901

This title is also available as an e-book.
ISBN-13: 978-1-57302-222-4   ISBN-10: 1-57302-222-5
Contact your Gale, Cengage Learning sales representative for ordering information.

Printed in Mexico
1 2 3 4 5 6 7 17 16 15 14 13

CONTENTS

Preface . . . . *vii*

Abortion 1
In Focus
   Will States be Able to Outlaw
      Abortion? 8
Admiralty and Maritime Law 11
Affirmative Action 13
Agricultural Law 15
Americans with Disabilities Act 17
Antitrust Law .19
Appellate Advocacy 22
Arbitration 24
Assassination .25
Attorney's Fees 26
Automobiles 29
Bankruptcy 33
Birth Control 35
Capital Punishment 39
Child Abuse 42
Child Custody .43
Civil Rights 45
Civil Service 46
Class Action 48
Congress of the United States 51
Conspiracy 53
Copyright 55
Counterfeiting .56
Criminal Law .57
Criminal Procedure 60
Debtor and Creditor 67
Department of Justice 68
Double Jeopardy 70
Drugs and Narcotics 71
Education Law .77

Election Law 78
Electronic Surveillance 81
Eminent Domain 83
Employment Discrimination 84
Environmental Law 86
ERISA 94
Establishment Clause 95
Estate Planning 100
Ex Post Facto Laws 101
Extortion 103
Family Law 105
Federal Communications Commission . . . 106
Federal Tort Claims Act 108
Fifth Amendment 110
First Amendment 112
Fourth Amendment 120
Fraud 125
Freedom of Speech 127
Gay and Lesbian Rights 131
Gun Control .137
In Focus
  The Future of Gun Control after
      Newtown 138
Habeas Corpus 141
Hate Crime 145
Immigration .147
International Law 150
Kidnapping 153
Labor Law 155
Lawyers 157
Limitations 160
Medicaid 163
Military Law .164

Murder 168
Patents 175
In Focus
  Courts Continually Grapple with
      Biotechnology Patent Issues 180
Plain-Error Rule 185
Preemption 186
Presidential Powers 187
Privacy 188
Privileges and Immunities 190
Product Liability 191
Search and Seizure 195
Second Amendment 196
Securities and Exchange Commission 199
Sentencing 201
Sex Offenses 204

Sovereign Immunity 208
Speedy Trial 208
Sports Law 210
Surrogate Motherhood 214
Taxation 217
Terrorism 218
Tobacco 223
Trademarks 228
Voting Rights Act 231
Appendix 237
Bibliography 249
Glossary 269
Abbreviations 279
Table of Cases Cited 297
Index by Name and Subject 299

The need for a layperson's comprehensive, understandable guide to terms, concepts, and historical developments in U.S. law has been well met by *The Gale Encyclopedia of American Law* (*GEAL*). Published in a third edition in 2010 (in e-book format, and 2011 in print) by The Gale Group, *GEAL* has proved itself a valuable successor to West's 1983 publication, *The Guide to American Law: Everyone's Legal Encyclopedia.* and the 1997 and 2004 editions of *The West Encyclopedia of American Law.*

Since 1998, Gale, Cengage Learning, a premier reference publisher, has extended the value of *GEAL* with the publication of *American Law Yearbook* (*ALY*). This companion volume series adds entries on emerging topics not covered in the main set. A legal reference must be current to be authoritative, so *ALY* is a vital companion to a key reference source. Uniform organization by *GEAL* term and cross-referencing make it easy to use the titles together, while inclusion of key definitions and summaries of earlier rulings in supplement entries whether new or continuations make it unnecessary to refer to the main set constantly.

UNDERSTANDING THE AMERICAN LEGAL SYSTEM

The U.S. legal system is admired around the world for the freedoms it allows the individual and the fairness with which it attempts to treat all persons. On the surface, it may seem simple, yet those who have delved into it know that this system of federal and state constitutions, statutes, regulations, and common-law decisions is elaborate and complex. It derives from the English common law, but includes principles older than England, along with some principles from other lands. The U.S. legal system, like many others, has a language all its own, but too often it is an unfamiliar language: many concepts are still phrased in Latin. *GEAL* explains legal terms and concepts in everyday language, however. It covers a wide variety of persons, entities, and events that have shaped the U.S. legal system and influenced public perceptions of it.

FEATURES OF THIS SUPPLEMENT

Entries

ALY 2013 contains 148 entries covering cases, laws, and concepts significant to U.S. law. Entries are arranged alphabetically and use the same entry title as in *GEAL* or *ALY* when introduced in an earlier *Yearbook* (e.g., September 11th Attacks). There may be several cases discussed under a given topic.

Profiles of individuals cover interesting and influential people from the world of law, government, and public life, both historic and contemporary. All have contributed to U.S. law as a whole. Each short biography includes a timeline highlighting important moments in the subject's life. Persons whose lives were detailed in *GEAL*, but who have died since publication of that work, receive obituary entries in *ALY*.

DEFINITIONS

Each entry on a legal term is preceded by a definition where applicable, which is easily distinguished by its sans serif typeface. The back of the book includes a Glossary of Legal Terms containing the definitions for a selection of the most important terms bolded in the text of the essays and biographies. Terms bolded but not included in the Glossary of Legal Terms in ALY can be found in the Dictionary volume of GEAL.

CROSS REFERENCES

To facilitate research, *ALY 2013* provides two types of cross-references: within and following entries. Within the entries, terms are set in small capital letters (e.g., First Amendment) to indicate that they have their own entry in *GEAL.*

APPENDIX

This section follows the main body and includes a selection of primary documents related to cases discussed in *ALY 2013.*

TABLE OF CASES CITED AND INDEX BY NAME AND SUBJECT

These features make it quick and easy for users to locate references to cases, people, statutes, events, and other subjects. The Table of Cases Cited traces the influences of legal precedents by identifying cases mentioned throughout the text. In a departure from *GEAL,* references to individuals have been folded into the general index to simplify searches. Litigants, justices, historical and contemporary figures, as well as topical references are included in the Index by Name and Subject.

CITATIONS

Wherever possible, *ALY* includes citations to cases and statutes for readers wishing to do further research. They refer to one or more series, called "reporters," which publish court opinions and related information. Each citation includes a volume number, an abbreviation for the reporter, and the starting page reference. Underscores in a citation indicate that a court opinion has not been officially reported as of *ALY'*s publication. Two sample citations, with explanations, are presented below.

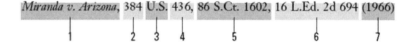

Miranda v. Arizona, 384 U.S. 436, 86 S.Ct. 1602, 16 L.Ed. 2d 694 (1966)

1   2 3 4   5   6   7

1. *Case title.* The title of the case is set in i and indicates the names of the parties. The suit in this sample citation was between Ernesto A. Miranda and the state of Arizona.

2. *Reporter volume number.* The number preceding the reporter abbreviation indicates the reporter volume containing the case. The volume number appears on the spine of the reporter, along with the reporter abbreviation.

3. *Reporter abbreviation.* The suit in the sample citation is from the reporter, or series of books, called *U.S. Reports,* which contains cases from the U.S. Supreme Court. Numerous reporters publish cases from the federal and state courts; consult the Abbreviations list at the back of this volume for full titles.

4. *Reporter page.* The number following the reporter abbreviation indicates the reporter page on which the case begins.

5. *Additional reporter citation.* Many cases may be found in more than one reporter. The suit in the sample citation also appears in volume 86 of the *Supreme Court Reporter,* beginning on page 1602.

6. *Additional reporter citation.* The suit in the sample citation is also reported in volume 16 of the *Lawyer's Edition,* second series, beginning on page 694.

7. *Year of decision.* The year the court issued its decision in the case appears in parentheses at the end of the cite.

Brady Handgun Violence Prevention Act, Pub. L. No. 103-159, 107 Stat. 1536 (18 U.S.C.A. § § 921-925A)

       1   2   3 4 5 6 7   8

1. *Statute title.*

2. *Public law number.* In the sample citation, the number 103 indicates this law was passed by the 103d Congress, and the number 159 indicates it was the 159th law passed by that Congress.

3. *Reporter volume number.* The number preceding the reporter abbreviation indicates the reporter volume containing the statute.

4. *Reporter abbreviation.* The name of the reporter is abbreviated. The statute in the sample citation is from *Statutes at Large.*

5. *Reporter page.* The number following the reporter abbreviation indicates the reporter page on which the statute begins.

6. *Title number.* Federal laws are divided into major sections with specific titles. The number preceding a reference to the U.S. Code stands for the section called Crimes and Criminal Procedure.

7. *Additional reporter.* The statute in the sample citation may also be found in the *U.S. Code Annotated.*

8. *Section numbers.* The section numbers following a reference to the *U.S. Code Annotated* indicate where the statute appears in that reporter.

COMMENTS WELCOME

Considerable efforts were expended at the time of publication to ensure the accuracy of the information presented in *American Law Yearbook 2013*. The editor welcomes your comments and suggestions for enhancing and improving future editions of this supplement to *The Gale Encyclopedia of American Law.* Send comments and suggestions to:

    American Law Yearbook

    Gale

    27500 Drake Rd.

    Farmington Hills, MI 48331-3535

ABORTION

Fifth Circuit Upholds Louisiana Abortion Clinics Law

State legislatures in a number of states have focused on regulating medical procedures used in ABORTION and on the clinics where abortions are performed. In Louisiana, the legislature enacted a law that imposes stringent conditions on abortion clinics, authorizing its department of health and hospitals to revoke a clinic's license if it violates any federal or state law or regulation, even if the violations do not deal with health and safety issues. Abortion providers challenged the law, arguing that it imposed a hardship on their operations. The Fifth **Circuit Court** of Appeals, in *Choice Incorporated of Texas v. Greenstein,* 691 F.3d 710 (2012), dismissed their case, concluding that their claims were not ripe for legal action.

In 2010, the Louisiana legislature passed Act 490, which amended the state's Outpatient Abortion Facility Licensing Law of 2001. Act 490 removed a provision that stated that the procedure for denial, suspension, or revocation of an outpatient abortion facility (OAF) license would be the same as the one in place for hospitals. The previous law authorized the health department to deny, suspend, or revoke a license only after finding a "substantial failure to comply." Act 490 only required a determination that there had been a "violation" to take action against an OAF. The law also granted the

secretary of the department of health new authority to deny, refuse to renew, or revoke a license if the applicant or licensee violated "any other federal or state law or regulation." Act 490 also removed a provision that gave an OAF the right to appeal to a **district court** for a trial on the secretary's action and have the action suspended during the pendency of the trial. Instead, the law allows an appeal to the secretary but does not suspend the execution of the secretary's judgment. In effect, a clinic would have to shut down after 30 days notice, while challenging the **state action**.

Act 490 also authorizes the secretary to issue an immediate suspension where the secretary finds that any state or federal law or regulation is violated and that the "violation or violations pose an imminent or immediate threat to the health, WELFARE, or safety of a client or patient." The secretary must give written notice of an immediate suspension and the suspension becomes effective upon receipt of this notice. The licensee has the right to file an appeal with the secretary, which does not block the suspension, or seek injunctive relief in district court. To obtain injunctive relief, the licensee must prove by clear and convincing evidence that the suspension was arbitrary and capricious. Act 490 removed from the 2001 law the requirement that the licensee be "given an opportunity to show compliance with all lawful requirements for the retention of the license."

Finally, Act 490 added a new provision that states that if a license is revoked or a renewal of a license is denied, "any owner, officer, member, manager, director, or administrator of the licensee may be prohibited from owning, managing, directing, or operating another out-patient abortion clinic in the state of Louisiana."

Five of the seven licensed OAFs in Louisiana and one doctor who performed abortions in the state filed a lawsuit in Louisiana federal district court, attempting to block the enforcement of Act 490. The plaintiffs sought a **declaratory judgment** and injunctive relief, arguing that Act 490 violated several constitutional provisions. They argued that the law violated the Fourteenth Amendment's Due Process and **Equal Protection** Clauses, as well as the FUNDAMENTAL RIGHT to terminate pregnancy guaranteed by the FOUR-TEENTH AMENDMENT. The district court granted the state's motion to dismiss before hearing these constitutional arguments, concluding that the claims were not ripe for judicial consideration. It determined the plaintiffs would not suffer any significant hardship because nothing in Act 490 required them to alter their conduct. Instead, it alters the state's conduct "in detecting and addressing violations." Although the act broadened the universe of laws the violation of which could result in adverse licensure decisions, the plaintiffs were legally obligated to adhere to these laws notwithstanding Act 490. The court concluded it was "pure speculation" whether the OAFs would one day be subjected to these new provisions.

The Fifth Circuit, in a 2-1 decision, upheld the district court ruling. Judge Priscilla Owen, writing for the majority, examined whether the plaintiffs had shown hardship that would demonstrate the case was ripe for a hearing on the merits of their constitutional arguments. The plaintiffs contended that they had been "forced to operate in a heightened state of vigilance" because they were unsure which laws the department would enforce and how they would be interpreted. Judge Owen rejected this argument, finding that actions violating Act 490 were already unlawful. No new affirmative obligations were imposed on the OAFs. By merely complying with all laws and regulations the OAFs would avoid any hardship.

The plaintiffs also argued that the new provision dealing with immediate suspension required them to demonstrate to a court by clear and convincing evidence that the action was arbitrary and capricious was a substantial hardship. Judge Owen disagreed, finding that an OAF could also challenge the constitutionality of this provision of the act in a lawsuit fighting the suspension. Such constitutional claims could prevail on the lesser preponderance of the evidence standard. In addition, the OAF could seek a **preliminary injunction** based on its constitutional claims in order to avoid being closed while it litigates them. Therefore, the case was not ripe for **judicial review**.

Judge James Dennis, in a lengthy DISSENT, argued that the majority had ignored a line of SUPREME COURT and circuit court decisions that allowed pre-enforcement challenges to anti-abortion statutes. In his view, the legal and practical hardships presented by the plaintiffs justified a hearing on the merits of their arguments, rather than waiting for the state to shut down an OAF based on Act 490.

Fifth Circuit Upholds Texas Regulations that Cuts Medicaid Funding to Abortion Providers

A number of states have sought to prevent any government funding of abortions. In 2005, Texas enacted the Women's Health Program (WHP) as a project to expand access to preventative health and family planning services for women. Under the program, Texas pays health care providers to provide an array of services, including counseling about contraceptives to women who meet certain financial criteria. The WHP, which is funded by Texas and the federal government's **Medicaid** program, derives most of its funding from MEDICAID. The law prohibits the state from contracting with entities or affiliates of entities that perform or promote elective abortions. This provision was not enforced until 2011, when the law was reauthorized and the state issued regulations that defined "promote" and "affiliate." Nine Planned Parenthood organizations that operate health clinics in Texas which do not provide abortions, sued the state, asking the court for a **preliminary injunction** to block enforcement of the regulations, which would cut off their Medicaid funding. The Fifth **Circuit Court** of Appeals, in *Planned Parenthood Association of Hildalgo County Texas, Inc. v. Suehs*, 592 F.3d 343 (2012), denied a PRELIMINARY INJUNCTION, ruling that

Texas had not infringed on the FIRST AMEND-MENT rights of the clinics.

After the passage of WHP in 2005, the Texas Health and Human Services Commission (THHSC) did not formally interpret the statute's restrictions on abortion-related activity and it did not exclude the nine clinics from receiving WHP funds. The commission paid the clinics for providing WHP services despite the fact they engaged in ABORTION advocacy and had some legal relationship with Planned Parenthood FEDERATION of America. The clinics understood the restriction on abortion-related activity to mean that if they did not recommend abortion as a health procedure, and if they maintained a separate legal identity from abortion-providing clinics, they could receive WHP funds. In 2011, THHSC issued regulations that interpreted WHP's restrictions on abortion-related activity. The regulations tracked the **statute**, denying funding to entities that performed or promoted elective abortions or are affiliates of entities that perform or promote elective abortions. Most importantly, THHSC defined the words "promote" and "affiliate" in the regulations.

The regulations defined "promote" as to "advocate or popularize, by, for example, advertising or publicity." They defined "affiliate" to include an **entity** that has a legal relationship with another entity that has been created or governed by at least one written document that demonstrates common ownership, management or control, a franchise, or the granting or extension of a license that authorizes the affiliate to "use the other entity's brand name, trademark, **service mark**, or other registered identification mark." The THHSC mandated that recipients of WHP funds certify their compliance with the new regulations. The nine clinics concluded that compliance was impossible and filed a federal lawsuit against THHSC Commissioner Thomas Suehs in federal **district court**. They sought a preliminary INJUNCTION that would stop the implementation of the regulations.

The clinics argued that the regulations violated their constitutional rights of free speech and association, and denied them **equal protection** of the laws. They implicitly conceded that under the new definitions in the regulations, they promoted elective abortions and were affiliates of entities that promoted elective abortions, and could not receive WHP funds.

The district court granted the clinics a preliminary injunction on April 30, 2012, blocking the enforcement of the THHSC regulations. The court concluded that the clinics had a substantial likelihood of succeeding on the merits of both constitutional claims. The state immediately appealed.

On August 21, 2012, a three-judge panel of the Fifth Circuit unanimously overturned the preliminary injunction. Judge E. Grady Jolly, writing for the court, stated that the district court had erred by analyzing the regulations as a whole, instead of separately examining the restriction on promoting elective abortions, and then the restriction on affiliating with entities that promote elective abortion. The legal principles differed between promotion and affiliation, which required treating them separately. As to the restriction on promoting elective abortion, it functioned as a speech-based funding condition but it also functioned "as a direct regulation of a state program." Under SUPREME COURT precedent, the direct regulation of a state program is constitutional. The government has authority to enact viewpoint-based restrictions on speech "when the government is, in effect, the speaker." Texas was entitled to disfavor abortion within its own subsidized program. To require the state to use providers that advocated abortion would make the state's policy meaningless. The court therefore ruled that Texas could deny WHP funds to organizations that promote elective abortions.

As to the restriction on affiliating with entities that promoted elective abortion, Judge

Social worker Amanda Winders at a Planned Parenthood rally at the Texas capitol building in Austin, March 7, 2013.
© AP PHOTO/ERIC GAY

Jolly addressed only one prong of the definition of affiliate: the authorization to use identifying marks. The court chose this prong because it implicated the same conduct as the restriction on promoting elective abortions: "Using a pro-abortion mark is, after all, a way of promoting abortions." The state had the authority to limit identifying marks that program grantees are authorized to use. Identifying marks are identifying messages. In this case the display of a pro-abortion Planned Parenthood mark would "eviscerate" Texas's choice to disfavor abortion, "just as it would be if the organizations promoted abortion through pamphlets or video presentations." As with the promotion definition, the affiliation definition was valid as a direct regulation of the content of a state program. As to the other prongs of the affiliation definition section, they limited affiliation in a "more conventional sense." The appeals court found these prongs problematic because they were not a direct regulation of the content of a government program. Judge Jolly stated, "Speech that organizations carry on in other capacities through affiliated entities is not speech within a government program in which the government has a direct say." However, he declined to examine these "potential constitutional infirmities," preferring to vacate the injunction and send the case back to the district court to decide that question for itself.

As to the EQUAL PROTECTION argument, the appeals court concluded that the district court's ruling on free speech and association had influenced its equal protection holding. Because the free speech holding was in error, the lower court's analysis and holding could not stand as well. The appeals court vacated the preliminary injunction and directed the district court to address the constitutionality of the prongs defining affiliation based on franchise and common ownership, management, or control.

Ninth Circuit Rules Arizona Abortion Law Unconstitutional

The U.S. SUPREME COURT has ruled that a woman has a constitutional right to choose to terminate her pregnancy before the fetus is viable. Medical technology has improved over the years, reducing the number of weeks before a fetus becomes viable to 23 or 24 weeks. However, viability can only be determined on a case-by-case basis. Despite this court precedent, the Arizona legislature passed a law that prohibited abortions when the fetus is 20 weeks old. The stated purpose of the law was to protect women's health and to avoid subjecting fetuses to pain during an ABORTION at that gestational age. Although the **district court** upheld the law, the Ninth **Circuit Court** of Appeals in *Isaacson v. Horne*, 716 F.3d 1213 (2013), struck down the law as unconstitutional. Supreme Court precedent did not allow Arizona to abrogate the right of women to terminate pregnancies prior to the viability of the fetus.

The state of Arizona had banned abortions after the fetus is viable, but in 2012 Governor Jan Brewer signed into law an abortion ban when the gestational age of the fetus has been determined to be at least 20 weeks, except for medical emergency. The stated purpose of the act was to ban abortions after 20 weeks of gestation "based on documented risks to women's health and the strong medical evidence that unborn children feel pain during an abortion at that gestational age." Physicians who performed abortions in violation of the law would be subjected to criminal prosecution.

Three board-certified obstetrician-gynecologists who practiced in Arizona file a lawsuit in Arizona federal district court against the state, seeking declaratory and injunctive relief against the enforcement of the new law on behalf of themselves and of their patients wishing to terminate pre-viability pregnancies at or after 20 weeks. The physicians, who performed abortions before fetal viability and at and after 20 weeks, asserted that their patients sought pre-viability abortions for a number of reasons. These included health concerns for the mother, a medical condition or anomaly affecting the fetus, or that the woman was about to miscarry. Under the new law, these women would be unable to terminate their pregnancies before fetal viability unless they had a medical emergency within the narrow exception of the law. Because of these restrictions, the physicians argued that the law violated their patients' FOURTEENTH AMENDMENT **substantive due process** rights.

The district court rejected the physicians' claims and denied all relief. The court held that the new law regulated, rather than prohibited abortion at and after 20 weeks gestational age because it contained a medical emergency exception permitting some abortions after 20 weeks gestation. The court also found that the law was a regulation because the law "may prompt a few women, who are considering abortion as an option, to make the ultimate decision earlier than they might have otherwise made it." The law did not impose a substantial obstacle to abortions because women still had the ability to terminate their pregnancies before 20 weeks. The legitimate state interests in fetal life and the health of pregnant women justified the "time limitation" on the right to pre-viability abortion. The physicians filed an emergency motion to the Ninth Circuit, asking for an INJUNCTION that would prevent enforcement of the law while they pursued their appeal with the appeals court. The court granted the motion.

In May 2013, a three-judge panel of the Ninth Circuit voted unanimously to overturn the Arizona law. Judge Marsha Berzon, writing for the court, stated that under Supreme Court precedent, a woman has a constitutional right to choose to terminate her pregnancy before the fetus is viable without undue interference by the state. In *Planned Parenthood v. Casey*, 505 U.S. 833, 112 S. Ct. 2791, 120 L. Ed. 2d 674 (1992), the Supreme Court stated that "Before viability, the State's interests are not strong enough to support a PROHIBITION of abortion or the imposition of a substantial obstacle to the woman's effective right to elect the procedure." The state argued that this statement was not controlling Supreme Court precedent but merely **dicta**. DICTA are statements or opinions expressed in a judicial decision that were not part of the legal basis for the resolution of the case. Judge Berzon disagreed, finding that this characterization was incorrect. She pointed to a string of abortion cases, starting with *Roe v. Wade*, 410 U.S. 113, 93 S. Ct. 705, 35 L. Ed. 2d 147 (1973), that identified fetal viability as the earliest point in pregnancy when the state's interest becomes "sufficiently compelling to justify not just *regulation* of the abortion procedure, but *proscription* of abortion unless necessary to preserve the life or health of the mother."

While viability is not a fixed point, it is the critical point. The Supreme Court had recognized that viability varied among pregnancies and that improvements in medical technology would "both push later in pregnancy the point at which abortion is safer than childbirth and advance earlier in gestation the point of fetal viability." Although viability is flexible, it is medically determinable and the attending physician must make that judgment. The Supreme Court had made clear that a state may not fix viability at a specific point in pregnancy. Arizona had admitted in court that no fetus is viable at 20 weeks gestational age and the district court declared it undisputed that viability occurs between 23 and 24 weeks of gestation. Therefore, the state's ban on abortion from 20 weeks "necessarily prohibits pre-viability abortions." Based on this conclusion the law was invalid.

Judge Berzon went on to point out the errors in the district court decision, finding that the **statute** imposed an undue burden on women seeking to terminate their pregnancies. The 20-week law deprived women of the right to choose abortion at all after 20 weeks gestation but prior to the viability of the fetus. The medical emergency exception did not save the statute, as it did not "transform it from a ban into a limitation as to the mode or manner of conducting abortions." Because the exception would not cover all women who seek pre-viability abortions at or after 20 weeks, the law continued to "operate as a complete bar to the rights of some women to choose to terminate their pregnancies before the fetus is viable."

North Carolina Judge Strikes Down Anti-Abortion License Plate

In 2011, the North Carolina General Assembly passed a bill that would allow individuals to purchase specialty plates with the message "Choose Life." The state's chapter of the AMERICAN CIVIL LIBERTIES UNION challenged the law in the U. S. **District Court** for the Eastern District of North Carolina on behalf of four automobile owners. U. S. District Judge James Fox concluded that the state's program violated the FIRST AMENDMENT. Accordingly, on December 7, 2012, the court permanently enjoined the state from issuing the plates. *ACLU of North Carolina v. Conti*, 912 F. Supp. 2d 363 (E.D.N.C. 2012).

Many states allow individuals to obtain plates with personalized messages at an extra cost in addition to the usual registration fees. North Carolina's system is different, however. The state's general assembly has approved issuance of a number of specialty license plates, and individuals and organizations may only select specialty plates that the general assembly has authorized.

A bill passed in 2011 authorized many new specialty plates, bringing the total number to 150. Among the new plates was one with the message "Choose Life." The general assembly considered six proposals for plates with alternative messages, including "Respect Choice" and "Trust Women. Respect Choice." However, the Republican-controlled general assembly rejected these proposals, leaving only the pro-life message. Governor Bev Purdue signed the bill into law in November 2011.

Those who would purchase the new "Choose Life" plate would have to pay a $25 annual fee in addition to the regular registration fees. Sixty percent of this additional fee, or $15 per plate, would help to fund the Carolina Pregnancy Care Fellowship, a private organization that supports crisis pregnancy centers in the state. The law specifically prohibited funds collected from the plate from being "distributed to any agency, organization, business, or other **entity** that provides, promotes, counsels, or refers to abortion." The law allowed the Division of Motor Vehicles to develop the plate if it received at least 300 applications.

The Carolina Pregnancy Care Fellowship is also the state contact for a national organization known as Choose Life, which has a mission of adding "Choose Life" plates in all 50 states. It spearheaded efforts for the state to approve the plate in North Carolina, setting up billboard advertisements throughout the state and supporting other promotions. Once the general assembly had passed the bill, the organization took applications for the specialty plate and reported that it had received more than 300. Thus, by the terms of the legislation, the Division of Motor Vehicles could have begun issuing plates once the governor signed the bill in 2011.

However, the state chapter of the ACLU filed a motion seeking a temporary INJUNCTION to prohibit the state from issuing the specialty plates. The ACLU represented four plaintiffs who wanted to purchase specialty plates bearing a pro-choice message. According to the ACLU, the state violated the plaintiffs' First Amendment rights because the state had created a forum that favored one viewpoint to the exclusion of another.

Had the state's issuance of the license plate been a matter of government speech, the state would not have violated the plaintiffs' First Amendment rights. This is because the First Amendment does not regulate government speech, allowing the government to select its own views and express what it wants. On the other hand, the First Amendment limits government regulation of private speech as well as "hybrid" speech that is both private and governmental at the same time. The government's restriction of hybrid speech must be viewpoint neutral.

On December 8, 2011, the district court concluded that the speech was private speech and that the state had violated the First Amendment by authorizing the "Choose Life" plate without offering a pro-choice alternative. Accordingly, the court temporarily enjoined the state from issuing the specialty plate. The court then reconsidered the issues before issuing a permanent injunction in its 2012 decision.

The Fourth **Circuit Court** of Appeals developed a test considering four factors to determine whether speech is private or governmental. These four factors include (1) the central purpose of the program in which the speech in question occurs; (2) the degree of editorial control exercised by the government or private entities over the content of the speech; (3) the identity of the literal speaker; and (4) whether the government or the private entity bears the ultimate responsibility for the content of the speech.

The defendants in the *Conti* case were public officials in North Carolina. They argued that the Fourth Circuit's test had been superseded by the U.S. Supreme Court's decision in *Johanns v. Livestock Marketing Ass'n*, 544 U.S. 550, 125 S. Ct. 2055, 161 L. Ed. 2d 896 (2005). At issue in the *Johanns* case was a program requiring private beef producers to fund what amounted to government speech in the form of a promotional campaign. The Court concluded that the program did not violate the First Amendment because the government effectively controlled the message, rendering the speech government speech.

According to the defendants, the Court in *Johanns* established a new test for determining whether speech is government speech or private speech, focusing solely on the degree of ultimate government control over a particular message. The district court disagreed, though. The court reviewed the decision in *Johanns* along with later SUPREME COURT decisions and concluded that the court had not established a one-factor test that should apply to the issue of government speech.

The district court therefore considered the factors in the Fourth Circuit's four-part test. Based on these factors, the court concluded that specialty license plates implicated private speech more than government speech. Thus, because the government had allowed only one viewpoint, the specialty plate violated the First Amendment. The court on December 7, 2012, permanently enjoined the state from "implementing, enforcing, or otherwise carrying out the program" for issuing the "Choose Life" plates.

North Carolina announced in January 2013 that it would appeal the district court's decision. An ACLU spokesperson expressed disappointment in the state's decision. Chris Brook, legal director for the ACLU of North Carolina Legal Foundation, commented, "It's unfortunate that the state has chosen to prolong what is really a very clear-cut First Amendment issue. The Fourth Circuit Court of Appeals has consistently ruled that any time the government creates an avenue for private speech, it cannot restrict that avenue to only one side of a contentious debate."

Oklahoma Supreme Court Strikes Down Abortion Law

A number of states have enacted laws that would make abortions more difficult to obtain and more expensive. Several of these laws have sought to limit medical abortions by requiring ABORTION providers to dispense the abortion-inducing drugs only in the ways tested and approved by the FOOD AND DRUG ADMINISTRATION (FDA) and described on the drug's label. Oklahoma passed the Abortion-Inducing Drugs Safety Act in 2011, which contained these restrictions. In 2012, the Oklahoma SUPREME COURT, in *Nova Health Systems v. Pruit*, 292 P.3d 28 (2012), ruled that the law was facially unconstitutional because it went against binding precedent by the U.S. Supreme Court in the case *Planned Parenthood v. Casey*, 505 U.S. 833, 112 S. Ct. 2791, 120 L. Ed. 2d 674 (1992).

The FDA approved medical abortion drugs in 2000. Since then an estimated one million women have selected this method to terminate pregnancy. The drug regimen known as RU-486 requires a woman to take two types of medications. A woman goes to a reproductive health facility during the first nine weeks of pregnancy and takes one tablet of the drug called mifepristone. This medication blocks progesterone, a hormone responsible for sustaining a pregnancy. As the drug takes effect, the pregnancy stops developing. Sometimes a woman will expel the fetus with no further action but more often she will need to take the drug misoprostol between 24 and 48 hours after the mifepristone to trigger the process. The process can take place in the privacy of her home.

Drug manufacturers must market a drug for a particular use with a particular regimen. However, many drugs are used for other medical conditions other than the original condition approved by the FDA or are administered in different dosages than originally called for. Approximately one out of every five drugs is commonly used for these "off-label" purposes. In the case of RU-486, researchers found that it could be more effective by adjusting the dosage of mifepristone. Studies showed that three tablets were not necessary. In addition, women did not need to take misoprostol at a health care facility. Using this new regimen, doctors concluded that the drugs had fewer side effects and were more effective. Cost was also a factor, as mifepristone costs $85 per tablet. However, the off-label use of RU-486 gave abortion opponents an opportunity to place conditions on medical abortions. These groups claimed that seven women in the United States had died after taking the medications according to the off-label regimen rather than the original regimen approved by the FDA in 2000.

In 2011, the Oklahoma legislature passed the Abortion-Inducing Drugs Safety Act. The law required abortion providers to dispense RU-486 drugs only in the way tested and approved by the FDA and described in the drug's label. The law also mandated that only physicians could dispense the drugs, that the physician must examine the woman before providing the drugs, and that physicians dispense the drugs according to the steps outlined on the drug's label. The Oklahoma Coalition for Reproductive Justice and Reproductive Services and the reproductive health care provider Nova Health Systems in Tulsa challenged the law after the governor signed the bill into law. The plaintiffs filed their action in state court, alleging that the act was unconstitutional and asking the court to issue a temporary INJUNCTION to prevent the implementation of the law until the legal challenge was over. The court granted the temporary injunction.

WILL STATES BE ABLE TO OUTLAW ABORTION?

In *Roe v. Wade*, 410 U.S. 113, 93 S. Ct. 705, 35 L. Ed. 2d 147 (1973), the U.S. SUPREME COURT declared that a woman has a right to terminate her pregnancy until the fetus becomes viable. At that point, the state may impose restrictions on when a late-term ABORTION may be performed and where. Opponents of abortion have fought unsuccessfully for a CONSTITUTIONAL AMENDMENT that would ban abortion. However, they have been successful in having state legislatures pass numerous laws that seek to make it more difficult and costly for a woman to obtain an abortion. The lower **federal courts** have struck down many of these laws as unconstitutional, but others have been allowed to go into effect.

Most of this legislation has been based on model laws drafted by national anti-abortion groups, such as the National Right to Life. According to the Guttmacher Institute, an organization that favors abortion rights, 2012 saw the second highest number of abortion restrictions ever enacted. Nineteen states enacted 43 laws to restrict access to abortion services. These laws included mandating invasive ultrasounds on women seeking abortions, blocking health insurance coverage, closing women's health clinics by defunding groups, restricting methods for medical abortions, requiring abortion providers to have admitting privileges at hospitals, requiring abortion clinics to become certified surgical centers, and banning abortions at or after 20 weeks gestational age.

Opponents of these laws, such as Planned Parenthood, contest the legitimacy of the reasons given by proponents as to why legislation is needed. Opponents contend that lawmakers have crafted these laws as a pretext for the elimination of abortion as a real-world option for women, especially poor women. Proponents see two benefits to their approach:

making abortions more difficult to obtain and providing legal cases that eventually will have to be addressed by the Supreme Court. With a more conservative Court, there is the possibility it will endorse some of these approaches and may even overturn *Roe v. Wade.*.

The Attack on Medical Abortions Since the FDA approved medical abortion drugs in 2000, it is estimated that one million women have chosen this method to terminate a pregnancy. The drug regimen known as RU-486 requires a woman to take two drugs. When the FDA approved the regimen, it set conditions on the dosages to be used. Over timer, researchers found that the procedure could be more effective by reducing the dosage of the medicines. In addition, women did not need to take the second drug at a health care facility. Reducing the dosage reduced the cost of the procedure and there were health benefits associated with the reduction.

The change in dosage is termed an "off-label" use and is legal under federal law. However, a number of states passed legislation that required abortion providers to dispense the RU-486 drugs only in the way tested and approved by the FDA. Legislators claimed that several women in the United States had died after taking the drugs using the off-label regimen. Oklahoma's version of the law also requires that only physicians may dispense the drugs and that they examine the woman before providing the drugs. Reproductive rights groups and a reproductive health care provider immediately challenged the law in state court. The Oklahoma Supreme Court, in *Nova Health Systems v. Pruit*, 292 P.3d 28 (2012), ruled the law unconstitutional, finding that it violated U.S. Supreme Court precedent and served no other purpose "than to prevent women from obtaining abortions and to punish

and discriminate against those women who do." The U.S. Supreme Court granted review after the state appealed, but in late June 2013, sent the case back to the Oklahoma Supreme Court for clarification of some issues.

Restricting Funding for Abortion Providers The Supreme Court has upheld federal and state laws that prohibit the spending of public funds to provide abortions for low-income women. However, for many years organizations such as Planned Parenthood, have separated their abortion services and clinics from all non-abortion services such as BIRTH CONTROL and medical services. In this way, these groups have been able to receive federal and state funding for non-abortion services. A number of states have recently enacted laws that remove this distinction, making it illegal to provide funding to any organization that is linked in any way to providing abortions.

In Texas, Planned Parenthood had for six years received funding from the state to provide preventative health and family planning services for women. The money came from the federal **Medicaid** program and the state. The 2005 law that authorized the program barred the state from contracting with entities or affiliates of entities that perform or promote elective abortions. State officials ignored this provision until 2011, when new regulations were put into place that ended Planned Parenthood's inclusion in the program. Though it had created separate legal entities for its abortion and non-abortion programs, Planned Parenthood conceded that under the law it promoted elective abortions and were affiliates of entities that promoted elective abortions. The Fifth **Circuit Court** of Appeals, in *Planned Parenthood Association of Hildalgo County Texas, Inc. v.*

Suehs, 592 F.3d 343 (2012), denied Planned Parenthood's request for a **preliminary injunction** that would allow it to continue to receive funding.

In 2011, Indiana passed a law that was similar to the Texas **statute,** barring abortion providers from receiving any state-administered funds, even if the services did not involve abortions. The aim of the law was to end the indirect subsidization of abortion. Planned Parenthood challenged the law. In *Planned Parenthood v. Commissioner of the Indiana* STATE DEPARTMENT *of Health,* 699 F.3d 962 (2012), the Seventh Circuit ruled that the law violated the MEDICAID Act's "free choice of provider" provision. Women were free to choose their own medical provider, even if it was Planned Parenthood. The court accepted Planned Parenthood's assertion that if the law went into effect, it would have to close one quarters of its clinics.

The conflict between the circuit courts over these funding restrictions is likely to continue as more cases are brought around the country. At some point the Supreme Court will have to accept review of one of these cases and resolve whether states may impose severe restrictions on organizations that provide both abortion and non-abortion services.

Imposing Strong Oversight on Outpatient Abortion Facilities Some states have enacted laws that impose HEIGHTENED SCRUTINY on outpatient abortion facilities. In 2010, Louisiana amended its law dealing with outpatient abortion facilities. Prior to the amendment, the procedure for denial, suspension, or revocation of an outpatient abortion facility was the same as for hospitals. A license could be revoked only after finding a "substantial failure to comply." The amended law only required a determination that there had been a "violation" to take action against an outpatient abortion facility. The law also gave the state the right to deny, refuse to renew, or revoke a license if the applicant or licensee violated "any other federal or state law or regulation."

Facilities would have to shut down in 30 days while challenging the **state action.** Finally, the law gave the state the authority to immediately suspend a facility if it found that any state or federal law or regulation was violated and that the violation posed an "imminent or immediate threat to the health, WELFARE, or safety of a client or patient."

Five of the seven licensed outpatient abortion facilities tried to block enforcement of the law. They were concerned that they could be shut down at any time for violating a law or regulation, even if it had nothing to do with their medical practice. The **district court** and the Fifth Circuit Court of Appeals, in *Choice Incorporated of Texas v. Greenstein,* 691 F.3d 710 (2012), refused to grant a PRELIMINARY INJUNCTION and instead dismissed the case. The appeals court found that the new law caused no hardship to the facilities because they merely had to comply with all laws and regulations to avoid any hardship. If and when a facility's license was revoked, the facility could make its constitutional arguments. However, the facilities contended that if they were put out of business during the course of LITIGATION, they would not have the financial means to press their case.

Laws Defining Fetal Viability at 20 Weeks Abortion opponents have had great success in passing laws that, in effect, define fetal viability at 20 weeks gestational age. They claim that fetuses feel pain at 20 weeks and that this alone justifies banning abortions at or after 20 weeks. This claim has been disputed by most in the medical community, who believe a fetus becomes viable between 23 and 24 weeks. These fetal pain laws challenge *Roe v. Wade* and *Planned Parenthood v. Casey,* 505 U.S. 833, 112 S. Ct. 2791, 120 L. Ed. 2d 674 (1992). Arizona's law tried to sidestep the issue of viability by stating the purpose of the act was "based on documented risks to women's health and the strong medical evidence that unborn children feel pain during an abortion at that gestational age."

The Ninth Circuit was the first to address these issues in *Isaacson v. Horne,* 716 F.3d 1213 (2013), where it struck down the Arizona law. Under Supreme Court precedent, a woman has a constitutional right to choose to terminate her pregnancy before the fetus is viable without undue interference by the state. Although viability is flexible, it is medically determinable and the attending physician must make that judgment. Arizona admitted that no fetus is viable at 20 weeks gestational age, just that the fetus feels pain. The court, finding that viability occurs between 23 and 24 weeks, ruled that the state could not restrict abortions for an additional three or four weeks of gestational age.

The fact that many states have passed a fetal pain law means that more lawsuits will be filed challenging their constitutionality. Over the next few years, as the cases move to the circuit courts, it is possible that some circuits will differ with the Ninth Circuit ruling. It is probable that the Supreme Court will have to resolve the constitutionality of such laws.

What Lies Ahead In 2013, Kansas enacted anti-abortion laws that directly challenge *Roe v. Wade.* Kansas, along with six other states, defines life as beginning with fertilization. Though supporters say the language is no more than a statement of principle, people on both sides of the abortion concede the wording could become important over time. Prospective parents or grandparents who want to prevent abortions could use the language.

Other states are more aggressive than Kansas in their opposition to abortion. In March 2013, Arkansas banned most abortions after the twelfth week of gestation. Two weeks later, North Dakota passed a law that prohibits abortions as early as the sixth week of gestation.

There appears to be no end to anti-abortion legislation and the litigation that inevitably follows. At some point in time the Supreme Court will be called on to determine how far the rights given to women in *Roe v. Wade* can be regulated by the states.

In April 2012, the trial court conducted a hearing and then asked for additional briefing on the legal issues before it. The plaintiffs contended that the off-label regimen of RU-486 was safe and effective, and disputed that the regimen had caused the death of eight women. They pointed out that clinics were following guidelines from the American Congress of Obstetricians and Gynecologists and the National Abortion FEDERATION. Moreover, by increasing the costs of medication and doctor visits, some women would be required to undergo unnecessary surgical procedures. The state contended it had a rational basis to regulate the use of the medication based on safety concerns. Abortion drugs are unique and subject to reasonable requirements for their use.

In May 2012, the trial court struck down the law and issued a permanent injunction. The court found that the law severely restricted "the ways in which doctors can treat women with abortion-inducing drugs" and therefore was unconstitutional. The court concluded the law violated a woman's right to privacy and bodily integrity. The restrictions were unconstitutional because "they are so completely at odds with the standard that governs the practice of medicine [that the law] can serve no purpose other than to prevent women from obtaining abortions and to punish and discriminate against those women who do." The law placed an undue burden on a woman's ability to make a decision about whether to have an abortion. The state appealed to the Oklahoma supreme court.

The state supreme court, in a unanimous ruling, upheld the trial court decision. The court issued a *per curiam* opinion, which meant that no member of the court attached his or her name to it. These types of opinions typically involve cases where the law is well settled and the facts are not in dispute. This was what happened with the abortion ruling. The court cited *Planned Parenthood v. Casey* as controlling its decision. This 1992 U.S. Supreme Court case announced a new standard to determine the validity of laws restricting abortions. The new standard looks at whether a state abortion regulation has the purpose or effect of imposing an "undue burden," which is defined as a "substantial obstacle in the path of a woman seeking an abortion before the fetus attains viability." The state supreme court

concluded that the law did impose an undue burden on women seeking an abortion. Under the Constitution's **Supremacy Clause**, the court was required to follow this federal decision. Therefore, on its face the law was unconstitutional and was "stricken in its entirety."

Seventh Circuit Strikes Down Law Banning State Funding to Abortion Providers

A number of states have sought to ban ABORTION providers, including Planned Parenthood, from receiving any state-administered funds, even if the money was earmarked for other services. Indiana passed such a law in 2011, but it was challenged in *Planned Parenthood v. Commissioner of the Indiana STATE DEPARTMENT of Health*, 699 F.3d 962 (2012). The Seventh Circuit agreed with Planned Parenthood that it had a right to sue the state over the defunding law and that Indiana did not have the authority to exclude a class of providers that received federal **Medicaid** funds.

In 2011, Indiana passed a law that prohibited state agencies from providing state or federal funds to "any **entity** that performs abortions or maintains or operates a facility where abortions are performed." The federal Hyde Amendment already banned states from using federal funds to pay for most non-therapeutic abortions and Indiana already had in a place a similar ban on the use of state funds; the law went further by prohibiting abortion providers from receiving any state-administered funds, even if the services did not involve abortions. The aim of the law was to eliminate the indirect subsidization of abortion. Planned Parenthood immediately challenged the law in federal court, arguing that as an enrolled MEDICAID provider, the law violated the Medicaid Act's "free choice of provider" provision. This provision requires state Medicaid plans to allow patients to choose their own medical provider. The federal government, in a **friend of the court** brief, supported this claim. Planned Parenthood also alleged the law was preempted by a federal block-grant **statute** that authorized the Secretary of Health and Human Services (HHS) to make grants related to sexually transmitted diseases. The **district court** agreed with Planned Parenthood on both claims and entered a **preliminary injunction** that prevented Indiana from enforcing the defunding law. The state appealed to the Seventh **Circuit Court** of Appeals.

A three-judge panel of the Seventh Circuit, in a 2-1 vote, upheld the Medicaid statute claim but reversed as to the block grant statute. Judge Diane Sykes, writing for the majority, noted that Medicaid was a joint federal-state program through which the federal government provided funding to the states so they could furnish medical care to needy individuals. Once a state elects to participate in Medicaid, it must follow all federal requirements and standards that are contained in the Medicaid Act. The act clearly stated that state Medicaid plans must permit any individual eligible for medical assistance to obtain assistance "from any institution, agency, community pharmacy, or person, qualified to perform the service or services required." This was known as the free-choice-of-provider requirement. Planned Parenthood was an enrolled provider in Indiana's Medicaid program. Though Planned Parenthood used private funding to support its abortion services, it received state-administered funds for other services regarding healthcare for women. The Indiana law was designed to cut off these funds. Planned Parenthood estimated that if the law went into effect, it would be forced to close one quarter of its clinics and lay off approximately 37 employees. This would also mean it would stop serving an unknown number of patients.

Judge Sykes concluded that these alleged harms were significant and pointed out that Indiana did not dispute this fact. To secure a PRELIMINARY INJUNCTION, plaintiffs must show irreparable harm, that there was a strong likelihood that they would prevail with their claims, and that the alleged harms would hurt the PUBLIC INTEREST. Having acknowledged the irreparable harm component, Judge Sykes found that there was a strong likelihood of success that Planned Parenthood would prevail on its free-choice-of-provider claim under the Medicaid Act. In addition, the federal government had threatened partial or total withholding of federal Medicaid funds to Indiana, which could total over $5 billion annually and affect as many as one million state residents. This prospect led the court to conclude that in assessing the balance of harms and public interest, the harms outweighed the state's interests in defunding abortion providers. The state had argued that any harm to Planned Parenthood's Medicaid patients was superficial because they had many other qualified Medicaid providers to choose from in every part of the state. Judge Sykes disagreed, finding that the law interfered with the Medicaid Act's free choice provision. As long as a provider was qualified, the state could not step between the provider and the patient. Therefore, the district court had properly analyzed the issues when it issued the INJUNCTION.

However, the appeals court disagreed with the district court ruling on the federal block-grant program for monitoring sexually transmitted diseases. In 2011, Indiana awarded Planned Parenthood $150,000 of grants from federal funds received by the state under the HHS program. It had received grants under this program continuously since 1996, but the new law led to the cancellation of the 2011 contracts. The district court found that the federal block-grant program preempted the defunding law. Judge Sykes disagreed. First, she found that the federal law did not create a private **right of action** for Planned Parenthood to challenge the contract cancellation. Second, she ruled that the block-grant program law "placed no conditions on recipient states other than the basic requirement that the block-granted money be used for the stated purposes." There was no evidence that Congress intended to preempt state authority to manage the block grant funds. Therefore, that part of the preliminary injunction was reversed, allowing Indiana to proceed with removing Planned Parenthood from the program.

ADMIRALTY AND MARITIME LAW

Lozman v. City of Riviera Beach, Florida

Under the U.S. Constitution, federal judicial power extends "to all Cases of **admiralty** and maritime jurisdiction." This means that if a case arises out of admiralty or maritime jurisdiction, the federal district courts have exclusive jurisdiction to resolve the dispute.

The Federal **Maritime Lien** Act, 46 U.S.C. § 31342, applies to allow a federal court to impose a maritime **lien**. The **statute** states:

(a) Except as provided in subsection (b) of this section, a person providing necessaries to a vessel on the order of the owner or a person authorized by the owner—

(1) has a MARITIME LIEN on the vessel;

(2) may bring a **civil action in rem** to enforce the LIEN; and

(3) is not required to allege or prove in the action that credit was given to the vessel.

Congress defined the term "vessel" elsewhere in the **U.S. Code**. Under 1 U.S.C. § 3, the term "vessel" includes "every description of watercraft or other artificial contrivance used, or capable of being used, as a means of transportation on water."

In *Lozman v. City of Riviera Beach, Florida*, 133 S. Ct. 735 (2013), the SUPREME COURT reviewed a case that focused on this definition. The case involved a floating home that was not self-propelled. In a 7–2 opinion, the Court ruled that the home was not a vessel because, as a practical matter, it was not capable of being used as a means of transportation on water. In reaching the conclusion, the Court adopted a "reasonable observer" standard to determine whether something is a vessel under federal law.

The decision concluded years of LITIGATION involving Fane Lozman. He purchased a floating home in 2002 and towed it from near Fort Myers to North Beach Village in Florida. He lived in the home until 2005 when Hurricane Wilma struck. He thereafter moved the home to the marina at the City of Riviera Beach, and he lived there until the city took possession of the home in 2009.

The marina provides storage for more than 500 types of commercial and recreational vessels. Those who store vessels at the marina can pay daily or monthly fees for use of the marina. Lozman paid a fee in March 2006 to store his floating home at the marina. However, his dispute with the city began shortly after he paid the dockage fee. The city began planning a multibillion-dollar redevelopment project, with city officials meeting with a private developer in May 2006.

Lozman attempted to challenge the redevelopment agreement by challenging the meeting between the city and the developer on grounds that the meeting violated Florida's sunshine law. Plans for redevelopment were eventually dropped, but the city nevertheless attempted to evict Lozman based on several violations of the city's ordinances. Lozman prevailed in the action, when a court denied the city's **summary judgment** because Lozman raised a genuine fact issue regarding whether his EVICTION was proper.

The dispute continued, however. The city approved new rules and regulations related to use of the marina, including requirements regarding insurance and documentation. The city claimed it had notified Lozman that he had not complied with these requirements. Lozman claimed he did not receive the notices, but the city nevertheless initiated **legal proceedings** against him. On April 20, 2009, the city filed a two-count complaint in the U.S. **District Court** for the Southern District of Florida to foreclose maritime liens the city said it held on Lozman's floating home. The court issued a warrant for the "arrest" of the home. The city eventually put the home up for public auction, bought the home at the auction, and had it destroyed.

When Lozman continued to challenge the city's actions, both the district court and the Court of Appeals for the Eleventh Circuit ruled in the city's favor. One particular conclusion related to the Supreme Court's decision: the lower courts both ruled that the floating home was a "vessel" under admiralty law. *City of Riviera Beach v. That Certain Unnamed Gray, Two-Story Vessel Approximately Fifty-Seven Feet in Length*, 649 F.3d 1259 (11th Cir. 2011).

Lower **federal courts** were split on the question of what constitutes a watercraft "capable of being used" as a means of transportation on water. The Eleventh Circuit had previously ruled that a vessel is capable of being used in this manner even if the owner intended to moor the craft indefinitely, so long as the craft were capable of moving over water under tow. On the other hand, the Fifth Circuit ruled that a structure is not a vessel when the craft is only theoretically but not practically capable of sailing.

Justice STEPHEN BREYER wrote for the 7-2 majority. Justice SONIA SOTOMAYOR, joined by Justice ANTHONY KENNEDY, dissented.

The majority disagreed with the Eleventh Circuit's broad interpretation of what a vessel could include. Breyer wrote: "Not every floating structure is a 'vessel.' To state the obvious, a wooden washtub, a plastic dishpan, a swimming platform on pontoons, a large fishing net, a door taken off its hinges, or Pinocchio (when inside the whale) are not 'vessels,' even if they are 'artificial contrivance[s]' capable of floating, moving under tow, and incidentally carrying even a fair-sized item or two when they do so."

The Court instead adopted a "reasonable observer" standard to determine whether a watercraft is a vessel. "[I]n our view," Breyer wrote, "a structure does not fall within the scope of this **statutory** phrase unless a reasonable observer, looking to the home's physical characteristics and activities, would consider it designed to a practical degree for carrying people or things over water."

The Court determined that no reasonable observer would conclude that Lozman's floating home was designed to transport anything over water. The home had no rudder or steering mechanism nor was it capable of self-propulsion. Moreover, the interior of the vessel looked nothing like a typical boat. In sum, "[t]he home has no other feature that might suggest a design to transport over water anything other than its own furnishings and related personal effects."

Sotomayor agreed with the majority that the Eleventh Circuit's test was "overinclusive." However, she also disagreed with the reasonable-observer test, calling it "novel and unnecessary." She would have remanded the case to the lower court for further analysis.

AFFIRMATIVE ACTION

Employment programs required by federal statutes and regulations designed to remedy discriminatory practices in hiring minority group members; i.e., positive steps designed to eliminate existing and continuing discrimination, to remedy lingering effects of past discrimination, and to create systems and procedures to prevent future discrimination; commonly based on population percentages of minority groups in a particular area. Factors considered are race, color, sex, creed, and age.

Sixth Circuit Strikes Down Michigan Constitutional Amendment Banning Affirmative Action

Affirmative action in college admissions has been long been a contentious issue. The full panel of the Sixth **Circuit Court** of Appeals ruled that a state CONSTITUTIONAL AMENDMENT that banned AFFIRMATIVE ACTION in public colleges and universities was unconstitutional. The decision in *Coalition to Defend Affirmative Action, INTEGRATION, and Immigrant Rights and Fight for Equality by Any Means Necessary (BAMN) v. Regents of the University of Michigan,* 701 F.3d 466 (2012), came on an 8–7 vote.

Proposal 2 was a successful voter-initiated amendment to the Michigan Constitution. Passed by voters in 2006, it was to take effect in December 2006. However, the federal district

barred its implementation pending the resolution of the lawsuit challenging its constitutionality. The amendment prohibited Michigan public colleges and universities from granting "preferential treatment to any individual or group on the basis of race, color, ethnicity, or national origin." The **district court** ruled that the amendment was constitutional and did not violate the **Equal Protection** Clause of the FOURTEENTH AMENDMENT.

A three-judge panel of the Sixth Circuit reversed the district court in a 2-1 decision. *BAMN v. Regents of Univ. of Michigan,* 652 F.3d 607 (2011). The majority opinion, written by Judge R. Guy Cole, Jr., ruled that the ban on affirmative action unconstitutionally altered Michigan's political structure by impermissibly burdening racial minorities. The panel's decision came eight years after the SUPREME COURT decisions, in *Gratz v. Bollinger,* 539 U.S. 244, 123 S. Ct. 2411, 156 L. Ed. 2d 257 (2003) and *Grutter v. Bollinger,* 539 U.S. 306, 123 S. Ct. 2325, 156 L. Ed. 2d 304 (2003), that universities cannot constitutionally establish quotas for members of certain racial groups, but universities could consider race as a "plus" factor in making its decisions. Both of these cases involved policies at the University of Michigan, which led opponents of affirmative action to file the ballot initiative known as Proposal 2.

Proposal 2 provided "The University of Michigan, Michigan State University, Wayne State University, and any other public college or university, community college, or school district shall not discriminate against, or grant preferential treatment to, any individual or group on the basis of race, sex, color, ethnicity, or national origin in the operation of public employment, public education or public contracting." The proposal also stated that "The state shall not discriminate against, or grant preferential treatment to, any individual or group on the basis of race, sex, color, ethnicity, or national origin in the operation of public employment, public education, or public contracting."

Proposal 2 prevailed by a vote of 58% to 42% on November 7, 2006. For the first time in nearly fifty years, public colleges and universities in Michigan could not consider race, sex, color, ethnicity or national origin while making admissions decisions. Because the proposal amended the state constitution, none of the colleges or universities could reconsider their policies without a **repeal** of Proposal 2.

Judge Cole based his reasoning that the amendment was unconstitutional on two Supreme Court decisions: *Washington v. Seattle Sch. Dist. No. 1*, 458 U.S. 457, 102 S. Ct. 3187, 73 L. Ed. 2d 896 (1982) and *Hunter v. Erickson*, 393 U.S. 385, 89 S. Ct. 557, 21 L. Ed. 2d 616 (1969). In the Seattle case, the Supreme Court stated that the Equal Protection Clause "guarantees racial minorities the right to full participation in the political life of the community. It is beyond dispute … that given racial or ethnic groups may not be denied the franchise, or precluded from entering into the political process in a reliable and meaningful manner." Moreover, the clause prohibits "a political structure that treats all individuals as equals, yet more subtly distorts governmental processes in such a way as to place special burdens on the ability of minority groups to achieve beneficial legislation." In *Hunter*, the Court held that the state "may no more disadvantage any particular group by making it more difficult to enact legislation in its behalf than it may dilute any person's vote or give any group a smaller representation than another of comparable size."

Judge Cole concluded that these rulings made clear that equal protection of the laws includes "an assurance that the majority may not manipulate the channels of change in a manner that places unique burdens on issues of importance to racial minorities." Ensuring a fair political process was especially important in education, where the Supreme Court has found a "paramount government objective" in making public institutions open and available to all segments of U.S. society. However, Judge Cole acknowledged that the Constitution does not protect minorities from political defeat. Therefore, the court applied the *Seattle* and *Hunter* benchmarks to determine the difference between the constitutional and the impermissible. Judge Cole found that in this case the majority had not only won, "but rigged the game to reproduce its success indefinitely."

The *Hunter/Seattle* rule stated that an enactment deprives minority groups of equal protection under the law when it has a racial focus, targeting a goal or program that primarily benefits a minority and works a reallocation of political power or reordering of the decision-making process that places special burdens on a minority group's ability to achieve its goals through that process. The amendment had a "racial focus" because Michigan's public universities' affirmative action programs primarily benefited minority students and were designed for that very purpose. Race-conscious admission policies increased minority enrollment. Judge Cole rejected the state's argument that because these policies also benefited students of other groups and the nation as a whole, minority students were not the primary beneficiaries. These wider benefits did not "undermine the conclusion that their primary beneficiaries are racial minorities."

The second part of the *Hunter/Seattle* rule required the appeals court to determine whether the constitutional amendment worked a reallocation of political power that placed special burdens on racial minorities. The state argued that Michigan university admissions committees were not "political" because they were not part of the electoral process. Judge Cole rejected this narrow reading of the word "political," concluding that the boards were "political" because they were governmental entities that were involved in governmental decision making. Therefore, there was "little doubt" that the amendment affected a political process under the two Supreme Court rulings.

The court then turned to the effect of the amendment: did it reorder the political process to place special burdens on racial minorities? Judge Cole concluded that it did. He pointed out the steps a Michigan citizen could take to change the admission policies on an issue unrelated to race. The person may lobby the admissions committee directly, petition higher administrative authorities at the university, work in an election to elect university board members who subscribe to similar views, and finally, campaign for an amendment to the state constitution. In contrast, a person seeking that Michigan universities adopt race-based admission policies "must now *begin*, by convincing the Michigan electorate to amend the Michigan Constitution." This would involve either convincing two-thirds of both the Michigan House of Representatives and Senate to support a proposal to abrogate the anti-affirmative action amendment, or obtain the signatures of ten percent of the electorate to get the proposal on the ballot. A majority of the voters would have to approve the amendment. Judge Cole stated that "Only after traversing this difficult and costly process would the now-exhausted Michigan citizen reach the starting point of his opponent who sought a non-race related admissions policy change."

The "stark contrast" between the avenues of political change following the passage of the anti-affirmative action amendment explained why the amendment could not be viewed as a "mere repeal of an existing race-related policy." If opponents of affirmative action had successfully lobbied the universities' admission units to change the policies there would have been no equal protection problem. Requiring racial minorities to "surmount more obstacles to achieve their political objectives than other groups face" was a violation of equal protection.

Shortly after the three-judge panel issued its ruling, the full court of appeals vacated the decision and agreed to rehear the case. In November 2012 the court issued its decision, again striking down the amendment. Judge Cole again authored the majority opinion. He employed the same reasoning based on the *Seattle* and *Hunter* decisions, which "expounded the rule that an enactment deprives minority groups of the equal protection of the laws" when it "has a racial focus, targeting a policy or program" that benefits minorities, and "reallocates political power or reorders the decision-making process in a way that places special burdens on a minority group's ability to achieve its goals through that process." Though Proposal 2 also banned the use of race in the state's employment policies and in public contracting, the decision dealt only with the way the proposal affected public education.

Judge Cole also noted that the amendment did not just repeal existing race-conscious admission policies. It went a step further by permanently barring any readoption of affirmative action policies. Moreover, the constitution would not bar college and university officials from deciding to do away with affirmative action programs, if the policy choice were left to them.

AGRICULTURAL LAW

Horne v. Department of Agriculture

The FIFTH AMENDMENT to the U.S. Constitution contains what is known as the Takings Clause, which prohibits the federal government from taking private property "for public use, without just compensation." In 2013, the U.S. SUPREME COURT was called upon to resolve an issue of whether a lower federal court had jurisdiction to review a takings claim related to a dispute over civil penalties imposed by a marketing order issued by the U.S. DEPARTMENT OF AGRICULTURE. The Court held that the Ninth **Circuit Court** of Appeals indeed had jurisdiction to review the takings dispute focused on the fines.

The case focused on the application of the Agricultural Marketing Agreement Act of 1937 (AMAA), 7 U.S.C. § 601 **et seq.**, a New Deal–era **statute** designed to avoid "unreasonable fluctuations in supplies and prices." Congress designed the statute to create a system for stabilizing prices for agricultural commodities. Under the AMAA, the U.S. secretary of agriculture may issue marketing orders to regulate the sale and delivery of agricultural goods. The Act establishes civil and criminal penalties for violations of a marketing order.

Agricultural "producers" are not subject to the provisions of the AMAA. The Act only regulates "handlers," defined as "processors, associations of producers, and others engaged in the handling" of agricultural commodities.

In 1949, the secretary of agriculture issued a marketing order that continues to apply to California raisins. The purpose of the marketing order was to stabilize prices of raisins by limiting the quantity of raisins sold domestically. The order defines a raisin "handler" as follows: "(a) Any processor or packer; (b) any person who places, ships, or continues natural condition raisins in the current of commerce from within the area to any point outside thereof; (c) any person who delivers off-grade raisins, other failing raisins or raisin residual material to other than a packer or other than into any eligible non-normal outlet; or (d) any person who blends raisins" (7 C.F.R. § 989.15).

The order also created a raisin administrative committee (RAC) consisting of a total of 47 members. The majority (35) represent producers, while others represent handlers, cooperative bargaining associations, and the public. The order authorizes the RAC to establish annual reserve pools of raisins that are not sold on the open market domestically. Portions of raisins that may be sold on the open market are referred to as "free-tonnage," while the portions that remain in the reserve pool are known as "reserve-tonnage."

A producer only receives payment for free-tonnage raisins. A handler holds the reserve-tonnage raisins in segregated bins, and the RAC may sell these reserve-tonnage raisins to handlers in overseas markets or secondary, noncompetitive domestic markets, such as school lunch programs. The RAC uses sales from the reserve pool to pay administrative costs. Remaining funds are divided among the producers, who receive a **pro rata** share.

Marvin and Laura Horne began producing raisins in California in 1969. They operated as raisin producers for more than 30 years but tried to find ways to avoid the mandatory reserve program. The Hornes brought their raisins to market without going through a traditional handler. They avoided paying assessments to the RAC for the 2002–2003 and 2003–2004 crop years. The Hornes also did not set aside reserve-tonnage raisins as the marketing order required.

The administrator of the Agriculture Marketing Service initiated an action against the Hornes and other businesses involved in the Hornes' operations. The administrator alleged that the Hornes were handlers of the raisins and that they were liable for the assessments and for the failure to hold the raisins in reserve as required by the order. The Hornes responded that they were not handlers because they did not actually take physical possession of other producers' raisins. The Hornes also argued that the order violated the Takings Clause of the Fifth Amendment.

In 2006, an **administrative law** judge ruled that the Hornes were indeed handlers and were subject to the marketing order. Moreover, the judge rejected the Hornes' argument based on the Takings Clause, concluding that "handlers no longer have a PROPERTY RIGHT that permits them to market their crop free of regulatory control." The Hornes appealed the decision to a judicial officer with the Agriculture Department, but the judge reached the same conclusions as the administrative law judge. The officer imposed penalties of nearly $700,000.

The Hornes then filed a complaint in the U.S. **District Court** for the Eastern District of California. The district court granted **summary judgment** in favor of the Agriculture Department, reaching the same conclusions as the administrative law judge and judicial officer

had. The district court also rejected the Hornes' argument based on the Takings Clause.

The Hornes appealed the decision to the Ninth Circuit Court of Appeals, which determined that the Hornes should have brought their claims based on takings grounds in the Federal **Court of Claims**. The court noted that had the Hornes brought their takings claims in their capacity as handlers, the Ninth Circuit would have jurisdiction to review the claim. However, in *Horne v. U.S. Department of Agriculture*, 673 F.3d 1071 (9th Cir. 2012), the court ruled that the Hornes had brought their claims as producers and should have initiated their action in the Court of Federal Claims based on jurisdiction provided in the Tucker Act, 28 U.S.C. § 1491.

In a unanimous decision, the Supreme Court reversed the Ninth Circuit. *Horne v. Department of Agriculture*, 133 S. Ct. 2053 (2013). Justice Clarence Thomas, writing for the Court, focused on the Ninth Circuit's characterization of the Hornes as producers instead of handlers in the context of the takings claim. According to the Supreme Court, the Ninth Circuit's characterization was not correct.

The Court stated: "Although petitioners argued that they were producers—and thus not subject to the AMAA or Marketing Order at all—both the USDA and the District Court concluded that petitioners were 'handlers.' Accordingly, the civil penalty, assessment, and reimbursement for failure to reserve raisins were all levied on petitioners in their capacity as 'handlers.' If petitioners' argument that they were producers had prevailed, they would not have been subject to any of the monetary sanctions imposed on them."

Based on the Court's conclusion that the Hornes were handlers for purposes of their constitutional argument, the Court then had to resolve whether a federal court has jurisdiction to adjudicate their takings claim. Previous cases had established that claims brought against the federal government based on the Takings Clause must be brought in the Court of Federal Claims under the Tucker Act, which establishes a waiver of the federal government's **sovereign immunity**. However, the cases have also established that Congress may withdraw the Tucker Act grant of jurisdiction, typically by creating a remedial scheme.

The Court concluded that the AMAA created a comprehensive remedial scheme that displaced jurisdiction under the Tucker Act. Thus, the Court ruled that the AMAA withdrew Tucker Act jurisdiction, allowing the Ninth Circuit to decide whether the Agriculture Department violated the Fifth Amendment.

AMERICANS WITH DISABILITIES ACT

Seventh Circuit Rules Employers Do Not Have to Automatically Fill Vacancies with Disabled Employees

The federal circuit courts of appeals are divided as whether the Americans with Disabilities Act (ADA) requires employers to automatically place disabled employees in vacant positions. The Tenth Circuit and the D.C. Circuit have ruled that the ADA requires reassignment to vacant positions, while the Seventh and Eighth Circuits have ruled that it does not. The U.S. SUPREME COURT has not addressed this issue directly but a 2002 decision by the Court led the EQUAL EMPLOYMENT OPPORTUNITY COMMISSION (EEOC) to believe the reasoning used in the Seventh and Eighth Circuit rulings had been undermined. In *Equal Employment Opportunity Commission v. United Airlines, Inc.,* 673 F.3d 543 (2012), the Seventh Circuit reaffirmed its decision as binding precedent but concluded the appeals court should reconsider the ruling in light of the 2002 Supreme Court case.

In 2003, United Airlines published Reasonable Accommodation Guidelines that dealt with accommodating employees who, because of their disability, could no longer perform the essential functions of their current jobs even with reasonable accommodations. The guidelines stated that transfer to an "equivalent or lower-level vacant position" might be a reasonable accommodation. However, the transfer process was to be competitive. An employee needing accommodation would be given preference by being allowed to submit an unlimited number of transfer applications, by being guaranteed an interview, and by receiving priority consideration over a similarly qualified applicant.

The EEOC filed a federal lawsuit against United, alleging that the guidelines policy violated the ADA. The Illinois **district court**, which is in the Seventh Circuit, granted

United's motion to dismiss the case because a 2000 Seventh Circuit decision, *EEOC v. Humiston-Keeling,* 227 F.3d 1024 (2000) was binding precedent. In *Humiston-Keeling,* the court held that a competitive transfer policy did not violate the ADA. The district court also rejected the EEOC's claim that the Supreme Court's decision in *US Airways, Inc. v. Barnett,* 535 U.S. 391, 122 S. Ct. 1516, 152 L. Ed. 2d 589 (2002) undermined the Seventh Circuit ruling. The EEOC then appealed to the Seventh Circuit, asking it to overturn its circuit precedent.

A three-judge panel of the Seventh Circuit unanimously upheld the district court decision. Judge Richard Cudahy, writing for the court, noted that *Humiston-Keeling* was directly on point in this case and it had not been overruled by the Seventh Circuit. *Humiston-Keeling* involved a worker who could no longer perform her conveyor job because of an injured arm. She applied for vacant clerical positions within the company but was never transferred. The EEOC brought suit, arguing that under the ADA, the reassignment form of reasonable accommodation required the employer to advance the disabled employee over a more qualified nondisabled person, "provided only that the disabled person is at least minimally qualified to do the job, unless the employer can show undue hardship." The appeals court rejected this interpretation of the ADA provided that it was the employer's "consistent and honest policy to hire the best applicant for the particular job in question."

Judge Cudahy pointed out that this controlling case required the EEOC to convince the court to OVERRULE its prior decision. The doctrine of *stare decisis* holds that "the mere existence of certain decisions becomes a reason for adhering to their holdings in subsequent cases." Though the EEOC's interpretation of the ADA was likely "more supportable" than that found in *Humiston-Keeling,* the EEOC had to provide the court with an "on-point" Supreme Court decision or a change in the ADA itself in order to prevail. The EEOC cited the 2002 *Barnett* decision to show the Supreme Court's ruling undercut the reasoning in *Humiston-Keeling.* In *Barnett,* the Court considered reassignment under the ADA in the context of a seniority system. Barnett, a disabled cargo handler, invoked seniority and transferred to a mailroom position. Later, at least two employees senior to Barnett intended to bid for the mailroom position. Barnett claimed that under the ADA, the mailroom job was a reasonable accommodation. The Supreme Court used a case-specific approach: Once the employee has shown he is seeking a reasonable accommodation, the employer must show special circumstances that demonstrate undue hardship in the "particular circumstances." While Barnett's request for assignment was a reasonable accommodation within the meaning of the ADA, the violation of the seniority system presented an undue hardship to any employer.

The EEOC pointed out that US Airways had relied heavily on *Humiston-Keeling* and that the Supreme Court "flatly contradicted much of the language" of the Seventh Circuit case. The Court had rejected the appeals court's conclusion that the ADA was "not a mandatory preference act" but only a "non-discrimination statute." Instead, the Court recognized that preferences would sometimes be necessary to further the ADA's "basic equal opportunity goal." US Airways had prevailed in 2002 *Barnett* not because it followed a "neutral rule" that allowed it an "automatic exemption" from the accommodation requirement of the ADA. Instead, it prevailed because its situation satisfied a much narrower exception based on the hardship that would be imposed on an employer using a seniority system.

Judge Cudahy acknowledged that the EEOC's argument might be persuasive, but cited a 2002 Seventh Circuit decision that relied on the recently handed down *Barnett* ruling as actually bolstering *Humiston-Keeling*. In this decision the Seventh Circuit equated seniority systems with any normal method of filling vacancies. The EEOC claimed this interpretation was wrong because the appeals court had enlarged the narrow exception set out in *Barnett* so as to swallow the rule. Judge Cudahy also cited a 2004 case and a 2008 case by the Seventh Circuit that relied on *Humiston-Keeling*. In his view their "mere existence and consistent interpretations compel this court to find that *Humiston-Keeling* remains good law."

Sixth Circuit Rules on Standard for Disability Claim

The circuit courts of appeals have interpreted parts of the Americans with Disabilities Act (ADA) differently. One issue in dispute has been the standard to be used to determine employer liability. The ADA prohibited DISCRIMINATION

"because of" the disability of an employee. However, the Sixth **Circuit Court** of Appeals ruled in the mid-1990s that interpreted this phrase to mean that an employee could only prevail if the company's decision to fire the employee was "solely" because of the employee's disability, a term that appears in the Rehabilitation Act but not in the ADA. Other circuit courts interpreted the phrase to mean that an employee could prevail if the disability was a "motivating factor" in the company's employment action, a phrase that appears in Title VII of the CIVIL RIGHTS Act of 1964 but not in the ADA. The Sixth Circuit Court, in *Lewis v. Humboldt Acquisition Corporation*, 681 F.3d 312 (2012), reversed itself and concluded its use of the "solely" standard was wrong and "out of sync" with other circuit courts. However, the appeals court rejected the use of the "motivating factor" standard and reverted to a "but-for" causation that dissenting members of the Sixth Circuit believed put too great a burden on individuals seeking to vindicate disability-based discrimination.

In 2006, Humboldt Acquisition Corporation dismissed Susan Lewis from her position as a registered nurse in one of the company's retirement homes. Lewis sued Humboldt in federal **district court**, claiming that the company fired her because she had a medical condition that made it difficult for her to walk and required her to sometimes use a wheelchair. Humboldt claimed it dismissed Lewis based on an outburst at work, in which she allegedly yelled, used profanity, and criticized her supervisor. The case went to a jury. Lewis requested the court to instruct the jury that if the alleged discrimination was a motivating factor in Humboldt's decision to fire her, then she should prevail. Humboldt countered by asking the court to instruct the jury that Lewis could only prevail if the fact that she was a qualified individual with a disability was the sole reason for Humboldt's decision to terminate her. The district court selected Humboldt's jury instruction because Sixth Circuit precedent required so. The jury found in Humboldt's favor. Lewis appealed to the Sixth Circuit, arguing that her motivating factor causation standard should have been used.

The entire Sixth Circuit heard the appeal. All 16 judges agreed with Lewis that the "sole" reason standard was wrong and should not have been used. In a 9–7 decision, the court refused to employ the "motivating factor standard." Judge

Jeffrey Sutton, writing for the entire court on the first issue and the majority on the second issue, acknowledged the "sole" reason standard was incorrect. In a 1995 decision that involved claims under the ADA and Rehabilitation Act (a law that pre-dated the ADA that deals with disability), the Sixth Circuit imported the Rehabilitation Act's "sole" reason causation into its reading of the ADA. When Congress enacted the ADA in 1990, it had borrowed many of the standards and requirements of the earlier law. However, the Sixth Circuit incorrectly concluded that the sole reason standard, which was not borrowed, should apply to the ADA. Judge Sutton noted that the ADA bars differential treatment "because of" the individual's disability. If Congress had meant to endorse the sole reason standard, it would have done so. Congress had amended both statutes "many times over the years but has never seen fit to join the causation standards." Therefore, the sole reason standard did not apply to the ADA.

As to Lewis's contention that the court adopt the "motivating factor" causation, the majority rejected it. Judge Sutton pointed out that the words "a motivating factor" did not appear in the ADA but appear in Title VII. For the same reasons the court refused to import "solely" from the Rehabilitation Act into the ADA, the court found it had "no license" to import "a motivating factor into the ADA. As originally enacted in 1964, Title VII made it unlawful for an employer to discriminate against any individual" because of "the individual's race, color, religion, sex, or national origin." In 1991, Congress added to the law after a SUPREME COURT decision considered how a because-of standard worked in mixed-motives cases. These cases involved permissible and impermissible considerations that played a role in the employer's adverse employment action. The Court concluded that if a Title VII PLAINTIFF could show that discrimination was the "motivating" factor in the employer's action, the employer had to show that it would have taken the same action regardless of that impermissible consideration. In Lewis's case, Humboldt would have to show that it fired her for her outburst at work, regardless of her disability. Congress changed Title VII by adding "a motivating factor" as a basis for discrimination liability

Judge Sutton concluded "a motivating factor" could not be read into the ADA. He cited a 2009 Supreme Court decision involving

the AGE DISCRIMINATION in Employment Act (ADEA) in which the Court refused to expand the reach of Title VII's "motivating factors" amendments to this civil rights **statute**. Although both laws concerned employment discrimination and shared common goals, the Court would not apply rules applicable under one statute to a different statute. Congress could have added the "motivating factor" language to the ADEA or the ADA but did not. When Congress amends one statute but not another, "it is presumed to have acted intentionally."

The appeals court, having disposed of both proposed causation standards, looked to the language of the ADA for the proper standard. The ADA bars discrimination "because of" an employee's disability, meaning that it prohibits discrimination that is a "but-for" cause of the employer's adverse decision.

The seven dissenting judges contended that the "motivating factor" should be used for ADA cases. Judge Eric Clay, in his DISSENT, noted that most of the other circuit courts had done so. Moreover, the ADA's "because of" phrase did not resolve what standard of causation should be applied. Instead of viewing the ADA in isolation, the court should consider "the broader purposes of the statute and its relationship to other civil rights statutes to determine the congressional intent as to the meaning of the phrase." The use of the "but-for" standard was "barely" more helpful to an ADA plaintiff than the "sole-cause standard." The "motivating factor" standard, which a majority of the circuits embraced, fulfilled Congress's purpose in enacting the ADA.

ANTITRUST LAW

Legislation enacted by the federal and various state governments to regulate trade and commerce by preventing unlawful restraints, price-fixing, and monopolies, to promote competition, and to encourage the production of quality goods and services at the lowest prices, with the primary goal of safeguarding public welfare by ensuring that consumer demands will be met by the manufacture and sale of goods at reasonable prices.

American Express Co. v. Italian Colors Restaurant

Historically, courts were hostile toward ARBITRATION agreements and were reluctant to enforce these agreements. In response to this hostility, in 1925 Congress enacted the Federal Arbitration Act (FAA), 9 U.S.C. §§ 1 **et seq.** The act establishes what the SUPREME COURT has called a "liberal federal policy favoring arbitration" and has stressed that the Act establishes a "fundamental principle that arbitration is a matter of contract." Thus, the courts will "rigorously enforce" arbitration agreements according to their terms.

Section 2 of the Act states as follows: "A written provision in any maritime transaction or a contract evidencing a transaction involving commerce to settle by arbitration a controversy thereafter arising out of such contract or transaction ... shall be valid, **irrevocable**, and enforceable, save upon such grounds as exist at law or in equity for the revocation of any contract." 9 U.S.C. § 2. The last phrase of this section allows a court to declare an arbitration agreement unenforceable on generally applicable contract defenses.

However, courts have been reluctant to invalidate arbitration agreements. Courts will generally enforce these agreements according to their terms in instances where the agreement specifies the rules under which parties must conduct arbitration. The Supreme Court has issued several rulings in the recent past that have sided with businesses who have wanted to enforce arbitration provisions.

In 2013, the Supreme Court reviewed a case in which a group of merchants wanted to bring a class-action lawsuit against American Express based on allegations that American Express had violated antitrust laws. The plaintiffs in the case were merchants who accept American Express cards. The agreement that the merchants signed with American Express contained a clause requiring the parties to submit disputes to be resolved through arbitration. The clause also stated: "There shall be no right or authority for any Claims to be arbitrated on a class-action basis." The plaintiffs argued that it was not economically feasible to bring individual complaints against American Express and asked the courts to waive agreements requiring the parties to arbitrate their claims. In a 5–3 decision, the Court rejected the merchants' arguments, concluding that nothing in the arbitration laws call for a waiver in such an instance. *American Express Co. v. Italian Colors Restaurant*, 133 S. Ct. 2304 (2013).

The merchants' claims were based on a policy employed by American Express whereby the merchants had to accept all versions of the company's credit cards. Several types of American Express cards do not require users to pay their full balance at the end of every month. The fees attached to these cards were about 30 percent higher than fees charged by competing companies such as Visa and MasterCard.

The merchants brought an antitrust suit as a **class action**, arguing that American Express used its **monopoly** power to force the merchants to accept the cards. American Express filed a motion to compel arbitration under the FAA. In response, the merchants submitted evidence showing that the cost of expert analysis to prove the antitrust claims could exceed $1 million. However, the maximum amount that any single merchant could receive through an award would be less than $40,000, so the plaintiffs argued that it was not economically feasible to bring individual claims.

LITIGATION continued for several years. The Second **Circuit Court** of Appeals ruled on two different occasions that the provision requiring arbitration was unenforceable. In 2012, the Second Circuit issued its last ruling, holding that the arbitration clause would completely preclude the antitrust claims against American Express. *In re American Express Merchants' Litigation*, 667 F.3d 204 (2d Cir. 2012).

The Supreme Court agreed to review the case. Justice SONIA SOTOMAYOR did not participate because she had previously served on the Second Circuit when the lower court had reviewed the dispute. In its 5–3 decision, the Court reversed the Second Circuit, with justices voting along ideological lines. Justice ANTONIN SCALIA wrote for the majority, while Justice ELENA KAGAN dissented.

Scalia focused his attention on Congress's intent when it passed the FAA. Scalia also reviewed provisions of the antitrust laws upon which the merchants' claims were based. Those antitrust laws are silent with respect to class-action claims.

Scalia wrote: "No contrary congressional command requires us to reject the waiver of class arbitration here. Respondents argue that requiring them to litigate their claims individually—as they contracted to do—would contravene the policies of the antitrust laws. But the antitrust laws do not guarantee an affordable procedural path to the vindication of every claim."

The fact that the antitrust laws were enacted decades before rules allowing class-action suits made no difference. Nothing in the Federal Rules of **Civil Procedure** suggested to the majority of the Court that waiver was proper in this type of case because of the high cost of complying with an arbitration clause.

Kagan argued that the Court should have applied a rule known as the effective-vindication rule, which effectively prevents arbitration clauses from "choking off a plaintiff's ability to enforce congressionally created rights."

Kagan wrote: "Here is the nutshell version of this case, unfortunately obscured in the Court's decision. The owner of a small restaurant (Italian Colors) thinks that American Express (Amex) has used its monopoly power to force merchants to accept a form contract violating the antitrust laws. The restaurateur wants to challenge the allegedly unlawful provision (imposing a **tying arrangement**), but the same contract's arbitration clause prevents him from doing so. That term imposes a variety of procedural bars that would make pursuit of the antitrust claim a fool's errand. So if the arbitration clause is enforceable, Amex has insulated itself from antitrust liability—even if it has in fact violated the law. The monopolist gets to use its monopoly power to insist on a contract effectively depriving its victims of all legal recourse."

She continued: "And here is the nutshell version of today's opinion, admirably flaunted rather than camouflaged: Too darn bad."

The U.S. CHAMBER OF COMMERCE cheered the decision, saying that the only parties who were losers in the case were "those in the plaintiffs' bar who want to cash in by forcing disputes into already overburdened courts."

Supreme Court Rules that Municipal Hospital Entity Does Not Have State-Action Antitrust Immunity

Federal antitrust laws generally are applied to private entities but in some cases to anticompetitive actions by state and local governments. However, the U.S. SUPREME COURT has applied state-action IMMUNITY to anticompetitive actions if the state legislature has clearly articulated and affirmatively expressed a policy that substantially lessens competition. In such cases, federal antitrust laws cannot be used to change the anticompetitive behavior. The Court, in FEDERAL TRADE COMMISSION v. Phoebe Putney Health System, Inc., 133 S. Ct. 1003, 185 L. Ed. 2d 43 (2013), concluded that state-action immunity did not apply to a Georgia public hospital authority that sought to acquire the second hospital in its county. The Court found that the Georgia state legislature had failed to include language in its law authorizing county hospital authorities that allowed authorities to have a **monopoly** of hospitals in the county.

In 1941, the state of Georgia amended its constitution to allow political subdivisions to provide health care services. The state legislature then enacted a law that authorized each county and municipality to create a hospital authority. These bodies, governed by 5-to-8-member boards, were given 27 powers. These include the power to acquire hospitals and other public health care facilities, to construct hospitals, and to establish rates and charges for the services provided. Hospital authorities are non-profit entities. In the same year the law was enacted, the city of Albany and Dougherty County established a hospital authority. It immediately purchased the Phoebe Putney Memorial Hospital, which had been in operation since 1911. In 1990, the authority restructured its operation by creating two private nonprofit corporations to manage the hospital: Phoebe Putney Health Systems, Inc. (PPHS) and its subsidiary, Phoebe Putney Memorial Hospital (PPMH). The authority leased the hospital to PPMH for $1 per year for 40 years. Under the lease, PPMH had the exclusive authority over the operation of the hospital, including the ability to set rates for services.

In 2010, PPHS began discussions with the for-profit owners of the other hospital in Dougherty County, Palmyra Medical Center. Palmyra, established in 1971, is two miles from Memorial Hospital. Together, the two hospitals accounted for 86% of the market for acute-care hospital services in the six counties surrounding Albany. Memorial accounted for 75% of that market on its own. PPHS presented the authority with a plan under which the authority would purchase Palmyra with PPHS controlled funds and then lease Palmyra to a PPHA subsidiary for $1 a year under the Memorial hospital lease agreement. The authority unanimously approved the transaction.

The Federal Trade Commission (FTC) soon issued an administrative complaint alleging that the proposed purchase-and-lease transaction would create a virtual monopoly and would substantially reduce competition in the market of acute-care hospital services. The FTC, along with the state of Georgia, then filed a federal lawsuit against the authority, and the various hospital entities, seeking an INJUNCTION to stop the transaction. The federal **district court** denied the request for the **preliminary injunction** and dismissed the case. The district court cited the state-action immunity doctrine, making the authority and other defendants immune from federal **antitrust law**. The Eleventh **Circuit Court** of Appeals upheld this ruling, finding that although the transaction would lessen competition, the state-action doctrine must prevail. It concluded that the challenged anticompetitive conduct was a "foreseeable result" of Georgia's hospital authority **statute**. The conduct was foreseeable because the state legislature "reasonably anticipated" such an action. The appeals court noted the numerous powers given to the hospital authorities clearly demonstrated the legislature had anticipated anticompetitive effects through consolidation of ownership.

The Supreme Court, in a unanimous decision, overturned the Eleventh Circuit ruling. Justice SONIA SOTOMAYOR, writing for the Court, reviewed only one question in its decision: whether the Georgia legislature, through the powers given to the hospital authorities, "clearly articulated and affirmatively expressed a state policy to displace competition in the market for hospital services." The Court concluded the legislature had not done so. Justice Sotomayor noted that state-action immunity is disfavored. Therefore, the defendants had to convince the Court that the state legislature clearly articulated its intent to approve anticompetitive behavior.

Justice Sotomayor concluded that state-action failed "because there is no evidence the State affirmatively contemplated that hospital authorities would displace competition by consolidating hospital ownership." The acquisition and leasing powers exercised by the authority, which the Eleventh Circuit thought pivotal in its immunity analysis, mirrored "general powers routinely conferred by state law upon private corporation." Private corporations also possessed other powers held by the authority. Such grants of general corporate

power did not demonstrate that the legislature "contemplated" that these powers would be used anticompetitively. Though the law allowed the authority to acquire the hospital, "it does not clearly articulate and affirmatively express a state policy empowering the Authority to make acquisitions of existing hospitals that will substantially lessen competition."

The Court found that the Eleventh Circuit had applied the concept of "foreseeability" from the clear-articulation test "too loosely." It was true that no legislature could be expected to list all of the anticipated effects of a law delegating authority to a lower governmental **entity**. Therefore, the Court required that a state policy to displace federal ANTITRUST LAW was "sufficiently expressed where the displacement of competition was the inherent, logical, or ordinary result of the exercised of authority delegated by the state legislature." The state must have foreseen and "implicitly endorsed" the anticompetitive effects as consistent with its policy goals. Justice Sotomayor stated that the authority failed this test because the law had given the authority the power to acquire "projects," which includes not only hospitals but also health care facilities, dormitories, office buildings, clinics, nursing homes and extended care facilities. The power to acquire hospitals "still does not ordinarily produce anticompetitive effects."

APPELLATE ADVOCACY

Supreme Court Rules Mentally Incompetent Inmates Cannot Stay Their Appeals

It is settled law that mentally incompetent defendants cannot be tried for their crimes until they are able to assist their legal counsel with their defense. However, the law has been unclear as to whether a person convicted of a crime and who is later deemed mentally incompetent could postpone an appeal of the trial verdict. Two federal circuit courts of appeal ruled that in federal **habeas corpus** proceedings, an inmate's **incompetency** must suspend the habeas proceedings. The U.S. SUPREME COURT, in *Ryan v. Gonzales,* 133 S. Ct. 696, 184 L. Ed. 2d 528 (2013), disagreed, ruling that the federal laws the appeals courts relied on were not applicable to the issue of mental incompetency at the appeal stage.

Ernest Gonzales was convicted by an Arizona jury of MURDER, armed **robbery**, and other crimes and sentenced to death. After he exhausted his state appeals, he filed a petition for a **writ** of **habeas corpus** in federal **district court**. While the petition was pending, Gonzales' lawyer asked the court to stay the proceedings because his client was no longer capable of rationally communicating with or assisting the lawyer. The lawyer cited a Ninth **Circuit Court** of Appeals decision that concluded the federal habeas **statute** required a stay of proceedings where an incompetent inmate raised claims that could potentially benefit from his ability to communicate rationally to his lawyer. The federal district court rejected Gonzales' motion, finding that his habeas claims were based on the trial record or were resolvable as matters of law. Neither would benefit from Gonzales's input. Gonzales appealed to the Ninth Circuit. While the case was pending, the Ninth Circuit issued a decision that held that incompetent habeas petitioners are entitled to a stay, even if the appeal is based entirely on the record. Not surprisingly, the Ninth Circuit overruled the district court and granted Gonzales a stay of proceedings.

In an Ohio case, Sean Carter was convicted of murder by a jury and sentenced to death. After he exhausted his state appeals, he filed a petition for a writ of HABEAS CORPUS and a motion to stay his proceedings because he was mentally incompetent. After several psychiatric evaluations and a competency hearing, the federal district court found Carter incompetent to assist his lawyer. The court applied the reasoning of the first Ninth Circuit court and ruled that Carter's assistance was required to develop four of his claims. Therefore, the court stayed the habeas proceedings. On appeal, the Sixth Circuit Court of Appeals noted that there was not a constitutional right to competence on a habeas appeal. However, it concluded that another federal statute, which deals with competency during trial proceedings, also applied to habeas appeals. The court stayed Carter's habeas proceedings indefinitely with respect to any claims that required his assistance.

The Supreme Court, in a unanimous decision, overruled the Ninth and Sixth Circuit decisions. Justice CLARENCE THOMAS, writing for the Court, concluded that the appeals courts had misapplied the federal laws in question. In the Gonzales case, the Ninth Circuit had used a law that guaranteed federal habeas petitioners

on death row the right to a federally funded lawyer. Justice Thomas pointed out that the statute did not direct district courts to stay proceedings when habeas petitioners were found incompetent. The Ninth Circuit had incorrectly reasoned that the RIGHT TO COUNSEL implied a right to competence. Prior Supreme Court rulings had made clear that the right to competence flowed from the Fifth Amendment's Due Process Clause and not from the Sixth Amendment's right to counsel provision.

Justice Thomas agreed that incompetency at trial could affect the right to counsel, such as the DEFENDANT identifying witnesses and deciding on trial strategy. Matters were much different in federal habeas proceedings, given their "backward-looking, record-based nature." He believed in most cases the inmate's lawyer provides "effective representation" regardless of the inmate's competence. Lawyers were "quite capable of reviewing the state-court record, identifying legal errors, and marshaling relevant arguments, even without their clients' assistance." Therefore, the Ninth Circuit's interpretation of the federal habeas statute provision was incorrect.

As to the Sixth Circuit's reading of the federal statute on competency in trial proceedings, Justice Thomas found it puzzling, as the statute does not apply to federal habeas proceedings. The statute applies only to trial proceedings prior to sentencing and "at any time after the commencement of PROBATION or supervised release." In contrast, federal habeas proceedings begin after sentencing, and inmates, by definition, are incarcerated rather than on probation. In addition, the statute only applies to federal defendants and probationers subject to prosecution in the **federal courts**. Carter had been convicted in Ohio state court. Therefore, he was a state prisoner challenging the basis of his conviction in a federal **civil action** for habeas relief. The statute was simply inapplicable to federal habeas proceedings.

Both Gonzales and Carter argued that federal district courts have the equitable power to stay proceedings when they determine that habeas petitioners are mentally incompetent. Justice Thomas agreed that such a power exists but declined to determine "the precise contours of the district court's discretion to issue stays." Instead, he addressed "only its outer limits." As to Gonzales, the district court correctly found that all of his claims were record based or resolvable as a MATTER OF LAW, irrespective of the inmate's competence. In addition, any evidence that Gonzales might be incompetent would be inadmissible because the record is limited to what was before the state court. The district court did not abuse its discretion in making this ruling.

In Carter's case, the district court ruled that four of his claims could potentially benefit from his assistance. However, three of the claims had been adjudicated in state postconviction proceedings. Therefore, any new evidence from Carter would be inadmissible. As to the fourth claim, the record was unclear whether it had been decided in the state court proceedings. Justice Thomas expressed concern about indefinite stays, noting that "At some point, the State must be allowed to defend its judgment of conviction." A district court could grant a stay if the petitioner's claim could "substantially benefit from the petitioner's assistance," but the court "should take into account the likelihood that the petitioner will regain competence in the foreseeable future." If there is "no reasonable hope of competence," a stay is inappropriate.

ARBITRATION

The submission of a dispute to an unbiased third person designated by the parties to the controversy, who agree in advance to comply with the award–a decision to be issued after a hearing at which both parties have an opportunity to be heard.

Oxford Health Plans v. Sutter

The U.S. SUPREME COURT has previously held, in the 2010 case of *Stolt-Nielsen v. AnimalFeeds International Corp.*, that "a party may not be compelled under the FAA [Federal ARBITRATION Act] to submit to class arbitration unless there is a contractual basis for concluding that the party *agreed* to do so." In that case, the parties' contract made no mention of class arbitration. Three years later, the Court was faced with a variation on that theme. In the case of *Oxford Health Plans v. Sutter*, 133 S. Ct. 2064 (2013), the parties *submitted* to arbitration the very question of whether their contract approved terms for class arbitration. In this case, the arbitrator's decision, whether correct or not, was not reviewable by a court because the arbitrator did not exceed his authority in interpreting the contract.

In 1986, John Sutter, a New Jersey physician, entered into a Primary Care Physicians

Agreement (PCPA) with Oxford Health Plans. Under its terms, Sutter would provide health care services for patients in Oxford's care network, and Oxford would reimburse Sutter for those services. The contract contained a general arbitration clause that stated, "No **civil action** concerning any dispute arising under this Agreement shall be instituted before any court, and all such disputes shall be submitted to final and binding arbitration in New Jersey, pursuant to the rules of the American Arbitration Association with one arbitrator." Slip Op., p. 4. As in the *Stolt-Nielsen* case, there was no explicit mention of class arbitration.

In 2002, Sutter filed suit on behalf of himself and also requesting class certification of other health care providers under the PCPA. The suit alleged breach of contract for various failures in reimbursement. Oxford moved to compel arbitration, and the court granted Oxford's motion and sent the case to arbitration.

In this case, unlike *Stolt-Nielsen*, Sutter and Oxford Health Plans both agreed to have the arbitrator decide whether their contract authorized class arbitration. The arbitrator focused on the "construction of the parties' agreement" by concentrating on the actual text (above). He concluded that it did authorize class arbitration, because it appeared to send to arbitration "the same universal class of disputes" that it barred the parties from bringing to court as "civil actions." Reasoning that a **class action** "is plainly one of the possible forms of CIVIL ACTION that could be brought in a court" but for the agreement, "on its face, the arbitration agreement clause ... expresses the parties' intent that class arbitration can be maintained." In other words, said the arbitrator, the intent of the clause was "to vest in the arbitration process everything that is prohibited from the court process."

Oxford returned to federal court and filed a motion to have the arbitrator's decision vacated, arguing that he had exceeded his authority under § 10(a)(4) of the Federal Arbitration Act (FAA). The **district court** denied the motion, and the Third **Circuit Court** of Appeals affirmed.

Meanwhile, the Supreme Court had decided *Stolt-Nielsen*. In that case, the parties had expressly stipulated that they had never reached an agreement on class arbitration. Therefore, the Court found that the arbitrators had "simply ... imposed [their] own view of sound policy" in approving class arbitration, and it vacated their decision.

Oxford next asked the arbitrator to reconsider his decision in light of *Stolt-Nielsen*. The arbitrator issued a new opinion holding that *Stolt-Nielsen* had no bearing because the parties in that case stipulated that there was no agreement on class arbitration, whereas in the present case, the parties disputed the meaning of their contract and agreed to arbitrate the question of whether class arbitration was included in their agreement.

Returning to federal district court, Oxford again tried to have the arbitrator's decision vacated, to no avail. Again, the Third Circuit affirmed. The **appellate court** emphasized that under § 10(a)(4) of the FAA, **judicial review** is strictly limited to determining whether an arbitrator exceeded his powers. If an arbitrator "makes a **good faith** attempt" to interpret a contract, his decision cannot be vacated, even if it contained "serious errors of law or fact."

The U.S. Supreme Court unanimously affirmed the Court of Appeals, further noting that under the FAA, courts may vacate arbitrators' decisions only in very unusual cases. Quoting from earlier **case law**, the Court said that if parties could take full-bore legal and evidentiary appeals, arbitration would be reduced to "merely a prelude to a more cumbersome and time-consuming JUDICIAL REVIEW process."

Here, the parties "bargained for the arbitrator's construction of their agreement." Therefore, his decision must stand, regardless of a court's view of its merits or demerits. "So," continued Justice ELENA KAGAN, writing for the majority, "the sole question for us is whether the arbitrator (even arguably) interpreted the parties' contract, not whether he got its meaning right or wrong." The Court went on to point out the "stark" differences between the present case and *Stolt-Nielsen,* including those mentioned. Quoting from *Enterprise Wheel,* 363 U.S. at 599, the Court added, "As we have held before, we hold again: 'It is the arbitrator's construction [of the contract] which was bargained for; and so far as the arbitrator's decision concerns construction of the contract, the courts have no business overruling him because their interpretation of the contract is different from his.'"

Justice SAMUEL ALITO filed a separate concurrence, joined by Justice CLARENCE THOMAS.

He added that an arbitrator may only authorize class-wide arbitration when given permission, and here, the absent plaintiffs did not consent to the arbitrator's authority. Nonetheless, said Justice Alito, Oxford Health Plans submitted to the arbitration, so the question of arbitrability cannot be raised.

ASSASSINATION

Gabrielle Giffords

The criminal case against Jared Lee Loughner, who was charged with the attempted ASSASSINATION of Arizona U.S. Representative Gabrielle "Gabbie" Giffords and the killing of six people, came to an end in August 2012, when Loughner pleaded guilty to 19 criminal counts. The plea came after the government forcibly medicated Loughner to treat his schizophrenia so that he could become mentally competent to stand trial. Though Giffords survived the shooting, she resigned from Congress in January 2012. However, in 2013 she reentered the public arena by starting a POLITICAL ACTION COMMITTEE focused on keeping guns out of the hands of criminals, terrorists, and the mentally ill.

On January 8, 2011, Giffords was conducting a constituents' meeting outside a grocery store in Casas Adobes, Arizona, a suburb of Tucson, when Loughner arrived. He opened fire on Giffords from close range and continued shooting others in crowd. He killed 6 people and wounded 13 others. Loughner was subdued by bystanders and taken into CUSTODY by police. Giffords, who had been shot in the head, was brought to a local hospital in critical condition. Doctors performed surgery to extract skull fragments from her brain and then placed her in an induced coma to allow her brain to recover. When she came out of the coma she could communicate with her hands and could move her arms. Giffords was transferred on January 21 to the Memorial Hermann Medical Center in Houston, Texas, where she underwent physical therapy, occupational therapy, and speech therapy. She was able to attend the May 16 launch of the space shuttle in Cape Canaveral, Florida. Mark Kelly, her **husband**, was a shuttle crewmember. Giffords was discharged from the medical center in mid-June but she continued to receive therapy. On August 1, she made her first public appearance on the floor of the House of Representatives, casting a vote to raise the debt ceiling. Giffords used a cane to walk and wrote with her left hand because she does not have full use of her right side due to the brain injury. The injury also robbed her of 50% of the vision in both eyes and made it difficult for her to speak and process language. On January 22, 2012, Giffords announced that she would resign her seat so she could focus on her recovery. She attended President Barack Obama's State of the Union Speech on January 24 and submitted her resignation the following day.

Legal proceedings against Loughner moved slowly. After being charged with the attempted assassination of Giffords and the MURDER of federal judge John Roll, Loughner was held in Tucson's federal prison. In light of Roll's death, all Arizona federal judges recused themselves from the case. The chief judge of the Ninth **Circuit Court** of Appeals appointed Judge Larry Burns, who was chambered in San Diego, California, to preside over the case. In March 2011, a federal **grand jury** indicted Loughner on 46 additional charges of murder and attempted murder. Loughner pleaded not guilty to all charges.

Loughner's mental competency to stand trial was questioned from the start. Two medical evaluations concluded that Loughner was suffering from paranoid schizophrenia. In May 2011, Judge Burns ruled Loughner was incompetent to stand trial. He was transferred to the U.S. Medical Center for Federal Prisoners in Springfield, Missouri to receive treatment. While at this center, Judge Burns ruled that authorities could forcibly medicate Loughner to treat his schizophrenia. Loughner's lawyer appealed this ruling and the Ninth Circuit agreed that because Loughner had not been convicted of a crime, he could refuse to take the medicine. However, the appeals court said that prison medical authorities could forcibly medicate him if the purpose was to protect the safety of prison personnel. A week after the ruling, Loughner was again forcibly given an antipsychotic drug. Authorities justified this action as a way to protect Loughner's safety and the safety of prison personnel. Loughner's lawyer again filed an appeal but in a March 2012 order, the Ninth Circuit ruled against him.

In September 2011, Loughner returned to court for a hearing on whether he was competent to stand trial. However, he was disruptive at the hearing and the judge ruled he was still not able to understand the charges against him and to assist his lawyer with his defense. Loughner remained at the Springfield medical center until August 7, 2012, when he appeared again in court. Doctors and psychologists on both sides filed evaluations on Loughner's mental state. One psychologist testified that Loughner had displayed depressive symptoms in 2006 and had been diagnosed with schizophrenia in 2011. She also testified that after a year of medication, Loughner had responded well to treatment. He understood the actions he had committed and had expressed remorse. Judge Burns ruled that Loughner was competent to stand trial but Loughner had agreed to a plea bargain. He pleaded guilty to 19 counts in exchange for the government agreeing not to pursue the death penalty. The plea agreement was approved by Giffords as well as by DEPARTMENT OF JUSTICE officials. Loughner was ordered to pay the 19 victims $1 million each and was required to forfeit any money earned by selling his story. On November 8, 2012, Judge Burns sentenced Loughner to seven consecutive life terms and an additional 140 years in prison without the possibility of PAROLE. Though the state of Arizona could have filed criminal charges against Loughner, the county attorney announced that she would not do so.

Following the December 14, 2012, mass murder of 20 children and six adults at the Sandy Hook Elementary School in Newtown, Connecticut, Giffords and Kelly returned to the public arena. In January 2013, they formed a political action committee called Americans for Responsible Solutions. The organization sought to enact tougher GUN CONTROL laws, even though both Giffords and Kelly are gun owners and believe in the SECOND AMENDMENT. Their proposed solutions include universal background checks to prevent criminals and the mentally ill from owning guns. They also endorsed limitations on the sale of high capacity magazines and **assault** weapons. Giffords testified before the SENATE JUDICIARY COMMITTEE on January 30, 2013, urging them to enact these proposals.

ATTORNEY'S FEES

Sebelius v. Cloer

The so-called "American Rule" with regard to costs of LITIGATION is that all litigants pay their own attorney's fees and costs. However, legislatures will sometimes decide to further the goals of a **statute** by requiring one party to pay the other party's costs and fees. For example, one of the common tort-reform proposals is to require the losing party to pay litigation costs for both parties (the so-called "English Rule").

When enacting the National Childhood Vaccine Injury Act of 1986 (NCVIA), 42 U.S.C. §§ 300aa-1 **et seq.**, Congress created a unique system for compensating attorneys for their fees. When the statute allows, a SPECIAL MASTER or court may award attorney's fees or costs from a government fund generated from a small tax on vaccines. The special master or court may award these fees and costs even to parties who file unsuccessful claims for compensation under the statute, so long as the parties awarded the fees and costs have not filed frivolous claims.

In *Sebelius v. Cloer*, 133 S. Ct. 1886 (2013), the Court reviewed a case involving a claimant who had filed her claim in an untimely manner. Although the Federal Circuit eventually determined that her claim was time-barred, the court held that the claimant was eligible for attorneys' fees and costs so long as the claimant brought the case in **good faith** and with a reasonable basis. In a unanimous decision, the SUPREME COURT affirmed the Federal Circuit.

Congress enacted the NCVIA in 1986 in part to stabilize the nation's vaccine market. Congress stated the purpose as follows: "The Secretary shall establish in the DEPARTMENT OF HEALTH AND HUMAN SERVICES a National Vaccine Program to achieve optimal prevention of human infectious diseases through immunization and to achieve optimal prevention against adverse reactions to vaccines. The Program shall be administered by a Director selected by the Secretary."

In previous cases, the Supreme Court has noted that Congress created a no-fault system of compensation when it enacted the NCVIA. Congress was concerned at the time with the efficiency of the civil tort system and designed the NCVIA to "work faster and with greater ease" than the general system. The Act was thus designed to compensate "injured parties after complaints mounted regarding the inefficiencies and costs borne by both injured consumers and vaccine manufacturers under the previous civil tort compensation regime."

Under § 300aa-15(e), a court or special master must award attorneys' fees and other costs that a party has incurred in any proceeding related to a petition filed pursuant to the NCVIA. The Act also states:

> If the judgment of the United States Court of Federal Claims on such a petition does not award compensation, the special master or court may award an amount of compensation to cover petitioner's reasonable attorneys' fees and other costs incurred in any proceeding on such petition if the special master or court determines that the petition was brought in GOOD FAITH and there was a reasonable basis for the claim for which the petition was brought

The case that reached the Supreme Court in 2013 involved Dr. Melissa Cloer. In 1996 and 1997, she received vaccination shots for hepatitis B. However, she soon developed symptoms for multiple sclerosis (MS). At the time of her vaccinations, the medical literature said nothing about connections between the hepatitis B shot and MS. She learned about this connection many years later at a time when her MS had progressed significantly.

She filed a claim for compensation under the NCVIA. However, her filing came more than 36 months after the first symptoms of MS had occurred. The Court of Federal Claims assigned the case to a chief special master, who determined that Cloer's claims were untimely based on the statute's 36-month limitations period. Cloer appealed the decision to a panel of the Federal Circuit, which reversed the decision. The panel decided that the clock did not start on her claim until "the medical community at large objectively recognize[d] a link between the vaccine and the injury."

The Federal Circuit then reviewed the case **en banc** and reviewed the panel's decision regarding the limitations period. The court determined that the period began to run when the first medically recognized symptom had occurred. Moreover, the court rejected other arguments raised by Cloer, including arguments based on a theory of equitable tolling. On the other hand, the court determined that even though Cloer's claim was untimely, she could still be eligible to recover fees and costs so long as she brought her claim in good faith and with a reasonable basis for her claim. *Cloer v. Secretary of Health & Human Services*, 675 F.3d 1358 (Fed. Cir. 2012).

The Supreme Court agreed to review the Federal Circuit's decision. The government argued that the Court should be reluctant to apply the provision on fees and costs broadly because Congress so rarely awards attorneys' fees to losing parties. The principal basis for the government's argument was that the provision on fees and costs only applies to "filings" and that the Court should construe a petition submitted after the limitations period as something other than a filing.

Justice SONIA SOTOMAYOR wrote for the unanimous Court, which rejected the government's arguments and affirmed the Federal Circuit's ruling. The Court reviewed the text of the statute and its use of the term "filed." In previous cases, the Court noted that an application is filed "when it is delivered to, and accepted by, the appropriate court officer for placement into the official record." Sotomayor noted, "When this ordinary meaning is applied to the text of the statute, it is clear that an NCVIA petition which is delivered to the clerk of the court, forwarded for processing, and adjudicated in a proceeding before a special master is a 'petition'" filed under the Act.

The Court determined that the Act's text did not support the government's argument. First, Congress used the term "filed" several times in the statute, but the statute does not distinguish between claims brought within the limitations period or not. Second, the government's argument would require the Court to consider Cloer's filing as something never filed at all because it was late. However, the statute repeatedly uses the word "filed" in its ordinary meaning.

The Court stated:

> The Government asks us to adopt a different definition of the term "filed" for a single subsection so that for fees purposes, and only for fees purposes, a petition filed out of time must be treated retroactively as though it was never filed in the first place. Nothing in the text or structure of the statute requires the unusual result the Government asks us to accept.

Justices CLARENCE THOMAS and ANTONIN SCALIA refused to join the Court's opinion for two parts that referred to the Act's LEGISLATIVE HISTORY.

Supreme Court Rules Plaintiff Entitled to Attorney's Fees By Obtaining Injunction

When a PLAINTIFF files a federal CIVIL RIGHTS lawsuit and prevails, the plaintiff is entitled to attorney's fees. Congress passed the Civil Rights Attorney's Fees Awards Act of 1976 for the purpose of encouraging lawyers to take on CIVIL RIGHTS CASES that might not be financially attractive. Since its enactment, the SUPREME COURT has been called on to determine in what circumstances lawyers may or may not be entitled to a fee award. In *Lefemine v. Wideman*, 133 S. Ct. 9, 184 L. Ed. 2d 313 (2012), the Court ruled that a plaintiff who was not awarded damages but obtained an INJUNCTION from the **district court** that forbade the police from arresting the plaintiff for public political protest, should be entitled to attorney's fees.

Steven Lefemine and members of Columbia Christians for Life (CCL) took part in demonstrations in which they carried photographs of aborted fetuses to protest the availability of abortions. In November 2005, Lefemine and approximately 20 other CCL members conducted a demonstration at a busy intersection in Greenwood County, South Carolina. After some residents complained about the graphic nature of the signs, a Greenwood County police officer told Lefemine that if the group did not put down their signs, Lefemine would be charged for **breach of the peace**. Lefemine objected and told the officer that he was infringing on his FIRST AMENDMENT rights. Eventually Lefemine cut the protest short and told the group to disband.

A year later, a lawyer representing Lefemine wrote a letter to Dan Wideman, the sheriff of Greenwood County. The lawyer told Wideman that CCL intended to return to the same intersection with the disputed signs. He also stated that if the police interfered again, Lefemine would "pursue all available remedies." Wideman's chief deputy responded that the police had not violated Lefemine's rights the year before and warned the lawyer that "should we observe any protester or demonstrator committing the same act, we will again conduct ourselves in exactly the same manner." Fearing sanctions by the police, CCL decided not to protest in the county for the next two years.

In October 2008, Lefemine filed a federal civil rights lawsuit against several Greenwood County police officers, claiming they had violated his First Amendment rights. He sought **nominal damages** (one dollar), a **declaratory judgment**, a permanent injunction, and attorney's fees. The South Carolina federal district court determined that the defendants had infringed on Lefemine's First Amendment rights. The court issued an injunction, permanently enjoining the defendants "from engaging in content-based restrictions on [Lefemine's] display of graphic signs." The court denied Lefemine's request for NOMINAL DAMAGES, concluding that the defendants were entitled to qualified IMMUNITY because the illegality of their conduct was not clearly established in 2005. The court also denied Lefemine attorney's fees under the Civil Rights Attorney's Fee Awards Act because under the "totality of the facts in this case the award of attorney's fees is not warranted."

Lefemine appealed the denial of attorney's fees to the Fourth **Circuit Court** of Appeals. That court upheld the district court decision on the ground that the district court's judgment did not make Lefemine a "prevailing party" under the Act. The appeals court concluded that the relief awarded to Lefemine did not alter the relative positions of the parties. The injunction prohibited only unlawful conduct by the defendants and merely "ordered [d]efendants to comply with the law and safeguard [Lefemine's] constitutional rights in the future. No other damages were awarded." Lefemine then petitioned the Supreme Court to hear his case.

The Supreme Court, in a unanimous decision, reversed the Fourth Circuit ruling. In a *per curiam* opinion, where no justice attaches his or her name to the opinion, examined the issue of who is a "prevailing party." In a previous case the Court had declared that a plaintiff "prevails" "when actual relief on the merits of his claim materially alters the legal relationship between the parties by modifying the defendant's behavior in a way that directly benefits the plaintiff." The Court also noted that it had repeatedly held that an injunction or DECLARATORY JUDGMENT will usually satisfy this test.

Turning to Lefemine's case, the Court found that under these established standards, Lefemine was a **prevailing party**. He desired to conduct demonstrations in the county with signs the police officers told him he could not carry. He brought his lawsuit in part to obtain an injunction that would protect him from the sanctions the defendants said awaited him. He succeeded in securing the injunction, which removed that threat. The district court had ruled that the defendants had violated his First Amendment rights and enjoined them from engaging in similar conduct in the future. This ruling produced the required "material

alteration in the parties' relationship." Before the ruling, the police intended to stop Lefemine from protesting with his signs. After the ruling, the police could not stop him from demonstrating. Therefore, when the district court ordered the police officers to comply with the law, the relief given supported the award of attorney's fees.

The Court pointed out that Lefemine should ordinarily recover an attorney's fee "unless special circumstances would render such an award unjust." Because neither the district court or appeals court addressed whether any special circumstances existed, the Court remanded the case to the lower courts for such a determination.

AUTOMOBILES

New Jersey Supreme Court Upholds Young Driver Sticker Law

In August 2012, the New Jersey SUPREME COURT upheld a state law requiring young drivers to place decals on their cars. Mothers of two younger drivers challenged the law on several grounds, but the state court ruled that the **statute** did not conflict with federal law nor violate either the U.S. or state constitutions.

Motor vehicle accidents cause more deaths among young men than any other cause. According to studies, these accidents account for more than 70 percent of all deaths in this age bracket. Concerns about the safety of young drivers have led lawmakers in every state to adopt graduated driver licensing laws, which phase in a young driver's privileges. These laws typically restrict young drivers from driving at night, driving with a certain number of nonparents or nondependents in the vehicle, or using wireless devices.

New Jersey's graduated-license law took effect on January 1, 2001. Under the law, a young driver first obtains a special learner's permit when the driver turns 16. Alternatively, if a driver does not obtain a license until turning 17, the driver obtains an examination permit. Once the driver has gained experience behind the wheel, the driver can apply for a probationary license. The driver must drive with the probationary license for at least 12 months before applying to receive a basic license.

In 2009, the New Jersey General Assembly approved a law that amended the statute establishing the graduated driver's license system. Under the new law, any driver who holds a special learner's permit, an examination permit, or a probationary license must display a "highly visible, reflective" decal on his or her vehicle. The law requires the chief administrator of the New Jersey Motor Vehicle Commission to issue the decals, which must be "clearly visible to law enforcement officers." In practice, state officials only require those under the age of 21 to display the decal.

Mothers of two young drivers challenged the law on several grounds. The Superior Court, Law Division, dismissed the action, and the mothers appealed. The **Appellate** Division of the Superior Court affirmed the lower court's decision, *Trautmann v. Christie*, 15 A.3d 22 (N.J. Super. 2011), and the New Jersey Supreme Court affirmed the intermediate court's decision on every ground. *Trautmann v. Christie*, 48 A.3d 1005 (N.J. 2012).

The mothers' first challenge was based on the Federal Drivers Privacy Protection Act, 18 U.S.C.A. §§ 2721–2725. This law forbids state motor vehicle departments to disclose or otherwise make available any driver's "personal information" or "highly restricted personal information" except in limited circumstances. The mothers argued that the federal law preempted the state law, alleging that the state law required drivers to reveal personal information in the form of the drivers' ages (i.e., under 21).

The APPELLATE Division rejected the mother's **preemption** argument, finding that Congress did not intend to restrict motor vehicle departments from revealing drivers' ages. The court wrote: "As a matter of common usage and ordinary understanding, a person's age group does not identify an individual. It identifies the person as a member of a large segment of the population." The court distinguished information identifying a driver's age with other personal information, such as the driver's name, address, telephone number, photograph, SOCIAL SECURITY number, or driver's identification number. The supreme court agreed with the lower court in rejecting the mothers' PREEMPTION argument.

The mothers also argued that the New Jersey law violated the **Equal Protection** Clause of the U.S. Constitution and the similar provision in the New Jersey Constitution.

According to the mothers, the statute treats in-state drivers differently from a class of other similar drivers, including drivers from other states. In other words, a younger driver who received a license in New Jersey must display the decal, while a younger driver who received a license from another state does not have to display the decal.

Both appellate courts likewise rejected this argument. The courts analyzed the issue under a rational-basis standing, meaning that the court had to uphold the law if the law were "rationally related to a legitimate government interest." Similarly, under the state constitution, the courts had to uphold the law if they determined that "there is an appropriate governmental interest suitably furthered by a differential treatment involved."

Both courts found that the state had a sufficient interest protected by the statute. The Appellate Division wrote: "The governmental interest furthered by enforcement of the system of restricted driving privileges established by the [graduated driver's license system, or GDLS] is safety on the roadways of this State. The decals which must be used by young drivers subject to the GDLS restrictions are a suitable means of furthering that interest. It would serve no purpose at all to impose the same obligation on young drivers licensed elsewhere who are not subject to the GDLS."

The state supreme court agreed, finding that the state decal law provided an enforcement mechanism for the state's graduated driver's license system. Because the decal system was rationally related to a legitimate government interest, the court upheld the law as constitutional.

The mothers' final challenge was based on the federal and state constitutions' prohibitions against unreasonable searches and seizures. According to both appellate courts, young drivers do not have a reasonable expectation of privacy regarding their age group. The Supreme Court noted that "a driver's age group can generally be determined by his or her physical appearance, which is routinely exposed to public view."

In January 2013, a group of researchers from the Children's Hospital of Philadelphia published the results of a study addressing the effect the decal law has had on the safety of young drivers. The study showed that the law resulted in a 14 percent increase in citations given to younger drivers during a one-year period. On the other hand, crashes among drivers in the age group affected by the New Jersey law fell by 9 percent. The researchers concluded that a total of 1,624 young people were not involved in crashes because of the new law.

The authors wrote: "These findings suggest that New Jersey's novel decal law is positively affecting the safety of probationary drivers, even with less-than-ideal driver compliance with [graduated driver's license, or GDL] restrictions and the decal law itself. Further, the fact that significant crash reductions were observed in New Jersey, a state that already has a strong GDL law and one of the lowest teen crash fatality rates, suggests that implementation of a decal law in states with higher teen crash fatality rates may lead to more marked reductions."

The study was published in the *American Journal of Preventive Medicine*.

Seventh Circuit Rules Parking Ticket Violates Federal Privacy Law

Congress passed the Driver's Privacy Protection Act (DPPA) in 1994, restricting the ability of STATE DEPARTMENTS OF MOTOR VEHICLES (DMVs) to disclose certain personal information contained in motor vehicles. Authorized recipients, such as law enforcement agencies, were further restricted in redisclosing information obtained from those records. If a person's information is disclosed illegally, the person may sue the violator for actual damages, but not less than $2,500 in **liquidated damages**. The Seventh Circuit, in *Senne v. Village of Palatine, Illinois*, 695 F.3d 597 (2012), ruled that a village could be held liable under the act for a parking citation placed on a motorist's automobile that revealed personal information in violation of the DPPA.

In August 2010, Jason Senne parked his vehicle overnight on a street in Palatine, Illinois, which violated a village **ordinance**. At 1:35 a.m., a village police officer placed a parking citation under a windshield wiper blade. The citation remained on the windshield, in public view, until Senne retrieved it around 6:30 a.m. The ticket had been printed electronically on a form. The printed information included a date and time stamp, the officer's name and badge number and the parking offense, which was

the basis for the citation. It also included information on the motor vehicle. However, it also included personal data about Senne, including his full name, address, driver's license number, date of birth, sex, height, and weight. The citation doubled as an envelope to remit payment of the fine. If used as an envelope, Senne's personal information would have been displayed on the outside.

Senne filed a lawsuit in federal **district court**, alleging that the parking ticket amounted to a disclosure by the village that violated the DPPA. He requested LIQUIDATED DAMAGES and injunctive relief for himself and others who had received these citation forms. The village asked the court to dismiss the case, arguing that the DPPA permitted this type of disclosure on the citation. The court agreed that the parking ticket was not a disclosure under the law. Senne appealed to the Seventh Circuit.

The full panel of the Seventh Circuit, in a 7-4 decision, overruled the district court, finding that the ticket was a disclosure regulated by the DPPA. Judge Kenneth Ripple, writing for the majority, acknowledged that the **statute** did not define a disclosure. However, the act did provide "sufficient information to discern the meaning of the term." The term "disclose" was first used in a subsection that forbids a state DMV from "knowingly disclos[ing] or otherwise mak[ing] available to any person or entity" protected personal information. According to Judge Ripple, this phrase left "little doubt about the breadth of the transactions Congress intended to regulate." It was clear to the appeals court that Congress intended to include with the DPPA's reach the kind of information published on the citation left on Senne's windshield. Placing the citation on the automobile in plain view on a public street was "certainly sufficient" to come within the scope of the law, regardless of whether another person viewed the information or whether the police officer intended it to be viewed only by Senne himself.

Judge Ripple, having determined that there was a disclosure, then examined whether the police department's disclosure of Senne's motor vehicle record violated the DPPA. The law contains a list of permissible uses of motor vehicle information. Permissive disclosures cover an array of purposes and recipients, including public entities, insurers, licensed private investigators, and commercial users such as bulk marketers. The village argued that the placement of the citation on the windshield was permitted either because the statute allows disclosure for use by a law enforcement agency or for use in connection with any civil or administrative proceeding, including the **service of process**. It did not describe how all the information printed on the ticket served either purpose because it did not believe the statute required that type of analysis. As long as the village could identify a subsection of the law under which some disclosure was permitted, any disclosure of information otherwise protected by the DPPA was exempt, whether it served an identified purpose or not.

The court rejected the village's position. The statute's purpose was to "prevent all but a limited range of authorized disclosures of information contained in individual motor vehicle records." The use of the words "for use" in both of the exceptions cited by the village performed a "critical function in the statute and contain the necessary limiting principle that preserves the force of the general PROHIBITION while permitting the disclosures compatible with that prohibition." Apart from the analysis of the **statutory** language, the court reviewed the LEGISLATIVE HISTORY of the DPPA.

From that review the court concluded, "safety and security concerns associated with excessive disclosures of personal information held by the State in motor vehicle records were the primary issue to be remedied by the legislation." Witnesses testified before Congress about this information being used by stalkers and the impact these disclosures of DMV records had on DOMESTIC VIOLENCE victims and law enforcement officers and their families.

Judge Ripple then applied the court's understanding of the DPPA to Senne's case. The court concluded that neither "for use" exception clearly applied to the information disclosed on the parking citation. With respect to the disclosure of some of the information, the court found it "difficult to conceive, even on a theoretical level, how such information could play a role in the excepted law enforcement purposes." Because the district court had improperly analyzed and applied the DPPA, the court remanded the case for further proceedings. The district was to apply the principles developed by the appeals court to Senne's case. The placement of the citation with protected personal information in view of the public constituted a disclosure under the statute, "regardless of whether Mr. Senne can establish that anyone actually viewed it."

BANKRUPTCY

A federally authorized procedure by which a debtor–an individual, corporation, or municipality–is relieved of total liability for its debts by making court-approved arrangements for their partial repayment.

Bullock v. BankChampaign

In *Bullock v. BankChampaign,* No. 133 S. Ct. 1754 (2013), the U.S. SUPREME COURT was asked to consider and describe the scope of the term "defalcation" in BANKRUPTCY law. Section 523(a)(4) of the Federal Bankruptcy Code declares that an individual cannot obtain a bankruptcy discharge of a debt "for **fraud** or **defalcation** while acting in a **fiduciary** capacity, **embezzlement**, or larceny." 11 U.S.C. § 523(a)(4). A unanimous Court held that the term includes a CULPABLE state of mind requirement "as one involving knowledge of, or gross recklessness in respect to, the improper nature of the relevant FIDUCIARY behavior."

In 1978, the father of petitioner Randy Curtis Bullock set up a trust for the benefit of his five children. He also named his son Randy as **trustee**. The trust contained a single asset, which was a life insurance policy. The trust instrument did allow the trustee to borrow funds against the insurance policy's value at an interest rate determined by the insurer.

Over the next several years, three loans were taken out against the policy's value, but all were repaid in full, along with interest. The first was at the request of the trustor, Randy's father, who wanted Randy's mother to repay a debt against the family business. The second involved Randy and his mother, who used the funds to pay for certificates of deposit, which in turn were used to buy a mill. The third, in 1990, again involved Randy and his mother, who used the funds to purchase real property for themselves.

Years later, in 1999, Randy's siblings sued him in Illinois state court for breach of fiduciary duty. The state court agreed, but noted that Randy "[did] not appear to have had a malicious motive in borrowing funds from the trust" but nonetheless "was clearly involved in self-dealing." The state court ordered Randy to pay the trust "the benefits he received from his breaches" (along with costs and attorney's fees). In order to secure payment for this judgment, the state court imposed constructive trusts on Randy's interest in the mill and his interest in the trust. Randy was removed as trustee of his father's trust, and BankChampaign was appointed to serve as trustee for all the trusts.

Randy then attempted to **liquidate** his interests in the mill and constructive trusts, in order to pay the court-ordered judgment, but was unable to. He then filed for bankruptcy in federal court.

In federal bankruptcy court, trustee BankChampaign opposed Randy's efforts to get the state court's judgment discharged, because that judgment was to be paid back into the trusts. The bankruptcy court agreed and granted **summary judgment** in BankChampaign's favor. It found that it could not discharge the SUMMARY JUDGMENT debt because of the above-cited § 523(a)(4), which excepts from discharge any debt "for defalcation while acting in a fiduciary capacity."

Reviewable in federal **district court**, the bankruptcy court's determination was affirmed, although the federal court said in its opinion that it was "convinced" BankChampaign was "abusing its power of trust by failing to liquidate the assets." The Eleventh **Circuit Court** of Appeals also affirmed. Its opinion held that "defalcation requires a known breach of a fiduciary duty, such that the conduct can be characterized as objectively reckless." The **appellate court** found that Randy's conduct satisfied that standard.

Randy Bullock appealed to the U.S. Supreme Court, effectively asking whether "defalcation" applied "in the absence of any specific finding of ill intent or evidence of an ultimate loss of trust principal." The Supreme Court accepted review, as it had long been debated among courts, with varying outcomes, as to whether defalcation included a **scienter** requirement, and if so, what kind of SCIENTER was required.

Justice STEPHEN BREYER delivered the opinion for a unanimous Court. It first noted that Congress included the term "defalcation" as an exception to bankruptcy debt discharge in 1867, but "legal authorities have disagreed about its meaning almost ever since." The Court then clarified that it would only address the confusion over the requisite state of mind (scienter) that accompanied the term, and would assume, and not decide, whether the term was broad enough to reach Randy's alleged conduct as a trustee who failed to "make a trust more than whole."

In answering the question about necessary state of mind, the Court reviewed dictionary meanings (to no avail), prior **case law**, and customary uses of the term, ultimately returning to Court precedent. Of particular import was the 1878 case of *Neal v. Clark,* 95 U.S. 704, in which Justice JOHN HARLAN interpreted the term "fraud" within the context of exceptions to discharge in bankruptcy court:

> [D]ebts created by "fraud" are associated directly with debts created by "embezzlement." Such association justifies, if it does not imperatively require, the conclusion that

the "fraud" referred to in that section means positive FRAUD, or fraud in fact, involving **moral turpitude** or intentional wrong, as does embezzlement; and not implied fraud, or fraud in law, which may exist without the imputation of **bad faith** or immorality.

"We believe that the **statutory** term 'defalcation' should be treated similarly," concluded the 2013 Court in *Bullock.* Thus, continued the Court, "where the conduct at issue does not involve bad faith, MORAL TURPITUDE, or other immoral conduct, the term requires an intentional wrong. We include as intentional not only conduct that the fiduciary knows is improper but also reckless conduct of the kind that the **criminal law** often treats as the equivalent." The Court then vacated the judgment of the court of appeals and remanded the case "to permit the court to determine whether further proceedings are needed and, if so, to apply the heightened standard that we have set forth."

Dewey & LeBoeuf Law Firm Files for Chapter 11 Bankruptcy

In the wake of the 2008 recession, many law firms across the country found themselves struggling for revenue. But perhaps none was more noteworthy than the 2012 filing for Chapter 11 BANKRUPTCY of one of the largest law firms in the nation, Dewey & LeBoeuf. Formed in 2007 after a merger of Dewey Ballantine and LeBoeuf, Lamb, Green & MacRae, the new firm boasted about 1,450 attorneys at its peak, according to the *National Law Journal.* It rendered worldwide services from two dozen offices, including New York, Washington, Los Angeles, London, and Paris. Clients included General Motors Corp., Novartis, and eBay. Just a year before, in 2011, the *American Lawyer* had ranked it fifth among the largest law firms for its commitment to **pro bono** work (public legal services without compensation). With Chapter 11 bankruptcy protection, the firm sought to **liquidate** its business in an organized manner with the least legal sequelae. In the end, according to the firm's December 31, 2012, "Amended Confirmation Plan Disclosure Statement," unsecured creditors would get approximately 5 to 15 cents on the dollar.

The bankruptcy filing followed an earlier failed attempt to find another merging partner. But instead of merging, Dewey & LeBoeuf (Dewey) found itself struggling with the loss of more than 160 of its nearly 300 partners to other firms, as news of compensation troubles and liquidity constraints surfaced. According to Reuters News Service, Dewey reported that negative economic conditions coupled with the firm's partnership compensation arrangements created the perfect storm, where its cash flow could no longer cover capital expenses and full compensation expectations.

That was putting it mildly, according to former partner Henry Bunsow, who filed the first lawsuit against the firm in California Superior Court in June 2012. The suit named five former members of Dewey's management team as defendants (plus several John Does), alleging they misrepresented Dewey's financial performance and stability in order to recruit top lawyers from other firms. Bunsow alleged in his complaint that defendants used the capital (investment) brought in by newly recruited partners to compensate favored partners at the firm, rather than use it for the benefit of the firm. In effect, they were "running a **Ponzi scheme** in order to enrich themselves and select partners of the firm," the complaint stated. Among the defendants was former chairman Steven Davis, who was removed after New York prosecutors began investigating "financial irregularities" at the firm. Other named defendants included former chief financial officer (CFO) Joel Sanders, former executive director Stephen DiCarmine, former office of the chairman member Jeffrey Kessler, and former executive committee member James Woods.

Bunsow painted a picture of financial excess for the chosen few within the firm's ranks. According to allegations contained in the complaint, Bunsow claimed he was guaranteed $5 million per year when he joined the firm in January 2011. At that time, he alleged, Dewey promised 2011 profits would be roughly $2 million per equity partner, which factored heavily in his decision. However, the complaint continued, Dewey failed to mention that at that time it already owed select partners about $300 million in promised compensation and bonuses stemming from previous years. The suit alleged that Bunsow lost $7.5 million in damages including capital he invested in the firm, and guaranteed compensation/benefits from 2011 and 2012.

According to Reuters, Steven Davis did inform, during a January 2012 partnership meeting, that 2011 profits would be roughly

$250 million, but that at least half of that amount was already committed to **pension** obligations and promises to partners for shortcomings in prior years' earnings. He reportedly told the partners that they would have to "own" the problem.

It is also taken as true, based on the firm's July 2012 "Statement of Financial Affairs," that a select cluster of partners continued to receive millions of dollars in compensation during this rough period. Overall, during the final five months prior to the bankruptcy filing, 25 Dewey partners received $21 million. In the last seven months of 2011, they had pocketed $49 million among themselves.

In February 2013, U.S. Bankruptcy Judge Martin Glenn approved a **liquidation** plan for the firm. *In re: Dewey & LeBoeuf LLP, Debtor*, No. 12-12321 (MG), U.S. Bankruptcy Court for the Southern District of New York. The plan included a "clawback settlement," wherein former Dewey partners agreed to pay $71.5 million back to the firm's estate, in exchange for IMMUNITY from LITIGATION. The partners in question each were to pay between $5,000 and $3.5 million. More than 450 former partners opted into the **settlement**.

Additionally, in April 2013, former chairman Davis, still under criminal investigation, agreed to pay more than $500,000 to Dewey's **trustee** in bankruptcy and insurer to settle civil charges that mismanagement led to the prestigious firm's fall from grace. In return, XL Specialty Insurance Co., which issued Dewey's management liability insurance policy, would contribute $19 million in the proposed settlement. Former CFO Joel Sanders and former executive director Stephen DiCarmine were not included in the settlement, and the trustee reserved the right to pursue nonsettled claims against them.

BIRTH CONTROL

Missouri Birth Control Law Struck by Federal Court

In March 2013, U.S. **District Court** Judge Audrey Fleissig struck down Missouri's SENATE Bill 749, requiring health care insurers to issue policies without contraception coverage if individuals or their employers objected, based on religious, ethical, or moral beliefs. The bill itself represented a contentious override by

Missouri's legislature, in September 2012, of State Governor Jay Dixon's earlier (July 2012) VETO of the "religious liberty" bill.

As background, in June 2012, the U.S. SUPREME COURT upheld the BARACK OBAMA administration's Patient Protection and Affordable Care Act of 2010 (ACA), part of which required new private health plans written on or after August 1, 2012, to include coverage for contraceptive counseling and services, without cost-sharing, to insureds. However, the U.S. DEPARTMENT OF HEALTH AND HUMAN SERVICES (DHHS) also promulgated regulations that exempted the contraceptives mandate for "religious employers." 45 C.F.R. § 147.130(a)(1)(iv)(B). Moreover, back in February 2012 (prior to the Court's decision upholding the law), President Obama announced a temporary (until August 2013) "safe harbor" accommodation (against prosecution for failure to comply) to deal with "conscience claims" of certain religious organizations not deemed to be "religious employers" under the regulation(s).

This mandate took effect in January 2013. It exempted existing plans that did not make significant changes to coverage—for example, cutting benefits or raising cost-sharing provisions—although DHHS projected that most would lose protected status within a few years.

As all this was happening, the Missouri Republican-controlled legislature, via Senate Bill 749, attempted to amend Mo. Rev. Stat. 376.1199 (2001), which already exempted religious entities, to now include individuals or employers who objected because of religious or moral beliefs. Referring to it as a "religious liberty bill," it hoped to ensure that no one would be forced to pay for contraceptive drugs or methods in their health insurance policies, if it violated their "moral, ethical, or religious beliefs." Vetoed by Missouri Governor Dixon in July 2012, the measure went back to the legislature, which then held a special veto session on September 12, where the governor's veto was overridden.

Meanwhile, the federal case was brought by insurance carriers, worried about being caught between federal and state laws. But Judge Fleissig's ruling found the state law was "in conflict with, and preempted by, existing federal law" under the U.S. Constitution's **Supremacy Clause** ("This Constitution, and the Laws of the United States in Pursuance thereof … shall be the supreme LAW OF THE LAND; and the Judges in every State shall be bound thereby, any Thing in the Constitution or Laws of any State to the Contrary notwithstanding"). Siding with the insurers, she noted that the state law "could force health insurers to risk fines and penalties by choosing between compliance with state or federal law." Prior to her final ruling in March 2013, she had issued a TEMPORARY RESTRAINING ORDER against the law in December 2012. "The Republican effort to deny contraceptive coverage cannot be supported by **case law** or sound public policy," she later ruled.

One month after the judge's ruling, Missouri Attorney General Chris Koster announced that he would not appeal the order. He did ask the court to amend the order to maintain the right for religious employers that are currently exempt under federal law.

The Guttmacher Institute reported that, as of June 1, 2013, 28 states had their own laws requiring insurers to comply with the mandate. But 20 states had laws that permitted certain employers and insurers to refuse to comply with the federal mandate, all of them variations on the extent of religious objection. Three states limit exemption to churches and church associations but require hospitals and other entities to comply. Seven states have a broader clause exempting not only churches and associations but also religiously affiliated schools and, potentially, some religious charities, but not hospitals. Nine states expand further to include some hospitals, and one state further exempts secular organizations with moral or religious objections. Nevada does not exempt employers but allows religious insurers to refuse coverage.

Sixth Circuit Upholds Ohio Law Limiting Abortion Medication

Until 2000, women who wished to end their pregnancy had to undergo a surgical ABORTION. That changed in 2000, when the FOOD AND DRUG ADMINISTRATION (FDA) approved the use of a drug that induces abortion. Since then an estimated one million women have used this method. The drug regimen known as RU-486 requires a woman to take two types of medications. Since 2000, Planned Parenthood has used RU-486 at its clinics, but it has modified the dosage and means of taking the medicine that the FDA put in place when it approved the drugs. Such a modification is legal under federal law. Opponents of abortion have enacted laws in several states that require the drugs to be administered under the original FDA requirements. The Sixth **Circuit Court** of Appeals, in *Planned Parenthood Southwest Ohio Region v. DeWine*, 696 F.3d 490 (2012), ruled that an Ohio **statute** that mandated these FDA requirements was constitutional.

In 2004, Ohio passed a law criminalizing the distribution of mifepristone, known as RU-486, unless the distribution mirrored certain protocols and gestational time limits identified by the FDA when mifepristone was first approved in 2000. Mifepristone, in combination with misoprostol, was the only form of medical abortion offered by Planned Parenthood in Ohio. RU-486 is a medication that terminates pregnancy by detaching the gestational sac from the uterine wall. Approximately 24 to 48 hours later, the woman takes misoprostol, which induces the contractions necessary to expel the fetus from the uterus. The mortality rate of mifepristone abortions is less than one per 100,000. Under the FDA's 2000 labeling requirement, the patient was to be given 600 mg of mifepristone followed by 0.4 mg of misoprostol administered orally two days later and the mifepristone could not be administered after 49 days of gestation.

Following FDA approval, additional clinical trials led to the development of new protocols for administering the drugs. One protocol called for 200 mg of mifepristone administered orally, followed one to three days later by 0.8 mg of misoprostol administered vaginally. In addition, the drugs could be administered up to 63 days of gestation. This new protocol, called the Schaff protocol, reduced the dosage of the drugs and number of days between drugs and changed the administration of misoprostol. A woman could take it vaginally at home, rather than taking it orally in a clinic. Planned Parenthood adopted this protocol at its Ohio clinics. Once a drug has been approved, the FDA does not ban the type of "off-label use" that Planned Parenthood used in its clinics. It is standard medical practice in the United States for doctors to prescribe FDA-approved drugs in dosages and for medical indications that were not approved or contemplated by the FDA. However, states may limit off-label use. This is what Ohio did when it passed the law that criminalized the use of the Schaff protocol.

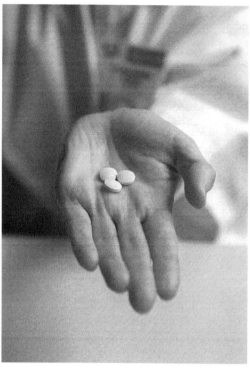

RU-486 was the focus of a 2012 suit that sought to overturn an Ohio law that limits administration of the drug to protocols mandated by the FDA.
MANOOCHER DEGHATI/ AFP/GETTY IMAGES

Shortly after the act passed in 2004, Planned Parenthood of Ohio sued the state in federal court, seeking an INJUNCTION that would prohibit the enforcement of the law. Planned Parenthood argued that the law was unconstitutional for four independent reasons, claiming it was vague, that it violated a woman's right to bodily integrity, that it imposed an undue burden on a woman's right to choose an abortion, and that it failed to adequately protect a woman's health and life. The **district court** ultimately ruled that the law was not unconstitutional as to the first three constitutional claims and dismissed those claims. As to the whether the law failed to adequately protect a woman's health and life, the court held that this claim should proceed to trial. However, it stayed the proceeding until the Sixth Circuit heard Planned Parenthood's appeal of the first three claims.

A three-judge panel of the Sixth Circuit voted 2-1 to uphold the district court's ruling denying an injunction on the three constitutional claims. Judge Karen Nelson Moore first examined whether the statute was unconstitutionally vague. The statute did not define the term "federal law" but the state argued that the term meant requiring compliance with the FDA requirements on the final printed labeling. This was confirmed by the Ohio SUPREME COURT, which responded to certified questions from the federal court by stating that the drug could only be administered through the woman's 49th day of pregnancy and at the dosage indications and treatment protocols expressly approved by the FDA in the drug's final printed labeling. Judge Moore concluded that in light of this "explicit interpretation" of the law, any facial vagueness concerns had been resolved.

As to the bodily-integrity claim, the appeals court pointed out that under the **substantive due process** clause of the FOURTEENTH AMENDMENT, "individuals possess a constitutional right to be free from forcible physical intrusions of their bodies against their will, absent a compelling state interest." Planned Parenthood contended that the law was similar to a forcible intrusion because a woman who desired a medical abortion between 50 and 63 days was "forced" to undergo surgery due to the unavailability of mifepristone during those days. Judge Moore rejected this claim because the Supreme Court had made clear that abortion regulations were to be analyzed under an undue-burden framework and not under the physical intrusion framework. A woman was not "forced" to have a surgical abortion. If that was "so undesirable as to make the woman choose to have no abortion at all, the undue-burden framework remains the appropriate remedy for addressing that concern."

Turning to the undue-burden claim, the court divided, with Judge Moore dissenting from her colleagues, believing there was an undue burden. Judge David McKeague, writing for the majority, concluded that the law did not impose an undue burden on a woman's ability to make the decision to have an abortion. The ban on medical abortions from 50-to-63 days of gestation was constitutional because it did not operate as a substantial obstacle to a woman's choice to have an abortion. Medical abortion was the preferred method for approximately 31% to whom it was available. While Planned Parenthood had submitted affidavits from women saying they preferred a medical abortion, all of the women proceeded to obtain a surgical abortion. The right to have an abortion was the "freedom to decide whether to terminate" a pregnancy. The Supreme Court had not extended this right to a woman's preferred method of terminating a pregnancy. As to the requirement that doctors followed FDA dosage requirements, Planned Parenthood argued that there would be a significant increase in the cost of a medical abortion due to the increased dosage of mifepristone. Judge McKeague noted that before the passage of the law, medical and surgical abortions were offered at the same price. Therefore, "unless the cost of surgical abortion is independently raised, the alleged cost of medical abortion would make surgical abortion a less-expensive option." The added cost of a medical abortion did not unduly burden the right to choose abortion "for a large fraction of affected women." Based on this conclusion, the court rejected the undue-burden claim.

CAPITAL PUNISHMENT

The lawful infliction of death as a punishment; the death penalty.

Arkansas Supreme Court Strikes Down State Execution Law

States that employ the death penalty have moved away from electrocution as the standard method of execution and have adopted the use of lethal injections of chemicals as the preferred method. The Arkansas state legislature passed the Method of Execution Act of 2008 (MEA), which gave the executive branch the authority to use lethal injections but did not specify what types of chemicals should be used. A death row inmate challenged the constitutionality of the law, arguing that the MEA's delegation of the precise chemicals to be used to the executive branch violated the separation-of-powers doctrine in Article IV of the Arkansas Constitution. The Arkansas SUPREME COURT, in *Hobbs v. Jones,* 212 Ark. 293 (2012), agreed with the inmate and struck down the law.

Jack Harold Jones was incarcerated on Arkansas's death row. He filed suit against Ray Hobbs, in his official capacity as director of the state's department of correction, alleging that the MEA was unconstitutional. Jones, who was scheduled to be executed on March 16, 2010, argued that under a recent Arkansas Supreme Court ruling, the MEA retroactively applied to currently incarcerated death row inmates. Nine other death-row inmates joined Jones's lawsuit and all asked that their execution dates be put on hold and that the court strike down the MEA. The trial court granted a **preliminary injunction** and ultimately found the MEA unconstitutional based on SEPARATION OF POWERS. It struck a portion of the law but preserved the remainder.

The Arkansas Supreme Court, in a 5-2 decision, upheld the trial court's reasoning but struck down the entire law. Justice Jim Gunter, writing for the majority, noted that the state believed the MEA could be applied so as to fully comport with the PROHIBITION on **cruel and unusual punishment** in both the federal and state constitutions. The state also contended the doctrine of separation of powers was not violated where the legislature "merely makes law and then confers authority or discretion with regard to execution of that law to the executive branch." Finally, it argued that because the state constitution was silent on which branch of government possessed the power to determine the precise conditions to carry out a criminal sentence, the legislature may delegate that power to the executive branch. In this case, the legislature did just that with the MEA, while giving significant guidance to the executive branch in how to accomplish that general purpose. The inmates, while agreeing with the trial court's decision that the MEA violated the separation-of-powers doctrine, argued that the trial judge erred by striking a portion. They believed that because the MEA provided no guidance for the department of correction in carrying out lethal-injection executions and allowed the department unfettered discretion in choosing the chemicals to be use and developing policies and procedures for administering lethal injection, it was an unconstitutional delegation of legislative power.

Justice Gunter stated that the inmates had the burden of proving the law was unconstitutional. The state constitution's separation-of-powers provision divided the powers into the legislative, executive, and judicial branches. It further stated that no department "shall exercise any power belonging to either of the others, except in the instances hereinafter expressly directed or permitted." Justice Gunter noted that although the court had held on many occasions that the legislature could not delegate its power to proclaim the law to the executive or judicial branches, the court had recognized that it could delegate discretionary authority to the other branches. The key issue was whether the MEA bestowed "an absolute, unregulated, and undefined discretion" on the department of correction. If so, the law bestowed "arbitrary powers and is an unlawful delegation of legislative powers." The MEA directed that the sentence of death be carried out by lethal injection of one or more chemicals, "as determined in kind and amount in the discretion of the Director of the Department of Correction." The **statute** listed specific chemicals that may be injected but also included a clause that stated "Any other chemical or chemicals, including but not limited to saline injection."

The court found that under the MEA the department had absolute discretion to determine the chemicals to be used for lethal injection. The list of chemicals included in the law was not mandatory. The use of the word "may" as employed implied "permissive or discretionary action or conduct." In addition, the list of chemicals was not exhaustive and included an option to select any other chemical or chemicals. Justice Gunter reasoned that the use of the word "may" in conjunction with a list of chemicals that is unlimited did not provide reasonable guidance to the department. The MEA gave the department "the power to decide all the facts and all the contingencies with no reasonable guidance given absent the generally permissive use of one or more chemicals." The

state argued that the bar on cruel and **unusual punishment** in the federal and state constitutions acted as a supplement to the **statutory** language found in the MEA. Justice Gunter disagreed. The central question was whether the legislature provided sufficient guidance.

The court concluded that the legislature had "abdicated its responsibility and passed to the executive branch the unfettered discretion to determine all protocol and procedures, most notably the chemicals to be used for a state execution." Therefore, the MEA was unconstitutional on its face. The next issue was whether the trial court's decision to remove a portion of the language dealing with chemicals corrected the constitutional issue. The court found that this decision to **excise** the clause "any other chemical or chemicals, including but not limited to" was incorrect. Even with the removal of the language, the department still had complete discretion in choosing the chemicals to be used. The statute was not severable because the MEA contained a single purpose: "to provide the procedures, or methods, by which the State may execute a DEFENDANT who was convicted of a capital offense and sentenced to death by lethal injection." The sections of the MEA were "interrelated and dependent" upon each other and the legislature had not included a severability clause, which suggested the legislature intended to pass the act as whole. Therefore, the court declared th entirety of the MEA unconstitutional.

Ninth Circuit Orders Idaho to Provide Full Media Access to Executions

Though the general public does not have access to executions, the press have a FIRST AMENDMENT right to be present as surrogates for the public. For example, the Ninth **Circuit Court** of Appeals in 2002 issued a decision that stated this requirement, insisting the public had a right to view executions from the moment the condemned was brought into the execution chambers, including those "initial procedures" that were "inextricably intertwined with the process of putting the condemned inmate to death." However, the state of Idaho refused to comply with this decision and prevented the press from viewing the proceedings until after the inmate was brought into the chamber and had intravenous lines inserted into his body. A coalition of media corporations sued the state for full access according to the Ninth Circuit ruling. In *Associated Press v. Otter*, 682 F.3d 821 (2012), the court reaffirmed its earlier ruling, concluding that none of the reasons offered by Idaho withstood constitutional scrutiny.

The media coalition asked the state to alter its execution procedure prior to the November 2011 execution of Paul Rhoades. The state failed to change the law in the days prior to the Rhoades execution and afterwards. The coalition filed suit against the state after Idaho set an execution date for Richard Leavitt. The plaintiffs argued that, as surrogates for the public, they had a right to witness all stages of the executions conducted by the state of Idaho. The state's refusal to allow such access violated the First Amendment. They asked the federal **district court** to issue a **preliminary injunction**, because without it they would be irreparably damaged by the denial of their right to view Leavitt's execution in its entirety. The district court rejected the plaintiffs' request for the INJUNCTION, leading them to appeal to the Ninth Circuit.

A three-judge panel of the Ninth Circuit unanimously reversed the district court decision. Judge Stephen Reinhardt, writing for the court, noted that a PLAINTIFF seeking a PRELIMINARY INJUNCTION must establish four elements: the likelihood the plaintiff will succeed on the merits; the likelihood the plaintiff will suffer irreparable harm if the injunction is not issued; whether or not the balance of equities tips in the plaintiff's favor; and whether or not the issuing of the injunction is in the PUBLIC INTEREST. The appeals court can only reverse a district court's denial of a preliminary injunction if the court abused its discretion in making its legal analysis. Based on these legal requirements, the appeals court concluded that the district court had abused its discretion with respect to each of the four elements the plaintiffs had to establish.

Judge Reinhardt found that the media coalition was quite likely to succeed on the merits of its First Amendment claim. The only issue as to the merits of the case was whether Idaho had asserted "legitimate penological interests sufficient" to overcome the First Amendment right of access declared by the Ninth Circuit in its 2002 decision. Idaho claimed that its interests were in protecting the dignity of condemned prisoners and the sensibilities of their families and fellow inmates.

The court rejected this assertion, finding that the state had failed to explain why the "modest expansion of witness access to include the insertion of intravenous lines would meaningfully affect them." Judge Reinhardt noted that the state already offended these sensibilities by allowing strangers to watch the execution. Idaho also claimed that it had an interest in preserving the anonymity of medical team members who participated in the execution. If doctors believed they would be more likely to be identified, they might not participate. Though this was a more substantial interest, the court found that the state had offered only speculation as to whether full access would make it unable to recruit and retain medical team members. Moreover, medical team members could use surgical garb to protect their identity. Because neither interest was sufficient, the plaintiffs satisfied the first element of the standard.

As to whether the plaintiffs had shown that they would suffer irreparable harm if they failed to gain a preliminary injunction, Judge Reinhardt ruled that the district court had abused its discretion. The district court concluded that witnesses would still see most of the execution process and that there would likely be other executions in the future. As to the first conclusion, the appeals court cited its 2002 decision as controlling: the press must see the execution from beginning to end. The second conclusion was incorrect because it ignored the rule that the loss of First Amendment freedoms for even short periods of time "unquestionably constitutes irreparable injury." The fact that the press might be able to observe future Idaho executions did not mean that they were unharmed "by the denial of their right to observe *this* execution."

The court then balanced the equities of issuing a preliminary injunction. The district court believed that an injunction would delay Leavitt's execution. Judge Reinhardt found that there was "minimal chance" Leavitt would secure a stay of execution if the injunction were issued. The appeals court did not see how making minimal changes to the procedure would require the state to alter its training procedures. Finally, Idaho's claim that members of the medical team might decline to participate in Leavitt's execution was no more than speculation.

As to the fourth element, the court had "no doubt that the entry of a preliminary injunction promotes the public interest." Courts have consistently recognized the significant public interest in upholding First Amendment principles when considering requests for preliminary injunctions. The district court's reliance on the public interest in the timely enforcement of criminal judgments "lacks any weight in light of our conclusion that no delay will occur." The appeals ordered the district court to issue the preliminary injunction requiring Idaho to allow witnesses to observe Leavitt's entire execution.

Richard Leavitt was executed June 12, 2012.

CHILD ABUSE

Fallout from Jerry Sandusky Child-Abuse Scandal Continues

More than a year after a Centre County, Pennsylvania, jury convicted former football coach Jerry Sandusky on 45 counts of CHILD ABUSE, a number of legal issues remained unresolved. Three officials from Pennsylvania State University face charges related to PERJURY, OBSTRUCTION OF JUSTICE, and endangering the WELFARE of children. Penn State has worked to settle claims brought by children who were abused on the university's campus. Moreover, the National Collegiate Athletic Association issued harsh sanctions against the university's football program stemming from a report about how university leaders handled the scandal.

Sandusky joined the coaching staff at Penn State in 1969. Eight years later, he and his **wife** formed the Second Mile, a charity designed to help children with absent parents or dysfunctional families. The Sanduskys became widely regarded for their charity work, and Sandusky had great success as a football coach. During his time as an assistant to Penn State head coach Joe Paterno, the Nittany Lions won national championships in 1982 and 1986.

Sandusky met most of his victims through the Second Mile. Several of those who testified against Sandusky at his trial in 2012 met Sandusky when they were less than 10 years old. Allegations that Sandusky was abusing children arose as early as 1998 when a mother reported to authorities that Sandusky had showered with her son. However, the investigation did not lead to criminal charges. About two years later, a janitor saw Sandusky performing a sexual act on a child in a shower at a Penn State locker room, but again no charges were filed.

In February 2001, a Penn State graduate assistant (and former quarterback) named Mike McQueary saw Sandusky engaged in a sexual **assault** of a child in a Penn State shower. McQueary then informed Paterno, who in turn reported the incident to athletic director Tim Curley and senior VICE PRESIDENT Gary Schultz, who oversaw the campus police. Curley and Schultz said they would investigate the matter further.

Exactly what McQueary told Curley and Schultz and exactly what those two men did in response to McQueary's report is subject to dispute. Curley and Schultz have maintained that McQueary was not specific about his allegations and that they did not realize the seriousness of his accusations. Curley and Schultz also submitted a report to President Graham Spanier. No further investigations took place nor were any criminal charges filed.

An investigation finally started in 2009 when a teenager's mother informed his school that Sandusky had sexually assaulted the boy. In early 2011, Curley, Schultz, Spanier, and Paterno testified before the **grand jury** assigned to Sandusky's case. Curley, Schultz, and Spanier later said they thought they were represented at the time by Penn State's general counsel, Cynthia Baldwin.

Sandusky was finally charged on November 5, 2011. Just days later, the university's board of trustees fired both Spanier and Paterno. Pennsylvania Attorney General Linda Kelly also announced that Curley and Schultz had been charged with perjury related to their testimony before the GRAND JURY and with failing to report child abuse as required by state law. Paterno, who was never charged, died from lung cancer in January 2012.

A jury convicted Sandusky on 45 of 48 charges related to his abuse that occurred between the years 1994 and 2009. In October 2012, Sandusky received a sentence of between 30 and 60 years in state prison. He is assigned to a maximum security prison. Sandusky has maintained that he is completely innocent of all charges, and he has announced plans to appeal his conviction. In January 2013, Judge John Cleland denied Sandusky's motion for a new trial.

Just weeks after the jury convicted Sandusky, former FBI director Louis Freeh released a report about the scandal. The university had hired Freeh to engage in a thorough review of the university's response to the abuse allegations. Freeh and his team conducted hundreds of interviews and concluded that Curley, Schultz, Spanier, and Paterno had intentionally covered up the abuse allegations to protect the reputation of the school's football program.

Based largely on the Freeh report, the National Collegiate Athletic Association (NCAA) announced that it would impose severe sanctions on the university. The sanctions included a significant loss of scholarships, a $60 million fine, and a ban on postseason play. Moreover, the NCAA vacated all Penn State wins dating back to 1998, the year that the first ALLEGATION arose.

At the time Freeh issued the report, the attorney general still had not charged Spanier with any crime. Nevertheless, Spanier's legal team attacked the report, calling it a "blundering indictment" and a "flat-out distortion of facts so infused with bias and innuendo that it is unworthy of the confidence placed on it." Spanier maintained that the only report he heard in 2001 was that Sandusky was "horsing around" with a child in a shower but did not know that anything sexual had occurred.

Freeh's team had found emails, however, suggesting that Spanier knew more. In one of the email exchanges, Curley suggested that he approach Sandusky one-on-one and insist that Sandusky seek help. Spanier appeared to agree with Curley but noted, "The only downside for us is if the message isn't 'heard' and acted upon, and we then become vulnerable for not having reported it."

On November 2012, Kelly announced that Spanier had been charged along with Curley and Schultz. Moreover, she said that Curley and Schultz would face additional charges of obstruction of justice and criminal CONSPIRACY. At her press conference, Kelly said, "If these men had done what they were supposed to do and legally required to do, several young men may not have been attacked by a serial predator."

Some of the charges against the men stem from testimony offered by Baldwin, who claimed that she only represented the university at Sandusky's grand jury **presentment**. If she had not represented the officials individually,

the officials were not entitled to claim **attorney-client privilege** to bar Baldwin's testimony against them. Attorneys for Curley, Schultz, and Spanier have argued that Baldwin had indeed represented each of them individually and that she should be barred from testifying. In April 2013, Judge Barry Feudale denied motion to have charges against Curley, Schultz, and Spanier dismissed, saying he lacked jurisdiction to grant the motion.

The Sandusky case has led to civil LITIGATION as well. Pennsylvania Governor Tom Corbett in January announced that the state would file a federal antitrust suit against the NCAA in an effort to set aside the NCAA's sanctions. Of particular concern to state officials is that the money collected from the $60 million in fines should remain within the state. The NCAA has argued forcefully against this position.

McQueary also has a suit pending before the university. He claims that he was wrongfully terminated for giving truthful testimony before the grand jury. He also claims the university defamed him. In April 2013, Judge Thomas Gavin denied the university's motion to dismiss McQueary's lawsuit, allowing it to proceed.

CHILD CUSTODY

Chafin v. Chafin

The United States is a party to the Hague Convention on the Civil Aspects of International Child Abduction. This treaty requires courts in a contracting state to order a child to be returned to his or her country of **habitual** residence when the child has been wrongfully removed to the contracting state. In 2011 a U.S. **district court** ruled that a child involved in a CUSTODY dispute should be removed from Alabama, where her father lived, and returned to Scotland with her mother. The child's father sought to appeal the decision, but the Eleventh **Circuit Court** of Appeals dismissed the case as moot because the child had already been removed to Scotland.

The U.S. SUPREME COURT agreed to review the case. In a unanimous decision, the Court reversed the Eleventh Circuit's decision, ruling that the case was not moot. According to the court, the father still had a concrete interest in the outcome of the case, meaning that the case was still ripe. *Chafin v. Chafin*, 133 S. Ct. 1017, 185 L. Ed. 2d 1 (2013).

The father is Jeffrey Lee Chafin, who was a sergeant in the U.S. Army. In 2006, he was stationed in Germany and married Lynne Hales. She was a citizen of the United Kingdom. They had a daughter, whom the court referred to as E.C. One year after E.C.'s birth, Mr. Chafin was stationed in Afghanistan. During this time, Ms. Chafin returned to Scotland. Mr. Chafin finally returned to the United States in 2010, and Ms. Chafin traveled to Alabama in February 2010.

However, Mr. Chafin filed for DIVORCE and also sought custody of E.C. from an Alabama state court. Ms. Chafin remained in Alabama throughout most of the year. Near the end of the year, though, she was arrested for DOMESTIC VIOLENCE, which came to the attention of U.S. Citizenship and IMMIGRATION Services. Ms. Chafin had stayed in the United States even though her visa had expired, and she was deported in February 2011. Mr. Chafin retained custody of E.C. at that time.

In 1980, the Hague Conference on **Private International Law** adopted the Hague Convention on the Civil Aspects of International Child Abduction, and a total of 89 nations are party to the convention. The United States adopted the treaty and ratified legislation to implement the treaty by passing the International Child Abduction Remedies Act (ICARA), 42 U.S.C. § 11601 **et seq.**

The treaty defines when removal or retention of a child is considered wrongful. This occurs when the removal or retention "is in breach of rights of custody attributed to a person, an institution or any other body, either jointly or alone, under the law of the State in which the child was habitually resident immediately before the removal or retention" and "at the time of removal or retention those rights were actually exercised, either jointly or alone, or would have been so exercised but for the removal or retention."

The treaty requires a court in a contracting state to order the return of a child wrongfully removed or retained when a period of less than one year has passed from the date of wrongful removal or retention. The treaty establishes several exceptions to its requirement for the child's return. For instance, the treaty establishes that a court does not need to order a child's return if a parent requesting return was not exercising custody rights at the time of the child's removal.

Under the ICARA, federal and STATE COURTS have **concurrent jurisdiction** over actions that arise under the Hague Convention. The **statute** requires a court to "decide the case in accordance with the Convention." A court that finds that a child has been wrongfully removed or retained must order the prompt return of the child. During the 2009 fiscal year, a total of 154 children were returned to other countries from the United States, while 324 children were returned to the United States from other countries.

Ms. Chafin filed suit in the U.S. District Court for the Northern District of Alabama in May 2011. After holding a **bench trial** in October 2011, the court determined that Scotland was E.C.'s habitual residence and ordered that the child should be returned to Scotland. Although Mr. Chafin asked the court to stay its order pending appeal to the Eleventh Circuit, the court denied the request. Ms. Chafin immediately left for Scotland.

In December 2011, a court in Scotland granted interim custody of E.C. to Ms. Chafin and enjoined Mr. Chafin from removing E.C. from Scotland. Meanwhile, Mr. Chafin pursued his appeal to the Eleventh Circuit Court of Appeals. The **appellate court**, however, dismissed the appeal, ruling that the case had become moot because the court was "powerless" to grant relief due to the Hague Convention. The Eleventh Circuit remanded the case to the district court, which ordered Mr. Chafin to pay more than $94,000 in court costs.

The Supreme Court granted **certiorari** to review the case, and a unanimous Court vacated the Eleventh Circuit's decision. Chief Justice JOHN ROBERTS wrote the opinion, with Justice RUTH BADER GINSBURG writing a concurring opinion. The Court heard oral arguments on December 5, 2012, and decided the case on February 19, 2013.

The principal issue in the case was whether the dispute between Mr. Chafin and Ms. Chafin remained a **case or controversy**, because Article III of the U.S. Constitution only grants **federal courts** jurisdiction over cases or controversies. Supreme Court decisions have established that a case becomes moot "when the issues presented are no longer 'live' or the parties lack a legally recognizable interest in the outcome." If the parties have a "concrete interest, however small, in the outcome of the LITIGATION, the case is not moot."

Both Mr. Chafin and Ms. Chafin continued to argue about where their daughter would be raised. To the Court, this showed that "this dispute is still very much alive." Roberts wrote, "This is not a case where a decision would address 'a hypothetical state of facts.' And there is not the slightest doubt that there continues to exist between the parties 'that concrete adverseness which sharpens the presentation of issues.'" (citations omitted)

The Court rejected Ms. Chafin's argument that the case was moot because the U.S. district court could not order the child's return to the United States. According to the Court, this argument confused mootness with the merits of the case. The Court also noted that Mr. Chafin had challenged the district court's award of court costs. The lower courts still had to rule on his appeal of the court costs, and even if his chances for success were slim, the issue was not moot. Based on its decision, the Court vacated the Eleventh Circuit's decision and remanded the case for further proceedings.

Justice Ginsburg concurred and was joined by Justices ANTONIN SCALIA and STEPHEN BREYER. Ginsburg wrote, "This case highlights the need for both speed and certainty in Convention decisionmaking," and she called on the lower court to resolve the dispute as "expeditiously as possible."

CIVIL RIGHTS

Personal liberties that belong to an individual owing to his or her status as a citizen or resident of a particular country or community.

D.C. Circuit Throws Out Torture Lawsuit Against Rumsfeld

The U.S. WAR ON TERRORISM that took troops into Afghanistan and Iraq led to the capture and detention of hundreds of suspected terrorists. Some of those detained were U.S. citizens, and most were eventually released from military CUSTODY. Several filed civil lawsuits against members of the Bush Administration, arguing that these officials had violated their constitutional rights by subjecting them to illegal detention and mistreatment. The **federal courts** rejected those suits for national security reasons. In *Doe v. Rumsfeld*, 683 F.3d 390 (2012), the District of Columbia **Circuit Court** of Appeals dismissed another such action that had been leveled against former Defense Secretary Donald Rumsfeld.

In December 2004, a U.S. citizen identified in the lawsuit as John Doe, traveled to Iraq as an employee of a U.S. defense contracting firm. Doe worked as a civilian Arabic translator and was assigned to a Marine Corps Human Intelligence Exploitation Team that operated on the Iraq-Syria border. Doe developed intelligence through contacts with local Iraqis and sought to discover threats to the Marine unit. In July 2005, he made contact and developed a relationship with an Iraqi sheikh. He became the point of contact for this person and cultivated him as a U.S. ally. In October 2005, Doe was about to depart for his annual leave. While waiting, he was interviewed by a Navy Criminal Investigative Service (NCIS) agent about his work. Two weeks later, three NCIS agents detained and interrogated him for four hours. The agents denied his request for a lawyer, confiscated his luggage, blindfolded him, kicked him in the back, and threatened to shoot him if he tried to escape.

Doe was transferred into the custody of the Marine Corps. After 72 hours of solitary confinement, he was flown to Camp Cropper, a U.S. military facility near Baghdad International Airport used to house high-value detainees. He was confined at Camp Cropper for 9 months, the first three months in solitary confinement. He was then placed in a cell with suspected hostile al Qaeda and Arab Socialist Ba'ath Party members. Military officers informed these inmates of Doe's DEFENSE DEPARTMENT affiliation to encourage his cellmates to attack him. Doe was subjected to extreme temperatures and sleep deprivation. During his detention, Doe was interrogated multiple times. In December 2005, the Detainee Status Board held a hearing and ruled that Doe was a threat to military forces in Iraq. The board held a second hearing in July 2006, after which Doe was transported to Jordan and ultimately to the United States, where he was released. Doe was never formally charged with a crime. Doe alleged that since his release he had been placed on watch lists, preventing contracting firms from hiring him and causing customs officials to interrogate him when he returns from international travel.

In November 2008, Doe filed a federal civil lawsuit against former Defense Secretary Donald Rumsfeld and other government officials, alleging that Rumsfeld violated his rights under the Detainee Treatment Act (DTA) and his constitutional rights that are guaranteed by the Fifth, Eighth, and Fourteenth Amendments. The latter ALLEGATION is known as a *Bivens* action and is based on the Supreme Court's decision in *Bivens v. Six Unknown Agents of the Federal Bureau of Investigation,* 403 U.S. 388, 91 S. Ct. 1999, 29 L. Ed. 2d 619 (1971). Rumsfeld asked the federal **district court** to dismiss the claims against him. The court dismissed the DTA claim because the law does not allow a private **cause of action**. Only the government may bring a lawsuit. The court also dismissed a procedural due process claim but allowed the *Bivens* action to proceed that was based on **substantive due process** violations. The court ruled that Rumsfeld was not entitled to qualified IMMUNITY, which would have shielded him from personal liability, because Doe had a right to be free from detention and interrogation practices that "shock the conscience." That right was clearly established at the time of Rumsfeld's alleged conduct. Rumsfeld appealed this part of the decision to the D.C. Circuit Court of Appeals.

A three-judge panel of the D.C. Circuit reversed the district court ruling concerning the *Bivens* action. Because it settled the matter on this issue, it did not rule on the issue of qualified immunity. Judge David Sentelle, writing for the court, stated that Doe's due process claims against Rumsfeld depended on whether the court was willing to extend the types of claims recognized in *Bivens.* In that case, the SUPREME COURT allowed a CAUSE OF ACTION against federal officials who violated a person's FOURTH AMENDMENT right to be secure from unreasonable searches and seizures, even if no **statute** authorizes such relief. However, the Court made clear that courts should not imply a cause of action if "special factors counsel hesitation." The district court in this case had found no special factors and concluded Doe had no other remedy for the alleged SUBSTANTIVE DUE PROCESS violations.

Judge Sentelle disagreed with these conclusions. A *Bivens* action "is not something to be undertaken lightly." Only twice in 42 years has the Supreme Court extended the reach of this cause of action: one was an employment due process claim and the other was a claim by a prisoner against prison officials for an EIGHTH AMENDMENT violation. Moreover, the Supreme Court "consistently has considered and rejected *Bivens* remedies

in all other contexts." The district court not only misread the **case law** but also missed special factors in this case that "counsel against the implication of a new *Bivens* remedy."

The appeals court found special factors pertaining to military, intelligence, and national security. First, the Supreme Court had never implied a *Bivens* remedy in a case involving these three areas of national concern. The Court had ruled that no *Bivens* remedy was available for injuries that arise out of military service. In addition, the judicial branch should not intrude on military decisions that were better left to the legislative and executive branches. Military detainee cases, in the view of the D.C. Circuit, implicate similar concerns regarding the conduct of war, the SEPARATION OF POWERS, and the public scrutiny of sensitive information. To allow Doe to proceed would require a court to examine military policies regarding the designation of detainees as "security internees" or "enemy combatants," as well as policies governing interrogation techniques. In addition, an inquiry into Rumsfeld's role in these policies would require "testimony from top military officials as well as forces on the ground, which would detract focus, resources, and personnel from the mission in Iraq." Finally, a *Bivens* remedy would hinder military members from acting decisively for fear of **judicial review** of every detention and interrogation. Therefore, the court ruled that Doe could not employ a *Bivens* action.

CIVIL SERVICE

The designation given to government employment for which a person qualifies on the basis of merit rather than political patronage or personal favor.

Supreme Court Clarifies Procedures for Federal Civil Service Appeals

Federal employees are granted certain rights under CIVIL SERVICE laws. The Civil Service Reform Act of 1978 (CSRA) permits a federal employee who is discharged or demoted to appeal her agency's decision to the MERIT SYSTEMS PROTECTION BOARD (MSPB). An appeal may be alleged that that the agency had insufficient cause for taking the action under CSRA but the appeal may instead charge the agency with DISCRIMINATION prohibited by a federal **statute**. When an employee alleges such discrimination, the appeal is known as a "mixed case." Mixed cases are governed by special procedures set out in the

CSRA and the regulations of the MSPB and the EQUAL EMPLOYMENT OPPORTUNITY COMMISSION (EEOC). The U.S. SUPREME COURT, in *Kloeckner v. Solis,* 133 S. Ct. 596, 184 L. Ed. 2d 433 (2012), was called on to clarify these special procedures. Specifically, the Court determined when an employee can seek **judicial review** in a federal **district court** when the employee brings a mixed case.

Carolyn Kloeckner worked at the DEPART-MENT OF LABOR (DOL). In 2005 she filed a complaint with the department's CIVIL RIGHTS office, alleging that the DOL had engaged in unlawful sex and AGE DISCRIMINATION by subjecting her to a hostile work environment. At this point her case was not appealable to the MSPB because she had not been subject to a serious personnel action such as demotion or discharge. Therefore, her case went forward not under the CSRA special procedures for mixed cases but under the EEOC's regulations for all other charges of discrimination. The department completed its internal investigation and report in June 2006, and Kloeckner requested a hearing before an EEOC **administrative law** judge. In July 2006, the department fired Kloeckner.

Having suffered a serious personnel action, Kloeckner appealed to the MSPB, as she now had a mixed case. However, with similar actions pending before both the EEOC and the MSPB, Kloeckner soon concluded that pursuing both cases would incur duplicative discovery expenses. She amended her EEOC complaint to include her claim of discriminatory removal and asked the MSPB to dismiss her case **without prejudice** for four months to allow the EEOC proceeding to be completed. The MSPB granted her request and instructed her to refile her claim after the EEOC case was resolved or by January 18, 2007, whichever occurred first.

The EEOC proceeding went well beyond the January 18 deadline. In April 2007, the EEOC judge dismissed Kloeckner's case because she had engaged in bad-faith conduct in connection with discovery. The judge returned the case to the DOL for a final decision. In October 2007, the department issued a ruling that rejected all of Kloeckner's claims. She appealed the DOL decision to the MSPB in November 2007, seeking review of a mixed case. The MSPB declined to hear her appeal, viewing it as an attempt to reopen her old MSPB case many months after the January deadline. Therefore, the board dismissed her appeal as untimely.

Kloeckner then brought a lawsuit in federal district court against the DOL, alleging unlawful discrimination. The court dismissed the case, concluding that under a ruling by the Eighth **Circuit Court** of Appeals, the dismissal of Kloeckner's MSPB case on procedural grounds meant that she should have filed an appeal with the Federal Circuit Court of Appeals in Washington, D.C. The district court could only hear discrimination cases where the MSPB decided the case on the merits. Kloeckner appealed to the Eighth Circuit, which upheld the lower court ruling. The Supreme Court agreed to hear Kloeckner's appeal because other circuit courts of appeal had ruled that district courts did have jurisdiction to hear mixed cases that were decided on procedural grounds.

The Court, in a unanimous decision, overturned the Eighth Circuit ruling. Justice ELENA KAGAN, writing for the Court, acknowledged that "the intersection of federal civil rights statutes and civil service law has produced a complicated, at times confusing, process for resolving claims of discrimination in the federal workplace." However, in this case some things were plain. Two sections of the CSRA, when read "naturally," directed employees like Kloeckner to file their cases in district court. It was true that one section of the CSRA directed appeals from the MSPB to the Federal Circuit, but there were exceptions. One exception stated that in cases of discrimination, an action could be filed directly in federal district court, bypassing the MSPB. The types of discrimination cases subject to district court jurisdiction were set out in the very next section of the CSRA. This section stated that a federal employee who suffered a serious personnel action and alleged discrimination that is known as a mixed case qualified for district court jurisdiction. In Kloeckner's case, she qualified under both of the CSRA provisions. It did not matter that the MSPB dismissed her claims as untimely or on the merits. Kloeckner "brought the kind of case that the CSRA routes, in crystalline fashion, to district court."

The government and the Eighth Circuit contended that the CSRA directed the MSPB's merits decisions to the district court, while procedural decisions were routed to the Federal Circuit. Though not explicitly described in the

CSRA, cases that were decided on procedural grounds were not decisions on the question of discrimination. Therefore, they were not "judicially reviewable actions" under the CSRA mixed case provisions. Therefore, the Federal Circuit had jurisdiction to hear an appeal from the procedural decision. Justice Kagan dismissed this argument, concluding that "It would be hard to dream up a more roundabout way of bifurcating JUDICIAL REVIEW of the MSPB's rulings in mixed cases." If Congress had wanted to implement such a scheme, it could have said so. Because it did not, the district courts have jurisdiction to hear all mixed cases.

CLASS ACTION

A lawsuit that allows a large number of people with a common interest in a matter to sue or be sued as a group.

Comcast Corp. v. Behrend

Rule 23 of the Federal Rules of **Civil Procedure** governs class-action lawsuits. A group of plaintiffs may maintain a class-action lawsuit only under certain conditions. One of those conditions is set forth in Rule 23(b)(3), which applies when "the court finds that the questions of law or fact common to class members predominate over any questions affecting only individual members, and that a **class action** is superior to other available methods for fairly and efficiently adjudicating the controversy."

In *Comcast Corp. v. Behrend*, 133 S. Ct. 1426, 185 L. Ed. 2d 515 (2013), the U.S. SUPREME COURT addressed whether a lower **district court** should have certified a class of more than two million subscribers who sought damages for alleged antitrust violations by Comcast Corporation, one of the largest CABLE TELEVISION companies in the United States. The Supreme Court determined that a federal district court had improperly certified the class because the plaintiffs could not prove that the plaintiffs' alleged damages could be measured on a class-wide basis.

Comcast began a series of transactions in 1998 to increase its share of the cable television market in the Philadelphia area. Comcast acquired some of the competing cable companies in the area. In other instances, Comcast "swapped" cable systems that it owned outside the Philadelphia area with systems inside the area. Plaintiffs in the case alleged that the transactions allowed Comcast to increase its market share in this area from 23.9 percent in 1998 to 77.8 percent in 2002.

Six plaintiffs sued Comcast in 2003, arguing that Comcast's actions had violated the Sherman Act, 15 U.S.C. § 1 **et seq.** The plaintiffs alleged that Comcast had violated § 1 of the Act for "imposing horizontal territory, market and customer allocations by conspiring with and entering into and implementing unlawful swap agreements, arrangements and devices." The plaintiffs also alleged that Comcast had created an illegal **monopoly** in violation of § 2 of the Act.

The plaintiffs alleged that Comcast's practices resulted in increased prices of nonbasic cable programming. The allegations focused on Comcast's alleged practices of eliminating competition, which deprived subscribers of lower prices that could result from increased competition.

The plaintiffs brought the suit as a CLASS ACTION. The plaintiffs proposed a class consisting of the following: "All cable television customers who subscribe or subscribed at any time since December 1, 1999, to the present to video programming services (other than solely to basic cable services) from Comcast, or any of its subsidiaries or affiliates in Comcast's Philadelphia cluster." This "cluster" included several counties near the Philadelphia area, including counties in Pennsylvania, Delaware, and New Jersey.

The U.S. District Court for the Eastern District of Pennsylvania held evidentiary hearings in 2009 to determine whether questions of law or fact common to class members predominated over questions affecting individual class members. The plaintiffs had proposed four theories about how Comcast's practices violated antitrust laws. One of those theories focused on "overbuilders," which are companies that build competing cable networks in areas where another dominant cable company already operates. The plaintiffs alleged that Comcast's practices reduced competition from these overbuilders. The district court accepted the overbuilder theory but rejected the others.

Following the four-day hearing, the district court certified the class. In summarizing its analysis of the evidence, the court noted:

> Having rigorously analyzed the expert reports, as well as the testimony presented by the parties during a four-day evidentiary hearing, we conclude that the class has met

its burden to demonstrate that the element of antitrust impact is capable of proof at trial through evidence that is common to the class rather than individual to its members, and that there is a common methodology available to measure and quantify damages on a class-wide basis.

Behrend v. Comcast Corp., 264 F.R.D. 150 (E.D. Pa. 2010)

A panel of the Third **Circuit Court** of Appeals reviewed the district court's decision. Comcast argued that the district court had improperly certified the class of plaintiffs because the plaintiffs had failed to attribute damages resulting from the overbuilder theory. However, the majority of the panel rejected the argument, stating that the court should not review the merits of the methodology of the damage calculation at the class certification stage. Instead, the panel found that the plaintiffs had shown damages capable of measurement, which was sufficient for class certification purposes. *Behrend v. Comcast Corp.*, 655 F.3d 182 (3d Cir. 2011).

The Supreme Court granted **certiorari** to review the case. In a 5–4 decision, the Court reversed the Third Circuit. Writing for the majority, Justice ANTONIN SCALIA stressed that the result of the case hinged on "straightforward application of class-certification principles" and not issues of substantive **antitrust law**.

The majority focused on the plaintiff's theory of resulting damages from the alleged antitrust violations. According to the Court, the plaintiffs' model for calculating damages did not focus specifically on the overbuilder theory but rather focused on the "alleged anticompetitive conduct as a whole." The lower courts had refused to consider arguments focusing on the damages model, but this failure led the majority to reverse the lower courts' decision.

Scalia wrote, "It is clear that, under the proper standard for evaluating certification, respondents' model falls far short of establishing that damages are capable of measurement on a classwide basis. Without presenting another methodology, respondents cannot show Rule 23(b)(3) predominance: Questions of individual damage calculations will inevitably overwhelm questions common to the class."

Scalia was joined by Chief Justice JOHN ROBERTS and Justices ANTHONY KENNEDY, CLARENCE THOMAS, and SAMUEL ALITO.

The majority's focus differed from the questions addressed during oral argument. The Court had granted CERTIORARI on the standard under which the expert's model should have been admissible to show predominance under Rule 23(b)(3). A DISSENT written by Justice RUTH BADER GINSBURG and joined by Justices STEPHEN BREYER, SONIA SOTOMAYOR, and ELENA KAGAN argued that the Court should have dismissed the case because the majority had effectively "abandon[ed] the question [the Court] instructed the parties to brief." The dissent also argued that the Court should not have disturbed factual findings of the lower courts related to the model used to measure the damages.

Genesis HealthCare v. Symczyk

A curious but important issue presented itself to the U.S. SUPREME COURT in *Genesis HealthCare Corp. v. Symczyk*, 133 S. Ct. 1523 (2013). It ended badly for the plaintiff/respondent and did little to resolve the conflict between circuits facing similar class actions/collective actions. The precise question before the Court was whether, under the FAIR LABOR STANDARDS ACT (FLSA), a case becomes moot and therefore must be dismissed when the lone PLAINTIFF in a yet-uncertified collective action receives an offer, under Rule 68 of the Federal Rules of **Civil Procedure**, from all defendants to settle her claim. By a narrow 5–4 decision, the Court held that the mootness of the plaintiff's individual claim was not properly before it, as the plaintiff/respondent had failed to file a cross-petition regarding this issue. She therefore had waived that argument, said the Court. Accordingly, the Court accepted, and let stand, the Third **Circuit Court** of Appeals' determination that her claim was now moot, even though she had not responded to the defendants' offer. This case did not, therefore, resolve existing disagreement among circuit courts of appeals as to whether an unaccepted Rule 68 offer that fully satisfies a plaintiff's individual claim is sufficient to render the individual's claim moot.

However, the Court reversed the Third Circuit's holding that her collective action (in behalf of yet-unnamed similarly situated claimants) was not moot and could continue. The Supreme Court held that well-settled principles of mootness instructed that when the plaintiff's individual claim became moot, the suit became moot, because the individual did not have a stake in the controversy sufficient to allow her to represent the group. Since she was the only named plaintiff, the entire case had been properly dismissed by the federal **district court** for lack of **subject matter jurisdiction**. (Moreover, because she had not responded to defendants' offers, which would have compensated her in full for her claim, she was left with neither **settlement** compensation nor a viable claim.)

The FLSA, 29 U.S.C. § 201 **et seq.** (not at issue here), provides for, among other things, standards for federal minimum wages, maximum work hours, and overtime guarantees that cannot be modified by COLLECTIVE BARGAINING or contract. Section 16(b) provides that employees may bring private causes of action on their own behalf, as well as on behalf of "other employees similarly situated" for FLSA violations. Such suits under FLSA are referred to as "collective actions" instead of class-action suits.

Plaintiff Laura Symczyk was formerly employed by Genesis HealthCare as a registered nurse at a nursing home in Philadelphia, Pennsylvania. Symczyk filed suit against her employer (defendants "Genesis," collectively) on behalf of herself and "all other persons similarly situated." The suit alleged violations under the FLSA because it automatically deducted 30 minutes of pay per shift worked for meal breaks, whether the employees took them or not. This was true, alleged the complaint, even if employees performed compensable work during those breaks. Symczyk sought **statutory** damages for the alleged violations, and during all proceedings relevant to this decision, she remained the sole plaintiff.

Simultaneously served with DEFENDANT Genesis's answer to the complaint was an offer of judgment (in favor of Symczyk), including $7,500 for alleged lost wages, along with "such reasonable attorneys' fees, costs, and expenses …" The offer of judgment also included a stipulation that if Symczyk did not accept the offer within 10 days of service, it was deemed withdrawn.

Symczyk did not respond to the offer that would have fully compensated her for her claim. Thereafter, Genesis filed a motion to dismiss the case for lack of jurisdiction. This was premised upon its argument that since it had offered complete relief to Symczyk, she no longer had a personal stake in the outcome of the suit, rendering the case moot. (No other individuals had joined the suit.) The district court granted the motion and the case was dismissed, starting the **appellate** process.

The Court of Appeals reversed. Symczyk had argued that a calculated "picking off" of named plaintiff(s) in a Rule 68 move like this, before collective action certification, frustrated the goals of collective actions. The **appellate court** agreed and remanded to the district court to allow Symczyk to seek "conditional certification" (parallel with a class action's joining of coplaintiffs).

But the U.S. Supreme Court disagreed and reversed. Citing copious **case law** precedent, the Court methodically showed how plaintiffs needed to show both "an actual controversy" and "a legally cognizable interest, or 'personal stake,' in the outcome of the action." Next, the Court cited *Lewis v. Continental Bank Corp.,* in instructing, "If an intervening circumstance deprives the plaintiff of 'a personal stake in the outcome of the lawsuit,' at any point during LITIGATION, the action can no longer proceed and must be dismissed as moot." 492 U.S. 469, 109 S. Ct. 3028 (1990). Symczyk being the sole plaintiff in the present case, the dismissal of her claim as moot (which the Court assumed, without deciding) was appropriate for lack of subject-matter jurisdiction. Various prior cases of the Court, raised in argument by Symczyk, were inapplicable, said the Court, because they involved collective or class actions in which a class had already been certified at the time of the representative plaintiff's dismissal.

Justice CLARENCE THOMAS delivered the opinion of the Court, joined by Chief Justice JOHN ROBERTS and Justices ANTONIN SCALIA, ANTHONY KENNEDY, and SAMUEL ALITO. Justice ELENA KAGAN, joined by Justices RUTH BADER GINSBURG, STEPHEN BREYER, and SONIA SOTOMAYOR, filed a DISSENT expressing that the majority opinion "got it wrong," from its assumption on the dismissal for mootness of the individual claim, to its interpretation of Rule 68. The dissent pointed out that Rule 68 expressly specifies that "[a]n unaccepted offer is considered withdrawn." Accordingly, opined the dissent, "Symczyk's individual claim was alive and well when the District Court dismissed her suit." Justice Kagan also advised, "A friendly suggestion to the Third Circuit: Rethink your mootness-by-unaccepted-offer theory."

Standard Fire Insurance Company v. Knowles

In a brief but succinct seven-page decision by a unanimous U.S. SUPREME COURT, PLAINTIFF Greg Knowles was not permitted to bind a precertified class of **putative** plaintiffs to damages under $5 million, thereby avoiding removal to federal court by DEFENDANT Standard Fire Insurance Company (Standard Fire) under the **Class Action** Fairness Act (CAFA) of 2005. 28 U.S.C. § 1332(d)(2). *Standard Fire Insurance Company v. Knowles,* 133 S. Ct. 1345 (2013). The Miller County **Circuit Court** in western Arkansas, where the lawsuit had been filed, was known as a "class-action magnet" by insurance companies because of sympathetic juries. Such stipulations had been upheld in the past by the U.S. Court of Appeals for the Eighth Circuit, and its similar holding in this case was reversed by the Supreme Court.

Under the CAFA, defendants in class-action lawsuits may remove the case to federal court if the potential damages (the "matter in controversy") exceed $5 million. To arrive at such determination as to whether a matter exceeds that amount, the **statute** requires that "claims of the individual class members must be aggregated." § 1332(d)(6).

Greg Knowles suffered damage to his house following a heavy storm that produced hail. In 2011, he filed suit in Arkansas state court against Standard Fire, alleging that the insurer had underpaid claims (insurance loss payments) by failing to include general contractors' fees. Knowles further sought to certify a class of "hundreds, and possibly thousands" of similarly situated and harmed Arkansas policyholders. As part of the petition for class certification, Knowles's complaint confined the class to Arkansas residents, alleged causes of action only under Arkansas law, and, by AFFIDAVIT, stipulated that representative Knowles would not seek damages for the class (in the aggregate) for more than $5 million.

Citing CAFA's jurisdictional provision, Standard Fire removed the case to the U.S. **District Court** for the Western District of Arkansas. However, the district court, based on Knowles's stipulation, found the **amount in controversy** to be below the threshold and remanded the case back to the state court in Miller County, Arkansas. The company appealed, but the Eighth Circuit Court of Appeals declined review. The U.S. Supreme Court granted **writ** of **certiorari** (review) "in light of divergent views in the lower courts."

Justice STEPHEN BREYER, writing for the unanimous Court, held that Knowles's affidavit of stipulation did not defeat federal jurisdiction under CAFA. While it could bind Knowles, he could not speak for those he proposed to represent because a proposed CLASS ACTION cannot legally bind members of the proposed class before the class is certified. Knowles lacked both authority and knowledge to assess the damages of unknown members of the proposed class, and he could therefore not concede the AMOUNT IN CONTROVERSY for absent class members.

The Court further noted that Knowles had conceded that federal jurisdiction cannot be based on contingent future events. Yet, because stipulations must be binding, together with the fact that a plaintiff cannot bind precertification class members, Knowles's stipulated amount of less than $5 million was effectually contingent. His own complaint contained estimates of how many class members there might be, "hundreds, and possibly thousands," yet he expected to bind the class of unknown plaintiffs with unknown damages to less than $5 million. Also contingent at this stage was Knowles's status as representative plaintiff, for the court might have found him to be an inadequate representative "due to the artificial cap he purports to impose on the class' recovery." (Slip Opinion, p. 5) Or, noted the Court, a different class member could come forward with an amended complaint without such stipulation, and the district court might permit the action to proceed with a new representative plaintiff.

In summary, said the Court, "We believe the District Court, when following the statute to aggregate the proposed class members' claims, should have ignored that stipulation. Because it did not, we vacate the judgment below and remand the case for further proceedings consistent with this opinion."

CONGRESS OF THE UNITED STATES

State Emergency Management Laws under the 2013 Sequester

In the wake of Congress's mandated "Sequestration," effective March 1, 2013, many states have been compelled to compensate for losses

in federal monies by reviewing, adapting, and in some cases, utilizing emergency funds to make up the difference.

The term "sequestration," as applied to governmental budget concerns, refers to the process of imposing largely automatic across-the-board spending cuts in order to enforce certain budget goals. The authority to utilize SEQUESTRATION stems from the Balanced Budget and Emergency Deficit Control Act of 1985 (BBEDCA, Title II of P.L. 99-177) commonly known as the Gramm-Rudman-Hollings Act.

As part of the Budget Control Act of 2011 (BCA), P.L. 112-25, bipartisan majorities in both houses of Congress voted in August 2011 for sequestration as a default means to facilitate compromise and compel Congress to act to reduce the budget by an agreed-upon deadline. One and a half years later, Congress had still failed to agree on balanced deficit reduction legislation. As a result, the law required President Obama to issue a sequestration order for **fiscal** year (FY) 2013, which he did on March 1, 2013. The order ("sequestration") canceled $85 billion in "across-the-board" budget resources spanning virtually all federal government branches, departments, and agencies.

Certain exemptions and special rules apply under sequestration, as provided for in §§ 255 and 256 of the BBEDCA (above). Mandatory exempt programs include SOCIAL SECURITY, Veterans Programs, military pay, federal retirement benefits, child nutrition, food stamps, and Pell Grants. Medicare/Medicaid benefits are limited to a 2% cap in reduction.

How the sequester trickles down to affect states and their citizens is less publicized but equally palpable in effect. This is because states receive huge amounts of funds and "block grants" from the federal government each year, but generally manage the money without federal interference, once they qualify and receive the funds.

Each state has its own "emergency management laws," with built-in plans to handle natural and man-made disasters, financial crises, health crises, education shortfalls, and infrastructure needs, in conjunction with federal grants, funds, and assistance. In other words, how states use federal monies remains discretionary within a range of specific limitations/purposes, according to an individual state's own resources and needs. But those "emergency" plans had to be tweaked and/or revamped in several states, in order to meet sequester shortfalls in funding.

One example of federal funding cut by the sequester is revenue generated from federal lands. Proportionally, the United States owns considerably more land in Western states than on the East Coast; it owns 81 percent of the land in Nevada and 0.3 percent of Connecticut's land. Those states and counties within states that contain or are surrounded by federal lands have less residents and more limited property tax bases to use for school funding, road construction, etc.

In addressing these inequities, the federal government administers programs such as Payment in Lieu of Taxes, which collects funds generated from oil and gas leasing, grazing, etc., on PUBLIC LANDS and returns it to rural states and communities for education, public safety, and infrastructure needs. In 2012, the U.S. DEPARTMENT OF INTERIOR announced a record $393 million in Payment in Lieu of Taxes funding.

Similar is the Secure Schools and Community Self-Determination Act, first passed in 2000. Under that program, roughly 25 percent of revenue generated from timber sales on federal lands is returned to states for rural counties. Communities in the Pacific Northwest and West have heavily relied on these programs because of declines in timber sales related to logging limitations and protection of endangered species such as the spotted owl. In January 2013, Secretary of Agriculture Tom Vilsack announced that $323 million in funding would go to 41 states to support local schools and road construction.

Shortly after the sequester was signed into law (March 2013), U.S. Forest Service Chief Thomas Tidwell sent letters to 41 state governments, demanding they return $17 million [aggregately] in money given to them that came from 2012 timber harvesting on federal lands. According to the letter, the move was necessary to meet a five percent obligatory spending cut for the Forest Service's 2013 budget, required by the sequester. States had received their proportional share of the timber funds in January 2013 without notice that they may be impacted by the sequester. For example, Gordon Cruickshank, chairman of Valley County Commission in Idaho, told CBS Local News that Valley County would have to return more than $128,000. This meant he would have to either not re-pave any of the county's 300 miles of road, defer maintenance on a bridge, or lay off two county employees.

The demand for return of some of the funds hit states two months after many had received and already dispersed the funds under the Secure Rural Schools program. The governors of Alabama, Alaska, and Wyoming publicly refused to return the funds, and challenged the legality of the demand. Meanwhile, in an April 2013 SENATE Energy and Natural Resources Committee meeting, Tidwell stated that non-compliant states would face interest, penalties, and administrative costs. (Other branches of government, such as the Bureau of Land Management, had not requested refunds for similar programs administered by them to rural states.)

A White House "Fact Sheet" reported that other federal program cuts that could affect state programs, i.e., cause states to compensate for, included cuts to education (impacting Head Start programs, teachers, and special education); food safety (up to 2,100 fewer food inspections); FBI and U.S. Attorneys (cuts of up to 1,000 persons could affect crime reporting, border security, national security); workplace safety (up to 1,200 fewer inspections by the Occupational Safety and Health Administration); social programs (Senior's Meals on Wheels, rental assistance from the DEPARTMENT OF HOUSING AND URBAN DEVELOPMENT [HUD] vouchers; programs for the homeless); and Native American programs under the DEPARTMENT OF THE INTERIOR. The Association of State and Territorial Health Officials (ASTHO) warned that federal cuts to state grants for public health programs would negatively impact child and adult vaccinations, HIV and AIDS treatments, disaster preparedness, foodborne outbreak prevention, mental health programs, and maternal and child health, in particular.

Finally, due to sequestration, the **disaster relief** section of the FEDERAL EMERGENCY MANAGEMENT AGENCY (FEMA) was scheduled to lose $1 billion for 2013. Following Hurricane Sandy, which hit the U.S. East Coast in spring 2012, FEMA was scheduled to pay out $10.8 billion to storm victims by the end of the fiscal year. This left just $2.5 billion in the DISASTER RELIEF fund for the remainder of the year. State emergency management funds would need to reapportion their own internal budget appropriations to accommodate any such disasters that might occur prior to year's end.

CONSPIRACY

An agreement between two or more persons to engage jointly in an unlawful or criminal act or an act that is innocent in itself but becomes unlawful when done by the combination of actors.

E-book Publishers Settle Price-Fixing Cases

Several of the largest book publishers in the United States, as well as the Apple computer company, faced lawsuits brought in 2012 alleging that the companies conspired to fix prices of electronic books, or e-books. The U.S. JUSTICE DEPARTMENT brought one of the suits in federal **district court** in New York. In a separate suit, 16 attorneys general made similar allegations. In August 2012, the publishers Hachette, HarperCollins, and Simon & Schuster agreed to pay $69 million in a **settlement** of the case brought by the states. Just days later, U.S. District Judge Denise Cote approved a settlement between the Justice Department and the same publishers. Other publishers negotiated settlements in early 2013.

The case stemmed from agreements made by the publishers and Apple. According to the allegations, the publishers named to the suits were unhappy with Amazon.com's pricing of e-books on the Amazon site. The publishers met with Apple and devised a scheme that would effectively raise the price of books by $2 to $3 per title. The publishers agreed to give Apple a 30 percent commission on e-books sold through Apple's iBooks site, and e-book retailers would be prevented from offering prices lower than Apple's. The DEPARTMENT OF JUSTICE alleged that the scheme cost customers about $100 million.

For many years, six large book publishers have dominated the publishing industry in the United States. In addition to Hachette, Harper-Collins, and Simon & Schuster, the other publishers are Macmillan, Penguin, and Random House. These six publishers generate about 60 percent of all revenue from print titles in the United States. These publishers are able to dictate wholesale prices for books by setting a list price and giving retailers a discount percentage. Thus, publishers may set a list price for a book at $50 and give retailers a 50 percent discount, making the wholesale price $25.

E-books are digital versions of books. Consumers can read e-books on a variety of devices, including computers, mobile phones, a variety of readers such as the Amazon Kindle, and tablets such as the Apple iPad. Consumers can purchase most of these e-books from their devices, meaning that the consumer does not need to visit a physical store or even a website through a browser to buy the title.

The market for e-books has been rising substantially. In 2007, e-books accounted for just 2 percent of the total number of titles sold. By 2011, this number had grown to 25 percent. According to filings in the cases, publishers sold about 114 million e-books in 2010, and these sales reached $441.3 million in revenues.

A significant reason why e-books became so popular was the introduction and rise in popularity of Amazon's Kindle device. The Kindle is a handheld electronic tablet used principally to read e-books. It debuted in November 2007, and each of the major publishers agreed to sell e-books to Amazon through the same model used to sell physical books. The publishers generally set lower prices for e-books compared with physical books. However, Amazon set a low price for e-books, charging $9.99 or less per title. In some cases, the price was lower than the wholesale price of the book. The reason for this strategy was that Amazon wanted to fuel sales of the Kindle and capture a large market share.

Fearful that Amazon's strategy would hurt sales of physical books, the major publishers decided to pursue some alternatives. Initially, the publishers delayed the release of e-book versions of new titles, hoping that consumers would buy the hardbound copies of the books. When this approach failed, the publishers decided to work with one of Amazon's competitors, Apple, to increase the price of the e-books.

Under the plan, Apple entered into contracts with each of the major publishers, agreeing to sell e-books through its new iBookstore starting in April 2010. Apple received a 30 percent commission for each title sold. The agreements also established a formula for setting the prices for e-books. The formula generally set the price for a new e-book at $12.99 to $14.99.

The publishers thereafter withheld e-books from other retailers, including Amazon, until the retailers agreed to follow the same model used by Apple. The result of this was that e-book sales rose by an average of 40 percent, even though the costs of these books did not increase. Moreover, prices of some e-books exceeded the corresponding prices of physical books because of the new pricing model.

Several individuals sued the publishers and Apple in different **federal courts**. The United States Panel on MULTIDISTRICT LITIGATION transferred all of the actions to the U.S. District for the

Southern District of New York. When the U.S. Department of Justice filed an action against the defendants, the case was also transferred to the federal court in New York. The claims alleged that Apple and the publishers conspired to violate the Sherman Antitrust Act, 15 U.S.C. § 1 **et seq.**, state antitrust and restraint-of-trade laws, state **consumer protection** statutes, and state law applying to UNJUST ENRICHMENT.

The second case was filed by the attorneys general of 16 states in the U.S. District Court for the Western District of Texas. The allegations made by the states were practically identical to those made in the case in New York. When the states filed the suit in April 2012, Connecticut Attorney General George Jepsen commented, "Publishers deserve to make money, but consumers deserve the price benefits of competition in an open and unrestricted marketplace. Those interests clearly collided in this case and we are going to work to ensure the eBook market is open once again to fair competition."

The defendants in the New York action filed a motion to dismiss, but District Judge Denise Cote held that the plaintiffs had stated plausible claims and denied the motion. *In re Electronic Books Antitrust Litigation*, 859 F. Supp. 2d 671 (S.D.N.Y. 2012). Less than four months later, three of the major publishers agreed to a $69 million settlement, which Cote approved on September 5, 2012. *United States v. Apple, Inc.,* 889 F. Supp. 2d 623 (S.D.N.Y. 2012). In December 2012 and February 2013, respectively, Penguin and Macmillan agreed to settlement agreements.

The trial began on June 3, 2013, and lasted more than two weeks. On July 10, 2013, Cote ruled that Apple violated anti-trust law by conspiring with publishers to fix e-book prices. Apple announced that it would appeal the ruling.

COPYRIGHT

An intangible right granted by statute to the author or originator of certain literary or artistic productions, whereby, for a limited period, the exclusive privilege is given to the person to make copies of the same for publication and sale.

Kirtsaeng v. John Wiley & Sons

In *Kirtsaeng v. John Wiley & Sons, Inc.,* 133 S. Ct. 1351 (2013), the U.S. SUPREME COURT held that, under COPYRIGHT law's "first sale" doctrine,

U.S. copyright owners cannot maintain control of, or stop the importation or reselling of, copyrighted material lawfully sold abroad. Under "copyright exhaustion," copyright owners maintain control of the first sale only. The 6–3 majority, 70-page opinion put to rest an issue left open by a previous term's case, *Costco Wholesale Corporation v. Omega*, 131 S. Ct. 565 (2010), where the newly appointed justice ELENA KAGAN took no part in consideration or decision, resulting in a split 4–4 decision.

The "first sale" doctrine, codified as Section 109(a) of the Copyright Act, 17 U.S.C. § 101 **et seq.**, essentially provides that after the first authorized sale or distribution of a copy of a copyrighted work, the copyright owner's right to control further distribution of that copy is "exhausted" (lost). For example, the purchase of a new book or DVD from a retail **entity** (that is authorized by the publisher or copyright owner) triggers the doctrine. Thereafter, the purchaser can resell the book to a used book dealer or resell the DVD to someone else, and there is no copyright INFRINGEMENT. The actual **statutory** language, in pertinent part, reads: "The owner of a particular copy or phonorecord lawfully made under this title, or any person authorized by such owner, is entitled, without the authority of the copyright owner, to sell or otherwise dispose of the possession of that copy or phonorecord." 17 U.S.C. § 109(a).

Supap Kirtsaeng, a Thai scholarship student who came to the United States in 1997, was accepted into a PhD program at the University of Southern California after receiving an undergraduate degree at Cornell University. To help pay for his studies, Kirtsaeng asked friends and family back in Thailand to purchase copies of foreign-edition English-language textbooks (where they sold at low prices) and send them to him. He then resold the books on eBay, reimbursed family and friends, and kept the profit. Some of the books resold by Kirtsaeng were textbooks published (printed) in Asia by John Wiley & Sons.

In 2008, Wiley sued Kirtsaeng in federal **district court** for copyright infringement. The complaint alleged violation of § 106(3)'s exclusive right to distribute and § 602(a), which provides that importation into the United States "without the authority of the owner of copyright under this title, of copies ... of a work that have been acquired outside the

United States" is a copyright infringement. Kirtsaeng defended that the books were "lawfully made" (i.e., not "bootleg" copies on the black market) and that he had legitimately acquired them. Thus, as lawful owner of the books, he could dispose of them or resell them as he saw fit under § 109(a) (see above).

The district court held that the "first sale" defense was not available to Kirtsaeng because it did not apply to "foreign-manufactured goods" (albeit manufactured under the authority of the copyright owner). He was found liable for copyright infringement and statutory damages of $600,000.

A split panel of the **Circuit Court** of Appeals for the Second Circuit affirmed. Since *Costco* left open questions, the Supreme Court accepted **certiorari** (review) to settle different views among circuits.

Writing for the majority, Justice STEPHEN BREYER reversed the district court and remanded the case. First, the opinion held, the "first sale" doctrine does apply to copies of copyrighted works lawfully manufactured abroad. Section 109(a) makes no reference to geography, noted the Court, referring to the statutory reference to works "lawfully made under this title." Rather, said the Court, "under" can mean "in accordance with" this title. This simple reading promotes the traditional objective of copyright law in combating PIRACY. Importantly, the historical context and language of the Copyright Act indicates that Congress was not referencing geography in writing the present version of § 109. The former version of the law referenced possessors who "lawfully obtained" a copy, whereas the new version refers to owners of a "lawfully made copy." Finally, as the Court generally presumes that the words "lawfully made under this title" carry the same meaning when they appear in different but related statutory sections, it is unlikely that Congress intended those words to have a different meaning in this section or Congress would have so said, noted the Court.

Justice Breyer was joined in the majority opinion by Chief Justice JOHN ROBERTS, JR., and Justices CLARENCE THOMAS, SAMUEL ALITO, SONIA SOTOMAYOR, and Kagan, who noted in a separate concurring opinion (somewhat addressing the DISSENT) that the majority's decision was no more restrictive to copyright owners than previous cases (e.g., *Quality King Distributors*

v. L'anza Research International, 523 U.S. 135, 118 S. Ct. 1125, 140 L. Ed. 2d 254 [1998]).

Justice RUTH BADER GINSBURG filed a dissenting opinion that was nearly as long as the majority opinion. She was joined by Justices ANTHONY KENNEDY and ANTONIN SCALIA. The dissent argued that the majority's decision was contrary to the purpose of the Copyright Act, which is to protect copyright owners from the importation of inexpensive versions of their products. Further, it gravely shrinks the protections afforded under § 602, and shifts the U.S. historical position of resisting international-exhaustion rules in international trade negotiations.

COUNTERFEITING

Five Charged with Importing Counterfeit Toys from China

On February 6, 2013, the U.S. JUSTICE DEPARTMENT announced that it had brought charges against five Chinese nationals and the corporations they had set up for importing COUNTERFEIT toys into the United States. The defendants each reside in Queens, New York. They allegedly violated not only federal INTELLECTUAL PROPERTY laws but also laws prohibiting the sale of hazardous products.

The five individuals charged include two naturalized citizens and three Chinese nationals. The two citizens are Guan Jun Zhang and Jun Wu Zhang. The other three are Cheng Hu, Hua Fei Zhang, and Xiu Lan Zhang. Four of the defendants were living at the same residence in Queens, New York, between 2009 and 2013. At various times, the defendants had set up several **closely held** corporations. These included Family Product USA, Inc.; HCC Wholesales, Inc.; Zy Wholesale, Inc.; HCL Lucky Toys, Inc.; and H.M. Import US Corp.

The INDICTMENT filed against each of these individuals and the corporations alleges that between July 2005 and January 2013, the defendants imported a variety of children's toys from the People's Republic of China. During this time period, U.S. Customs and Border Protection seized 33 items imported by the defendants.

Seventeen of these seizures involved toys that could not be distributed in the United States because the toys were potentially hazardous. The hazards included high phthalate levels, accessible **battery** compartments, small parts that presented choking or ingestion hazards, and excessive lead content. The other sixteen seizures involved items containing images that violated U.S. COPYRIGHT or trademark laws.

On each occasion of **seizure**, the specific toy company that violated federal law received a notice of the seizure. A representative of the respective toy company signed each of these notices and abandoned the seized item. The indictment alleges:

> Due to the number and volume of the seizures, the individual defendants kept forming and shifting their use of the violator toy companies and taking turns as principals, in order to continue importing and distributing violative and infringing toys. Each time the number of seizures accumulated for one violator toy company, the individual defendants formed a new violator toy company to continue importing the violative and infringing toys.

Prosecutors have charged the defendants with violating a series of **consumer protection** statutes. The statutes include the Consumer Product Safety Act (CPSA), 15 U.S.C. §§ 2051–2089; the Consumer Product Safety Improvement Act of 2008 (CPSIA), Pub. L. No. 110-314, 122 Stat. 3016; the Federal Hazardous Substances Act (FHSA), 15 U.S.C. §§ 1261–1278; and agency regulations based on these statutes. The CPSIA contains specific restrictions on the sale, distribution, or import of children's toys that contain more than .1 percent phthalates, which is used on coatings for plastics. Exposure to phthalates, especially by young children, can cause serious health risks. The CPSIA also prohibits the sale, distribution, or import of children's toys that contain BATTERY components accessible without the use of a coin, screwdriver, or other common household tool.

"The people and companies involved in this illegal trade ... placed the lives of innocent children in danger," said James T. Hayes, special agent with Homeland Security Investigations (HSI). "They allegedly sold toys with high lead content and cheap knock offs with substandard parts that break easily and pose a choking hazard. HSI is firm on using its unique customs expertise and law enforcement partnerships to put an end to the importation and sale of dangerous goods."

A second set of charges focuses on alleged violations of federal copyright and trademark laws. According to prosecutors, the defendants imported and sold knockoff versions of toys featuring popular children's characters, including Winnie the Pooh, Dora the Explorer, SpongeBob Square Pants, Betty Boop, Teenage Mutant Ninja Turtles, Power Rangers, Spiderman, Tweety, Mickey Mouse, Pokemon, and other characters from movies such as "Toy Story," "Cars," and "High School Musical."

The Copyright Act of 1976, 17 U.S.C. § 102, protects "original works of authorship fixed in any tangible medium of expression, now known or later developed, from which they can be perceived, reproduced, or otherwise communicated." Additionally, the Trademark COUNTERFEITING Act of 1984, 18 U.S.C. § 2320, applies to a mark that is "identical with, or substantially indistinguishable from, a mark registered on the principal register in the United States Patent and Trademark Office" The Trademark Counterfeiting Act makes it a crime to use such a mark when the use is "likely to cause confusion, to cause mistake, or to deceive."

"The defendants are accused of importing and selling toys that posed significant health hazards to children or were the product of blatant intellectual property theft," said Lanny Breuer, assistant attorney general. "They allegedly retooled their operations many times in order to avoid detection, and despite repeated citations by the authorities, they continued to peddle counterfeit toys featuring Dora the Explorer, SpongeBob SquarePants and other popular children's characters. Today's actions reflect a Justice Department focused on ensuring that consumers receive safe and legitimate goods."

The investigation involved the Justice Department; the U.S. attorney's office for the Eastern District of New York; HSI; the New York field operations director of Customs and Border Protection; the CONSUMER PRODUCT SAFETY COMMISSION; and the New York City Police Department. Prosecutors in the case will include Evan Williams of the Justice Department's Criminal Division along with U.S. attorneys Claire Kedeshian and William Campos from the Eastern District of New York.

CRIMINAL LAW

A body of rules and statutes that defines conduct prohibited by the government because it threatens and harms public safety and welfare and that establishes punishment to be imposed for the commission of such acts.

BP Corporation Agrees to Plead Guilty to Criminal Charges in Gulf Oil Spill

In April 2012, the first criminal charges against an individual connected with the April 2010 Gulf of Mexico oil spill were filed by federal prosecutors in the U.S. **District Court** for the Eastern District of Louisiana. Kurt Mix, a former BP Oil Company engineer, was charged with OBSTRUCTION OF JUSTICE for allegedly deleting emails and text messages relating to the flow rate of petroleum oil leaking from a damaged underwater well. *United States v. Mix,* No. 12-cr-00171. The explosion of the Deepwater Horizon drilling rig at BP's Macondo Well off the Gulf Coast south of Louisiana killed 11 and caused the largest marine oil spill in U.S. history.

A little more than six months later, in November 2012, the U.S. DEPARTMENT OF JUSTICE (DOJ) announced that BP Exploration and Production, Inc. had agreed to plead guilty to **felony manslaughter**, obstruction of Congress, and environmental crimes in connection with the Deepwater Horizon incident. As part of the plea deal, BP agreed to pay a record $4 billion in criminal fines and penalties. Additionally, two top-ranking BP supervisors were charged with MANSLAUGHTER and a former senior BP executive was charged with obstruction of justice. The individuals were not part of the plea agreement or monetary fines. That case is *In re: Oil Spill by the Oil Rig "Deepwater Horizon,"* No. 10-md-02179.

The DOJ referred to the agreement as "the single largest criminal resolution in the history of the United States." U.S. Attorney General ERIC HOLDER, delivering the lengthy press release to media reporters, said that the agreement "constitutes a major achievement toward fulfilling a promise that the JUSTICE DEPARTMENT made nearly two years ago to respond to the consequences of this epic environmental disaster and seek justice on behalf of its victims." Holder went on to say that "we specifically structured this resolution to ensure that more than half of the proceeds directly benefit the Gulf Coast region so that residents can continue to recover and rebuild."

In detail, BP pleaded guilty in the agreement to 11 counts of felony manslaughter (for the 11 deaths), one count of felony obstruction of Congress, and violations of the Clean Water and Migratory Bird Treaty Acts. Assistant Attorney General Lanny A. Breuer of the DOJ's Criminal Division remarked that the Gulf disaster was the result of "BP's culture of privileging profit over prudence." He also opined that "we hope that BP's acknowledgment of its misconduct—through its agreement to plead guilty to 11 counts of felony manslaughter—brings some measure of justice to the family members of the people who died onboard the rig."

American legal **jurisprudence** recognizes corporate liability for criminal acts, especially when based on the misconduct of key corporate officials. In this case, BP's criminal liability was premised on the conduct of three key individuals within the company (who were also being criminally charged individually). Robert Kaluza, 62, of Henderson, Nevada, and Donald J. Vidrine, 65, of Lafayette, Louisiana, who were the highest-ranking supervisors onboard the oil rig on April 20, 2010, were individually charged with negligent and grossly negligent conduct in a separate 23-count INDICTMENT listing violations of the federal **involuntary manslaughter** and seaman's manslaughter statutes as well as the CLEAN WATER ACT. A third person, David I. Rainey, 58, a former BP executive and second-highest-ranking executive at Unified Command during the spill response, was charged with obstruction of Congress and making false statements to law enforcement officials.

In the plea agreement, BP admitted that it (through senior executive Rainey) obstructed an inquiry by Congress as to the amount of oil being spilled into the Gulf as the crisis was occurring. Specifically, BP admitted to withholding documents and providing false and misleading information in response to House of Representative requests for flow-rate information. BP specifically admitted that Rainey manipulated internal estimates in order to underestimate the actual amount of oil flowing from the gaping hole in the well, and also withheld data that contradicted BP's public announcement of leaks amounting to 5,000 barrels per day. Government and independent scientists later determined that more than 60,000 barrels per day were leaking at the site.

Pursuant to an order presented to the court, approximately $2.4 billion of the $4 billion criminal recovery would go to acquiring, restoring, preserving, and conserving the marine and coastal environments, ecosystems, and bird and wildlife habitat in the Gulf of Mexico and bordering states. Some of the recovery would also be dedicated to significant restoration of the barrier islands and/or river diversion along the coast of Louisiana. An additional $350 million would go to funding improved oil spill prevention and response efforts in the Gulf.

The resolution of criminal liability did not resolve the government's continued efforts to recover civil penalties under the Clean Water Act, which could amount to additional billions in civil fines and penalties based on pollution. However, concurrent with resolution of the criminal aspects of the case, the SECURITIES AND EXCHANGE COMMISSION (SEC) announced its resolution of SECURITIES fraud charges with BP in a $525 million settlement.

For its part, BP reported that prior to the agreement, it had already spent more than $14 billion in operational response and cleanup costs and another $1 billion on early restoration projects, in addition to the more than $9 billion it had paid out to settle civil claims from individuals, businesses, and local governmental entities.

In the end, government officials estimated that 25 percent of the spilled oil was recovered; roughly another one-fourth washed ashore, and 36 percent was naturally dispersed or evaporated. About 16 percent was broken down by chemical dispersants. BP had originally asserted that it believed the amount of oil spilled was 20–50 percent less than government estimates.

Smith v. United States

At **common law**, a DEFENDANT wanting to raise an **affirmative defense** bears the burden of proving the defense. For instance, a defendant charged with MURDER may argue that he acted in SELF-DEFENSE, which is an AFFIRMATIVE DEFENSE to the crime. Under the COMMON LAW rule, the defendant would bear the burden of proving the elements of self-defense by a preponderance of the evidence.

In some cases, the courts have ruled that the government must disprove the elements of a defense rather than require the defendant to bear the burden to prove those elements. In *Mullaney v. Wilbur*, 421 U.S. 684, 95 S. Ct. 1881, 44 L. Ed. 2d 508 (1975), the SUPREME COURT reviewed a rule from the State of Maine that required a defendant to prove that he had acted in the **heat of passion** after he was provoked by an **assault**. The Court found that if

the defendant acted in the heat of passion, the act negated an element of a murder charge, which required the state to prove that the defendant had acted with **malice aforethought**. However, requiring the defendant to prove the affirmative defense of heat of passion meant that the state would no longer have to prove **malice**. Therefore, the Court held that the Due Process Clause of the FOURTEENTH AMENDMENT required the state to disprove the defendant's defense.

A defendant in the case of *Smith v. United States*, 133 S. Ct. 714, 184 L. Ed. 2d 570 (2013) relied on *Mullaney* in arguing that the government should bear the burden of disproving the defendant's defense that he had withdrawn from a CONSPIRACY related to an illegal drug business. In a unanimous decision, the Court rejected the defendant's argument, ruling that Congress must have intended to preserve the common-law rule.

The 2013 case involved Calvin Smith. The government indicted him for crimes related to his participation in a crime business that sold cocaine, crack cocaine, heroin, and marijuana in the Washington, D.C., area. The INDICTMENT included 158 counts and alleged a conspiracy involving 16 coconspirators. According to the indictment, the coconspirators committed violent crimes in addition to running the drug business. Among these violent crimes were 31 alleged murders. The time period spanned from the 1980s until 2000.

Smith faced a trial with five other coconspirators in the U.S. **District Court** for the District of Columbia. A jury convicted him on charges of conspiracy to possess and distribute narcotics, conspiracy under the Racketeer Influenced and Corrupt Organizations Act (RICO), continuing criminal enterprise, and murder. Smith received a life sentence for these convictions.

Smith raised a defense based on a five-year **statute of limitations** contained in 18 U.S.C. § 3282. The basis of his argument was that the conspiracy counts were time-barred because he had spent the last six years of the alleged conspiracy in prison on another **felony** conviction. Smith had not yet raised the defense that he had withdrawn from the conspiracy. The final jury charge instructed the jury to find Smith guilty if the government had proven **beyond a reasonable doubt** that (1) the conspiracies existed; (2) Smith was a member of the conspiracies; and (3) the conspiracies continued to exist within five years before the indictment. Smith had been incarcerated since June 1, 1994, and was indicted in 2000.

During the jury's deliberations, the jury sent the judge a note. It asked, "If we find that the Narcotics or RICO conspiracies continued after the relevant date under the **statute** of limitations, but that a particular defendant left the conspiracy before the relevant date under the STATUTE OF LIMITATIONS, must we find the defendant not guilty?" The judge responded, "Once the government has proven that a defendant was a member of a conspiracy, the burden is on the defendant to prove withdrawal from a conspiracy by a preponderance of the evidence." Smith challenged this instruction.

Smith appealed his convictions to the U.S. Court of Appeals for the District of Columbia Circuit. In a lengthy and complex opinion, the court rejected Smith's arguments regarding the jury instruction. The court followed prior precedent from the D.C. Circuit establishing that "the defendant, not the government, 'has the burden of proving that he affirmatively withdrew from the conspiracy if he wishes to benefit from his claimed lack of involvement.'" *United States v. Moore*, 651 F.3d 30 (D.C. Cir. 2011).

The federal circuits were divided on the issue of whether the government or the defendant should bear the burden of proving withdrawal or lack of withdrawal from a conspiracy. The Second, Fifth, Sixth, Tenth, and Eleventh Circuits had ruled that the defendant should always bear the burden to prove withdrawal. The First, Third, Fourth, and Ninth Circuits ruled that once a defendant has produced evidence of withdrawal, the burden to disprove withdrawal shifts to the government.

To resolve the split among the circuits, the Supreme Court granted **certiorari**. In a relatively short opinion written by Justice ANTONIN SCALIA, the Court affirmed the D.C. Circuit's decision.

Scalia's opinion noted that though the government has the burden to prove each fact necessary to constitute the crime that the government has accused the defendant of committing, the same principle does not apply to affirmative defenses. The government may not shift the BURDEN OF PROOF to the defendant "when an affirmative defense does negate an element of

the crime." However, when the defendant raises a defense based on argument that certain conduct excuses a defense, "the Government has no constitutional duty to overcome the defense beyond a reasonable doubt."

The Court concluded that the defense of withdrawal from a conspiracy does not negate an element of the conspiracy crime. The government must prove that two or more people have agreed to commit a crime and that the defendant knowingly and willfully participated in such a crime. Scalia wrote, "Far from contradicting an element of the offense, withdrawal presupposes that the defendant committed the offense."

The Court noted that Congress could have chosen to shift the burden back to the government, but Congress chose not to do so. The opinion said this decision by Congress was "both practical and fair" because where one party is in the position to know the facts and the other party is not, the party with knowledge "is best situated to bear the burden of proof." In the context of a conspiracy, the Court stated: "The defendant knows what steps, if any, he took to dissociate from his confederates. He can testify to his act of withdrawal or direct the court to other evidence substantiating his claim. It would be nearly impossible for the Government to prove the negative that an act of withdrawal never happened."

In a rather harshly worded concluding paragraph, the Court added a further reason why Smith should have to bear the burden of proving his defense. The Court stated: "Having joined forces to achieve collectively more evil than he could accomplish alone, Smith tied his fate to that of the group. His individual change of heart (assuming it occurred) could not put the conspiracy genie back in the bottle. We punish him for the havoc wreaked by the unlawful scheme, whether or not he remained actively involved. It is his withdrawal that must be active, and it was his burden to show that."

CRIMINAL PROCEDURE

The framework of laws and rules that govern the administration of justice in cases involving an individual who has been accused of a crime, beginning with the initial investigation of the crime and concluding either with the unconditional release of the accused by virtue of acquittal (a judgment of not guilty) or by the imposition of a term of punishment pursuant to a conviction for the crime.

Chaidez v. United States

In the 2010 case of *Padilla v. Kentucky*, 130 S. Ct. 1473, 176 L. Ed. 2d 284, the U.S. SUPREME COURT decided that a criminal DEFENDANT receives ineffective assistance **of counsel** when the defendant's attorney fails to inform the client that a guilty plea carries the risk of DEPORTATION. Under the Supreme Court's precedent, the ruling would not apply retroactively if the Court had announced a new rule. In 2013, the Court reviewed the decision in *Padilla* and determined that the Court had indeed announced a new rule. The Court ruled that a woman who filed a motion to attack her conviction just before the Court decided *Padilla* could not rely on *Padilla* as authority.

Many commentators thought that the Supreme Court had broken new ground when it decided *Padilla*. In that case, a defendant's counsel gave erroneous advice that PLEADING guilty to a drug distribution charge would not impact the defendant's IMMIGRATION status. The defendant argued that he had received ineffective assistance of counsel in violation of the SIXTH AMENDMENT to the U.S. Constitution. The Kentucky Supreme Court rejected his argument, holding that consequences of a guilty plea were outside the scope of the rights protected by the Sixth Amendment.

The U.S. Supreme Court reversed. In an opinion written by Justice JOHN PAUL STEVENS, the Court concluded that "advice regarding deportation is not categorically removed from the **ambit** of the Sixth Amendment right to counsel." The Court applied the case of *Strickland v. Washington*, 466 U.S. 668, 104 S. Ct. 2052, 80 L. Ed. 2d 674 (1984), in which the Court had established the modern rules addressing ineffective assistance of counsel claims. The Court in *Padilla* determined that the rule from *Strickland* has an important application in deportation cases.

To determine whether a case applies retroactively, the Court uses the framework established in the case of *Teague v. Lane*, 489 U.S. 288, 109 S. Ct. 1060, 103 L. Ed. 2d 334 (1989). Under *Teague*, a constitutional rule applies to all cases if the rule is not a new one and is instead only an old rule that applies to

new facts. Conversely, a new rule only applies to cases that are on direct review. A new rule applies retroactively only in limited circumstances. This meant that if the Court in *Padilla* had announced a new rule, the rule as a general matter could not apply retroactively.

The case of *Chaidez v. United States* involved a native of Mexico, Roselva Chaidez, who had become a lawful permanent U.S. resident in 1977. She was indicted in 2003 on three counts of **mail fraud** related to an insurance scheme. Her counsel advised her to plead guilty to two counts, which she did on December 3, 2003, and she was sentenced in April 2004 to four years' PROBATION.

Chaidez's crimes involved **fraud** that led to losses of more than $10,000. Under 8 U.S.C. § 1227, an alien "convicted of an aggravated **felony** at any time" after admission to the United States may be deported. Because of the nature of her crime, the U.S. government in 2009 initiated deportation proceedings after Chaidez had been unsuccessful in applying for U.S. citizenship.

On January 25, 2010, Chaidez filed a motion for a **writ** of coram nobis, which allowed Chaidez to attack her conviction even though she was not in CUSTODY. A court can grant the writ only in narrow circumstances when the court needs to provide **collateral** relief to address an ongoing civil disability that results from a conviction. The writ of **coram** nobis is functionally similar to a writ of **habeas corpus**.

The Supreme Court decided *Padilla* on March 31, 2010, which was less than three months after Chaidez had filed her writ. In the U.S. **District Court** for the Northern District of Illinois, Chaidez argued that *Padilla* should apply retroactively to her case, asserting that the Court had not announced a new rule. The district court judge Joan B. Gottschall agreed and ruled in Chaidez's favor, vacating Chaidez's conviction on grounds that she had received ineffective assistance of counsel.

The government appealed the decision to the Seventh **Circuit Court** of Appeals. The court stated that Judge Gottschall had written a "thoughtful opinion" but reversed Gottschall's decision. The Seventh Circuit reviewed the circumstances surrounding *Padilla*, including concurrences and dissents filed in the case. The court also noted that "numerous courts had failed to anticipate the holding" in *Padilla*, providing "strong evidence that reasonable jurists could have debated the outcome." *Chaidez v. United States*, 655 F.3d 684 (7th Cir. 2011).

The Supreme Court agreed to review the case and, in a 7–2 decision, affirmed the Seventh Circuit. Writing for the majority, Justice ELENA KAGAN focused first on the rule from *Teague v. Lane*. According to the majority, the opinion in *Teague* "makes the retroactivity of our criminal procedures decision turn on whether they are novel." Based on this principle, a case establishes a new rule "when it breaks new ground or imposes a new obligation" on the government.

When the Court decided *Padilla*, it did "something more" than apply rules from previous cases such as *Strickland* and its progeny. Prior to the Court's decision, nearly all **federal courts** had held that the Sixth Amendment did not require attorneys to advise clients of the deportation consequences of pleading guilty. After the Court's decision, failure of counsel to give such advice does constitute ineffective assistance in violation of the Sixth Amendment.

Based on the Court's conclusion, the Court determined that criminal defendants "whose convictions became final prior to *Padilla* . . . cannot benefit from its holding." Accordingly, the Court affirmed the Seventh Circuit's decision. *Chaidez v. United States*, 133 S. Ct. 1103, 185 L. Ed. 2d 149 (2013).

Justice SONIA SOTOMAYOR, joined by Justice RUTH BADER GINSBURG, dissented, arguing that the Court in *Padilla* had merely applied *Strickland* in a new setting. Justice CLARENCE THOMAS concurred, asserting that the Court had decided *Padilla* wrongly and *Padilla* should not apply in a case such as Chaidez's.

Florida v. Harris

The FOURTH AMENDMENT to the U.S. Constitution prohibits a police officer from engaging in unreasonable searches and seizures and requires an officer to show **probable cause** to obtain a warrant to conduct a **search**. The SUPREME COURT has established rules that govern when an officer may search certain places, such as a car. Under the rules, an officer may conduct a search of an automobile when the officer has PROBABLE CAUSE to believe that CONTRABAND or evidence of a crime is present.

Many cases have focused on whether an officer has had probable cause to search for drugs or similar contraband. To determine whether an officer has probable cause to conduct the search, the courts looked to the totality of the circumstances. The Supreme Court has "rejected rigid rules, bright-line tests, and mechanistic inquiries in favor of more flexible, all-things-considered approach."

The Florida Supreme Court in 2011 reviewed a case involving the search of a man's car. An officer believed he had probable cause because of his drug-sniffing dog. The Florida Supreme Court ruled that the officer lacked probable cause and established a long checklist of items that officers needed to consider before determining that probable cause existed. However, the U.S. Supreme Court reversed the decision after rejecting the standard that the Florida court had established.

The DEFENDANT in the case was Clayton Harris. On June 24, 2006, he was stopped by an officer named William Wheetley, who had determined that the tag on Harris's car had expired. Wheetley saw that Harris was breathing rapidly and shaking. Moreover, Wheetley observed an open can of beer in Harris's car. Harris refused Wheetley's request to consent to a search, so Wheetley employed his drug-sniffing dog named Aldo to determine whether any drugs were present in Harris's car. Aldo sniffed around the car and alerted Wheetley about a scent near one of Harris's door handles.

Based on this alert, Wheetley searched Harris's car. Wheetley found more than 200 pseudoephedrine pills contained in a plastic bag. After arresting Harris, Wheetley continued the search and found chemicals used to make methamphetamine. Harris later admitted that he was addicted to the drugs and had cooked some at home two weeks before the search.

Wheetley testified that he had been an officer for three years and had handled a drug dog since 2004. He had completed a drug detection training course that took 120 hours. Aldo had been certified as a drug-detection dog in February 2004. The dog was trained and certified to detect such drugs as cannabis, cocaine, ecstasy, heroin, and methamphetamine. However, Aldo could not detect alcohol or pseudoephedrine, which is what the officer had found in Harris's car.

Wheetley had worked with Aldo since July 2005, or about 11 months before the Harris arrest. Wheetley and the dog had completed a 40-hour training seminar, and Wheetley had spent additional time every week continuing training. Wheetley testified that Aldo had a "really good" success rate in detecting drugs. Wheetley maintained records of Aldo's performance when the dog found drugs. However, Wheetley did not keep records of instances where Aldo alerted the officer about drugs but no drugs were found.

Two months after Wheetley had originally stopped Harris, Wheetley stopped Harris again. Aldo once again alerted the officer to the same door as the original search. However, Wheetley only found an open liquor bottle and no drugs. Harris produced evidence of this search at trial as part of his argument that Aldo was unreliable with regard to his ability to sniff for drugs.

Despite Harris's arguments, a trial court ruled that Wheetley had probable cause to search Harris's car, and a **district court** of appeals summarily affirmed the trial court's decision.

Harris then appealed the decision to the Florida Supreme Court. A divided court reversed the lower court's decision. The court acknowledged that the totality-of-the-circumstances test applied but that the lower court should have considered more factors when determining whether probable cause existed. The court stated that the lower court should have considered instances in the past when the dog may have falsely alerted the officer about the presence of drugs. The court rejected the state's argument that a dog's field-performance test was meaningless because dogs cannot distinguish between odors suggesting that drugs are present and other residual odors where drugs are not present. The court said that these facts should have been part of the court's determination of whether probable cause existed. *Harris v. State,* 71 So. 3d 756 (Fla. 2011).

The U.S. Supreme Court agreed to review the case, and a unanimous Court reversed the Florida Supreme Court's decision. Justice ELENA KAGAN wrote the Court's opinion. *Florida v. Harris,* 133 S. Ct. 1050, 185 L. Ed. 2d 61 (2013).

The Court stressed that previous decisions had not reduced the test for probable cause to a "precise definition or quantification." Likewise, the Court has rejected "rigid rules, bright-line tests, and mechanistic inquiries..." Instead, the Court has adopted a flexible approach that considers all factors related to the search.

The Court completely disagreed with the Florida Supreme Court's analysis. Kagan wrote: "The Florida Supreme Court flouted this established approach to determining probable cause. To assess the reliability of a drug-detection dog, the court created a strict evidentiary checklist, whose every item the State must tick off. Most prominently, an alert cannot establish probable cause under the Florida court's decision unless the State introduces comprehensive documentation of the dog's prior 'hits' and "misses' in the field."

Using the correct approach, the court should take into account all of the facts to determine "what all the circumstances demonstrate." The Court reviewed the evidence in the case, including Aldo's training and proficiency. The training record showed that Aldo was reliable in detecting drugs, and when the dog detected drugs in Harris's car, it provided Wheetley with probable cause to search the vehicle.

Maryland v. King

Collection and analysis of DNA EVIDENCE has become a common practice in law enforcement in the United States. The SUPREME COURT has acknowledged that DNA testing "may significantly improve both the criminal justice system and police investigative practices." This is true because the testing makes it "possible to determine whether a biological tissue matches a suspect with near certainty." Every state now requires the collection of DNA from those convicted of felonies. Moreover, a total of 28 states and the federal government have passed laws allowing law enforcement to collect DNA evidence automatically when a person is arrested.

The Supreme Court in 2013 addressed the question of whether the practice of collecting DNA evidence at the time of an arrest when officers do not have a warrant violates the FOURTH AMENDMENT of the U.S. Constitution. In *Maryland v. King,* 133 S. Ct. 1958 (2013), the Court concluded that it is reasonable for law enforcement to follow the procedure of collecting the DNA evidence.

The case focused on the application of a Maryland **statute.** Under Public Safety Code § 2-504(a)(3)(i), law enforcement authorities may collect DNA samples from "an individual who is charged with...a crime of violence or an attempt to commit a crime of violence." In April 2009, Alonzo Jay King was arrested in

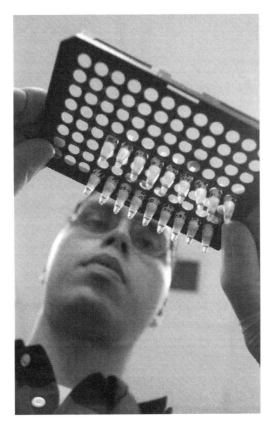

A forensic analyst processes DNA samples as part of a criminal invetsigation.

MARIO VILLAFUERTE/
GETTY IMAGES

Maryland on first- and second-degree **assault** charges. Because prosecutors charged him with a crime of violence, the statute allowed law enforcement to collect a DNA sample. An agent with a county booking facility collected a DNA sample from King by using a buccal swab and taking a sample of saliva from King's cheek.

Personnel with the county facility sent the DNA sample to the Maryland State Police **Forensic** Sciences Division. The division later sent the evidence to a private lab for testing. Lab personnel uploaded the DNA test results to the Maryland DNA database. This occurred in July 2009 and allowed detectives to cross-reference King's DNA with evidence found in unsolved cases.

Less than a month after King's DNA was uploaded to the database, an officer with the state police contacted a Detective Barry Tucker of the Salisbury (Maryland) Police Department. King's DNA proved to be a match to an unsolved RAPE case. The rape occurred on September 21, 2003, and involved a 53-year-old woman. The man who committed the rape wore a scarf over his head and carried a handgun. After the man raped the woman, she underwent a sexual ASSAULT forensic

examination, and the **examiner** collected semen from the vaginal swab. The woman was not able to identify the man after the attack.

Tucker presented the DNA database hit to a **grand jury** in Wicomico County on August 4, 2009, and the GRAND JURY returned an INDICTMENT on ten charges against King related to the attack on the woman. One of those charges included first-degree rape. The hit in the database was the only evidence that supported the indictment. In November 2009, officers took another DNA sample from King, and the DNA again matched the vaginal swab taken from the victim in 2003.

King claimed that collecting his DNA evidence amounted to an illegal **search and seizure** and filed a motion to suppress the evidence. A hearing judge in February 2009 denied King's motion to suppress the DNA evidence. The same judge later presided over a second hearing to consider King's motion. The second motion focused on whether the state had followed proper protocols when collecting the DNA. However, the judge again denied King's motion. King pleaded not guilty to the charges but was convicted of rape. He was sentenced in 2010 to life in prison without PAROLE.

The Maryland Court of Appeals (the state's highest court) agreed to review the case. The court considered two questions. First, the court reviewed whether the trial court erred when it denied King's motion to suppress the DNA evidence "obtained through a warrantless **search** conducted without any individualized suspicion of wrongdoing." Second, the court determined whether the lower court improperly shifted "the BURDEN OF PROOF to the defense to demonstrate that a search or **seizure** made without individualized suspicion is unreasonable."

In 2012, the Maryland Court of Appeals ruled that the collection of the DNA violated King's Fourth Amendment rights. The court considered the totality of the circumstances and concluded that King's "expectation of privacy is greater than the State's purported interest in using King's DNA to identify him." *King v. State*, 42 A.3d 549 (Md. 2012). The court relied on decisions from California and Arizona that had reached the same conclusion.

The U.S. Supreme Court granted **certiorari** to review the case. In a 5–4 decision, the Court reversed the Maryland court. The case featured an unusual split among the justices. Justice ANTHONY KENNEDY wrote for the majority and was joined by Chief Justice JOHN ROBERTS along with Justices CLARENCE THOMAS, STEPHEN BREYER, and SAMUEL ALITO. Justice ANTONIN SCALIA dissented and was joined by liberal justices RUTH BADER GINSBURG, SONIA SOTOMAYOR, and ELENA KAGAN.

The majority noted that although the Court had not addressed the constitutionality of the swab procedure, "the framework for deciding the issue is well established." The Court reviewed cases that addressed intrusions into the body, such as a "venipuncture to draw blood." Comparatively, the swab procedure to collect DNA evidence is a "far more gentle process" and involves a "negligible" intrusion into the defendant's body.

The Court nevertheless considered the intrusion a search, meaning that the procedure needed to be "reasonable in its scope and manner of execution." The Court balanced the interests of privacy with the law enforcement–related concerns to determine whether the procedure was reasonable. The Court concluded that the procedure was indeed reasonable.

Kennedy wrote: "When officers make an arrest supported by **probable cause** to hold for a serious offense and they bring the suspect to the station to be detained in CUSTODY, taking and analyzing a cheek swab of the arrestee's DNA is, like fingerprinting and photographing, a legitimate police booking procedure that is reasonable under the Fourth Amendment."

Scalia took the unusual step of summarizing his DISSENT from the bench. He noted that the Court has "insisted upon a justifying motive apart from the investigation of crime." In the context of the collection of DNA evidence, Scalia argued that "no such noninvestigative motive exists." He added, "Make no mistake about it: because of today's decision, your DNA can be taken and entered into a national database if you are ever arrested, rightly or wrongly, and for whatever reason."

United States v. Davila

Federal Rule of **Criminal Procedure** 11(b) provides for *vacatur* (vacating) of a defendant's guilty plea under certain circumstances. In *United States v. Davila*, 133 S. Ct. 2139 (2013), the U.S. SUPREME COURT held that a magistrate's error was harmless and did not warrant vacatur under F.R.Crim.P. 11(b), as the record failed to show prejudice to the defendant's decision to plead guilty.

In 2009, Anthony Davila was indicted by the U.S. government on multiple tax **fraud** charges, including filing over 120 false tax returns and receiving more than $423,000 from the U.S. Treasury as a result. Davila sent a letter to the federal **district court** in Georgia, where his case was pending, and expressed dissatisfaction with his court-appointed counsel. He complained that his attorney offered no defense strategies and simply advised that he plead guilty. He requested new court-appointed counsel.

In response, a U.S. **magistrate** judge held an in-camera hearing with Davila and his attorney, without the presence of government prosecution. At the onset, the magistrate judge advised Davila that he was free to represent himself but that he would not be getting another court-appointed counsel. Addressing Davila's complaint that his defense counsel had no defense strategy and wanted him to plead guilty, the magistrate judge responded that often this was the best advice counsel could give a client, and "there may not be a viable defense to these charges." As to defense counsel's alleged attempt to urge Davila to plead guilty, the magistrate judge advised that, in view of whatever evidence there might be, "it might be a good idea for the DEFENDANT to accept responsibility for his criminal conduct" and go to the sentencing phase with the best arguments available without wasting the government's time and the court's time.

The magistrate judge counseled Davila on prosecution's ability to suggest a downgraded penalty from that in the Federal Sentencing Guidelines if he cooperated. "You've got to tell the PROBATION officer everything you did in this case regardless of how bad it makes you appear to be," said the magistrate, "because that is the way you get that three-level reduction for acceptance [of responsibility], and believe me, Mr. Davila, someone with your criminal history needs a three-level reduction for acceptance." He urged Davila to cooperate with the government, "to come to the cross," in order to "get the [sentence] reduction for acceptance [of responsibility]."

More than three months after that in-camera hearing before the magistrate judge, Davila agreed to plead guilty to a CONSPIRACY charge in exchange for dismissal of the other

33 counts in the INDICTMENT. Six days after that, he entered his plea before a district court judge. Under oath, he stated that he had not been forced or pressured to plead guilty. Importantly, Davila did not mention the in-camera hearing before the magistrate judge, nor did the record reflect whether the district court judge was aware of that hearing.

Prior to the sentencing hearing, however, Davila moved to vacate his plea and dismiss the charges, telling the district court that his move was "strategic." Aware that prosecution had made time-frame errors in the indictment, and that prosecution had a duty to disclose all information relevant to a court's determination as to whether to accept a plea bargain, Davila intended, by PLEADING guilty, to make the court aware that the prosecution was "vindictive."

The district court denied Davila's motion, citing his statement at the plea hearing that he was under no "pressure, threats, or promises [made] by the government in the plea agreement." The court also noted that Davila had been fully advised of his rights and the consequences of his plea. Accordingly, the district court found his plea "knowing and voluntary." Furthermore, in light of Davila's extensive criminal history, the court sentenced him to 115 months in prison. Again, at the sentencing, neither Davila nor the judge mentioned the in-camera hearing.

On appeal, Davila's court-appointed counsel sought leave to withdraw from the case, asserting that there were no issues of arguable merit to be raised. However, the **Circuit Court** of Appeals for the Eleventh Circuit denied counsel's motion following its own "independent review" of the record. That review, said the court, "revealed an irregularity in the statements of a magistrate judge, made during a hearing prior to Davila's plea, which appeared to urge [him] to cooperate and be candid about his criminal conduct to obtain favorable sentencing consequences." The **appellate court** then asked counsel to address whether this "irregularity" constituted reversible error under F.R.Crim.P. 11(c)(1). That rule prohibits courts from participating in plea discussions.

The Eleventh Circuit ultimately held that Davila's plea must be vacated because the magistrate's violation of F.R.Crim.P. 11(c)(1) required automatic vacatur. The **appellate** court applied its "bright line rule," eliminating the need for inquiry into whether the error was prejudicial.

Justice RUTH BADER GINSBURG, writing for the seven-justice majority, reversed and vacated the judgment of the Eleventh Circuit. While acknowledging that the magistrate judge's conduct (in participating in plea discussions) was indeed improper and a violation of F.R.Crim.P. 11(c)(1), Rule 11(h) clearly provides that "a variance from the requirements of [Rule 11] is **harmless error** if it does not affect substantial rights." The Court went on to dissect and discuss the advisory committee's note at the time of the 1983 amendment that enacted Rule 11(h), "reject[ing] the extreme sanction of automatic reversal" and clarifying that Rule 52(a)'s provision for HARMLESS ERROR also applied to plea errors.

Here, the record showed no prejudice to Davila's decision to plead guilty. Because Davila failed to raise the issue of the magistrate judge's comments when he offered his plea, he had the burden to show that, but for the misconduct, he would not have pleaded guilty. Moreover, noted the Court, three months had elapsed between that discussion with the magistrate judge, in front of defense counsel, and his plea.

The Court cited numerous precedent that defined "structural errors" ("fundamental constitutional errors that defy analysis by harmless error standards"), which would trigger automatic reversal because "they undermine the fairness of a criminal proceeding as a whole." Rule 11(c)(1) errors do not belong in that highly exceptional category, said the Court. Automatic vacatur of a guilty plea is incompatible with Rule 11(h)'s test for harmless error, not done in this case.

Justice Ginsburg was joined by Chief Justice JOHN ROBERTS, JR., and Justices ANTHONY KENNEDY, STEPHEN BREYER, SONIA SOTOMAYOR, ELENA KAGAN, and SAMUEL ALITO. Justice ANTONIN SCALIA, joined by Justice CLARENCE THOMAS, concurred in part and concurred in the judgment. He opined that the majority could have simplified the matter by merely relying on the plain language of the harmless error rule, without the need to laboriously cover the LEGISLATIVE HISTORY.

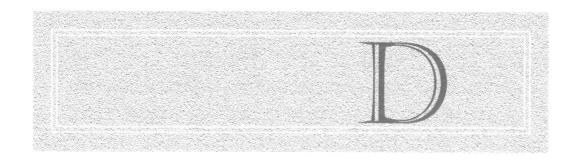

DEBTOR AND CREDITOR

A debtor is one who owes a debt or the performance of an obligation to another, who is called the creditor; one who may be compelled to pay a claim or demand; anyone liable on a claim, whether due or to become due.

In bankruptcy law, a person who files a voluntary petition or person against whom an involuntary petition is filed. A person or municipality concerning which a bankruptcy case has been commenced.

Marx v. General Revenue Corporation

Congress enacted the Fair Debt Collection Practices Act (FDCPA), 15 U.S.C. §§ 1692–1692p to address the problem of abusive practices employed by debt collectors. Under 15 U.S.C. § 1692(e), the purpose of the **statute** was "to eliminate abusive debt collection practices by debt collectors, to insure that those debt collectors who refrain from using abusive debt collection practices are not competitively disadvantaged, and to promote consistent **State action** to protect consumers against debt collection abuses."

One provision of the Act allows courts to award attorney's fees to the DEFENDANT. The Act in 15 U.S.C. § 1692k states: "On a finding by the court that an action under this section was brought in **bad faith** and for the purpose of harassment, the court may award to the defendant attorney's fees reasonable in relation to the work expended and costs."

In *Marx v. General Revenue Corporation*, 133 S. Ct. 1166, 185 L. Ed. 2d 242 (2013), the SUPREME COURT addressed the question of whether a **district court** could award costs to a defendant without a finding that the PLAINTIFF brought the action in bad faith and for the purpose of harassment. In a 7–2 decision, the Court held that the Act did not displace a rule in the Federal Rules of **Civil Procedure** that allows courts to award costs to the **prevailing party**.

The case focused on Olivea Marx. She had taken out a loan guaranteed by EdFund, a division of the California Student Aid Commission. After Marx defaulted on her loan, EdFund hired General Revenue Corporation (GRC) in September 2008 to collect on Marx's account. Marx alleged that a GRC agent called her several times a day and threatened to garnish 50 percent of her wages. Moreover, according to Marx, an agent with GRC sent a facsimile to Marx's employer to request information about Marx's employment status. An agent then called the employer to verify Marx's status and was told that the agent would have to send a written request for information. The agent sent the written request on a standard employment verification form that contained GRC's name, local address, and telephone number, along with a number identifying Marx's account.

Marx sued GRC in October 2008, alleging that collectors with GRC had violated the FDCPA. Shortly thereafter, GRC made an offer of judgment to settle Marx's claims. The offer included $1,500 plus reasonable attorney's fees and costs. However, Marx did not respond to the **settlement** offer.

The U.S. District Court for the District of Colorado held a one-day **bench trial**. The district judge Richard P. Matsch determined that Marx had failed to show any violation of the FDCPA. GRC submitted a bill of costs that included witness fees, witness travel expenses, and DEPOSITION transcript fees. The total of these costs was $7,779.16. Although Matsch denied some costs, he ordered Marx to pay $4,543.03.

The district court based its award of costs on Rule 54(d)(1) of the Federal Rules of CIVIL PROCEDURE. This rule states: "Unless a federal statute, these rules, or a court order provides otherwise, costs—other than attorney's fees—should be allowed to the prevailing party." On appeal to the Tenth **Circuit Court** of Appeals, Marx argued that the FDCPA in 15 U.S.C. § 1692k only allows an award of costs upon a finding that the plaintiff had brought the case in bad faith and for the purpose of harassment.

The Tenth Circuit disagreed. The court stated that § 1692k(a)(3) "unambiguously provides for two cost-shifting scenarios: one for a prevailing plaintiff and the other for a prevailing defendant. When a plaintiff prevails, he or she recovers costs and reasonable attorney's fees." The court stated that "[w]hen a defendant prevails *and* the court finds that the suit was brought in bad faith and for the purpose of harassment, then (in the court's discretion) that defendant may *also* recover attorney's fees." The real issue, the court said, was whether § 1692k(a)(3) supersedes Rule 54(d) and effectively limits the court's ability to award costs.

The **appellate court** held that § 1692k(a)(3) does not supersede Rule 54(d). The court stated, "We believe § 1692k(a)(3)—in both its prevailing-plaintiff and bad-faith provisions—merely recognizes that the PREVAILING PARTY is entitled to receive the costs of suit as a matter of course. Nothing in the language of the statute purports to exclude Rule 54(d) costs from being taxed and awarded in FDCPA suits." *Marx v. General Revenue Corporation*, 668 F.3d 1174 (10th Cir. 2011).

The Supreme Court agreed to review the case, limiting the review to the question of costs. Justice CLARENCE THOMAS wrote for the

7–2 majority, which affirmed the Tenth Circuit's decision. Justice SONIA SOTOMAYOR, joined by Justice ELENA KAGAN, dissented.

The majority noted that Rule 54(d)(1) gives district courts the discretion to award costs, but the rule also allows a federal statute or different rule of civil procedure to provide otherwise. Several federal statutes effectively displace Rule 54 and limit a court's discretion in awarding costs. For instance, in the context of damages related to commodity exchanges, Congress in 7 U.S.C. § 18 explicitly established that plaintiffs are not liable for costs.

However, the Court concluded that § 1692k (a)(3) is not contrary to and does not displace Rule 54(d)(1). The majority reviewed the context of the language in § 1692k(a)(3) as well as the language of other provisions in the FDCPA. The Court determined that this context suggested that Congress did not intend to displace Rule 54(d)(1). Moreover, the language in § 1692k(a)(3) stands in contrast to other statutes in which Congress has displaced Rule 54(d)(1).

Thomas wrote, "Although Congress need not use explicit language to limit a court's discretion under Rule 54(d)(1), its use of explicit language in other statutes cautions against inferring a limitation in § 1692k(a)(3). These statutes confirm that Congress knows how to limit a court's discretion under Rule 54(d)(1) when it so desires." In sum, the Court found no reason to infer that Congress in § 1692k(a)(3) intended to limit the ability of a court to award costs under Rule 54(d)(1).

Sotomayor in DISSENT argued that the plain meaning of § 1692k(a)(3) dictated a result different from the one reached by the majority. She noted that Rule 54(d)(1) states that the rule does not apply when another federal statute "provides otherwise," and in her opinion, the FDCPA provides otherwise.

DEPARTMENT OF JUSTICE

Operation Fast and Furious "Gun-Walking" Scandal

Although media coverage did not focus on the "Operation Fast and Furious" matter until June 2012, in fact, the controversy had been polarizing Washington, D.C., for almost a year prior to that. What triggered media attention in June was President Barack Obama's exercise of **executive privilege** (for the first time in his presidency) over documents related to the covert operation, at the same time that House Oversight Chair Darrell Issa scheduled a CONTEMPT vote against Attorney General ERIC HOLDER for withholding similar related documents. Ultimately, a September 2012 DEPARTMENT OF JUSTICE (DOJ) inspector general report led to sanctions against 14 U.S. DOJ and Bureau of Alcohol, Tobacco, and Firearms (ATF) officials.

Operation Fast and Furious was the code name for a program initially launched in 2009 through a collaborative effort among the DOJ, the FBI, and the ATF. The program was intended as part of a larger strategy to identify and eliminate illegal firearms trafficking, particularly among gang "cartels." In the past, law enforcement had spent many hours and taxpayer dollars prosecuting individuals ("straw purchasers") who bought guns from or for the cartels. Instead, the gist of Operation Fast and Furious was to allow guns to "walk" across the border into Mexico, eventually tracing them to the "top bosses" of Mexico's powerful drug cartels.

While the program looked good on paper, things went terribly wrong. Between 2009 and 2011, ATF agents ostensibly allowed nearly 2,000 firearms to "walk" across the border. However, ATF lost track of and/or failed to track the guns. Ultimately it was alleged that as many as 1,700 of the weapons had been lost, and more than 100 of them had shown up at violent crime scenes on both sides of the border.

The misbegotten program came to light after December 2010, when Border Patrol Agent Brian Terry was shot and killed by Mexican bandits during a border shootout. Two of the guns recovered at the scene turned out to have serial numbers linked to Fast and Furious guns "walked" across the border.

This led to a politically polarized congressional investigation directed mostly at Attorney General Holder for his reluctance to disclose DOJ's involvement and response to Fast and Furious. The House Republican–led investigation ultimately led to Holder being the first U.S. cabinet member held in contempt of Congress for not disclosing the documents. While the House investigation labeled the program as a failed fiasco for the Obama administration, in

Department of Justice Inspector General Michael Horowitz testifies before House members during the DOJ's investigation of "Operation Fast and Furious."
CHRIS MADDALONI/CQ ROLL CALL

truth, the "gun-walking" strategy actually started in 2006 under the Bush administration. At that time, it was labeled Operation Wide Receiver. (The Wide Receiver program had also "devolved into a fiasco," reported Paul M. Barnett in a May 2013 article for *Bloomberg Businessweek*.) In any event, the Fast and Furious operation was the biggest that the DOJ had ever been involved in.

As the investigation continued, more and more guns were tracked to scenes of violent murders and massacres, primarily in Mexico, where the timing of Operation Fast and Furious coincided with an upsurge of wars among Mexico's strongest drug cartels.

Media coverage of Fast and Furious accelerated after the House focus on Holder's information holdout became increasingly politicized in the early summer of 2012. In September 2012, ABC News published a report revealing "new details" about the Fast and Furious "scandal," relying heavily on a Mexican army document obtained exclusively by Univision News. According to the ABC report, Univision News had identified a total of 57 previously unreported firearms that were purchased by "straw purchasers" ostensibly monitored by ATF during Operation Fast and Furious. These guns were eventually recovered in Mexico at the scenes of various murders, kidnappings, and at least one massacre.

One incident reported in the article occurred on January 30, 2010, when a local commando of at least 20 hit men parked outside a birthday party of high school and college students in Villas de Salvárcar, Ciudad Juárez. As the party continued toward midnight, several of the gunmen broke into a one-story residence and opened fire on the nearly 60 partying teenagers. Lookout gunmen stationed outside gunned down a screaming neighbor and several teenagers attempting to escape. Ultimately, 14 teenagers were killed and 12 more wounded. The gunmen were later identified as hired hit men for the Mexican **cartel** La Linea. At least three of the weapons fired that night were linked to those being tracked by the ATF under Fast and Furious. A similar massacre had occurred just four months earlier at El Aliviane, a rehabilitation center also in Ciudad Juárez, where 18 young men were killed.

According to documents obtained by Univision, close to 175 weapons from Operation Fast and Furious inadvertently ended up in the hands of drug traffickers in wars in the northern Mexican states between the Sinaloa and Juárez factions, as well as the expanding Zetas.

The point of origin for guns ostensibly tracked in the program came primarily from ATF offices in Arizona, but Texas and Florida ATF offices were also used. According to Univision, high-powered firearms from Florida's Operation Castaway ended up in Columbia, Honduras, and Venezuela, according to a prison interview with the lead informant.

DOUBLE JEOPARDY

Evans v. Michigan

A basic tenet of American **constitutional law** and **jurisprudence** is the Fifth Amendment's protection against double jeopardy—that is, the risk of facing another trial for a crime previously acquitted of. Prior U.S. SUPREME COURT decisions have defined an ACQUITTAL as encompassing any ruling that determines the prosecution's proof is insufficient to establish criminal liability for an offense. Further, the Court has long held that such is true even where an acquittal "is based upon an egregiously

erroneous foundation." *Fong Foo v. United States,* 369 U.S. 141, 143, 82 S. Ct. 671. (The Court has, however, distinguished substantive rulings of acquittals from procedural rulings that lead to mistrials or dismissals unrelated to factual guilt or innocence, and which therefore do not bar retrial.)

In *Evans v. Michigan,* 133 S. Ct. 1069 (2013), the U.S. Supreme Court reversed the Michigan Supreme Court and held that a midtrial acquittal based on defendant's motion for a **directed verdict**, even though based on the trial judge's error regarding an evidentiary element of the crime, nonetheless constitutes an acquittal for purposes of **double jeopardy**. The Court's 8–1 ruling was premised on the trial court's determination (albeit erroneous), that the state had not provided sufficient evidence for a particular element of the **statutory** offense. In fact, the unproven element was not a required element at all, and the prosecution had met its actual burden.

Michigan's Compiled Laws define two separate crimes of ARSON. MCL § 750.72 requires that the structure burned be a dwelling, while § 750.73 covers all other real property. Lamar Evans was picked up by Detroit police in September 2008 as he was running away with a gasoline can from a burning vacant house. It was later determined that gas had been poured inside the house, which was destroyed. Evans was charged with burning "other real property" under § 750.73.

After the state rested its case at the criminal trial, Evans moved for a DIRECTED VERDICT, citing Michigan Criminal Jury Instruction § 31.3 that listed as a "fourth" element of the charged offense (§ 750.73) "that the building was not a dwelling house." He also cited the commentary to the instructions, which emphasized, "an essential element is that the structure burned is not a dwelling house." The trial judge, noting that the testimony of the structure's owner identified the structure as a dwelling house, found that the nondwelling requirement of § 750.73 had not been met by the state. He granted Evans a directed verdict of acquittal and dismissed the case.

Under Michigan case precedent, the burning of "other real property" is a LESSER INCLUDED OFFENSE under the cited Michigan **criminal law**. Therefore, disproving the greater offense is not required. Accordingly, on the state's appeal, the

Michigan Court of Appeals reversed and remanded. The **appellate court** noted that the trial court had indisputably "misperceived" the elements of the offense under which Evans had been charged and had obviously erred in directing a verdict. Therefore, said the **appellate** court, retrial was not barred.

The Michigan Supreme Court, divided, nonetheless concluded that "when a trial court grants a defendant's motion for a directed verdict on the basis of an error of law that did not resolve any factual element of the charged offense, the trial court's ruling does not constitute an acquittal for purposes of double **jeopardy** and retrial is therefore not barred." 491 Mich. 1,4.

To resolve conflict among state and **federal courts** on this matter, the U.S. Supreme Court granted **certiorari** (review). Precisely, the sole question before the Court was framed as "whether retrial is barred when a trial court grants an acquittal because the prosecution had failed to prove an 'element' of the offense that, in actuality, it did not have to prove."

The Court, in an opinion delivered by Justice SONIA SOTOMAYOR, responded in the affirmative, reversing Michigan's highest court. Citing and distinguishing a long list of Supreme Court cases (including *Fong Foo*), the Court concluded that the DOUBLE JEOPARDY Clause barred retrial of Evans's offense.

The Michigan Supreme Court had justified its conclusion by holding that there was a "constitutionally meaningful difference" between Supreme Court precedent and *Evans*. It argued that the Court's cases "involve[d] evidentiary errors regarding the proof needed to establish a factual element of the . . . crimes at issue" and ultimately involved "a resolution regarding the sufficiency of the factual elements of the charged offense." 491 Mich. at 14–15.

But the Court's 8–1 majority perceived no such distinction. To the contrary, it noted that the trial court, following Michigan's Rule of **Criminal Procedure** 6.19(A), granted Evans's motion for the court "to direct a verdict of acquittal on any charged offense as to which the evidence is insufficient to support a conviction." Moreover, the trial judge expressly cited the prosecution's evidence (including the testimony of the homeowner) as basis for his determination that the state had failed to prove

its case. The fact that the judge's ruling was in error and a clear misunderstanding of what facts the state needed to prove does not change the result that his ruling was an acquittal based on insufficient evidence. Said the Court, "Seeing no meaningful constitutional distinction between a trial court's 'misconstruction' of a **statute** [as in *Arizona v. Rumsey*, 467 U.S. 203, 104 S. Ct. 2305] and its erroneous addition of a statutory element, we hold that a midtrial acquittal in these circumstances is an acquittal for double jeopardy purposes as well."

Finally, the Court addressed an argument raised by the lone dissenter, Justice SAMUEL ALITO, who echoed arguments raised by the state as well as an **amicus curiae** brief from the U.S. DEPARTMENT OF JUSTICE. Collectively, they protested that the rules have become unworkable, effectively denying prosecution a "full and fair opportunity" to present its evidence to a jury, while reaping a "windfall" on the DEFENDANT from the trial court's unreviewable error. But the Court responded that sovereigns (in this case, Michigan) have the power to disallow the practice of midtrial acquittals through their own rules, including ones that may defer consideration of motions for acquittal until the end of trial, or providing for mandatory continuances, expedited **interlocutory** appeals, and so forth.

DRUGS AND NARCOTICS

Drugs *are articles intended for use in the diagnosis, cure, mitigation, treatment, or prevention of disease in humans or animals, and any articles other than food intended to affect the mental or body function of humans or animals.* Narcotics *are any drugs that dull the senses and commonly become addictive after prolonged use.*

Big Pharmaceutical Settlements in 2012

Despite hefty fines and civil/criminal penalties, the pharmaceutical industry ("Big Pharma") continued making record profits through 2012, according to numerous media reports. In a September 2012 *Time* magazine article, journalist Maia Szalavitz reported that the July 2012 $3 billion judgment against pharmaceutical giant GlaxoSmithKline (the largest fine ever imposed on a drug company), represented just 11 percent of its associated revenues.

Also in September 2012, the Public Citizen's Health Research Group, a research and watchdog organization, updated its December 2010 report documenting all major financial settlements and court judgments between pharmaceutical manufacturers and federal or state governments. The information was of value because many of the settlements received little or no media coverage, compared with coverage for civil or criminal trials against the companies. The Public Citizen's report listed 74 settlements, totaling $10.2 billion in financial penalties that had been reached in the roughly 20 months from November 2010 through July 18, 2012. (Only settlements totaling $1 million or more were included in the report.) In just the first six months of 2012 alone, $5 billion in federal settlements and $1.6 billion in state settlements were documented.

The settlements involved charges for numerous violations, both criminal and civil, including illegal off-label marketing and the deliberate overcharging of tax-funded healthcare programs such as **Medicare** and **Medicaid**. Drug pricing **fraud** against state MEDICAID programs was one of the most common violations, while the largest penalties were associated with the unlawful promotion of drug products. Roughly two-thirds of all settlements were the result of whistle-blower-initiated investigations.

The huge $3 billion federal **settlement** with GlaxoSmithKline (GSK) involved criminal charges of illegal marketing of its antidepressant drugs Paxil (paroxetine) and Wellbutrin (bupriopion) for uses not approved, and Lamictal (lamotrigine). It also faced charges for withholding data on the health risk of its diabetes medication Avandia. The company was additionally charged with making payments or offering lavish gifts (expensive vacations) to doctors for dispensing its drugs, including television's "Dr. Drew," who allegedly received $275,000 indirectly from GSK. The payment was for his promotion of Wellbutrin as treatment for sexual dysfunction, despite a lack of data on its use for this purpose. He failed to disclose this payment when he discussed Wellbutrin on the air. Finally, the settlement covered allegations of overcharging government health care programs for its products.

Drug-maker Abbott Industries settled (for $1.5 billion) both criminal and civil charges in 2012, for illegally marketing its product Depakote (valproic acid) as a treatment for aggression and agitation, despite no approval for those uses. Moreover, the drug was found to cause severe side effects like anorexia (loss of appetite) in the elderly. Abbott also marketed Depakote as an add-on treatment for schizophrenia, when in fact internal company research showed no additional benefit for that condition and it was not approved for that use. It also settled charges for illegal kickbacks.

In 2012, Johnson & Johnson (J & J)settled with the state of Texas for $158 million and the state of Arkansas for $1.2 billion, both for illegal promotion/marketing of its products. (The year before, it settled with the state of South Carolina for $327 million for the same thing.) Still pending but near settlement was the settlement of pending federal charges ($1.5 to $2 billion) for illegal marketing of its atypical antipsychotic drugs Risperdal (risperidone) and Invega (paliperidone). Despite lack of data showing any benefit, in addition to known risks, these drugs were illegally marketed to child psychiatrists and doctors treating geriatric patients. The company also faced charges for concealing data involving both drugs' link to weight gain and diabetes. Some of these charges came to light years after Johnson & Johnson funded the writing of national treatment guidelines (the Texas Medical Algorithm Project) intended as a broad model for doctors providing evidence-based psychiatric care. However, a whistleblower lawsuit later alleged that the company paid state officials for preferred placement of its drugs in the guidelines. For example, the guidelines cited Risperdal as a treatment for attention-deficit hyperactivity disorder (ADHD) in children. The FDA had never approved the drug for this use, nor had there been any evidence that the drug proved beneficial for children with this condition.

Amgen, already treading water in a 2013 U.S. SUPREME COURT SECURITIES FRAUD case (*Amgen Inc. v. Connecticut Retirement Plans and Trust Funds*, 133 S. Ct. 1184 [2013]) was also facing a whistleblower lawsuit, accusing it of BRIBERY (for doctors to prescribe its drugs) and for conspiring with doctors to overfill vials of the anemia-treating drug Aranesp (darepoetin alfa). According to the claim, doctors would then give the excess "free" drugs to patients but bill insurance companies for them. Federal investigations were also pending against the company in 2013 for the marketing, pricing, and dosing of Aranesp, along with the promotion of clinical data on the drug's safety and effectiveness. Amgen reported that it had set aside funds to settle these investigations.

In May 2013, Indian generic drugmaker Ranbaxy Laboratories, Ltd., majority-owned by Japanese drugmaker Daiichi Sankyo, pleaded guilty to federal **felony** charges stemming from 2010-2011 investigations by the U.S. DEPARTMENT OF JUSTICE regarding drug safety. The guilty plea and settlement payment of $500 million resolved both criminal and civil charges relating to drug safety and selling adulterated products. The DOJ investigations found evidence that Ranbaxy manufactured and distributed generic drugs that were substandard, i.e., below U.S. FOOD AND DRUG ADMINISTRATION (FDA) standards. The drugs were made at two plants in India, and included prescription products intended for children, such as the antibiotic amoxicillin. Ranbaxy had reached a related settlement with the FDA in 2011. A 2008 ban by the FDA prohibited Ranbaxy from selling about 30 different drugs in the United States and in 2009 the FDA alleged that Ranbaxy had falsified data and test results. As part of the 2013 settlement, Ranbaxy pleaded guilty to three felony counts related to the manufacturing of substandard, unsafe products and then selling the adulterated drugs. It also pleaded guilty to four counts of making material false statements. Of the $500 million in settlement funds, $350 million was to settle civil claims (largely from states and their Medicaid programs) and $150 million in criminal fines and penalties.

Voters in Colorado and Washington Legalize Marijuana

Colorado and Washington in 2012 became the first states to legalize possession and use of marijuana for recreational use. Voters in both states approved measures during the November elections allowing users to possess a certain amount of the drug. The number of states allowing possession and use of marijuana for medical purposes also increased when Massachusetts voters approved a measure during the elections.

The Colorado law was titled Amendment 64: The Regulate Marijuana Like Alcohol Act of 2012. The proposal amended Article XVIII of the state's constitution (miscellaneous provisions) by adding a new section that applies to the personal use and regulation of marijuana. The amendment begins with the following statement of purpose: "In the interest of the efficient use of law enforcement resources, enhancing revenue for public purposes, and individual freedom, the people of the state of Colorado find and declare that the use of marijuana should be legal for persons twenty-one years of age or older and taxed in a manner similar to alcohol."

More than 55 percent of voters approved the law during the November 6 election. This number was consistent with polls showing that a majority of voters supported the proposal before the election. Among those advocating against the proposal, though, was the editorial board of the *Denver Post*, arguing that marijuana policy did not belong in the state's constitution. Nevertheless, more than 1.3 million voters approved Amendment 64.

Amendment 64 allows those 21 years or older to possess, use, display, purchase, and transport one ounce or less of marijuana. The law also allows users to possess "marijuana accessories." Users may grow up to six marijuana plants in their homes, but the law forbids users to sell the homegrown marijuana. The law forbids users from consuming marijuana in public.

Amendment 64 contains provisions that allow the state to regulate marijuana cultivation facilities. The amendment required the state's department of revenue to establish regulations to implement the new law no later than July 1, 2013. The department of revenue may not "prohibit the operation of marijuana establishments" and must establish "[p]rocedures for the issuance, renewal, suspension, and revocation of a license to operate a marijuana establishment."

Amendment 64 requires the department to establish requirements for applications to cultivate or manufacture marijuana; qualifications to become licensed to operate a marijuana establishment; security measures; labeling of marijuana products; prevention of sale to those under the age of 21; and restrictions on advertising and display of marijuana and marijuana products. Moreover, the department must establish health and safety regulations for the manufacture and cultivation of marijuana, and the department must establish civil fines for failure to comply with the department's regulations.

On December 10, 2012, Colorado Governor John Hickenlooper created the Amendment 64 Implementation Task Force. Hickenlooper's

The performer Snoop Lion exhales marijuana smoke onstage at the Fillmore Auditorium in Denver, CO, April 19, 2013.

SETH MCCONNELL/THE DENVER POST/GETTY IMAGES

EXECUTIVE ORDER charged the task force with identifying the "legal, policy and procedural issues that need to be resolved, and to offer suggestions and proposals for legislative, regulatory and executive actions that need to be taken, for the effective and efficient implementation of Amendment 64." The task force submitted its findings in a report issued to Hickenlooper on March 13, 2013. The report addressed 17 topics related to Amendment 64, including issues related to regulatory structure, financing and taxation, licensing and operational requirements, consumer safety, education, and other issues.

Washington voters approved a similar measure in November. The state's proposal to legalize marijuana was known as Initiative 502. A summary of the initiative, prepared by the Washington attorney general's office, stated as follows:

> This measure would remove state-law prohibitions against producing, processing, and selling marijuana, subject to licensing and regulation by the liquor control board; allow limited possession of marijuana by persons aged twenty-one and over; and impose 25% **excise** taxes on wholesale and retail sales of marijuana, earmarking revenue for purposes that include substance-abuse prevention, research, education, and healthcare. Laws prohibiting driving under the influence

would be amended to include maximum thresholds for THC blood concentration.

Initiative 502 was approved by 56 percent of Washington State voters on November 6. Provisions of the law have phased in during a one-year period. Possession of marijuana, as well as criminal provisions applying to driving under the influence of the drug, became effective on December 6, 2012. The law delegates implementation authority to the Washington State Liquor Control Board.

Not all marijuana proposals passed in 2012, however. Oregon voters rejected a proposal to legalize marijuana for recreational use, while Arkansas citizens voted against a proposal to allow marijuana for medical uses. The proposal in Oregon was less restrictive than the proposals in Colorado and Washington, but sheriffs and **district attorneys** in the state opposed the measure. According to the opponents, the law would have led to more problems with intoxicated drivers among other issues.

Supporters of the laws in Colorado and Washington have been unsure about how the federal government will react to the new marijuana laws. Marijuana is still listed as a Schedule I drug under the Controlled Substances Act, 21 U.S.C. § 812, meaning that federal authorities could still legally arrest users in either state notwithstanding the new marijuana laws. Nevertheless, neither state experienced friction with federal authorities in the first several months after voters approved those laws. In April 2013, Representative Dana Rohrabacher (R.-Cal.) introduced a bill in Congress that would ensure the federal government would respect state marijuana laws.

The new laws in Colorado and Washington will likely provide a significant revenue boost for both states. Taxation of marijuana could produce as much as $100 million in revenues, and lawmakers in other states have said they are interested in pursuing similar laws for the revenue potential from taxes. Moreover, Colorado expects a boost in tourism as individuals who want to use marijuana are more likely to visit the state, which already attracts many tourists thanks to the Rocky Mountains and other features.

Oregon and Washington were two of the first states to allow marijuana use for medical purposes in 1998. Colorado approved medical marijuana in 2000. Other states that allow medical marijuana as of 2013 include Alaska, Arizona, California, Connecticut, Delaware, Hawaii, Maine, Michigan, Montana, Nevada, New Jersey, New Mexico, Rhode Island, Vermont, and Washington. The District of Columbia also allows its use.

Results of a poll conducted by the Pew Research Center and published in the *Los Angeles Times* in April 2013 shows that Americans favor laws legalizing marijuana. A total of 52 percent voted in favor, compared with 45 percent who voted against. Moreover, 72 percent of respondents said the federal government's efforts to crack down on marijuana possession "cost more than they are worth."

EDUCATION LAW

The body of state and federal constitutional provisions; local, state, and federal statutes; court opinions; and government regulations that provide the legal framework for educational institutions.

Federal Government Struggles with Student-Loan Interest Rates

The federal government in 2012 and 2013 continued to struggle with questions about how to address student-loan interest rates. President BARACK OBAMA signed a bill in 2012 that kept interest rates for federally subsidized loans at 3.4 percent for at least one more year. However, Congress did not act before July 1, 2013, meaning that the rates doubled until the House was able to reach a compromise that brought the rate down to 3.86 percent. In addition, the bill included a clause that protects borrowers impacted by the doubled rate from paying the steeper fees.

Student-loan debt in the United States has been growing exponentially. One report indicated that national student-loan debt grew by almost 300 percent between 2004 and 2012. As of 2012, the total amount of student loan debt in the United States was $1.1 trillion. Americans owe more in student-loan debt than they owe on credit cards or cars. In fact, only mortgage debt exceeded student-loan debt in 2013.

For many years, student loans subsidized by the federal government had variable interest rates. During the early 2000s, however, the variable rate was consistently below 6 percent, leading to calls to create a fixed interest rate. In 2007, Congress approved a plan to establish a fixed interest rate of 6.8 percent with plans to reduce this rate during several phases. Under this plan, loans fell from 6.8 percent to 5.6 percent in 2009–2010, 4.5 percent in 2010–2011, and 3.4 percent in 2011–2012. Because this was a five-year plan, though, the rate would return to 6.8 as of July 1, 2012, unless Congress acted.

The average college graduate owes more than $26,000 in student-loan debt. However, the job market has not improved during the past five years, so many of the college graduates owing this debt have struggled to pay their loans. In fact, the U.S. DEPARTMENT OF EDUCATION reported in 2012 that the default rate for student loans was 13.4 percent, the highest level in 14 years. The number is higher among graduates of for-profit colleges.

In an effort to ease some of the burden, Congress approved a provision in a bill passed in 2012 to extend the interest rate of 3.4 percent for one more year. The extension was part of a transportation bill known as Moving Ahead for Progress in the 21st Century Act, Pub. L. No. 112-141, 126 Stat. 405. Title III of the Act applied to the Federal Direct Stafford Loan Interest Rate, extending the 3.4 percent rate until July 1, 2013. Reports estimate that the rate change would have affected 7.4 million college graduates with student-loan debt.

President Barack Obama delivers a speech on student loans in the White House Rose Garden, May 31, 2013.
MANDEL NGAN/AFP/ GETTY IMAGES

Concerns about the rising cost of education and the growing student-loan debt were topics raised during the 2012 presidential race. Just before the election in November, the Department of Education announced the launch of a new program designed to help students repay their loans. The program is known as the "Pay As You Earn" repayment plan, and it is designed to limit monthly payments to an amount that is more affordable based on the borrower's income and family size. Specifically, the plan limits payments to 10 percent of a borrower's discretionary income. Loans eligible for the plan include Direct Subsidized Loans, Direct Unsubsidized Loans, Direct PLUS Loans, and Direct Consolidation Loans; the program is limited to borrowers who took out their initial loans after October 1, 2007 and received a disbursement after October 1, 2011.

For those eligible, the Pay As You Earn plan ensures that a borrower's monthly payment will be lower than if the borrower followed a standard repayment plan. Moreover, the plan also provides that the federal government will pay a borrower's unpaid accrued interest while the borrower makes the lower payments for up to three years. The plan has additional provisions for loan cancellations after a borrower makes 20 years of payments and loan forgiveness for those who hold public-service jobs. The Department of Education established an online calculator that estimates whether a borrower is eligible for the plan. The calculator is available at http://studentaid.ed.gov/PayAsYouEarn.

The Pay As You Earn plan is only available to those who took out a loan after October 1,

2007, and who have taken out a loan after October 1, 2011. Thus, the plan only affects current students and recent graduates. Those who took out loans before October 2007 may still be eligible for an older version of the plan, which set payments at 15 percent of a borrower's discretionary income.

The level of student-loan debt is still a concern, however. Economists and other commentators have stressed fears that widespread defaults of student loans could cause a financial crisis similar to the one caused by homeowners defaulting on their mortgages in 2007. The Consumer Finance Protection Bureau (CFPB) has solicited comments about how to address student-loan issues. Of particular concern to the CFPB are private loans, which account for about 15 percent of all student loans.

Student borrowers had more reason to worry because of Congress's failure to extend the student interest rate for at least another year. With members of Congress debating other budgetary issues, maintaining the lower interest rates for student loans was not a priority in 2013. Budget proposals submitted by SENATE Democrats did not allocate money to keep interest rates at the 3.4 percent level. Moreover, House Republicans wanted interest rates to return to the 6.8 percent level as part of an effort to balance the budget. Although change in interest rates will reportedly save the government $6 billion, lawmakers ultimately faced public pressure to reach a compromise, and voted 392-31 on the new legislation.

President Obama is expected to sign the bill into law.

ELECTION LAW

Arizona Upholds English Proficiency Requirement for Public Officeholders

An Arizona law prohibits individuals from running for public office if they are not proficient in the English language. In 2012, a candidate for a city council seat was disqualified from appearing on the election ballot because a state trial court concluded that she was not sufficiently proficient in English to perform as a city council member. In *Escamilla v. Cuello*, 282 P.3d 403 (2012), the Arizona SUPREME COURT rejected the candidate's claim that the trial court had read the proficiency requirement more broadly than intended and that the law itself was unconstitutional.

In late 2011, Alejandrina Cabrera filed as a candidate for the San Luis city council. Soon after, San Luis Mayor Juan Carlos Escamilla brought a special action seeking to disqualify Cabrera as candidate. He named in the lawsuit Sonia Cuello, in her capacity as city clerk. The mayor alleged that Cabrera should be excluded from the March 2012 election ballot because she could not read, write, and speak the English language as required by Arizona state law. The trial court appointed an expert to evaluate Cabrera's English proficiency. The expert concluded that she could not function on the city council because her command of English was deficient. Based on this EXPERT TESTIMONY, the court ordered Cuello not to put Cabrera's name on the election ballot. Cabrera immediately appealed to the Arizona Supreme Court.

The court, in a unanimous decision, upheld the trial court. Justice Robert Brutinel, writing for the court, noted that Cabrera disputed several trial court actions. She first alleged that the trial judge erred in issuing its order 29 days after the mayor filed the complaint. Under the Arizona law, trial courts are to hear and make a decision on an election matter within 10 days after the action was filed. Justice Brutinel relied on an earlier decision by the court, which interpreted this time limit as directive and not jurisdictional. When a non-jurisdictional deadline is not met, the key question was whether a party suffered prejudice because of the delay. Cabrera alleged that the filing and prosecution of the case left her little time to appeal and that the mayor failed to diligently prosecute this case. Brutinel rejected these claims, finding that the trial court's handling of the case left sufficient time for expedited **appellate** review before the ballot-printing deadline. In addition, the court concluded that the mayor moved in a timely manner to serve Cabrera with the lawsuit and promptly moved the court to appoint an expert to test Cabrera. Moreover, the court found that some of the delay was caused by Cabrera's tardiness in filing an answer to the action. Because there was prejudice to Cabrera, there were no grounds to throw out the ruling.

Turning to the proficiency standard, Justice Brutinel pointed out that Arizona law had required English proficiency as a qualification for public office since before statehood. The territorial code stated that no person who could not read and write English was eligible to run for public office. The state's enabling act of 1910 included a similar qualification, which was incorporated in the state constitution. It also stated that the person had to understand English "sufficiently well to conduct the duties of the office without the aid of an interpreter." The territorial code proficiency requirement was carried forward in early versions of the state code and was reenacted in 1956. The law states that a "person who is unable to speak, write and read the English language" was not eligible to hold a state, county, city, town or precinct office, whether elected or appointed. The trial court had ruled that the **statute** would be meaningless if it only required "minimal or bare proficiency at speaking, reading, and writing the English language." Therefore, it narrowly construed the statute to require "sufficient proficiency in speaking, reading, and writing the English language" to understand and perform the duties of the office sought. Cabrera contended the trial court improperly expanded the statute by requiring some degree of fluency in addition to the required ability to read, write, and speak English. She could read aloud city council meeting minutes printed in English and was able during her testimony to engage in basic conversation using English. In her view, that was enough to meet the **statutory** requirement.

Justice Brutinel relied on the enabling act and state constitution provisions that stated all state officers and legislators had to know English well enough to conduct business without an interpreter as setting the standard for proficiency. Though the Arizona law that dealt with all elected officials did not include this language, the court reasoned that it implicitly included those requirements. This was the "most plausible and harmonious reading of the statute." The testimony at the trial level supported the conclusion that Cabrera failed to comprehend questions posed to her in English. Her testimony showed "minimal English language comprehension." For example, she could read aloud city council documents but could not answer elementary questions about what she had read or what had occurred at council meetings. While Cabrera could read English at a ninth or tenth grade level, the statute required that she have the ability to speak English. The expert who tested

Cabrera concluded that she had "minimal survival proficiency" in spoken English. She could perform certain "courtesy requirements and maintain simple face-to-face conversation on familiar topics," but she could not otherwise follow a conversation.

The court rejected Cabrera's attacks on the qualifications and testing methods of the court-appointed expert. It also rejected her constitutional challenge to the statute. She argued the law violated her right to participate in government. Justice Brutinel found no merit in this argument because there is no general constitutional right to seek or hold public office. The state may require a citizen to meet more strict requirements to hold office than to vote for that office. Cabrera also cited the court's 1998 decision striking down a CONSTITUTIONAL AMENDMENT adopting English as the state official language in support of her argument. The court rejected this as well, stating that the key problem with the amendment was that it would have made it illegal for public officials to communicate with non-English-speaking constituents. These constituents would have been impeded in obtaining access to their government and limited the political speech of public officials. There were "no similar concerns" in this case. The law did not prohibit speech in languages other than English. Instead, the law required public officials to have sufficient proficiency in English, which enhanced rather than impeded their ability to communicate with their constituents and the public.

Lavin v. Husted

The Sixth **Circuit Court** of Appeals in 2012 struck down an Ohio **statute** that prevented doctors who treated **Medicaid** patients from contributing to certain campaigns for public office. A group of doctors wanted to donate to the campaign of the state's attorney general, but the candidate declined the donations because the doctors were MEDICAID providers. The Sixth Circuit determined that the state law prohibiting these donations violated the doctors' FIRST AMENDMENT rights.

Calls for campaign finance reform date back to the WATERGATE scandal in 1974. The investigations by Congress following the scandal revealed that special-interest groups were able to bypass laws limiting donations. Some donors would give millions to political candidates in an effort to persuade candidates to adopt policies favorable to the donors. Congress enacted a series of laws that reformed financing of presidential elections and created greater transparency in terms of actual donations given to candidates.

Several states also approved campaign-finance laws in a variety of forms. In 1978, the State of Ohio approved a bill designed to address **fraud** among Medicaid providers. The law prohibited these providers from fraudulently claiming Medicaid payments for services never actually rendered. The law, codified at Ohio Rev. Code § 3599.45, also included the following provision: "No candidate for the office of attorney general or county PROSECUTOR or such a candidate's campaign committee shall knowingly accept any contribution from a provider of services or goods under contract with the department of job and family services pursuant to the [federal] medicaid program...." At the time the Ohio General Assembly enacted § 3599.45, a series of scandals had occurred in which contractors offered bribes and kickbacks to state officials, and the contractors received state contracts in return.

In July 2010, several doctors who are Medicaid providers contacted campaign officials for Ohio Attorney General Richard Cordray. The doctors wanted to contribute to his reelection campaign. However, the campaign officials learned that the doctors were Medicaid providers and informed the doctors that Cordray could not accept donations because of § 3599.45. Moreover, Cordray's website informed potential donors that his campaign could not accept money from Medicaid providers or any person with an ownership interest in a provider.

Two months after being turned down by Cordray's campaign officials, the doctors filed suit in the U.S. **District Court** for the Northern District of Ohio. Arguing the case before District Judge Donald C. Nugent, the doctors asserted that the Ohio law violated their First Amendment rights and sought a **preliminary injunction** that would allow them to donate to Cordray's 2010 campaign. However, Judge Nugent denied the motion for a PRELIMINARY INJUNCTION, holding that the doctors failed to show a strong likelihood that they would succeed on the merits of their case.

The district court did not resolve the case until after the November 2010 elections. The

DEFENDANT in the case was Jon Husted, the Ohio SECRETARY OF STATE. He moved for **summary judgment**, arguing that state statute did not violate the First Amendment. Specifically, the defendant asserted that the statute was closely drawn to advance sufficiently important state interests of preventing corruption and the appearance of corruption.

Judge Nugent granted Husted's summary-judgment motion. The judge rejected the doctors' argument that the state law was not closely drawn to a legitimate **state interest** because it amounted to a complete ban across the state. Nugent wrote, "While § 3599.45 places a ban rather than a limit on direct campaign contributions by Medicaid providers and their owners to candidates for county prosecutor and attorney general, it does not prevent Medicaid providers and their owners from making contributions to a POLITICAL ACTION COMMITTEE or political party that supports a candidate for county prosecutor or attorney general." Moreover, the judge noted, the law did not prevent potential donors from giving money to candidates through family members or from making "symbolic expressions of support" to a candidate. *Lavin v. Husted*, 803 F. Supp. 2d 756 (N.D. Ohio 2011).

The doctors appealed the decision to the Sixth Circuit, which reversed the district court's decision in an opinion written by Circuit Judge Raymond Kethledge. Husted argued the doctors could not **redress** their injuries in a lawsuit against the secretary of state because the secretary lacks any authority to enforce § 3599.45. However, the court noted that the secretary is Ohio's chief election officer, and Ohio law charges the secretary with investigating the administration of election laws and reporting violations to appropriate officials. The court also rejected Husted's argument that the case was moot because the elections had occurred two years before. The court found that the dispute was one "capable of repetition, yet evading review," meaning that the case was not moot.

Kethledge's opinion then turned to the question of whether § 3599.45 violated the First Amendment. The state had to prove how its ban on contributions furthered a sufficiently important interest and how the ban was "closely drawn" to further that interest. The court concluded that Husted could prove neither.

The court rejected Husted's argument that the statute furthered the state's interest in corruption, noting that three previous attorneys general had signed sworn declarations saying that campaign contributions would not have influenced their decision-making. The court likewise concluded that § 3599.45 was not closely drawn, stressing that the statute established a complete ban on contributions and not just a limitation on amounts given.

"The statute here restricts the First Amendment rights of nearly 100,000 Medicaid providers who do not commit FRAUD, based on an attenuated concern about a relative handful of providers who do," wrote Kethledge. "There is no avoiding the conclusion that the contribution ban set forth in § 3599.45 is not closely drawn. The ban is therefore unconstitutional." *Lavin v. Husted*, 689 F.3d 543 (6th Cir. 2012).

The Sixth Circuit is among several **federal courts** that have struggled with issues surrounding the constitutionality of campaign finance laws. Several cases have focused on the effects of the Supreme Court's decision in *Citizens United v. Federal Election Commission*, 558 U.S. 310, 130 S. Ct. 876 (2010), which struck down portions of the Bipartisan Campaign Reform Act of 2002.

ELECTRONIC SURVEILLANCE

Clapper v. Amnesty International USA

The U.S. SUPREME COURT has established that for a party to bring a claim in federal court, the party must have standing. This means that the party must have suffered an injury so that the dispute presents a "case or controversy" over which a federal court has jurisdiction.

In 2013, the Supreme Court applied the doctrine of standing to a dispute involving 2008 amendments to the Foreign Intelligence Surveillance Act of 1978 (FISA), 50 U.S.C. § 1881a. Several groups and individuals challenged the law on the grounds that it violated the FOURTH AMENDMENT of the U.S. Constitution. However, in a 5–4 opinion written by Justice SAMUEL ALITO, the Court ruled that none of the plaintiffs had suffered an injury that gave them standing to challenge the **statute**. Accordingly, the Court reversed a ruling by the Second Circuit that the plaintiffs could challenge the law.

Congress enacted FISA in 1978 to allow the government to conduct ELECTRONIC SURVEILLANCE for purposes of acquiring foreign intelligence information. The officials who must obtain approval are the attorney general and the director of national intelligence. Under FISA, the Foreign Intelligence Surveillance Court can approve surveillance after determining that there is **probable cause** for the government to believe that "the target of the electronic surveillance is a foreign power or an agent of a foreign power." The court must also determine that each of the specific "facilities or places at which the electronic surveillance is directed is being used, or is about to be used, by a foreign power or an agent of a foreign power." If the Foreign Intelligence Surveillance Court denies an application, the FOREIGN INTELLIGENCE SURVEILLANCE COURT OF REVIEW has jurisdiction to review the denial.

Following the September 11 attacks in 2001, President GEORGE W. BUSH gave the National Security Agency the authority to conduct warrantless WIRETAPPING of communications between a party located outside the United States and a suspected member of al Qaeda or an affiliated terrorist organization. The Foreign Intelligence Surveillance Court issued orders in February 2007 allowing electronic surveillance where PROBABLE CAUSE existed to believe that a member of al Qaeda or a related organization would participate in the communication. However, the court later narrowed the scope of the authorization.

Under amendments passed in 2008, the government must still seek approval from the Foreign Intelligence Surveillance Court before conducting the surveillance. However, the amendments changed the procedure followed to seek the court's approval. The government does not need to demonstrate probable cause when the government targets non-U.S. individuals located abroad. Moreover, the amended FISA "does not require the government to specify the nature and location of each of the particular facilities or places at which the electronic surveillance will occur."

A group of plaintiffs immediately challenged the 2008 amendments to FISA. The plaintiffs included AMNESTY INTERNATIONAL and the AMERICAN CIVIL LIBERTIES UNION. Other plaintiffs included journalists and lawyers who represented clients at Guantanamo Bay. Defendants in the case were James R. Clapper, Jr., the director of national intelligence; ERIC HOLDER, the U.S. attorney general; and other government officials.

The plaintiffs challenged the statute on constitutional grounds. They argued that the statute violated the Fourth Amendment because the process through which the government can seek authorization for a warrantless **search** does not comply with cases construing the warrant requirement in the Fourth Amendment.

The plaintiffs brought the case in the U.S. **District Court** for the Southern District of New York. In 2009, the district court granted **summary judgment** in favor of the government, ruling that the plaintiffs lacked standing to proceed with their claim. AMNESTY *International USA v. McConnell*, 646 F. Supp. 2d 633 (S.D.N.Y. 2009). The plaintiffs then appealed the decision to the Second **Circuit Court** of Appeals, and the **appellate court** reversed the district court's decision. According to the Second Circuit, the plaintiffs suffered "*present injuries in fact—economic and professional harms—stemming from a reasonable fear of future harmful government conduct.*" *Amnesty International USA v. Clapper*, 667 F.3d 163 (2d Cir. 2011).

The Supreme Court agreed to review the Second Circuit's judgment, and in a 5–4 opinion, the Supreme Court reversed. Writing for the majority, Justice Alito summarized the standing doctrine, stressing that the "standing inquiry has been especially rigorous when reaching the merits of the dispute would force us to decide whether an action taken by one of the other two branches of the Federal Government was unconstitutional." The Court has often ruled that plaintiffs lack standing when the PLAINTIFF has asked the Court to "review actions of the political branches in the fields of intelligence gathering and foreign affairs."

To establish that they had standing, the plaintiffs had to show a "concrete, particularized, and actual or imminent" injury. The injury had to be "fairly traceable" to the action challenged and had to be "redressable by a favorable ruling." The plaintiffs could not show standing by alleging possible future injuries. Instead, the plaintiffs had to show that the threatened injury was certainly impending.

The majority concluded that the plaintiffs could not establish injuries sufficient to meet the standing requirement. The plaintiffs argued that they had suffered injuries because they had taken steps to avoid surveillance. The majority rejected this argument, with Alito noting that the plaintiffs "cannot manufacture standing by incurring costs in anticipation of nonimminent harms."

Joining Alito were Chief Justice JOHN ROBERTS and Justices ANTONIN SCALIA, ANTHONY KENNEDY, and CLARENCE THOMAS. *Clapper v. Amnesty International USA*, 133 S. Ct. 1138, 185 L. Ed. 2d 264 (2013).

Justice STEPHEN BREYER dissented and was joined by three other justices. Breyer argued that the Court has found in similar circumstances that plaintiffs have had standing to challenge potential future injury. After the Court reached its decision, ACLU lawyer Jameel Jaffer criticized the Court's decision, saying that the ruling "insulates the statute from meaningful **judicial review** and leaves Americans' privacy rights to the mercy of the political branches."

EMINENT DOMAIN

The power to take private property for public use by a state, municipality, or private person or corporation authorized to exercise functions of public character, following the payment of just compensation to the owner of that property.

Koontz v. St. Johns River Water Management District

The FIFTH AMENDMENT to the U.S. Constitution protects against actual or constructive "taking" of private property by the government. Over the years, the U.S. SUPREME COURT has relied on the Fifth Amendment's Takings Clause to ensure important protections against the misuse of governmental power when it comes to land regulation. In several cases, the Court has found land-use regulations to be effective "takings" of property from a land owner, because they so constrict or limit the use of the land that it becomes useless to the owner. In *Koontz v. St. Johns River Water Management District*, 133 S. Ct. 2586 (2013), the U.S. Supreme Court invoked previous Court precedent to restrict a governmental land management agency from using regulations to compel compliance with its unconstitutional demands involving a land-use permit.

In 1972, Coy A. Koontz, Sr., purchased an undeveloped parcel of land (just under 15 acres) along Florida State Road 50, a divided four-lane highway east of Orlando. The property is located less than 1,000 feet from an intersecting road, Florida State Road 408, which is a toll expressway and a major thoroughfare in the Orlando area. The parcel is also encumbered with a 100-foot wide ditch along its western border and high-voltage power lines across its middle. This, in combination with its proximity to the highway and other construction on nearby land parcels, serves to isolate the northern section of the property from any other undeveloped land.

In the same year that Koontz purchased the property, 1972, Florida enacted the Water Resources Act, dividing the state into five water/land management districts. Under the Act, each district is tasked with regulating "construction that connects to, draws water from, drains water into, or is placed in or across the waters in the state" (codified as amended at Fla. Stat. § 373.403[5]). The Act specifies that landowners who want to construct on such lands must obtain (from the local jurisdictional "land management district") a Management and Storage of Surface Water (MSSW) permit. Permits may impose "such reasonable conditions" on the permit as are "necessary to assure" that construction will "not be harmful to the water resources of the district." § 373.414(1).

Despite these restrictions, Florida's wetlands continued to diminish. In 1984, the Florida legislature passed the Warren S. Henderson Wetlands Protection Act, making it illegal to "dredge or fill in, on, or over surface waters" without a Wetlands Resource Management (WRM) permit. Fla. Stat. § 403.905(1). Under this Act, permit applicants are required to provide "reasonable assurance" that proposed construction on wetlands is not "contrary to the public interest" (as defined by enumeration **within the statute**).

Consistent with the Act, one of the five districts, St. Johns River Water Management District (St. Johns), required that permit applicants who wanted to build on wetlands had to offset the resulting environmental damage by creating, enhancing, or preserving wetlands elsewhere.

Koontz, whose property fell within the general wetlands area of St. Johns District, decided to develop the 3.7-acre northern section of it, and in 1994, he applied for both MSSW and WRM permits. His proposal was to raise the elevation of that area (to make it suitable for a building), grade the land from there down, in a southerly direction, and install a dry-bed pond for retaining (and gradually releasing) storm water runoff from the building and proposed parking lot. To mitigate any environmental effects, he offered to foreclose any possible future development of the remaining 11 acres by deeding to St. Johns District a conservation **easement** on those remaining acres. St. Johns considered the 11-acre conservation easement (out of Koontz's 14.9-acre parcel) to be inadequate and denied permit.

For more than eleven years, Koontz tried to reach agreement with St. Johns. In summary, St. Johns ultimately gave Koontz two choices if he wanted a permit: (1) he could reduce the size of his development to just one acre and deed St. Johns a conservation easement on the remaining 13.9 acres, forego the retention pond, and instead install a more costly subsurface stormwater drain system beneath the building site, plus install retaining walls, or (2) Koontz could proceed with the 3.7-acre development he proposed, deed a conservation easement on the remaining 11.2 acres to St. Johns, plus agree to hire contractors to improve 50 acres of another parcel of St. Johns's land several miles away, by either replacing culverts or filling in ditches, or an "equivalent" improvement.

Koontz filed suit in state court under Fla. Stat. § 373.617(2), claiming money damages under the **statute** because St. Johns's ultimatum to him was an "unreasonable exercise of the state's POLICE POWER constituting a taking without just compensation."

On **appellate** remand to the Florida trial court, the court concluded that even Koontz's northern section (the proposed construction site) had been so "seriously degraded" over the past years, by extensive construction on surrounding parcels, that any further mitigation (St. Johns's request for offsite improvements to other parcels) "lacked both a nexus and proportionality to the environmental impact of the proposed construction." It found St. Johns's actions unlawful. The Florida **District Court** affirmed. The Florida Supreme Court reversed. It held that the U.S. Supreme Court precedent's "nexus" requirement did not apply here because the permit was denied, and further held that St. Johns's demand for money for improvement on other St. Johns's land did not give rise to a **cause of action** under Koontz's claim.

The "nexus" language quoted in the courts' decision(s) comes from two Supreme Court cases that are relevant. Both *Nollan v. California Coastal Commission*, 483 U.S. 825, 107 S. Ct. 3141 (1987), and *Dolan v. City of Tigard*, 512 U.S. 374, 114 S. Ct. 2309 (1994) involved special applications of the "unconstitutional conditions" doctrine that protects the Fifth Amendment right to **just compensation** for property that the government "takes" when landowners apply for land-use permits. Together, the cases provide what is referred to as the *Nollan/Dolan* test when reviewing the "permit" process.

A very divided U.S. Supreme Court reversed the Florida Supreme Court. Justice SAMUEL ALITO, writing for the narrow 5–4 majority, held that indeed, *Nollan/Dolan* still applies. St. Johns' demand for property from Koontz in conjunction with Koontz's request for a land-use permit must still meet the above test, even when the permit is denied. Second, the majority held that the *Nollan/Dolan* test also applies when St. Johns' exaction/demand was for money (i.e., in this case, demanding that Koontz pay hired contractors to improve other St. Johns land).

All nine justices agreed on the first part of the majority's decision. The DISSENT, led by Justice ELENA KAGAN, focused on the second question the Court addressed, strongly disagreeing that *Nollan/Dolan* is also applicable when the government conditions a permit on the payment or expenditure of money.

EMPLOYMENT DISCRIMINATION

Supreme Court Clarifies Who Is a Supervisor under Title VII

Under Title VII of the CIVIL RIGHTS Act of 1964, an employer's liability for workplace harassment may depend on the status of the harasser. If the harassing employee is the victim's co-worker, the employer is liable only if it was negligent in overseeing working conditions. However, if the harasser is a "supervisor," different rules apply that can make the employer strictly liable for the harassment. For fifteen years the lower courts came to different conclusions as to how to determine who is a "supervisor." The SUPREME COURT, in *Vance v. Ball State University*, 133 S. Ct. 2434 (2013), settled the issue by declaring an employee is a "supervisor" for Title VII purposes only if he or she is empowered by the employer to take tangible employment actions against the victim, such as discipline, demotion, or termination.

Maetta Vance, an African-American woman, began working for Ball State University (BSU) in 1989 as a substitute server in the university's catering division. In 1991, BSU promoted her to a part-time catering assistant position, and in 2007 she was selected as a full-time catering assistant. During her years working at BSU, Vance lodged many complaints of racial DISCRIMINATION and retaliation, but the court case dealt with Vance's interactions with fellow BSU employee, Saundra Davis. Davis, a white woman, was employed as a catering specialist in the catering division. She did not have the power to hire, fire, demote, promote, transfer, or discipline Vance. In late 2005 and early 2006, Vance filed internal complaints with BSU and charges with the EQUAL EMPLOYMENT OPPORTUNITY COMMISSION (EEOC), alleging racial harassment and discrimination. Many of the complaints and charges pertained to Davis. Vance complained that Davis glared at her, smiled at her, intimidated her, and often gave her "weird" looks.

BSU tried to address the problem but Vance's workplace strife continued. As a result, Vance filed a lawsuit in 2006 in Indiana federal **district court**, claiming that she had been subjected to a racially hostile work environment in violation of Title VII. In her complaint she alleged that Davis was her supervisor and that BSU was vicariously liable for Davis's creation of the racially hostile work environment. The district court dismissed the lawsuit against BSU, concluding that the university was not vicariously liable because Davis was not Vance's supervisor. The court also held that BSU could not be liable in NEGLIGENCE because it responded reasonably to the incidents of which it was aware. The Seventh **Circuit Court** of Appeals affirmed these rulings and Vance appealed to the Supreme Court. The Court agreed to hear the case because other circuit courts of appeals had followed the EEOC's more open-ended approach in defining who is a supervisor.

The Supreme Court, in a 5-4 ruling, agreed with the Seventh Circuit that Davis was not a supervisor. Justice SAMUEL ALITO, writing for the majority, noted that there are different liability rules for employers if a supervisor is involved with harassment of an employee. An employer is vicariously liable for a supervisor's creation of a hostile work environment when the supervisor takes a "tangible employment action, such as hiring, firing, failing to promote, or reassignment with significantly different responsibilities." Even if the supervisor's harassment did not result in a tangible employment action, the employer can still be vicariously liable if the employer was unable to establish an **affirmative defense**. Such a defense would be a showing that the employer used reasonable care to prevent and promptly correct any harassing behavior and that the PLAINTIFF unreasonably failed to take advantage of any preventive or corrective opportunities that were provided. Therefore, defining the term "supervisor" is of great consequence in a Title VII action.

Justice Alito concluded that an employee is a "supervisor" only when the employer has empowered the employee to take tangible employment actions against the victim. The Court rejected the EEOC's "nebulous definition" of a "supervisor." The EEOC took the position that an employee, in order to be classified as a supervisor, must wield authority "of sufficient magnitude so as to assist the harasser explicitly or implicitly in carrying out the harassment." The Court found this interpretation too broad, because any authority over the work of another employee provides "at least some assistance." The EEOC in its briefs stated that the authority had to be more than occasional and that an employee who directs "only a limited number of tasks or assignments" for another employee would not qualify as a supervisor. Justice Alito found this standard vague, and if applied in a courtroom, difficult to decide. Under the Court's definition of "supervisor," the question of supervisor status could "very often be resolved as a MATTER OF LAW before trial." This would simplify the trial process and give the plaintiff clear direction as to whether she needs to prove negligence or **vicarious liability**. The EEOC's approach would make matters more complicated and difficult, requiring evidence of negligence, VICARIOUS LIABILITY, employer affirmative defenses, and two sets of jury instructions.

The Court concluded that its definition of supervisor reflected the realities of the workplace. Justice Alito noted that many modern organizations have abandoned a "highly hierarchal management structure, where employees have overlapping authority with respect to the assignment of work tasks." Employees may direct each other depending on the particular aspect of the work.

Justice RUTH BADER GINSBURG, in a dissenting opinion joined by Justices STEPHEN BREYER, SONIA

SOTOMAYOR, and ELENA KAGAN, argued that the Court should have followed the EEOC's guidance that the "authority to direct an employee's daily activities establishes supervisory status under Title VII." The majority's decision removed from the supervisory category employees "who control the day-to-day schedules and assignments of others."

ENVIRONMENTAL LAW

An amalgam of state and federal statutes, regulations, and common-law principles covering air pollution, water pollution, hazardous waste, the wilderness, and endangered wildlife.

American Trucking Associations, Inc. v. City of Los Angeles

The U.S. Constitution grants specific, enumerated powers to the federal government. Additionally, Article VI of the Constitution contains the **Supremacy Clause**, which states: "This Constitution, and the Laws of the United States which shall be made in Pursuance thereof; and all Treaties made, or which shall be made, under the Authority of the United States, shall be the supreme LAW OF THE LAND; and the Judges in every State shall be bound thereby, any Thing in the Constitution or Laws of any State to the Contrary notwithstanding."

Based on its constitutional powers, the federal government can enact laws that preempt conflicting state law. This **preemption** can be express or implied. In an instance where Congress has expressly preempted state law in a certain area, the courts focus on whether the PREEMPTION provision applies to a particular state law. If the federal law preempts the particular state law, the court will not enforce the state law in question.

In *American Trucking Associations, Inc. v. City of Los Angeles*, 133 S. Ct. 2096 (2013), the SUPREME COURT addressed whether a federal law preempts provisions of a contract imposed by the Port of Los Angeles on trucks operating on the port's premises. The Court concluded that the FEDERAL AVIATION ADMINISTRATION Authorization Act (FAAAA), 49 U.S.C. § 14501(c)(1) indeed preempted the contract's provisions.

The port is a division of the City of Los Angeles and owns marine terminal facilities. The port leases these facilities to terminal operators that load and unload cargo onto and from docking ships. Short-haul trucks known as "drayage trucks" transport the cargo into and out of the port. The companies operating the drayage trucks are licensed by the federal government.

During the 1990s, the board that operates the port decided to accommodate more ships by enlarging the port's facilities. This plan met resistance from neighborhood and environmental groups, which objected to the plans because of concerns over increased air pollution and congestion as well as a decrease in safety in the area surrounding the port. The groups sued the port to enjoin the expansion effort, and this lawsuit effectively prevented the board from implementing the plan for more than a decade.

The board addressed the groups' concerns by implementing the Clean Truck Program in 2007. The board developed a concession agreement that trucking companies had to sign to operate on the port's premises. This agreement contained two provisions relevant to the case before the Supreme Court. First, the agreement required each truck to have a placard containing a telephone number that a person could call to report environmental or safety concerns. Second, the companies had to submit a plan that listed the off-street parking locations for each truck when those trucks were not being used.

To ensure that each company that provided drayage services signed a concession agreement, the port enacted an **ordinance** (known as a "tariff") establishing criminal penalties related to the concession agreement. Under the **tariff**, the criminal penalties applied to a terminal operator that permitted access by a drayage truck to any terminal in the port unless the drayage truck was registered under a concession agreement. An operator could violate the tariff "each and every day" that an operator allowed access to an unregistered truck. Violations of the tariff could result in a fine of up to $500 or a prison sentence of up to six months.

American Trucking Associations, Inc. (ATA), a national trade association that represents the trucking industry, filed suit against the port and the City of Los Angeles. The ATA argued that § 14501(c)(1) of the FAAAA preempted requirements in the concession agreements.

Section 14501(c)(1) states: "[A] State [or local government] may not enact or enforce a law, regulation, or other provision having the force and effect of law related to a price, route, or service of any motor carrier . . . with respect to the transportation of property." Much of the LITIGATION focused on the language "having the force and effect of law." The U.S. **District Court** for the Central District of California in 2010 ruled that the FAAAA did not preempt the concession agreement.

In *American Trucking Associations, Inc. v. City of Los Angeles*, 660 F.3d 384 (9th Cir. 2011), the Ninth **Circuit Court** of Appeals agreed with this conclusion, holding that the placard and parking requirements in the agreements did not have "the force and effect of law." The court determined that the agreements were "designed to address specific **proprietary** problems." Because of this conclusion, the lower court ruled that the agreement did not have the force and effect of law.

The Supreme Court unanimously reversed the Ninth Circuit's decision. Justice ELENA KAGAN wrote for the Court, with Justice CLARENCE THOMAS writing a concurring opinion.

The Court's decision came down to the question of whether the port was acting with its regulatory authority when it approved the tariff or whether the port was simply acting as a market participant. The lower courts concluded the port had acted just as any private party to a contract would have acted. The port argued before the Supreme Court that § 14501(c)(1) excludes ordinary contractual arrangements from the preemption clause.

However, the Court rejected the argument. Kagan wrote: "[T]hat **statutory** reading gets the Port nothing, because it exercised classic regulatory authority—complete with the use of criminal penalties—in imposing the placard and parking requirements at issue here." The Court stressed that the port had accomplished its objective of ensuring that drayage trucks would all be registered under a concession agreement by imposing criminal sanctions on parties that did not comply with the tariff. "So the contract here functions as part and parcel of a governmental program wielding coercive power over private parties, backed by the threat of criminal punishment," Kagan wrote.

The lower courts had also addressed whether the port could restrict a federally licensed carrier from operating in the port. In *Castle v. Hayes Freight Lines, Inc.*, 348 U.S. 61, 75 S. Ct. 191, 99 L. Ed. 68 (1954), the Court held that the State of Illinois could not prevent a federally licensed motor carrier from using the state's highways because of prior violations of state safety regulations. In *American Trucking Associations, Inc.*, the Court declined to decide what result the decision in *Castle* dictated, because the Court had already concluded that the port's tariff was preempted.

In his concurrence, Thomas argued that Congress lacked power to enact the provision in § 14501 because the **statute** only applied to intrastate commerce as opposed to interstate commerce. He stated, however, that because the parties did not raise the constitutional challenge in the lower courts, he agreed that the Court had reached the correct result regarding the preemption provision.

Arizona Voters Veto Ownership of Grand Canyon

In addition to the important presidential election in November 2012, several states had proposal issues ("ballot measures") on their respective state ballots, asking citizens to vote on them. One such initiative was Arizona's Proposition 120, asking voters to amend the state constitution to declare Arizona's sovereignty and jurisdiction over the "air, water, PUBLIC LANDS, minerals, wildlife, and other natural resources within the state's boundaries." "Public lands" included nearly 73 million acres of federally owned land within the state, including national park lands. Among them is the Grand Canyon National Park. The measure was an unabashed attempt to sidestep federal environmental laws and open up at least 25 million acres to mining, logging, and livestock grazing interests. Arizona voters defeated Proposition 120 by a 2–1 margin.

Proposition 120 was essentially a REPUBLICAN PARTY initiative intended to bolster the state's economy. Also fueling the effort was a perceived frustration with federal management of federal lands within the state. The sponsor of the legislation who put the issue on the ballot, Rep. Chester Crandell (R-Heber), was quoted in the area's *East Valley Tribune* as citing forest areas as a prime example. "We had a thriving forest industry back in the 70s and 80s," said Crandell, referring to timber companies harvesting logs

A view of Grand Canyon National Park, AZ.
NAVÉ ORGAD/ALAMY

and drilling interests against those seeking to protect the pristine environment and keep it intact for future generations.

Proponents saw the measure as an important message to counter overreaching federal control of more than 50 percent of the land in the Western United States. But opponents found the measure unenforceable, unconstitutional, environmentally irresponsible, and "typical of a state known for high-profile confrontations with national authorities on illegal immigration," said Amanda J. Crawford in her reporting for Bloomberg News. She also found this measure reminiscent of the old "sagebrush rebellion" of the 1970s stemming from restrictions on the use of public lands and wilderness designations at that time. Among Crawford's commentators on the subject was Paul Bender, dean emeritus of the SANDRA DAY O'CONNOR College of Law and a **constitutional law** professor at Arizona State University. "If you want to start a war, this is the way," Bender commented. "When the state passes its own IMMIGRATION law, people say, 'Well, that is crazy Arizona.' But if people go to the Grand Canyon and find a uranium mine there, they are going to be very upset."

Although many strategists, speculating on the sentiments of Arizona's populace, deemed the initiative a failure from the beginning, it was not without legislative precedent. In March 2013, Governor Gary Herbert of Utah signed into law similar legislation demanding that some federal lands be conveyed to the state by 2014. Utah state attorneys, however, warned that the law would likely be found unconstitutional and would trigger costly, protracted, and ultimately futile legal battles. Also, earlier in 2013, Arizona Governor Jan Brewer had vetoed a prior attempt by legislators calling for the relinquishment of approximately 48,000 square miles. She cited the creation of uncertainty for existing leaseholders on federal lands during tough economic times as the reason for her VETO.

on federal lands. "That's when all the [environmental] lawsuits started." According to Crandell, federal agencies then became hesitant to approve not only new logging projects, but also forest thinning. Crandell blames the huge wildfires that have plagued the state on the lack of forest thinning and timbering.

Among those against the measure, a wall of opposition came from environmental groups, concerned about management practices of state agencies reporting to elected state officials. Also quoted in the *Tribune* article was Steve Arnquist of the Arizona League of Conservation Voters. He argued that it made no sense for each of 50 states to have its own environmental rules and regulations regarding public lands, without a standardized baseline representing a safe level for clean air and clean water. States might have different standards for the CLEAN AIR ACT, "[b]ut the air doesn't know when to stay in the state," he said, and "human lungs are the same in all the states." Arnquist noted that the state had already had problems managing its own state lands without the addition of federal lands. The SIERRA CLUB, actively in opposition to the initiative, estimated that targeted lands comprised between 39,000 and 46,700 square miles, or roughly 34 to 41 percent of the entire state.

The failed measure was largely referred to in the media as part of the "sagebrush revolt" by Republicans in Western states. According to the Thomson Reuters Foundation, the initiative stemmed from decades-old federal-versus-state tugs-of-war over control of a wide range of natural resources that faced-off mining, logging,

Decker v. Northwest Environmental Defense Center

In *Decker v. Northwest Environmental Defense Center*, 133 S. Ct. 1326 (2013) (consolidated with *Georgia-Pacific West v. Northwest Environmental Defense Center*), the U.S. SUPREME COURT deferred to the ENVIRONMENTAL PROTECTION

AGENCY (EPA) for interpretation of its own regulations, which the Court found to be reasonable. The consolidated cases involved stormwater runoff under the 1972 CLEAN WATER ACT, 33 U.S.C. § 1251 **et seq.** The decision reversed that of the Ninth **Circuit Court** of Appeals, which had found the complained-of activity not exempt under the Act or related regulations.

A short review of relevant statutes and regulations is necessary to understand both cases. The Clean Water Act requires that before any pollutants are discharged from any point source into the NAVIGABLE WATERS of the United States, a National Pollutant Discharge Elimination System (NPDES) permit must first be obtained. 33 U.S.C. §§ 1311(a), 1362(12). The relevant EPA implementing regulation is the Silvicultural Rule, 40 CFR § 122.27(b)(1), which specifies which types of logging-related discharges are "point sources" under the Act. (Those discharges designated as point sources under the Silvicultural Rule must obtain NPDES permits unless another **statutory** provision exempts them from coverage.) "Discharges composed entirely of stormwater" are exempted under 33 U.S.C. § 1342(p)(1) *unless* the discharges are associated with "industrial activity." § 1342(p)(2)(B). Under the EPA's Industrial Stormwater Rule, the term "associated with industrial activity" is limited (i.e., is not exempted from permit requirements) to discharges "from any **conveyance** that is used for collecting and conveying storm water and that is directly related to manufacturing, processing or raw materials storage areas at an industrial plant." 40 CFR § 122.26(b)(14).

After the filing of appeals in the present cases, but prior to oral arguments before the Court, the EPA issued a final version to the Industrial Stormwater Rule, clarifying that NPDES permit requirements applied only to logging operations that involved rock crushing, gravel washing, log sorting, and log storage facilities, which are all listed in the Silvicultural Rule.

Georgia-Pacific had a contract with the state of Oregon to harvest timber from state forests. Two logging roads used by Georgia-Pacific (and other logging companies), owned by the Oregon Department of Forestry and the Oregon Board of Forestry, are parallel to rivers in the area. A series of ditches, culverts, and channels are used to direct stormwater runoff into the

nearby rivers, bringing copious amounts of sediment along with the stormwater. Research has shown that these sedimentary deposits are harmful to the environment, in that they adversely affect fish and other wildlife that depend on the water.

The nonprofit Northwest Environmental Defense Center filed civil suit against Oregon state local governments and officials, including Decker, as well as Georgia-Pacific and other logging companies. For jurisdiction and standing, Northwest Environmental invoked the Clean Water Act's citizen-suit provision, 33 U.S.C. § 1365. The gist of the complaint characterized the ditches and channels as "point sources," and defendants therefore had not obtained the required NPDES permits. Defendants (Decker, Georgia-Pacific, et al.) successfully argued that the ditches, culverts, and channels were not "point sources" under the Act or Silvicultural Rule, and the **district court** granted the motion and dismissed the case.

The U.S. Circuit Court of Appeals for the Ninth Circuit reversed, finding that the complained-of ditches and channels were indeed "point sources" under the Silvicultural Rule. Moreover, said the court, the discharges were "associated with industrial activity" under the Industrial Stormwater Rule, contrary to the EPA's own conclusion.

The U.S. Supreme Court reversed and remanded. First, it disposed of a jurisdictional challenge to Northwest's ability to file suit. The Court found the Act's provision utilized by Northwest (citizens' suit provision) was appropriate. Second, and more substantively, the Court, while deferring to the EPA's explanation of the scope of its regulatory reach, held that the EPA's amendment to the Industrial Stormwater Rule (exempting the complained-of activity) did not make this case moot. An actionable controversy continued to exist regarding whether defendants could be liable for unlawful discharges that occurred during the earlier version of the Industrial Stormwater Rule. The earlier version would govern the discharges complained of, and whether permits were required, even if, in the future, those types of discharges would be exempt.

That having been said, the Court went on to note that the earlier version of the Industrial Stormwater Rule did in fact exempt (from permit requirements) channeled stormwater runoff from logging roads. The Court then expressly held that this exemption was a "reasonable interpretation" of the statutory term, "associated with industrial activity." When an agency interprets its own regulation, said the Court, it is entitled to deference by the courts. It was reasonable for the EPA to conclude that the "conveyances" of defendants referred only to the actual harvesting of raw materials, and not to the "manufacturing, processing or raw material storage areas at an industrial plant." Moreover, the EPA has been consistent over the years in its view that these types of discharges were exempt from permitting, and the interpretation did not represent a change from prior practice.

Justice ANTHONY KENNEDY delivered the opinion of the Court, in which all justices either joined or filed separate concurring opinions, excepting Justice STEPHEN BREYER, who took no part in consideration or decision. Justice ANTONIN SCALIA concurred in part, but dissented on Part III, showing displeasure in the manner in which the Court has given agencies the authority to interpret their own rules.

EPA Wins Multiple Challenges to Sulfur Dioxide Rules

In July 2012, the U.S. **Circuit Court** of Appeals for the D.C. Circuit in Washington upheld the 2010 ENVIRONMENTAL PROTECTION AGENCY (EPA) rules limiting emissions of sulfur dioxide, a highly reactive colorless gas, mostly generated by power plants that burn fossil fuels to produce electricity. *National Environmental Development Association's Clean Air Project v. EPA*, 686 F.3d 803 (D.C. Cir. 2012). The captioned case was consolidated with at least 10 others, including ones filed by North Dakota, Texas, and three other states. The decision came just days after the same court upheld the EPA's 2010 rules limiting emissions of nitrogen dioxide near major roadways, and three weeks after its decision upholding the EPA's rules on greenhouse gas emissions for industries and vehicles (mainly carbon dioxide and other pollutants).

In January 2013, the U.S. SUPREME COURT, without comment, denied review of the D.C. Circuit's earlier ruling on still another challenge to the 2010 rule on sulfur dioxide, *Asarco LLC v. U.S. Environmental Protection Agency*, No. 12-510, leaving intact the decision of the **appellate court**. Collectively, the cases were not wholly

redundant because some challenged the EPA regulations on a different ground or theory, but the **appellate** court ultimately upheld the EPA's rules in total.

As background, under the 1972 CLEAN AIR ACT, the EPA is authorized to promulgate standards necessary to protect public health, while still allowing an "adequate margin of safety." 42 U.S.C. § 7408–7409. In 2007, the U.S. Supreme Court held that the Clean Air Act provided for the EPA's authority to regulate greenhouse gases as pollutants. *Massachusetts v. EPA*, 549 U.S. 497, 127 S. Ct. 1438. Since that time, the EPA has faced several legal challenges to the rules, primarily led by industry. (The EPA has determined that power plants account for approximately 70 percent of sulfur dioxide in the air.)

Specific to the captioned case, the 2010 regulation restricts sulfur dioxide (SO2) emissions to 75 parts per billion (ppb) over a one-hour period. 75 Fed. Reg.35520. This substantially lowered the previous standard for maximum sulfur dioxide emissions, which was 140 ppb over 24 hours, set in 1971. The change, it was alleged, could cost companies $1.5 billion.

In the captioned case, the rule was challenged by a trade group, the National Environmental Development Association's Clean Air Project, representing several energy giants including Exxon Mobil Corp., ConocoPhillips, and General Electric. The suit alleged that the EPA's new rule on sulfur dioxide was unconstitutional because it violated notice-and-comment rule-making provisions, in that it failed to inform that it was considering changing the methods of attaining sulfur dioxide standards. Moreover, the complaint(s) alleged, the new standard of 75 ppb was "arbitrary" in that it was lower than needed to protect the public from harm.

The APPELLATE court first ruled that it did not have jurisdiction over the rule-making issue. More importantly, the court found that the EPA had acted within its authority to promulgate such regulations, and that the new established maximum (of 75 ppb) was not arbitrary.

For its part, the EPA (with several, mostly environmental, groups coalesced behind it for amicus support) responded that the new maximum level was necessary to protect the public, especially the elderly or those with asthmatic conditions who were more sensitive to sulfur dioxide exposure, and who were vulnerable to more severe injury from such exposure. To back its determination of appropriate maximum levels, the EPA cited research that showed that even short-term exposure to sulfur pollution posed greater health risks than previously accounted for under the prior rules. Special segments of the general population, including children, the elderly, and those with asthmatic conditions were particularly susceptible to harm, said EPA.

Said Judge David Sentelle in his decision, "EPA cites evidence that current levels of SO2 in the ambient air, even when the air quality meets the current SO2 [standards] . . . still cause respiratory effects in some areas."

In the *Asarco* case (declined for review by the Supreme Court), the PLAINTIFF was Gruppo Mexico SAB's Asarco LLC, and the claims were similarly grounded in alleged arbitrary standards and unconstitutionally defective rulemaking notice. Asarco runs a copper smelting facility in Hayden, Arizona, that is one of the three main U.S. copper smelting operations. The U.S. DEPARTMENT OF JUSTICE (DOJ), in an amicus brief, had urged the Supreme Court to deny review, but Freeport-McMoRan Copper & Gold, Inc., the world's largest publicly traded copper producer, filed an amicus brief in support of Asarco.

In a telephone interview with the *Chicago Tribune*, the University of Michigan law professor David Uhlmann, a former chief of the DOJ's Environmental Crimes Section, said that the string of favorable rulings for the EPA was a good sign for proponents of climate change regulation. He added that courts were often reluctant to get involved with the "nuts-and-bolts" of environmental decision-making, acknowledging the EPA's greater subject-matter expertise. But "the Supreme Court is far more likely to get involved when the issue is the authority to regulate," he said.

Speaking to the claims of arbitrariness, Professor Zygmunt Plater, a law professor at Boston College Law School, also in a telephone interview with the *Tribune*, suggested that "the phrase 'adequate margin of safety' [42 U.S.C. § 7408–7409] provides a needed buffer, given that the line where environmental harms become significant is too often very difficult to predict until after a harmful situation occurs."

Los Angeles County Flood Control District v. Natural Resources Defense Council, Inc.

Congress created the primary law directed at addressing control of WATER POLLUTION through the enactment of the CLEAN WATER ACT (CWA), 33 U.S.C. § 1251 **et seq.**, in 1972. The CWA's goals are "to restore and maintain the chemical, physical, and biological integrity of the Nation's waters." The CWA prohibits discharge of pollutants into water unless this discharge is done in compliance with the provisions of the **statute**.

In 2013, the U.S. SUPREME COURT reviewed a case addressing whether the CWA requires a city to obtain a permit when polluted water flows from a portion of a river, into a concrete channel, and back into another portion of the same river. In other words, the question before the Court was whether the transfer of the water from the channel and back into the river constituted a discharge. In a unanimous decision, the Court ruled that this did not constitute a discharge, reversing the Ninth **Circuit Court** of Appeals. *Los Angeles County Flood Control District v. Natural Resources Defense Council, Inc.*, 133 S. Ct. 710, 184 L. Ed. 2d 547 (2013).

The decision was unusual in that both parties and the federal government agreed that the act constituted a discharge. The **respondent** in the case, the Natural Resource Defense Council (NRDC), argued that the Supreme Court should affirm the lower court because the Ninth Circuit had "reached the right result, albeit for the wrong reason." The Supreme Court rejected the argument, limiting its focus to the question upon which the Court granted **certiorari**.

The case focused on stormwater runoff in Los Angeles County, which covers a 4,500-square-mile area. This runoff is caused when water from rain and other precipitation flows over streets, parking lots, and various other sites. The water will run over paved areas and collect various pollutants, including metals, sediments, motor oil, trash, raw sewage, pesticides, and so forth. This runoff is one of the major causes of water pollution in Southern California.

Los Angeles County developed a massive storm-sewer system to carry off stormwater runoff. The water is collected by thousands of storm drains from each municipality and unincorporated area, and the water is channeled into the storm-sewer system. The municipal separate storm-sewer systems (MS4s) only collect the untreated stormwater. These systems eventually drain into a flood-control and storm-sewer infrastructure. The water collected into the MS4 is channeled through various rivers in the Los Angeles County area and eventually into the Pacific Ocean.

The CWA and regulations implementing the statute require any operator of an MS4 that serves a population of more than 100,000 to obtain a permit through the National Pollutant Discharge Elimination System before the operator can discharge stormwater into NAVIGABLE WATERS. The district in charge of operating the MS4 in Los Angeles County obtained the necessary permit for its MS4 in 1990. The permit was renewed several times thereafter.

Data from stations in the Los Angeles River and the San Gabriel River showed that the water exceeded quality-control standards for several pollutants, including aluminum, copper, cyanide, fecal coliform bacteria, and zinc. The MS4 discharges into these rivers, but previous cases have established that "thousands of permitted dischargers" also feed water into these rivers.

The NRDC and the Santa Monica Baykeeper filed a citizen suit under 33 U.S.C. § 1365. This section allows any citizen to bring a **civil action**

> against any person (including (i) the United States, and (ii) any other governmental instrumentality or agency to the extent permitted by the ELEVENTH AMENDMENT to the Constitution) who is alleged to be in violation of (A) an effluent standard or limitation under this chapter or (B) an order issued by the Administrator or a State with respect to such a standard or limitation.

The plaintiffs named the Los Angeles County Flood Control District and several other defendants in the action.

The U.S. **District Court** for the Central District of California granted **summary judgment** in favor of the defendants, concluding that the record established by the PLAINTIFF was insufficient to support a finding that the district's MS4 had discharged the stormwater that caused the pollution. However, the Ninth Circuit reversed the district court. The Ninth Circuit focused on concrete channels constructed along the rivers for flood-control purposes. According to the **appellate court**, when water flowed out of the concrete channels and back into the rivers, the flow was a "discharge" of polluted water for purposes of the CWA. *Natural Resources Defense Council, Inc. v. County of Los Angeles*, 673 F.3d 880 (9th Cir. 2011).

The Supreme Court agreed to review the case on the question of whether a "discharge of pollutants" takes place when polluted water "flows from one portion of a river that is navigable water of the United States, through a concrete channel" and then "into a lower portion of the same river."

All of the parties agreed that answer to this question was "no." The Court focused solely on its decision in *South Florida Water Management District v. Miccosukee Tribe*, 541 U.S. 95, 124 S. Ct. 1537, 158 L. Ed. 2d 264 (2004). The Court in that case held that a transfer of polluted water from two parts of the same body of water did not constitute a discharge of pollutants under the CWA. The Court concluded that the facts in *Miccosukee* were analogous to the facts from the Los Angeles District and therefore concluded that the transfer of water from the concrete channel to the river was not a discharge.

Justice SAMUEL ALITO concurred in the judgment but did not write a separate concurring opinion.

Tarrant Regional Water District v. Herrmann

In *Tarrant Regional Water District v. Herrmann*, 133 S. Ct. 2120 (2013), the U.S. SUPREME COURT was asked to resolve a dispute over the distribution of scarce water resources, pursuant to an existing agreement among four states. A question arose as to whether, under the Constitution's Interstate **Commerce Clause**, the congressionally approved agreement would preempt individual state laws that restricted water access to other signatory states to the agreement. In this case, the Court found that an Oklahoma **statute** favoring in-state applicants over out-of-state applicants for water appropriation permits was not preempted.

The Red River begins on the border between New Mexico and Texas, runs through the Texas Panhandle, forms the border between Texas and Oklahoma, then continues easterly until it reaches the shared border with Arkansas. From there, it turns south into Louisiana, eventually emptying into the Great Mississippi and Atchafalaya Rivers. The topography and geography of the river's course and distribution flow tends to favor upstream states like Oklahoma and Texas, to the disadvantage of downstream states like Arkansas and Louisiana. Louisiana suffers its own peculiar disadvantage as it lacks the capability of having sufficiently large reservoirs in which to store water.

Disputes over the **allocation** or distribution of water between states in this arid region would be commonplace but for the existence of the Red River Compact, an agreement among the states of Arkansas, Louisiana, Oklahoma, and Texas to equitably apportion the water of the Red River basin among themselves. Congress expressly authorized the formation of such agreements among states in 1955, to circumvent future disputes over scarce water resources, which would likely result in costly and protracted **legal proceedings**. In 1980, the above states signed the Red River Compact, and Congress signed it into law.

The Compact divided the area it governs into five subdivisions ("Reaches"), which are further divided into smaller "subbasins." The Compact acknowledged that downstream Louisiana lacked reservoir sites to store water during high-flow periods, and that upstream states were unwilling to release their own stored water. Therefore, as to Reach II, the Compact expressly granted control over the water in subbasins 1–4 to the states in which the subbasins are located but required the water in subbasin 5 to be allowed to flow down to Louisiana at certain minimum levels. However, when the water flow exceeded 3,000 cubic feet per second (cfs), the Compact gave the states "equal rights" to the use of subbasin 5's water, "provided no state is entitled to more than 25 percent of the water in excess of 3,000 [cfs]." This provision, under § 5.01(b)(1) of the Compact, became central to the ensuing dispute that followed.

The Texas state-established Tarrant Regional Water District (Tarrant), which supplies water to north-central Texas, anticipated a growing water shortage due to increased land use. It then sought permits from the state of Oklahoma (the Oklahoma Water Resources Board, or OWRB) to appropriate water from Oklahoma for use in Texas. Tarrant anticipated that Oklahoma would deny the permits, citing state laws that effectively prevented out-of-state

applicants from taking Oklahoma's water outside its borders. It therefore, simultaneously with permit applications, filed suit in federal **district court**. It sought an INJUNCTION against Oklahoma from enforcing state statutes, arguing that those restrictive statutes were preempted by the Red River Compact. It further argued that Oklahoma's statutes interfered with, and discriminated against, the interstate commerce of shipments of water as a commodity—particularly, excess water left unallocated under the Compact.

The district court disagreed and granted **summary judgment** to Oklahoma's OWRB. The U.S. Court of Appeals for the Tenth Circuit affirmed.

Also affirmed, said an unanimous U.S. Supreme Court. Writing for the Court, Justice SONIA SOTOMAYOR first dispelled the matter of **preemption**, holding that the Compact did not preempt Oklahoma's water statutes. Tarrant argued that 5.01(b)(1) of the Compact creates a "borderless common" in subbasin 5, in which each of the states may cross each other's boundaries in order to access a shared pool of water (subject to the 25 percent limitation). Conversely, OWRB argued that under the Compact, the "equal rights" afforded to each state means that each has an equal opportunity to use any excess water in subbasin 5 within its own borders. The silence in language regarding cross-border rights, argued OWRB, means that the Compact's drafters had no intention of creating any such rights.

The Court affirmed the latter view. As interstate compacts are construed under contract law principles, and the Compact is silent on cross-border diversions, the Court construed the intent to be that the Compact intended to leave intact a respect for state borders. Moreover, long-standing precedent supports the principle that states generally do not cede WATER RIGHTS from within their own territories. Any other reading of the Compact would create jurisdictional and administrative confusion.

Even though silent on cross-border diversions, the Compact's express language also supports this conclusion. It declares, in relevant part that its provisions should not "be deemed to . . . [i]nterfere with or impair the right or power of any Signatory State to regulate within its boundaries the appropriation, use, and control of water, or quality of water, not inconsistent with its obligations under this Compact."

Other interpretive clues existed in the facts that (1) since 1980, no other signatory state had pressed for a cross-border diversion until Tarrant sued in 2007; and (2) Tarrant had previously tried to purchase water from Oklahoma, which undermined its argument that it was constitutionally entitled to it.

As to the COMMERCE CLAUSE arguments regarding excess "unallocated" water, the Compact makes clear that regarding flowing water in excess of 3,000 cfs in subbasin 5, "all states are free to use whatever amount of water they can put to beneficial use," subject to the limitation that if all those uses cannot be met, "each state will honor the other's right to 25% of the excess flow."

In sum, Oklahoma's statutes are not preempted because "the Compact creates no cross-border rights in its signatories for these statutes to infringe," said the Court. Moreover, there is no Commerce Clause conflict because Tarrant's assumption that the Compact leaves some excess water "unallocated" is incorrect. If more that 25 percent of subbasin 5's water is in Oklahoma, the Court continued, "that water is not 'unallocated'; rather, it is allocated to Oklahoma unless and until another State calls for an accounting and Oklahoma is asked to refrain from utilizing more than its entitled share."

ERISA

U.S. Airways v. McCutchen

In addition to governing retirement **pension** plans, the EMPLOYEE RETIREMENT INCOME SECURITY ACT of 1974 (ERISA), 29 U.S.C. § 1001 **et seq.**, also contains many provisions that relate to health benefits plans. The health benefits plan established for its employees by employer U.S. Airways entitled it to be reimbursed for any medical expenses paid on behalf of employees if they later recovered monetary damages from a **third party** (as in a private lawsuit). Moreover, under § 502(a)3 of ERISA, health plan administrators are authorized to bring civil lawsuits "to obtain . . . appropriate equitable relief . . . to enforce . . . the terms of the plan."

In *U.S. Airways v. McCutchen*, No. 133 S. Ct. 1537 (2013), the U.S. SUPREME COURT held that ERISA terms prevailed over equitable defenses (such as UNJUST ENRICHMENT), even where an employee may have a net gain of $0 after reimbursing the health plan administrator. However, where terms of the plan leave gaps or are silent, such as terms addressing how to pay for the costs of recovery against a THIRD PARTY, equitable relief such as the common-fund doctrine (where both employee and plan administrator share attorneys' costs and expenses) may be the best indication of the parties' intent.

James McCutchen was a covered BENEFICIARY under his employer U.S. Airways' health care plan when he suffered serious injuries caused by another driver who collided with McCutchen's vehicle. Three other persons were killed or seriously injured in the accident. The benefits plan paid $66,866 in medical expenses for McCutchen's injuries. Later, McCutchen filed a private lawsuit against the other driver, and retained legal counsel for a 40 percent contingency fee to represent him in this matter. Even though his accident-related damages were estimated at $1 million, his attorneys recovered only $110,000, mostly due to limited insurance coverage and defendants' liabilities to the others killed or injured. In any event, after deducting $44,000 for attorneys' fees, McCutchen was left with $66,000.

But the plan administration for U.S. Airways demanded reimbursement of the $66,866 paid on behalf of McCutchen for his medical expenses. It cited express language from its summary plan description to employees:

> If [U.S. Airways] pays benefits for any claim you incur as the result of NEGLIGENCE, willful misconduct, or other actions of a third party, . . . [y]ou will be required to reimburse [U.S. Airways] for amounts paid for claims out of any monies recovered from [the] third party, including, but not limited to, your own insurance company as the result of judgment, **settlement**, or otherwise.

McCutchen protested, but his attorneys put $41,500 in **escrow** (representing the $66,866 minus a proportional share of attorneys' fees/ costs) pending outcome of the dispute. U.S. Airways then filed suit under ERISA § 502(a)3 (above), requesting "appropriate equitable relief" to enforce the plan's reimbursement provision. It requested an equitable **lien** of $66,866 against both the ESCROW account ($41,500) and $25,366 more from McCutchen.

After paying the agreed 40 percent attorney fee ($44,000), this would have left McCutchen with $0 from the entire $110,000 recovered in his lawsuit against the third party.

McCutchen defended that U.S. Airways was not entitled to the relief it sought because he had recovered only a small percentage of his total damages. He argued that U.S. Airways could recover only if he (McCutchen) over-recovered damages due him. Second, McCutchen argued "undue enrichment"—that is, that U.S. Airways got a free ride to reimbursement while he and his attorneys did all the work. He requested that U.S. Airways pay its fair share for the costs and attorneys' fees incurred for the recovery.

The **district court** rejected both arguments, holding that the clear and unambiguous language of the ERISA plan provided for full reimbursement for expenses paid. This ruling was vacated by the Court of Appeals for the Third Circuit. The **appellate court** reasoned that in a suit for "appropriate equitable relief," a court must look to any responsive "equitable doctrines and defenses" that might limit the requested recovery. Here, the **appellate** court indeed found "unjust enrichment" with a "windfall" to U.S. Airways. It remanded to the district court to determine an amount less than the requested $66,866 that would qualify as "appropriate equitable relief."

There being a split among circuit courts of appeals on this subject, the U.S. Supreme Court accepted review on whether such equitable defenses can override an ERISA plan's reimbursement provision. The answer was no.

Justice ELENA KAGAN, writing for the majority, vacated the Third Circuit decision. In its stead, the Court held that the ERISA plan's terms governed, and no equitable defenses could override those contractual terms, not even unjust enrichment. The Court methodically distinguished **case law** cited by McCutchen and the government's amicus brief as inapplicable to the present case.

However, the Court found that the terms of the plan were silent on the **allocation** of recovery costs. This gave opportunity to apply by default rule the common-fund doctrine of proportionally sharing the costs to fill that gap. U.S. Airways had the opportunity to depart from such a well-established rule by drafting

terms in the contract. But it did not. This doctrine does not address how to allocate a third-party recovery (not applicable here), but rather, how to pay for the costs associated with obtaining the recovery.

Said the Court,

Without cost sharing, the insurer free rides on its beneficiary's efforts—taking the fruits while contributing nothing to the labor. Odder still, in some cases—indeed, in this case—the beneficiary is made worse off by pursuing a third party...US Airways claimed $66,866 in medical expenses. That would put McCutchen $866 in the hole; in effect, he would pay for the privilege of serving as US Airways' collection agent.

In sum, because U.S. Airways' reimbursement provision did not address costs of recovery, "it will be properly read as having retained the common fund doctrine." After vacating the APPELLATE judgment, the Court remanded for further proceedings consistent with its opinion.

Justices ANTHONY KENNEDY, RUTH BADER GINSBURG, SONIA SOTOMAYOR, and STEPHEN BREYER joined in the majority. Justice ANTONIN SCALIA dissented, joined by Chief Justice JOHN ROBERTS, JR., and Justice CLARENCE THOMAS. The DISSENT, while agreeing with the majority on ERISA prevailing, noted that the case was accepted for review on a question that presumed unambiguous language in the provision. Loud and clear, said the dissent, the provision calls for a beneficiary to reimburse any amounts the plan has paid, out of monies recovered from a third party, without any contribution to attorneys' fees or expenses.

ESTABLISHMENT CLAUSE

Eighth Circuit Allows Ten Commandments Lawsuit to Proceed

There have been numerous lawsuits filed challenging government displays of the Ten Commandments. Sometimes the displays violate the First Amendment's Establishment Clause, while other times they do not. The Eighth **Circuit Court** of Appeals, in *Red River Freethinkers v. City of Fargo*, 679 F.3d 1015 (2012), examined whether a display of the Ten Commandments that had been ruled constitutional could be challenged again when the city reversed its decision to remove the display. The appeals court concluded that the plaintiffs had raised sufficient constitutional objections and new facts that to proceed with their lawsuit.

In 1958, the Fraternal Order of Eagles, a non-religious civic organization, donated a Ten Commandments monument to the city of Fargo, North Dakota. In 1961, the monument was installed in its current location, a grassy, open mall on city property. No objections were raised about the monument until 2002, when a group of Fargo residents sued the city in federal **district court**. The residents were all members of the Red River Freethinkers, a nonprofit corporation dedicated to the promotion of atheism and agnosticism. They asked the court to declare the city's display of the monument a violation of the Establishment Clause and order its removal from the mall. The court considered the display a "passive monument." A reasonable observer could not perceive the city as adopting or endorsing the religious message of the display because the monument came from a private organization and the display contained a message from the Eagles that described the secular purpose of the display. Moreover, the lack of community complaints or legal challenges over the monument's nearly fifty year history demonstrated that the community did not perceive the display as an endorsement by the city of a religion. Therefore, the court dismissed the lawsuit.

The plaintiffs did not appeal the decision but adopted a new strategy. The district court had relied on the fact the city had received the monument from a private organization, so the Freethinkers offered the city a monument for installation on the mall with an inscription that included the statement "The government of the United States of America is not, in any sense, founded on the Christian religion." The group said it preferred that its offer be accepted but if the city decided to remove the Ten Commandments display to a private location, it would withdraw its offer. The city attorney advised the city commissioners they could decline the offer, decline the offer and move the Ten Commandments display, accept the Freethinkers' offer and allow it to be installed, or establish a committee to create "diversity" or "freedom" displays. He said from a purely legal standpoint, the commission should choose the second option and remove the display. To do otherwise would risk costly LITIGATION with the Freethinkers.

The commission voted to reject the Freethinkers' offer and to donate the Ten Commandments monument to a private **entity**. A great many Fargo residents wanted the monument to remain where it was. They circulated a petition to change the municipal code to provide that "A marker or monument on City of Fargo property for 40 or more years may not be removed from its location on City of Fargo property." Over 5,000 residents signed the petition. The commission adopted the **ordinance** unanimously and rescinded its prior vote. The Freethinkers then filed a federal lawsuit, contending that the city's ADOPTION of the ordinance and its refusal to accept their monument violated the Establishment Clause. The district court dismissed the lawsuit, finding that the Freethinkers had already litigated and lost its Establishment Clause claim. As to the asserted new injury—"the magnification of its members' sense of exclusion and anger"—that was caused by the continued presence of the monument, the judge found no evidence that the city commission had engaged in "impermissibly religious expression." The Freethinkers did not have standing to bring the lawsuit.

A three-judge panel of the Eighth Circuit ruled unanimously that the Freethinkers did have standing to bring their lawsuit. Judge Roger Wollman, writing for the court, examined the elements of standing. The first was injury. The Freethinkers alleged that the city's actions after the initial lawsuit now violated the Establishment Clause. Its members had come into unwanted contact with the monument and as a result had suffered feelings of "exclusion, discomfort, and anger." However, none of its members had altered their behavior to avoid the monument. Judge Wollman concluded that having unwelcome contact with the monument was a sufficient injury.

The second element of standing is causation. The alleged injury to Freethinkers members must be "fairly traceable" to the city's allegedly unlawful conduct. Judge Wollman found that injury was a "direct consequence of the city's allegedly unlawful conduct." The Freethinkers provided sufficient facts to make an Establishment Clause violation: the city displayed a Ten Commandments monument; the city passed an ordinance prohibiting the removal of the monument; the city had a policy of not accepting other monuments in the mall where the Ten

Commandments monument stands. Therefore, this element of standing had been met.

The third element of standing is redressability. This goes to the question of whether the court can provide relief for the alleged injury. Judge Wollman noted that the Freethinkers had asked the court to invalidate the ordinance, to order the removal of the Ten Commandments monument from city property, and had requested monetary damages and attorney's fees. He assumed, without deciding, that invalidating the ordinance would not **redress** the injury to the Freethinkers members. Their request for monetary damages and attorney's fees likewise would not redress the alleged injury of direct and unwelcome contact with the monument. Judge Wollman did find that removal of the monument from public property would remedy the alleged injury. The district court had made the same finding but ruled that Freethinkers had already had their day in court on the issue of removal. The appeals court disagreed, as the current case presented an issue that could not have been raised or decided in the first case: whether city's action after the first lawsuit "transformed the Ten Commandments from a permissible display into an impermissible violation of the Establishment Clause." If things had changed since the end of the first lawsuit, and if those changes resulted in an Establishment Clause violation, the court could remedy the violation by ordering the removal of the monument from city property. Because Freethinkers had proved the three elements of standing, the appeals court remanded the case for further proceedings on the merits of the case.

Fourth Circuit Rules Upholds Public School Credits for Off-Campus Religious Classes

Since the 1950s, the SUPREME COURT has permitted public schools to release their students for part of the school day to attend off-campus religious instruction. In 2006, the state of South Carolina amended its law dealing with school release programs to allow students to earn grades and academic credit for this type of religious instruction. The parents of two children who attended a South Carolina high school challenged the law, arguing that it violated the Establishment Clause of the FIRST AMENDMENT. The Fourth **Circuit Court** of Appeals, in *Moss v. Spartanburg County School District Seven*, 683 F.3d 599 (2012), upheld the constitutionality of the act, finding that the award of academic credit by public schools did not excessively entangle them with religion or express an endorsement of Christianity.

In 2007, the Spartanburg County School District Seven adopted a policy allowing public school students to receive two academic credits for off-campus religious instruction offered by private educators. The policy came about because of the passage of the Released Time Credit Act by the South Carolina legislature the previous year. The law gave school districts the authority to award no more than two academic credits to high school students who completed released time classes in religious instruction off-campus. These classes were to be evaluated on the basis of purely secular criteria that have been used to evaluate similar classes at private high schools when students transfer from a private to a public high school. The term "secular criteria" included the number of hours of classroom time, a review of the course syllabus, the methods of assessment used in the course, and whether the course was taught by a certified teacher.

Soon after Spartanburg put in place its credit policy, Spartanburg Bible Education in School Time, a local bible school, approached the school district, requesting that they allow students to attend a released time religious course for academic credit. The two-semester course dealt with the Christian worldview. The district agreed but only if the unaccredited bible school agreed to let an accredited private school review the course using secular criteria. The accredited school would then award course credits given by the bible school and submit them to Spartanburg High School for academic credit. The bible school made an arrangement with Oakbrook Preparatory School, an accredited private Christian school, to carry out this plan. Oakbrook reviewed syllabi, spoke with instructors, suggested minor curricular changes, and concluded the course was academically rigorous. The Spartanburg school district preferred this arrangement because school officials would not have to become involved in assessing the "quality" of religious released-time courses. Over a three-year period, 20 Spartanburg High School students, out of 1,500 students each year, elected to take the course. The high school did not actively or directly promote the religious course.

Robert Moss, the parent of Melissa Moss, who attended Spartanburg High School, and

Ellen Tillett, for herself and on behalf of her minor child who attends the high school, filed a federal lawsuit in 2009. They contended the school's released time credit policy violated the Establishment Clause. Neither of the student plaintiffs took the bible school course, nor did they claim they were harassed for not participating in the class. The students did not claim the high school promoted the course but the Mosses received a promotional letter in the mail from the bible school, which indicated the course would be available for elective credits and that it would teach students "the basic tenets of the Christian worldview." The school district provided the addresses of students to the bible school, but public school officials did not review or approve the letter that was sent. The **district court** ruled in favor of the school district. It found that the stated purpose of the **release time program**, the accommodation of religion, was plausible and was secular. The effect of the RELEASE TIME PROGRAM was not to advance religion but to merely accommodate students' desire to "partake in religious instruction." Finally, the school district had not become entangled with religion because it accepted credits from the bible school like it did for students transferring from a private school. The plaintiffs appealed.

A three-judge panel of the Fourth Circuit unanimously upheld the lower court decision and the released time policy. Judge Paul Niemeyer, writing for the court, first ruled that Ellen Tillett and her child had no standing to be part of the lawsuit because they had no personal exposure to the bible school course apart from "their abstract knowledge of the School District's released time policy." The Tilletts did not receive the promotional letter that the Moss family did. Therefore, Tillett was not injured by the policy and lacked standing. Robert and Melissa Moss did have standing because they received the letter and they were not Christians. They claimed they felt like "outsiders" in their own community, viewing the letter as an endorsement of Evangelical Christianity by the school district. Therefore, they had standing to bring the lawsuit.

Turning to the merits of the case, Judge Niemeyer noted that off-campus released time initiatives are generally constitutional. The Mosses argued that the released time program

at issue was different than the kind approved by the Supreme Court because it provided academic credit for released time coursework. The awarding of credit advanced religion more than does traditional released time. The court rejected these claims, pointing out that the released time policy took place off campus and expressly prohibited any use of public staff or funds for its execution. The released time grades were handled "much like the grades of a student who wishes to transfer from an accredited private school into a public school within the School District." The public school accepted the grades without individually assessing the quality or subject matter of the course.

Judge Niemeyer emphasized the "governing principle that private religious education is an integral part of the American school system." The acceptance of transfer credits by public schools accommodated the choice among "options public and private, secular and religious." In addition, the school district had not become excessively entangled with the bible school. The district did not actively promote the bible school course. School officials "carefully maintained a neutral relationship" with the bible school. Therefore, the policy did not violate the Establishment Clause.

Second Circuit Strikes Down Town Board Led Prayer

Numerous lawsuits have been filed in the past twenty years over prayers that have been said aloud at public school events and government meetings. Critics of the practice allege that most of the religious leaders offering the prayers are Christian and that many of the prayers refer to Christianity. In *Galloway v. Town of Greece*, 681 F.3d 20 (2012), the Second **Circuit Court** of Appeals examined a town board's long-standing practice of opening its meetings with a short **prayer**. Based on the fact that the prayer practice violated the First Amendment's Establishment Clause because it affiliated the town with a single creed, Christianity, the appeals court ruled that the practice was unconstitutional.

The town of Greece, New York has approximately 94,000 residents. It elects a five-member town board that governs and conducts official business at monthly public meetings. Before 1999, town board meetings began with a moment of silence. That year, at the direction of the town supervisor, the town began inviting local clergy to offer an opening prayer. Prayer-givers often asked members of the audience to participate by bowing their heads, standing, or joining in the prayer. After the conclusion of the prayer, the town supervisor typically thanked the prayer-givers for being the town's "chaplain of the month." Sometimes the "chaplain" was presented with a plaque. Between 1999 and 2010, the town did not adopt any formal policy concerning the process of inviting prayer-givers, the permissible content of prayers, or any other aspect of its prayer practice. The town claimed that anyone could request to give an invocation, including adherents of any religion, atheists and the nonreligious, and that it had never denied such a request. The town also did not review the language of prayers before they were delivered, and it did not censor any invocation. The town did not, however, publicize to town residents that anyone could volunteer to deliver prayers or that any type of invocation would be permissible.

In 2007, Susan Galloway and Linda Stephens, who had been attending town meetings for many years, began complaining about the prayer practice to town officials, sometimes during public comment periods at town board meetings. They objected to the fact that the prayers aligned the town with Christianity and that the prayers were sectarian rather than secular. The town did not make any official response to these objections, which lead Galloway and Stephens to file a federal lawsuit against the town, challenging aspects of the prayer practice under the Establishment Clause. They argued that the town's procedure for selecting prayer-givers unconstitutionally preferred Christianity over other faiths and the prayers were impermissibly sectarian. The federal **district court** dismissed the lawsuit, finding no evidence that town employees intentionally excluded representatives of other faiths. As to the content of the prayers, the court held that under SUPREME COURT **case law**, the Establishment Clause did not foreclose denominational prayers. Therefore, the prayer practices did not have the effect of establishing the Christian religion. Galloway and Stephens appealed to the Second Circuit.

A unanimous three-judge panel reversed the district court's decision. Judge Guido Calabresi, writing for the appeals court, noted that the

Supreme Court had issued just one decision ruling on the constitutionality of legislative prayer. In *Marsh v. Chambers,* 463 U.S. 783, 103 S. Ct. 3330, 77 L. Ed. 2d 1019 (1983), the Court ruled that the Nebraska legislature's practice of beginning its sessions with a prayer, delivered by a state-employed clergyman, did not violate the Establishment Clause. It conducted a largely historical analysis and found that the First Congress appointed paid chaplains and opened legislative sessions with prayers. However, six years later the Court suggested in a case that did not involve legislative prayers that legislative prayers invoking sectarian beliefs may, on the basis of those references alone, violate the Establishment Clause. The Court noted that the prayers in *Marsh* did not violate the Establishment Clause because the "particular chaplain had 'removed all references to Christ.'" In the years since, a number of circuit courts of appeals questioned the validity of all forms of "sectarian" prayers, as they affiliate government with one specific faith or **belief**.

Judge Calabresi concluded that the court must ask "whether the town's practice, viewed in its totality by an ordinary, reasonable observer, conveyed the view that the town favored or disfavored certain religious beliefs." Viewing the town's prayer practices, he found them to be an endorsement of a particular religious viewpoint. The town's process for selecting prayer-givers "virtually insured a Christian viewpoint." Christian clergy delivered every one of the prayers for nine years, a result of the town inviting only clergy who lived within the town's borders. As to the content of the prayers, most of them contained "uniquely Christian references," but they were not "inherently a problem" because they did not "preach conversion, threaten damnation to nonbelievers, downgrade other faiths, or the like." However, the prayers confirmed that the town's prayer practice identified the town with Christianity in violation of the Establishment Clause.

The appeals court acknowledged that the town or its leaders had religious **animus** to other faiths. The desire to open the meetings with a prayer was "understandable," as "Americans have done just that for more than two hundred years." However, when "one creed dominates others," there are important constitutional concerns. Judge Calabresi also found relevant the fact that most of the prayer-givers appeared to speak on behalf of the town and its residents, rather than only on behalf of themselves. Prayer-givers often asked that the audience participate, and spoke in the first-person plural: let "us" pray, "our" savior, and "we" ask. Town officials contributed to the impression that these prayer-givers spoke on the town's behalf by stating they were "our chaplain of the month."

Therefore, the appeals court held that an objective, **reasonable person** would believe the town's prayer-practice "had the effect of affiliating the town with Christianity." It pointed out that the town could open its meetings with prayers and invocations, but only if the town included multiple beliefs and made clear that the volunteer prayer-givers did not express an official town religion and "did not purport to speak on behalf of all the town's residents."

ESTATE PLANNING

Hillman v. Maretta

Many people make common estate-planning mistakes. For an estimated 70 percent of Americans, the mistake is a complete lack of an estate plan. For others, mistakes may relate to a lack of planning for estate taxes or failing to plan for potential disability or incapacity. Another common mistake is a person's failure to control the beneficiaries on assets such as retirement accounts and life insurance policies.

In *Hillman v. Maretta*, 133 S. Ct. 1943 (2013), the Supreme Court reviewed a case in which a former federal employee had made one of those estate-planning mistakes. He had failed to change the name of a beneficiary on his life insurance policy from his former **wife** to his current wife. After he died, his former wife collected the proceeds of the policy, and his widow sued the former wife to recover those proceeds. However, a unanimous Supreme Court ruled that a federal law preempts a Virginia **statute** that would allow the widow to recover, meaning that the former spouse was allowed to keep all of the proceeds.

The federal law in question was the Federal Employees' Group Life Insurance Act (FEGLIA), 5 U.S.C. § 8701, which establishes the order of preference in terms of the beneficiaries entitled to recover the proceeds

of a life insurance policy covered by the Act. The Act states:

> [T]he amount of group life insurance and group accidental death insurance in force on an employee at the date of his death shall be paid, on the establishment of a valid claim, to the person or persons surviving at the date of his death, in the following order of precedence:
>   First, to the beneficiary or beneficiaries designated by the employee in a signed and witnessed writing received before death in the employing office....
>   Second, if there is no designated beneficiary, to the widow or widower of the employee.

Moreover, the Act contains a provision establishing that the Act preempts state law. The statute in 5 U.S.C. § 8709(d)(1) states:

> The provisions of any contract under this chapter which relate to the nature or extent of coverage or benefits (including payments with respect to benefits) shall supersede and preempt any law of any State or political subdivision thereof, or any regulation issued thereunder, which relates to group life insurance to the extent that the law or regulation is inconsistent with the contractual provisions.

Virginia law contains provisions designed to ensure that former spouses do not receive payments of death benefits following a DIVORCE. Section 20.111.1(A) annuls "any revocable beneficiary designation contained in a then existing written contract owned by one party that provides for the payment of any death benefit to the other party." The Virginia law also anticipates the possibility that § 20.111.1 (A) could be preempted by federal law. Under § 20.111.1(D), if § 20.111.1(A) is preempted "with respect to the payment of any death benefit, a former spouse who, not for value, receives the payment of any death benefit that the former spouse is not entitled to under this section is personally liable for the amount of the payment to the person who would have been entitled to it were this section not preempted."

These sections of federal and state law were at issue in the case involving Warren Hillman. In December 1996, he named his wife Judy Maretta as the beneficiary under his Federal Employees' Group Life Insurance policy. However, he and Maretta divorced in 1998. According to Warren Hillman's daughter, he and Maretta had no contact after the divorce. He married Jacqueline Hillman in 2002 but never changed the beneficiary designation in the life insurance policy.

Warren Hillman died in July 2008. Jacqueline Hillman filed a claim for the benefits under the life insurance policy, but she was told that the proceeds would go to the named beneficiary, who was Maretta. Maretta received the death benefits, which amounted to $124,558.03.

Jacqueline Hillman filed a lawsuit against Maretta in Virginia state court. Hillman argued that Maretta was liable to Hillman under § 20.111.1(D) because Maretta was not Warren Hillman's spouse at the time of his death. Jacqueline Hillman sought either a judgment against Maretta or an order directing Maretta to pay the proceeds to Hillman. Maretta responded by arguing that FEGLIA entirely preempted the Virginia law and that Hillman was entitled to nothing.

The **Circuit Court** of Fairfax County in Virginia ruled in Jacqueline Hillman's favor, holding that FEGLIA did not preempt the Virginia law. Maretta then appealed the decision to the Virginia Supreme Court, which reversed the Circuit Court's ruling. The Virginia Supreme Court determined that Congress intended for FEGLI benefits be paid to the designated beneficiary, so FEGLIA preempted the conflicting state law. *Maretta v. Hillman,* 722 S.E.2d 32 (Va. 2012).

A unanimous Supreme Court affirmed the Virginia Supreme Court's ruling. Justice SONIA SOTOMAYOR wrote the opinion for the Court. Justices CLARENCE THOMAS and SAMUEL ALITO each wrote concurring opinions.

The majority noted that Congress had the authority to expressly preempt state law under the **Supremacy Clause** of the U.S. Constitution. When Congress has enacted a statute preempting state law, the state law is preempted to the extent that the state law conflicts with the federal law. One way in which a conflict can arise is when a state law "stands as an obstacle to the accomplishment and execution of the full purposes and objectives of Congress."

In this instance, Congress created a system that is not only easier to administer but also one that honors an insured's wishes with regard to paying the beneficiary named on the policy. FEGLIA establishes that the insured's right to designate the beneficiary "cannot be waived or restricted." Section 20.111.1(D) directly conflicts with this policy because it allows a person other than a named beneficiary to recover proceeds of a policy.

The Court said that Congress could have conveyed a different policy if it wanted to ensure that the named beneficiary was not somehow incorrect. "But that is not the judgment Congress made," Sotomayor wrote. "Rather than draw an inference about an employee's probable intent from a range of sources, Congress established a clear and predictable procedure for an employee to indicate who the intended beneficiary of his life insurance shall be."

Thomas agreed with the Court's conclusion but did not agree with the specific analysis the Court employed. In particular, he disagreed that the Court should look to Congress's purposes and objectives in determining whether a federal statute preempts state law. Alito also disagreed with the Court's analysis, saying the Court went "well beyond what is necessary" to find that FEGLIA preempts the Virginia law.

EX POST FACTO LAWS

[Latin, "After-the-fact" laws.] *Laws that provide for the infliction of punishment upon a person for some prior act that, at the time it was committed, was not illegal.*

Supreme Court Rejects Criminal Sentence for Violating the Ex Post Facto Clause

Under the U.S. Constitution, **ex post facto laws** are prohibited. This means that laws cannot be changed retroactively in a criminal case to alter the definition of a crime or increase the punishment for a criminal act. A DEFENDANT who committed his crimes in 1999 and 2000 was sentenced under the 2009 Federal Sentencing Guidelines rather than the 1998 version that was in effect when the crimes occurred. This resulted in an increase in his prison sentence from a maximum of 37 months under the 1998 guidelines to a sentence of 70 months imprisonment using the 2009 guidelines. He argued that this violated the bar on EX POST FACTO LAWS. The U.S. SUPREME COURT, in *Peugh v. United States,* 133 S. Ct. 2072 (2013), agreed, reversing the sentence and directing the lower court to use the 1998 guidelines to resentence him.

Marvin Peugh and his cousin, Steven Hollowell, operated two farming-related businesses in

Illinois. Grainery, Inc. bought, stored, and sold grain, while Agri-Tech, Inc., provided farming services to landowners and tenants. When Grainery began experiencing cash-flow problems, the two men engaged in two **fraudulent** schemes. They obtained a series of bank loans by representing falsely the existence of contracts for future grain deliveries from Agri-Tech to Grainery. When they failed to repay the **principal** on these loans, the bank suffered losses of over $2 million. Second, they artificially inflated the balances of accounts under their control by writing bad checks between their accounts. This "check kiting" scheme allowed them to overdraw an account by $471,000. They engaged in this illegal conduct in 1999 and 2000. Their actions were not uncovered immediately but eventually they were charged with nine counts of bank **fraud**, in violation of federal **criminal law**. Hollewell pleaded guilty to one count of check kiting, but Peugh pleaded not guilty and went to trial. He testified that he had not intended to DEFRAUD the banks but the jury convicted him on five of the bank FRAUD counts.

At sentencing, Peugh argued that the Constitution's Ex Post Facto Clause required that he be sentenced under the 1998 version of the Federal Sentencing Guidelines in effect at the time of his offenses, rather than the 2009 version of the guidelines in effect at the time of his sentencing. The two versions produced significantly different results. Under the 1998 guidelines, the range of imprisonment for Peugh was from 30 to 37 months. Under the 2009 guidelines the sentencing range rose to 70 to 87 months. The **district court** rejected Peugh's request and sentenced him under the 2009 guidelines, noting that it was required to do so under binding Seventh **Circuit Court** of Appeals precedent. The court sentenced him to 70 months' imprisonment, the bottom of the 2009 guidelines range. The Seventh Circuit upheld this decision based on its precedent. The Supreme Court agreed to hear Peugh's appeal because other circuit courts of appeals had ruled contrary to the Seventh Circuit.

The Supreme Court, in a 5-4 decision, reversed the Seventh Circuit, concluding that the application of the 2009 guidelines was an ex post facto law. Justice SONIA SOTOMAYOR, writing for the majority, reviewed the history of the Federal Sentencing Guidelines. Congress enacted the guidelines in 1984 to impose more uniformity on criminal sentences. Federal district court judges no longer had much discretion to fashion criminal sentences. Instead, the Federal Sentencing Guidelines Commission established formulas based on the seriousness of the crime and the criminal history of the defendant. For 21 years the **federal courts** were required to follow these mandatory guidelines. However, in 2005 the Supreme Court ruled that mandatory guidelines violated the SIXTH AMENDMENT. The guidelines were to remain in existence and courts were to consult them, but could make sentencing decisions on a case-by-case basis. If the district court departs from the sentencing guidelines range, it must explain the basis for its chosen sentence. On appeal, the district court's sentence is reviewed for reasonableness under an abuse-of-discretion standard. Justice Sotomayor also pointed out that under federal law, district courts are instructed to apply the sentencing guidelines that are "in effect on the date the defendant is sentenced." However the guidelines themselves include a provision that if the court determines using the guidelines in effect at the time of sentencing would violate the Ex Post Facto Clause, the court must use the guidelines "in effect on the date that the offense of conviction was committed."

Peugh argued that the Ex Post Facto Clause was violated because the 2009 guidelines called for a greater punishment than attached to bank fraud in 2000, when his crimes were completed. The government contended that because the more punitive guidelines applied to Peugh's sentence were only advisory, there was no ex post facto problem. Justice Sotomayor admitted that both parties could point to prior decisions of the Court to support their views. For instance, the Court had never accepted the proposition that a law must increase the maximum sentence for which a defendant is eligible in order to violate the clause. On the other hand, the Court had made "it clear that mere speculation or conjecture that a change in law will retrospectively increase the punishment for a crime will not suffice to establish a violation" under the clause. The key inquiry for the Court was whether a given change in the law presents a "sufficient risk of increasing the punishment attached to the covered crimes."

Justice Sotomayor looked to a 1987 Court decision involving Florida's state sentencing guidelines. The Court ruled that applying amended sentencing guidelines that increased a defendant's recommended sentence could violate the Ex Post Facto Clause, even though the sentencing courts had discretion to deviate from the recommended sentencing range. Though the federal guidelines were now advisory, district courts were still required to give deference to the sentencing ranges. The federal rules imposed "a series of requirements on sentencing courts that cabin the exercise of that discretion." Therefore, a retrospective increase in the guidelines range applicable to a defendant "creates a sufficient risk of a higher sentence to constitute" an ex post facto violation.

EXTORTION

The obtaining of property from another induced by wrongful use of actual or threatened force, violence, or fear, or under color of official right.

Sekhar v. United States

The federal Hobbs Act, 18 U.S.C. § 1951(a), prohibits obtaining property by threat (EXTORTION). In *Sekhar v. United States*, 133 S. Ct. 2720 (2013), the U.S. SUPREME COURT unanimously held that an attempt to compel a person to recommend to his employer the approval of an investment did not constitute "the obtaining of property from another" under the Hobbs Act.

Under the Act, extortion is defined as "the obtaining of property from another, with his consent, induced by wrongful use of actual or threatened force, violence, or fear, or under color of official right." § 1951(b).

Giridhar Sekhar was a managing partner of FA Technology Ventures, which managed various investment funds. The state of New York sought worthy investments for its Common Retirement Fund (CRF), which covers **pension** funds for employees of the state and its local governments. The CRF's sole **trustee**, the state **comptroller**, is tasked with finding and choosing investments for the CRF.

In 2009, the state comptroller's office was considering whether to invest in a certain fund that was managed by FA Technology Ventures. The investment would have given FA Technology millions of dollars in service fees. However, the state comptroller's general counsel made a written recommendation to the comptroller advising against investing in the fund, based on

news that the state attorney general was investigating another fund that was being managed by FA Technology. The comptroller then decided not to issue a "commitment," which would have allowed the parties to proceed to the next level (a limited partnership agreement between the CFR and the recipient of the investment). The comptroller notified a partner of FA Technology of his decision. That partner at FA Technology was aware of rumors that the general counsel (who had recommended against the investment) was having an extramarital affair.

Soon thereafter, the general counsel began to receive a series of emails demanding that he recommend moving forward with the FA Technology fund investment. The emails threatened that if he did not, his extramarital affair would be exposed to his **wife**, to government officials, and to the media. He contacted law enforcement, who traced some of the emails to Sekhar's home computer and others to offices of FA Technology Ventures.

Sekhar was indicted and convicted by a jury of attempted extortion, in violation of the Hobbs Act, which subjects a person to criminal liability if he or she "in any way or degree obstructs, delays, or affects commerce or the movement of any article or commodity in commerce, by **robbery** or extortion or attempts or conspires to do so." § 1951(b)(2). The Act also defines extortion (see above).

On the verdict form at Sekhar's criminal trial, the jury was asked to specify the property that petitioner attempted to extort. They were given three options: (1) the Commitment; (2) the Comptroller's approval of the Commitment; (3) the General Counsel's recommendation to approve the Commitment. The jury chose only the third option.

Sekhar appealed his conviction, arguing that the general counsel's recommendation was not "property" under the Hobbs Act. The **district court** held that general counsel's right to make professional decisions without external influence constituted "intangible personal property." The U.S. Court of Appeals for the Second Circuit affirmed. The U.S. Supreme Court granted **certiorari** (review) of the case.

Justice ANTONIN SCALIA delivered the opinion for an unanimous Court. He started with the established principle of interpretation that "Congress intends to incorporate the well-settled meaning of the common-law terms it uses." *Neder v. United States*, 527 U.S. 1, 119 S. Ct. 1827 (1999). The Court then summarized that "[w]hether viewed from the standpoint of the **common law**, the text and genesis of the **statute** at issue here, or the **jurisprudence** of this Court's prior cases, what was charged in this case was not extortion."

The Court went on to explain that extortion requires the obtaining of items of value, typically cash, from the victim. Extortion requires not only the deprivation of property (from the victim) but also the acquisition of property (by the perpetrator). Accordingly, property extorted must be transferable—that is, "capable of passing from one person to another." In the present case, no such property existed.

While implying that what occurred in the present case was "coercion," not extortion, the Court noted that New York courts had consistently held that the type of interference with rights as occurred in this case was coercion.

Thus finding no "extortion" under the Hobbs Act, the Court reversed the decision of the Second Circuit.

FAMILY LAW

Statutes, court decisions, and provisions of the federal and state constitutions that relate to family relationships, rights, duties, and finances.

Adoptive Couple v. Baby Girl

What made this family-law ADOPTION case different from others was the biological parentage of the father, who was a registered member of the Cherokee [Indian] Nation. In *Adoptive Couple v. Baby Girl*, 133 S. Ct. 2552 (2013), the U.S. SUPREME COURT used the express language of the INDIAN CHILD WELFARE ACT (ICWA) of 1978 to reverse the lower court's ruling that awarded CUSTODY of a baby up for adoption to its biological father. The lower court's award of custody was notwithstanding the fact that the father ostensibly had relinquished parental rights and had never met the 27-month-old child. The trial court, as well as the South Carolina Supreme Court, had relied on precisely the same Act (the ICWA) to award custody to the biological father, who first came forward during adoptive proceedings.

The Indian Child WELFARE Act (ICWA), 25 U.S.C. §§ 1901–1963, was enacted after Congress found that "an alarmingly high percentage of Indian families [were being] broken up by the removal, often unwarranted, of their children from them by nontribal public and private agencies." § 1901(4). This "wholesale removal of Indian children from their homes" prompted the legislation, which establishes federal standards that govern state-court CHILD CUSTODY proceedings involving Native American children.

In this case, while the birth mother was pregnant, her relationship with the biological father ended, although they had originally intended to marry. In June 2009, the mother sent the biological father a text message, asking if he would rather pay CHILD SUPPORT or relinquish his parental rights. He responded via text message that he relinquished his rights. The mother then decided to put the baby girl up for adoption. The mother's attorney, based on information from the mother, contacted the Cherokee Nation to determine if the father was enrolled therein; however, his first name was misspelled and his birthday incorrect, causing the Cherokee Nation to respond that his membership could not be verified via tribal records.

Proceeding on, the mother chose Adoptive Couple, non-Indians living in South Carolina, to adopt the baby girl through a private adoption agency. Adoptive Couple provided both emotional and financial support to the mother during the pendency of her pregnancy and were present at the birth in Oklahoma on September 15, 2009, where Adoptive Father cut the umbilical cord. The very next morning, the birth mother signed forms relinquishing her parental rights and consenting to the adoption. Adoptive Couple and baby returned to South Carolina a few days later and began formal adoption proceedings in that state, although they allowed the birth mother to communicate and visit.

Four months after the birth of the baby girl, Adoptive Couple served the biological father with notice of the pending adoption. He signed and returned the papers, stating that he was "not contesting" the adoption. (He later testified that, at the time of signing, he believed he was relinquishing his rights to the birth mother, not to Adoptive Couple.) One day after signing, the biological father contacted an attorney and subsequently requested a stay of the adoption proceedings. Later, in the actual adoption proceedings, he stated that he did not consent to the adoption and took a PATERNITY test, positively identifying him as the biological father.

In September 2011, trial proceedings began in the South Carolina family court; by then, the baby was two years old and only knew Adoptive Couple as parents. The family court determined that Adoptive Couple failed to carry the heightened burden of proving that Baby Girl would suffer serious emotional or physical harm if the biological father had custody; it denied the petition for adoption and awarded custody to the biological father. Baby Girl was handed over to him in December 2011. At the age of 27 months, she had never seen or met him before.

The South Carolina Supreme Court affirmed the decision, bringing in the ICWA as supportive backdrop. First, it held that ICWA governed the situation because it was undisputed that the case involved a child custody proceeding of an Indian child. It further determined that under ICWA, the biological father fell within the definition of parent. Finally, it cited two provisions within the ICWA that would prohibit the termination of the biological father's parental rights. First, Adoptive Couple had failed to show that "active efforts ha[d] been made to provide remedial services and rehabilitative programs designed to prevent the breakup of the Indian family." ICWA § 1912(d). Second, Adoptive Couple had failed to show that the biological custody of Baby Girl to the biological father would result in "serious emotional or physical harm to her beyond a reasonable doubt." ICWA § 1912(f). Finally, said the **appellate court**, even if parental rights of the biological father were terminated, § 1915(a) adoption-placement preferences would have applied.

On appeal to the U.S. Supreme Court, Justice SAMUEL ALITO delivered the opinion for the majority five justices, reversing the state supreme court. The opinion's opening paragraph summed the Court's thoughts on the matter:

> This case is about a little girl (Baby Girl) who is classified as Indian because she is 1.2% (3/256) Cherokee. Because Baby Girl is classified in this way the South Carolina Supreme Court held that certain provisions of the federal Indian Child Welfare Act of 1978 required her to be taken, at the age of 27 months, from the only parents she had ever known and handed over to her biological father, who had attempted to relinquish his parental rights and who had no prior contact with the child. The provisions of the federal **statute** at issue here do not demand this result.

First, said the Court, ICWA § 1912(f) (barring involuntary relinquishment of parental rights in the absence of the heightened showing that serious harm to the Indian child is likely to result from the parent's "continued custody" of the child) does not apply, because the biological father never had custody of the child, indeed, never met her. Second, ICWA § 1912(d) (remedial efforts to avoid breaking up the Indian family) also was inapplicable to a situation where the biological father abandoned the Indian child before birth and never had custody of the child. Finally, the Court clarified that § 1915(a)'s adoption-placement preferences are also inapplicable because no alternative party had come forward to adopt the baby; custody was never sought by the baby's paternal grandparents, other members of the Cherokee Nation, or other Native American families.

Noting that the biological father never offered financial support during the mother's pregnancy, even though he well was able to, in addition to other facts specific to this case, the Court expressed concern that a different result—that is, adopting the lower court's rationale—could lead to an absentee biological Indian father playing the "ICWA trump card" to override the mother's decision and the child's best interests. The Court remanded the case back to the STATE COURTS for further determinations consistent with its ruling.

FEDERAL COMMUNICATIONS COMMISSION

City of Arlington v. FCC

The U.S. Constitution grants powers to the three branches of government. These branches—particularly the legislative branch—delegate power in turn to administrative agencies. The legislative branch may have different reasons for delegating this authority. For instance, Congress may want to take advantage of an agency's expertise in carrying out a legislative directive, or Congress may want to employ agencies to address local concerns.

Congress creates agencies and delegates legislative authority through enactment of enabling statutes. When Congress delegates authority to an agency, the agency is often required to interpret the very **statute** that delegates the authority to the agency. The SUPREME COURT has developed principles that apply to the way that a court reviews an agency's interpretation of the statute that the agency administers. Under the case of *Chevron U.S.A., Inc. v. Natural Resources Defense Council, Inc.*, 467 U.S. 837, 104 S. Ct. 2778, 81 L. Ed. 2d 694 (1984), a court generally defers to an agency's construction of the statute administered by the agency.

In 2013, the Court was called upon to review how *Chevron* deference applies when an agency interprets the scope of the agency's own regulatory authority. The Court in *City of Arlington v. FCC*, 133 S. Ct. 1863 (2013), ruled that a court should defer to an agency's construction in such an instance just as a court would defer to other agency interpretations.

The dispute in *City of Arlington* focused on the way the FEDERAL COMMUNICATIONS COMMISSION (FCC) constructed the TELECOMMUNICATIONS Act of 1996. In the statute, Congress addressed the location, construction, and modification of facilities, such as towers and antennas, required for wireless telecommunications. Before Congress enacted the Telecommunications Act of 1996, local authorities made **zoning** decisions related to these telecommunications facilities.

The 1996 Act delegated considerable authority to the FCC to "prescribe such rules and regulations as may be necessary in the PUBLIC INTEREST to carry out" the Act's provisions. One of the provisions of the Act, codified at 47 U.S.C. § 332(c)(7)(B), requires local governmental entities to act on applications for wireless sites "within a reasonable period of time after the request is duly filed." Congress's clear goal in enacting this provision was to require local ZONING authorities to act promptly on applications related to wireless facilities.

However, wireless providers who submitted applications for facilities often faced long delays when seeking approval. An association representing wireless service providers asked the FCC to issue a rule clarifying the meaning of "reasonable period of time" stated in the statute. In November 2009, the FCC issued a declaratory ruling to clarify the language in the statute. The ruling stated: "[T]he record evidence demonstrates that unreasonable delays in the personal wireless service facility siting process have obstructed the provision of wireless services." Moreover, the ruling stated that these delays "impede the promotion of advanced services and competition that Congress deemed critical in the Telecommunications Act of 1996." Accordingly, the FCC ruled that a reasonable period of time is presumptively 90 days to process some applications and 150 days for other applications.

Several state and local governments filed suit to oppose the agency's ruling. More particularly, these governments argued that the FCC exceeded its authority to issue the ruling because Congress had not demonstrated intent to grant the FCC wide authority. The case reached the Fifth **Circuit Court** of Appeals, which ruled that the FCC's ruling was entitled to deference under *Chevron*, even though the ruling was based on the agency's interpretation of its own **statutory** authority. *City of Arlington v. FCC*, 668 F.3d 229 (5th Cir. 2012).

The Supreme Court granted **certiorari** to review the case. The Court's four liberal justices joined Justices ANTONIN SCALIA to form a 6–3 majority, which ruled that the FCC's ruling was entitled to *Chevron* deference. Justice STEPHEN BREYER filed a concurring opinion, while Chief Justice JOHN ROBERTS filed a dissenting opinion, joined by Justices Anthony Kennedy and Samuel Alito.

Scalia repeated one of the basic premises that underlies the doctrine that emerged from *Chevron*. The Court in that case stated that "if [a] statute is silent or ambiguous with respect to [a] specific issue, the question for the court is whether the agency's answer is based on a permissible construction of the statute." The Court established that when Congress leaves a term in a statute ambiguous and also calls on an agency to construe the statute, Congress has left resolution of the ambiguity to the agency. According to Scalia's opinion, "Congress knows to speak in plain terms when it wishes to circumscribe, and in plain terms when it wishes to enlarge, agency discretion."

The governments challenging the FCC's authority argued that the Court should distinguish between jurisdictional questions and nonjurisdictional questions when determining whether an agency's interpretation is entitled to deference. The governments argued that when an agency's interpretation relates to a jurisdictional issue, a court should not afford deference to the interpretation.

However, the majority determined that this premise of jurisdictional versus nonjurisdictional questions in the context of *Chevron* deference was "false" and a "mirage." The real question was instead "whether the agency has stayed within the **bounds** of its statutory authority." Scalia referred to a number of examples of instances where the agencies have construed the scope of their own jurisdictions, and the Supreme Court has regularly ruled that these constructions were entitled to deference.

Breyer agreed that the key question was not whether the key distinction in the case was whether the agency had made a jurisdictional or nonjurisdictional interpretation. However, he noted that a number of factors should play a role in a court's decision about whether Congress delegated authority to an agency to fill any gaps in the legislation the agency administers.

Roberts said his disagreement with the Court's decision was "fundamental", because he did not believe that a court should defer to an agency's interpretation until the court decides, on its own, that the agency is entitled to deference. He stated "An agency cannot exercise interpretive authority until it has it; the question whether an agency enjoys that authority must be decided by a court, without deference to the agency." Roberts would have remanded the case to the Fifth Circuit, instructing the lower court to determine on its own whether the FCC had authority to administer and interpret the statute.

FEDERAL TORT CLAIMS ACT

Levin v. United States

As the sovereign, the United States is immune from suit unless it consents to be sued. The government can waive **sovereign immunity** through the enactment of a **statute**. Courts have established that this waiver cannot be implied and must instead be "unequivocally expressed." Congress enacted the FEDERAL TORT CLAIMS ACT

(FTCA), 28 U.S.C. §§ 1346, 2671–2680, in 1948 as one of the statutes that establishes a waiver of SOVEREIGN IMMUNITY. Other statutes also affect the government's IMMUNITY.

The SUPREME COURT in *Levin v. United States*, 133 S. Ct. 1224, 185 L. Ed. 2d 343 (2013), reviewed a case involving the question of whether the federal government has consented to suit for a medical **battery** claim. A member of the U.S. Navy brought a BATTERY suit (among other claims) against the United States based on an eye surgery that navy surgeons performed on the PLAINTIFF. Two lower courts ruled that the government had not waived immunity for the claim. However, the Supreme Court ruled that the government had consented to suit for this type of battery claim.

The plaintiff who brought the case was Steven Levin. He was referred to the Ophthalmology Department at the U.S. Naval Hospital in Guam in 2003. Levin had developed a cataract in his right eye. A surgeon recommended a procedure known as "phacoemulsification with intraocular lens placement." Levin signed two consent forms related to anesthesia necessary for the surgery as well as the surgery itself. The procedure took place in March 2003. However, Levin claimed that he had orally withdrawn his consent before the surgery took place. The surgery caused complications that required continued treatment.

Levin then filed suit against the United States in the U.S. **District Court** for the District of Guam. He alleged that surgeons committed MEDICAL MALPRACTICE (based on NEGLIGENCE) as well as battery. Levin argued that the FTCA established the basis of federal jurisdiction.

After discovery, Levin was unable to produce evidence from experts to support his claims, and the United States filed a motion for **summary judgment** on Levin's claims. The district court determined that the lack of EXPERT TESTIMONY meant that Levin's claim did not present a genuine issue of material fact to support his medical MALPRACTICE claim, and the court granted SUMMARY JUDGMENT on that particular claim. However, the district court determined that a genuine fact issue existed about whether Levin had consented to the surgery. Thus, the district court denied summary judgment regarding Levin's battery claim.

The United States then filed a new motion, arguing that the district court lacked subject-matter jurisdiction to hear the case. The government argued that the FTCA expressly retained sovereign immunity for battery claims. The district court agreed with the government, granted the motion, and dismissed Levin's remaining claim. Levin then appealed the decision to the Ninth **Circuit Court** of Appeals, but the Ninth Circuit affirmed the lower court's decision.

The case hinged in part on the language of the FTCA, which does not waive immunity for every tort claim. In 28 U.S.C. § 2680(h), the FTCA does not waive immunity for "[a]ny claim arising out of **assault**, battery, **false imprisonment**, **false arrest**, **malicious prose- cution**, **abuse of process**, **libel**, **slander**, MISREPRESENTATION, deceit, or interference with contract rights." Levin conceded that this section by itself would bar his battery claim.

However, Levin's argument focused on language in the Gonzalez Act, 10 U.S.C. § 1089. This statute is one of several that protects government employees from individual tort liability. The Act applies specifically to military medical personnel and allows a plaintiff to pursue remedies under the FTCA against the United States but not against individual health care providers. The Supreme Court previously determined that the Gonzalez Act "functions solely to protect military medical personnel from malpractice liability."

Levin pointed to a specific provision in 10 U.S.C. § 1089(e). This section establishes that the FTCA's preservation of immunity against battery claims "does not apply to any **cause of action** arising out of negligent or wrongful act or omission in the performance of medical, dental, or related health care functions." Levin argued that this section negated the FTCA's preservation of immunity against battery claims.

Both lower **federal courts** rejected Levin's reading of the FTCA and the Gonzalez Act. The Ninth Circuit said that Levin's construction of the Gonzalez Act was "not the best reading of the statute" and instead read the statute to establish an "expression of personal immunity" for claims brought against military medical personnel. The court also concluded that Congress had not given an unequivocal waiver of immunity regarding the nature of Levin's claim. *Levin v. United States*, 663 F.3d 1059 (9th Cir. 2011).

The Supreme Court agreed to review the case, and in a unanimous decision, the Court reversed the Ninth Circuit. Justice RUTH BADER GINSBURG wrote for the Court. Justice ANTONIN SCALIA refused the join the majority opinion with regard to two footnotes that refer to LEGISLATIVE HISTORY.

The Court recited the two arguments related to § 1089(e) of the Gonzalez Act. The govern- ment reiterated its argument accepted by the lower courts that the Gonzalez Act provision related to battery claims was designed to ensure that if a claim for medical battery were available against the United States, a private plaintiff could not pursue a claim against an individual DEFENDANT.

The Court rejected the government's read- ing of the statute. The Court stressed that an operative clause in the Gonzalez Act states that the intentional tort exception in the FTCA "shall not apply" and that another clause limits the **abrogation** of the FTCA to medical personnel. The Court characterized the govern- ment's reading of the Gonzalez Act as "most unnatural," because the reading would require the Court to construe the words "shall not apply" as "shall apply."

The government made several other argu- ments, but the Court found all of them unpersuasive. The Court concluded that the Gonzalez Act allows a plaintiff to bring a claim based on medical battery against the United States based on actions taken by a military medical doctor acting within the scope of his employment. Accordingly, the Court reversed the Ninth Circuit's decision.

Supreme Court Clarifies Exception to the Federal Tort Claims Act

The FEDERAL TORT CLAIMS ACT (FTCA), waives the federal government's **sovereign immunity** in certain circumstances to permit persons to sue the government for damages. The FTCA contains a section that prevents a suit for damages involving intentional torts by federal employees, but there is a provision in this section that allows lawsuits involving inten- tional torts like **assault and battery** for "acts or omissions" of an "investigative or law enforce- ment officer." The lower **federal courts** could not agree as to whether this meant that federal correctional officers came under this provision or whether it was limited to **tortious** conduct that occurs during the course of executing a **search**, seizing evidence, or making an arrest.

The U.S. Supreme Court, in *Millbrook v. United States*, 133 S. Ct. 1441, 185 L. Ed. 2d 531 (2013), resolved the question, holding that the law enforcement provision applied to any federal law enforcement officers' acts or omissions.

Kim Milbrook, a prisoner in custody of the federal Bureau of Prisons (BOP), filed suit under the FTCA, asserting claims of negligence, **assault**, and **battery**. He alleged that in 2010 he had been forced to perform oral sex on a BOP correctional officer, while another officer held him in a chokehold, and a third officer stood watch nearby. Millbrook claimed the officers threatened to kill him if he did not comply. He alleged he suffered physical injuries as a result of the assault and sought compensation for his injuries.

The government asked the federal court to dismiss Millbrook's case, arguing that the FTCA did not waive sovereign immunity from suit on Millbrook's intentional tort claims. The government based its argument on the intentional tort exception in the FTCA and the **belief** that the law enforcement provision did not apply. Under binding Third **Circuit Court** of Appeals precedent, the law enforcement provision applied only to tortious conduct that occurred during the course of executing a search, seizing evidence, or making an arrest. Therefore, the acts and omissions of correctional officers were immune from an FTCA lawsuit. The **district court** agreed and dismissed Millbrook's lawsuit. Not surprisingly, the Third Circuit affirmed the lower court ruling. The Supreme Court agreed to hear Millbrook's appeal because other circuit courts based immunity on different grounds or waived it whenever an investigative or law enforcement officer committed one of the specified intentional torts.

The Supreme Court, in a unanimous ruling, reversed the Third Circuit decision. Justice Clarence Thomas, writing for the Court, found that the plain language of the law enforcement provision "answers when a law enforcement officer's 'acts or omissions' may give rise to an actionable tort claim under the FTCA." The provision lists six intentional torts and indicates that the officer's "acts or omission" fall "within the scope of his office or employment." Justice Thomas concluded that nothing in the text of the **statute** further qualified the category of "acts or omissions" that may trigger FTCA liability. He acknowledged that the Ninth

Circuit had narrowed the scope of the law enforcement provision by finding that the provision did not apply unless the tort was "committed in the course of investigative or law enforcement activities." The Third Circuit had narrowed the provision even more narrowly in holding that it applied only to conduct during the course of a search, a **seizure**, or an arrest. These interpretations did not find any support in the text of the statute. The FTCA's only mention of searches, seizures, and arrests was found in the **statutory** definition of an "investigative or law enforcement officer." Justice Thomas found that his provision focused on the status of "persons whose conduct may be actionable, not the types of activities that may give rise to a tort claim against the United States." The provision distinguished between the acts for which immunity was waived and the class of persons whose acts may give rise to an actionable FTCA claim. Thomas stated that the plain text confirmed that Congress "intended immunity determinations to depend on a federal officer's legal authority, not on a particular exercise of that authority."

The text of the law enforcement provision did not indicate that the officer must be engaged in "investigative or law enforcement activity." Congress could have limited the scope of the provision to claims arising from "acts or omissions of investigative or law enforcement officers *acting in a law enforcement or investigative capacity*," but it did not do so. Therefore, the Court declined to read such a limitation into unambiguous text.

FIFTH AMENDMENT

Salinas v. Texas

During any judicial term, the U.S. Supreme Court might review a case that represents a new variation or nuance to the general principles against self-incrimination under the Constitution's Fifth Amendment. In *Salinas v. Texas*, 133 S. Ct. 2174 (2013), the Court considered whether evidence of a person's *silence* when asked a question by police during a voluntary interview at the police station, prior to any arrest or being read his *Miranda* rights, could be used as part of prosecution's case-in-chief at trial? A **plurality** of the Court said yes.

In 1992, police in Houston, Texas, found two homicide victims, brothers, shot inside their residence. There were no witnesses, but police recovered six shotgun shell casings at the scene, and a neighbor observed a man fleeing the area in a dark-colored car after the neighbor had heard gunfire.

The investigation led police to Genovevo Salinas, who had been a guest at a party hosted by the victims on the night before the murders. Police visited Salinas at his house, where they observed a dark blue vehicle in his driveway. He voluntarily spoke with them, agreed to hand over his shotgun for ballistics testing, and voluntarily accompanied them back to the police station for further questioning.

During the interview, Salinas appeared cooperative and answered the officer's questions. However, when asked whether his shotgun "would match the shells recovered at the scene of the murder," Salinas fell silent and offered no answer. Police made note of his body language when asked this particular question (downcast eyes, biting bottom lip, clenching fists in his lap, etc.). He did not ask for an attorney; he did not affirmatively assert his right to remain silent. Importantly, after a few moments of silence, police proceeded with other questions, which Salinas answered. The interview at the police station lasted approximately one hour. (Although Salinas was not read *Miranda* warnings, all parties later agreed that the interview was noncustodial and the eventual trial proceeded on the assumption that he was not given any *Miranda* warnings.)

After the interview, police placed Salinas under arrest for unrelated charges (outstanding traffic warrants). Meanwhile, prosecutors came to the conclusion they had insufficient evidence to charge him with the murders, and he was released. Within days of his release, police obtained a statement from a man who said he heard Salinas confess to the killings. Police then decided to charge Salinas, but he had disappeared. Years later, in 2007, police discovered Salinas was living in the Houston area under an assumed name. He was arrested for the 1992 murders.

The first trial ended in a MISTRIAL. At the retrial, over defense objections, prosecutors introduced evidence of Salinas's silence when asked by officers about the shell casings. This time, Salinas was found guilty by the jury and subsequently sentenced to 20 years in prison.

On direct appeal in state court, Salinas argued that the use of his silence as part of

prosecution's case-in-chief violated the Fifth Amendment against self-incrimination. However, the argument was rejected by the **appellate court** based on the premise that his prearrest, pre-*Miranda* silence was not "compelled" within the meaning of the Fifth Amendment. The Texas Court of Criminal Appeals affirmed on the same ground. The U.S. Supreme Court accepted review to resolve conflict in the lower courts. The Court affirmed the state **appellate court's** decision.

Justice SAMUEL ALITO, writing for the majority, concluded that the Fifth Amendment claim failed because Salinas did not invoke the privilege (against self-incrimination) in response to the officer's question. The Court has previously recognized two exceptions to the requirement that a person must invoke the privilege. First, a criminal DEFENDANT need not take the stand and assert the privilege at his own trial. Second, a failure to invoke the privilege may be excused where governmental coercion makes his **forfeiture** of the privilege involuntary. Neither of these exceptions was available or applicable to Salinas.

It was undisputed that Salinas voluntarily accompanied police to the station for questioning and was free to leave any time during the interview. Further, he was not totally silent and offered responses to police questions but for the one question about shell casings, Justice Alito continued. The critical question for the Court, therefore, was whether, under these circumstances, Salinas was deprived of the ability to voluntarily invoke the Fifth Amendment. He was not, said the Court.

One final argument raised by Salinas addressed the fairness of requiring a person unschooled in legal doctrine to know that he had to affirmatively assert his right to remain silent, rather than just remain silent. But, reminded the Court, the Fifth Amendment guarantees that no person may be compelled to be a witness against himself, not the right for a person to remain silent. In any event, concluded the majority, it is well settled that FORFEITURE of the **privilege against self-incrimination** does not need to be knowing. *Minnesota v. Murphy*, 465 U.S. 420 at 427–428.

Justice Alito was joined by Chief Justice JOHN ROBERTS, JR., and Justice ANTHONY KENNEDY. Justice CLARENCE THOMAS filed an opinion concurring in the judgment, noting that Salinas's claim would fail even if he invoked the privilege, because the prosecutor's comments at trial did not compel him to give self-incriminating testimony. Justice Scalia joined in the concurrence. Justice STEPHEN BREYER filed a dissenting opinion, joined by Justices SONIA SOTOMAYOR, RUTH BADER GINSBURG, and ELENA KAGAN. Justice Breyer opined that, knowing that the question about shell casings was accusatory and a response could be incriminating, "Salinas' silence derived from an exercise of his Fifth Amendment rights."

FIRST AMENDMENT

Agency for International Development v. Alliance for Open Society International, Inc.

In *Agency for International Development v. Alliance for Open Society International, Inc.*, 133 S. Ct. 2321 (2013), the U.S. SUPREME COURT held that a government agency, which required recipients of grant monies for the fight against HIV/AIDS to have a policy explicitly opposing PROSTITUTION, violated the FIRST AMENDMENT of the U.S. Constitution. The U.S. Agency for International Development (USAID), along with the DEPARTMENT OF HEALTH AND HUMAN SERVICES (HHS), were among the defendants in the case; the plaintiffs were nongovernmental organizations (NGOs) qualified to receive this funding only if they met the prerequisite conditions.

Through the U.S. Leadership Against HIV/AIDS, Tuberculosis, and Malaria Act of 2003, 22 U.S.C. § 7601 **et seq.**, Congress appropriated and apportioned billions of dollars toward funding NGOs to help curb the worldwide pandemic spread of deadly HIV/AIDS in the most severely affected regions. According to congressional findings, more than 65 million people had been infected with HIV worldwide, and more than 25 million had perished, 19 million of them in sub-Saharan Africa alone. Another congressional finding linked the "sex industry, the trafficking of individuals into such industry, and sexual violence" to the spread of the HIV/AIDS epidemic.

Within the language of the Act are 29 different objectives, reflecting several approaches to the problem. One of those identified strategies "make[s] the reduction of HIV/AIDS behavioral risks a priority of all

prevention efforts," including "measures to address the social and behavioral causes of the problem." § 7601(15), § 7611(a)(12). In implementing the Act, Congress recruited and enlisted the assistance of NGOs "with experience in health care and HIV/AIDS counseling" to "provide treatment and care for individuals infected with HIV/AIDS." § 7601(18).

The funds came with two conditions. First, no funds made available to carry out the Act could be used "to promote or advocate the legalization or practice of prostitution or sex trafficking." § 7631(e). Second, no funds made available could be used to "provide assistance to any group or organization that does not have a policy explicitly opposing prostitution and sex trafficking, except ... to the Global Fund to Fight AIDS, Tuberculosis and Malaria, the World Health Organization, the International AIDS Vaccine Initiative or to any UNITED NATIONS agency." § 7631(f).

The HHS and USAID are the federal agencies tasked with primary responsibility for the implementation of the Act. Accordingly, the agencies directed that the actual award documents (granting specific monies to specific NGOs) contain an express agreement that recipients of the funds would commit to opposing "prostitution and sex trafficking because of the psychological and physical risks they pose for women, men, and children." USAID, Acquisition & Assistance Policy Directive 12-04.

In 2005, a group of domestic NGOs that were engaged in combating HIV/AIDS overseas, led by the Alliance for Open Society International and Pathfinder International, brought suit against the federal government. They expressed a fear that by adopting a policy explicitly opposing prostitution, they might **alienate** certain host governments and might diminish their effectiveness by making it more difficult to work with prostitutes. They also expressed concern that the policy requirement might require them to censor some of their statements in publications, conferences, and other forums that are funded by private donations, especially when discussing how best to prevent the spread of HIV/AIDS among prostitutes. The lawsuit expressly sought a **declaratory judgment** that implementation of the policy requirement violated their First Amendment **freedom of speech** rights, along with a **preliminary injunction** barring the government from cutting off their funding for the duration of the LITIGATION. They prevailed and the government appealed.

While the appeal was pending, HHS and USAID issued guidelines permitting fund recipients to work with affiliated organizations not bound by the policy requirement, as long as the fund recipients retained "objective integrity and independence from any affiliated organization." 44 CFR § 89.3. This became the subject prompting a remand. Ultimately, however, the **Circuit Court** of Appeals for the Second Circuit affirmed the **district court** after remand, concluding that the policy requirement, as implemented, violated the NGOs' FREEDOM OF SPEECH.

The U.S. Supreme Court, by a 6–2 margin (with Justice ELENA KAGAN taking no part in discussion or decision) affirmed. It held that the policy requirement, by making the affirmation of a **belief** "that by its nature cannot be confined within the scope of the Government program" a condition of federal funding, violated the First Amendment. The First Amendment, the Court reminded, "prohibits the government from telling people what they must say" (quoting from *Rumsfeld v. Forum for Academic and Institutional Rights, Inc.,* 547 U.S. 47, 126 S. Ct. 1297).

Chief Justice JOHN ROBERTS, JR., writing for the majority, acknowledged that, as a general matter, recipients who object to conditions can always decline funds, even where the exercise of First Amendment rights may be affected. But in some cases, he noted, funding conditions can result in unconstitutionally burdensome INFRINGEMENT on First Amendment rights. Over the years, Supreme Court precedent has recognized a distinction between conditions that define the limits of a government spending program (e.g., those that identify the activities Congress wishes to subsidize), and those conditions "that seek to leverage funding to regulate speech outside the contours of the program itself."

This dilemma fit within the present case, the Court found. Recipients of the Act's funds could not avow to the belief dictated by the policy agreement when spending the Act's funds, and then assert a contrary belief while participating in activities funded on their own or through private donations. Further, said the Court, "the Policy Requirement goes beyond

preventing recipients from using private funds in a way that would undermine the federal program. It requires them to pledge ALLEGIANCE to the Government's policy of eradicating prostitution."

Justice ANTONIN SCALIA, in his DISSENT, argued that the government had the right to choose financial aid for only those groups that shared its view on how to address the problem for which the funds were slated. Further, he opined, the fact that the government must often choose between policy options does not imply that it is coercing groups to adopt its views. Justice CLARENCE THOMAS joined the dissent.

Eighth Circuit Upholds Law Banning Picketing at Funerals

Westboro Baptist Church, located in Topeka, Kansas, has become nationally known for its PICKETING of funerals and other public places, where members hold signs disparaging gay people. Members believe that God punishes the United States by deaths of its citizens for tolerating homosexuality. The have displayed signs at funerals of fallen soldiers with messages such as "God Hates Fags," "Thank God for 9/11," and "Thank God for Dead Soldiers." This has led communities, states, and the federal government to enact laws that restrict picketing at funerals and military funerals. These laws bar demonstrators from being within a certain distance of a funeral location in the hours before and after the funeral. Two members of Westboro challenged a Missouri city's **ordinance** that restricted such picketing, arguing that the law violated their FIRST AMENDMENT right to display their messages at the time and place of their choosing. The Eighth **Circuit Court** of Appeals, in *Phelps-Roper v. City of Manchester,* 697 F.3d 678 (2012), upheld the ordinance, finding that its time, place, and manner regulations were consistent with the First Amendment.

In 2007, Manchester, Missouri, a city with approximately 19,000 residents, adopted an ordinance designed to limit the time and place of picketing and other protest activities around funerals or burials. The city said the purpose of the ordinance was the need to protect the dignity that is inherent in funerals in U.S. society and the dignity which "inures to the physical and psychological benefit of the family of the deceased." The ordinance set certain time and

place restrictions in connection with funerals and burials. Picketing and other protest activities were barred within 300 feet of any funeral or burial site during or within one hour before or one hour after the conducting of the funeral or burial service. The term "protest activities" was defined in the ordinance as "any action that is disruptive or undertaken to disrupt or disturb a funeral or burial service." The law did not, however, restrict picketing or protesting funeral processions. A violation of the ordinance carried with it a fine of up to $1,000 and/or up to three months imprisonment.

In 2009, Shirley and Megan Phelps-Roper, members of Westboro Church, filed a lawsuit in federal court challenging the constitutionality of the ordinance on First Amendment grounds. They argued that the First Amendment protects their right to display their messages at a time and place of their choosing. Even though the plaintiffs had never gone to Manchester to picket a funeral or burial, they sought a permanent INJUNCTION against its enforcement. They also sued seven other Missouri municipalities with funeral protest ordinances. These cases were dismissed after the ordinances were repealed. The federal **district court** granted **summary judgment** to the Phelps-Ropers, finding that the ordinance was content based and therefore presumptively invalid. The ordinance was flawed because it was not narrowly tailored to advance a significant government interest or to allow for ample alternative channels of communication. The city then appealed to the Eighth Circuit.

The 11 members of the Eighth Circuit heard the appeal, ruling unanimously that the ordinance was valid. Judge Dianna Murphy, writing for the court, noted that Manchester defended the ordinance as a valid time and place restriction. The ordinance was content neutral, as it was not directed at the content of the protestor's speech or at the manner of its delivery. The city contended the restrictions were narrow and that the ordinance did not restrict funeral processions. The Phelps-Ropers argued that the ordinance impermissibly restricted their right to picket. They claimed that church members abandoned plans to picket at two funerals in or about Manchester because of the ordinance, and that they had not considered picketing there since.

A key question was whether the ordinance was or was not content neutral. If the ordinance was content based, then the court had to apply the **strict scrutiny** standard of constitutional review, which is the highest level of scrutiny. Under this test a law is presumptively invalid. The government must prove it had a compelling interest to enact the law and that the law was narrowly tailored to address the issue at hand. If the ordinance was content neutral, the court must apply intermediate scrutiny. Under this standard, the law must be narrowly tailored to serve a significant government interest and allow for ample alternative channels for communication. Judge Murphy rejected the Phelps-Ropers' claim that the law was content based because their protests prompted its passage. The SUPREME COURT has allowed restrictions on where ABORTION protesters could picket near abortion clinics, finding these laws content neutral because they did not regulate speech but rather "the places where some speech may occur." These restrictions applied equally to all demonstrators, regardless of viewpoint, and made no reference to the content of the speech. In addition, the Sixth Circuit concluded that an Ohio **statute** identical to Manchester's ordinance was content neutral. Therefore, the Eighth Circuit applied intermediate scrutiny to the ordinance.

The court first found that the city had a significant government interest in protecting the privacy of funeral attendees. The Supreme Court had expanded the protected area of privacy beyond the home when it considered First Amendment challenges to an injunction prohibiting certain picketing and noise near clinic entrances and the homes of abortion providers. The law was clear that government restrictions on First Amendment rights could be justified as a significant interest in confrontational settings and in certain instances when the offensive speech was so intrusive that the "unwilling audience cannot avoid it." Judge Murphy concluded that the government had a significant interest in protecting the privacy of mourners because "mourners are in a vulnerable emotional condition and in need of 'unimpeded access' to a funeral or burial."

The court also found that the ordinance was narrowly tailored. Judge Murphy stated that it was narrowly tailored "because it places very few limitations on picketers" and the city's significant interest in protecting the privacy of mourners justified the 300 foot restriction "for a specific limited time and a short duration." Picketers could still communicate their message to funeral attendees. The ordinance did not place limits on the number of picketers or the noise level, including the use of amplification equipment, or on the numbers, size, text, or images of placards.

Judge Murphy then examined whether the ordinance left open "ample alternative channels" for speakers to disseminate their message. She noted that Manchester did not bar door-to-door proselytizing. Church members were free to mail literature to Manchester residents or contact them by telephone. Dissemination of letters to the editor or the Internet was also available. Judge Murphy concluded that Westboro Church members had "ample alternative channels" to convey their message. Because the ordinance met the three elements of intermediate scrutiny, the ordinance was constitutional.

Indiana Federal Court Allows Taliban Prayer in Prison

In January 2013, U.S. **District Court** for the Southern District of Indiana Judge Jane Magnus Stinson ruled that a prison warden had violated the religious freedom rights of American Taliban prisoner John Walker Lindh at the federal prison in Terre Haute, Indiana. Lindh and nearly two dozen other Muslim prisoners are being held at the "high-risk" facility where prisoners have limited contact with the outside world. The 31-year-old California-born Lindh, dubbed by the media as the "American Taliban," is serving a 20-year sentence for supporting terrorists after he was captured in Afghanistan by U.S. troops in 2007 and later pleaded guilty to the lesser charges.

The lawsuit was originally filed in 2007 by two Muslim prisoners at that facility, and Lindh joined the suit in 2010. The two original plaintiffs, no longer at that prison, dropped out of the suit, but Lindh, represented by the AMERICAN CIVIL LIBERTIES UNION (ACLU), continued. As of early 2013, the 55-cell facility housed approximately 42 prisoners, more than half of whom are Muslim.

Lindh, who was sentenced in 2002, came to the Terre Haute facility in 2007. The complaint alleged that prior to 2007, Muslim prisoners were allowed to hold group prayers at least three times a day (group **prayer** being a belief of the Hanbali school of the religion, to which Lindh adhered

after he converted). Since then, the complaint alleged, with the exception of the holy month of Ramadan, they are permitted just one weekly group prayer gathering. (Muslims in general are required to pray five times daily, but not necessarily in congregate form.) The complaint further alleged that private prayer in the individual cells does not meet Quran requirements and is inappropriate because persons are forced to kneel in close proximity to their toilets.

Prison officials responded to the complaint by saying that it was Lindh's own behavior, after coming to the facility in 2007, that prompted the change in policy. Lindh is housed in the Communications Management Unit (CMU), where he has limited opportunity to communicate with the outside world. The inmates housed therein are under open as well as covert audio and video surveillance, and all telephone calls are monitored, except those with legal counsel. They are not allowed to touch or have any physical contact with family members who visit, and they must speak English at all times except when reciting ritual prayers.

The government countered that, without such limitations, prisoners would be enabled to conspire with outsiders to commit terrorist or criminal acts. In fact, said the government in court documents, Lindh had delivered a "radical, all-Arabic sermon" to other Muslim prisoners that was loyal to techniques described in a manual seized from al Qaeda members which detailed how they should conduct themselves when they are imprisoned. Lindh's sermon, said the government, proves "that religious activities led by Muslim inmates are being used as a vehicle for radicalization and violence in the CMU." The government further argued that Lindh was permitted to pray as many times as he wanted, every day, wherever he happens to be "as his religion suggests to him that he should." Also, argued the government, daily group prayers were allowed until May 2007 when Muslim inmates refused to stop in the middle of a prayer to return to their cells during a fire emergency.

Citing the 1993 Religious Freedom Restoration Act, P.L. 103-141, 42 U.S.C. § 2000bb **et seq.**, which was specifically designed to protect religious speech in prison where internal policies may burden such rights, the district court found a violation of rights, without a compelling **state interest** for doing so. By not allowing group prayer, said the judge, while at the same time allowing other group activities, such as board games, the government impermissibly curtailed the religious freedoms of the plaintiffs. Further, said the judge, the "multi-purpose" room was used by Muslim prisoners for listening to, or watching recorded Quran verses. Allowing them to pray together, therefore, was not significantly different and should be allowed, ruled the judge. The court order issued an INJUNCTION "prohibiting the warden from enforcing the policy against daily congregate prayer for Muslims, including Mr. Lindh, for whom daily prayer is a sincerely held religious belief."

In May 2013 the parties were back in court. Ken Falk, legal director of the ACLU in Indiana, filed a motion asking the court to find the prison warden in CONTEMPT for failure to meet the requirements of the order. Since the January order, Prison Warden John Oliver told the court, he first developed a policy allowing groups of ten inmates to pray together three times a day. But, according to him, the new policy created security concerns after Muslim inmates allegedly began exhibiting gang-like behavior, such as extorting and bullying other prisoners and defying the staff.

He then changed the policy to permit them, in groups of two, to pray together in their cells. The warden argued that he believed he was complying with the court's order, while balancing the security needs of this high-risk prison unit with the religious rights of the Muslim prisoners. He further told the court that in March, the prison had converted a recreation room to a "meditation room," to accommodate all prisoners. He then stated that several Muslim prisoners began shunning others by banning them from group prayer, controlling access to food, and claiming the room territorially, leaving prayer rugs and other religious items lying around. The warden also informed the court that a group of Catholic inmates stopped using the room, calling it the "Muslim room."

The judge did not indicate when a decision would be forthcoming.

President Signs Law Restricting Protests at Veterans' Funerals

In August 2012, President BARACK OBAMA signed into law the Honoring America's Veterans and Caring for Camp Lejeune Families Act of 2012, P.L. 112-154. Despite its name, the bill is a comprehensive one covering a multitude of veterans' affairs. It also incorporated the provisions of the Sanctity of Eternal Rest for Veterans Act, intended to keep protesters from using veterans' cemeteries and funerals as forums for free speech on many topics.

The new law, first and importantly, extended care to a group of military service members who were stationed at Camp Lejeune, with their families, during a period when contaminated water was later implicated in major medical issues for several people. Second, and as relevant here, the new law extended the existing 2006 law that prohibited public protesting within 300 feet of national cemeteries, starting one hour before a funeral and terminating one hour after it ends.

Republican Senator Olympia Snowe (R-Me.) introduced the bill after the U.S. SUPREME COURT ruled that the FIRST AMENDMENT barred the father of Matthew Snyder, a U.S. Marine killed in Iraq, from obtaining damages for emotional distress when members of the Westboro Baptist Church appeared and launched a public protest at the marine's funeral. *Snyder v. Phelps*, 131 S. Ct. 1207, 179 L. Ed. 2d 172 (2011). The narrow high court ruling, specific to the facts of the case, reversed a jury award for the grieving family. The Court held that the Westboro church has a First Amendment right to promote their "broad-based message" on public matters such as war. The small Topeka, Kansas, church congregation did not know Snyder and traveled to Maryland to use the occasion of Snyder's funeral as a public forum to launch general protests. They shouted and flashed signs bearing messages such as "Thank God for Dead Soldiers!" and "God Blew Up the Troops" and "AIDS Cures Fags."

Snowe, who had complained about the partisan politics of Washington, and who later announced that she would not run for reelection, expressed gratitude to Congress for passing the bill "to protect the solemn moments of military funerals from outside disruption." The two sides to the First Amendment argument could not have been more polarized. Snowe, in a public statement, said, "Protests that encroach upon the funerals and burials of our fallen soldiers are repugnant and inappropriate—and they undermine the respect military families and loved ones undeniably deserve."

But the Westboro Baptist Church, whose entire congregation consists mostly of family members, believes that God punishes the United States for tolerating "the sin of homosexuality" by taking the lives of soldiers. Said church spokesperson Steve Drain (about protesting at a military funeral), "The Lord has just granted us another round of preaching opportunity here." He also accused Congress of enabling homosexuality by attempting to "keep Bible preaching away from funerals."

Because government may regulate the "time, place, and manner" of public speech under the First Amendment, Snowe designed the bill's provisions to do just that. The new law, adding to the existing ban on protests near national cemeteries, now requires that protesters must be at least 300 feet from military funerals, from two hours before the funeral service until two hours after it ends. Violators face fines and up to two years' imprisonment.

Meanwhile, the Westboro Baptist Church continued to revel in its notoriety, an effect it expressly appreciated as part of its mission to spread the word of the Bible. Spokesperson Drain said, in a CNN report, that funerals were one of the few events where "people will take a really serious look at really moral matters of heaven and hell." The church declared that the new law would not stop its protests at these events, but that the church would "obey all laws." He also said that the purpose for the protests was to influence the people attending the funerals.

"Influence" was probably not the word most attendees would have chosen. A majority of states now have their own laws responding to such protests, one of the latest being that passed in March 2013 by the state of North Carolina. The Alabama state HOUSE OF REPRESENTATIVES also passed a bill that says protesters must stay at least 1,000 feet or two blocks away from funerals; as of mid-2013, that bill was advancing to the state SENATE.

Additionally, private citizens have taken matter into their own hands, forming human chains around funerals to keep back such protesters. Many veterans' funerals have been blocked off by a show of force of other veterans on motorcycles providing a shield. In early 2013, the White House received five related petitions, containing nearly 700,000 signatures, asking that the Westboro Baptist Church be

Soldiers at the funeral of a U.S. Army private in Elwood, IL, November 2010.
SCOTT OLSON/GETTY IMAGES

declared a "hate group" and its tax-exempt status be revoked. The White House released a statement informing that it did not maintain a list of such groups. But it released a map visually demonstrating where most of the petition-signers came from. High-density areas of petitioners showed up in Kansas, where Westboro Baptist Church is based (Topeka).

The church's congregation consists primarily of pastor Fred Phelps, his 13 children, at least 54 grandchildren, and 7 great-grandchildren, along with their accompanying spouses, relatives, and some friends. Church members travel the country to protest at highly visible funeral events. In July 2013, the church announced, via Twitter messages, that it intended to appear at the funerals of 19 firefighters who died together while attempting to contain an Arizona wildfire that had destroyed thousands of acres and several homes.

Seventh Circuit Rules Illinois Law Barring Audio Recording of Police Officers Violates First Amendment

The First Amendment's grant of the right to free expression is not unlimited. The SUPREME COURT has allowed restrictions on speech for a variety of reasons, including the right to privacy. The Seventh **Circuit Court** of Appeals confronted an unusual question: does the FIRST AMENDMENT protect the right of a person to audio record the public speech of law enforcement officers performing their duties? The state of Illinois eavesdropping **statute** made it a **felony** to audio record all or any part of a conversation unless all parties to the conversation give their consent. Individuals could take silent video of police officers but if they turned on their microphones they could face a prison term of four to fifteen years. The appeals court, in AMERICAN CIVIL LIBERTIES UNION v. Illinois, 679 F.3d 583 (2012), ruled that the ban on audio recordings did violate the First Amendment.

The American Civil Liberties Union (ACLU) filed suit against Cook County State's Attorney Anita Alvarez, asking an Illinois federal **district court** to declare the eavesdropping statute unconstitutional and bar Alvarez from enforcing the law. The ACLU planned to carry out a "police accountability program," in which it would openly audio record police officers without their consent when the officers were performing their public duties in public places and the officers were speaking at a volume audible to the unassisted ear. The organization intended to record policing at protests and public demonstrations in public places in and around the Chicago area. The recordings would be published online and through other forms of electronic media. The ACLU contended its planned audiovisual recording was protected under the First Amendment's speech, press, and petition clauses. However, because it feared prosecution, the ACLU had not proceeded with the program.

Alvarez asked the court to dismiss the case, arguing the ACLU could not show a threat of prosecution and therefore did not have standing to bring the lawsuit. The district court disagreed and found the ACLU had standing, but ruled that the ACLU could not show a First Amendment injury because the First Amendment did not protect "a right to audio record." The court believed that the ACLU's claim was an "unprecedented expansion of the First Amendment." The ACLU appealed the decision to the Seventh Circuit.

A three-judge panel of the Seventh Circuit, voting 2-1, overturned the district court decision. Judge Diane Sykes, writing for the majority, agreed with the lower court that the ACLU had standing to bring the lawsuit because it had demonstrated a credible threat of prosecution. The eavesdropping statute clearly prohibited the ACLU's proposed audio recording and the ACLU had identified many recent prosecutions against individuals who recorded encounters with on-duty police officers. In fact,

Alvarez had filed three such prosecutions and had not stated that she would decline to prosecute the ACLU or its employees and agents if they audio recorded police officers without consent. Judge Sykes acknowledged that the "ACLU does not know precisely when or if its employees would face prosecution or which officers would be involved." However, pre-enforcement lawsuits always "involved a degree of uncertainty about future events." In this case that uncertainty did not undermine the credible threat of prosecution.

Turning to the substantive claim, Judge Sykes noted that Alvarez had taken an extreme position, arguing that openly recording what police officers say while performing their duties in public was wholly unprotected by the First Amendment. This extreme position did not make sense because the act of making an audio or audiovisual recording was "necessarily included within the First Amendment's guarantee of speech and press rights as a corollary of the right to disseminate the resulting recording." The right to publish or broadcast these recordings would be "largely ineffective" if the prior act of making the recording were wholly unprotected. Banning photography or note taking at a public event would raise serious First Amendment concerns and the same was true of a ban on audio and audiovisual recording. The law, restricting a medium of expression, interfered "with the gathering and dissemination of information about government officials performing their duties in public." Because of this fact, the eavesdropping statute burdened speech and press rights and was subject to heightened First Amendment scrutiny.

Judge Sykes pointed out that under HEIGHTENED SCRUTINY, a law that restricts the First Amendment can only survive if it is content neutral, if there is an important public justification for the challenged regulation, and if there is a reasonably close fit between the law's means and ends. The last requirement means that the "burden on First Amendment rights must not be greater than necessary to further the important governmental interest at stake." The court agreed that the eavesdropping statute was content neutral because it banned all audio recordings, regardless of the subject matter. However, as applied in this case, the court concluded that the law likely failed the other two parts of the scrutiny standards. Alvarez argued that the law was necessary to protect conversational privacy, which is an important government interest. Surreptitiously recording private communications clearly implicated privacy expectations, but such expectations were not at issue in this case. The ACLU wanted to openly audio record police officers performing their duties in public places and speaking at a volume audible to bystanders. This type of communication lacked any "reasonable expectation of privacy." Lacking this expectation, the state could not identify any other substantial government interest that would be served by banning audio recording. The breadth of the statute was also troubling to Judge Sykes. It was not narrowly tailored to the government's interest in protecting conversational privacy because it dealt with public rather than private or confidential speech. Therefore, the court reversed and remanded the case to the district court with instructions to issue a **preliminary injunction** barring the state from applying the eavesdropping statute against the ACLU while the case proceeded to a conclusion.

Third Circuit Rules News Media Has No First Amendment Right to Report from Polling Places

The media has the FIRST AMENDMENT right to report on what happens in society. This right to gather news was called into question as the result of a Pennsylvania state law that restricts the public's access to polling places. A publisher brought suit in federal court, challenging the law under the First Amendment and the **Equal Protection** Clause of the FOURTEENTH AMENDMENT. The Third **Circuit Court** of Appeals, in *PG Publishing Company v. Aichele,* 705 F.3d 91 (2013), upheld the law, finding that under a constitutional balancing test, there was no historical presumption of openness in the voting process and that allowing the public and the press into polling places could "concern, intimidate, or even turn away potential voters."

PG Publishing Company (PG), doing business as the *Pittsburgh Post-Gazette* newspaper, filed suit prior to the November 6, 2012 election against Carol Aichele, in her capacity as Pennsylvania's SECRETARY OF STATE, and the Allegheny Board of Elections. The company challenged a Pennsylvania election law that required everyone except election officials,

police officers, and persons in the course of voting to "remain at least ten (10) feet distant from the polling place during the progress of voting." A "polling place" was defined as "the room provided in each election district for voting at a primary or election." PG asserted that the law infringed on its First Amendment right to access and gather news at polling places. It also contended that the law had been selectively enforced in different election districts, which violated the EQUAL PROTECTION Clause of the Fourteenth Amendment. PG alleged that its reporters and photographers had been denied access to polling places in Alleghany County. The newspaper contended that reporting from polling places during the upcoming 2012 election was particularly important because a new Voter ID law requiring voters to present photo ID was to be enforced. PG asked the court to declare the law unconstitutional as applied.

The defendants moved to dismiss the PG lawsuit and the federal **district court** granted their motion. As to the First Amendment claim, the court applied it to an individual's physical location and not his speech. This meant there was no need to decide whether a polling place was a public forum. Instead, the court analyzed the law as content-neutral in a nonpublic forum. The court concluded that PG's First Amendment rights were not abridged because the law sought to protect a voter's right to cast a ballot "free from the taint of intimidation and fraud." As to the equal protection claim, the court held that the examples PG provided of inconsistent application of the law did not rise to the level of a constitutional violation. PG had failed to show that a single election official had discriminated against its reporters in applying the challenged law. PG then appealed to the Third Circuit Court of Appeals.

In a unanimous ruling, a three-judge panel of the Third Circuit upheld the district court decisions but based its First Amendment ruling on different grounds. Judge Joseph Greenaway, writing for the court, noted that the U.S. SUPREME COURT, while recognizing that the First Amendment bars the government from interfering in any way with a free press, has never ruled that the First Amendment guarantees "the press a constitutional right of special access to information not available to the public generally." Therefore, the appeals court declined to hold that the press was entitled to any greater protection under its right of access for news-gathering purposes that is accorded the general public. That right to access did not extend to all information.

Judge Greenaway applied a balancing test to evaluate PG's First Amendment right to access challenge. The test, which he labeled the "experience and logic test," was applicable to the voting process and polling places. Access to government proceedings must be evaluated "with an eye toward the historical and structural role of the proceeding." As for public access to polling places, the court had to determine whether polling places were presumptively open to the press and the general public. He first examined the history of elections in the United States. In the colonial era, voting was conducted by voice vote. After the United States was formed, the states adopted a paper ballot election system. However, paper balloting was corrupted by voter intimidation and **fraud**, with the polling place often an "open auction space." By the later 1800s, states began adopting "the Australian system" of voting, which placed all candidates on a single ballot, provided for the erection of polling booths open only to election officials, two representatives of each candidate, and the electors about to vote. By 1900, almost all of the states had adopted this system and at least 34 of the 45 states had enacted laws that banned election-day speech within 100 feet of the polling places. The Pennsylvania law at issue had been enacted in 1937, which in Judge Greenaway's view cemented the fact that the state had a history of preserving secrecy in voting. Therefore, the historical record was insufficient "to establish a presumption of openness in the context of the voting process itself."

The court then applied the "logic" prong of the access test. The question was whether public access played a significant positive role in the voting process. Judge Greenaway pointed to the prevention of election FRAUD, voter intimidation, and other electoral evils that came through openness in the voting process. Yet he found no "tangible or discernible evidence of how the public good would benefit so much more" if the press was inside the room, rather than 10 feet away. There was also the problem of limiting this new access just to PG's reporters, as there was no constitutionally valid way of doing so. If PG gained access, then all other members of the

press must share in this right. On top of it all, there was the question of who was a member of the press. In the court's view, "the class of persons to whom such a right is applicable is almost boundless." Finally, there was the real possibility that the presence of reporters during the sign-in period, when individuals are exchanging personal information with the voting official could intimidate or even turn away potential voters. Therefore, the "logic" prong disfavored finding a constitutionally protected right of access to the voting process.

FOURTH AMENDMENT

Massachusetts High Court Upholds Warrantless Search of Cellphone

The technological advances made in cellphones have transformed these devices from mere telephones to powerful computers containing large amounts of personal data. Courts have begun examining the actions of law enforcement officers who search cellphones that were seized incident to a lawful arrest, to determine whether these warrantless searches violate a defendant's FOURTH AMENDMENT rights. Massachusetts' highest court, the Supreme Judicial Court, in *Commonwealth v. Phifer*, 979 N.E.2d 210 (2012), upheld the validity of a cellphone search but limited its decision to the facts in the case. It declined to address whether such a warrantless search was always valid, and if so, the permissible extent of such a search.

Demetrius Phifer was charged with selling drugs near a school or park. Two Boston police officers, assigned to a drug control unit, were conducting a drug investigation in the East Boston section of the city. The officers saw Phifer standing on a street corner and talking on a cellphone. They believed he was waiting for or looking for someone. The officers recognized Phifer and knew he had two outstanding warrants relating to drug offenses. A few minutes later, Phifer got into a car driven by a woman that one of the officers recognized as a drug user. The front seat passenger, Dennis Claiborne, was also recognized by the officer as a drug user. While the car drove around the block, the officer observed what he thought to be a drug transaction between Phifer and Claiborne. After Phifer was dropped off, the officer approached Phifer and placed him under arrest on the outstanding warrants. The other officer approached the car and recovered cocaine from Claiborne. Claiborne gave the officer his cellphone telephone number.

The officers took Phifer to the police station for booking. They seized $364 in cash that Phifer had with him, as well as his cellphone. After booking, one of the officers conducted a search of the "flip phone" to check the list of incoming and outgoing calls. He discovered that the recent phone log displayed several received calls from the phone number associated with Claiborne's cellphone. The officer knew that cellphones were often used in the drug business. Prior to trial, Phifer's lawyer filed a motion to suppress the evidence from the warrantless search of Phifer's cellphone. The lawyer contended that the cellphone was searched without **probable cause** or Phifer's consent, in violation of Fourth Amendment.

The trial judge denied Phifer's motion, concluding that the search of his cellphone was a lawful search incident to an arrest. Because the arrest was lawful, the officer had the right to perform a search and the right to search its contents. Though some **federal courts** had ruled similarly, the judge noted that no **appellate** decision in Massachusetts addressed the issue. Therefore, it was not surprising that the Supreme Judicial Court agreed to hear Phifer's pretrial appeal of his Fourth Amendment claim.

In a unanimous decision, the court upheld the trial court decision. Justice Margot Botsford, writing for the court, noted that U.S. SUPREME COURT has allowed a few established and well-delineated exceptions to the Fourth Amendment's warrant requirement. One of these exceptions is a search incident to a lawful arrest. This exception has been justified by the reasonableness of searching for weapons, instruments of escape, and evidence of a crime when a person is taken into official CUSTODY and lawfully detained. Phifer did not challenge these general principles but contended that cellphones are different from other types of items a person might carry on his body at the time of arrest because they have the capacity to store vast quantities of private information. Because they are different, they must be treated differently under the Fourth Amendment.

Justice Botsford emphasized that neither her court nor the U.S. Supreme Court had addressed whether the contents of cellphones may be searched in whole or in part incident to a lawful arrest. In the present case, the state court declined "the defendant's invitation to venture very far into this thicket because there is no need to do so in order" to decide Phifer's argument. The court found that the facts in this case made clear that the limited search of the recent call list on Phifer's cellphone did not violate the FOURTEENTH AMENDMENT. Justice Botsford cited a 1988 decision by her court that found a search of a gym bag by the DEFENDANT at the time of his arrest as a lawful search incident to an arrest. Police were entitled to examine the contents of the bag. This decision controlled the present case because the **seizure** of the phone itself—the physical object—was permissible as an incident to Phifer's lawful arrest. The police had PROBABLE CAUSE to believe the cellphone's recent call list would contain evidence relating to the crime for which Phifer had been arrested. The officers had observed Phifer using the phone just prior to the drug transaction with Claiborne and knew that cellphones were commonly used in the drug trade.

The court emphasized the limited nature of its ruling. Justice Botsford stated, "We do not suggest that the assessment necessarily would be the same on different facts, or in relation to a different type of intrusion into a more complex cellular telephone or other information storage device." She recognized cellphones had become "essentially computers," which were capable of storing large quantities of personal and private information. The expectation of privacy that individuals have for the information on their cellphones might lead to greater Fourth Amendment protections, but the court declined to consider this question.

Supreme Court Limits Search Warrant Detention by Police

When police execute a **search** warrant and enter a person's home, they are entitled to detain anyone in the home while the search is being made. The U.S. SUPREME COURT, in *Michigan v. Summers*, 452 U.S. 692, 101 S.Ct. 2587, 69 L.Ed.2d 340 (1981), authorized this procedure. However, in later years the question arose as to whether police could detain individuals who were not in the immediate vicinity of the premises to be searched. The Court, in *Bailey v. United States*, 133 S. Ct. 1031, 185 L. Ed. 2d 19 (2013), ruled that detention incident to a search was limited to the immediate vicinity of the premises.

On the evening of July 28, 2005, police in Wyandanch, New York obtained a warrant to search a residence for a handgun. The residence was a basement apartment. A confidential informant had told police he saw the gun when he was at the apartment to buy drugs from a heavyset black male with short hair known as "Polo." As police prepared for the search, two detectives were watching the apartment in an unmarked car. They observed two men, later identified as Chunon Bailey and Bryant Middleton, leave the apartment and drive off in a car that was parked in the driveway. The detectives followed the car, while informing the search team that they were following the car and intended to detain the occupants. The search team then entered the apartment and began the search.

The detectives tailed the car for about a mile before pulling it over in a parking lot. They ordered Bailey and Middleton out of the car and did a patdown search of each man. The officers found no weapons but discovered a ring of keys in Bailey's pocket. Bailey identified himself and said he lived at the address where the search was taking place. However, his driver's license listed his residence as Bayshore, New York, the town where the confidential informant told the police the suspect Polo used to live. Middleton said Bailey was giving him a ride home and that they had come from the apartment. Police handcuffed both men and explained they were being detained incident to the execution of a SEARCH WARRANT at the apartment. Bailey switched his story, telling the detectives he did not live at the apartment and "Anything you find there ain't mine." A patrol car took both men back to the apartment. By the time they returned, the search team had found a gun and drugs in plain view inside the apartment. Bailey and Middleton were placed under arrest and Bailey's keys were seized incident to the arrest. Officers later found that one of the keys opened the apartment door.

Bailey was charged with three federal offenses, including possession of cocaine with an intent to distribute, possession of a firearm by a felon, and possession of a firearm in furtherance of drug trafficking. Bailey sought to suppress the apartment key and the statements he made to the detectives when they stopped his car. He argued that this evidence derived from an unreasonable **seizure**. The federal **district court** denied his motion, concluding that Bailey's detention was permissible under *Michigan v. Summers,* as a detention incident to the execution of a search warrant. A jury found Bailey guilty on all three counts. The Second **Circuit Court** of Appeals upheld the district court ruling on the seizure of Bailey. The Supreme Court agreed to hear Bailey's appeal because other circuit courts of appeal had reached differing conclusions as to whether *Michigan v. Summers* justified the detention of occupants beyond the immediate vicinity of the premises covered by a search warrant.

The Court, in a 6-3 decision, reversed the Second Circuit. Justice ANTHONY KENNEDY, writing for the majority, noted that the Court gave "some latitude for police to detain" where the intrusion on a person's privacy is "so much less severe" than that involved in a traditional arrest. In *Summers,* the Court had allowed detention without **probable cause** to arrest for a crime when executing a search warrant. It found the additional intrusion caused by detention to be "slight." However, in that case the DEFENDANT was detained on a walk leading down from the front steps of his house. For Bailey's detention to be lawful, it had to be shown that it was consistent with the "purpose and rationale" announced in *Summers.*

Justice Kennedy pointed to three important law enforcement interests contained in the *Summers* decision. The first interest was "minimizing the risk of harm to officers." The execution of a search warrant may give rise to sudden violence or "frantic efforts to conceal or destroy evidence." Detaining occupants minimizes the risk of harm to officers and occupants alike. If, for example, Bailey had returned to his apartment, the police could have detained him under *Summers.* However, in this case Bailey was well away from his residence at the time the search began. If the Second Circuit reasoning were applied, it would "justify detaining anyone in the neighborhood who could alert occupants that the police are outside." Such an extension of *Summers* was not consistent with this first interest.

A second law enforcement interest relied on in *Summers* was that "the orderly completion of the search may be facilitated if the occupants of the premises are present." If occupants are permitted to wander, they might conceal or destroy evidence, try to distract officers, or "simply get in the way." In Bailey's case those risks were not present. He was not a threat to the proper execution of the search. Justice Kennedy concluded that Bailey's detention "served no purpose in ensuring the efficient completion of the search."

The third law enforcement interest addressed in *Summers* was "preventing flight in the event that incriminating evidence is found." If officers had to keep close supervision of occupants who were not restrained, the search might be rushed, causing damage to property or compromising its execution. Justice Kennedy emphasized that the "concern over flight is not because of the danger of flight itself but because of the damage that potential flight can cause to the integrity of the search." This was not a factor in Bailey's detention away from his residence.

Justice Kennedy concluded that none of the interests in *Summers* applied in Bailey's case. He stated that "Where officers arrest an individual away from his home, however, there is an additional level of intrusiveness." A public detention resembles a "full-fledged arrest." Moreover, Bailey was subjected to a detention away from the scene and a second one at his apartment: "In between, the individual will suffer the additional indignity of a compelled transfer back to the premises, giving all the appearances of an arrest." Therefore, *Summers* was limited to detentions in the immediate vicinity of the premises searched.

Supreme Court Strikes Down Drug-Sniffing Dog Search

The U.S. SUPREME COURT, in a major ruling, found that police may not use a drug-sniffing dog to "search" the exterior of a home if the police lack **probable cause** for such a **search**. In *Florida v. Jardines,* 133 S. Ct. 1409, 185 L. Ed. 2d 495 (2013), the Court held that the area immediately surrounding and associated with a home, known as **curtilage**, is part of the home itself. As with the interior of the home, police may not legally enter this space without a warrant if they lack PROBABLE CAUSE that a crime has been committed.

In 2006, Miami-Dade Police Department detective William Pedraja received an unverified tip that Joelis Jardines was growing marijuana in his home. A month later the department and the federal DRUG ENFORCEMENT ADMINISTRATION sent a joint surveillance team to Jardines' home. Detective Pedraja, a member of the team, watched the home for fifteen minutes and saw no vehicles in the driveway or activity around the home. He could not see inside the home because the blinds were closed. He then approached the home with a trained canine handler who brought with him a drug-sniffing dog. The dog was trained to detect the scent of marijuana, cocaine, heroin, and several other drugs. The dog indicated the presence of these drugs through particular behavioral changes recognized by his handler. The handler had the dog on a six-foot leash as he approached Jardines' front porch. The dog sensed one of the odors he had been trained to detect and began exploring the area for the strongest presence of that odor. The dog tracked back and forth, engaging in what the handler called "bracketing." After sniffing the base of the front door, the dog sat. This indicated that this was the odor's strongest point. The handler then brought the dog back to his vehicle. He informed Pedraja that there had been a positive alert for narcotics. Pedraja applied for and received a warrant to search Jardines' home. Upon searching the home, police found marijuana plants.

Jardines was charged with trafficking in cannabis. At trial he asked the court to suppress the marijuana plants on the ground that the canine investigation was an unreasonable search under the FOURTH AMENDMENT. The trial court granted the motion but the Florida Third District **Court of Appeal** reversed it. However, the Florida Supreme Court overturned the appeals court ruling, finding that the canine investigation was a Fourth Amendment search unsupported by probable cause, making invalid the warrant based upon information gathered in that search.

The U.S. Supreme Court agreed to hear the state's appeal as the question of whether the officer's behavior was a search within the meaning of the Fourth Amendment. The Court, in a 5-4 ruling, concluded that the canine investigation was indeed a search. Justice ANTONIN SCALIA, writing for the majority, noted that the Fourth Amendment provided that when the government obtains information by physically intruding on persons, homes, papers, or effects, a "search" has "undoubtedly occurred." In the majority's view, this principle "renders this case a straightforward one." The officers had gathered information in the CURTILAGE of the home, which in this case was the front porch. The Court had previously ruled that this area enjoys the same protection as part of the home itself. The officers gained their information by "physically entering and occupying the area to engage in conduct not explicitly or implicitly permitted by the homeowner."

Justice Scalia stated that the "very core" of the Fourth Amendment stands "the right of a man to retreat into his own home and there be free from unreasonable governmental intrusion." This principle would be "of little practical value if the State's agents could stand in a home's porch or side garden and trawl for evidence with impunity." There was no doubt in this case that police had entered the curtilage of Jardines' home, as the front porch "is the classic exemplar of an area adjacent to the home." The activities of home life extended to the front porch.

The next issue was whether the officers' investigation was accomplished through an unlicensed physical intrusion. Law enforcement officers may view a home as they pass by on a public thoroughfare, but an officer's ability to gather information is "sharply circumscribed when he steps off those thoroughfares and enters the Fourth Amendment's protected areas." In this case the detectives had their feet and the feet of the dog "firmly planted on the constitutionally protected extension of Jardines' home." The only question was whether Jardines had given his leave for them to do so. Justice Scalia concluded that he had not given the officers license to investigate his home. An implicit license exists for a stranger to approach a home by its front path, knock promptly, wait briefly to be received, and then, absent an invitation to stay longer, leave. Having a drug-sniffing police dog "explore the area around the home in hopes of discovering incriminating evidence is something else." There is no customary invitation to do *that*. In Scalia's view the "background social norms that invite a visitor to the front door do not invite him there to conduct a search."

Florida had argued that investigation by drug-sniffing dog by definition could not implicate any legitimate privacy interest. It pointed out that the Court had allowed canine inspections of luggage in an airport, chemical testing of a substance that had fallen from a parcel in transit, and canine inspection of an automobile during a lawful traffic stop. In these cases the Court ruled that these searches did not violate a person's reasonable expectation of privacy. Justice Scalia found this line of reasoning irrelevant because the "reasonable expectations test" did not address situations where law enforcement officials intrude on a person's property to gather evidence.

Supreme Court Warrantless Blood Test Unconstitutional

The FOURTH AMENDMENT protects citizens from unreasonable searches and seizures. Under the amendment, law enforcement officers must obtain a **search** warrant from a **magistrate** before performing the search. However, the U.S. SUPREME COURT allows warrantless searches when exigent circumstances require quick action. In a 1966 case, the court held that a warrantless blood test of an individual arrested for driving under the influence of alcohol was permitted where the officer was confronted with an emergency and feared that the delay necessary to obtain a warrant threatened the destruction of evidence. In *Missouri v. McNeely,* 133 S. Ct. 1552, 185 L. Ed. 2d 696 (2013), the Court refused to classify the natural metabolization of alcohol in the bloodstream as an exigency that would allow an exception to the Fourth Amendment's warrant requirement for nonconsensual blood testing in all drunk-driving cases.

A Missouri highway patrol officer stopped Tyler McNeely's truck at 2 a.m. after he exceeded the speed limit and repeatedly crossed the center line. The officer observed that McNeely appeared to be intoxicated, as he had blood-shot eyes, his speech was slurred and he had the smell of alcohol on his breath. McNeely admitted that he had consumed "a couple of beers" at a bar. McNeely was unsteady on his feet and performed poorly on a **battery** of field-sobriety tests. After McNeely declined to use a portable breath-test machine to measure his blood alcohol concentration (BAC), the officer placed him under arrest and began to transport him to the station house. The officer changed his mind after McNeely said he would refuse to take a breath sample at the station house, instead driving him to a nearby hospital for a blood test. The officer did not try to secure a warrant. At the hospital, McNeely refused to consent to the blood test. The officer directed the lab technician to take a blood sample, which was completed around 2:35 a.m. The test revealed that McNeely's BAC measured 0.154, almost twice the legal limit of 0.08.

McNeely was charged with driving while intoxicated (**DWI**). He asked the trial court to suppress the blood test results, arguing that, under the circumstances, taking the blood without first obtaining a SEARCH WARRANT violated his Fourth Amendment rights. The trial court agreed, concluding that the exigency exception to the Fourth Amendment did not apply because, apart from the fact that as in all cases of intoxication, McNeely's liver was metabolizing blood alcohol, there were no circumstances suggesting the officer faced an emergency that made obtaining a warrant impracticable.

The Missouri Supreme Court upheld the trial court ruling, using the U.S. Supreme Court's decision in *Schmerber v. California*, 384 U.S. 757 , 86 S. Ct. 1826, 16 L. Ed. 2d 908 (1966) as the backdrop to its analysis. *Schmerber* required lower courts to use a totality of the circumstances analysis when determining whether exigency permits a nonconsensual, warrantless blood test. The Missouri court concluded that *Schmerber* "requires more than the mere dissipation of blood-alcohol evidence to support a warrantless blood draw in alcohol-related cases." In McNeely's case there were no "special facts," such as whether the officer was delayed by the need to investigate an accident and transport an injured suspect to the hospital, as had been the case in *Schmerber*. Finding that this was a "routine DWI case," the court ruled that the warrantless blood test violated the Fourth Amendment.

The U.S. Supreme Court, in a 5-4 decision, upheld the Missouri Supreme Court ruling. Justice SONIA SOTOMAYOR, writing for the majority, noted that the Court had created a number of exceptions to the Fourth Amendment's warrant requirement. A well-recognized exception applied when the exigencies of the situation make the needs of law enforcement "so compelling that a warrantless search is objectively reasonable under the Fourth Amendment." A variety of circumstances may give rise to an exigency sufficient to justify a warrantless search, including the prevention of the imminent destruction of evidence. To determine whether an officer faced such an emergency that justified a warrantless search, the Court looked to the totality of the circumstances. In *Schmerber*, the Court applied this approach. Schmerber had suffered injuries in an automobile accident and was taken to the hospital. While he was receiving treatment, an officer arrested him and ordered a blood test over his objection. The Court allowed the warrantless search because time had already been taken to investigate the accident and bring Schmerber to the hospital. Justice Sotomayor also pointed that the Court's decision was strictly based "on the facts of the present record."

Missouri asked the Court to abandon the totality of the circumstances approach when dealing with drunk-driving cases. It sought a *per se* rule that would allow warrantless blood tests as standard operating procedure because BAC evidence is "inherently evanescent." As long as the officer had **probable cause** and the blood test is conducted in reasonable manner, it would be "categorically reasonable for law enforcement to obtain the blood sample without a warrant." Justice Sotomayor agreed that the human body's natural metabolic processes dissipated the alcohol level in a person's blood until it is fully absorbed and eventually eliminated. However, it did not follow that the Court should depart from "case-by-case assessment of exigency" and adopt a categorical rule. In those cases where law enforcement can reasonably obtain a warrant before a blood sample can be drawn without "significantly undermining the efficacy of the search, the Fourth Amendment mandates that they do so."

Justice Sotomayor concluded that Missouri had failed to account for advances in the 47 years since *Schmerber* was decided. She pointed out that the majority of states allow police officers or prosecutors to apply for search warrants remotely, using telephonic or radio communication as well as email and video conferencing. In addition, some jurisdictions have streamlined the warrant process by using standard-form warrant applications for drunk-driving investigations. In McNeely's case, the county in which his arrest took place had such a form and the arresting officer admitted he had used it in the past.

FRAUD

A false representation of a matter of fact—whether by words or by conduct, by false or misleading allegations, or by concealment of what should have been disclosed—that deceives and is intended to deceive another so that the individual will act upon it to her or his legal injury.

Amgen, Inc. v. Connecticut Retirement Plans and Trust Funds

In the 2013 case of *Amgen, Inc. v. Connecticut Retirement Plans and Trust Funds*, 133 S. Ct. 1184 (2013), the U.S. SUPREME COURT held that "materiality" need not be proven at the class-certification stage of pending SECURITIES **fraud** lawsuits (filed by groups of shareholders seeking to be united as plaintiffs in a single class-action suit). The Court's 6–3 decision upheld that of the Ninth **Circuit Court** of Appeals, which had reached a similar conclusion. *Amgen* did not alter the elements ultimately needed to establish a viable **cause of action**; it merely established that not all elements need be proven at the class-certification stage of LITIGATION.

As background, under § 10(b)of the Securities Exchange Act of 1934, 15 USC § 78j(b) (2006 ed.), and the **correlative** SECURITIES AND EXCHANGE COMMISSION Rule 10b-5, 17 CFR § 240.10b-5 (2011), plaintiffs in a private securities–fraud lawsuit must prove (among other things) they relied on material misrepresentations or omissions made by DEFENDANT when purchasing defendant's stock, ultimately causing them economic harm or loss.

There are several theories under which shareholders may sue corporations for securities FRAUD. One such theory, endorsed by the U.S. Supreme Court in its 1988 decision of *Basic, Inc. v. Levinson*, 485 U.S. 224, 108 S. Ct. 978, 99 L. Ed. 2d 194, is known as "fraud-on-the-market."

In order to lessen the evidentiary burden on securities fraud plaintiffs, the Court, in *Basic*, endorsed the fraud-on-the-market theory to permit certain Rule 10b-5 plaintiffs to invoke a **rebuttable presumption** of reliance on material misrepresentations that have been made known to the general public. As the Court explained, this theory "rests on the premise that certain well developed markets are efficient processors of public information. In such markets, the 'market price of shares' will 'reflec[t] all publicly available information.'" 425 U.S. at 246. Accordingly, the Court held that if a market were shown to be efficient, courts could presume that investors trading securities in that market relied on public, material misrepresentations about those securities.

California-based Amgen, Inc., a biotechnology manufacturer, had secured approval from the U.S. FOOD AND DRUG ADMINISTRATION (FDA) for two new drug products that purportedly stimulated red blood cell production, effectively reducing the need for blood cell transfusions in anemic patients. According to plaintiffs' lawsuits, Amgen allegedly misrepresented to the FDA certain facts that affected the safety and efficacy of its products.

PLAINTIFF Connecticut Retirement Plans and Trust Funds ("Connecticut Retirement") brought a fraud-on-the-market suit against Amgen and several of its officers (collectively, "Amgen") for misrepresenting (to shareholders) the nature of several FDA committee meetings. The complaint alleged that Amgen's misrepresentations about its two new drugs artificially inflated the price of its stock. The complaint further alleged that plaintiff shareholders purchased Amgen stock correlative with the time of the misrepresentations. When the truth about the safety of the new drugs became public, Amgen's stock dropped sharply in value, resulting in financial loss to plaintiffs who purchased the stock at the inflated prices.

Connecticut Retirement requested the federal district (trial) court to certify a class of plaintiffs representing all shareholders who purchased Amgen's stock between April 22, 2004, and May 10, 2007. (The latter date allegedly represented the meeting when Amgen made corrective disclosures about the subject products, after which the stocks declined in value.) As a key named plaintiff, Connecticut Retirement sought to represent and protect the interests of the entire class in this matter.

Amgen opposed class certification. However, unlike in the earlier *Basic* decision, which dealt with presumptive reliance, Amgen objected to what it saw as presumptive "materiality" applicable to the whole class of potential plaintiffs.

The precise issue before the Court concerned one of the prerequisites of class certification under Rule 23(b) of the Rules of Federal Procedure—to wit, that "the questions of law or fact common to class members predominate over any questions affecting only individual members." In this regard, Amgen argued that to meet this "predominance" requirement, Connecticut needed to more than merely plead (in its complaint) that Amgen's misrepresentations and omissions materially affected Amgen's stock price. Otherwise, how could the court determine that plaintiffs shared a "common" **question of law** or fact that predominated over their individual claims or issues?

The federal **district court** declined to accept Amgen's argument. It further refused to consider Amgen's attempt to introduce substantive rebuttal evidence which, according to Amgen, showed that the market was well aware of the truth regarding alleged misrepresentations and omissions at the time that the plaintiffs purchased Amgen stock. The court granted the class certification but granted Amgen an **interlocutory** appeal. In November 2011, the U.S. Circuit Court of Appeals for the Ninth Circuit upheld the district court.

Amgen's case, as before the Supreme Court, represented a conflict between lower circuit courts of appeals "over whether district courts must require plaintiffs to prove, and must allow defendants to present evidence rebutting, the element of materiality before certifying a class action," wrote Justice RUTH BADER GINSBURG in the Court's majority opinion. In affirming the Ninth Circuit opinion, the Court stated that

> [w]hile Connecticut Retirement certainly must prove materiality to prevail on the merits, we hold that such proof is not a prerequisite to class certification. Rule 23(b)(3) requires a showing that *questions* common to the class predominate, not that those questions will be answered, on the merits, in favor of the class. Because materiality is judged according to an objective standard, the materiality of Amgen's alleged misrepresentations and omissions is a question common to all members of the class Connecticut Retirement would represent.

Further, said the Court, even failure of proof on the common question of materiality would not result in individual members' questions therefore predominating. If Connecticut Retirement failed to present sufficient evidence of materiality at the later stage of a summary-judgment motion or at trial, it would end the case for all members of the class.

Finally, the Court noted that Congress has expressly rejected petitions to undo the fraud-on-the-market theory.

Justices ANTONIN SCALIA and CLARENCE THOMAS wrote separate dissenting opinions (with Justices ANTHONY KENNEDY and Scalia also joining in Thomas's DISSENT). Both dissents opined that, without proof of materiality (at the class-certification stage), there can be no evidence that the claim has class-wide relevance.

FREEDOM OF SPEECH

Arizona Supreme Court Extends First Amendment Protection to Tattoo Parlors

The Arizona SUPREME COURT in 2012 became the first state supreme court to rule that tattoos and the process of tattooing are entitled to full protection by the FIRST AMENDMENT. The case involved an Arizona city's denial of a permit for a couple to open a tattoo parlor. The court's decision reversed a lower court's judgment that the owners had failed to state a claim on which the court could grant relief.

Modern tattooing requires the use of an electronic tattooing machine. The machine motors a needle that moves up and down rapidly, puncturing a person's skin between 50 and 3,000 times per minute. When the needle punctures the skin, it deposits insoluble ink into the skin, creating the mark that forms the tattoo. As a general matter, the tattooing process is safe, so long as the equipment used is sterilized and maintained in sanitary condition. On the other hand, tattooing can carry the risk of causing infection or spreading disease if the operator does not handle the equipment correctly.

Most states, to some extent, regulate tattoo parlors to ensure that the operators maintain the equipment correctly and perform the tattooing safely. For example, in some states, only a licensed physician can apply a facial tattoo. Other regulations include prohibitions on applying tattoos on intoxicated customers or requiring a state agency to inspect tattoo parlors.

Arizona state law defines "tattooing" as "mark[ing] the skin with any indelible design, letter, scroll, figure, symbol, or any other mark that is placed by the aid of needles or other instruments upon or under the skin with any substance that will leave color under the skin and that cannot be removed, repaired or reconstructed without a surgical procedure." The state prohibits tattooing of minors but has few other restrictions or regulations.

Ryan and Laetitia Coleman owned a tattoo parlor in Nice, France, and wanted to open a branch in Mesa, Arizona. Mesa's city code requires tattoo parlors, pawns shops, body-piercing salons, and some other institutions to obtain a council use permit from the Mesa City Council before opening one of these types of businesses. The process requires Mesa's planning and **zoning** board to review each application and recommend whether the city council should approve the application. The Colemans applied for the permit in July 2008, and the city's ZONING staff in February 2009 recommended that the planning and zoning board approve the application.

When the planning and zoning board met in 2009, however, the board voted 3–2 to recommend that the city council deny the Colemans' permit. The city council then held a public hearing, and on March 30, 2009, the council denied the Colemans' permit application. The only council member to vote in the Colemans' favor was Mayor Scott Smith, who reportedly thought opponents of the permit had not proven their case. However, several residents spoke at the public hearing and expressed concern that the tattoo parlor would introduce unwelcome individuals into the community.

The Colemans sued the City of Mesa in Arizona state court, arguing that the city had violated their rights to **freedom of speech**. However, Maricopa County Superior Court Judge Larry Grant dismissed the lawsuit, holding that the Colemans had not stated a claim on which the judge could grant relief. Specifically, the judge ruled that the council's decision was a "reasonable and rational regulation of land use."

The Colemans then appealed the case to a division of the court of appeals of Arizona. On November 3, 2011, the **appellate court** reversed the superior court's decision. Presiding Judge Ann Scott Timmer wrote: "We hold that obtaining a tattoo, applying a tattoo, and engaging in the business of tattooing are exercises of free speech entitled to protection as a FUNDAMENTAL RIGHT under the Arizona Constitution and the U.S. Constitution. As such, any restriction on that right must be highly scrutinized by our courts." By holding that the City of Mesa had violated the Colemans' rights to FREEDOM OF SPEECH, due process, and **equal protection**, the **appellate** court

reversed the superior court's decision and remanded the case for additional proceedings. *Coleman v. City of Mesa*, 265 P.3d 422 (Ariz. App. 2011).

The APPELLATE court was persuaded by the Ninth **Circuit Court** of Appeals' decision in *Anderson v. City of Hermosa Beach*, 621 F.3d 1051 (9th Cir. 2010). In *Anderson*, the court held "The tattoo itself, the process of tattooing, and even the business of tattooing are not expressive conduct but purely expressive activity fully protected by the First Amendment." However, other state and **federal courts** have held that the practice of tattooing itself is not expressive conduct.

The City of Mesa argued that the Arizona Supreme Court should follow the reasoning that the act of tattooing itself is not expressive conduct protected by the First Amendment. The court disagreed, however. Vice Chief Justice Scott Bales wrote, "A tattoo involves expressive elements beyond those present in a 'a pen-and-ink' drawing, inasmuch as a tattoo reflects not only the work of the tattoo artist but also the self-expression of the person displaying the tattoo's relatively permanent image." The court also concluded that the process or act of tattooing is expressive conduct, much like the art of writing a book is expressive conduct. In other words, Bales wrote, "the art of writing is no less protected than the book it produces; nor is painting less an act of free speech than the painting that results."

The court decided that the Colemans had a constitutionally protected interest in the business of tattooing. However, the court limited its holding to the motion that the superior court had granted. The City of Mesa could impose reasonable time, place, or **manner restrictions** on the Colemans' speech and not violate the First Amendment. The superior court had not considered whether the City of Mesa's denial was a permissible regulation of speech, so the court reversed the judgment of the superior court and remanded the case. The supreme court also vacated the opinion of the court of appeals. *Coleman v. City of Mesa*, 284 P.3d 863 (Ariz. 2012).

The Colemans' attorney, Clint Bolick, called the decision "very significant" because no other state supreme court had held that tattooing was expressive conduct protected by the Constitution. Attorneys for the City of Mesa said they hoped the superior court would rule that the council's denial of the Colemans' application was reasonable under the circumstances.

Eighth Circuit Strikes Down St. Louis Traffic Ordinance

The Eighth **Circuit Court** of Appeals in August 2012 ruled that an **ordinance** in the City of St. Louis, Missouri, violated the FIRST AMENDMENT and due process rights of a group trying to display a message over a busy overpass. The case involved an advocacy group that questions the official account of the September 11 attacks from 2001. The court ruled that the ordinance failed to provide fair notice of the activities that the ordinance prohibited.

A group of individuals who believe that the government may have been responsible for the terrorist attacks on September 11, 2001, established the 9/11 Questions Group. The group claims that photographic evidence from the sites of the terrorist attacks refutes the versions of the events offered by the government. The group also believes that the government is withholding evidence from the public. The group's website indicates that the group has chapters in 65 cities in the United States as well as in Europe and Australia. Collectively, the group consists of more than 10,000 members.

Donald E. Stahl is a member of the St. Louis chapter of the 9/11 Questions Group. He and other members sought to communicate the group's message to a wide audience by sponsoring public service announcements on a local public access cable channel, distributing leaflets, and displaying signs.

On February 6, 2009, Stahl and two others decided to display signs at a busy pedestrian overpass near the merger of two interstate highways. Stahl had previously displayed signs at this location during rush hour in the evening, but on February 6, he and the others displayed the signs starting at 6 a.m. One of the other members of the group held a three-foot-by-four-foot sign with the message "9/11 was an inside job."

More than an hour after Stahl and the others arrived, a police officer named Fred B. Cox received a request to drive to the area where Stahl and the others were holding their signs. Cox did not see any disruption of traffic because of the signs and instead only saw a moderate amount of cars moving at a slow pace.

Nevertheless, he asked the men to leave because they were disrupting traffic on one of the interstate highways. When Stahl and one of the other men refused to leave, Cox arrested both men.

Cox and another officer issued summons to Stahl and the other man based on § 17.16.270 of the Revised Code of the City of St. Louis. The city enacted the ordinance in 1979. The text of the section read as follows: "No person shall sell or offer for sale any goods or merchandise, display any sign or pictures, participate in or conduct an exhibition or demonstration, talk, sing or play music on any street or abutting premises, or alley in consequences of which there is such a gathering of persons or stopping of vehicles as to impede either pedestrians or vehicular traffic."

Stahl and the other DEFENDANT answered the summons some time later, but they were informed that the charges against both men had been dropped. Stahl then brought suit in the U.S. **District Court** for the Eastern District of Missouri seeking a declaration that § 17.16.270 violated the First Amendment of the U.S. Constitution. He did not seek any personal relief for alleged violations of his constitutional rights and instead only asked the court to enjoin the city from enforcing the ordinance in the future.

U.S. **Magistrate** Judge Frederick R. Buckles rejected Stahl's arguments. Buckles concluded that the ordinance created a content-neutral restriction with reasonable limitations on the time, place, and manner of the speech. Buckles determined that the city had an interest in protecting the free flow of traffic and that the ordinance was narrowly tailored to serve this interest. Buckles also ruled against several other claims, including arguments that the ordinance was overly broad and vague. Accordingly, the court granted the motion for **summary judgment** filed by the city. *Stahl v. City of St. Louis, Mo.*, No. 4:09CV712 FRB, 2010 WL 4781482 (E.D. Mo. Nov. 17, 2010).

A panel of the Eighth Circuit reviewed the case and reversed the district court's decision. An opinion written by Senior Circuit Judge Michael Joseph Melloy focused first on the Due Process Clause of the FOURTEENTH AMENDMENT rather than the First Amendment itself. Several cases have established that a law violates the Due Process Clause when the law fails to "give fair warning that the allegedly violative conduct was prohibited." In other words, the clause requires the law to provide adequate notice of conduct the law prohibits.

The St. Louis ordinance failed to provide adequate notice. Melloy's opinion noted,

> [the ordinance] offends the Due Process Clause because it fails to provide fair notice of what is forbidden. We note that the ordinance is not vague in the traditional sense that its language is ambiguous; the language is fairly clear that speech and activities that actually cause a pedestrian or traffic obstruction are prohibited. Rather, the problem is that the ordinance does not provide people with fair notice of when their actions are likely to become unlawful.

Of particular concern to the court was that "a person only violates the ordinance if his or her action evokes a particular response from a third party." In other words, to violate the ordinance, the demonstration would have to impede traffic. The court found that the ordinance had a "chilling effect on core First Amendment speech." Because the law violated the Due Process Clause and implicated First Amendment rights, the court struck down the ordinance as unconstitutional. *Stahl v. City of St. Louis, Mo.*, 687 F.3d 1038 (8th Cir. 2012).

The 9/11 Questions Group remained in the news later in 2012. In December, the Missouri DEPARTMENT OF TRANSPORTATION approved the group's application to "adopt" a stretch of highway in the St. Louis area. Under this Adopt-a-Highway program, the group agreed to pick up litter on the stretch of highway at least four times per year for the next three years. The group's name appears on a sign along the highway.

GAY AND LESBIAN RIGHTS

Chatterjee v. King

While the issue of same-sex marriage has dominated the legal and political debates in recent years, same-sex couples who have adopted children and then decided to end their relationship have faced uncertainty as to CHILD CUSTODY and VISITATION RIGHTS. The Uniform Parentage Act (UPA), which many states have adopted in some form, contains language that suggests presumptions establishing a father and child relationship can be applied to women. Critics of this position believe a mother and child relationship can only be established through biology or ADOPTION. The New Mexico SUPREME COURT, in *Chatterjee v. King,* 280 P.3d 283 (2012), concluded that the state's UPA should be read to make the father-child relationship presumptions applicable to the mother-child relationship.

Bani Chatterjee and Taya King entered into a long-term, committed relationship that lasted from 1993 to 2008. In 2000, they traveled to Russia so King could adopt a female child. Chatterjee held out the child as her daughter ever since she arrived from Russia. The child believed Chatterjee was her parent, as they lived together with King until 2008. Chatterjee provided the child with financial and emotional support during the eight years the three were together but she never adopted the child. After the relationship ended, King moved to Colorado and tried to prevent Chatterjee from having any contact with the child.

Chatterjee filed a petition in New Mexico state court, seeking to establish parentage and determine CUSTODY and timesharing. She alleged that under the New Mexico UPA she was a presumed natural parent. King filed a motion to dismiss, arguing that Chatterjee was a **third party** who was seeking custody and visitation under the New Mexico Dissolution of Marriage Act. This law prohibits a THIRD PARTY from receiving custody rights absent a showing of unfitness of the natural or adoptive parent. The **district court** dismissed Chatterjee's petition for FAILURE TO STATE A CLAIM upon which relief could be granted.

Chatterjee appealed to the New Mexico Court of Appeals, which affirmed part of the district court's decision and reversed another part. The appeals court ruled that Chatterjee did not have standing to seek joint custody without showing that King was unfit because she was not the biological or adoptive mother of the child. It also held the UPA presumptions establishing a father and child relationship could not be applied to women, and that a mother and child relationship could only be established through biology or adoption. The court did reverse the district court's dismissal concerning the opportunity for Chatterjee to seek standing for visitation and remanded this issue to the district court. The district court appointed a **guardian ad litem** for the child and accepted the guardian ad litem's recommendation that contact and visitation with Chatterjee would be in the best interest of the child. Chatterjee appealed to the New Mexico Supreme Court on the UPA issues.

The supreme court, in a unanimous ruling, reversed the court of appeals, concluding that Chatterjee had standing to pursue joint custody of the child. Justice Edward Chavez, writing for the court, found that Chatterjee had standing to establish parentage as an "interested party" under the UPA. A section of the UPA stated that any interested party may bring an action to determine the existence or nonexistence of a mother and child relationship and that "insofar as practicable, the provisions of the Uniform Parentage Act applicable to the father and child relationship apply." Though this was a case of **first impression**, Justice Chavez concluded that the legislature clearly intended that the UPA have broad application. As for the way to treat cases under the UPA, the supreme court agreed that a case-by-case analysis was the best way to determine whether an action is appropriate under the UPA. Chatterjee claimed that she openly held out the child as her natural child from the moment she and King brought the child to New Mexico from Russia. Based on this claim, she argued that she should be able to establish a parent and child relationship under the UPA presumptions of PATERNITY. Under that provision, a man is presumed to be the natural father of a child "if he openly holds out the child as his natural child and has established a personal, financial, or custodial relationship with the child." Any person who is able to establish presumed natural parenthood is an interested party under the UPA.

Justice Chavez agreed with Chatterjee that the same presumptions that govern paternity also apply to maternity. The plain language of the UPA, the purpose of the act, the application of paternity provisions to women in other states with similar UPA provisions, and **public policy** all supported Chatterjee's argument. The act clearly stated that as far as practicable the provisions of the UPA governing the determination of a father and child relationship apply to the determination of a mother and child relationship. Justice Chavez determined that it was practicable to apply the presumptions of a natural father of a child to that of the natural mother and child.

The court concluded that the drafters of the UPA intended that provisions relating to the father and child relationship apply to women in appropriate situations. Justice Chavez noted that the drafters of the UPA provided in a comment that masculine terminology was used for the sake of simplicity and that the act did not limit application of its provisions to males. There was no indication that the New Mexico legislature, when it adopted the UPA with just minor revisions in 1986, intended a different reading.

Justice Chavez pointed to the decisions by other STATE COURTS that supported the supreme court's interpretation of the UPA provisions as applicable to women as well as men. Courts in California, Colorado, and Oregon, when interpreting parentage laws, concluded that provisions applicable to men were equally applicable to women. The New Mexico court also believed that PUBLIC POLICY justified its reading of the UPA. The state had a strong interest in ensuring that a child will be cared for financially and emotionally by two parents. Moreover, the UPA was written to address the "interest that the children have in their own support" and that "every child should be treated equally, regardless of the marital status of their parents."

Having established that Chatterjee was an "interested party" under the UPA, the court said she had standing to bring an action to establish a parent and child relationship with the child. Assuming that all of her facts were true, Chatterjee would have standing to seek joint custody as a natural parent. The court remanded the case to the district court for further proceedings as to the facts that Chatterjee alleged.

Hollingsworth v. Perry

Many parts of American society since the 1990s have begun not only to tolerate gay and lesbian individuals but also to recognize that gays and lesbians deserve equal rights in all respects, including marriage. Although 32 states ban same-sex marriage through amendments to state constitutions, a growing number of states now recognize these marriages.

The debate over same-sex marriages was especially contentious in California, where a decision by the California SUPREME COURT was effectively overruled by a ballot initiative approved by voters in 2008. For five years, advocates on both sides of the debate fought

Plaintiffs Sandy Stier (left) and Kris Perry during a June 2013 press conference after the U.S. Supreme Court declined to rule on the constitutionality of Proposition 8, effectively allowing gay marriage to resume in California.
JOSHUA ROBERTS/ BLOOMBERG/GETTY IMAGES

over whether this ballot initiative, known as Proposition 8, was constitutional.

In one of the landmark rulings of the 2012 term, the Supreme Court in *Hollingsworth v. Perry*, No. 12-144, 2013 WL 3196927 (June 26, 2013) ruled that the parties attempting to defend the California ban on same-sex marriage did not have standing. The effect of the ruling was that same-sex marriages could continue in California. The Court decided *Hollingsworth* on the same day that it decided *United States v. Windsor*, 133 S. Ct. 2675 (2013), and both cases have been viewed as significant victories for the gay-rights movement.

The Supreme Court has decided few cases on gay rights. In *Romer v. Evans*, 517 U.S. 620, 116 S. Ct. 1620, 134 L. Ed. 2d 855 (1996), the Court ruled that a state could not single out gays and lesbians for disparate treatment. That decision focused on an amendment to the Colorado constitution that forbade a state agency or court from considering gay or lesbian individuals as a protected class. Seven years later, the Court in *Lawrence v. Texas*, 539 U.S. 558, 123 S. Ct. 2472; 156 L. Ed. 2d 508 (2003), struck down a Texas **sodomy** law aimed at homosexual individuals.

The Court avoided the gay-rights debate for nearly a decade after its decision in *Lawrence*.

During that time, state legislatures wrestled with decisions about whether to grant marriage rights to gays and lesbians or, conversely, whether to amend state constitutions to ban these marriages. State and **federal courts** have also issued a number of rulings related to gay and lesbian rights.

The California Supreme Court was one of those courts. In 2008, the court ruled that the state's ban on same-sex marriage violated the **equal protection** clause contained in the state's constitution. Almost immediately, county clerks began to issue marriage licenses to same-sex partners, and these marriages have remained legal. However, voters in November 2008 considered Proposition 8, which amended the California Constitution to read, "Only a marriage between a man and a woman is valid or recognized in California." About one year later, the California Supreme Court ruled that the amendment was properly enacted under California law.

Two same-sex couples who wanted to marry in California filed a lawsuit in the U.S. **District Court** for the Northern District of California. These plaintiffs argued that Proposition 8 violated the FOURTEENTH AMENDMENT of the U.S. Constitution. The defendants named in the case included several state officials, including the governor and attorney general. The named officials refused to defend the law during the trial, and the district court ruled that Proposition 8 was unconstitutional. The court also enjoined the state officials from enforcing the law.

The officials refused to appeal the order. However, the official proponents (as established under California law) of Proposition 8 did appeal the ruling to the Ninth **Circuit Court** of Appeals. The Ninth Circuit asked the proponents why the court should not dismiss the action for lack of Article III standing. After the parties submitted briefs and argued before the court, the Ninth Circuit certified the question to the California Supreme Court. The California court answered that the proponents indeed had standing to defend the law. The Ninth Circuit relied on this answer and ruled that the proponents indeed had standing.

When the Ninth Circuit decided the case on its merits, the court affirmed the lower court's ruling that Proposition 8 violated the EQUAL PROTECTION Clause of the Fourteenth Amendment. Relying on the Supreme Court's ruling in *Romer v. Evans*, the Ninth Circuit ruled that the state could not take away the official designation of marriage from same-sex couples while retaining the designation for heterosexual couples. The court noted that Proposition 8 served no purpose "but to impose on gays and lesbians, through the **public law**, a majority's private disapproval of them and their relationships." *Perry v. Brown*, 671 F.3d 1052 (9th Cir. 2012).

The public widely followed the case during oral arguments in March 2013. Justices ANTHONY KENNEDY and SONIA SOTOMAYOR asked questions suggesting that it may be premature for the Court to review the case. Sotomayor asked whether it would be more appropriate to allow the states to experiment with their laws and society as a whole to debate the issue before the Court should render a decision. On the other hand, several justices asked questions focused on the standing issue.

In a 5–4 decision, the Court vacated the Ninth Circuit's decision by ruling that the proponents did not have standing to defend the law. Chief Justice JOHN ROBERTS wrote for the majority, which included Justices ANTONIN SCALIA, STEPHEN BREYER, RUTH BADER GINSBURG, and ELENA KAGAN. Justice Anthony Kennedy dissented, joined by Justices CLARENCE THOMAS, SAMUEL ALITO, and Sotomayor.

The majority recited the basic principles underlying the standing doctrine. Article III of the Constitution grants authority to the federal courts to decide "cases" or "controversies." The standing requirement, which relates directly to Article III, "requires the litigant to prove that he has suffered a concrete and particularized injury that is fairly traceable to the challenged conduct, and is likely to be redressed by a favorable judicial decision."

The proponents of Proposition 8 had to prove that they had suffered injuries that affected them in a personal and individual way. It was not enough that the proponents had a "generalized grievance." They had to have an official role in enforcing the law. The Court rejected the proponents' argument that they had such a role because these proponents were the ones who collected signatures and filed the ballot initiative pursuant to California law. According to the majority, once voters approved Proposition 8, the proponents had no role in enforcing it. The proponents simply had no more of a "personal stake" in defending the law than any other citizen in California. The Court also rejected the proponents' argument that they were agents of the State of California.

Justice Roberts summed up the opinion as follows: "We have never before upheld the standing of a private party to defend the constitutionality of a state **statute** when state officials have chosen not to. We decline to do so for the first time here."

Kennedy argued that the Court should have followed the California Supreme Court's lead and rule that the plaintiffs indeed had standing because of the ballot initiative system in California. He wrote,

> In my view Article III does not require California, when deciding who may appear in court to defend an initiative on its behalf, to comply with . . . this Court's view of how a State should make its laws or structure its government. The Court's reasoning does not take into account the fundamental principles or the practical dynamics of the initiative system in California, which uses this mechanism to control and to bypass public officials—the same officials who would not defend the initiative, an injury the Court now leaves unremedied.

Same-sex marriages resumed in California almost immediately after the Supreme Court issued its opinion. In fact, the two couples who

originally challenged the law were both married within days of the decision. However, on June 27, the Court declined to review two other cases addressing gay rights, meaning that the STATE COURTS and lower federal courts will have to wrestle with the Supreme Court's 2013 rulings.

United States v. Windsor

Few cases garnered as much attention and media coverage during the U.S. Supreme Court's 2012-2013 term than that of *United States v. Windsor,* 133 S. Ct. 2675 (2013), which struck down the federal Defense of Marriage Act (DOMA) as unconstitutional for its exclusion of legally-married same-sex spouses for federal benefits. Even Justice Antonin Scalia, in his DISSENT, stated, "Few public controversies touch an institution so central to the lives of so many, and few inspire such attendant passion by good people on both sides." The historic decision affirmed that of the U.S. **Circuit Court** of Appeals for the Second Circuit, which had reached the same conclusion.

Section 3 of the 1996 Defense of Marriage Act (DOMA), 110 Stat. 2419, states in relevant part that, for the purposes of federal law, the words "marriage" and "spouse" refer to legal unions between one man and one woman. By so stating, Section 3 expressly amended the

Dictionary Act, 1 U.S.C. § 7 (a law providing rules of construction for more than 1,000 federal laws and all federal regulations) to substitute the new definitions.

The PLAINTIFF, Edith Windsor, married her longtime partner Thea Clara Spyer in Toronto, Canada in 2007. The State of New York, where both resided, recognized the marriage. But under DOMA, the federal government did not. When Spyer died in 2009, she left her estate to her spouse, Windsor. Windsor sought to claim the federal estate tax exemption for surviving spouses, but was barred by DOMA. Under protest, she paid the $363,053 in federal estate taxes, then asked for a refund. When the INTERNAL REVENUE SERVICE denied her request, she filed federal suit against the government in 2010, arguing that DOMA violates the Fifth Amendment's **Equal Protection** principles.

While the tax lawsuit was still pending, in February 2011, the U.S. Attorney General, by order of President Obama, notified the Speaker of the HOUSE OF REPRESENTATIVES that the U.S. DEPARTMENT OF JUSTICE (DOJ) would no longer defend the constitutionality of DOMA's § 3. Although it had defended it in the past, the President now believed that "classifications based on sexual orientation should be subject to a heightened standard of scrutiny."

Recognizing "the judiciary as the final **arbiter** of the constitutional claims raised," the President, while instructing the DOJ not to defend DOMA's § 3, nonetheless decided that "Section 3 will continue to be enforced by the Executive Branch." He further expressed that the United States had an "interest in providing Congress a full and fair opportunity to participate in the LITIGATION of those cases."

In response to the Attorney General's letter, the Bipartisan Legal Advisory Group (BLAG) of the House of Representatives voted to intervene in the litigation to defend DOMA.

Deciding the case on the merits of the tax refund, the federal **district court** ruled against the United States, finding DOMA's § 3 unconstitutional and ordering a tax refund to Windsor, with interest. Before the SUPREME COURT could act on petitions for "certiorari before judgment," the Court of Appeals for the Second Circuit, applying HEIGHTENED SCRUTINY to classes based on sexual orientation, affirmed the district court's judgment. The United States did not comply with the judgment and Windsor did not receive her refund. The Supreme Court expressly granted **certiorari** on the question of the constitutionality of § 3 of DOMA.

As a preliminary matter, the Court needed to address jurisdictional Article III standing of the government and BLAG. Windsor was an **aggrieved party** and clearly had standing, but the Executive's decision that DOJ would not defend the constitutionality of DOMA's § 3, while still enforcing DOMA, complicated the issue of the government's standing as a party defending DOMA. (The district court had permitted BLAG status as an intervening party.) The fact that Windsor and the government's Executive *agreed* on the unconstitutionality of DOMA's § 3 undermined the need for the parties to present adversarial sides to the issues in order for the Court to exert judicial power (decision-making).

Ultimately, the Court's majority concluded that, despite the Executive's agreement regarding DOMA's unconstitutionality, the government still stood to suffer real economic injury (the adverse judgment to refund the taxes) and therefore maintained standing in the case. As to BLAG, the Court found that it had raised substantial arguments in support of the constitutionality of DOMA (where the Executive Branch did not) reflecting an actual controversy

under Article III; this allowed the Court to address the case without needing to decide whether BLAG would have had standing in the district court.

Moving, then, to the constitutional merits of the case, the narrow 5-4 majority held that DOMA was unconstitutional as a deprivation of the equal liberty of persons—equal liberty being one of the protections of the FIFTH AMENDMENT. First, the Court recognized that by history and tradition, the definition and regulation of marriage has always been within the **purview** of the States. But, whereas states that give same-sex partners the right to marry are giving them a dignity and status of immense import, the federal government uses the same class distinction to impose restrictions and disabilities.

Moreover, DOMA's provisions are directed toward a class of persons that the State of New York and 11 other states have sought to protect. By seeking to injure the very class New York seeks to protect, DOMA violates basic due process and EQUAL PROTECTION principles applicable to the federal government, said the Court. In fact, DOMA's avowed purpose, and certainly its practical effect, are to impose a separate status, and so a stigma, upon a prescribed set of individuals (those who enter into same-sex marriages), commensurate with the imposition of disabilities on that prescribed set. Said the Court,

> DOMA instructs all federal officials, and indeed all persons with whom same-sex couples interact, including their own children, that their marriage is less worthy than the marriages of others. The federal **statute** is invalid, for no legitimate purpose overcomes the purpose and effect to disparage and to injure those whom the State, by its marriage laws, sought to protect in personhood and dignity. By seeking to displace this protection and treating those persons as living in marriages less respected than others, the federal statute is in violation of the Fifth Amendment. This opinion and its holding are confined to those lawful marriages.

Justice ANTHONY KENNEDY delivered the opinion of the Court, joined by Justices RUTH BADER GINSBURG, STEPHEN BREYER, SONIA SOTOMAYOR, and ELENA KAGAN. Chief Justice JOHN ROBERTS, JR. wrote a dissenting opinion essentially grounded in doubt that the Court had jurisdiction over the case. He further opined that, in the interests of uniformity and stability, Congress had the power to enact DOMA. Justice Scalia questioned the power of the Supreme Court to invalidate democratically-enacted legislation, and the Chief Justice and Justice CLARENCE THOMAS joined in that dissent. Justice SAMUEL ALITO also filed a separate dissent, arguing that the definition of marriage is up to the people/states to decide, and that DOMA did not interfere with that.

GUN CONTROL

Fifth Circuit Upholds Law Banning Commercial Handgun Sales to Persons Under 21

Emboldened by the Supreme Court's SECOND AMENDMENT decision in *District of Columbia v. Heller*, 554 U.S. 570, 128 S. Ct. 2783, 171 L. Ed. 2d 637 (2008), the NATIONAL RIFLE ASSOCIATION (NRA) filed a federal lawsuit challenging a law that bans federal firearms licensees (FFLs) from selling handguns to persons under the age of 21. The NRA argued that the law restricted the Second Amendment rights of 18-to-20-year old adults to keep and bear arms under the Second Amendment. The Fifth **Circuit Court** of Appeals, in *National Rifle Association v. Bureau of Alcohol, Tobacco, Firearms, and Explosives*, 700 F.3d 185 (2012), rejected the NRA's claim, finding that the law did not infringe on the core Second Amendment right announced in *Heller* of a responsible, law-abiding adult to possess and use a handgun to defend his or her home and family.

The NRA and a group of persons under the age of 21 filed a federal lawsuit in Texas, challenging the federal law and regulations which prohibit federally licensed firearms dealers from selling handguns to persons under the age of 21. The plaintiffs contended that the PROHIBITION violated the Second Amendment. The **district court** rejected their constitutional claims and granted **summary judgment** for the government. The plaintiffs then appealed to the Fifth Circuit.

A three-judge panel of the Fifth Circuit unanimously affirmed the lower court decision. Judge Edward Prado, writing for the court, noted that the federal laws at issue were enacted as part of the **Omnibus** Crime Control and Safe Streets Act of 1968, Pub. L. No. 90-351, 82 Stat. 197. The laws regulate the sale of firearms by FFLs and were part of a larger **statutory** package that seeks to control the manufacture and sale of firearms in the U.S. by licensing dealers.

However, other federal laws touch upon the transfer and possession of handguns to persons under the age of 21. Under the law, 18-to-20-year-olds may possess and use handguns. Parents or guardians may gift handguns to 18-to-20-year-olds. This same age group may lawfully acquire handguns through unlicensed, private sales and they may possess and use long guns, and may purchase them from FFLs or non-FFLs. The only restriction on purchasing a handgun for 18-to-20-year-olds is the law banning purchases from FFLs.

Judge Prado stated that the "crux" of the plaintiffs' position was that the federal ban violated their rights under the Second Amendment, as interpreted by the SUPREME COURT in the *Heller* decision. The case was one of **first impression**, as no other circuit court had addressed federal laws in light of *Heller*. Because of this, the appeals court needed to establish a framework for evaluating post-*Heller* Second Amendment challenges. Judge Prado pointed out that *Heller* established the central right of the Second Amendment that responsible citizens may use arms "in defense of hearth and home." The District of Columbia could not ban home handgun possession but the Supreme Court also stated "the right secured by the Second Amendment is not unlimited." The Court said its decision did not "cast doubt on longstanding prohibitions on the possession of firearms by felons and the mentally ill ... or laws imposing conditions and qualifications on the commercial sale of arms."

Judge Prado established a two-step inquiry into the constitutionality of the federal firearms law. The court must first assess whether the conduct at issue falls within the scope of the Second Amendment right to possess a handgun in the home. If the challenged law burdens conduct outside the Second Amendment's scope, then the law passes constitutional muster. If the law does burden conduct that falls within the Second Amendment's scope, "we must then proceed to apply the appropriate level of means-end scrutiny." The appropriate level of scrutiny "depends on the nature of the conduct being regulated and the degree to which the challenged law burdens the right."

The court concluded that a "longstanding, presumptively lawful regulatory measure would likely fall outside the **ambit** of the

IN FOCUS

THE FUTURE OF GUN CONTROL AFTER NEWTOWN

The nation was shocked on December 14, 2012, when it was reported that 20-year-old Adam Lanza entered the Sandy Hook Elementary school in Newtown, Connecticut and fatally shot 20 children and six adult staff members. Lanza, who killed himself as police arrived, had shot and killed his mother prior to the school shootings. He used his mother's Bushmaster rifle and several high-capacity ammunition magazines during the crimes. In the wake of the shooting, President BARACK OBAMA stated that he would make GUN CONTROL a "central issue" at the start of his second term of office. He formed a Gun Violence Task Force to examine the causes of gun violence in the United States and in mid-January 2013, proposed universal background checks on firearms purchases, an **assault** weapons ban, and limiting ammunition magazine capacity to 10 rounds. Relatives of the Newtown massacre victims lobbied Congress and public opinion appeared to support new gun control measures, yet after the second worst mass shooting in U.S. history, the SENATE defeated a watered-down bill on April 17, 2013.

The national debate over gun control, which revived after the mass shooting at Virginia Tech University in 2007, again after the shooting of Representative Gabrielle Giffords and 19 others in Tucson, Arizona in 2011, and yet again after the mass shooting at an Aurora, Colorado movie theater in 2012, followed a predictable pattern. Gun control advocates argued that the federal ASSAULT weapons ban, which had expired in 2004, should be reinstated and that universal background checks must be instituted to prevent criminals and mentally ill people from purchasing them. Gun rights advocates countered that those who sought these controls were politicizing these tragedies and that state and federal officials were not enforcing the laws currently on the books. Commentators noted that the NATIONAL RIFLE ASSOCIATION (NRA) continued to exert strong influence over state and federal legislators, despite opinion polls that showed strong support for some gun control reforms. A few commentators sought to go beyond the black-and-white positions of either side and look at gun violence in the United States to see what role gun control could effectively play in reducing assaults and murders.

The U.S. Gun Economy It has been assumed that the NRA and its absolutist interpretation of SECOND AMENDMENT gun rights have prevailed in the gun control debate because of its effective LOBBYING efforts. Though this is likely true, gun control has also been affected by the U.S. gun economy. According to the business research firm Hoovers, the U.S. gun and ammunition industry generates $6 billion in annual revenues. There are over 200,000 people employed in jobs related to the firearms industry, who earn $9.8 billion in annual wages. The U.S. government estimates there were 310 million firearms in the U.S. In 2011, almost 5.5 million firearms were manufactured in the U.S., 95 percent of which were sold domestically. There are almost 132,000 federally licensed firearms and ammunition dealers. There are four times as many firearms dealers than there are grocery stores in the United States.

With this large economic footprint, the firearms industry and the NRA have worked together since 1999, when gun manufacturers and distributors were being sued by cities and municipalities for the gun violence. The NRA aligned itself with the firearms industry and successfully lobbied for a 2005 federal law that gave the industry IMMUNITY from these types of lawsuits. That same year the NRA began a fundraising drive to obtain corporate partners, which has attracted millions of dollars from the firearms industry. Since 2005, the drive has raised between $14 and $38 million from the firearms industry, according to a 2011 study by the Violence Policy Center, a group that favors gun control. The gun industry has benefited from the NRA's lobbying efforts that prevented the renewal in 2004 of the federal ban on assault weapons. Since that time, the annual rifle production of U.S. gun manufacturers has risen by almost 38%.

The symbiotic relationship between the NRA and the firearms industry has meant that anti-gun control efforts have been well funded in comparison to organizations seeking more restrictions on guns. In 2011, gun rights lobbyists outspent gun control lobbyists by a 17-to-1 ratio, according an analysis by Republic Report. Gun rights groups spent $4.2 million, while gun control groups spent just $240,000. In the 2012 presidential election, the NRA spent $14 million to try to defeat President Obama.

Since the Newtown killings, gun control advocacy groups have become aggressive in raising money for lobbying. Former U.S. Representative Gabbie Giffords and her **husband**, Mark Kelly, launched a new POLITICAL ACTION COMMITTEE, Americans for Responsible Solutions, which will lobby Congress and state governments for universal background checks, the banning of assault weapons, and limitations on ammunition magazine capacity. Unlike members of other gun control groups, Giffords and Kelly have proclaimed themselves defenders of the Second Amendment and have emphasized that they own and shoot guns. New York Mayor Michael Bloomberg created "Mayors Against Guns," an action fund through which Bloomberg has funneled over $14 million. In addition, a super PAC funded by Bloomberg, Independence USA PAC, spent $8 million in the 2012 elections to defeat legislators who were opposed to gun control. In the weeks leading up to the April 17, 2013 Senate vote, Bloomberg spent $12 million in ads targeting key lawmakers.

Protesters march in Washington, D.C. in support of gun control restrictions, April 2013.

MANDEL NGAN/AFP/ GETTY IMAGES

It is unclear whether gun control advocates can build organizations that can compete with the financial and volunteer resources of the NRA. It is clear that money alone will not change the balance of power for gun control advocates.

Lack of Data on Gun Violence The ability to make informed choices on effective gun control measures has been hampered by a federal ban on funding research on gun violence. A 1993 scholarly article on gun ownership as a risk factor for HOMICIDE in the home drew widespread public attention. The research had been funded by the federal Centers for Disease Control and Prevention (CDC). The NRA responded by campaigning for the elimination of the center that had funded the study, the CDC's National Center for Injury Prevention. Though the center was not eliminated, in 1996 Congress inserted into a crime bill a provision that barred the center from funding research that would "advocate or promote gun control." Congress took $2.6 million from the center's budget, which had been used the previous year to fund firearm injury research, and reallocated it to research on the prevention of traumatic brain injury. Though Congress did not explicitly bar firearms injury research, the law was unclear enough that federal employees did not want to risk their careers or the agency's funding.

A report released in January 2013 by Mayors Against Illegal Guns found that since 1996 the CDC's funding of firearms injury prevention had fallen 96% and was just $100,000 of the agency's $5.6 billion budget. In 2011 it was revealed that the CDC asks researchers to notify it if their studies have anything to do with firearms. The CDC then relayed this information to the NRA as a courtesy. In 2013, Congress added language to the appropriations legislation that funds the National Institutes of Health, stating that none of the funds could be used to advocate or promote gun control. Mark Rosenberg, a former director of the National Center for Injury Control and Prevention, stated in 2012 that the scientific community had been "terrorized" by the NRA.

In January 2013, President Obama appointed a panel of experts to determine what should be done with research on gun issues. He had previously included $10 million in his 2014 budget for gun-related research, the first federal financing for the topic in 17 years. In June 2013, the panel released its recommendations. The panel called for better data on guns. It noted that there is no accurate national count on how many guns there are in the U.S. and that "Basic information about gun possession, distribution, ownership, acquisition, and storage is lacking." Without such information, "it is virtually impossible to answer fundamental questions" about gun violence or to evaluate efforts intended to reduce that violence. The panel recommended that researchers look into patterns of gun ownership across demographic groups, how young people gain access to guns, and the potential risks and benefits of having a gun at home.

The NRA and other gun rights groups have opposed additional reporting requirements, which they believe would lead to a national gun registry. The expert panel denied that there was intent, pointing out that publicly available databases could have individual identities removed. Though public health officials applauded the panel's recommendations, they cautioned that it would be difficult to get Congress to appropriate the funds that President Obama proposed in his budget.

What Lies Ahead Supporters of gun rights overcame the emotional response to the Newtown shootings due to their effective lobbying. The NRA's 4.5 million members are a potent force, writing letters to legislators and lobbying in person. Members of Congress are wary about going against the NRA's positions on gun rights. Grover Norquist, anti-tax activist and NRA director, stated "It's intensity versus preference. While 90 percent will tell you, 'Sure, I'm for that,' 5 percent will really hate that, and on Election Day the only people who remember your position are the 5 percent."

Some supporters of gun control see better days ahead. They believe that the NRA was out of touch with many of its members, who support universal background checks. They point to public outrage directed at senators who voted against the bill. Some public opinion polls showed a steep decline in approval for some of these senators. There is also the matter of demographics: According to the University of Chicago's General Social Survey, fewer than one-third of U.S. households owned guns in 2011, down from 54 percent in 1977. A shrinking gun ownership base over time will eventually dilute the power of the NRA. Finally, gun control advocates point to the growing number of representatives and senators who have been targeted for defeat by the NRA yet managed to be reelected.

Second Amendment." This would mean the law would likely be upheld at step one of the framework. Turning to the firearms law at issue, the court concluded that the Second Amendment did not protect the burdened conduct—the ban on FFLs selling handguns to 18-to-20-year-olds. From the very beginnings of the United States, the right to keep and bear arms has not been unlimited. By the end of the nineteenth century, 19 states restricted the ability of persons under 21 to purchase or use particular firearms. Other states passed similar restrictions in the early twentieth century. This longstanding, historical tradition suggested that the conduct at issue fell outside the Second Amendment's protection.

The appeals went further, assuming that even if the challenged law burdened the Second Amendment, the law still survived constitutional scrutiny. Because the law did not burden the core of the amendment's guarantee that persons could possess and use firearms in the defense of their home, the court must employ the "intermediate scrutiny" standard of constitutional review. This standard "requires the government to show a reasonable fit between the law and an important government objective." The government argued that the law enacted in 1968 attempted to manage an important public safety problem: the ease with which young persons were purchasing handguns through FFLs. A multi-year investigation told Congress that there was a causal relationship between the easy availability of firearms to persons under 21 and the rise in crime. Based on this and other evidence, the court concluded that the government had satisfied its burden of showing a "reasonable means-ends fit between the challenged federal law and an important government interest."

As to the second part of intermediate scrutiny, Judge Prado found that the means that Congress selected were "reasonably adapted to achieving" the government interest at stake. Congress "reasonably tailored a solution to the problem." Alternatively, Congress could have banned all persons under 21 from possessing handguns, but instead "deliberately adopted a calibrated approach." Since 1968, this means-end fit has retained its reasonableness, as the threat posed by "18-to-20-year-olds with easy access to handguns endures." Therefore, the **statute** was not unconstitutional.

HABEAS CORPUS

[Latin, "You have the body."] *A writ (court order) that commands an individual or a government official who has restrained another to produce the prisoner at a designated time and place so that the court can determine the legality of custody and decide whether to order the prisoner's release.*

Johnson v. Williams

A **writ** of *habeas corpus* (guaranteed under Article I, Section 9 of the U.S. Constitution as well as state constitutions) permits a prisoner to collaterally challenge the legality of his conviction or imprisonment (not his guilt or innocence). In 1996, Congress enacted the Antiterrorism and Effective Death Penalty Act of 1996 (AEDPA), 28 U.S.C. § 2254 *et seq.*, which provided that a federal habeas court could not grant relief to a state prisoner whose claim had already been "adjudicated on the merits in State court." (There are exceptions for decisions that are "contrary to, or involve[] an unreasonable application of, clearly established Federal law, as determined by [this] Court," or when "based on an unreasonable determination of the facts in light of the evidence presented in the State Court proceeding." § 2254[d][2]).

But what constitutes **adjudication** "on the merits" if there is no language in a decision that expressly addresses a particular federal claim, but other claims are discussed at length? In *Johnson v. Williams,* 133 S. Ct. 1088 (2013),

Williams, through federal habeas **corpus**, appealed a state **appellate court** ruling that dismissed her appeal without expressly addressing the merits of her federal claim. The U.S. SUPREME COURT overwhelmingly concluded that, in cases such as this, there is a **rebuttable presumption** that the state court did in fact adjudicate the federal claim on the merits as well.

In 1999, Tara Williams was charged in the robbery-murder of a store clerk. While she admitted at a California state trial that she was the getaway driver of a vehicle waiting outside the store, she denied entering the store and also denied knowledge that her accomplices were planning to rob the store or kill the clerk. The prosecution responded that under California law (as in many states), Williams need only to agree to help commit a **robbery**, regardless of whether she knew where or when, to provide sufficient predicate for **felony** MURDER.

Within hours of closing arguments, the 12-member jury disbelieved her testimony 11-1. Still, during jury deliberation, the jury foreman sent the judge two notes. One queried about one of the jury instructions on CONSPIRACY. In the other, the foreman informed the trial judge that the single holdout juror had "expressed an intention to disregard the law...and...has expressed concern relative to the severity of the charge (first degree murder)." When the situation was not resolved by the next morning,

141

the judge, over Williams' objection, questioned the jury foreman, along with lawyers for both parties. The foreman testified that Juror 6 had specifically mentioned JURY NULLIFICATION and the foreman expressed doubt that Juror 6 was willing to apply **felony-murder rule**.

The judge then ordered questioning of Juror 6, who first denied then later admitted bringing up jury nullification. The juror further testified that he would convict only if he was "very convinced . . . beyond a reasonable doubt." The judge took testimony from the eleven remaining jurors, who generally corroborated the foreman's testimony. Then the judge dismissed Juror 6 for bias, and a replacement juror was placed in deliberations. All 12 jurors then convicted Williams.

Williams appealed to the California **Court of Appeal**, arguing (as relevant here) that the dismissal of Juror 6 violated both her SIXTH AMENDMENT right to an unanimous jury (her federal claim) and the California state Penal Code (which, among other things, allows dismissal of a juror who, upon **good cause** shown, is unable to perform his or her duty under the law). Williams' appeal cited both authorities as having been violated but did not distinguish between the two as to the alleged violation.

The California **appellate** court dedicated several pages of its opinion to a discussion of the juror's dismissal, including the judge's questioning prior to the dismissal. The court concluded that Juror 6 had been properly dismissed for bias and affirmed the trial court's decision without specifically mentioning that it was deciding a Sixth Amendment issue. After Williams petitioned the California Supreme Court, which remanded for consideration in light of a recent state decision in another case with similar but not identical issues. On remand, the state APPELLATE court reaffirmed its prior decision without expressly referring to Williams' federal claim.

Williams later sought federal habeas relief, but the federal **district court** applied AEDPA's deferential standard under § 2254 (see above) and denied relief. However, the Ninth **Circuit Court** of Appeals concluded that the deferential standard did not apply because the California appellate court decision had not mentioned Williams' federal claim. Moreover, the Ninth Circuit then proceeded to review the federal claim *de novo*, finding that dismissal of the juror had violated the Sixth Amendment.

All nine justices of the U.S. Supreme Court disagreed (Justice ANTONIN SCALIA writing a separate concurring opinion). Justice SAMUEL ALITO, delivering the opinion of the Court, reversing the Ninth Circuit Court held that, despite specific language in the state appellate court's decision, Williams' Sixth Amendment federal claim had been adjudicated on the merits along with the other claims. A state court is only required to evaluate the evidence and arguments, said the Court, and need not expressly note every enumerated claim.

Although ADJUDICATION on the merits is a REBUTTABLE PRESUMPTION, noted the Court, several facts in the present case support adjudication, despite the absence of express language. Most importantly, on remand, the state appellate court expressly dissected and discussed California's newest decision, *People v. Cleveland* (which held that a juror had been improperly dismissed because he had disagreed with other jurors over the evidence), and distinguished the present case. Even though *Cleveland* was a state supreme court case, it in turn had examined three federal appellate cases that concerned Sixth Amendment analysis. Whether or not Williams' state and federal claims were co-extensive, their similarity made it unlikely that the state appellate court would have considered one while overlooking the other, said the Court. Moreover, the state appellate court expressly discussed and quoted from *United States v. Wood*, 299 U.S. 123, 57 S. Ct. 177, 81 L. Ed. 78 (1936), a Sixth Amendment case concerning juror impartiality.

Although all nine justices agreed on the judgment of reversal of the Ninth Circuit for the reasons stated, Justice Scalia, in a separate concurring opinion, expressed concern over the majority's note that a federal claim rejected as a result of "sheer inadvertence" is not adjudicated on the merits. He opined that this might represent a "newly-sponsored enterprise of probing the judicial mind," in other words, inviting more LITIGATION in future suits.

McQuiggin v. Perkins

A **writ** of *habeas corpus* (guaranteed under Article I, Section 9, of the U.S. Constitution as well as state constitutions) permits a prisoner to challenge the legality of his conviction or imprisonment (not his guilt or innocence). In enacting the Antiterrorism and Effective Death Penalty Act of 1996 (AEDPA), 28 U.S.C. § 2254 *et seq.*, Congress provided that state prisoners ordinarily have one year to petition for a writ (starting from the date "on which the judgment became final by the conclusion of direct review or the expiration of the time for seeking such review"). § 2254(d)(1)(D). The **statute** extends the limitations period for newly-discovered evidence, to one year from the date that the new evidence "could have been discovered through the exercise of due diligence."

In *McQuiggin v. Perkins*, 133 S. Ct. 1294 (2013), prisoner Floyd Perkins filed his petition 11 years after his conviction became final, and six years after the "discovery" of new evidence of "actual innocence," presented in the form of ostensibly-exonerating affidavits. He sought not an extension, but an exception to § 2254(d), claiming that there should be equitable tolling of the limitations period for claims of "actual innocence." The term "actual innocence" is from Sixth **Circuit Court** of Appeals precedent (*Souter v. Jones*, 395 F.3d 577 [2005] in which the **appellate court** held that "a habeas petitioner who demonstrates a credible claim of actual innocence based on new evidence may, in exceptional circumstances, be entitled to equitable tolling of habeas limitations." Perkins asserted that a plea of actual innocence can overcome AEDPA's one-year **statute of limitations**.

In the end, the U.S. Supreme Court supported this view, with caveats. A credible showing of actual innocence may allow a petitioner to pursue habeas relief regardless of procedural bars such as AEDPA's statute of limitations, under a "miscarriage of justice" exception, ruled the Court. However, unjustifiable delay on a petitioner's part should still be a factor in determining whether actual innocence has been reliably shown. In other words, the delay does not unequivocally bar relief, but may impact the petitioner's credibility. Any petitioner invoking a miscarriage of justice exception "must show that is more likely than not that no reasonable juror would have convicted him in the light of the new evidence" (the Court quoting from *Schlup v. Delo*, 513 U.S. 298, 115 S. Ct. 851, 130 L. Ed. 2d 808 [1995]).

Putting all this in perspective with the facts before the Court, the record reflected that on March 4, 1993, Perkins had attended a party in Flint, Michigan and left with friend Rodney Henderson and an acquaintance, Damarr Jones. Henderson was found dead in a wooded area, and Jones became prosecution's key witness against Perkins. Other prosecution witnesses (friends of both Perkins and Henderson) testified that Perkins had confessed to them. But at trial, Perkins testified in his own defense, implicating Jones instead. To the point, he testified that an hour after parting with Henderson and Jones, he observed Jones under a streetlight with blood on his pants, shoes, and plaid coat. He never saw Henderson again.

The jury convicted Perkins and he was sentenced to life without parole in 1993. After all state appeals were completed, Perkins' conviction became final in 1997. More than 11 years later, in 2008, he filed a federal habeas petition in federal court, alleging, among other things, ineffective counsel. To overcome the AEDPA's statute of limitations, Perkins asserted newly discovered evidence of actual innocence, comprising three separate affidavits. These affidavits, dated 1997, 1999, and 2002 respectively, identified Jones as the killer, and offered first-hand accounts of either Jones' **confession** to them or observations of Jones disposing of blood-stained clothing.

The **district court** found that characterizing the affidavits as newly-discovered evidence was "dubious" considering facts known to Perkins at the time of his trial in 1993. Further, even accepting that characterization, Perkins's petition was still untimely as the date of the last affidavit was 2002, and the petition was not filed until six years later in 2008. Even under the Sixth Circuit precedent described above, said the district court, Perkins still failed to show the due diligence needed to invoke equitable tolling. Alternatively, the district court found that Perkins had not shown that, in light of this "newly-discovered" evidence, it was more likely than not that no reasonable juror would have convicted him.

The Sixth Circuit limited its review to address whether the district court properly imposed the precondition of "diligence" to allow a claim of actual innocence to defeat the statute of limitations. The **appellate** court reversed the district court, instead holding that Perkins' "gateway" actual innocence claim allowed him to go forward with his ineffective counsel claim as though it had been timely filed. There being a divide among circuit courts of appeals on this matter, the U.S. Supreme Court granted review.

Writing for the majority in the divided 5-4 decision, Justice RUTH BADER GINSBURG held that actual innocence, if proved, can provide a gateway through which a habeas petitioner may proceed, irrespective of the procedural bar, including the AEDPA statute of limitations. The Court had previously applied this "fundamental miscarriage of justice" exception in similar contexts, e.g. failure to observe state procedural rules including filing deadlines. Notwithstanding, a federal habeas court, faced with an actual innocence claim, should approach unjustifiable delay (in filing) not as a threshold inquiry to bar relief, but rather, as a factor in determining whether actual innocence has been reliably shown. In other words, the gateway should open only where a petition claiming actual innocence presents "evidence of innocence so strong that a court cannot have confidence in the outcome of the trial unless the court is also satisfied that the trial was free of nonharmless constitutional error," *Schlup* 513 U.S. at 316.

Justice Ginsburg was joined by Justices ANTHONY KENNEDY, ELENA KAGAN, STEPHEN BREYER, and SONIA SOTOMAYOR. Justice ANTONIN SCALIA filed a strong DISSENT, joined by Chief Justice JOHN ROBERTS, JR. and Justices SAMUEL ALITO and CLARENCE THOMAS. The dissent opined that the Court lacked the power to OVERRULE Congress by creating a legislative exception to § 2254 that does not exist.

Trevino v. Thaler

Prior to 2012, if a state prisoner were to challenge his conviction or sentence by alleging unconstitutionally ineffective counsel, and the STATE COURTS denied relief because he did not follow established state rules for raising this claim ("procedural default"), a federal judge generally could not utilize **habeas corpus** to reach the claim and overturn the state's ruling. But in *Martinez v. Ryan,* 566 U.S. 1 (2012), the U.S. SUPREME COURT held that ineffective counsel at state post-conviction-initial-review-collateral-hearings claims (i.e., ineffective for not raising the ineffective-counsel-at-trial claim) may qualify as "cause" to excuse procedural defaults. In the 2013 case of *Trevino*

v. Thaler, 133 S. Ct. 1911 (2013), a narrow 5-4 majority of the Court expanded application of the *Martinez* holding.

The earlier case of *Martinez* was fact- and circumstance-specific. To start, if state procedural rules require a prisoner to raise an ineffective-assistance-of-counsel-at-trial claim during the first state **collateral** review proceeding, and there is either no counsel or ineffective counsel at the state collateral review proceeding as well, such lack of counsel or ineffective counsel on collateral review may excuse the procedural default. (Prior to *Martinez,* attorney error in post-conviction proceedings did not qualify as "cause" to excuse procedural default. *Coleman v. Thompson,* 111 S. Ct. 2546, 115 L. Ed. 2d 640 [1991].) However, the *Martinez* Court qualified its holding by limiting it to instances where state **procedural law** *required* a DEFENDANT to initially raise claims of ineffective-counsel-at-trial at an initial-review collateral proceeding. Now, in *Trevino,* the Court held that *Martinez*'s exception holds true even where state law (Texas) does not require a defendant to raise such claims in the first collateral proceeding, but ostensibly allows it to be raised on direct appeal.

The relevant facts in *Trevino* started with his conviction of capital MURDER in Texas state court. At the penalty-phase hearing, defense counsel presented a single witness (Trevino's aunt) to present evidence of **mitigating circumstances**, which might have warranted a sentence of life without PAROLE instead of execution. Finding insufficient MITIGATING CIRCUMSTANCES (among other things), the judge imposed a sentence of death.

The trial judge appointed new counsel for Trevino's direct appeal, but this second counsel did not raise the issue of ineffective-counsel-at-trial as part of his appeal. Before this appeal was decided, a third attorney was appointed to represent Trevino in state collateral relief. While this third attorney did raise an issue of ineffective-counsel-at-trial-at-the-penalty-phase, he did not include a claim that the ineffective trial counsel claim consisted of a failure to adequately investigate and present mitigating circumstances during the penalty phase. The state collateral relief was denied and the Texas Court of Criminal Appeals affirmed.

Next, Trevino petitioned for a **writ** of federal **habeas corpus**. The federal **district court** appointed yet another new counsel to represent him. This attorney raised for the first time that Trevino's counsel at trial was constitutionally ineffective for failing to adequately investigate and present mitigating circumstances during the penalty phase. New counsel advised the federal court of copious evidence found during his own investigation (about Trevino's background, including allegedly impaired cognitive abilities). The federal district court then stayed habeas proceedings to permit Trevino to go back to state court and raise this claim, but the state court held that Trevino had not raised this claim during initial postconviction proceedings; hence, he had procedurally defaulted. Back in district court, the judge held that, despite the fact that "even the most minimal investigation...would have revealed a wealth of additional mitigating evidence," the state court's ruling represented "an independent and adequate state ground" for denying relief which barred the federal court from considering it under federal habeas relief. The Fifth **Circuit Court** of Appeals affirmed the district court's mention of "an independent, adequate state ground" as justification for denying federal relief.

While all this was occurring below in the *Trevino* matter, the Supreme Court had not yet decided *Martinez*. Even so, as the Fifth Circuit later reasoned in another Texas case, *Martinez* would not have applied in Texas because *Martinez* narrowed its "for good cause" exception to circumstances where state law *requires* a criminal defendant to raise his claim of ineffective-counsel-at-trial claim in initial state collateral review proceedings. Texas law does not explicitly state this, and on its face, appears to permit such claims to be raised on direct appeal.

The U.S. Supreme Court accepted review to resolve this. Writing for the narrow majority, Justice STEPHEN BREYER expanded the *Martinez* rationale to reach Trevino's circumstance. The Court failed to find sufficient reason to distinguish between Texas law (*Trevino*), which theoretically granted permission to bring such claims on direct appeal but in practice denied a meaningful opportunity to do so, and Arizona law (*Martinez*), which required the claim to be raised at the initial collateral review proceeding. The bottom line is that the right to adequate assistance of trial counsel is the same, and critically important, in both.

In both circumstances, the Court continued, practical considerations such as the need for new counsel, the need to expand the trial record, and the need for sufficient time to develop the claim, support the need for collateral rather than direct review. In both circumstances (under both states' rules), ineffective counsel during an initial-review collateral proceeding will deprive a defendant of any opportunity for review of an ineffective-counsel-at-trial claim. Thus, a distinction between the two state procedural rules is not meaningful.

Justice Breyer was joined by Justices ANTHONY KENNEDY, ELENA KAGAN, RUTH BADER GINSBURG, and SONIA SOTOMAYOR. Chief Justice JOHN ROBERTS, JR. filed a dissenting opinion, joined by Justice SAMUEL ALITO. His DISSENT found the majority's decision an "invitation to litigation" that further undermined state sovereignty and further created a malleable, rather than narrowly-circumscribed exception in *Martinez*. Justice ANTONIN SCALIA filed his own dissent, joined by Justice CLARENCE THOMAS, reaffirming his disagreement and dissent in the *Martinez* decision ("That line lacks any principled basis, and will not last").

HATE CRIME

A crime motivated by racial, religious, gender, sexual orientation, or other prejudice.

Rutgers Student Convicted for Webcam Spying on Homosexual Roommate

In March 2012, former Rutgers University student Dharun Ravi was convicted on all 15 counts charged, after Webcam (computer-mounted camera) spying on his male roommate's gay tryst. The freshman roommate, Tyler Clementi, committed SUICIDE three days later, after learning that Ravi sent out Twitter and text messages encouraging others to watch the Webcam video. While Ravi was not charged with Clementi's death, he was prosecuted under state **hate crime** statutes for bias intimidation. The New Brunswick, New Jersey jury also convicted him of invasion of privacy, lying to investigators, attempting to influence a witness, hindering arrest, and tampering with evidence (for trying to conceal the Twitter and text messages). The trial lasted 13 days, and the seven-woman, five-man jury deliberated for 13 hours over three days.

The verdict set in motion a legal debate over hate crimes in general and their application in a tech-savvy, social-media-connected world. It cemented the reality that ages-old "boys will be boys" pranks and defenses are no longer considered youthful indiscretions. Instead, the conduct may be prosecuted as "bullying" (bias intimidation) and/or illegal invasion of privacy under most hate-crime laws. The incident left two young and gifted college roommates irreversibly changed: one dead, the other a convicted criminal.

The case was considered rare, given that few facts were in dispute. Ravi's legal counsel agreed to facts that he set up a Webcam (camera) on his computer in the shared dorm room to peek at Clementi's date with a man in the dorm room on September 19, 2010. He then exited to a friend's room and watched remotely as Clementi and his guest engaged in intimate kissing. When Clementi invited the man back two days later, Ravi sent Twitter and text messages to others, telling them he had seen his roommate "kissing a dude" and urging them to spy through his Webcam. He then deleted the messages after Clementi committed suicide. Records showed that Clementi had checked Ravi's Twitter account 38 times after the first Webcam viewing, then left the Rutgers campus and drove to the George Washington Bridge, where he jumped to his death. He was an 18-year-old freshman at the University.

Even though the messages were essentially deleted by Ravi, there was a long trail of electronic evidence, including Twitter feeds and cell phone records, dining hall swipe cards, dormitory surveillance cameras, and a "net flow" analysis showing when and how computers in the dormitory were connected. Evidence at trial showed that Ravi had used his computer skills to plug Clementi's email address into various computer programs to discover what websites Clementi frequented and to learn that he was gay. Records also revealed that Clementi had gone online to request a room change and had complained to a resident assistant.

On behalf of their client, defense counsel had argued that Ravi set up the Webcam because he feared that Clementi's guest would steal something. The verdict resulted in mixed comments from gay media sources, some of whom opined that Ravi had been excessively charged because Clementi was dead. Others opined that he had become a scapegoat for gay-bullying, and that he should face a lighter sentence.

In May 2012, Ravi, who was facing as much as five to ten years of prison for some of the charges, was sentenced to 30 days in jail, three years PROBATION, 300 hours of COMMUNITY SERVICE, and attendance at counseling sessions for cyber-bullying and alternative lifestyles. He also was ordered to pay a $10,000 assessment to the probation department, payable in monthly increments of $300 starting in August 2012. The money would go to victims of bias crimes. Ravi was ordered to report to Middlesex Adult Correctional Center on May 31, 2012. Judge Glenn Berman further recommended that Ravi, born in India and in the United States on a "green card," not be deported.

At the sentencing hearing, Middlesex County Superior Court Judge Berman berated Ravi for his "colossal insensitivity." He further told Ravi that most defendants stand when a judge speaks to them, then sarcastically told Ravi to keep his seat. He also referred to Ravi's pre-sentencing letter as "unimpressive."

Clementi's family, understandably bitter, spoke at the sentencing hearing in a packed courtroom and asked that Ravi receive prison time. Clementi's father told the court that Ravi's conduct was "cold and calculating," and then he tried to "cover it up," showing no remorse. Clementi's mother stated that she assisted her "excited" son in moving into the Rutgers dorm, and she described Ravi's "coldness" upon meeting Clementi, not getting up from his computer to say hello or even pause to acknowledge Clementi's presence. "No greeting, no smile, no recognition, no nothing," she told the court. She referred to Ravi's conduct toward her son as "arrogant and mean-spirited."

Conversely, Ravi's mother delivered an emotional plea for leniency, saying that her son had suffered enough from media coverage and that his dreams were shattered. She then flung herself on her son, sobbing and hugging him.

After the initial verdict, Clementi's father, director of public works in a Northern New Jersey town, read a brief statement that he hoped would reach middle and high school students,

> You're going to meet a lot of people in your lifetime…Some of these people you may not like. Just because you don't like them doesn't mean you have to work against them. When you see somebody doing something wrong, tell them: "That's not right. Stop it." The change you want to see in the world begins with you.

IMMIGRATION

The entrance into a country of foreigners for purposes of permanent residence. The correlative term emigration *denotes the act of such persons in leaving their former country.*

Arizona v. Inter Tribal Council of Arizona, Inc.

One of the more closely-watched cases before the U.S. SUPREME COURT in its 2012-2013 term was the challenge to Arizona's voter registration laws. Decision in this case stood to potentially affect similar laws in several other states. The controversy invoked issues of the U.S. Constitution's **Supremacy Clause**, Elections Clause, **equal protection**, and several other legal theories and doctrines. The underlying subject was Arizona's "concrete evidence" requirement of proving U.S. citizenship before being permitted to register to vote, particularly by mail. Federal law only requires that, when registering by mail using the standard Federal Form, the applicant **aver**, under penalty of PERJURY, that he or she is a citizen of the United States. The quintessential question before the Court was whether Arizona's requirement demanding proof of citizenship is preempted by the National Voter Registration Act of 1993 (NVRA), 107 Stat.77, as amended, 42 U.S.C. § 1973gg, *et seq.*

The short answer is yes. Ultimately, in June 2013, the Court announced its decision, affirming the Ninth **Circuit Court** of Appeals decision

that found Arizona's law preempted, effectively striking it and similar laws in other states. *Arizona v. Inter Tribal Council of Ariz. Inc.,* 133 S. Ct. 2247 (2013). Notwithstanding, the Court reaffirmed Arizona's ability to request the federal Election Assistance Commission (EAC) to incorporate state-specific instructions on the Federal Form for voter registration, and to have court review of any rejection or declination of such request.

The National Voter Registration Act (NVRA) requires that states "accept and use" a uniform Federal Form for voter registration in upcoming federal elections (most importantly, for U.S. congressional seats). The contents of that Form are prescribed by the EAC (above), a federal agency under the authority of the NVRA, § 1973gg-7(a)(1), and "in consultation with the chief election officers of the States," § 1973gg-7(a)(2). Thus, the Federal Form contains many state-specific instructions regarding what information registrants must provide and where they may submit the Form, etc. However, each state-specific instruction requires approval by the EAC before it is included on the Federal Form.

The Federal Form does not require documentary proof of citizenship, but the NVRA does require states to provide simplified systems for registering to vote in *federal* elections. The Act further requires states to permit prospective voters to "register to vote in elections for Federal

San Carlos Apache Tribal Chairman Terry Rambler speaking with reporters at the U.S. Supreme Court after attending oral arguments in Arizona v. Inter Tribal Council of Arizona, *March 2013.*

CHIP SOMODEVILLA/
GETTY IMAGES

office" by any of three methods: simultaneously with a driver's license application, in person, or by mail. § 1973gg-2(a).

In 2004, the State of Arizona passed a ballot initiative, Proposition 200, ostensibly designed to "combat voter fraud." It required registrants to present proof of citizenship at the time they registered to vote; it also required them to present identification when they voted on election day. Proposition 200 amended Arizona's election code by requiring county recorders to "reject any application for registration that is not accompanied by satisfactory evidence of United States citizenship." Ariz. Rev. Stat. Ann. § 16-166(F).

The EAC did not grant Arizona's 2005 request to include this new requirement on the Federal Form, which only requires an **attestation** of citizenship under penalty of perjury. Consequently, several groups of plaintiffs filed separate suits to enjoin the voting provisions of Proposition 200, particularly, registration by mail. The federal **district court** consolidated the cases, then denied **preliminary injunction** (which would have stopped the law from taking effect until the challenge was adjudicated on the merits). There followed several decisions, reversals, and remands, until finally, in 2010, a panel

of the Ninth Circuit Court of Appeals (which included guest retired Supreme Court justice SANDRA DAY O'CONNOR), held that Arizona Proposition 200's proof of citizenship requirement "conflicts with the NVRA's text, structure, and purpose." The full *en banc* Ninth Circuit Court of Appeals agreed in 2012. It is this part of the final **appellate** decision that became the subject of Supreme Court review.

In affirming the Ninth Circuit's finding that NVRA preempts Arizona's proof of citizenship requirement, the Court first looked to the Constitution's Elections Clause, Article I, Section 4, Clause 1, which imposes on states the duty to prescribe the "time, place, and manner" of electing Representatives and Senators. However, the Constitution's express language further states that "Congress may at any time by Law make or alter such Regulations, except as to the places of chusing [sic] Senators." Congress precisely did this with the enactment of the NVRA, which empowers the EAC to create a Federal Form for federal elections, and to require states to "accept and use" that form. The Court concluded that the implication of this mandate was that the Federal Form is to be accepted as sufficient for the requirement it is meant to satisfy. Arizona's requirement of further proof improperly usurps that.

Arizona also argued that under the Constitution's SUPREMACY CLAUSE, there is a presumption against **preemption**. But, said the Court, the precise power afforded by Congress to the EAC is the power to preempt. When Congress acts under the Supremacy Clause, it is on clear notice that its legislation is likely to displace some element of pre-existing law in one or more of the states.

Still, while the NVRA would preempt any state attempt to require additional information beyond that required by the Federal Form (without EAC approval), the NVRA does not prohibit states from denying registration based on information in their possession that establishes an applicant's ineligibility. The Court noted that after Arizona, in 2005, had requested EAC to include the evidence-of-citizenship requirement in the state-specific instructions of the Federal Form, the EAC divided 2-to-2 on the request (a minimum of three votes are needed), but Arizona did not challenge the inaction by seeking **judicial review**, which was available to it. In sum, Arizona still has the opportunity to establish, in a judicial court review, that mere oath is not sufficient to "effectuate" the citizenship requirement. The Court further noted that Arizona might assert that EAC's inaction or refusal to accept its request is/was arbitrary, since the EAC had accepted a similar instruction requested by Louisiana.

Justice ANTONIN SCALIA delivered the opinion for the 7-2 majority, with Justice ANTHONY KENNEDY concurring in part and dissenting in part (questioning the Court's statement that "there exists a hierarchy of federal powers" such that PREEMPTION varies according to which power Congress has exercised. Justice CLARENCE THOMAS filed a dissenting opinion, arguing that states have the right to determine voter qualification for federal elections. Justice SAMUEL ALITO also filed a separate DISSENT opining that voter qualification determination rests with the states, and further opining that the NVRA does not require that states treat the federal requirements as the sole requirements.

Moncrieffe v. Holder

In April 2013, the U.S. SUPREME COURT, by a 7-2 majority, held that a non-citizen's state conviction for a marijuana offense did not rise to the level of "aggravated felony" for purposes of the IMMIGRATION and NATURALIZATION Act (INA). The significance of this holding is that if the offense had met the INA's criteria for an aggravated **felony**, the convicted non-citizen would be removable and the U.S. Attorney General would be prohibited from canceling removal via discretionary relief. *Moncrieffe v. Holder,* 133 S. Ct. 1678 (2013).

As background, one of the provisions under the INA, 66 Stat. 163, 8 U.S.C. § 1101 *et seq.* states that certain non-citizens may be deported for offenses such as expired visas and conviction of certain crimes, including "aggravated felonies." One of the crimes listed by INA as an aggravated felony is the "illicit trafficking in a controlled substance," including any drug offense that the Controlled Substances Act makes punishable as a felony. The Supreme Court has previously ruled that a conviction under state drug offense laws "constitutes a 'felony punishable under the [CSA]' only if it proscribes conduct punishable as a felony under that [CSA] federal law." *Lopez v. Gonzales,* 549 U.S. 47, 127 S. Ct. 625, 166 L. Ed. 2d 462 (2006).

Adrian Moncrieffe, a lawfully-admitted permanent resident from Jamaica, was arrested by police during a 2007 traffic stop, when police found 1.3 grams of marijuana (about enough for two to three cigarettes) in his car. He pleaded guilty in Georgia state court to possession of marijuana with the intent to distribute under Ga. Code Ann. § 16-13-30(j)(1). Under Ga. Code Ann. § 42-8-60(a), allowing more lenient treatment for first-time offenders, the Georgia court's judge withheld entering a judgment of conviction or imposing any imprisonment. Instead, he ordered five years PROBATION, after which the charge would be expunged altogether.

In 2010, the U.S. DEPARTMENT OF HOMELAND SECURITY initiated removal proceedings against Moncrieffe, as an alien convicted of an aggravated felony under the INA. As authority, it cited CSA's 21 U.S.C. § 841(a), in this case, possession of marijuana with intent to distribute, punishable by up to five years imprisonment, § 841(b)(1)(D).

Moncrieffe raised as defense another subsection, § 841(b)(4), which makes marijuana distribution punishable as a **misdemeanor** (instead of a felony) if it involves a small amount of substance and there is no remuneration. Both an immigration judge and the Board of Immigration Appeals rejected this argument and upheld removal. On appeal, the U.S. Court of Appeals for the Fifth Circuit denied his petition for review, holding that § 841(b)(1) provided the default punishment for his offense.

The U.S. Supreme Court reversed. Justice SONIA SOTOMAYOR, writing for the majority, held that since the Controlled Substance Act (CSA) contained categories for both a felony and a misdemeanor for possession of marijuana, a "categorical approach" must be used to determine which category the Georgia state offense was comparable to. Importantly, the actual conduct of the offender is irrelevant. Instead, the state **statute** which defines the crime is examined to determine if it fits within the "generic" federal (CSA) definition of an aggravated felony.

Using this approach, the question becomes whether Georgia's law necessarily proscribes conduct punishable as a felony under the [CSA] federal law. *Lopez,* above. As to the actual crime, the state and federal provisions corresponded. But CSA's § 841 has two subsections, one [§ 841(a)] entitled "Unlawful Acts," and the other, [§ 841(b)], "Penalties." This is where

Moncrieffe's defense came in. He had argued that his offense qualified as a misdemeanor under § 841(b)(4) (a "small amount" of marijuana, for no remuneration).

Standing alone (not looking to the underlying facts), his conviction under Georgia's general statute, for possession with intent to distribute, neither revealed the quantity found nor whether there was remuneration. Accordingly, Moncrieffe's offense could correspond with either CSA's felony or its misdemeanor provisions. That ambiguity alone meant that the conviction did not necessarily involve facts that corresponded to a CSA offense punishable as a felony. The Court reversed the judgment of the Court of Appeals and remanded.

The Court also noted,

This is the third time in seven years that we have considered whether the Government has properly characterized a low-level drug offense as "illicit trafficking in a controlled substance," and thus an "aggravated felony." Once again we hold that the Government's approach defies the "commonsense conception" of these terms.

Citation omitted.

The majority opinion included Chief Justice JOHN ROBERTS, JR. and Justices ANTONIN SCALIA, ANTHONY KENNEDY, RUTH BADER GINSBURG, STEPHEN BREYER, and ELENA KAGAN. Justice CLARENCE THOMAS dissented, opining that since Georgia punished convictions under its statute as felonies, Moncrieffe's conviction should be considered an "aggravated felony." Justice SAMUEL ALITO also filed a separate DISSENT, saying that the majority opinion provided opportunity for non-citizen drug traffickers to remain in the country.

INTERNATIONAL LAW

The body of law governing the legal relations between states or nations.

Kiobel v. Royal Dutch Petroleum

The Alien Tort **Statute** (ATS), 28 U.S. C. § 1350, part of the JUDICIARY ACT OF 1789, was invoked twice in the 18th century (1793 and 1795) and then not again for 167 years (1908), then again in 1960. It does not prohibit anything or establish any **cause of action**. It merely provides district courts with jurisdiction, and non-citizen ALIENS with a legal forum, for certain tort claims to be heard. Those tort claims must allege a wrong "committed in

violation of the **law of nations** or a treaty of the United States."

In 1980, a Second **Circuit Court** of Appeals decision permitted two Paraguayan non-citizens to proceed under ATS against a former Paraguayan law enforcement officer who allegedly killed a member of their family. Since that time, ATS has been invoked more frequently, and some circuits broadened the scope of defendants to include corporations. Alien residents in the United States began increasingly utilizing ATS to bring suits against alleged wrongdoers in their native countries. This expansion of ATS caused both concern and controversy among circuits. In 2004, the U.S. SUPREME COURT, attempting to contain the flood of these cases, clarified that the grant of jurisdiction was instead "best read as having been enacted on the understanding that the **common law** would provide a CAUSE OF ACTION for [a] modest number of international violations." *Sosa v. Alvarez-Machain*, 542 U.S. 692, 124 S. Ct. 2739, 159 L. Ed. 2d 718 (2004). (In that case, the Court rejected plaintiff's claim for "arbitrary arrest and detention" because it failed to state a violation of the LAW OF NATIONS with the requisite "definite content and acceptance among civilized nations." *Id.*, at 699,732.

Finally a case presented itself which would give the U.S. Supreme Court the opportunity to dispositively address confusing questions about the use of ATS among the circuits. In *Kiobel v. Royal Dutch Petroleum*, 133 S. Ct. 1659 (2013), arguments were originally heard in early 2012, on the question of whether corporations were proper defendants under ATS. Without deliberating, the Court set the case for re-argument on the question of whether and when the ATS allowed courts to adjudicate actions involving alleged violations that occurred outside of the United States and within the territory of other sovereigns. Following briefs and re-argument, the Court decided, in April 2013, that there was a presumption against the ATS conferring jurisdiction over alleged violations that occur "extraterritorially," i.e., outside the United States.

In *Kiobel*, a group of Nigerian nationals, led by Esther Kiobel, filed suit in federal **district court** against Royal Dutch Petroleum, Shell Petroleum Development Company, and others under ATS. They alleged that the petroleum companies were complicit with the Nigerian government in violence against them for protesting environmental harm caused by oil exploration and production in their homeland area of Ogoniland, in the Niger delta area of Nigeria. The DEFENDANT corporations are British and Dutch corporations with limited contacts to the United States. The complaint alleged that the defendants enlisted the Nigerian government to suppress demonstrations (with alleged beatings, killings, rapes, looting and destruction of property, etc.) It further alleged that defendants aided and **abetted** the Nigerian government in these violent suppressions by providing them with food, transportation, compensation, and use of their property to launch military attacks.

The federal District Court for the Southern District of New York dismissed claims against corporate defendants, then certified its order for **interlocutory** appeal (conducted while the remainder of the case was pending the appeal's outcome). Both parties cross-appealed to the U.S. Court of Appeals for the Second Circuit. In September 2010, a majority of the Second Circuit affirmed the dismissal of the entire complaint, holding that the "law of nations" did not recognize corporate defendants. Following 2011 oral arguments, the parties were directed to provide supplemental briefs on the additional question of territoriality.

After careful consideration of the history and text of the statute, the Court ultimately concluded that there was no evidence to support the application of ATS to attempt to regulate foreign conduct (excepting PIRACY on the high seas). The majority found that proper use and purpose of the ATS was for claims that had substantial territorial connections to the United States. While the conduct alleged in the complaint may have violated the law of nations, the Court shifted focus of the test for jurisdiction under ATS to the location of the conduct, rather than the citizenship (lack thereof) of the plaintiffs or presence of the defendants (sufficient contacts). The majority expressly pointed out that mere presence of a corporation within the United States was an insufficient connection to support jurisdiction under ATS. Further, anticipating the argument raised by other plaintiffs in other cases that extraterritorial conduct nonetheless has produced effects in the United States, the Court noted that "even where the claims touch and concern the territory of the United States, they must do so with sufficient force to displace the presumption against extraterritorial application." Explaining the exception for piracy on the high seas, the Court said that regulating this was a right claimed by every nation and therefore "carries less direct foreign policy consequences" than an attempt to regulate conduct occurring within the territories of other sovereigns/nations.

Chief Justice JOHN ROBERTS, JR. delivered the opinion of the Court, joined by Justices SAMUEL ALITO, ANTONIN SCALIA, ANTHONY KENNEDY, and CLARENCE THOMAS. Justices Kennedy and Alito also filed separate concurring opinions, Justice Thomas joining Justice Alito's opinion as well. Justice STEPHEN BREYER filed an opinion concurring in the judgment, joined by the remaining Justices RUTH BADER GINSBURG, SONIA SOTOMAYOR, and ELENA KAGAN.

KIDNAPPING

New York Court of Appeals Rules that Custodial Parent Can Be Convicted of Kidnapping

The crime of KIDNAPPING is usually associated with the abduction of a person by a stranger. In New York, the question arose of whether it was possible for a parent who has custodial rights to a child to be guilty of kidnapping that child. The state's highest court, the New York Court of Appeals, in *People v. Leonard,* 970 N.E.2d 856 (2012), ruled that it was possible. The court found that a father, who used his baby daughter as a hostage and who threatened to kill her if the police approached him, was guilty of kidnapping.

Leo Leonard had a romantic relationship with a woman (the court called her Mary) that ended a few days after their daughter was born. Mary moved with the baby from Brooklyn, where she and Leonard had been living, to Ulster County. There was no court order affecting the CUSTODY of the child, so Leonard and Mary were equally entitled to custody. When the baby was six weeks old, Leonard showed up unexpectedly at Mary's new home. The couple got into a verbal altercation, which escalated when Leonard pulled out a knife and cut Mary. Leonard calmed down and allowed Mary to leave for work, while the baby remained with him. Mary called her mother and a friend from her car and the friend called the police.

Mary's mother and stepfather arrived at Mary's home and found Leonard sitting outside, holding the baby. Shortly after that, Mary and the police arrived. Seeing the police, Leonard took out his knife and gestured toward the baby with it, before retreating into the house. Police and Leonard maintained a tense standoff in a bedroom, during which Leonard held the knife near the baby's chest and throat. He told officers that if they came closer he would kill the child. Police finally persuaded Leonard to give the baby, unharmed, to them. Leonard was convicted of **burglary**, endangering the WELFARE of a child, two weapons offenses, and kidnapping in the second degree. The New York **Appellate** Division upheld the convictions, finding that the evidence of kidnapping was legally sufficient. Leonard then appealed to the New York Court of Appeals.

The court, in a 4-3 decision, upheld the kidnapping conviction. Judge Robert S. Smith, writing for the majority, examined the statutes involving the definition of kidnapping. The kidnapping **statute** stated "A person is guilty of kidnapping in the second degree when he abducts another person." The **statutory** definition of "abduct" means to "restrain a person with intent to prevent his liberation by either (a) secreting or holding him in a place where he is not likely to be found, or (b) using or threatening to use deadly physical force." Judge Smith then looked to the statutory definition of the word "restrain," which "means to restrict a person's movements intentionally and unlawfully," as well as interfering the person's liberty.

Judge Smith, concluded that the "decisive question" was whether Leonard "restrained" the child, according to the statutory definition of that term. Leonard had intentionally moved the child from one place to another and confined her to the bedroom to which she had been moved. Leonard contended that he did not restrict her movements or interfere with her liberty because a six-week-old child is incapable of going or remaining anywhere voluntarily. The court rejected this argument, as it implied that "no infant could ever be kidnapped." Leonard had restricted the child's movement and interfered with the child's liberty; the child's lawful movement had been hindered.

The next question was whether Leonard restricted the child's movements unlawfully, without consent, and with knowledge that the restriction was unlawful. Leonard claimed that as a custodial parent with rights equal to those of Mary to control the child, it was impossible for him to act unlawfully, without consent, and with knowledge that his actions were unlawful. As a custodial parent, he could lawfully take the child anywhere he wanted, and the only consent he needed was his own. Judge Smith conceded that Leonard had, in general, a right to control his child's movements, but "there comes a point where even a custodial parent's control over a child's movements is unlawful, and obviously so." The court concluded, "a kidnapping by a custodial parent of his own child is not a legal impossibility." It was possible in cases like Leonard's where a "defendant's conduct is so obviously and unjustifiably dangerous or harmful to the child as to be inconsistent with the idea of lawful custody."

However, the court cautioned that this holding "should not be too readily extended." Not every parent who disciplines a child inappropriately becomes a kidnapper when "he or she causes the child to move from place to place, or to remain stationary." It was much different when a person holds a knife to a child's throat and threatens MURDER. In that case a "line has been crossed."

Judge Theodore T. Jones, in a dissenting opinion joined by two other members of the court, contended that the state had failed to prove all elements of kidnapping in the second degree. In addition, the majority had taken Leonard's threatened use of force, which amounted to endangering the welfare of a child, an offense Leonard had been convicted of, "and contrived a scenario whereby an individual whose actions constitute child endangerment may be punished for second-degree kidnapping, an offense which carries significantly greater punishment." This type of "bootstrapping" was unacceptable.

LABOR LAW

Michigan Passes Right to Work Law

In December 2012, the state of Michigan—the core of organized labor and birth place of the United Auto Workers (UAW) international union—became the 24th right-to-work state. Right to Work laws prohibit employers and unions from compelling workers to join unions or pay union membership dues (even if not union members) as a condition of employment. (Also in 2012, Indiana expanded its right to work law to include all private sector employment, from previously applying only to school employees. Michigan and Indiana remained the only two states in the heavily unionized Midwest to have right to work laws.) During the 2012 legislative session, 19 states debated right to work legislation; laws were passed in four states, either expanding existing right to work laws, or in the case of Michigan, establishing the right.

Right to Work laws create "open shop" free labor states. With workers no longer compelled to join unions in order to get employment in unionized companies, or forced to contribute mandatory membership dues, union membership declines, along with commensurate negotiating power.

This was the second loss for Michigan's unions. In November 2012, voters defeated Proposal 2, a ballot measure to write COLLECTIVE BARGAINING into the state constitution (which would effectively thwart later efforts to pass right to work legislation). The proposal was defeated 58 percent to 42 percent.

There was outrage at the state capital in Lansing, Michigan as union workers stormed the capitol building and were joined by teachers walking out of school and even some DEMOCRATIC PARTY state senators, who walked out on the final vote to approve the initial bills.

That scene at the state capital on December 6, 2012 played out in Ingham County **Circuit Court** when an emergency complaint was filed after state police allegedly closed the capitol building at approximately noon on December 6 just prior to legislators gathering for a vote. A Lansing *State Journal* reporter who was in the House chamber on that day had reported observing that the gallery appeared to be filled for most of the day with both (what looked like) union members and people dressed in business attire, who he assumed were legislative aides or staff. Media sources then reported that Republican staffers were taking up seats (in the gallery seating for the public) as much as four hours before the day's legislative session. The complaint alleged that the right to work legislation was passed in violation of the state's Open Meetings Act.

The capitol was closed off for approximately five hours during the initial legislative meeting/hearing. However, those who were inside the gallery were permitted to stay.

Following this publicity, an amended complaint was filed on January 31, 2013, adding as plaintiffs a coalition that included the Michigan Education Association, the Michigan AFL-CIO, the AMERICAN CIVIL LIBERTIES UNION (ACLU), and several Democratic state legislators.

In June 2013, Ingham County Judge William Collette rejected a motion filed by the state's Attorney General, Bill Shuette (a Republican), to dismiss the lawsuit. The judge stated on record that the coalition of plaintiffs had presented sufficient evidence to meet their burden of presenting a viable **cause of action** (i.e., on the basis of factual allegations construed in a light most favorable to them, at this stage). The judge did not determine whether a violation had actually occurred, only denied the motion for dismissal of the case at this early stage.

Judge Collette first advised both sides of weaknesses in their respective positions. He further requested that Assistant Attorney General Michelle Brya explain what appeared to be "a concerted effort" by Republican leadership to prevent members of the general public from observing the initial legislative action on the right to work law, by having their staff members take up all the seats in the public gallery at the state building on December 6. Finally, the judge ordered the attorney general to file a formal answer to the complaint, which Schuette had failed to do. (Michigan **civil procedure** does permit a motion for summary disposition/ judgment in lieu of an answer to the complaint, but since the motion was denied, an answer was now required.)

The first right to work laws were passed in the 1940s, Florida and other southern states leading in the movement. Most were enacted by **statute**, but several states incorporated them by CONSTITUTIONAL AMENDMENT. Interest surged in the 1970s and again in the 1990s, but has since slacked off. Federal law (primarily the Labor-Management Reporting and Disclosure Act of 1959) provides for union elections, finances, management, etc., but right to work has remained a state issue.

NLRB: Facebook Postings Were Protected Activities

The NATIONAL LABOR RELATIONS BOARD (NLRB) in December 2012 ruled that a nonprofit company violated the National Labor Relations Act (NRLA) by firing five employees. These employees had posted negative comments about a fellow employee on Facebook. The NLRB ruled that the employees were engaged in an activity protected by the Act.

An employee complaining to others about workplace issues is certainly not a new phenomenon. In a typical office setting, employees might discuss their jobs or their employer in a break room or around a water cooler. In the past, the NLRB has addressed issues that arise when an employer has punished or fired an employee for making negative comments about the employer or another employee.

More recently, social media has become ubiquitous in most aspects of American life, and individuals often turn to social media as an outlet for communication. Within the employment context, some consider sites such as Facebook and Twitter to be the "new water cooler," because employees will engage in informal online discussions that are similar to the discussions the employee would have around a water cooler. Companies have adopted policies to try to regulate employee communication on social media sites, often prohibiting employees from criticizing the company or fellow employees.

The NLRB case focused on the Facebook activities of employees at Hispanics United of Buffalo, Inc. (HUB), a nonprofit group in New York. Marianna Cole-Rivera and Lydia Cruz-Moore worked for HUB, providing assistance to domestic-violence victims. According to Cole-Rivera, Cruz-Moore was often critical of fellow employees, saying that the other employees provided poor assistance to clients.

On Friday, October 9, 2009, Cruz-Moore sent Cole-Rivera a text message saying that Cruz-Moore was going to report her concerns to Lourdes Iglesias, HUB's executive director. After the two employees had exchanged further communications, Cole-Rivera posted a message on her personal Facebook account using her personal computer. The message read: "Lydia Cruz, a coworker feels that we don't help our clients enough at [HUB]. I about had it! My fellow coworkers how do u feel?" Four other employees responded to the message from their personal computers, with each objecting to Cruz-Moore's report about their work performances.

Cruz-Moore saw the posting and also responded, calling the content of other messages "lies." Cruz-Moore then complained to Iglesias about the Facebook messages. On

Monday, October 12—the first workday after Cole-Rivera posted her message—Iglesias fired Cole-Rivera and each of the other four employees. Iglesias said the Facebook comments amounted to "bullying and harassment" and that HUB had a zero-tolerance policy regarding this type of conduct. HUB conceded that the sole reason for firing the employees was because of the Facebook postings.

One of the employees filed a charge that HUB had engaged in an UNFAIR LABOR PRACTICE by firing the five employees. A regional director of the NLRB then issued a complaint, alleging that the firings violated the NLRA. Under § 7 of the NLRA, 29 U.S.C. § 157, "Employees shall have the right to self-organization, to form, join, or assist labor organizations, to bargain collectively through representatives of their own choosing, and to engage in other concerted activities for the purpose of COLLECTIVE BARGAINING or other mutual aid or protection." Section 8(a)(1) of the Act, in turn, establishes that it is an unfair labor practice for an employer "to interfere with, restrain, or coerce employees in the exercise of the rights guaranteed in section 7."

An **administrative law** judge reviewed the case and ruled in the employees' favor in September 2011. The judge, Arthur Amchan, first determined that the NLRB has jurisdiction over the case. He then reviewed authority under previous NLRB decisions and determined that the employees had engaged in activities protected by § 8(a)(1). Amchan also concluded that the employees were harassing Cruz-Moore in their messages.

Amchan relied in part on the NLRB's decision in *Myers Industries*, 268 N.L.R.B. 493 (1984), which established four elements that must be proven to establish a violation under § 8(a)(1): "(1) the activity engaged in by the employee was 'concerted' within the meaning of Section 7 of the Act; (2) the employer knew of the concerted nature of the employee's activity; (3) the concerted activity was protected by the Act; and (4) the discipline or discharge was motivated by the employee's protected, concerted activity." Amchan concluded that HUB's actions met each of these four elements.

HUB appealed Amchan's decision to the full Board. A 3–1 majority adopted Amchan's recommendations that HUB had interfered with the employees' rights. Like Amchan, the majority determined that *Myers Industries*

applied to determine whether a violation had occurred. Specifically, the Board had to determine whether the Facebook comments constituted a concerted activity and whether the NLRA protected the activity.

The Board in *Meyers* defined a concerted activity as one "engaged in with or on the authority of other employees, and not solely by and on behalf of the employee itself." A later decision expanded the definition to include "circumstances where individual employees seek to initiate or to induce or to prepare for group action, as well as individual employees bringing truly group complaints to the attention of management."

The majority decided there was "no question" the activities of the group posting on Facebook was for the purpose of mutual aid or protection. The comments were part of a common cause, said the Board, and the group was taking a first step toward group action with their posts.

The Board also decided that the activity was one protected by the Act. The majority stated as follows:

> The Board has long held that Section 7 protects employee discussions about their job performance, and the Facebook comments plainly centered on that subject. As discussed, the employees were directly responding to allegations they were providing substandard service to the Respondent's clients. Given the negative impact such criticisms could have on their employment, the five employees were clearly engaged in protected activity in mutual aid of each other's defense to those criticisms." *Hispanics United of Buffalo*, 359 N.L.R.B. No. 37 (Dec. 14, 2012).

The Board upheld Amcham's remedies, which included full reinstatement of each of the employees along with back pay and benefits lost plus interest.

LAWYERS

A person, who through a regular program of study, is learned in legal matters and has been licensed to practice his or her profession. Any qualified person who prosecutes or defends causes in courts of record or other judicial tribunals of the United States, or of any of the states, or who renders legal advice or assistance in relation to any cause or matter.

Florida Supreme Court Approves New Lawyer Advertising Rules

Florida has traditionally had strict limits on lawyer advertising, especially compared with limits in other states. In 2013, the Florida SUPREME COURT loosened some of these regulations but also extended the rules so that they apply to lawyer websites. The court was divided on whether to adopt the rules, with three judges dissenting to at least part of the rule changes.

Florida's regulations on lawyer advertising were almost infamous among lawyers. For example, these regulations prohibited lawyers from using certain types of music or "manipulative" visual portrayals. Moreover, the rules forbid use of advertisements that created "suspense." In one case, the Florida Supreme Court ruled that a lawyer's use of a pit bull wearing a spiked collar violated the rules because of what the image suggested.

Attorneys in the state complained about the regulations in the past. In 2008, a lawyer named William Harrell, Jr., challenged whether the regulations were constitutional. His case arose when the Florida bar rejected his use of the slogan "Don't settle for less than you deserve." A bar committee first concluded that the slogan violated the state's rules but later changed its conclusion to allow the ad. Nevertheless, Harrell pursued his challenge to the advertising rules in federal court. In 2011, U.S. District Judge Marcia Morales Howard ruled in Harrell's favor. She concluded that the rules that applied to Harrell's ad were vague and violated his FIRST AMENDMENT rights. *Harrell v. Fla. Bar*, No. 3:08-cv-15-J-34TEM, 2011 WL 9754086 (M.D. Fla. Sept. 30, 2011).

In 2007, the Florida Supreme Court requested that the Florida bar conduct a comprehensive study of the advertising rules. *In re: Amendments to the Rules Regulating the Florida Bar—Advertising*, 971 So. 2d 763 (Fla. 2007). The bar studied U.S. Supreme Court decisions addressing free-speech concerns regarding lawyer advertising restrictions. Moreover, the bar surveyed attorneys and members of the public.

The bar concluded that the state should completely restructure the rules addressing advertising. According to the supreme court, "The proposals are designed to make the advertising rules more cohesive, easier for lawyers to understand, and less cumbersome for the Bar to apply and enforce." The Florida Bar Board of Governors approved the new rules after publishing the rule proposals in the *Florida Bar News* in 2011 and 2012. The bar then submitted the rules to the Florida Supreme Court for full approval.

Under the new rules, a lawyer may include references to results of previous cases. The former rules prohibited advertisements from including any testimonials or references to previous cases. The new rules allow a lawyer to refer to previous results so long as the results are "objectively verifiable." The rule requires the lawyer to obtain the consent of the client affected by the prior result.

The new Rule 4-7.13 defines a testimonial as "a personal statement, affirmation, or endorsement by any person other than the advertising lawyer or a member of the advertising lawyer's firm regarding the quality of the lawyer's services or the results obtained through the representation." A lawyer may include some testimonials but the ruling lists several instances in which the lawyer may not. For example, the lawyer may not draft the testimonial used in the ad nor may the lawyer exchange anything of value for the testimonial.

Several of the new rules prohibit certain types of advertisements. Rule 4-7.14 prohibits "potentially misleading" advertisements, including one that is "literally accurate, but could reasonably mislead a prospective client regarding a material fact." Rule 4-7.15 forbids a lawyer from displaying an "unduly manipulative or intrusive" advertisement. An example of an advertisement that is "unduly manipulative" is one that uses the voice or image of a celebrity, except for local announcer who does not endorse the lawyer.

Several of the previous restrictions remain in the new rules. Under Rule 4-7.17, a lawyer in one firm may not pay advertisement costs of a lawyer in another firm. The new rules also prevent a nonlawyer from paying advertising costs of a lawyer. The new rules prohibit in-person **solicitation** of clients, as did the old rules. Under the new rules, any written communication, including email, from a lawyer seeking professional employment must include the word "Advertisement" on each page of the communication."

One the more controversial rule changes involved changes to Rule 4-7.11, which addresses the application of the rules. The previous rules stated that lawyer websites were exempt from advertising rules because the information contained on the sites were "information upon request." The new rule applies to "all forms of communication in any print or electronic forum," including "websites, social networking, and video sharing sites."

Four of seven justices on the Florida Supreme Court approved the amended rules. The Court responded to several concerns raised during the public comment period. One concern raised involved the term "objectively verifiable," which commenters said was unclear. The Court disagreed, noting as follows:

> If the attorney can show, by objective facts, that the statement is true, then he has presented an objectively verifiable statement in the advertisement. On the other hand, making a subjective statement such as 'the best trial lawyer in Florida' is a misleading statement that fails to meet the requirement because it is neither objective nor verifiable. The advertising statement must be supported by verifiable facts. *In re: Amendments to the Rules Regulating the Florida Bar—Subchapter 4-7, Lawyer Advertising Rules*, 108 So. 3d 609 (Fla. 2013).

The Florida bar continued to address advertising rules after the supreme court approved the rule changes. In April 2013, the Standing Committee on Advertising issued a proposed **advisory opinion** about use of "hidden text" and meta tags on an attorney's website. The opinion cautioned against a lawyer's improper use of "false, deceptive and misleading **search** engine optimization techniques" by hiding text such that a search engine could see the text but a human eye could not. An attorney could accomplish this through the use of meta tags, which are part of a website's coding but which do not appear in a web browser. Although the proposed opinion would not prohibit use of meta tags, an attorney is prevented from using tags in a false, deceptive, or misleading manner.

New York Lawyer Disbarred for Stealing Client Money

A New York attorney named Douglas Arntsen in 2012 pleaded guilty to several **felony** charges related to his theft of more than $10 million from accounts of corporate clients. He received a sentence of between 4 to 12 years, and in 2013, the State of New York disbarred him.

Arntsen graduated from St. John's University before attending the law school at Seton Hall University. He was admitted to the New York bar in 2003. He worked at large law firms, including Buchanan Ingersoll, before joining Crowell & Moring in 2007. Arntsen worked as a REAL ESTATE lawyer and commercial litigator.

Fellow workers later said they had no reason to think that Arntsen was the type who would steal from clients or otherwise commit a felony. Arntsen is married with a young child and reportedly lived in a modest home on Staten Island. One lawyer said of Arntsen, "The guys in the office, we'd go out for a few drinks after a long day, but not Doug. He'd have one Coke and go home."

One of Crowell & Moring's clients was Regal Real Estate, and Arntsen had access to Regal's **escrow** account. Around September 2011, some of Regal's managers complained about money missing from the account and confronted Arntsen about the missing money. Arntsen admitted to taking the money from the account and agreed to take Regal managing partner William Punch to several banks in Manhattan to retrieve the money. During this time, Arntsen returned $1.8 million to Punch.

Arntsen told Punch that the remaining money was held in banks in Miami and Hong Kong. Arntsen asked to meet Punch at a designated meeting place the next day, but Punch became concerned and notified authorities. Arntsen never showed up the next day at the meeting place and instead fled to Hong Kong. He was quickly arrested in Hong Kong, and authorities extradited him back to the United States. After Arntsen's arrest, Regal filed a $6 million lawsuit against Crowell & Moring.

Crowell & Moring faced a second lawsuit by another realty company even before Arntsen's arrest. Aristone Realty Capital accused Crowell & Moring of conspiring with Regal in an illegal KICKBACK scheme involving property in Manhattan. The original suit sought $1 million in damages, but in light of Arntsen's arrest, Aristone amended its complaint to allege $6 million in damages. Aristone accused the law firm of trying to cover up Arntsen's **malfeasance** before his arrest in September 2011. The legal problems for Crowell & Moring continued in November 2011 when the real estate company BCN 16th St. sued the law firm, alleging that Arntsen stole more than $1 million from BCN's ESCROW account.

Other allegations arose late in 2011 that executives with Crowell & Moring knew about Arntsen's misdeeds several months before he was arrested. In November 2011, Xun Energy, Inc., sued a woman who had intended to buy a stake in Xun. Arntsen had been asked to manage a $25,000 escrow fund related to the Xun deal. When the deal fell through, Xun's chief executive officer asked Arntsen to return the escrow funds. Arntsen did not immediately respond to the request, so the CEO copied Crowell & Moring's executive committee on a second demand for the escrow funds. When Arntsen finally returned the funds, they came from a different account than the one used for the original transfer, suggesting that Arntsen might have misappropriated those funds.

Crowell & Moring settled its dispute with Regal in December, agreeing to reimburse the real estate company for all of the funds that Arntsen had taken. While announcing the return of the escrow funds, Crowell & Moring issued the following statement:

> We were appalled to learn that a former employee seems to have been involved in an elaborate plot to DEFRAUD our client and his colleagues at Crowell & Moring. The alleged conduct of this former employee is in stark contrast to everything we stand for as a firm and is entirely inconsistent with the strong reputation of trust we have built among our clients over the years. We are grateful to our client Regal for their patience in this matter and are pleased finally to be in a position to honor our obligations to them through this **settlement**.

The allegations hurt Crowell & Moring's business. The firm had nearly 500 attorneys at the time the allegations arose but lost the heads of two of its practice groups in February 2012. Reports indicated that the firm was going to lose a "slew of lawyers," including partners, because of the allegations. On the other hand, the firm announced that it had made several lateral hires to make up for the lawyers it lost. Moreover, the firm settled its disputes with Aristone and BCN in May 2012.

Prosecutors alleged that Arntsen had stolen a total of $7 million from the various firms. He was represented during his prosecution by the prominent white-collar defense attorney Alan Lewis of Carter, Ledyard & Milburn. Prosecutors charged Arntsen on charges of first-degree **larceny** and first-degree scheme to defraud. He could have faced up to 25 years in prison on the charges.

On October 3, 2012, Arntsen pleaded guilty to the charges. Manhattan District Attorney Cyrus Vance said that Arntsen had betrayed the sacred trust between lawyer and client "to support a lavish lifestyle that included visits to expensive restaurants, sporting events, and strip clubs." Moreover, said Vance, Arntsen had purchased businesses for himself, friends, and family members.

On October 18, 2012, Arntsen received a sentence of between 4 and 12 years in prison. He became tearful during his sentencing hearing, saying, "I'm so sorry for what I did, for the money I took and I spent, for the trust that I squandered. As much as I've dreaded this day, I've also longed for it. I am ready to take responsibility for my actions."

Under New York law, Arntsen's felony convictions were cause for an automatic disbarment. A disciplinary committee of the New York SUPREME COURT, **Appellate** Division, initiated disbarment proceedings, but Arntsen did not respond. On March 19, 2013, the APPELLATE Division ruled that Arntsen was disbarred as of the date of his conviction.

LIMITATIONS

Sebelius v. Auburn Regional Medical Center

The issue before the U.S. SUPREME COURT in *Sebelius v. Auburn Regional Medical Center,* 133 S. Ct. 817 (2013) was one of "equitable tolling," or the extension of the period of time for filing an action under certain narrow circumstances. This case involved the competing interests of internal agency deadlines and the doctrine of equitable tolling. Ultimately, the Court ruled that equitable tolling was not available to hospitals filing administrative appeals to contest the amounts of **Medicare** reimbursements, where the agency had its own internal regulation allowing a three-year extension for **good cause**.

The federal MEDICARE program provides hospitals with reimbursement compensation, the amount for which is based on the disproportionate number of low-income patients (receiving SOCIAL SECURITY Income [SSI]) that they serve. The Center for Medicare & **Medicaid** Services (CMS) is charged with formulating and deciding the amount of these reimbursements (usually through a **fiscal** intermediary, e.g., a private insurance company). By **statute**, hospitals have 180 days to appeal these determinations to the administrative Provider Reimbursement Review Board (PRRB). 42 U.S.C. § 1395oo(a)(3). Notwithstanding, by internal agency regulation, the Secretary of Health and Human Services, Kathleen Sebelius, permitted that period to be extended, up to three years, for good cause. 42 CFR 405.1841(b).

In a totally unrelated case (*Baystate Medical Center v. Mutual of Omaha Insurance Company*) the PRRB ruled that CMS had systematically understated the number of SSI (low income) patients in its calculations for reimbursement to providers, resulting in shortchanging hospitals of reimbursements due. It further found that CMS was aware of these errors but did not correct them. The PRRB's (*Baystate*) decision was made public in 2006.

Following the publication of the above decision, a group of hospitals, including Auburn Regional Medical Center ("Auburn"), filed claims with the PRRB for additional reimbursements, based on the findings in the *Baystate* case. For Auburn, the filing of the claim was more than ten years after a fiscal intermediary had made its determination as to the amount of reimbursement due. But Auburn alleged in its appeal that the 180-day appeal period should be equitably tolled because it was not able to identify the underpayments until now, due to lack of access to data used by CMS to calculate the amounts. (Because of privacy laws, hospitals do not have direct access to the SSI database. CMS gets its data directly from the Social Security Administration, then matches data with hospital inpatient records.)

The PRRB concluded that it lacked jurisdiction to extend the 180 days because it had no equitable powers (other than those expressly conferred by statute or regulation). It then dismissed the case as untimely filed. **Judicial review** followed. The federal **district court** likewise dismissed the case. However, the U.S. Court of Appeals for the D.C. Circuit found that the 180-day **statutory** limitations period was subject to equitable tolling because Congress indicated nothing to the contrary in the relevant PRRB statute (42 U.S.C. § 1395oo[a][3]).

The Supreme Court was unanimous in its decision. Justice Ruth Bader Ginsburg, writing for the Court, reversed the **appellate court**. First, the Court covered the predicate "jurisdictional" question, holding that the 180-day limitation was not jurisdictional. (If it were, the Court would not have the power to apply equitable tolling.) Relying on, and citing from, earlier Court precedent, Justice Ginsburg reiterated that unless Congress has clearly stated that a statutory limitation is jurisdictional, it should be treated as nonjurisdictional, meaning that a court may then apply the doctrine of equitable tolling as called for.

That having been said, the Court next determined that Congress had vested in Secretary Sebelius "large rulemaking authority" to administer the Medicare program. Accordingly, courts lack authority to second-guess or undermine this rulemaking unless there is evidence that it is arbitrary, capricious, or manifestly contrary to the statute. Limiting its review under a deferential standard, therefore, the Court found the Secretary's regulation regarding a three year extension for good cause to be a reasonable and permissible interpretation of Congress' 42 U.S.C. § 1395oo(a)(3).

Finally, to the question of whether equitable tolling could extend the limitation even further, the Court rejected application of the doctrine. To impose equitable tolling that would allow appeals barred by the Secretary's own internal regulation would essentially usurp the rulemaking authority and "gut" the agency's requirement that an appeal will be dismissed if filed later than 180 days unless the provider shows good cause and requests an extension for no longer than three years.

The hospitals had argued a failure to adhere to the "fundamentals of fair play," since the agency allows the reopening of a fiscal intermediary's reimbursement determination "at any time" if the determination was the result of **fraud** or fault of the hospitals. But the Court rejected this final argument. Fiscal intermediaries must process tens of thousands of determinations. Giving them more time to discover overpayments than giving hospital providers time to discover underpayments was simply an "administrative reality" of the system.

Justice Sonia Sotomayor did file a separate concurring opinion, in which she noted that the Court was not establishing that equitable tolling principles are irrelevant or never applicable to internal administrative deadlines.

MEDICAID

WOS v. E.M.A.

Most health care insurers have a right not only to subrogate claims of their insureds, but also to be reimbursed for medical expenses paid by them on behalf of the insured, from any third-party settlements received by the insured. In *Wos v. EMA*, 133 S. Ct. 1391 (2013), the U.S. SUPREME COURT held that federal **Medicaid** law preempted North Carolina **statute** to the extent that the statute permitted recovery by the state MEDICAID program of amounts received by a Medicaid BENEFICIARY in a third-party tort **settlement** that were not specifically designated as for medical expenses.

E.M.A. a minor, was born in 2000, but suffered birth-related serious injuries resulting in mental retardation, cerebral palsy, and other medical injuries and impairments. Starting within weeks of her birth, her parents applied for and received assistance from North Carolina's state Medicaid program (which will continue to pay part of her ongoing medical care for life).

On her behalf in 2003, her parents and **guardian** filed a MEDICAL MALPRACTICE suit against a hospital and the doctor who delivered her at birth. Expert witnesses at trial estimated damages in excess of $42 million, including medical and skilled nursing care expenses, loss of future earning capacity, and miscellaneous

damages such as architectural handicap renovations to her parents' home, specially-equipped motorized transportation, etc as well as her pain and suffering. The largest itemized estimated damage ($37 million) was for skilled home care over her lifetime (13–18 hours per day). Her parents also sought recovery for their own emotional distress over her injury. Despite the EXPERT TESTIMONY (and the undisputable fact that she would need care for her lifetime), the suit was settled in **mediation** for $2.8 million, partly due to insurance policy limits. In any event, the settlement did not **itemize** damages or allocate portions of the total settlement amount toward any particular medical or non-medical claim for damages.

The federal Medicaid anti-lien provision, 42 U.S.C. § 1396p(a)(1) preempts any state effort to recoup any portion of a Medicaid beneficiary's third-party tort settlement or judgment that is "not designated as payments for medical care." *Arkansas Dept. of Health and Human Servs. v. Ahlborn*, 547 U.S. 268, 126 S. Ct. 1752, 164 L. Ed. 2d 459 (2006). By comparison, N.C. Gen. Stat. Ann. § 108A-57 creates an irrefutable **statutory** presumption that the state program may recoup up to 1/3 of the total settlement amount, or the actual medical expenses, whichever is less.

As part of settlement approval, the state court placed 1/3 of the settlement amount in **escrow** pending a judicial determination of the amount recoverable by the state Medicaid program (which at that time had already paid $1.9 million for E.M.A.'s medical bills and continued care). Her parents protested and filed suit in federal **district court**, arguing that the above federal Medicaid anti-lien provision preempted, and therefore did not permit, North Carolina's **lien**.

While that case was pending, the North Carolina Supreme Court decided in another case that the state's 1/3 statutory presumption was a reasonable method to determine the state's recovery of medical expenses in such cases. The district court agreed. However, the U.S. **Circuit Court** of Appeals could not reconcile this holding with the *Ahlborn* case and reversed.

By a 6-3 margin, the U.S. Supreme affirmed. Writing for the majority, Justice ANTHONY KENNEDY reiterated that the federal Medicaid anti-lien provision preempted North Carolina's statutory effort to declare that one-third of any tort recovery is recoverable as medical expenses. In *Ahlborn*, the Court held that federal law required an assignment to states of "the right to recover that portion of a settlement that represents payments for medical care," but it also "precludes attachment or encumbrance of the remainder of the settlement." 547 U.S. at 282,284. Notwithstanding, *Ahlborn* did not resolve the question of how to determine what portion of a settlement represented payment for medical care.

But neither did North Carolina's statute resolve this question. To the contrary, it directly conflicted with the federal law, said the Court, in that it chose the arbitrary percentage of one-third to represent medical expenses, then established a conclusive presumption that that percentage represents its share of any tort recovery. Prior to the *Ahlborn* decision, North Carolina interpreted its statute to permit recovery even when the funds received by the beneficiary did not represent reimbursement for medical expenses. Following *Ahlborn*, the North Carolina Supreme Court put forward a new interpretation of its statute that allowed recovery for "the portion of the settlement that represents payment for medical expenses" as the lesser of the state's past medical expenditures or one-third of the plaintiff's total recovery. *Andrews v. Haygood*, 362 N.C. 599 (2008).

Unfortunately, said the Court, "[u]nder this reading of the statute the presumption operates even if the settlement or a jury verdict expressly allocates a lower percentage of the judgment to medical expenses." Accordingly, North Carolina's statute is preempted to the extent that it would operate to allow the state to make a claim to any part of a Medicaid beneficiary's tort recovery not "designated as payments for medical care." *Ahlborn* at 284.

Chief Justice JOHN ROBERTS, JR. dissented, joined by Justices ANTONIN SCALIA and CLARENCE THOMAS. The DISSENT opted for giving more latitude to states to devise their own regulations, as the majority "could point to no statutory or regulatory requirement, much less an unambiguous one, requiring such an approach" (as the majority held).

MILITARY LAW

The body of laws, rules, and regulations developed to meet the needs of the military. It encompasses service in the military, the constitutional rights of service members, the military criminal justice system, and the international law of armed conflict.

Bradley Manning Acquitted of Aiding the Enemy, Found Guilty of Espionage Violations

To military prosecutors, the actions of Private First Class Bradley Manning amounted to ESPIONAGE, among other charges, and should subject him to life in prison. Manning's supporters, however, painted the small-framed former intelligence analyst as a courageous whistle-blower. Manning's case continued in 2013 when he pleaded guilty to 10 of 22 charges related to information he leaked to WikiLeaks, a website that publishes documents that are often classified or confidential. In July 2013, Manning was acquitted by military judge Col. Denise Lind of aiding the enemy, but was found guilty on 20 counts of violating portions of the Espionage Act.

Manning had been promoted from private first class to specialist in November 2009, at which time he had been deployed to Iraq. He worked as a computer analyst at a base near Baghdad and had access to networks containing classified information. Reports indicate that Manning is gay, and he was struggling with a number of personal issues. Several reports have stated that Manning planned to seek gender reassignment.

Manning joined the U.S. Army in 2007 after growing up in Oklahoma. He was apparently homeless for some time before enlisting in the service. His mental and emotional problems interfered with his military career. With his small frame—5'2", 105 pounds—he was allegedly the subject of bullying, and he often lashed back. He struck another solider and at one point overturned a table in a conference room. His actions led the army to demote Manning to the rank of private first class.

During his time in Baghdad, Manning had come into contact with Adrian Lamo, a computer hacker known for breaking into the secured computer networks of Microsoft and the *New York Times*. Manning introduced himself to Lamo as "an army intelligence analyst, deployed to eastern Baghdad, pending discharge for 'adjustment disorder.'" Manning also stated that he had nearly full access to the military's classified network for the previous eight months.

During their online conversations, Manning bragged to Lamo about the amount of information Manning could access. Lamo later gave logs of messages to the *Washington Post*. In those messages, Manning said he could retrieve documents from "a database of half a million events during the Iraq war...from 2004 to 2009...with reports, date time groups, lat-lon locations, [and] casualty figures." Manning also claimed he could obtain files related to some 260,0000 diplomatic cables "explaining how the first world exploits the third, in detail, from an internal perspective."

Manning told Lamo that he had already supplied classified information to WikiLeaks, the website created by the Australian Julian Assange and designed to publish secret information. Manning claimed to Lamo he had provided WikiLeaks with access to video footage of Army airstrikes in 2007 and 2009, each of which allegedly involved the shooting of civilians. Other information given to WikiLeaks included about 500,000 military reports as well as 250,000 diplomatic cables.

Concerned with the information Manning was releasing, Lamo in May 2010 contacted military authorities to report Manning. According to an article in *Wired* magazine, Lamo said "I wouldn't have done this if lives weren't in danger. He was in a war zone and basically trying to vacuum up as much classified information as he could, and just throwing it up into the air." WikiLeaks published much of this information during 2010.

Private Bradley Manning is escorted from a military court in Fort Meade, MD on June 6, 2012.
ALEX WONG/GETTY IMAGES

On July 6, 2010, the army issued a press release stating that army prosecutors had charged Manning with violating **Articles** 92 and 134 of the Uniform Code of Military Justice. The army alleged that Manning violated Article 92 by "transferring classified data onto his personal computer and adding unauthorized software to a classified computer system." The charges under Article 134 included eight different specifications, alleging the following: (1) violating 18 U.S.C. § 793 by communicating, transmitting, and delivering national defense information to an unauthorized source; (2) violating 18 U.S.C. § 1030(a)(1) by disclosing classified information concerning the national defense with reason to believe that the information would cause injury to the United States; and (3) violating 18 U.S.C. § 1030(a)(2) by exceeding authorized access to obtain classified information from a U.S. department or agency.

On March 1, 2011, the Army replaced the original charges with a total of 22 charges. Among the new charges were that Manning had aided the enemy, stolen public records, and illegally transmitted defense information. Although the espionage violations were lesser charges, together they carry a maximum sentence of 136 years in prison.

Manning's trial was scheduled to begin in February 2013. On February 28, 2013, he pleaded guilty to 10 of the charges. At his hearing, Manning said to the judge, "No one associated with [WikiLeaks] pressured me into sending any more information. I take full responsibility." However, he did not plead guilty to aiding the enemy or committing espionage, and convictions of those offenses would be more serious than the charges to which he pleaded guilty. He told the judge that he thought the release of information "might be embarrassing" to the United States but did not think the information would damage the country.

Manning has become something of a folk hero among those who have opposed the U.S. military presence in Iraq and elsewhere. Supporters have created a website known as "Free Bradley Manning," and Facebook and Twitter members have set up similar support pages on those sites. An editorial in the *Los Angeles Times* opined that military prosecutors should have considered backing off of the additional charges and just required Manning to serve the sentence based on the charges to which he pleaded guilty. Others, however, said that Manning damaged national security through his actions and should face all of the potential consequences.

On July 31, 2013, Manning was acquitted of the charges of aiding the enemy and unauthorized possession of information relating to national defense. He was found guilty on 20 counts of violating the Espionage Act, including the theft of U.S. Southern Command records and STATE DEPARTMENT cables, among other charges. The judge sentenced Manning to thirty-five years in a military prison on August 21. Just prior to his sentencing, he issued an apology for his actions to the military court, saying "I'm sorry that my actions hurt people ... I'm sorry that they hurt the United States" (Savage, August 15, 2013).

In a related action, several news organizations petitioned the military courts to request access to documents filed in Manning's trial. The U.S. Army Court of Criminal Appeals denied the petition, and the U.S. Court of Appeals for the Armed Forces dismissed the appeal. The latter court ruled that it lacked jurisdiction to compel the trial court to give access to the documents. *Center for Constitutional Rights v. United States*, 72 M.J. 126 (2013).

Military Sexual Assaults Create Jurisdictional Debate

Still waters run deep, and the undercurrent of dissatisfaction with the military's handling of sexual **assault** allegations over the years was exactly that: an undercurrent. Then it surfaced in 2013. What first caused the focus was the Pentagon's release of the U.S. Department of Defense's (DOD) massive study (based on a confidential survey of 108,000 active duty members of the armed forces) of sexual assaults within the military. It revealed that, of the 26,000 members of the military who said they were sexually assaulted in 2012 alone, the military reported only 3,374 incidents.

And then, as if on cue and nearly concurrent with the release of the report, came the 2013 poster child for the alarming statistic. Shortly after midnight on May 5, 2013, outside a Crystal City, Virginia bar, Air Force Lt. Col. Jeffrey Krusinski was arrested for sexual **battery** after groping a woman's breasts and buttocks in the bar's parking lot. She beat him off with her cell phone until Arlington County police came. The 41-year-old arrestee, Col. Krusinski, happened to be the officer in charge of the U.S. Air Force's Sexual ASSAULT Prevention Program.

Although the Air Force made known that Col. Krusinski was "removed from his position immediately" upon information of his arrest, DEFENSE DEPARTMENT officials attempted to take the case away from Arlington authorities, asking that they "relinquish prosecution" and turn the matter over to the military. "We didn't," said Arlington County Commonwealth Attorney Theo Stamos (PROSECUTOR) in a *Washington Post* article reporting the story. Stamos also believes that this was the first time, in her nearly two decades of locally prosecuting members of the military ("being where we are in Arlington"), that the military had asked for a case. It surprised her.

Krusinski had no comment for media reporters after his ARRAIGNMENT in Arlington County court. Trial was set for late July 2013 on the **misdemeanor** charge of sexual BATTERY. He faced a maximum punishment of $2,500 in fines and up to one year in jail. On the day following Krusinski's arrest, the *Washington Post*'s Craig Whitlock learned (and reported) that Air Force Lt. Gen. Susan J. Helms granted **clemency** in 2012 to an Air Force captain convicted of sexual assault, explaining in an internal memo that she found his testimony more credible than that of his accuser. Just weeks earlier, in February 2013, Air Force Lt. Gen. Craig A. Franklin dismissed a jury verdict convicting a star fighter pilot of sexual assault and ordered his release from prison. An Air Force spokesperson said the general reviewed the entire trial record and determined that the evidence did not prove guilt **beyond a reasonable doubt**. In early June 2013, a Navy judge, residing over a pretrial hearing, ruled that two military defendants in sexual assault cases could not be punitively discharged because President Obama, in public remarks to the media, exercised "unlawful command influence" when he said offenders should be "prosecuted, stripped of their positions, court-martialed, fired, dishonorably discharged. Period."

This type of internal self-policing and self-redeeming within the military was precisely what led to heated Congressional debate in Washington. At a White House news conference, President BARACK OBAMA, expressing ZERO TOLERANCE, told reporters that he had ordered Defense Secretary Chuck Hagel to "step up" investigation and response. Hagel told reporters that the Pentagon was instituting a new plan that orders service chiefs to incorporate sexual assault programs into their commands. Under Hagel's plan (to which commanders had until November 1, 2013 to report back), the military was to propose new ways to hold commanders more accountable for sexual assaults occurring within their services.

But that was not enough for Congress. In June, the House passed a defense bill that would strip commanders of their authority to dismiss COURT-MARTIAL findings, would establish minimum sentences for sexual assault convictions, permit victims to apply for a permanent change of station or unit transfer, and ensure that convicted offenders left the military. The SENATE Armed Forces Committee had its own wish list, including mandatory review of internal decisions by commanders to not prosecute sexual assault, making retaliation (for reporting an assault) a crime, and automatic dishonorable discharges for convicted offenders. Further, military commanders would no longer be able to unilaterally overturn jury convictions.

Despite the tough talk and legislative intent to act on the matter in an expedited

manner, one main stumbling block impeded the momentum. There remained strong disagreement over whether military prosecutors rather than military commanders should have the power to decide which sexual assault cases to prosecute. Senator Kirsten E. Gillibrand (D-NY) garnered an impressive coalition of bipartisan support for giving military prosecutors the power. However, longtime Armed Forces Committee Chairman Carl Levin (D-MI) rejected it, hinting that he would not go against Defense Secretary Hagel and top military brass who did not want commanders' powers removed. "It is the chain of command that can and must be held accountable if it fails to change a military culture," he said during one hearing. Meanwhile, Senator Claire McCaskill (D-MO), also on the Armed Forces Committee, was holding up the nomination of Lt. Gen. Helms for vice commander of the Air Force Space Command, pending additional information about Helms's decision to overturn a jury conviction in a sexual assault case.

Some key findings in the released 300+ page DOD report ("2012 Workplace and Gender Relations Survey of Active Duty Members") included one that showed 6.1 percent of women and 1.2 percent of men indicated experiencing unwanted sexual contact in 2012. The most complained-of conduct was unwanted sexual touching. Sixty-seven percent of the negative experiences occurred at a military installation, 41 percent during work day/duty hours. Males were identified as the offenders in 94 percent of the experiences, females in one percent, and five percent indicated that the offenders were both male and female.

Former service members and military sexual assault victims Anu Bhagwati, BriGette McCoy, Rebekah Havrilla, and Brian Lewis testify before the Senate Armed Services Committee in Washington, D.C., March 2013.
WIN MCNAMEE/GETTY IMAGES

The top three categories of offenders were military coworkers (57 percent), another military person (40 percent), and another military person of higher rank or grade who was not in their chain of command (38 percent). Exactly half (50 percent) indicated the offender had used some degree of physical force, with 17 percent also reporting that the offender threatened to ruin their reputation/career if they did not consent. Alcohol (mostly) or drugs (minorly) were involved in roughly half of all incidents.

MURDER

The unlawful killing of another human being without justification or excuse.

Connecticut Elementary School Shooting Kills 20 Children

On the morning of December 14, 2012, a young man forcefully entered an elementary school in Sandy Hook, Connecticut. He shot the school's principal and school psychologist before heading to classrooms. He shot children and teachers during the rampage. By the time the shootings ended, 20 young children were dead along with six adults. The shooter, 20-year-old Adam Lanza, committed SUICIDE before authorities could apprehend him.

It was one of the most deadly mass shootings in U.S. history. The killings occurred just five years after a gunman killed 32 people at Virginia Polytechnic Institute and State University. The Sandy Hook slaughter was the deadliest shooting that has occurred in a public school in U.S. history. The nation spent weeks mourning the victims.

Sandy Hook Elementary School had 456 enrolled students as of early December 2012. The school developed a policy under which its doors were locked at 9:30 a.m. Just before that time, though, teachers and administrators reportedly heard gun shots near the front of the school. School principal Dawn Hochsprung and school psychologist Mary Sherlach, along with a teacher named Natalie Hammond, confronted the shooter, Lanza.

Lanza was dressed in black clothing and wore a vest. He was armed with a semiautomatic Bushmaster .223-caliber rifle as well as two handguns and a shotgun. He had 10 magazines that contained 30 rounds each, along with bullets for the handgun and the shotgun. He was a thin young man who was reportedly withdrawn and lived at home with his mother. He was also at one time a student at Sandy Hook.

Lanza shot and killed both Hochsprung and Sherlach. He also shot and injured Hammond. By the time he had shot the women, they had alerted others that a shooter was in the building. He walked toward a first-grade classroom, where students were trying to hide in a bathroom. Most of those students as well as a substitute teacher named Lauren Rousseau were shot and killed. The lone surviving child was able to lay still and play dead.

Lanza then went to another first-grade classroom. Several students were hiding under desks, while others hid in a closet. Victoria Leigh Soto, the teacher, was walking toward the door to lock it when Lanza entered. Lanza killed the children hiding under the desks. One of the children who was soon shot yelled at others to run away, and six of the children who did so survived. Soto attempted to protect other children who had left their hiding places to try to run to safety. Lanza shot her and several of those students. Eleven students in Soto's class survived, including five children who hid in a closet.

Moments later, Lanza shot and killed a teacher's aide named Anna Marie Murphy, who was trying to protect a six-year-old special needs child. Another teacher's aide named Rachel D'Avino was also murdered while she tried to protect her students. Other teachers in the building were able to protect students by hiding the children in bathrooms, closets, or part of the school's library. Lanza bypassed some rooms and was unable to enter other parts.

The entire slaughter lasted less than 15 minutes. Lanza shot every victim with more than one shot. He shot one of the children 11 times. He killed a total of 20 children in the two first-grade classrooms, and he murdered six adults. He shot a total of 154 rounds during that time. When Lanza saw police officers enter the building, he hid before shooting himself in the head with one of his handguns.

The killing had actually begun before Lanza headed to the elementary school. His mother, Nancy, had purchased all of the guns Lanza used plus several more. She had also reportedly taken her sons to a shooting range to teach them to shoot. On the morning of December 14, Adam Lanza shot his mother multiple times, killing her as she lay in her bed.

Investigators soon tried to determine what could make a 20-year-old commit such unspeakable acts. Lanza had no criminal record and lived five miles from the school where he shot the children. He had once attended Sandy Hook for a time, but his mother removed him from the public school and enrolled him at a Catholic school. He became an honors student at Newtown High School and later attended Western Connecticut State University.

Although intelligent, he was also socially awkward. He was diagnosed at a young age with a form of autism, and other reports suggested that he had a personality disorder. He also reportedly had been bullied in high school, and his mother had expressed concern over his mental state. His mother and father divorced when he was young, and his mother reportedly supported herself and her two sons with ALIMONY payments and her DIVORCE **settlement**.

Lanza's father made the following statement one day after the killings:

> Our hearts go out to the families and friends who lost loved ones and to all those who were injured. Our family is grieving along with all those who have been affected by this enormous tragedy. No words can truly express how heartbroken we are. We are in a state of disbelief and trying to find whatever answers we can. We too are asking why.

Authorities found disturbing evidence when they visited Lanza's home. Officers found more than 1,600 rounds of ammunition along with 11 knives, 3 samurai swords, a pistol, and a bayonet. He had a military-style uniform in his bedroom, and he had saved pictures of a corpse from a shooting at Northern Illinois University in 2008.

Lanza spent much of his time in his basement playing violent video games such as "Call of Duty." Investigators found gun targets in his basement as well as books related to autism. Just weeks before the shootings at the elementary school, Lanza's mother found sketches of dead bodies in his room, and she told friends that she was concerned about his mental state.

Some parents of the young victims blamed Lanza's upbringing as a cause for the shooting. David Wheeler lost his six-year-old son in the massacre. He told a reporter, "It was like a set of

An informal memorial for the victims of the Newtown, CT school shooting, December 2012.
EMMANUEL DUNAND/ AFP/GETTY IMAGE

dominos, in many ways, just waiting for the first one to tick over. I think it is pretty obvious to anyone who looks that something was very, very wrong in there."

The Sandy Hook shooting, along with the killings at a movie theater in Aurora, Colorado, renewed the debate about GUN CONTROL in the United States. Many called on Congress and state legislatures to enact stricter limits on gun ownership, especially with regard to **assault** weapons and background checks. Other groups, such as the NATIONAL RIFLE ASSOCIATION, have opposed such efforts, arguing that strict gun control laws would not have prevented the tragedy at Sandy Hook.

Former Murder Suspect Casey Anthony Faces Numerous Legal Challenges

Former MURDER suspect Casey Anthony continued to have legal problems in 2012 and 2013. Her two-year-old daughter, Caylee, died in 2008, but Anthony was acquitted of murder and **manslaughter** charges in 2011. She was convicted on other grounds based on evidence that she provided false information to police and investigators, and she faces a civil suit brought by a former nanny based on a **libel** claim. Faced with nearly $800,000 in liabilities, Anthony filed for BANKRUPTCY.

Caylee Anthony was last seen alive on June 15, 2008. During the investigation into Caylee's whereabouts, Anthony had supplied investigators with numerous stories that turned out to be false. For instance, Anthony told police that she worked at Universal Orlando Resort, but deputies discovered that she did not. Anthony also alleged that she had dropped Caylee off with a nanny named Zenaida Gonzalez on June 9. However, Gonzalez denied that she knew Anthony or that she had taken possession of Caylee. Police arrested Anthony on July 17, 2008, and detained her on charges of murder, child neglect, lying to investigators, and interfering with a criminal investigation.

In 2008, Gonzalez brought her civil suit against Anthony, claiming that Anthony committed **defamation** by telling investigators that Gonzalez had taken possession of Caylee. Gonzalez's lawyers were unable to depose Anthony before her criminal trial, though, so the case did not proceed until after Anthony's ACQUITTAL.

Anthony's murder trial in 2011 created a media frenzy. News and talk shows devoted many hours to the trial's coverage. Many were convinced that Anthony was guilty, and when a jury of five men and seven women acquitted her, the verdict sparked an outrage. Prosecutors were able to convict Anthony on four counts related to false information and interference with the criminal investigation, and Anthony received a one-year PROBATION period. Anthony went into hiding after her acquittal, making no public appearances until she appeared in court in 2013.

Anthony could not remain out of the news while she was effectively in hiding. She received a SUBPOENA to give a DEPOSITION in Gonzalez's civil case just one day after the 2011 acquittal. Anthony's attorneys filed numerous motions to delay a trial in the case, while Gonzalez's attorneys proceeded in their efforts to issue a subpoena to Anthony to require her to appear in person at the trial. In April 2012, Gonzalez appeared on the "Dr. Phil" show, saying she wanted Anthony to apologize.

One year after Anthony's acquittal, her attorney Jose Baez released a book titled *Presumed Guilty—Casey Anthony: The Inside Story*. He claimed in the book that Anthony's father, George Anthony, had sexually abused her starting at a young age. The book also alleged that the abuse escalated into INCEST and that Anthony's father may have impregnated Anthony. In other words, Casey Anthony's father may have also been Caylee Anthony's father. According to Baez, Anthony learned to lie at a young age because of the abuse, which was a point that Baez had raised before the jury at Anthony's trial. Baez likewise suggested that George Anthony had actually killed Caylee to hide the incest.

Anthony appealed her four convictions, and Florida's Fifth **District Court** of Appeals heard the appeal on January 8, 2013. At her trial, Anthony's lawyers argued that several statements made to police should be suppressed because they were made before she received *Miranda* warnings. On appeal, Anthony argued that her convictions for making false statements should be set aside because the trial court erred in not suppressing the statements. The **appellate court** disagreed, finding that Anthony was not in police CUSTODY and subject to interrogation at the time she made the statements.

On the other hand, the court agreed with Anthony that the trial court should not have convicted her on four separate counts for each of the statements that proved to be false. Two of the statements that led to convictions related to her employment at Universal Studios Orlando. A third statement related to Anthony's allegations that she left Caylee with Gonzalez, while a fourth related to a statement that Caylee had called Casey Anthony on July 15, 2008. The court concluded that the state had failed to prove four separate instances of providing false information, and on January 25, 2013, the court set aside two of Anthony's convictions. *Anthony v. State*, No. 5D11-2357, 2013 WL 275533 (Fla. App. Jan. 25, 2013).

Anthony's legal problems only continued after the **appellate** court's decision, though. On the same day that the APPELLATE court set aside her convictions, Anthony filed for bankruptcy. The filing indicated that Anthony owed creditors a total of $792,119.23. At the same time, Anthony had assets of only $1,084. Many of the creditors listed were consultants hired for Anthony's trial, but the filing did not list specific amounts owed for many of these creditors. She owed Baez a total of $500,000 for his legal fees. She also owed money to several agencies for investigative fees and costs. These agencies included the Orange County Sheriffs Office ($145,660.21 owed), the Florida Department of Law Enforcement ($61,505.12 owed), and the Metropolitan Bureau of Investigation in Orlando ($10,283.90 owed). Moreover, Anthony owed $68,540 to the INTERNAL REVENUE SERVICE, along with other smaller fees to a variety of other creditors.

Critics suggested that Anthony filed the bankruptcy petition to avoid liability in the civil lawsuits she faces. In addition to the suit brought by Gonzalez, Anthony also faced a lawsuit brought by a search-and-rescue organization known as Texas EquuSearch, which allegedly spent $100,000 searching for Caylee. Moreover, a meter reader named Roy Kronk, who found Caylee's body in 2008, sued Anthony when Anthony's lawyers suggested that Kronk was responsible for the killing.

Anthony claimed to have no regular income and that she lived off the generosity of others. One item of Anthony's "property" that could have significant value, though, is the rights to her life story. Bankruptcy **trustee** Stephen Meininger proposed that he should be able to sell these rights and claimed that two individuals had already offered as much as $12,000 for these rights.

George Zimmerman Acquitted in the Death of Trayvon Martin

It has become increasingly common for the American public to become engrossed with high-profile MURDER cases nearly every year. Examples of those include the 1995 trial of O.J. SIMPSON for the murders of his ex-wife, Nicole, and an acquaintance named Ronald Goldman; the 2005 trial of Scott Peterson for the murder of his **wife**, Laci; the 2011 trial of Casey Anthony for the death of her daughter, Caylee; and the 2013 trial of Jodi Arias for the murder of her boyfriend, Travis Alexander.

One of the most anticipated trials of 2013 began in June with the state's case against George Zimmerman for the death of teenager Trayvon Martin. Zimmerman pleaded not guilty to a charge of murder, claiming he acted in SELF-DEFENSE when he shot Martin outside of an apartment building in Sanford, Florida. On July 13, 2013, a jury of six women acquitted Zimmerman on all charges, sparking a national debate about whether race played a role in the verdict.

Neither the state nor Zimmerman disputed many of the facts, which occurred on February 26, 2012. Shortly after his 17th birthday, Martin visited his father in Sanford, which is near Orlando. While wearing a hooded sweatshirt commonly known as a "hoodie," Martin returned from 7-Eleven store and headed to the apartment of his father's fiancée. The teen carried a can of iced tea and a bag of Skittles.

What happened on the grounds of the apartment complex was the principal focus in the case against Zimmerman. He was part of a

George Zimmerman on trial in a Sanford, FL courtroom, June 24, 2013.
JOE BURBANK/ORLANDO SENTINEL/MCT VIA GETTY IMAGES

community watch program, and he called 911 to report Martin as a "suspicious guy." Zimmerman claims that when he encountered Martin, the teen knocked Zimmerman to the ground and began to slam Zimmerman's head into the concrete of a sidewalk. Zimmerman has claimed that he shot Martin in self-defense. Zimmerman's nose was bloody after the altercation, and he had marks on the back of his head. When officers originally detained Zimmerman, they found no evidence to contradict Zimmerman's account. Moreover, the police report noted that the back of Zimmerman's clothes were wet, suggesting that Zimmerman was on his back.

Police soon discovered, though, that some evidence contradicted Zimmerman's version of the story. Two neighbors told officers that Zimmerman was on top of Martin. Moreover, police discovered that Martin was on the phone with his girlfriend at the time of the skirmish. Eyewitnesses told police that Zimmerman did not appear to have a broken nose, and surveillance showed that Zimmerman had not been seriously injured.

The state formally charged Zimmerman with second-degree murder on April 11, 2012. He was released on bail after posting a $1 million bond on July 6, 2012. By that time,

Zimmerman's wife, Shellie, was charged with PERJURY based on statements she had made about their family finances. Because of these allegedly false statements, Zimmerman had been held in CUSTODY during the month of June. Shellie Zimmerman asked a Seminole County judge to dismiss the charge, but the judge in February 2013 denied the request.

In August 2012, George Zimmerman focused his attention on Judge Kenneth R. Lester, Jr. According to Zimmerman's lawyers, Lester made "gratuitous, disparaging remarks about Mr. Zimmerman's character; advocated for Mr. Zimmerman to be prosecuted for additional crimes; offered a personal opinion about the evidence for the prosecution; continued to **hold over** Mr. Zimmerman's head the threat of future CONTEMPT proceedings, and ultimately set a bond at $1,000,000." A Florida **appellate court** on August 2012 agreed with Zimmerman's motion to remove Lester from the case and appointed Circuit Judge Debra Nelson to preside over the trial.

While still awaiting trial in December 2012, Zimmerman filed a **defamation** suit against NBC based on allegations that the network had edited the content on a 911 recording. When the recording aired on NBC's *Today* show, it omitted a question asked by the 911 dispatcher about Martin's race. The edited version sounded as if Zimmerman had volunteered the information that Martin was black, possibly suggesting that Zimmerman had targeted Martin because of the teen's race. However, the dispatcher had asked whether Martin was white, black, or Hispanic, and Zimmerman responded to the question by stating, "He looks black."

Florida has adopted a "stand-your-ground" law, which allows a person to use DEADLY FORCE in self-defense when presented with an unlawful threat. The law does not require the DEFENDANT to retreat before acting. The defendant can request that the court hold a pretrial hearing to consider the self-defense. However, Zimmerman ultimately decided to forgo the hearing and argue his defense before the jury.

Zimmerman's trial began on June 24, 2013, with the parties arguing before six female jurors. PROSECUTOR John Guy opened the case by stating, "We are confident that at the end of this trial you will know in your head, in your heart, in your stomach that George Zimmerman did not shoot Trayvon Martin because he had to. He shot him

for the worst of all reasons, because he wanted to." In the OPENING STATEMENT for the defense, Zimmerman's attorney, Don West, told the jury that Martin had used a deadly weapon in the form of the concrete sidewalk, which was "no different than if he picked up a brick or smashed his head against a wall."

One of the key prosecution witnesses was Martin's girlfriend, Rachel Jeantel, who said she was on the phone with Martin just before the shooting. She said that Martin told someone to "get off" before the call abruptly ended. The prosecution also relied heavily on the tape of Zimmerman's 911 call. The recording revealed a voice screaming in the background. The prosecution called Martin's mother, Sybrina Fulton, to verify that the voice was Martin's.

On CROSS-EXAMINATION, Jeantel admitted to using the term "cracker" to refer to whites. Moreover, on cross-examination, a neighbor said that he saw Martin on top of Zimmerman while throwing punches in a manner described as "ground and pound," a term used in mixed martial arts.

The defense began to present its case on Friday, July 5. Zimmerman did not take the stand. His lawyers presented EXPERT TESTIMONY to establish that Zimmerman had suffered injuries that would make him fear for his life. Other witnesses indicated that Zimmerman was not physically able to defend himself in a fight. The defense otherwise focused on Zimmerman's dedication to the community.

During his **closing argument**, Zimmerman's attorney, Mark O'Mara, said that Zimmerman was "completely innocent." He noted, "I wish the verdict had guilty, not guilty, and completely innocent. I would ask you to check the last two." Regarding the evidence presented, O'Mara commented, "If it hasn't been proven, it's just not there. You can't fill in the gaps. You can't connect the dots. You're not allowed to."

The jury deliberated for less than two days before returning a verdict of not guilty. After the verdict's announcement, a crowd outside the courtroom protested, with several arguing that racism played a major role in the outcome. President BARACK OBAMA responded to the controversy by focusing on the struggles that African Americans often face. He stated:

There are very few African-American men in this country who haven't had the experience of being followed when they were shopping in a department store. That includes me. And there are very few African-American men who haven't had the experience of walking across the street and hearing the locks click on the doors of cars. That happens to me, at least before I was a senator. There are very few African-Americans who haven't had the experience of getting on an elevator and a woman clutching her purse nervously and holding her breath until she had a chance to get off. That happens often.

Following the verdict, the U.S. JUSTICE DEPARTMENT announced that it would review the case to decide whether to file federal charges against Zimmerman based on allegations that he committed a **hate crime**.

James Holmes Kills 12 and Injures 58 in Theater Shooting

Beginning at midnight on July 20, 2012, a movie theater in Aurora, Colorado, showed the premiere of the *Batman* sequel, *The Dark Knight Rises*. Some in the crowd were dressed in costumes similar to characters in the movie. Just minutes after the movie began, a person dressed in black threw a canister of tear gas into the audience and started shooting into the crowd. By the time the massacre had ended, 12 people were dead and another 58 were injured.

Police soon arrested and charged James Holmes, a former doctoral student at the University of Colorado. The slaughter at the theater stunned the nation, as did the revelation that Holmes had rigged his apartment to explode if anyone entered it. When police arrested him, Holmes claimed he was "The Joker," a villain in the Batman movies. Holmes had dyed his hair orange, and many of the pictures in the media showed Holmes with dyed hair and a disturbed look on his face. In May 2013, Holmes pleaded not guilty to the charges by reason of insanity.

A native of San Diego, Holmes graduated from the University of California, Riverside, with high honors in 2006. He was reportedly a very bright student, and he enrolled at the University of Colorado's School of Medicine in 2011 as a doctoral candidate in the school's neuroscience program. Other than a speeding ticket at the University of Colorado, authorities have no record that Holmes engaged in any wrongdoing while he was a student. Friends said that Holmes was shy but funny. Neighbors

reported that Holmes was laid back and usually kept to himself.

Holmes began to display alarming behavior months before the theater attack. In April 2012, he created an account on Match.com, which later featured pictures of him with orange hair, in which the headline of his account asked, "Will you visit me in prison?" His profile on AdultFriendFinder.com contained the same headline. On June 7, 2012, Holmes failed oral exams at the University of Colorado, and he began the process of withdrawing from the school that summer. Prosecutors later said that his failures on his exams directly led to his acts in the movie theater.

In May 2012, Holmes purchased several weapons, including canisters of tear gas, a .40-caliber pistol, a tactical shotgun, and a pair of handcuffs. On the same day he failed the exams in June, he bought a semiautomatic rifle along with bullets and a gun case. By the end of June, Holmes had purchased thousands of rounds for his various guns as well as hearing protection and a laser sight. He completed his purchases in July, buying enough armor that it covered his neck, arms, torso, legs, and groin. He bought additional guns just weeks before the shooting, plus gun powder and other materials.

Evidence showed that Holmes visited the Aurora theater several times before the July 20 shooting. Authorities found pictures on his phone from June 29. The pictures showed close-up shots of a door latch. He took more pictures of the theater's emergency doors on July 11. By that time, he had already purchased

James Holmes (left) sits with defense attorney Daniel King during a hearing in Arapahoe County, CO on June 4, 2013.
ANDY CROSS/THE DENVER POST VIA GETTY IMAGES

a ticket to the midnight showing of *The Dark Knight Rises* on July 20.

Surveillance video revealed that Holmes entered the Century 16 theater in Aurora at about midnight on July 20. He wore dark clothing, including a skull cap, but wore a light-colored shirt. An attendant retrieved the ticket on Holmes's phone, and Holmes then headed to the concession stand. He stood there for several minutes, according to one witness, before heading toward the theater showing the Batman movie.

Another witness said that just before the movie began at 12:20 a.m., a man dressed with a dark cap or bandana received a phone call and then propped open the emergency exit with his foot. Holmes apparently entered through that emergency door. Holmes tossed a canister of tear gas into the crowd, causing everyone to start screaming and running. Holmes then opened fire and hit many people in the audience. He killed 12, while 70 others were injured because of the bullets, tear gas, or other injuries that occurred in the commotion.

Holmes gathered his arms and left the theater. He returned to his car, and police arrested him while he stood next to the car. When the officers approached him, Holmes was still wearing the gas mask. He complied with all requests but appeared to be "very detached" from the situation. His behavior returned to bizarre, though, after being taken to the police station. At one point, he tried to take a staple out of a table and stick it into an electrical outlet.

Holmes admitted to officers that he had rigged his apartment to explode. The purpose of this was to have authorities send officers to the scene of the fire rather than the theater. When officers arrived at the apartment, they found materials containing glycerin, gun powder, and homemade napalm. Holmes had also soaked his carpet with gas and oil. He told police that he had developed systems that would trigger the explosives to detonate if someone had stepped on a trip wire. Holmes had also constructed a remote control that would cause the materials to explode.

Prosecutors originally charged Holmes on a total of 152 counts, including 24 counts of first-degree MURDER and 116 counts of attempted first-degree murder. The media showed images of the orange-haired Holmes appearing confused or dazed. Prosecutors added more attempted-murder counts to the charges in October. Holmes appeared at a three-day hearing in January 2013, where prosecutors presented the evidence that showed **probable cause** for the charges. A PUBLIC DEFENDER represented Holmes.

Holmes initially pleaded not guilty. Holmes's lawyers filed a one-page motion in May 2013, informing the court that Holmes would plead not guilty by reason of insanity and asking the court to accept the change in pleas. On June 4, Judge Carlos Samour, Jr., accepted Holmes's plea and ordered Holmes to undergo mental testing. Moreover, the judge ruled that the prosecution should have access to a notebook Holmes sent to his psychiatrist.

An internal review conducted by the Aurora fire department showed there were critical delays between the time that the shootings were reported and the time that the department contacted emergency medical workers. Moreover, ambulances became trapped by other cars along with about 1,400 people fleeing the theater. Police resorted to using their own cars to drive the most critically injured up a grassy hill behind the theater.

PATENTS

Rights, granted to inventors by the federal government, pursuant to its power under Article I, Section 8, Clause 8, of the U.S. Constitution, that permit them to exclude others from making, using, or selling an invention for a definite, or restricted, period of time.

Apple Wins $1 Billion in Patent Suit Against Samsung

Global electronics/smartphone competitors Apple Inc. (iPad, iPhone, etc.) and Samsung (Galaxy tablet, etc.) have been facing off in court with each other for years. At any given time, there are likely a dozen pending suits between them in several countries (including Germany and Australia), and still another U.S. patent INFRINGEMENT trial was scheduled for March 2014 in California. But on August 24, 2012, Apple won a decisive victory against Samsung when a nine-member jury awarded Apple Inc. $1.049 billion in damages in the case *Apple Inc. v. Samsung Electronics Co. Ltd.* No. C11-1846, N.D. Cal. The case stems from a lawsuit filed by Apple in 2011 for patent infringement. The parties made strange legal bedfellows, as Apple was the largest customer for components manufactured by Samsung, and both are among the most recognized consumer brand names in the global market.

Following a trial that lasted just under three weeks, three days of deliberations, and a jury verdict form that asked them more than 700 questions, the seven-men, two-women federal jury found that Samsung had infringed on several Apple PATENTS on mobile devices. The victory was near complete for Apple, as the jury also rejected all of Samsung's counterclaims. (Samsung had asked for more than $422 million, also alleging patent infringement by Apple on five of Samsung's patents.) Moreover, its verdict concluded that Samsung's infringement had been willful, and Samsung could have been liable for treble damages. Samsung had also challenged the validity of the patents themselves, but the jury found all seven subject patents to be valid.

Korea-based Samsung is the world's largest maker of smartphones, selling roughly three times as many smartphones using Android (the Google operating system) as Apple sells iPhones. But the gist of the case involved how much Apple's iPhone had inspired Samsung to overhaul its own mobile phones. One of the key patents allegedly infringed in this case covered a method of distinguishing between one-finger scrolling on a touch-screen device, and two-fingered gestures such as pinching to zoom out of an image. (It did not cover the actual pinch-to-zoom feature itself.)

As to physical design of the actual phone, the jury found that Samsung had infringed on Apple patents with at least one phone or tablet in relation to iPhone's face, screen, and speaker

An Apple iPad 2 and iPhone 4S (left) sit side by side with a Samsung Galaxy Tab 10.1 tablet and S3 smartphone.
SEONGJOON CHO/
BLOOMBERG/GETTY
IMAGES

slot; the shape of iPhone's face, rounded corners and bezel; and the icon arrangement on the home screen. As to software design, the jury found that Samsung had infringed on Apple patents for the bounce-back effect (when a user tries to scroll beyond the end of a list or image); scrolling, pinching, and zooming; and tap-to-zoom and center. One minor loss for Apple: the jury found no infringement of Apple's D'889 patent by Samsung's Galaxy Tab 10.1.

Following the verdict, Apple filed for preliminary injunctions prohibiting Samsung from selling the infringing products. But Apple's legal battle was also to sandbag the exponential growth of Google's Android operating system used by Samsung and other smartphone makers. Android phones made up roughly 68 percent of global smartphone shipments, compared to Apple's 17 percent share, according to IDC market research. Global smartphone revenues were expected to exceed $250 billion, according to a *Wall Street Journal* article quoting estimates from Credit Suisse.

This patent case was particularly complex, as it involved software features, hardware design, and high-speed communication features, as well as "trade-dress," a claim concept for the overall look and feel of a device. The trial also added to the debate about the future of U.S. intellectual PROPERTY LAW. Critics have complained that the U.S. PATENT AND TRADEMARK OFFICE grants too many patents; others question whether laymen juries can correctly decide such complex cases. In the *Wall Street Journal* article following the verdict, Christal Sheppard, assistant professor of law at the University of

Nebraska College of Law, said, "Software patents are clogging the system at every possible point . . . This could be the bellweather case that goes to the SUPREME COURT to decide what invention in the 21st century really means for software."

.

Association for Molecular Pathology v. Myriad Genetics, Inc.

In an important case with far-reaching consequences, the U.S. SUPREME COURT, in *Association for Molecular Pathology v. Myriad Genetics, Inc.,* 133 S. Ct. 2107 (2013), was asked to determine whether the Patent Act allowed PATENTS on human genes. Despite the complexity of the subject, a unanimous Court held that naturally-occurring gene sequences, and their natural derivative products, were not patentable. However, the creation of new (not naturally-occurring) products produced in a laboratory exempts them as being products of nature. Accordingly, laboratory manipulation of gene sequences refined by synthetic processes to create molecules not found in nature are patent-eligible.

Human genes that form the basis for hereditary traits are encoded as deoxyribonucleic acid (DNA), taking the shape of a double helix. Each "cross-bar" in the DNA helix is made up of two chemically joined nucleotides: each of the four different types of nucleotides binds with one of the other types naturally to form a cross-bar. If the bonds between two types of nucleotides separate, the DNA double helix unwinds into two single strands.

DNA and its informational sequences, along with processes that create amino acids and proteins, are naturally-occurring within cells. However, scientists can extract DNA from cells, using well-known laboratory methods, to isolate, study, and often, manipulate the sequences. Scientists also know how to create synthetic DNA, referred to as complementary DNA, or cDNA.

Changes in genetic sequences are referred to as mutations, and can be as small as the alteration of a single nucleotide, which affects only a single letter in the genetic code. Larger changes, conversely, involving deletion, rearrangement, or duplication of hundreds or thousands of nucleotides, have more wide-reaching consequences, including the elimination, misplacement, or even duplication of entire genes. Mutations may be harmless or may cause or increase risk of disease and malformation. Hence, the study of genetics and gene manipulation can lead to significant and valuable medical discoveries.

Myriad Genetics claimed such a medical breakthrough. It discovered the precise location and sequence of the BRCA1 and BRCA2 genes, mutations of which can dramatically increase risk of breast and ovarian cancer. Prior to discovery of these genes, scientists knew that heredity played a role in cancer risk, but they did not know which genes were associated with those cancers. Now, knowledge of the precise location of BRCA1 and BRCA2 gave Myriad the opportunity to determine their nucleotide sequence. That information, in turn, enabled Myriad to develop medical tests capable of detecting mutations in a person's BRCA1 and BRCA2 genes.

Once it found the precise location and sequence of BRCA1 and BRCA2 genes, Myriad applied for and was granted several patents on those genes, including mutations. Myriad's theory of patent-eligibility was that of isolating and identifying the genes from the human body. From there, Myriad claimed several DNA molecules, variations, or sequential mutations associated with BRCA1 and BRCA2 genes, e.g., from U.S. Patent No. 5,747,282, Myriad claimed "6. An isolated DNA molecule coding for a mutated form of the BRCA2 polypeptide set forth in SEQ ID NO:2, wherein said mutated form of the BRCA2 polypeptide is associated with susceptibility to cancer."

Section 101 of the Patent Act (35 U.S.C. § 101) states,

> Whoever invents or discovers any new and useful . . . composition of matter, or any new and useful improvement thereof, may obtain a patent therefore, subject to the conditions and requirements of this title.

According to Myriad, the patents would give it exclusive right to isolate an individual's BRCA1 and BRCA2 genes, as well as the exclusive right to synthetically create the BRCA cDNA. Under the Patent Act's 35 U.S.C. § 154(a)(1), Myriad would have the right to "exclude others from making" its patented composition of matter. Moreover, it would effectively have exclusive rights over diagnostic testing and further scientific research of these genes.

A rendering of the double helix structure formed by a DNA molecule.
FRITZ GORO/TIME & LIFE PICTURES/GETTY IMAGES

After obtaining the patents, Myriad began sending patent INFRINGEMENT letters to other entities that were offering BRCA testing services to women, resulting in settlements declaring that all "infringing activity" would cease. However, several years later, one of the settling researchers, along with several other doctors, medical associations, the Association for Molecular Pathology, and even medical patients, filed suit. The suit named as defendants not only Myriad, but also the U.S. PATENT AND TRADEMARK OFFICE, and sought a declaration that the patents were invalid because they covered "products of nature."

The **district court** granted **summary judgment** in favor of the plaintiffs. It ruled that isolating a gene does not alter its naturally-occurring fundamental properties. The U.S. **Circuit Court** of Appeals for the Federal Circuit reversed, holding that isolated genes were chemically distinct from their natural state found in the human body. After remand on a matter of standing, the **appellate court** held that both isolated DNA and cDNA were patent-eligible. All three **appellate** justices, however, had differing views on whether the act of isolating DNA, i.e., separating a gene or sequence of nucleotides from the rest of the chromosome, was an inventive act eligible for patent.

A unanimous Supreme Court affirmed in part and reversed in part. Justice CLARENCE THOMAS, writing for the Court, walked through the Constitutional basis of the patent grant, Congress's broad definition of patent eligibility, and the Court's imposition of limitations (excluding laws of nature, natural phenomena, and abstract ideas). Such exclusions "are basic tools of scientific and technological work" that lie beyond the domain of patent protection. *Mayo Collaborative Services v. Prometheus Laboratories*, 132 S. Ct. 1289, 182 L. Ed. 2d 321 (2010).

Summarizing all facts, the Court then noted that it was undisputed that Myriad did not create or alter any genetic information encoded in the BRCA1 and BRCA2 genes (the location and order of the nucleotides existed in nature before Myriad "discovered" them), but merely claimed patent for identifying their precise location and genetic sequence.

Ultimately, the Court held that a naturally occurring DNA segment was a product of nature and Myriad's DNA claim of patent for this was erroneously granted. Notwithstanding, the Court further found that the creation of new products, such as gene sequences created in a laboratory by synthetic processes to create molecules that do not occur naturally, are patent-eligible. Accordingly, cDNA is patent-eligible because its creation results in an exons-only molecule, which is not naturally occurring.

The Court took important note to declare what it was *not* deciding in this case. The matter before it did not involve method claims, patents on new applications of knowledge about the BRCA1 and BRCA2 genes, or the patentability of DNA wherein the order of naturally-occurring nucleotides has been altered, as such scientific alteration of the genetic code presents a different inquiry entirely.

(Justice ANTONIN SCALIA filed a separate concurrence in part and concurrence in the judgment.)

Bowman v. Monsanto

Sometimes, litigants may be too clever for their own good, implied Justice ELENA KAGAN, writing for a unanimous U.S. SUPREME COURT in *Bowman v. Monsanto Company*, 133 S. Ct. 1761 (2013). Indiana farmer Vernon Bowman had claimed a loophole in his purchase

agreement with Monsanto that prohibited him from saving genetically patented soybean seeds from his harvested crop for reuse in later crops. Instead, he bought bulk seed from a grain elevator (used for animal feed, food products, industrial use, etc.), hoping that some of Monsanto's patented seeds would be in the mix. They were. After culling out the valuable Monsanto seeds, he kept their progeny going for eight growing seasons. After discovering this practice, Monsanto sued him for patent INFRINGEMENT. He lost, to the tune of $84,456. The Supreme Court affirmed.

The legal question before the Court in *Bowman* invoked the patent law doctrine of "patent exhaustion." The specific question was whether a farmer who bought patented seeds may reproduce them through planting and harvesting, without infringing on the patent holder. The Court unequivocally confirmed that he may not.

Monsanto is one of three corporations controlling more than half of the global seed market (along with DuPont and Syngenta). Monsanto is also the creator and patent-owner of Roundup, trade-name for a ubiquitous glyphosate-based herbicide (e.g., weed killer) sold globally. Monsanto invented and was granted a U.S. patent for its genetically-modified soybean seed, known as Roundup Ready, because its genetic alteration allows it to survive exposure to glyphosate-based herbicides. Thus, farmers who use this seed can use glyphosate-based weed killers without damaging their crops.

Growers who purchase the desirable Roundup Ready soybean seed must sign Monsanto's special licensing agreement that restricts the use of the seeds to one growing season, and prohibits the saving or harvesting of soybeans for replanting (since soybeans are in themselves the "seeds" that are planted). The agreement's terms limit growers to either consuming or selling their soybean crop as a commodity, generally to grain elevators or agricultural processors. Likewise, the terms effectively prevent farmers from reproducing their own Roundup Ready seeds, forcing them instead to purchase from Monsanto each season.

Vernon Bowman purchased Roundup Ready each year for his first crop of the season. In accordance with Monsanto's agreement, he used all of the seed for planting and sold his entire grain crop to a grain elevator. However, considering a second crop "risky" because of late-season unpredictability, he was unwilling to pay the premium price for Roundup Ready again. Knowing that the majority of local farmers used Roundup Ready seed, Bowman went to a local grain elevator and purchased bulk "commodity soybeans" intended for animal or human consumption or agricultural processing. But Bowman instead planted the soybeans, treated his fields with glyphosate-based weed killer, and culled the surviving plants, which in turn, produced a new crop of soybeans carrying the Roundup Ready trait. These seeds he saved for his late-season plantings, continuing until he had produced eight crops in this manner.

Monsanto sued Bowman for patent infringement. Bowman defended by raising the doctrine of patent exhaustion. Under such doctrine, the legal **purchaser** or subsequent owner of a patented product may resell or dispose of the product as he sees fit. Bowman argued that Monsanto could not control his use of the soybeans because they were the subject of a prior authorized sale (from local growers to the grain elevator).

The **district court** granted judgment to Monsanto and awarded damages of $84,456. This was affirmed by the U.S. Court of Appeals for the Federal Circuit (which handles most patent appeals). The **appellate court** explained that a purchaser's "right to use" following an authorized sale does not include "the right to construct an essentially new article on the template of the original, for the right to make the article remains with the patentee." 657 F.3d 1344 at 1348.

In affirming that decision, the Supreme Court summarized the "patent exhaustion" doctrine by noting that the initial authorized sale of a patented item terminates all patent rights to that item. Thus, by "exhausting" the patent-holder's **monopoly** in that item, the sale gives the purchaser or subsequent owner "the right to use or sell" it as he sees fit. But, the doctrine terminates patent-holders' rights only as to the particular item sold. It does not affect the patent-holder's right to prevent a purchaser from making new copies of the patented item. In this case, Bowman reproduced Monsanto's patented invention, so the exhaustion doctrine

Seed chipping technology at a Monsanto facility in St. Louis, MO.
BRENT STIRTON/GETTY IMAGES

did not protect him. Although he had the right to re-sell the patented soybeans or consume them himself (or feed to his animals), he could not copy or reproduce them without Monsanto's permission.

To hold otherwise would gut the entire purpose of patent protection: after years of research, Monsanto would only receive reward from the first seed sold, and other seed companies could reproduce the product at will and market it to growers *ad infinitum*. Accordingly, said the Court, "The exhaustion doctrine is limited to the 'particular item' sold to avoid just such a mismatch between invention and reward."

Bowman further contended that soybeans were self-replicating and/or sprouted on their own when not properly stored, and so "it was the planted soybean, not Bowman" himself, that made replicas of Monsanto's patented product. The Court humorously referred to this as the failed "blame-the-bean" defense, for Bowman was not a passive observer of this process. Rather, he purchased beans intended for consumption or processing from a grain elevator, planted them, applied a glyphosate-based weed-killer to cull out any plants that did not have the Roundup Ready genetic trait, saved the surviving beans for the next season, planted them, harvested more seeds, and continued this process for eight growing seasons.

The Court, in affirming the judgment, was quick to note that its holding herein was "limited," addressing only the situation before it, and not "every one involving a self-replicating product."

COURTS CONTINUALLY GRAPPLE WITH BIOTECHNOLOGY PATENT ISSUES

As recently as the 1970s, the biotechnology industry was practically nonexistent. Since that time, the industry has grown exponentially. By the mid-1990s, the industry had created more than 100,000 jobs and generated nearly $8 billion in revenues. This growth continued in the 2000s, as the biotechnology industry grew by an estimated 6.4 percent between 2001 and 2010.

In fact, a report of the Industrial College of the Armed Forces stated that this industry generated $92.4 billion in revenues in 2010 and had a short-term projected growth rate of 9.4 percent. The report stated that the industry "is only now emerging on the world stage with the real prospect of providing solutions to some of the most difficult challenges of our time—global food security and safety; spiraling healthcare costs and personalized medical demands; and, the need for alternative energy sources as well as energy independence."

Companies within the biotechnology industry rely heavily on the patent system in the United States. This system is based on a **quid pro quo** theory through which the government gives an inventor the exclusive right to manufacture and sell an invention for a period of time in exchange for complete disclosure about the invention. The purpose of this system is to give the inventor financial incentive to invest in research and discovery of new advancements.

Biotechnology companies invest millions or billions of dollars in their research and development departments. The companies earn back their investments largely through enforcement of

their PATENTS. Nearly all of the companies in the medical, agricultural, and industrial biotechnology subsectors have relied on patent enforcement to generate a significant portion of revenues.

Legal issues frequently arise about what type of inventions these biotechnology companies may patent. In fact, some companies have reportedly spent tens of millions of dollars in LITIGATION costs to protect patents, which are often worth many times that amount in terms of the revenue they generate.

In 2013, two cases came before the SUPREME COURT, with one focusing on an issue related to agricultural biotechnology and the other addressing an issue from the field of medical biotechnology.

Agricultural Biotechnology Patents and the Monsanto Disputes One of the biotechnology companies frequently involved in litigation over patents is Monsanto. The company has annual revenues of nearly $12 billion, and the company's many patents are central to its financial success. However, the company has been involved in many disputes involving the farming industry dating back to the 1980s and has been heavily criticized in many sectors because of its business practices.

Many of the disputes involving Monsanto patents have related to the patents for genetically modified seeds. Farmers historically would save seeds to reuse in subsequent seasons. Moreover, these farmers would also share the seeds with each another. However, Monsanto forbids the reuse of its seeds, forcing the farmers to purchase new seeds each season. In one case in 2003, a farmer

from Tennessee received a prison sentence of eight months for CONSPIRACY to commit **fraud** when he hid a truckload of cotton seed. Monsanto wanted to use these seeds as evidence in a proceeding brought against the farmer for reusing the seeds in violation of an agreement signed between the parties.

A number of disputes have arisen from Monsanto's so-called "Roundup Ready" gene. This involved a genetic modification to a soybean seed that allows the seed to survive the active ingredient contained in herbicides such as Roundup (which is also, incidentally, a Monsanto product). A farmer who uses a Roundup Ready seed may kill weeds with an herbicide, but the herbicide will not kill the actual soybean crop. A farmer who uses a Roundup Ready seed must sign an agreement not to reuse the seed in subsequent seasons. Without the agreement, it would be possible (and rather easy) for farmers to produce their own Roundup Ready seeds by replanting the soybeans produced by the original Monsanto seed.

A farmer from Indiana named Vernon Bowman thought he found a way around buying Monsanto seeds. After purchasing the seeds from Monsanto at the start of the season, he decided to plant a second crop and purchased seeds from a grain elevator at a price significantly less than what Monsanto charged. Bowman correctly guessed that many of the seeds in the grain elevator would be Roundup Ready seeds, and this allowed him to produce several crops from seeds purchased at the grain elevator.

Monsanto sued Bowman for patent INFRINGEMENT, and a federal **district court** awarded the company $84,456. Bowman appealed the case all the way to the Supreme Court, but a unanimous Court sided with Monsanto. Writing for the Court, Justice ELENA KAGAN stated: "Bowman planted Monsanto's patented soybeans solely to make and market replicas of them, thus depriving the company of the reward patent law provides for the sale of each article. Patent exhaustion provides no haven for that conduct." *Bowman v. Monsanto Co.*, 133 S. Ct. 1761 (2013).

Monsanto was involved in yet another dispute in 2013, only the dispute involved Congress. As part of the Consolidated and Further Continuing Appropriations Act, Pub. L. No. 113-6, a section known as the Farmer Assurance Provision was added. The section effectively limits the ability of federal judges from stopping the growth or harvesting of crops from genetically modified seeds, even if evidence shows that the seeds and resulting crops present potential health risks. Because Congress rushed to consider the appropriations bill, several members of Congress said they were unaware that the section had been added.

Critics dubbed the section the "Monsanto Protection Act," and some members of Congress vowed to effectively **repeal** it. As of July 2013, those efforts had failed. However, the appropriations bill is set to expire on its own terms on September 30, 2013, giving members of Congress the opportunity to reconsider the provision.

Patenting the Human Gene The Supreme Court had to tackle a more challenging issue when the Court addressed a case involving the patentability of the human gene. The case focused on patents owned by Myriad Genetics, Inc., which has reportedly spent $500 million on research to create tests for hereditary breast cancer and ovarian cancer. To do so, the researchers isolated the location and sequence of two genes. Mutations of these genes—known as the BRCA1 and BRCA2 genes—greatly increase the risk of breast or ovarian cancer. Myriad also isolated and created synthetic molecules, and these synthetically created molecules can be used to create tests for cancer. The synthetically created DNA is known as cDNA.

The question that reached the Supreme Court was, as a general matter, whether the human gene can be patented. The answer to that could have had a wide-reaching impact. Those who own medical biotechnology patents feared the Court could issue a decision preventing patent protection for any genetic material. Firms that had spent many millions of dollars on innovations would lose their patents and could potentially lose their investments.

On the other hand, those who oppose patenting of human genes argued that the patents present a "roadblock to discovery" because researchers hesitate to study patented genes in laboratories, fearing patent infringement suits. Supporters of the lawsuit brought against Myriad believed that eliminating the patents for human genes could, in effect, reduce health care costs.

The plaintiffs that sued Myriad included a group of medical organizations, genetic counselors, and cancer patients. The U.S. Court of Appeals for the Federal Circuit distinguished between DNA found in the human body and isolation of DNA. The court determined that DNA found within the human body is not patentable but that isolated DNA and the methods for analyzing DNA sequences are patentable. *Association for Molecular Pathology v. United States Patent and Trademark Office*, 653 F.3d 1329 (Fed. Cir. 2011).

On June 13, 2013, the Supreme Court issued a unanimous ruling on the case. An opinion written by Justice CLARENCE THOMAS concluded that isolated DNA that involved a naturally occurring segment of DNA was not eligible to be patented. This meant that Myriad could not patent the location and genetic sequence of the BRCA1 or BRCA2 genes because the information existed in nature. However, the Court ruled, the synthetically created cDNA did not occur naturally, and Myriad could patent the cDNA. *Association of Molecular Pathology v. Myriad Genetics, Inc.*, 133 S. Ct. 2107 (2013).

Myriad viewed the decision as a victory. In a piece published in *USA Today*, Myriad's president and CEO, Peter D. Meldrum, offered an explanation of what the case was about. He wrote

> There are several misconceptions about this case. We did not patent the genes in anyone's body. That is not possible under U.S. patent law. Instead, we patented our own discoveries— the synthetic molecules we isolated and created in the lab to provide life-saving tests.
>
> Those isolated synthetic molecules are different from the DNA in your cells. They do not exist in nature by themselves. As our legal brief outlines, "They were never available to the world until Myriad's scientists applied their inventive faculties to a previously undistinguished mass of genetic matter and created a new chemical entity."

Myriad's investors feared a ruling that would invalidate patents for all genetic material. After the Court's decision, Myriad's stock rose 10 percent to $37.29 per share.

FTC v. Actavis, Inc.

As a general matter, the holder of a patent has the exclusive right to make, use, or sell an invention for a certain period of time. The right given through the patent is, in effect, a **monopoly**. A patent holder has the right to bring a lawsuit in federal court against a person or **entity** that is accused of infringing the patent. A party accused of infringing the patent has two basic defenses. First, the party can argue that the patent is invalid. Second, the party can argue that a product does not infringe the patent holder's rights.

In the area of pharmaceutical drugs, Congress created a revised system for resolving disputes between patent holders that manufacture brand-name drugs and competing generic drug manufacturers. Under the Drug Price Competition and Patent Term Restoration Act of 1984, Pub. L. No. 98-417, 98 Stat. 1585 (commonly known as the Hatch-Waxman Act), Congress created a regulatory framework under which a generic drug manufacturer may challenge the validity of a patent owned by a brand-name manufacturer. This process is designed to be faster than general challenges to a patent's validity.

Some brand-name drug manufacturers sought to avoid competition by creating a "reverse settlement" agreement. This happens when a generic drug manufacturer sues the brand-name drug manufacturer that holds the patent. In the agreement, the generic drug manufacturer promises not to produce a patented product until the patent expires. In exchange, the patent holder agrees to pay millions of dollars to the generic drug manufacturer. The result is that the brand-name drug remains the only drug on the market, allowing the patent holder to make more money without the competition.

In *FTC v. Actavis, Inc.*, 133 S. Ct. 2223 (2013), the SUPREME COURT was called upon to resolve a question about whether this type of agreement could violate federal antitrust laws. The FEDERAL TRADE COMMISSION filed a complaint against parties who had entered into a reverse payment system. Two lower courts dismissed the complaint, ruling that the **settlement** agreement was immune from attack. The Supreme Court disagreed, however, ruling that such an agreement can "sometimes violate antitrust laws." The Supreme Court therefore ruled that the courts should allow the FTC's complaint to proceed.

The case focused on several pharmaceutical drug companies. In 1999, Solvay Pharmaceuticals filed a new drug application with the FOOD AND DRUG ADMINISTRATION for a brand-name drug known as AndroGel, which is designed to increase testosterone in men. Solvay obtained a patent for the drug in 2003 and disclosed the patent to the FDA pursuant to the terms in the Hatch-Waxman Act.

A drug manufacturer known as Watson Pharmaceuticals (later known as and referred to below as Actavis, Inc.) subsequently filed a new drug application for a generic drug modeled after AndroGel. Another generic drug manufacturer known as Paddock Laboratories also filed an application for a generic version of the product. Both Actavis and Paddock claimed that Solvay's patent was invalid and that their drugs did not infringe on Solvay's patent. Solvay later sued Actavis and Paddock for patent INFRINGEMENT. Thirty months after Solvay filed suit, the FDA approved Actavis's generic-drug application.

In 2006, the parties entered into a reverse-settlement agreement. The agreement provided that Actavis and Paddock would not bring their products to the market until August 31, 2015, which would be 65 months before Solvay's patent was set to expire. Moreover, Actavis agreed to promote Solvay's product to doctors, including urologists. In exchange, Solvay agreed to pay millions of dollars to each of the generic drug manufacturers, including an estimated $19 to $30 million annually to Actavis.

The FTC filed a complaint against each of the parties who entered into the reverse settlement agreement. The FTC alleged that the parties violated the Federal Trade Commission Act, 15 U.S.C. § 45, because the parties agreed "to share in Solvay's monopoly profits, abandon their patent challenges, and refrain from launching their low-cost generic products to compete with AndroGel for nine years."

The U.S. **District Court** for the Northern District of Georgia dismissed the case after concluding that the FTC had not established an antitrust violation. The FTC appealed the decision to the Eleventh **Circuit Court** of Appeals, which affirmed the district court's decision. The Eleventh Circuit ruled that in the absence of "sham LITIGATION or fraud," the FTC could not attack a reverse settlement agreement on antitrust grounds "so long as [the agreement's] anticompetitive effects fall within the scope of the exclusionary potential of the patent." *FTC v. Watson Pharmaceuticals, Inc.*, 677 F.3d 1298 (11th Cir. 2012).

The FTC again appealed the decision, and the Supreme Court agreed to review the case. In a 5–3 decision, the Court reversed the Eleventh Circuit. Justice ANTHONY KENNEDY joined the Court's four liberal justices in the majority. Justice STEPHEN BREYER wrote the majority opinion. Chief Justice JOHN ROBERTS, JR., dissented, while Justice SAMUEL ALITO did not take part in the decision.

The majority decided that the case should not be decided solely on patent-law grounds without consideration of the antitrust laws designed to promote competition. Previous cases had established that some patent-related settlement agreements had violated antitrust laws. Moreover, the Court noted, the Hatch-Waxman Act established a general procompetition policy and required parties to report patent settlement agreements to federal antitrust regulators.

The Court acknowledged that antitrust scrutiny of settlement agreements could lead to litigation that would be time-consuming, complex, and expensive. The Court acknowledged that the Eleventh Circuit's decision had some support in a general policy supporting settlements of disputes. However, the Court identified several reasons why the FTC should be allowed to pursue its complaint. Among those reasons was that the reverse settlement agreements have the "potential for genuine adverse effects on competition." Moreover, the Court stated the Eleventh Circuit had misjudged the feasibility of an antitrust action in this context.

The Court refused to rule that the reverse settlement agreements are presumptively unlawful. Moreover, the Court rejected the FTC's argument that courts should apply a "quick look" approach to these settlement agreements, which would effectively require a DEFENDANT to meet a burden of proving that an agreement has procompetitive effects.

In reversing the Eleventh Circuit, the Court allowed the FTC's case to proceed. The Court instructed the lower courts to follow the "rule of reason" standard established in 15 U.S.C. § 4302.

Roberts disagreed with the majority's approach, arguing that a "patent carves out an exception to the applicability of antitrust laws." He said that the Court carved out a novel approach to addressing antitrust claims brought in the context of settlement agreements. He would have rejected this approach and affirmed the lower courts' dismissal of the FTC's action.

Gunn v. Minton

In the LEGAL MALPRACTICE case of *Gunn v. Minton*, 133 S. Ct. 1059 (2013), the underlying case (the "case within the case") was one for patent INFRINGEMENT. In other words, Vernon Minton was suing his former attorney, Jerry Gunn, for mishandling his patent infringement case, which he lost. In matters of legal MALPRACTICE such as this, one must prove that, but for the alleged NEGLIGENCE on the part of legal counsel, one would have prevailed in the underlying case.

Federal courts have exclusive jurisdiction over actual patent cases. By the time this case got to the U.S. SUPREME COURT, the issue was neither one of patent infringement nor legal malpractice, but rather, one of jurisdiction. The Texas Supreme Court had upheld dismissal of Minton's legal malpractice case, finding that it belonged in federal and not state court. But the U.S. Supreme Court reversed in a unanimous opinion which relied upon a factual test endorsed in previous precedent. It held that there was no federal subject-matter jurisdiction over legal malpractice suits arising out of LEGAL REPRESENTATION in an underlying patent case.

Minton, a former SECURITIES BROKER, had developed computer program software and appurtenant TELECOMMUNICATIONS networking that facilitated independent stock trading. He named it the Texas Computer Exchange Network, or TEXCEN. In 1995, Minton leased TEXCEN to R. M. Stark & Co., a securities brokerage.

More than a year later, Minton applied for a patent involving an interactive securities trading system substantially based on TEXCEN. The U.S. PATENT AND TRADEMARK OFFICE issued a patent to Minton in 2000. Following receipt of said patent, Minton, represented by attorney Gunn and others, filed suit for patent infringement in federal **district court** against the National Association of Securities Dealers, Inc. (NASD) and the NASDAQ STOCK MARKET, Inc. Both defendants moved for **summary judgment**, arguing that under the "on sale" bar of 35 U.S.C. § 102(b), a patent is invalid if the invention it covers is sold more than a year before a patent application is filed. Minton argued discreet differences between TEXCEN and his newly-patented system, but the district court dismissed his suit and further declared his patent invalid.

On a motion for reconsideration in the district court, Minton raised for the first time the argument that the lease agreement with R.M. Stark was actually part of ongoing testing of TEXCEN, thereby constituting an "experimental use" exception to the on-sale bar. The federal district court denied his motion and he appealed to the U.S. Court of Appeals for the Federal Circuit. Holding that Minton had waived the experimental-use argument by not raising it earlier, the federal **appellate court** affirmed the district court's decision.

Minton then brought a legal malpractice action against his original attorneys ("Gunn," *et al.*) in Texas state court. His former attorneys defended that the lease of TEXCEN to R.M. Stark was not in fact for "experimental use." Therefore, the experimental-use argument would have failed, even if it had been timely raised in the underlying patent suit. Finding that Minton had produced "less than a **scintilla** of proof" that the lease of TEXCEN was for experimental use, the Texas state court granted SUMMARY JUDGMENT in favor of Gunn and dismissed the legal malpractice suit. (Since Minton would not have prevailed in his underling patent infringement case, the malpractice case also failed.)

Minton appealed to the Court of Appeals of Texas, raising an entirely new argument. This time, he argued that because his legal malpractice claim was based on alleged negligence in an underlying patent lawsuit, it "aris[es] under" federal patent law for purposes of federal jurisdiction under 28 U.S.C. § 1338(a). Under this provision, "[n]o State court shall have jurisdiction over any **claim for relief** arising under any Act of Congress relating to patents." Minton then argued that the Texas courts therefore lacked subject-matter jurisdiction over his legal malpractice suit. He petitioned the **appellate** court to vacate the trial court's order and then, instead, dismiss for lack of jurisdiction. This would leave him free to start all over again with a clean slate in federal court.

The Texas APPELLATE court carefully considered this new argument, but a divided court

ultimately rejected it. It did so by relying on U.S. Supreme Court precedent, namely *Grable & Sons Metal Products v. Darue Engineering*, 545 U.S. 308, 125 S. Ct. 2363, 162 L. Ed. 2d 257 (2005), which articulated a test to apply in such cases. After so doing, the Texas appellate court concluded that the federal interests articulated in Minton's state law claim for legal malpractice, though they involved an underlying case of alleged federal patent infringement, were not sufficiently substantial to trigger the "arising under" federal jurisdiction of 28 U.S.C. § 1338 (a). The appellate court then proceeded to the merits of Minton's malpractice case and affirmed the trial court's dismissal for failure to prove "experimental use."

But the Texas Supreme Court, applying the same test, came to a different conclusion, finding that Minton's claim involved "a substantial federal issue" under *Grable* because the success of the legal malpractice claim was dependent upon the resolution of the federal patent law question. Citing some federal circuit cases, it reversed.

Ultimately, a unanimous U.S. Supreme Court agreed with the dissenting justices on the Texas high court. Writing for the Court, Chief Justice JOHN ROBERTS, JR., reversed the majority opinion of the Texas Supreme Court, first noting that the Constitution certainly permits Congress to extend federal jurisdiction over a case such as this; the question was whether Congress had done so.

Federal (patent) law did not create the **cause of action** in Minton's legal malpractice claim, said the Court. Therefore, under *Grable*, the malpractice claim can "aris[e] under" federal law only if it "necessarily raises a stated federal issue, actually disputed and substantial, which a federal forum may entertain without disturbing any congressionally approved balance of federal and state judicial responsibilities." *Grable*, 55 U.S. at 314. Applying such inquiry to the present case, the Court acknowledged that resolution of a federal patent question was "necessary" to Minton's claim. Moreover, the stated federal issue was "actually disputed." However, the "substantial[ity]" of the federal issue failed the *Grable* test. Irrespective of how the STATE COURTS resolved the hypothetical "case within a case" to settle the state malpractice claim, it would have no real-world effect or impact on federal patent law or precedent.

Nothing in the state court can change the outcome of Minton's federal patent case. Accordingly, the Court unanimously concluded that 28 U.S.C. § 1338(a) did not deprive state courts of **subject matter jurisdiction**.

PLAIN-ERROR RULE

The principle that an appeals court can reverse a judgment and order a new trial because of a serious mistake in the proceedings, even though no objection was made at the time the mistake occurred.

Henderson v. United States

To preserve an objection for an appeal, a litigant must generally raise the issue at the trial level or it is held to be waived. An **appellate court** generally will not correct legal error made during a criminal trial unless the DEFENDANT had brought the error to the trial court's attention. Federal Rule of **Criminal Procedure** 52(b) does provide an exception for "[a] plain error that affects substantial rights [to] be considered even though it was not brought to the [trial] court's attention."

In the 1997 case of *Johnson v. United States*, 520 U.S. 461, 117 S. Ct. 1544, 137 L. Ed. 2d 718 (1997), the U.S. SUPREME COURT held that, when controlling law is settled at the time of trial but later changes in the defendant's favor at the time of appeal, "it is enough that an error be 'plain' at the time of **appellate** consideration." 520 U.S. at 468. In the 2013 case of *Henderson v. United States*, 133 S. Ct. 1121 (2013), the U.S. Supreme Court, by a 6-3 divide, expanded that holding to include circumstances under which governing law is still *unsettled* at the time of trial but a trial judge's decision would be in plain error at the time of APPELLATE review, the exception of Rule 52(b) would still apply.

In early 2010, 26-year-old Amarcion Henderson pleaded guilty in federal **district court** to a single count of being a felon in possession of a firearm. The approved national Sentencing Guidelines advise a sentence of 33 to 41 months imprisonment for such an offense. Neither defense counsel nor the prosecution raised any objection to the sentencing range. However, when the district court accepted Henderson's plea, defense counsel urged the court to consider Henderson's drug problem and to order drug treatment as part of his sentence. The district court then sentenced Henderson to

a prison term of 60 months to "try to help" Henderson qualify for the Bureau of Prisons 500-hour in-house drug rehabilitation program. Defense counsel did not object, even though the sentence greatly exceeded the maximum 41-month sentencing guidelines.

Henderson's counsel later appealed, arguing that the court had erred in sentencing Henderson to a term greater than the sentencing guidelines solely for rehabilitation. In 2011, before the appeal had been heard, the U.S. Supreme Court decided *Tapia v. United States*, 131 S. Ct. 2382, which held that sentences greater than those in the guidelines could not be imposed for rehabilitative purposes. Accordingly, the district court's decision in Henderson's case would have been plain error if *Tapia* had already been decided. But the earlier *Johnson* case could not help Henderson because it applied only to *settled* law. As the U.S. Court of Appeals for the Fifth Circuit put it, "Henderson cannot show that the error in his case was plain . . . because an error is plain only if it was clear under current law *at the time of trial*." 646 F.3d 223, 225.

Up until this case, the First, Second, Sixth, Tenth, and Eleventh Circuit Courts of Appeals had applied a time-of-the-appeal standard, while the Fifth, Ninth, and D.C. Circuit had applied the time-of-trial standard (as to settled law). To resolve this conflict among circuits, the U.S. Supreme Court granted review.

Writing for the majority, Justice STEPHEN BREYER reversed and remanded to the Fifth Circuit. The majority held that if a trial judge's decision would be plain error at the time of appellate review, Rule 52(b) would apply, even though the decision was not in plain error at the time it was made. This expands *Johnson* to the extent that there is no longer a distinction between settled and unsettled law at the time the decision is made: if it constitutes plain error at the time it is being reviewed by an appellate court, Rule 52(b) will apply.

Justice Breyer was joined by Chief Justice JOHN ROBERTS, JR. and Justices ANTHONY KENNEDY, RUTH BADER GINSBURG, SONIA SOTOMAYOR, and ELENA KAGAN. Justice ANTONIN SCALIA filed a dissenting opinion, in which he was joined by Justices CLARENCE THOMAS and SAMUEL ALITO. The lengthy DISSENT opined that when the law was unsettled at the time an error was committed, the error was not "plain" within the meaning of Rule 52(b). To hold otherwise, continued the dissent, "disregards the importance of claim preservation and deprives Rule 52(b)'s plainness limitation of all conceivable purpose."

PREEMPTION

Dan's City Used Cars v. Pelkey

What at first blush appeared to be a simple case of unfair and illegal disposal of a towed vehicle turned into a full-blown federal issue when the DEFENDANT towing company invoked the FEDERAL AVIATION ADMINISTRATION Authorization Act (FAAAA) of 1994. In *Dan's City Used Cars v. Pelkey*, 133 S. Ct. 1769 (2013), a unanimous U.S. SUPREME COURT ruled that the Act did not preempt the state law claim because the claim was not related to the "transportation of property" (under the Act), but rather to the sale and disposal of property.

In 2007, Robert Pelkey was seriously ill and bedridden. The apartment building complex where he resided had a policy requiring tenants to move their cars from the parking lot during snowstorms. Pelkey's 2004 Honda remained in the lot during and after a February snowstorm. The landlord, not knowing whose vehicle was in the lot, requested that Dan's City Used Cars (Dan's City) tow and store the vehicle. Pelkey did not know it had been towed. Soon after the removal of his car, Pelkey was admitted to a hospital for a foot amputation, during which operation, he suffered a heart attack. He survived but remained under hospital care until April 2007.

Meanwhile, Dan's City, not knowing Pelkey's identity or of his hospitalization, sought permission from the state's (New Hampshire) Department of Public Safety to sell the Honda at auction. The department responded by notifying Dan's City of the last known owner of the vehicle. Dan's City then attempted to contact Pelkey by letter, but the post office returned it, checking the box "moved, left no address." Dan's City then scheduled an auction sale for April 19.

In the days following Pelkey's hospital discharge, his attorney learned from the apartment complex's counsel what happened to Pelkey's vehicle. On April 17, the attorney contacted Dan's City and advised that Pelkey wanted to reclaim the vehicle and would pay any associated towing/storage charges. Notwithstanding, Dan's City

proceeded with the auction but got no bidders. It then disposed of the car by trading it to a **third party**. Pelkey was not notified of the trade and received no proceeds from the sale.

Pelkey filed suit against Dan's City in New Hampshire state court, alleging various violations of the state's **consumer protection** act. He also brought **statutory** and common-law claims regarding breaches of duties for bailees/bailments. But the state court concluded that his state claims were preempted under FAAAA and granted **summary judgment** to Dan's City.

As relevant here, FAAA's **preemption** clause, 49 U.S.C. § 14501(c)(1), preempts state laws "related to a price, route, or service of any motor carrier . . . with respect to the transportation of property." Conversely, New Hampshire's CONSUMER PROTECTION Act, § 358-A:2 makes it unlawful for "any person to use any unfair method of competition or any unfair or deceptive act or practice in the conduct of any trade or commerce within [the state]."

The New Hampshire Supreme Court reversed, finding FAAAA's PREEMPTION clause inapplicable because Pelkey's claims related to the storage and disposal of Pelkey's car, not to "the transportation of property." The U.S. Supreme Court then granted review to resolve conflict in state supreme courts on the preemption issue.

Justice RUTH BADER GINSBURG delivered the opinion of the Court, in which all justices joined. When Congress supersedes state legislation by **statute**, she wrote, the Court's task is to "identify the domain expressly pre-empted," quoting from *Lorillard Tobacco Co. v. Reilly*, 533 U.S. 525, 121 S. Ct. 2404, 150 L. Ed. 2d 532 (2001). Focusing on the statute's express language, the Court concluded that Pelkey's state claims were not preempted by the FAAAA because they were not "related to" the service of a motor carrier "with respect to the transportation of property."

Dan's City argued that because the statute's definition of "transportation" included "storage" and "handling," Pelkey's claims fell under preemption. But, said the Court, the statute's reference to services such as "storage" and "handling" fall under the statute's definition of "transportation" only as those services relate to the movement of property, as in temporary storage of property while in transit to its final destination. Here, property stored after delivery was no longer in transit, nor did storage occur in the course of transporting Pelkey's vehicle. Finally, Dan's City's "service" of removing and transporting Pelkey's car from the parking lot ended months before the conduct Pelkey complained of, which related to the disposal of abandoned vehicles under state law.

PRESIDENTIAL POWERS

D.C. Circuit Strikes Down Obama Recess Appointments

Under Article II, Section 2, Clause 2 of the Constitution, the "President shall have Power to fill up all Vacancies that may happen during the Recess of the SENATE, by granting Commissions which shall expire at the end of their next Session." Known as the "Recess Appointments Clause," it has been used by recent administrations to appoint individuals whose confirmations have been blocked by the Senate. President BILL CLINTON made 139 recess appointments, while President GEORGE W. BUSH made 179 appointments. President BARACK OBAMA has made 32 recess appointments, three of which were challenged in court by an employer who objected to a ruling by the NATIONAL LABOR RELATIONS BOARD (NLRB). The employer argued that three members of the NLRB who had been appointed were not valid appointees because the Senate had not gone into recess when the President appointed them. The District of Columbia **Circuit Court** of Appeals agreed in *Noel Canning v. National Labor Relations Board*, 705 F.3d 490 (2013). The court overturned the NLRB ruling, finding that without the three members, the board lacked a **quorum** of three to make a valid decision. Two members of the three-judge panel held that only vacancies that occurred during a valid recess could be filled with recess appointments.

The NLRB heard a dispute between Noel Canning and the International Brotherhood of Teamsters over allegations that the company had reneged on a promise to let union members decided how much of their proposed raise would go to their **pension** fund. The NLRB sided with the Teamsters, leading Noel Canning to appeal the decision to the D.C. Circuit. The company alleged that the five-member NLRB did not have the authority to issue the decision for lack of a quorum, as three members were

never validly appointed because they took office under supposed recess appointments that were made when the Senate was not in session. Second, it argued that these three vacancies did not happen during a Senate recess.

A three-judge panel of the D.C. Circuit agreed unanimously with Noel Canning's first argument, but split 2-1 in favor of the second argument. Chief Judge David Sentelle, writing for the court, noted that President Obama appointed three members of the board on January 12, 2012. Sharon Block filled a spot that became vacant on January 3, 2012. Terence Flynn filled a seat that became vacant on August 27, 2010, while Richard Griffin filled a seat that became vacant on August 27, 2011. Judge Sentelle also found that at the time the purported recess appointments were made, the Senate was operating pursuant to a unanimous consent agreement, which provided that the Senate would meet in **pro forma** sessions every three business days from December 20, 2011 through January 23, 2012. The agreement stated that the Senate would not conduct business during those sessions. However, during the December 23 session, the Senate overrode its prior agreement and passed a temporary extension to the payroll tax holiday. During the January 3, 2012 PRO FORMA session the Senate acted to convene the second session of the 112th Congress and to fulfill its constitutional duty to meet on January 3.

Noel Canning argued that the term "the Recess" in the Recess Appointments Clause referred to the intersession recess of the Senate, which is the period between sessions of the Senate when the Senate is by definition not in session and therefore unavailable to receive and act upon nominations from the president. The NLRB countered that appointments could be made during intrasession "recesses" or breaks in Senate business when it is otherwise in a continuing session. Judge Sentelle sided with Noel Canning, finding that the NLRB had failed to differentiate between "recesses" and the constitutional language of "the Recess." Calling it "the Recess" was not an "insignificant decision. In the end it makes all the difference." The "inescapable conclusion" was that the Framers' use of "the Recess" meant something different than "a generic break in the proceedings." The Senate is either in session or it is in the recess. If the Senate breaks for three days within an ongoing session, it is not in "the Recess."

The court noted that it was universally accepted that "Session" here referred to the usually two or sometimes three sessions per Congress. Therefore, "the Recess" occurred only when the Senate is not in one of those sessions. Historically, presidents only made three intra-session appointments before 1947. The infrequency of intrasession recess appointments during the first 150 years of the republic suggested an assumed absence of the power to make such appointments. This was important for the court. Judge Sentelle concluded that the appointment practices of the first Presidents and their understanding of the Constitution was "more **probative** of its original meaning than anything to be drawn from administrations of more recent vintage." To employ the NLRB's intrasession interpretation of "the Recess" "would wholly defeat the purpose of the Framers in the careful SEPARATION OF POWERS structure reflected in the Appointments Clause." It would "demolish" the checks and balances inherent in the advice-and-consent requirement, giving the President "free rein to appoint his desired nominees at any time he pleases, whether that time be a weekend, lunch, or even when the Senate is in session and he is merely displeased with its action. This cannot be the law."

A unanimous court decision on the first issue was enough to compel a ruling vacating the NLRB's order against Noel Canning. However, Judge Sentelle and another member of the panel also addressed and sided with Noel Channing's argument that only vacancies occurring during a recess were subject to recess appointments. The Clause permitted only the filling up of "Vacancies that may happen during the Recess of the Senate." Judge Sentelle fixed on the word "happen," finding that a simple reading of the clause "could not logically have encompassed any vacancies that happened to exist during the 'the Recess.'" In his view a vacancy happens or "comes to pass" only "when it first arises." Therefore, a President may only exercise the Recess Appointment Clause when a vacancy occurs during an intersession recess.

PRIVACY

Maracich v. Spears

When a person applies for a driver's license or registers a vehicle, state motor vehicle departments generally require the applicant to disclose sensitive personal information. This information usually includes the applicant's name, address, telephone number, SOCIAL SECURITY number, and medical information. Concerns about this information in the 2010s focus on the dangers associated with IDENTITY THEFT. However, in the early 1990s, concerns focused on use of this information for STALKING purposes. For instance, some individuals used information available through state motor vehicle offices to identify and later harass ABORTION providers and their patients. Other issues focused on the use of the information by businesses to solicit customers.

Congress enacted the Driver's Privacy Protection Act of 1994 (DPPA), 18 U.S.C. §§ 2721-2725, to protect information contained in driver's license databases. Congress designed the Act to establish "a regulatory scheme that restricts the States' ability to disclose a driver's personal information without the driver's consent." The Act establishes liability for a person "who knowingly obtains, discloses or uses personal information, from a motor vehicle record, for a purpose not permitted under the chapter."

The Act establishes 14 exceptions to the Act's ban on disclosure. Under 18 U.S.C. § 2721 (b)(4), a person may disclose information "[f]or use in connection with any civil, criminal, administrative, or arbitral proceeding in any Federal, State, or local court or agency or before any self-regulatory body, including the **service of process**, investigation in anticipation of LITIGATION, and the execution or enforcement of judgments and orders, or pursuant to an order of a Federal, State, or local court." Another provision contained in 18 U.S.C. § 2721(b)(12) allows disclosure "[f]or bulk distribution for surveys, marketing, or solicitations if the State has obtained the express consent of the person to whom such personal information pertains."

In *Maracich v. Spears*, 133 S. Ct. 2191 (2013), the U.S. SUPREME COURT reviewed a case involving the question of whether the exception contained in 18 U.S.C. § 2721(b)(4) allowed disclosure of information to a lawyer if the lawyer uses the information to solicit clients. The Court ruled that this type of use fell outside the exception because the information was not used "in connection with" litigation or "in anticipation of litigation."

The case focused on a group of lawyers from South Carolina. They had instituted several lawsuits in South Carolina in 2006 and 2007 against car dealerships. The suits alleged that the dealerships engaged in unfair practices related to certain fees the dealerships charged. To identify potential clients, the lawyers requested personal information about drivers held by the South Carolina DEPARTMENT OF MOTOR VEHICLES through the state's freedom of information **statute**. The department complied and supplied personal information to the lawyers, including information about cars purchased.

The lawyers drafted several letters used to solicit clients for the cases focused on fees charged by car dealerships. The letters contained a phrase stating clearly that the letter was "advertising material." The letters also clearly indicated that the lawyers had obtained information about fees charged to potential clients through the freedom of information requests. The lawyers filed copies of the letters with the South Carolina Office of Disciplinary Counsel as required by state rules of professional conduct. In 2006 and 2007, the lawyers had mailed letters to tens of thousands of purchasers.

Three years after the lawyers commenced the litigation against the car dealerships, a group of buyers brought a **class action** lawsuit against the plaintiffs' lawyers who had obtained the personal information. The buyers alleged that the lawyers had violated the DPPA by acquiring and using the personal information. The buyers alleged that the lawyers had obtained information under **false pretenses** and had violated the Act through the **solicitation**.

The lawyers moved to dismiss the case, arguing that the exception in 18 U.S.C. § 2721 (b)(4) allowed them to obtain and solicit clients with the personal information. The lawyers stressed that the buyers in the CLASS ACTION were represented by the same counsel that represented the car dealerships. The lawyers asserted that the DPPA litigation was an "obstructionist legal tactic" designed to undermine the litigation against the car dealerships.

The U.S. **District Court** for the District of South Carolina ruled in favor of the lawyers by concluding that the litigation exception in the DPPA applied to the information obtained. The buyers appealed the decision to the Fourth

Circuit Court of Appeals, which affirmed the district court's decision. The Fourth Circuit concluded that the letters sent by the lawyers constituted "solicitation" under the DPPA. However, the court determined that when "solicitation is an accepted and expected element of, and is inextricably intertwined with, conduct satisfying the litigation exception under the DPPA, such solicitation is not actionable." *Maracich v. Spears*, 675 F.3d 281 (4th Cir. 2012).

The Supreme Court disagreed with both lower courts, ruling in a 5–4 decision that the solicitation of clients did not fall within an exception under the DPPA. Justice ANTHONY KENNEDY wrote for the majority, joined by Chief Justice JOHN ROBERTS, JR., and Justices CLARENCE THOMAS, STEPHEN BREYER, and SAMUEL ALITO. Justice RUTH BADER GINSBURG dissented.

The majority noted that "[i]f considered in isolation, and without reference to the structure and purpose of the DPPA," the exception in 18 U.S.C. § 2721(b)(4) could apply broadly to personal information used for soliciting clients in the manner the lawyers used the information in the case. However, the majority read the exception more narrowly based on the purpose and structure of the DPPA.

Kennedy wrote: "If (b)(4) were read to permit disclosure of personal information whenever any connection between the protected information and a potential legal dispute could be shown, it would undermine in a substantial way the DPPA's purpose of protecting an individual's right to privacy in his or her motor vehicle records. The 'in connection with' language in (b)(4) must have a limit. A logical and necessary conclusion is that an attorney's solicitation of prospective clients falls outside of that limit."

The Court noted that lawyers operate in different capacities. They are OFFICERS OF THE COURT and agents for their clients, but they also operate businesses. The majority concluded that Congress did not intend to give lawyers access to sensitive personal information when the lawyers were acting in an entrepreneurial capacity rather than in the capacity as an advocate or officer of the court.

The Court established a standard focusing on the purpose of the letters. If the use of the information has the "predominant purpose of solicitation" the use is not protected by the exception in 18 U.S.C. § 2721(b)(4). The Court remanded the case to the Fourth Circuit to determine whether the predominant purposes of the lawyers' letters was to solicit clients for the litigation against the car dealerships.

Ginsburg disagreed with the majority, finding that the **statutory** language allows the lawyers to use the personal information in the manner they did. She stated that nothing in the DPPA "warrants the massive liability this Court's judgment authorizes."

PRIVILEGES AND IMMUNITIES

Concepts contained in the U.S. Constitution that place the citizens of each state on an equal basis with citizens of other states in respect to advantages resulting from citizenship in those states and citizenship in the United States.

Supreme Court Upholds Virginia's Bar on Providing Public Information to Non-Virginians

The Constitution's **Privileges and Immunities** Clause states that the "Citizens of each state [are] entitled to all **Privileges** and **Immunities** of Citizens in the several states." The purpose of the clause is to place the citizens of each state upon the same footing with citizens of other states, so far as the advantages of citizenship in those states are concerned. However, the U.S. SUPREME COURT has said that a state does not need to apply its laws equally to nonresidents. In *McBurney v. Young,* 133 S. Ct. 1709, 185 L. Ed. 2d 758 (2013), the Supreme Court addressed whether Virginia's FREEDOM OF INFORMATION ACT (FOIA), which allows only citizens of that state to access public records, violated the rights of nonresidents. The court concluded that it did not violate the PRIVILEGES AND IMMUNITIES Clause.

Mark McBurney, a citizen of Rhode Island, and Roger Hulbert, a citizen of California, each requested documents under the Virginia FOIA, but their requests were denied because they were not citizens of Virginia. The FOIA states that "all public records shall be open to inspection and copying by any citizen of the Commonwealth," but it grants no such right to non-Virginians. McBurney, a former resident of Virginia, asked the state's CHILD SUPPORT enforcement agency to file a petition for child support on his behalf after his ex-wife, a Virginia resident, defaulted on her child support obligations. The agency complied but only after a nine-month delay. McBurney believed the delay was due to agency error and that it cost him nine months of support. To discover the reason for the agency's delay, he filed a FOIA request seeking all emails, notes, files, memos, reports, letters, policies, and opinions pertaining to his family and all documents pertaining to the handling of child support claims like his. The agency denied his request because he was not a Virginia citizen. McBurney later requested the same documents under Virginia's Government Data Collection and Dissemination Practices Act and received most of the information he had sought about his case. However, he did not receive any general policy information about how the agency handled claims like his.

Hulbert ran a business that requests REAL ESTATE tax records on clients' behalf from state and local governments across the United States. In 2008, Hulbert was hired by a land and title company to obtain real estate tax records for properties in Henrico County, Virginia. He filed a FOIA request for documents with the county's real estate assessor's office, but his request was denied because he was not a Virginia citizen.

McBurney and Hulbert filed a federal CIVIL RIGHTS lawsuit in Virginia federal **district court**, seeking declaratory and injunctive relief for violations of the Privileges and Immunities Clause. The district court dismissed the lawsuit and the Fourth **Circuit Court** of Appeals affirmed this decision. The Supreme Court agreed to hear the case because the Third Circuit Court of Appeals had ruled that Delaware's FOIA, which limited access to citizens of that state, did violate the Privileges and Immunities Clause.

The Court, in a unanimous decision, upheld the constitutionality of the Virginia FOIA. Justice SAMUEL ALITO, writing for the court, noted that the Court had long held that the Privileges and Immunities Clause protected only those privileges and immunities that are "fundamental." The plaintiffs alleged that the Virginia citizens-only FOIA provision violated four different "fundamental" privileges or immunities: the opportunity to purse a common calling, the ability to own and transfer property, access to the Virginia courts, and access to public information.

Hulbert argued that the FOIA provision abridged his ability to earn a living in his chosen profession, which was obtaining property records from state and local governments on behalf of his clients. Justice Alito agreed that the Privileges and Immunities Clause protected the rights of citizens to "ply their trade, practice their occupation, or pursue a common calling." However, the Virginia FOIA did not abridge Hulbert's right to engage in a common calling because the Court had only struck down laws under the clause when those laws were enacted for the "protectionist purpose of burdening out-of-state citizens." The Virginia FOIA was not enacted to provide a competitive economic advantage for Virginia citizens, but to provide Virginians with access to public records. In addition, the provision limiting the use of the FOIA to Virginia citizens "recognizes that Virginia taxpayers foot the bill for the fixed costs underlying recordkeeping in the Commonwealth." The clause did not require a state to "tailor its every action to avoid any incidental effect on out-of-state tradesmen."

Hulbert also alleged that the FOIA provision abridged the right to own and transfer property in Virginia. Justice Alito agreed that the right to take, hold, and dispose of real and PERSONAL PROPERTY is one of the privileges of citizenship. If a state prevented out-of-state citizens from accessing real estate records that are necessary to the transfer of property, it would violate the Privileges and Immunities Clause. However, that was not the case in Virginia. Under Virginia law, any records and papers of every circuit court are open to inspection by any person and the clerk of court must furnish copies upon request. While tax assessment records were not required by **statute** to be made available to noncitizens, the practice of local governments was to make these records available to all. Henrico County, from which Hulbert sought real estate tax assessments, posts this information online. In the Court's view, "Requiring noncitizens to conduct a few minutes of Internet research in lieu of using a relatively cumbersome state FOIA process" did not impose any significant burdens on noncitizens to own or transfer property in Virginia.

McBurney alleged that the FOIA provision impermissibly burdened his access to public proceedings by creating an "information asymmetry between adversaries based solely on state citizenship." Justice Alito pointed to a prior Court decision which made clear that there is no constitutional violation if the non-resident "is given access to the courts of State upon terms which in themselves are reasonable and adequate for the enforcing of any rights" of the non-resident. The FOIA provision did not deprive McBurney of "reasonable and adequate" access to the Virginia courts. Virginia's rule of **civil procedure** provided for discovery and the issuing of subpoenas. In addition, the Government Data Collection and Dissemination Practices Act provided McBurney most of the information he wanted.

The Court rejected the plaintiffs' "sweeping claim" that the FOIA provision denied them the right to access public information on equal terms with citizens of Virginia. Justice Alito concluded that the Privileges and Immunities Clause covered this "broad right." He pointed to prior Court rulings that made clear there was no constitutional right to obtain all the information provided by FOIA laws.

PRODUCT LIABILITY

The responsibility of a manufacturer or vendor of goods to compensate for injury caused by a defective good that it has provided for sale.

Mutual Pharmaceutical Co. v. Bartlett

In *Mutual Pharmaceutical Company v. Bartlett*, 133 S. Ct. 2466 (2013), a woman suffered terrible side effects from a generic drug. The U.S. SUPREME COURT, in a very narrow 5-4 decision with strong opposition in the DISSENT, held that her state-law claim for **product liability** damages was preempted by federal law covering generic drugs, ultimately leaving her without a viable claim.

The prescription pain medication sulindac is a generic version of the branded version, Clinoril. It is a non-steroidal anti-inflammatory drug (NSAID).

In December 2004, Karen Bartlett began taking sulindac, after her doctor prescribed Clinoril for her shoulder pain and her pharmacist dispensed the generic form. Within months, she developed a rare but serious side effect known as Stevens-Johnson Syndrome, a skin sensitivity that causes epidermal skin tissue to die/become necrotic. The medical term is "toxic epidermic necrolysis." Ultimately, Bartlett spent months in a medically-induced coma, as "[s]ixty to sixty-five percent of the surface of [her] body deteriorated, was burned off, or turned into an open wound," according to court documents. She also endured 12 eye surgeries, but ended up disabled, disfigured, and nearly blind.

At the time of the prescription, sulindac's label did not include any warnings about toxic epidermal necrolysis, although the package insert did contain such warning. One year later, in 2005, the FOOD AND DRUG ADMINISTRATION (FDA) recommended changing all NSAID labels to include express warnings about this condition.

The labeling issue, and FDA's directives, were key to this case. The federal Food, Drug, and Cosmetic Act requires manufacturers to obtain Food and Drug Administration (FDA) approval before marketing any brand-name or generic drug in interstate commerce. 21 U.S.C. § 355(a). Once approval is obtained, a manufacturer is prohibited from making any major changes to the "qualitative or quantitative formulation of the drug product, including active ingredients, or in the specifications provided in the approved application." 21 CFR § 314.70(b)(2)(i). Important to this case, generic drug makers are also prohibited from unilaterally making any changes to a drug's label. 21 CFR § 314.150(b)(10).

Bartlett sued the manufacturer of sulindac, Mutual Pharmaceutical, in New Hampshire state court, primarily relying upon state PRODUCT LIABILITY laws (design defect) for the **cause of action**. Mutual removed the case to federal court, but nonetheless was found liable by jury trial for damages in excess of $20 million. The **Circuit Court** of Appeals for the First Circuit affirmed. The U.S. Supreme Court granted review.

New Hampshire's design-defect product liability laws require manufacturers to design their products to be "reasonably safe" for their intended and foreseeable uses. In determining whether a product is "reasonably safe," New Hampshire courts employ a "risk/utility approach," which asks whether the gravity of the danger outweighs the product's utility. Three factors are examined to determine this: (1) the usefulness and desirability of the product to the public as a whole; (2) whether the risk of any danger can be reduced without significantly impacting either the product's effectiveness or its cost; and (3) the presence and efficacy of any warning to avoid unreasonable risk of harm from hidden dangers or other foreseeable uses.

An important U.S. Supreme Court case came into play here. In *PLIVA, Inc. v. Messing,* 131 S. Ct. 2567, 180 L. Ed. 2d 580 (2011), the Court held that failure-to-warn claims against generic drug manufacturers were preempted by the FDCA's prohibitions against making any changes to generic drug labels.

In the present case, Justice SAMUEL ALITO, writing for the narrow majority, dissected New Hampshire's three risk/utility factors relevant to Bartlett's claim. As for the first two of the factors, the product's "usefulness" and the reduction of any "risks of danger," either of these would require Mutual Pharmaceutical to redesign the drug, because each of those factors is a result of the drug's chemical design and active ingredients. But redesign is not possible, first, because FDCA requires that generic drugs have the same active ingredients, route of administration, dosage form, strength, and labeling as their brand-name drug equivalents. Second, this particular drug's simple composition makes it chemically incapable of being re-designed.

Accordingly, the only way for sulindac to meet the "risk/utility" test under New Hampshire law was to strengthen its warnings, a consideration under the third factor. This is where Supreme Court precedent, specifically, *Messing* (above), came into play. *Messing* made clear that generic drug manufacturers were prohibited from making changes to their labels. The essence of **preemption** is that, when federal law prohibits an action required by state law, the state law is "without effect." Having failed to meet New Hampshire's requirements without violating federal law, and being incapable of re-designing the drug's components, Mutual was left with the "impossibility" of complying with both federal and state law.

The First Circuit had affirmed the $21 million jury verdict because it created a fourth alternative for Mutual: stop selling sulindac. But the Court dismissed this as against the Court's previous PREEMPTION cases holding that actors attempting to meet both state and federal obligations are not required to cease activity altogether.

The dissent, strong as it was, did not technically disagree with the correctness of preemption in this case. Rather, in the dissent by Justice STEPHEN BREYER, joined by Justice ELENA KAGAN, a company could comply with both state and federal requirements "either by not doing business in the relevant State or by paying the state penalty, say damages, for failing to comply with, as here, a state-law tort standard."

Justice Sonia Sotomayor's dissent was stronger, joined by Justice RUTH BADER GINSBURG, blaming the Court for depriving 20-year-old Bartlett of legal remedy. This dissent essentially accused the majority of "unnecessarily" and "unwisely" extending *Messing*'s rule to this case, which serves to "immunize generic drug manufacturers from state-law failure-to-warn claims." The dissent cited various flaws in the majority's reasoning, including its assumption that this was a failure-to-warn case, when, in fact, the trial court had dropped the warning part of the claim after the physician indicated he had not read the label, and proceeded on the design defect claims. Also, said Sotomayor, New Hampshire law did not require a change in label; it only considered, as a factor, the adequacy of warnings. Therefore, said the dissent, this case was not like *Messing,* and did not meet the strict "impossibility" criteria needed to avoid liability.

SEARCH AND SEIZURE

In international law, the right of ships of war, as regulated by treaties, to examine a merchant vessel during war in order to determine whether the ship or its cargo is liable to seizure.

A hunt by law enforcement officials for property or communications believed to be evidence of crime, and the act of taking possession of this property.

ACLU Requests FBI Memoranda About GPS Tracking

In 2012, the U.S. SUPREME COURT ruled that law enforcement's use of a global positioning system (GPS) tracking device was a **search** under the FOURTH AMENDMENT of the U.S. Constitution. The ruling did not completely resolve the issue of when the state may use a GPS device without a warrant, however, leaving many questions about policies law enforcement agencies should adopt. In a speech, general counsel with the FEDERAL BUREAU OF INVESTIGATION (FBI) referred to two internal memoranda addressing the issues, but when the AMERICAN CIVIL LIBERTIES UNION (ACLU) requested copies of those memoranda, the FBI refused. This led the ACLU to file a freedom of information request to obtain the memoranda.

The Supreme Court's decision in *United States v. Jones*, 132 S. Ct. 945, 181 L. Ed. 2d 911 (2012), focused on whether the police must obtain a warrant before using a GPS device to track a suspect. The case involved the use of a GPS device to track a suspected drug dealer named Antoine Jones. Agents with the FBI and officers with the District of Columbia police attached a GPS device to Jones's car and tracked his movements for nearly a month.

The Court addressed whether the government's use of the device constituted a search, meaning that the agents and officers needed to obtain a warrant. A majority opinion written by Justice ANTONIN SCALIA concluded that because the agents and officers had not obtained the warrant, the evidence against Jones was inadmissible, and the Court overturned his conviction. However, concurring opinions by Justices SAMUEL ALITO and SONIA SOTOMAYOR noted that the Court had not completely answered the questions in the case. Most notably, Scalia's majority opinion did not resolve whether Jones had a reasonable expectation of privacy in the tracking of his movements.

The FBI and other agencies were not sure what standards the case established. About a month after the Court decided *Jones*, FBI General Counsel Andrew Weissmann spoke at a symposium sponsored by the University of San Francisco LAW REVIEW and titled "Big Brother in the 21st Century? Reforming the Electronic Communications Privacy Act." He said that the decision "changes the landscape" with regard to the use of the GPS devices. When the Court decided the case, the FBI had about 3,000 GPS devices in use. However, the FBI had to turn off most of those devices because of the decision in *Jones.*

According to Weissmann, the Court "did not wrestle with the problems their decision creates." He added, "the real problem from a law enforcement perspective is that the clarity that people look for…doesn't come from the decision naturally." Weissmann also addressed the concurring opinions, which suggested that individuals have expectations of privacy in their overall movements, which would mean that the Fourth Amendment would protect their privacy interests in such movement. Weissmann noted, "From a law enforcement perspective, even though it's not technically holding, we have to anticipate how it's going to go down the road."

FBI Director Robert Mueller also criticized the Court's opinion. Speaking before the House Appropriations Committee in March, Mueller said, "It will inhibit our ability to use this in a number of surveillances where it has been tremendously beneficial. We have a number of people in the United States whom we could not indict, there is not **probable cause** to indict them or to arrest them who present a threat of terrorism.… [They] may be up on the Internet, may have purchased a gun, but have taken no particular steps to take a terrorist act."

During the symposium, Weissmann referred specifically to two memoranda the FBI was scheduled to issue in late February. These memos were designed to set forth official FBI policy on the use of GPS tracking devices in light of the Court's decision. According to Weissmann's comments, one memo addressed whether the decision would apply to such transportation modes as airplanes and boats and also whether the decision would apply across international borders. A second memo addressed whether and how the decision may apply to other methods of gathering evidence.

On July 18, 2012, the ACLU sent a letter to the FBI requesting copies of both memoranda. The ACLU submitted the request based on provisions in the FREEDOM OF INFORMATION ACT, 5 U.S.C. § 522. The FBI acknowledged that it had received the ACLU's request but did not immediately supply copies of the memoranda. This led the ACLU to file an action in the U.S. **District Court** for the Southern District of New York. The ACLU has sought injunctive relief, asking the court to issue an INJUNCTION ordering the FBI to disclose the memos.

In its complaint for injunctive relief, the ACLU stated: "The American public has a strong interest in the disclosure of the memoranda. The FBI is the nation's premier law enforcement agency. How the FBI implements the Supreme Court's decision in *Jones* will shape not only the conduct of its own agents but also the policies, practices and procedures of other law enforcement agencies—and, consequently, the privacy rights of Americans."

ACLU staff attorney Catherine Crump added the following: "Collecting personal data is increasingly easy for the government to do but hard for citizens to detect, so it's more important than ever for the American public to know the rules that law enforcement is operating under, especially when it comes to location tracking. Knowing the FBI's position on what it can and can't do in investigations is essential if America's privacy laws are going to keep up with technology."

In January 2013, the FBI released the memos. However, the contents of both memoranda were almost entirely redacted. Many of the pages consisted of nothing but large black boxes covering the substance of the memo. The ACLU said in response that it would continue to insist that the FBI release both memos in their entirety.

SECOND AMENDMENT

Second Circuit Upholds New York Concealed Carry Law

Since the early twentieth century, the state of New York has required applicants who wish to carry a concealed handgun in public to demonstrate "proper cause." A group of New York handgun owners, who failed to obtain licenses because they failed to demonstrate such a special need for self-protection, filed a federal lawsuit. The group contended that under the Supreme Court's recent ruling in *District of Columbia v. Heller,* 554 U.S. 570, 128 S. Ct. 2783, 171 L. Ed. 2d (2008), the New York law violated the SECOND AMENDMENT. The Second **Circuit Court** of Appeals, in *Kachalsky v. County of Westchester,* 701 F.3d 81 (2012), upheld the law, concluding that the concealed carrying of handguns in public was not addressed in *Heller.* That case only looked at the possession of handguns used for SELF-DEFENSE in the home.

New York has had a long history of regulating the possession and use of firearms.

Like most states during the nineteenth century, New York heavily regulated the carrying of concealable firearms. Due to a rise in violent crimes associated with concealable firearms, New York enacted the Sullivan Law in 1911, which made it unlawful for any person to possess without a license "any pistol, revolver, or other firearm of a size which may be concealed upon the person." The law was upheld as constitutional in 1913 and in the same year it was amended to impose a statewide standard for the issuance of licenses to carry firearms in public. To obtain a license to carry a concealed pistol or revolver, the applicant was required to demonstrate "good moral character, and that proper cause exists for the issuance [of the license]." New York also has a general PROHIBITION on the possession of any firearm, except rifles and shotguns, absent a license. Most licenses are limited by place or profession. Licenses "shall be issued" to possess a registered handgun in the home or in a place of business by a merchant or storekeeper. Licenses also shall be issued for a messenger employed by a bank or express company to carry a concealed handgun, as well as for certain state and city judges and those employed by a prison or jail.

The plaintiffs in this case only challenged the provision that requires proper cause for obtaining a license to carry a concealed handgun. The term "proper cause" is not defined in the law but New York STATE COURTS have defined the term to include carrying a handgun for target practice, hunting, or self-defense. When an applicant demonstrates proper cause to carry a handgun for target practice or hunting, the licensing officer may restrict the license to cover those two categories. To establish proper cause to obtain a license without any restrictions, an applicant must "demonstrate a special need for self-protection distinguishable from that of the general community or of persons engaged in the same profession." A number of state court cases made clear that a generalized desire to carry a concealed weapon to protect one's person and property did not constitute proper cause.

The federal **district court** upheld the use of "proper cause." A three-judge panel of the Second Circuit did as well. Judge Richard Wesley, writing for the court, noted that the plaintiffs believed the *Heller* decision guaranteed them the right to possess and carry weapons in public to defend themselves from dangerous confrontations. In addition the plaintiffs argued that New York could not constitutionally force them to demonstrate proper cause to exercise that right. Judge Wesley concluded that *Heller* provided "no categorical answer to this case." The SUPREME COURT confined itself to ruling that the District of Columbia could not ban the possession of firearms in the home. It did not define the scope of the Second Amendment or the standard of review for laws that burden Second Amendment rights.

The plaintiffs argued that *Heller* demonstrated that there is a "fundamental right" to carry handguns in public and though a state may regulate open or concealed carrying of handguns, it cannot ban both. Judge Wesley pointed out that many states have imposed similar restrictions as New York, while others have not. This "highly ambiguous history and tradition" did not resolve the issue at hand. Moreover, New York's proper cause requirement did not operate as a complete ban on the possession of handguns in public.

Judge Wesley rejected the plaintiffs' second argument, in which they asked the court to apply the First Amendment's prior-restraint analysis when analyzing the proper cause requirement. The plaintiffs argued that the nature of the rights guaranteed by each amendment is identical. One has a right to speak and a right to bear arms. Therefore, "just as the FIRST AMENDMENT permits everyone to speak without obtaining a license, New York cannot limit the right to bear arms to only some law-abiding citizens." The court declined to apply substantive First Amendment principles "wholesale" into the Second Amendment **jurisprudence**. Moreover, no court has done so. Judge Wesley stated that even if the court did so, "this case would be a poor vehicle for its maiden voyage." Under prior-restraint law, the plaintiffs would have to show that officials had "unbridled discretion in making licensing determinations." This was not the case in New York, where judicial precedent had mandated an objective standard for licensing officers to follow.

The court did not believe that strict judicial scrutiny should be the standard of review in this case. HEIGHTENED SCRUTINY was more appropriate because the proper cause requirement did not burden the "core" Second Amendment right identified in *Heller* as the "right of law-abiding, responsible citizens to use arms in defense of hearth and home." The state's ability to regulate firearms "is qualitatively different in public than in the home." The history of the regulation of firearms in public showed that the Second Amendment allows state regulation. New York has compelling interests in public safety and crime prevention. Most importantly, the proper cause requirement was substantially related to these interests, thereby justifying the constitutionality of the law.

Seventh Circuit Panel Strikes Down Ban on Concealed Weapons

By 2012, 49 of the 50 states had passed laws allowing citizens to carry concealed weapons outside of the home. The only state with an almost complete ban on concealed weapons was Illinois. However, citizens and organizations challenged the Illinois statutes creating the ban, and a panel of the Seventh **Circuit Court** of Appeals in December 2012 ruled that the state had violated the SECOND AMENDMENT by prohibiting the weapons. The court gave the state legislature 180 days to approve a law that would comply with the Constitution, but state lawmakers could not reach an agreement.

The two Illinois laws in question were the Unlawful Use of Weapons (UUW) **statute**, 720 I.L.C.S. 5/24-1, and the Aggravated Unlawful Use of a Weapon (AUUW) statute, 720 I.L.C.S. 5/24-1.6. The UUW provides that a person commits an offense if the person "[c]arries or possesses in any vehicle or concealed on or about his person, except when on his land or in his own abode, legal dwelling, or fixed place of business, or on the land or in the legal dwelling of another person as an invitee with that person's permission, any pistol, revolver, stun gun or taser or other firearm." The UUW further prohibits possession of a weapon "on or about his person, upon any public street, alley, or other PUBLIC LANDS within the corporate limits of a city, village or incorporated town." Exceptions under the statute apply only when the weapon is unloaded and enclosed in a case, not immediately accessible to the user, or broken down in a nonfunctioning state.

The AUUW is similar to the UUW. Under the AUUW, a person commits another offense for carrying a weapon in a vehicle or in public and one of these two factors is present: "(A) the firearm possessed was uncased, loaded and immediately accessible at the time of the offense; or (B) the firearm possessed was uncased, unloaded, and the ammunition for the weapon was immediately accessible at the time of the offense."

Private citizens and several organizations brought suits in two federal district courts in Illinois to challenge the law. The organizations included the Second Amendment Foundation, Illinois Carry, and the Illinois State Rifle Association. In *Moore v. Madigan*, 842 F. Supp. 2d 1092 (C.D. Ill. 2012), and *Shepard v. Madigan*, 863 F. Supp. 2d (S.D. Ill. 2012), the plaintiffs requested that the courts enjoin enforcement of both the UUW and the AUUW based on Second Amendment arguments.

The principal focus in both cases was on the U.S. Supreme Court's decisions in *District of Columbia v. Heller*, 554 U.S. 570, 128 S. Ct. 2783, 171 L. Ed. 2d 637 (2008), and *McDonald v. Chicago*, 130 S. Ct. 3020, 177 L. Ed. 2d 894 (2010). In *Heller*, the Court concluded that individuals generally have the "right to possess and carry weapons in case of confrontation." The Court in *McDonald* extended this rule to apply to the states through the Due Process Clause of the FOURTEENTH AMENDMENT.

Both U.S. district judges ruled that the Illinois statutes did not violate the Second Amendment. In *Shepard*, Judge William D. Stiehl reviewed the statutes in light of the historical foundation of the Second Amendment. Stiehl concluded that the historical right to bear arms did not necessarily extend beyond the home. According to his analysis, the Supreme Court's decision in *Heller* focused on the right to possess a firearm within a home, and the Illinois statute did not prohibit a person from carrying a firearm for this purpose.

Similarly, in *Moore*, Judge Sue E. Myerscough concluded that the Illinois statutes did not restrict an activity that the Second Amendment protects. Like Stiehl, Myerscough focused her attention on the Supreme Court's reference to "in the home" when discussing the right to bear arms protected by the Constitution. She concluded that the Illinois statutes satisfied an intermediate level of scrutiny, meaning that she concluded the law served an important government interest of public safety and that the statutes were substantially related to the government interest.

The plaintiffs appealed both decisions to the Seventh Circuit Court of Appeals. In a 2–1 panel decision, the court reversed both **district court** rulings. Writing for the majority, Judge RICHARD POSNER disagreed with both district courts that the Second Amendment principally applies in the home. He wrote: "The right to 'bear' as distinct from the right to 'keep' arms is unlikely to refer to the home. To speak of 'bearing' arms within one's home would at all times have been awkward usage. A right to bear arms thus implies a right to carry a loaded gun outside the home."

Posner also disagreed with both district court's reliance on the history of the right to bear arms. He stated: "We are disinclined to engage in another round of historical analysis to determine whether eighteenth-century America understood the Second Amendment to include a right to bear guns outside the home. The SUPREME COURT has decided that the amendment confers a right to bear arms for SELF-DEFENSE, which is as important outside the home as inside."

The majority said that it would remand the cases to the respective district courts with instructions for those courts to declare the Illinois statutes unconstitutional. However, the majority agreed to stay the remand order for 180 days "to allow the Illinois legislature to craft a new gun law that will impose reasonable limitations, consistent with the public safety and the Second Amendment as interpreted in this opinion, on the carrying of guns in public." *Moore v. Madigan*, 702 F.3d 933 (7th Cir. 2012).

Judge Ann Claire Williams dissented, noting evidence of the dangers caused by stray bullets and the lack of clear evidence that carrying a gun provides more personal safety. She would have deferred to the Illinois Legislature to make its own laws on the matter.

Illinois Attorney General Lisa Madigan asked the full Seventh Circuit court to review the case, but the court denied the request. Lawmakers discussed ways to pass a new law to comply with the decision, but gun-control advocates were unable to reach a compromise with gun-rights advocates.

SECURITIES AND EXCHANGE COMMISSION

Gabelli v. SEC

Legislatures enact statutes of limitations to limit the period of time during which a party can

Michael Moore, the lead plaintiff in a 2012 suit that sought to overturn Illinois' concealed weapons ban.
ZBIGNIEW BZDAK/CHICAGO TRIBUNE/MCT/GETTY IMAGES

bring a claim. Ordinarily, the **statute** requires the party to bring a claim within a certain number of years after a **cause of action** "accrues." For instance, a CAUSE OF ACTION in tort accrues when the tort occurs, and the PLAINTIFF must bring a tort claim within a prescribed time period (such as two years) after accrual.

Courts have created some exceptions that allow parties to bring claims after the period of time stated in the **statute of limitations**. One of the most significant exceptions is known as the discovery rule. The discovery rule applies when the plaintiff could not discover the fact of injury because of the nature of the injury. For example, a defendant's acts may expose a plaintiff to a substance that causes the plaintiff to contract cancer several years after exposure. If the STATUTE OF LIMITATIONS applies strictly, the plaintiff would have to bring the claim within the prescribed period, even though the plaintiff may have no means to determine that she had suffered injury. However, if the discovery rule applies, the cause of action would not accrue until the plaintiff discovered or should have discovered with the exercise of reasonable diligence the fact of injury.

Federal agencies also have to bring actions within a time period established in statutes of limitations contained in the **U.S. Code**. Congress established a five-year statute of limitations codified at 28 U.S.C. § 2462. This statute provides as follows: "Except as otherwise provided by Act of Congress, an action, suit or proceeding for the enforcement of any civil fine, penalty, or **forfeiture**, **pecuniary** or otherwise, shall not be entertained unless commenced within five years from the date when the claim first accrued if, within the same period, the offender or the property is found within the United States in order that proper service may be made thereon."

In 2013, the U.S. Supreme Court reviewed a case about how 28 U.S.C. § 2462 applies to an enforcement action brought by the Securities and Exchange Commission. The SEC had brought an enforcement action against investment advisors who had allegedly committed **fraud**. The Allegation said that the **fraudulent** activity occurred between 1999 and 2002, but the SEC did not bring its action until 2008. The SEC argued that the discovery rule should apply to delay the accrual date in the SEC's action. However, a unanimous Court rejected the SEC's argument, holding that the government had to bring the action within five years of alleged Fraud. *Gabelli v. SEC*, 133 S. Ct. 1216, 185 L. Ed. 2d 297 (2013).

The SEC's case focused on the activities of officials with Gabelli Funds, L.L.C., which was an investment advisor for a **mutual fund** known as Gabelli Global Growth Fund (GGGF). These officials included Bruce Alpert, Gabelli's chief operating officer, and Marc Gabelli, the portfolio manager for the GGGF.

The SEC alleged that Alpert and Gabelli had allowed one investor in the GGGF to engage in a practice known as "market timing." The Supreme Court described market timing as "a trading strategy that exploits time delay in mutual funds' daily valuation system." The practice allows an investor to buy an undervalued fund at a low price and then sell at a higher price the next day. The practice is not illegal but can harm long-term investors.

According to the SEC's complaint, one of the GGGF's investors, Headstart Advisers, Ltd., was allowed to engage in market timing while other investors in the fund were not. Headstart Advisers in turn invested in a Hedge Fund run by Gabelli. Alpert and Gabelli did not disclose the agreement with Headstart to any of the other investors in GGGF. In fact, Alpert and Gabelli stated that they would not tolerate the practice of market timing by the other investors.

The SEC's complaint was based on the Investment Advisers Act of 1940, 15 U.S.C. § 80b-6(1), (2). This Act prohibits an investment advisor from employing "any device, scheme, or artifice to DEFRAUD any client or prospective client" or engaging "in any transaction, practice, or course of business which operates as a fraud or deceit upon any client or prospective client." The statute allows the SEC to seek civil penalties, and the five-year statute of limitations in 28 U.S.C. § 2462 applies to these actions.

Alpert and Gabelli argued that the limitations period had expired because the alleged fraud occurred no later than August 2002 but the SEC had not brought the complaint until April 2008. The U.S. **District Court** for the Southern District of New York agreed with the defendants and dismissed the claim. However, the Second **Circuit Court** of Appeals applied the discovery rule and determined the claim had not accrued until the SEC had discovered the fraud. *SEC v. Gabelli*, 653 F.3d 49 (2d Cir. 2011).

The Supreme Court granted **certiorari** to review the case, and the Court unanimously reversed the Second Circuit's decision. Chief Justice John Roberts, Jr., wrote the Court's opinion.

The Court noted that a claim accrues and the limitations period begins to run "when the plaintiff has a complete and present cause of action." The Court acknowledged that the discovery rule had a distinct application in the context of fraud. Older Supreme Court decisions established that "where a plaintiff has been injured by fraud and 'remains in ignorance of it without any fault or want of diligence or care on his part, the bar of the statute does not begin to run until the fraud is discovered.'"

However, the Court was not willing to extend the reasoning for applying the discovery rule to a case involving an enforcement action brought by the government. No lower court case before 2008 had ever applied the discovery rule to such an action. In fact, the Court noted that the government had failed to point to any case in the first 160 years of the enactment of 28 U.S.C. § 2462 where the discovery rule extended the accrual period for a government enforcement action.

The Court concluded that the reasons for applying the discovery rule to a private fraud case do not extend to the government's action.

A private citizen who has been defrauded likely has no reason to know of the fraud because the injury is self-concealing. Thus, it is just to extend the period of time to bring an action until the plaintiff discovered or should have discovered the injury. However, the SEC's "very purpose" is to root out fraud, and the SEC has considerable authority to investigate fraudulent acts.

Justice Roberts wrote: "In a civil penalty action, the Government is not only a different kind of plaintiff, it seeks a different kind of relief. The discovery rule helps to ensure that the injured receive recompense. But this case involves penalties, which go beyond compensation, are intended to punish, and label defendants wrongdoers."

Because the Court was unwilling to apply discovery rule, the cause of action accrued no later than 2002. Therefore, the Court remanded the case, and the Second Circuit affirmed the district court's dismissal of the claims.

SENTENCING

The postconviction stage of the criminal justice process, in which the defendant is brought before the court for the imposition of a penalty.

Alleyne v. United States

The U.S. SUPREME COURT in 2013 revisited an issue addressing whether a judge should be able to increase a defendant's mandatory minimum sentence based on facts determined by the judge and not a jury. The Supreme Court decided in 2002 that a judge could determine from a preponderance of the evidence that facts existed to support an increase in the minimum sentence. Critics of the 2002 case called on the Court to OVERRULE the prior case, and in *Alleyne v. United States*, 133 S. Ct. 2151 (2013), the Court did so.

The SIXTH AMENDMENT to the U.S. Constitution states: "In all criminal prosecutions, the accused shall enjoy the right to a speedy and public trial, by an impartial jury of the State and district wherein the crime shall have been committed." Courts have read this provision, along with the Due Process Clauses of the Fifth and Fourteenth Amendments, to require the government to prove each element of an offense to a jury **beyond a reasonable doubt**.

However, the Supreme Court has decided that the government does not need to submit this proof to a jury to resolve all questions. In *McMillan v. Pennsylvania*, 477 U.S. 79, 106 S. Ct. 2411, 91 L. Ed. 2d 67 (1986), the Court introduced the term "sentencing factor" as a fact that a judge could find and affect a defendant's sentence without the jury's involvement.

Fourteen years after the decision in *McMillan*, the Court addressed which types of facts that a judge may decide and those that a court must submit to a jury. The Court's opinion in *Apprendi v. New Jersey*, 530 U.S. 466, 120 S. Ct. 2348, 147 L. Ed. 2d 435 (2000), addressed a case questioning whether a judge could sentence a DEFENDANT beyond the maximum allowed by **statute**. The Court ruled that a court could not, establishing a rule that "any fact that increased the prescribed **statutory** maximum sentence must be an 'element' of the offense to be found by the jury."

Two years after the Court decided *Apprendi*, the Court reached a different answer when confronted with the issue of whether a judge could increase a defendant's mandatory minimum sentence based on facts not submitted to the jury. The Court in *Harris v. United States*, 536 U.S. 545, 122 S. Ct. 2406, 153 L. Ed. 2d 524 (2002), distinguished circumstances related to mandatory minimum sentences and those related to maximum sentences, ruling that the Sixth Amendment did not apply to determinations of the mandatory minimum sentences. Therefore, judges were free under *Harris* to base sentences beyond the mandatory minimum on facts not proven BEYOND A REASONABLE DOUBT.

In August 2009, Allen Ryan Alleyne's girlfriend suggested that he rob the store manager of the convenience store where she worked while the manager made his daily deposits at a local bank. The girlfriend provided details about the store, and Alleyne and his girlfriend rented a car to carry out the **robbery**. On October 1, Alleyne and an ACCOMPLICE pulled their car to the side of the road ahead of the store manager's car. The store manager pulled his car over to render aid. The accomplice left the rental car and approached the store manager's car. When the manager rolled his window down, prosecutors alleged that the accomplice put a gun to the manager's neck and demanded the manager's money. The accomplice took $13,201.99, and he and Alleyne sped away. Federal prosecutors charged Alleyne with one count of ROBBERY affecting interstate commerce and one count of using, carrying, brandishing, and possessing a firearm in furtherance of a crime of violence. The jury in the U.S. **District Court** for the Eastern District of Virginia found Alleyne guilty of both crimes.

Alleyne's conviction on the charge of using or carrying a firearm in relation to a crime of violence was based on 18 U.S.C. § 924(c)(1)(A). This statute is a discrete offense in and of itself. Violation of its statutory provision(s) carries a minimum prison term of five years, in addition to "any other term of imprisonment imposed on the [offender]." § 924(c)(1)(A) and (D). It establishes different sentences depending on how the defendant used the firearm. The general sentence for a violation is five years. However, if the jury finds that the defendant "brandished" a firearm, the statute extends the mandatory minimum sentence to seven years. The statute extends the sentence to ten years if the defendant discharges the firearm. The jury found that Alleyne had "used" or "carried" a firearm, but the jury did not decide that he had brandished a firearm.

Alleyne's robbery charge carried a sentence of between 46 and 57 months. A presentencing report recommended an additional sentence of seven years based on the conclusion that Alleyne had brandished the weapon during the robbery. Alleyne objected to the sentence, stressing that the jury had only found that he had carried or used a firearm. However, the district court judge found by preponderance of the evidence that Alleyne reasonably had foreseen that his accomplice would brandish the weapon. Therefore, the court sentenced Alleyne to seven years on the weapons charge, giving Alleyne a total sentence of 130 months in prison.

Alleyne appealed his conviction to the Fourth **Circuit Court** of Appeals. However, the Fourth Circuit cited *Harris* to support its conclusion "that Supreme Court precedent forecloses any argument that Alleyne's constitutional rights were violated by the district court's finding that he was accountable for brandishing the firearm despite the jury's finding that he was not guilty of that offense." *United States v. Alleyne*, 457 F. App'x 348 (4th Cir. 2011).

The Supreme Court agreed to review the decision. The Court's more liberal justices— STEPHEN BREYER, RUTH BADER GINSBURG, SONIA SOTOMAYOR, and ELENA KAGAN—each agreed that the Court should overrule the previous decision in *Harris*. The deciding vote came from Justice CLARENCE THOMAS, who voted to vacate Alleyne's conviction because the jury had not found the critical fact beyond a REASONABLE DOUBT.

Thomas wrote the majority opinion, which focused on Alleyne's argument that the Court had wrongly decided *Harris* in 2002. Thomas relied to an extent on historical precedent from cases decided in the 17th and 18th centuries. These cases typically connected facts with certain punishments, meaning that if a fact was by law something essential to a penalty, the fact was an element of an offense.

Thomas then reviewed the decisions in *Apprendi* and *Harris*. Thomas had concurred in the former but dissented in the latter. He stressed that it is "impossible to dissociate the floor of a sentencing range from the penalty affixed to the crime." Thomas also noted that facts that increase a defendant's sentence aggravate the defendant's punishment. Allowing a judge to increase the mandatory minimum was not a matter of limiting a judge's discretion in sentencing. Instead, the Court ruled that a fact that aggravates the range of allowable sentences is a element of an offense that the court must submit to a jury to determine proof beyond a reasonable doubt.

Justice Sotomayor concurred in the opinion, noting that the Court had properly followed its precedent in *Apprendi*. Justice Breyer also concurred, agreeing that *Apprendi* should control sentencing questions involving both mandatory minimum and mandatory maximum sentences.

Chief Justice JOHN ROBERTS, JR., and Justice SAMUEL ALITO both filed dissenting opinions. Roberts argued that he could find no support for the decision in the history or purpose of the Sixth Amendment, while Alito suggested that the Court's decision in *Apprendi* was wrongly decided.

Descamps v. United States

The Armed Career Criminal Act (ACCA), 18 U.S.C. § 924(e), was designed by Congress to keep repeat offenders of violent crimes off the streets. Under the Act, criminals who have three prior convictions for violent felonies must receive a minimum sentence of 15 years for any subsequent **felony** conviction. The ACCA defines a violent felony as any crime involving the threatened use of physical force, or a **burglary**, which is punishable by imprisonment for greater than one year. In *Descamps v. United States*, 133 S. Ct. 2276 (2013), the U.S. SUPREME COURT was asked to determine whether lower courts had correctly determined that Matthew Descamps' three prior felony convictions were predicate felonies under the ACCA and warranted the Act's enhanced sentence? The Court decidedly said "No" and reversed the ruling of the U.S. **Circuit Court** of Appeals for the Ninth Circuit.

In September 2007, following jury trial in a federal **district court**, Descamps was found guilty of felony possession of a firearm. At sentencing, the U.S. District Court for the Eastern District of Washington (state) concluded that Descamps' prior convictions for **robbery**, BURGLARY, and felony harassment constituted three predicate violent felonies under the ACCA. Accordingly, it sentenced him to 262 months in prison followed by five years of supervised release.

Descamps appealed, arguing that his prior burglary conviction, which occurred in California, could not be counted as a predicate felony under ACCA. He had pleaded guilty to a violation of California Penal Code Ann. § 459, which provides that a "person who enters" certain locations "with intent to commit grand or **petit larceny** or any felony is guilty of burglary." Importantly, the California **statute** does not require that the "person who enters" do so unlawfully, and it does not require that the entry itself be done in an unlawful manner, such as burglary statutes that generally require a "breaking and entering." Thus, California's statute is more expansive in its sweep, covering more crimes than would normally be considered under a "generic" definition of burglary.

As noted above, the ACCA does include "burglary" as one of its predicate felonies toward an enhanced sentence. In determining whether a prior conviction counts under the Act, courts use what has become known as a "categorical approach." This involves comparing the elements of the statute under which the person was convicted with the elements of the "generic" crime, i.e. the offense as commonly understood. If the statute's elements are the same or narrower than those of the generic offense, the conviction constitutes one that qualifies for an enhanced sentence.

The Supreme Court had previously approved a "modified" version of that approach when a prior conviction is under a "divisible statute," or one that enumerates alternative elements of an offense, e.g., a burglary involving entry into a building *or* a vehicle. In such a case, where one of the elements matches that found in a generic offense (e.g., entry of a building), but the other does not (e.g., entry of a vehicle), sentencing courts may consult certain documents, such as indictments or jury instructions, to determine which alternative element formed the basis for the defendant's prior conviction. They can then proceed to compare elements as in a regular categorical approach.

Returning to the California statute in question, the *Descamps* case asked whether sentencing courts may also consult those additional documents when a DEFENDANT was convicted under an "indivisible statute" that did not contain alternative elements but criminalized a broader swath of conduct than its generic counterpart.

The federal district court determined that the modified categorical approach applied, and it examined certain documents, including the record of the plea, in order to discover whether Descamps had "admitted the elements of a generic burglary" when entering his plea. (Without objection from defense counsel, the PROSECUTOR at the plea hearing had stated on record that the crime "involve[d] the breaking and entering of a grocery store.") The district court determined that the prior conviction qualified as a predicate felony under ACCA. The Ninth Circuit Court of Appeals affirmed, taking generally the same "modified categorical approach" to permit review of certain underlying documents to determine the factual basis of a prior conviction.

The Supreme Court accepted review to resolve a split among circuits as to whether the modified approach (encompassing the review of underlying documents) applies when a statute contains an indivisible single set of elements, but they encompass more offenses than the relevant corresponding "generic" offense.

There was prior Supreme Court precedent to instruct in this case, namely *Taylor v. United States*, 495 U.S. 575, 110 S. Ct. 2143, 109 L. Ed. 2d 607 (1990), which first adopted the categorical approach, and *Shepard v. United States*, 544 U.S.

13, 125 S. Ct. 1254, 161 L. Ed. 2d 205 (2005), wherein a burglary statute covered entries into "boats and cars" as well as buildings.

Justice ELENA KAGAN, writing for the 8-1 majority, held that a felony burglary conviction under California's Penal Code (§ 459) was not a generic burglary conviction as it did not match traditional elements of the generic offense, e.g., "breaking and entering a building," or "unlawful entry." Moreover, the Court found the Ninth Circuit's review of outside documents exceeded its authority, as sentencing courts may only review them in cases where the underlying statute included alternative elements, which California's statute did not. Therefore, the "modified" approach was not applicable. Such unwarranted review of the underlying record "raises serious SIXTH AMENDMENT concerns," said the Court.

Justice SAMUEL ALITO, the lone dissenter, opined that the majority's decision artificially limited the ACCA by examining the sometimes arbitrary wording of a statute. Instead, he would recommend a more practical approach. "When it is clear that a defendant necessarily admitted or the jury necessarily found that the defendant committed the elements of generic burglary, the conviction should qualify," the DISSENT read.

SEX OFFENSES

Seventh Circuit Rules Indiana Sex Offender Registry Violates Due Process

Most states have public databases of persons convicted of SEX OFFENSES. These databases provide the public with information as to convicted sex offenders in their communities. An Indiana sex offender filed a federal civil lawsuit against the state, alleging that the state had failed to provide a process for the correction of errors in the registry. The Seventh **Circuit Court** of Appeals, in *Schepers v. Commissioner, Indiana Department of Correction,* 691 F.3d 909 (2012), agreed that the state had violated the Fourteenth Amendment's Due Process Clause by failing to provide a procedure for correcting these errors.

Indiana maintains what it calls the "Sex and Violent Offender Registry." People visiting the registry's website find on each registrant's page a recent photograph, home address, the height, weight, age, race, and sex of the registrant, and information about the particular offense that led the person's being placed on the registry. Some registrants' pages also carry the label "sexually violent predator," if they had committed certain serious offenses or had multiple previous convictions for certain sex and violent offenses. The status of being a sexually violent predator imposes extra burdens on offenders. They must register more frequently and cannot live, work, or volunteer within 1,000 feet of a school, public park, or youth program center. Violating these conditions is a **felony**. In addition, if a sexually violent predator plans to be absent from his/her home more than 72 hours, s/he must inform local law enforcement in both the county where s/he resides and the county where s/he intends to visit about his/her travel plans.

David Schepers filed a lawsuit in Indiana federal **district court**, alleging that the state had failed to provide a procedure for correcting errors in the registry's information about a sex offender. Schepers, one of an estimated 24,000 sex offender registrants in Indiana, had been convicted in 2006 of two counts of child exploitation. These two convictions were listed in the registry along with the designation "Offender Against Children." However, Schepers was also erroneously designated as a "sexually violent predator," which made him subject to the more burdensome requirements and restrictions required by **statute**. Schepers attempted to correct this error but discovered the Indiana Department of Corrections (DOC) provided no official channel or **administrative procedure** allowing him to do so. He tried telephoning DOC officials to get the label removed but was unsuccessful.

After he filed his lawsuit, the DOC instituted a new policy that tried to provide some process to correct registry errors. Under the new appeal policy, the DOC must send prisoners notice before they are released from their institution that explains what information will be published on the registry. The prisoner has 20 days to seek review by submitting an appeal. The person deciding the appeal can then request additional information or consult with the prisoner. However, the policy does not require that a hearing be conducted. After 30 days have passed, all appeals are "deemed denied." If not denied, the prisoner is informed of the decision to grant an appeal in full or in part. The prisoner has no right to further review after the appeal decision. This new policy did not apply to persons who already had been released or who had never been incarcerated in a DOC facility. Based on this new policy, the DOC asked the district court to dismiss Schepers' lawsuit, contending that the new policy provided sufficient due process. In addition, it contended that the Due Process Clause did not apply at all because registry mistakes did not infringe any constitutionally protected liberty interest. The district court rejected the latter argument but agreed that the new policy was sufficient to satisfy the Due Process Clause. The court dismissed the lawsuit and Schepers appealed.

A three-judge panel of the Seventh Circuit unanimously ruled that the DOC policy was not sufficient to satisfy due process. Judge Diane Wood, writing for the court, pointed out that for Schepers to show the DOC's action injured his reputation under the Due Process Clause, the action had to alter his legal status or rights. The DOC did not challenge the district court's holding that mislabeling Schepers as a sexually violent predator further stigmatized his reputation and implicated a liberty interest protected by the Due Process Clause.

The only issue on appeal was whether Indiana was "providing whatever process is 'due.'" Judge Woods needed to balance three factors to reach an answer: (1) the private interest that will be affected by the official action; (2) the risk of an erroneous deprivation of this interest through the procedures used; and, (3) the government's interest, including the additional **fiscal** and administrative burdens that additional procedural requirements would entail. The DOC contended its process adequately balanced these three factors but the court found a "glaring problem" with this position: "it ignores the fact that the policy provides *no process* whatsoever to an entire class of registrants—those who are not incarcerated." In addition, those who are incarcerated and get the benefit of the new policy have "no guarantee that later mistakes will not be made." The court also noted that a brief review of the registry revealed that registrants are sometimes given sentences that are suspended, sentences of PROBATION, and sentences with terms so low that they receive credit for time served and

never move to a DOC facility. Though the DOC argued that it made no sense for it to be the agency responsible for furnishing notice and review to people who were not located in their institutions, Judge Wood concluded that the Indiana legislature had decided just that when it gave the DOC control over the entire registry. Therefore, the DOC's current procedures were inadequate.

Judge Woods found that this deficiency alone required the court to reverse the district court, but expressed concern with the fact that the appeal process "never actually requires the DOC to review a registrant's complaint." Under the 30-day "deemed denied" policy, an appeal never had to be considered before it was rejected. This means an offender could "mail the appeal to the DOC appeal authority, only to have it sit on a desk unread." This was not sufficient to satisfy the Due Process Clause. The appeals court returned the case to the district court, encouraging the parties "to work together to come to an agreement that fits within the boundaries" of the court's decision.

Seventh Circuit Strikes Down Sex Offender Social Media Ban

Many states have enacted laws restricting the lives of convicted sex offenders who are no longer under the supervision of the courts. The importance of the Internet in everyday life led some legislatures to make it a crime for adults to solicit children to engage in sexual intercourse or other sexual acitvities. The state of Indiana took the issue further when it passed a law that banned most registered sex offenders from using social networking sites like Facebook, instant messaging, and chat programs. A sex offender, on behalf of a class of similarly situated sex offenders, challenged the law on FIRST AMENDMENT grounds. The Seventh **Circuit Court** of Appeals, in *Doe v. Marion County, Indiana*, 705 F.3d 694 (2013), struck down the law, finding it was not narrowly tailored to serve a significant government interest.

The Indiana law prohibited certain sex offenders from knowingly or intentionally using a social networking website, instant messaging, or chat room program that "the offender knows allows a person who is less than eighteen years of age to access or use ..." A violation constituted a **misdemeanor**, while subsequent convictions constituted felonies. A convicted sex offender, John Doe, challenged the law in federal **district court**. He had been convicted of two counts of child exploitation in 2000 and had been released from prison in 2003. Doe was required to register as a sex offender on Indiana's registry. Under the law, Doe was prohibited from using social network sites. He claimed the law violated his First Amendment rights and asked the court to grant his request to proceed anonymously and to grant his motion to certify the case as a **class action**. The court granted both motions but upheld the law. The court found that the law did implicate Doe's First Amendment rights but held that the regulation was narrowly tailored to serve a significant **state interest** and left open sufficient alternative channels of communication. The court pointed out that Doe could attend civic meetings, write letters to the newspaper, comment on online stories that did not require a Facebook account, email friends and family, publish a blog, or use social networking sites that do not allow minors. Doe appealed to the Seventh Circuit.

A three-judge panel of the Seventh Circuit unanimously reversed the district court and threw out the law as an abridgment of Doe's First Amendment rights. Judge Joel Flaum, writing for the court, noted that the U.S. SUPREME COURT has ruled that a complete ban on certain expressive activities can be narrowly tailored, "but only if each activity with the proscription's scope is an appropriately targeted evil." On the other hand, the Supreme Court has invalidated bans on expressive activity that are not the substantive evil if the state has alternative means of combating the evil. Indiana agreed that there was nothing dangerous about Doe's use of social media as long as he did not improperly communicate with minors. Moreover, the state agreed that illicit communication comprised "a minuscule subset of the universe of social network activity." Based on these agreements, Judge Flaum found that the Indiana law targeted "substantially more activity than the evil it seeks to redress."

The appeals court pointed out that Indiana has other methods to combat unwanted and inappropriate communication between minors and sex offenders. The state made it a **felony** for persons over 21 to solicit children under 16 to engage in sexual intercourse, deviant sexual conduct, or any fondling intended to arouse the child or the older person. Another Indiana law punishes "inappropriate communication with a child" and communication "with the intent to gratify the sexual desires of the person or the individual." In addition, both statutes have enhanced penalties for using a computer network. Judge Flaum concluded that these laws better advanced Indiana's "interest in preventing harmful interaction with children by going beyond social networks." Both statutes were "neither over- nor under-inclusive like the **statute** at issue here."

The district court had suggested the law was narrowly tailored to serve purposes different from the existing **solicitation** and communication laws. The existing laws sought to punish those who had already committed the crime of solicitation, while the social network law aimed to prevent and deter the sexual exploitation of minors by barring sexual offenders from entering a "virtual world where they have access to minors." Judge Flaum found that the "immediate problem" was that all criminal laws generally punish those who have already committed a crime. Therefore, characterizing the new law as preventative and the existing laws as reactive was "questionable." The goal of deterrence did not "license the state to restrict far more speech than necessary to target the prospective harm."

The court made clear that the state might be able to draft a more narrowly tailored law that would survive First Amendment scrutiny. Judge Flaum speculated that such a law would have to target certain types of sex offenders who present an "acute risk." For example, the law could be tailored to those individuals "whose presence on social media impels them to solicit children."

United States v. Kebodeaux

In *United States v. Kebodeaux*, 133 S. Ct. 2496 (2013), the U.S. SUPREME COURT ruled on constitutional challenges to the Sex Offender Registration and Notification Act of 2006 (SORNA), 42 U.S.C. § 16901 *et seq.*, which created both a federal requirement to register and a federal penalty for failure to register. In this case, the question centered on how the law might affect a former sex offender who no longer was in government CUSTODY or on supervised release at the time the law was enacted. By a 7-2 margin, the Court's majority held that the Fifth **Circuit Court** of Appeals had erred in holding that Kebodeaux was not under federal obligation (to register) until SORNA was enacted, because pre-SORNA federal law also obligated him. The Fifth Circuit also erred in holding that Congress lacked the authority to criminally penalize a person (for failure to register) who, although convicted of a federal sex offense, had already completed his criminal sentence prior to SORNA.

In 1999, while Anthony Kebodeaux was serving in the U.S. Air Force, he was court-martialed and convicted of a federal sex offense. He served a three-month sentence and was dishonorably discharged from the military service. After moving to Texas, he registered with Texas authorities in 2004. Congress passed SORNA in 2006. In 2007, Kebodeaux moved from San Antonio to El Paso, Texas, and updated his sex offender registration. However, within months he returned to San Antonio. He did not re-register/update his new address.

Acting under SORNA, the federal government prosecuted him and a federal **district court** convicted him of violating SORNA. A panel of the Fifth Circuit Court of Appeals originally upheld the conviction, but later, a full court, on appeal, voted 10-6 to reverse the conviction. The full court stated that, by the time SORNA was enacted in 2006, Kibodeaux had "fully served" his sentence several years prior, and he was "no longer in federal custody, in the military, under any sort of supervised release or PAROLE, or in any other special relationship with the federal government."

According to the Fifth Circuit, the past commission of a federal crime did not give the federal government open-ended criminal authority over the offender, once he had completed his punishment/sentence. Importantly, the **appellate court** limited its decision to the facts of this case, i.e., that both offense and sentence occurred prior to SORNA. It did not question the authority of Congress to compel intra-state changes to registration or otherwise **place restrictions** on federal prisoners, post-release from prison, after SORNA. But looking to the record before it, the **appellate** court found that SORNA did not apply to Kebodeaux because he had been "unconditionally let . . . free."

The U.S. Supreme Court disagreed. Justice STEPHEN BREYER, delivering the opinion for the majority, held that the U.S. Constitution's NECESSARY AND PROPER CLAUSE gave Congress the power to both enact the registration provisions of SORNA, and to apply them to Kebodeaux, even though his conviction and prison time both occurred prior to SORNA's enactment.

The Military Regulation and Necessary and Proper Clauses, both in Article I, grant power to Congress to create federal crimes and to regulate punishment for the crimes' offenders. Contrary to the Fifth Circuit's assumption that Kebodeaux's release was "unconditional," the Court found that relevant statutes and regulations made it clear that at the time of Kebodeax's release, he was subject to the Wetterling Act, a federal law with similar registration requirements as SORNA. His court martial and conviction expressly contained two sentencing requirements: three months' confinement, and registration as a sex offender in the state where he resided, with a continued need to keep that information current.

Because Kebodeaux was subject to those federal registration requirements at the time of his prison release, Congress had the authority to modify those registration requirements through SORNA and apply them to him. Further, the fact that meeting these federal-law requirements involved compliance with state-law requirements (in this case, Texas) made them no less federal law requirements. Therefore, Kebodeaux could be prosecuted for failure to meet the federal law requirements.

Justice Breyer was joined in the majority opinion by Justices ANTHONY KENNEDY, RUTH BADER GINSBURG, SONIA SOTOMAYOR, and ELENA KAGAN. Chief Justice JOHN ROBERTS, JR. and Justice SAMUEL ALITO filed separate opinions concurring in the judgment. (Justice Roberts felt the conclusion was clear and simple, and the majority unnecessarily expounded on extraneous discussions, e.g., the benefit of registration to public safety.) Justice ANTONIN SCALIA dissented in that, SORNA aside, "[t]hat does not establish, however, that the Wetterling Act's registration requirement was itself a valid exercise of any federal power, or that SORNA is designed to carry the Wetterling Act into execution." Justice Scalia also joined in the DISSENT of Justice CLARENCE THOMAS, who opined that SORNA does not "carr[y] into Execution" any federal power that is enumerated in the Constitution. Therefore, as applied to Kebodeaux, it was unconstitutional.

SOVEREIGN IMMUNITY

The legal protection that prevents a sovereign state or person from being sued without consent.

United States v. Bormes

In 2000, the U.S. Treasury Department launched a website, Pay.gov, that enabled consumers to make online payments to government agencies by using credit or debit cards. In August 2008, attorney James Bormes, who was filing a lawsuit on behalf of a client in U.S. **District Court** for the Northern District of Illinois, utilized Pay.gov to pay the court's $350 filing fee with a credit card. The confirmation page displayed the expiration date of Bormes' American Express credit card, along with the last four digits of his credit card.

Bormes then filed a **putative class action** suit against the U.S. government, for himself and all others similarly harmed, for violations of the Fair Credit Reporting Act (FCRA), 15 U.S.C. § 1681 *et seq. United States v. Bormes*, 133 S. Ct. 12 (2012). The complaint alleged that the printed receipt bearing such personal information violated § 1681c(g)(1), and he and thousands of others were entitled to damages under § 1681n. The cited § 1681c(g)(1) states that:

> no person that accepts credit cards or debit cards for the transaction of business shall print more than the last 5 digits of the card number *or* the expiration date upon any receipt provided to the cardholder at the point of the sale or transaction.

The Act defines "person" broadly (e.g., individuals, partnerships, corporations, trusts, etc.) and expressly includes "government or governmental subdivision or agency, or other entity." It also provides that actions may be brought "in any appropriate United States district court, without regard to the **amount in controversy**, or in any other court of competent jurisdiction."

Bormes asserted jurisdiction of the case under FCRA's § 1681p as well as under the Little Tucker Act, 28 U.S.C. § 1346(a)(2). The Little Tucker Act provides that district courts "shall have **original jurisdiction**, concurrent with the United States Court of Federal Claims, of . . . [a]ny . . . civil action or claim against the United States, not exceeding $10,000 in amount, founded . . . upon . . . any Act of Congress."

In response to the government's motion to dismiss for lack of **subject matter jurisdiction** and failure to state a claim, the district court concluded that it did have jurisdiction under the FRCA. However, it dismissed the case because FCRA did not waive governmental (sovereign) immunity, which is necessary to permit a damages suit against the United States. It also found that invoking the Little Tucker Act was moot, because it already had jurisdiction under the FRCA.

The U.S. **Circuit Court** of Appeals for the Federal Circuit vacated the district court's decision, holding that the Little Tucker Act provided the government's consent to suit, as the underlying FCRA could be interpreted as mandating a right of recovery in damages (as against the United States).

A unanimous U.S. Supreme Court disagreed. In vacating the decision of the Federal Circuit, Justice Antonin Scalia, writing for the Court, held that the Little Tucker Act did not waive the **sovereign immunity** of the United States in damage actions under the FCRA. It did not create any substantive rights. Therefore, it was inapplicable to cases where the underlying law (FCRA) imposing monetary liability had its own specific judicial remedies. Rather, the Little Tucker Act was intended to fill the gap left open in more general statutes where monetary relief might be warranted. The lower court should have referred directly to the text of the FCRA itself to decide whether sovereign immunity was waived. Justice Scalia offered no opinion as to whether FCRA waived sovereign immunity. "Since FCRA is a detailed remedial scheme, only its own text can determine whether the damages liability Congress crafted extends to the federal government," he wrote.

The Court then remanded the case to the Seventh Circuit, as the government had petitioned, since the Little Tucker Act's jurisdictional grant did not apply to this case. The remand required a determination as to whether the FCRA itself waives the federal government's immunity to damages actions under its § 1681n (see, above).

SPEEDY TRIAL

Supreme Court Dismisses Appeal on Right to a Speedy Trial

The Sixth Amendment gives criminal defendants the right to a speedy trial. When a defendant claims a violation of this right, the Supreme

COURT has applied a four-part test to assess whether there was such a violation. In *Boyer v. Louisiana*, 133 S. Ct. 1702, 185 L. Ed. 2d 774 (2013), the Court examined whether a state funding crisis that delayed a trial for seven years should be considered in assessing a speedy trial claim. In an unusual move, the Court dismissed the appeal without an opinion after both sides submitted briefs and presented oral arguments. In a concurring opinion, Justice SAMUEL ALITO placed most of the blame for delay on the defendant. In a dissenting opinion, Justice SONIA SOTOMAYOR contended that the Court should have addressed the issue.

In February 2002, Jonathan Boyer and his brother were hitchhiking in Calcasieu Parish, Louisiana. A driver picked up the pair, whereupon Boyer demanded the man give them his money. When the man refused, Boyer shot and killed him. After his brother helped him cover up the crime, Boyer fled to Florida where he was captured about a month later. The police had a strong case against Boyer, as he gave a detailed **confession** and his brother agreed to testify about the crime. Other witnesses came forward saying they had heard Boyer confess to the crime. In addition, his fingerprints were found in the victim's truck.

The state prosecutors announced they would seek the death penalty and the state court appointed Thomas Lorenzi, an experienced trial attorney, to serve as Boyer's primary defense counsel. However, state law required that in death penalty cases, two lawyers must represent the defendant. Therefore, a less experienced lawyer from the Louisiana Capital Assistance Center (LCAC) assisted Lorenzi. The LCAC lawyer was paid by the state but there was confusion about which branch of the state government should pay Lorenzi's fees. The trial court scheduled a hearing on this matter but the hearing was repeatedly put off at the urging of the defense. For the next three years the defense requested that the hearing be continued on eight separate occasions, causing a total delay of approximately 20 months. The trial judge issued other continuances without any objection from the defense, delaying the hearing another 15 months. When the matter was scheduled for hearing, Hurricane Rita forced the parish courthouse to close.

The trial court held the hearing in March 2006, at which time the state revealed that Lorenzi's fees could not be paid until the start of the next **fiscal** year. Ten months later, the state announced it would no longer seek the death penalty, which allowed Lorenzi to withdraw from the case and have lawyers from the LCAC handle Boyer's defense. Justice Alito, in his concurring opinion, noted that the case then proceeded "at a plodding pace." The defense filed pre-trial motions and took pre-trial appeals. The court halted the proceedings for 11 months after concluding that Boyer was temporarily incompetent to stand trial. The case finally went to trial in September 2009. A jury found Boyer guilty of second-degree MURDER and armed **robbery**. The Louisiana Third Circuit **Court of Appeal** upheld Boyer's conviction, finding that there had been no violation of Boyer's right to a speedy trial under the Sixth Amendment. The appeals court recognized that the more than seven-year delay from arrest to trial was "presumptively prejudicial." It found the reason for the delay was caused by "lack of funding" for Boyer's defense, but declined to weigh this period of the delay against the state at all for the purposes of its analysis under a four-part Supreme Court speedy trial test. It concluded that during the first three years Boyer was incarcerated for first-degree murder, "the progression of the prosecution was 'out of the State's control.'" The Louisiana Supreme Court denied review of this decision and Boyer successfully petitioned his case to the U.S. Supreme Court.

After oral arguments the Supreme Court dismissed the petition as improvidently granted, with no other explanation. However, Justice Alito, in a concurring opinion joined by Justices ANTONIN SCALIA and CLARENCE THOMAS, offered his viewpoint on why the Court acted as it did. He concluded that after examining the case record, the majority found that the "single largest share of the delay in this case was the direct result of defense requests for continuances, that other defense motions caused substantial additional delay, and that much of the rest of the delay was caused by events beyond anyone's control." In addition, the delay caused by the defense worked in Boyer's favor, as the murder charge was reduced and the death penalty removed in a "very strong case of first-degree murder." As to Boyer's claim that the majority of the delay was caused by "lack of funding," Justice Alito argued that the appeals court statement should be read in context. What the statement most likely meant was "not that the delay in question was caused by the State's failure to provide funding but simply that the delay was attributable to the funding issue." In his view, the record did not support the proposition that much, if not most, of the delay was caused by the state's failure to fund the defense.

Justice Sonia Sotomayor, in a dissenting opinion joined by Justices RUTH BADER GINSBURG, STEPHEN BREYER, and ELENA KAGAN, stated that the Court accepted Boyer's petition to answer whether a delay caused by a state's failure to fund legal counsel for an indigent's defense should be weighed against the state in determining whether there was a deprivation of the defendant's Sixth Amendment right to a speedy trial. There was no reason to dismiss the case because prior Court precedents clearly stated that such a delay should weigh against the state. In prior speedy trial cases, the Court had used a balancing test that identified four factors a court should consider. These included the length of delay, the reason for the delay, the defendant's assertion of his right, and prejudice to the defendant. The key factor was the second one: the reason for delay. Justice Sotomayor looked to the Louisiana appeals court ruling that the "majority of the seven-year delay" was caused by the "lack of funding" made available to the defense. She contended the Court should have deferred to this factual determination instead of imposing its reading of the record on the case. The court should have remanded the case to the appeals court and have it apply the four-part test correctly. Under the balancing test, Boyer still might not have succeeded, but the court needed to follow the correct analysis in weighting each of the four factors.

SPORTS LAW

Cyclist Lance Armstrong Admits to Years of Doping

The cyclist Lance Armstrong ended years of denials when he admitted in January 2013 that he had taken performance-enhancing drugs (a practice known as "doping") during his racing days. The admission came months after the U.S. Anti-Doping Agency had released hundreds of pages of evidence showing that Armstrong had indeed doped. The agency had already stripped Armstrong of his seven Tour de France titles and banned him for life from competitive cycling. Armstrong also faces a lawsuit based on the False Claims Act, and the result of the case could bankrupt him.

Although cycling has never had the same type of high profile in the United States as other sports, some figures within the cycling world have become household names. For instance, Greg LeMond became a celebrity throughout the world when he became the first non-European to win the Tour de France in 1986, and he won the event two more times in 1989 and 1990. LeMond's success helped to lead a new generation of American cyclists to compete at a high level in the international arena.

Armstrong competed in amateur triathlons during the 1980s. He eventually focused on cycling and became the U.S. national amateur champion by 1991. He competed in the Olympics in 1992 and his first Tour de France in 1993. The Tour de France is widely considered the most prestigious and difficult bicycle race in the world.

In 1996, Armstrong's world came crashing down. He was coughing up blood and had a large growth on one of his testicles. Doctors diagnosed him with stage 3, or advanced, testicular cancer, which had already spread to his brain, lungs, and abdomen. Doctors immediately performed surgery on him and administered chemotherapy. His chance for survival at the time of the surgery was reportedly less than 40 percent. He had an additional surgery to remove a brain tumor.

Armstrong completed his chemotherapy treatment in December 1996, and doctors declared him to be cancer-free just months later. In 1997, he announced the formation of a foundation to benefit cancer research. Armstrong's foundation was originally known as the Lance Armstrong Foundation, and it later became known as Livestrong. The organization is well known for selling yellow bracelets that helped raise funds for Livestrong.

Armstrong returned to the world of competitive cycling after his recovery. By 1999, he was the leader of a racing team sponsored by the U.S. POSTAL SERVICE. He competed in the Tour de France and became the second American to win it. Over the next seven years, his legend grew as he won the race a record seven times. By the time he won his final Tour de France in 2005, he was one of the most recognizable athletes in the world. He had endorsements from many major sponsors, and

Lance Armstrong in the 2010 Tour de France, three years before he admitted to using performance-enhancing drugs during his racing career.
SPENCER PLATT/GETTY IMAGES

reports indicate that his NET WORTH is more than $100 million. He announced his first retirement from professional cycling in 2005.

Even during the height of his success, though, allegations of doping haunted him. In 2004, authors David Walsh and Pierre Ballester published a book titled *L.A. Confidential: Les Secrets de Lance Armstrong*, which alleged that Armstrong had started taking drugs as early as 1995. In 2004 and 2005, several other stories of Armstrong's use of performance-enhancing drugs arose, including allegations that he had tested positive for the drug cortisone in 1999, when Armstrong won his first Tour de France.

Other cyclists had also become embroiled in doping scandals. Armstrong's former teammate Floyd Landis won the Tour de France but was stripped of the title after he failed a drug test. Alberto Contador of Spain, who had won the Tour in 2007 and 2008, lost his 2010 title because of a failed drug test as well. Of the Tour winners since 1995, only two have not been implicated in doping scandals, according to an editorial in the *Washington Post*.

Armstrong consistently issued strong denials that he had ever doped. In an interview with CBS reporter Bob Schieffer (also a cancer survivor),

Armstrong said, "I was on my death bed. You think I'm going to come back into a sport and say 'OK, OK doctor give me everything you got. I just want to go fast?' No way. I would never do that." Nike also featured Armstrong in several advertisements where he would refer to his work ethic. In a 2001 ad, Armstrong is quoted as saying, "This is my body and I can do whatever I want to it. I can push it, and study it, tweak it, listen to it. Everybody wants to know what I'm on. What am I on? I'm on my bike, busting my ass six hours a day. What are you on?"

Amid the allegations, Armstrong returned to competitive cycling. He competed in the Tour de France in 2009 and 2010 but was unable to win. The doping rumors did not end, either. Former teammates told reporters that Armstrong not only doped but that he was the so-called ringleader of a widespread doping program used by his racing team. One teammate, Tyler Hamilton, told a CBS reporter that he and Armstrong had used erythropoietin, or EPO, together while competing in the 1999, 2000, and 2001 Tour de France races. Other racers confirmed Hamilton's story.

Armstrong faced a federal investigation in 2011, and during that year, he announced his final retirement from professional cycling. In February 2012, federal prosecutors announced that they would not charge Armstrong with any criminal wrongdoing. Nevertheless, the U.S. Anti-Doping Agency pressed forward, collecting evidence of Armstrong's doping activities. The agency announced in June 2012 that it was officially charging him with accusations of doping and trafficking drugs. Armstrong attempted to enjoin the agency's action by filing a lawsuit in federal court. However, his case was dismissed twice. On August 23, 2012, he announced that he would not pursue ARBITRATION to challenge the agency's charges.

The U.S. Anti-Doping Agency is a quasi-governmental organization charged with policing the use of drugs in Olympic sports. The agency's head, Travis Tygart, sparred verbally with Armstrong and Armstrong's representatives in the press. At the time that he announced he would not fight the charges, Armstrong still enjoyed significant public support. In fact, donations to Livestrong increased in August and September 2012.

However, public opinion regarding Armstrong turned mostly negative in October, when the agency released hundreds of pages of evidence showing how widespread Armstrong's use of drugs had been. The evidence showed that Armstrong had pressured teammates into taking drugs and hiding their drug use. He pressured others not to inform authorities about this drug use. According to the agency, "The [U.S. Postal Service] Team doping CONSPIRACY was professionally designed to groom and pressure athletes to use dangerous drugs, to evade detection, to ensure its secrecy and ultimately gain an unfair competitive advantage through superior doping practices. A program organized by individuals who thought they were above the rules and who still play a major and active role in sport today."

The agency stripped Armstrong of all seven of his Tour de France titles. He was also banned for life from competing in any sports governed by the agency. This prevents Armstrong from competing in marathons and triathlons in addition to cycling. In January 2013, Armstrong finally admitted to his drug use in an interview with Oprah Winfrey. The admission was reportedly part of an effort to convince the agency to change the ban so that Armstrong can eventually return to competition.

Meanwhile, Armstrong faces a lawsuit filed by the federal government and based on the False Claims Act. Armstrong received $40 million in sponsorship money from the U.S. Postal Service, a government agency. The government alleges that Armstrong obtained the money fraudulently because he doped throughout the time the Postal Service sponsored him.

National Football League Suspends New Orleans Saints Players and Coaches for Bounty System

National Football League Commissioner Roger Goodell handed down some of the harshest punishments in league history when he suspended several players and coaches involved in a scandal while associated with the New Orleans Saints. The NFL determined that the players and coaches had established a bounty system through which players received cash awards for injuring players on opposing teams. This alleged conduct violated league rules. Nevertheless, former NFL commissioner Paul Tagliabue, whom the league appointed to hear appeals, later vacated suspensions of four players.

The bounty controversy came at a time when the NFL faced hundreds of lawsuits brought by former players accusing the league of NEGLIGENCE in addressing concussion and other head injuries. These former players have said that the league "glorified" violence associated with the sport but concealed dangers associated with concussions caused by the violent collisions in football.

Gregg Williams joined the Saints as a defensive coordinator in 2009. The defense improved under Williams, and the Saints as a whole had their best season in franchise history, winning 13 regular-season games and winning Super Bowl XLIV. Williams's defenses were known for their aggressive play.

In 2010, the NFL began an investigation into allegations that Williams had helped to establish a bounty system to reward players for injuring players on opposing teams. Williams and the rest of the Saints organization denied the allegations, and the investigation proceeded slowly. However, multiple independent sources verified that the Saints had indeed put the system in play.

On March 2, 2012, the league announced the results of the investigation, concluding that between 22 and 27 defensive players on the Saints had participated in the bounty program during the 2009, 2010, and 2011 seasons. Players would regularly contribute money into a pool and then receive payments based on performances during previous games. Some payments were made for legal actions, such as interceptions and fumble recoveries. However, other payments were made for such actions as knocking a player out of a game. The league said the total amount of funds involved may have reached as high as $50,000 in 2009. Payoffs were typically between $1,000 and $1,500.

Goodell made the following statement about the bounty program in March 2012: "The payments here are particularly troubling because they involved not just payments for 'performance,' but also for injuring opposing players. The bounty rule promotes two key elements of NFL football: player safety and competitive integrity. It is our responsibility to protect player safety and the integrity of our game, and this type of conduct will not be tolerated."

The bounty system violated the NFL's constitution and **bylaws**. Moreover, the system violated the **collective bargaining agreement** between the league and the NFL Players Association. In a memo sent from the league to NFL teams in 2011, Goodell wrote: "No bonus or award may directly or indirectly be offered, promised, announced, or paid to a player for his or his team's performance against a particular team or opposing player or a particular group thereof. No bonuses or awards may be offered or paid for on field misconduct (for example, personal fouls to or injuries inflicted on opposing players)."

The league's investigation concluded that Saints owner Tom Benson was unaware of the bounty program and had ordered the team's general manager, Mickey Loomis, to end the program. However, the league concluded that Loomis, head coach Sean Payton, and Williams did nothing to end the program. By the time the league had made its announcements, Williams had already joined the St. Louis Rams as their defensive coordinator. Williams admitted to his role in the system.

Just weeks after the league announced its findings, Goodell announced the first suspensions. Williams received an indefinite suspension that caused him to miss the entire 2012

season. Payton also missed the entire season with a one-year suspension. Loomis was suspended for eight games, while assistant head coach Joe Vitt was suspended for six games. The league also fined the Saints $500,000 and made the team forfeit two draft picks. Each of these individuals and the organization appealed their suspensions and punishments, but Goodell upheld the punishments.

Goodell turned his attention to players involved. On May 2, 2012, the NFL announced that it had suspended Jonathan Vilma, Scott Fujita, Anthony Hargrove, and Will Smith for their roles in the bounty system. The league determined that Vilma was the most heavily involved player and suspended him for the entire 2012 season. The other players' suspensions lasted several games. At the time, Fujita had signed to play for the Cleveland Browns, while Hargrove was a member of the Green Bay Packers. The players appealed their suspensions, but Goodell upheld them in July 2012.

Vilma was vocal in his own defense and sued Goodell in May 2012 for **defamation**. According to papers filed in the lawsuit, Vilma claimed that Goodell had made "false, defamatory and injurious" statements regarding Vilma and that Goodell had engaged in "willful and **wanton** misconduct." However, in January 2013 a federal judge in New Orleans dismissed Vilma's suit.

On June 4, 2012, an arbitrator ruled that Goodell had the authority under the collective-bargaining agreement to issue the punishments in the cases. However, an internal **appellate**

New Orleans Saints linebacker Jonathan Vilma was suspended for part of the 2012 season as a result of his role in the bounty system scandal.
HEINZ KLUETMEIER/
SPORTS ILLUSTRATED/
GETTY IMAGES

panel in September 2012 reviewed the arbitrator's decision and vacated the suspensions. The panel concluded that Goodell could still suspend the players based on charges that the players' conduct was detrimental to the league. In October, Goodell reissued the suspensions for all four players.

Vilma appealed his suspension yet again and requested that Goodell RECUSE himself from the matter during the appeal. Goodell agreed to do so, and the league appointed former commissioner Tagliabue to review the player suspensions. After holding a hearing and listening to testimony in late November, Tagliabue on December 11, 2012, vacated each player's suspension. Tagliabue affirmed Goodell's conclusion that the bounty system was in place, but Tagliabue concluded that the conduct justified fines but not the suspensions.

Vilma ended up playing in 11 games in 2012, while Smith played in all 16 and Fujita played in 4. Loomis and Vitt returned to their roles with the Saints, but Payton and Williams missed the entire season. The Saints had a disappointing season, finishing with a losing record for the first time in five seasons.

SURROGATE MOTHERHOOD

New Jersey Supreme Court Upholds Law Preventing Infertile Women from Being Legal Parents

While SURROGATE MOTHERHOOD is legal in the state of New Jersey, the legal rights of married men and women who are infertile are different. A man who is infertile and whose **wife** becomes pregnant using ARTIFICIAL INSEMINATION with the sperm of another man is recognized as the natural father at birth. However, the law does not grant a comparable right to an infertile married woman, where the husband's sperm is used to artificially inseminate the egg of a surrogate mother. The infertile married woman is required to go through court proceedings to adopt the child. A couple challenged the law, arguing that it violated the **equal protection** guarantee of the New Jersey Constitution. In *In the Matter of the Parentage of a Child by T.J.S. and A.L.S., h/w,* 54 A.3d 263 (2012), an evenly divided New Jersey SUPREME COURT upheld an appeals court decision that ruled the law was constitutional.

T.J.S. and A.L.S arranged to have the husband's sperm fertilize anonymous eggs through in vitro fertilization and then to have the eggs implanted in a gestational surrogate willing to bear the child for the couple. Under New Jersey law, A.L.S., the infertile wife, did not have the right to have her name placed on the birth certificate as the natural mother. If roles had been reversed, T.J.S., the **husband**, would have had the right to be named as the natural father. A.L.S. was required to file a petition for ADOPTION to gain legal recognition as the child's mother. Prior to the child's birth, the couple filed a lawsuit in state court requesting an order that would require their names be printed on the child's birth certificate "as the biological parents of the child" after the surrogate surrendered her parental rights. The court issued the pre-birth order on July 2, 2009. On July 7, the surrogate gave birth. Three days later she signed an AFFIDAVIT surrendering all legal rights to the child to the married couple. A birth certificate was issued listing T.J.S. and A.L.S as the child's parents.

However, the state's Department of Health and Senior Services, Bureau of Vital Statistics and Registration had not been given notice of the couple's application for a pre-birth order. The state asked the court to vacate the order allowing A.L.S. to be listed as the mother on the birth certificate. The trial court granted the state's request and vacated its previous order. The court recognized that similar pre-birth orders had been approved in the county and other counties in the state but concluded there was no legal basis for them in the state's Parentage Act or the Artificial Insemination Act. The court also ruled that not allowing A.L.S.'s name to be placed on the birth certificate did not deny her EQUAL PROTECTION under the state constitution.

The couple appealed to the **Appellate** Division, which affirmed the trial court decision. The court held that the state constitution did not require that an infertile wife be given the same benefits conferred on the infertile husband under the Artificial Insemination Act. Similarly, the Parentage Act did not violate equal protection because the situations of infertile men and women were not parallel and that the legislature was entitled to take these differences into account "in defining additional means of creating parenthood." A.L.S. was not similarly situated to the infertile man because "the surrogate mother whose parental rights are deemed worthy of protection ... stands in the way of the infertile wife's claim to automatic motherhood." The distinctions between A.L.S. and the infertile husband were rationally based on account of "the State's valid interest in making identification of the father easier when the child is born during the marriage for CHILD SUPPORT purposes and its equally sound interest in requiring more than a shared intent before effectuating a legal change in the parental relationship between adult and child."

The couple then appealed to the New Jersey Supreme Court. The court deadlocked on a 3-3 vote. In such cases, an evenly divided court must uphold the appeals court decision. Justice Helen Hoens, in a concurring opinion joined by two other justices, stated she would have affirmed the APPELLATE Division decision. She agreed with that court's reasoning that the Parentage Act's presumption of PATERNITY could not "be understood or interpreted to create a presumption of maternity." The plain language of the act provided that the status of maternity was grounded on either a biological or genetic connection to the child. Because A.L.S. lacked either connection, she could only require that status through adoption. In addition, the availability of adoption defeated the equal protection argument. A.L.S.'s "desire to create a more expedient method that will effectuate her intent does not represent a FUNDAMENTAL RIGHT nor one of constitutional magnitude."

Judge Hoens noted that the plaintiffs wanted the court to look at them "not as one man and one woman, but as an infertile couple." Through this redefinition as infertile people they claimed to have "attained a status of equivalence that supports their equal protection challenge." Hoens rejected this argument because it ignored the "plain and unavoidable biological fact" that their child is biologically related to the surrogate mother, who under state law had legal rights and protections. This biological connection trumped the plaintiffs' desire to avoid the adoption process. The proper course for the plaintiffs was to seek a change in the law through the legislature. She noted that such a bill had been passed by the New Jersey legislature in 2012 but had been vetoed by Governor Chris Christie. The governor believed there had been insufficient study of the larger social questions implicated by the legislation. In light of the debate within the legislative and executive branches over this issue the present need was for the court to take no action.

Justice Barry Albin, in a dissenting opinion joined by two other justices, contended that the laws in question clearly violated equal protection. The two laws treated husbands and wives differently, with infertile wives "granted inferior rights of parenthood."

TAXATION

The process whereby charges are imposed on individuals or property by the legislative branch of the federal government and by many state governments to raise funds for public purposes.

PPL Corp. v. Commissioner of Internal Revenue

Every tax year, many U.S. corporations pay taxes to other sovereigns for the privilege of doing business in their countries, for earned incomes or profits, etc. Some of those taxes represent real "bargains" compared to what they would have paid in the United States. But other foreign taxes are "creditable" toward earning tax credits in the United States on corporate tax returns filed with the U.S. INTERNAL REVENUE SERVICE.

In May 2013, the U.S. SUPREME COURT unanimously sided with PPL Corporation in ruling that PPL could claim $39 million in foreign tax credits against its U.S. tax liability, getting credit for a 1997 British windfall tax. *PPL Corp. v. Commissioner of Internal Revenue,* 133 S. Ct. 1897 (2013).

The tax followed a 1997 one-time "windfall tax" under the newly-elected British Labour Party in the United Kingdom (U.K.), imposed on 32 U.K. companies privatized between 1984 and 1996 by the then-Conservative government. During this period, companies formerly owned by the government were sold to private parties via an initial sale of shares known as "flotation." As part of privatization, the companies were required to offer services at the same rates they had offered when government controlled, for a set period. As a result, many became dramatically more efficient, earning substantial profits in the process. Taxing these windfall profits became a platform issue for the Labour Party, which defeated the Conservative Party in 1997. PPL Corp. was part-owner of one of these privatized U.K. companies subject to the British windfall tax.

In its 1997 federal TAX RETURN, PPL claimed credit for its share of the windfall tax, relying on INTERNAL REVENUE CODE §§ 901–(b)(1). That section states, in relevant part, "[i]n the case of . . . a domestic corporation," any "income, war profits, and excess profit taxes" paid overseas are creditable against U.S. income taxes. Treasury regulations, which "flesh out" the Code, interpret this section to mean that, a foreign tax is creditable if its "predominant character" "is that of an INCOME TAX in the U.S. sense." §§ 901–2(a)(1).

The Commissioner of Internal Revenue rejected, but the **Tax Court** accepted the British windfall tax as creditable against U.S. taxes under § 901. That decision was reversed again by the U.S. Court of Appeals for the Third Circuit. To resolve a split among circuit courts of appeals, the U.S. Supreme Court accepted **certiorari** (review).

Justice CLARENCE THOMAS delivered the opinion for an unanimous Court, which reversed the Third Circuit and concluded that the U.K tax was creditable. The Court found that the "predominant character" of the windfall tax was that of an excess profits tax, comparable to a category of income tax in the U.S. sense.

Although the Court's conclusion was clear and brief, its analysis was more complex, as it dissected the manner in which the British government had not only calculated but also applied the tax. As the Court noted, "It is undisputed that net income is a component of the U.K.'s 'windfall tax' formula...It is also undisputed that there is no meaningful difference for our purposes in the accounting principles by which the U.K. and the U.S. calculate profits...The disagreement instead centers on how to characterize the tax formula the Labour Party adopted."

There followed, in the COURT OPINION, mathematical algebraic equations and variables of the Labour Party's taxation formula. According to testimony from the treasurer of South Western Electricity Board, "In effect, the way the tax works is to say that the amount of profits you're allowed in any year before you're subject to tax is equal to one-ninth of the flotation price [the amount investors paid for the company when the government sold it]. After that, profits are deemed excess, and there is a tax."

Continuing its own dissection and analysis, the Court summarized:

> The annual profits are then multiplied by 4.0027, giving the total "acceptable profits" (as opposed to windfall profit) that each company's flotation value entitled it to earn during the initial period given the artificial price-to-earnings ratio of 9. This fictitious amount is finally subtracted from *actual* profits, yielding the excess profits, which were taxed at an **effective rate** of 51.71 percent.

After comparing other models of taxation presented, the Court concluded,

> The economic substance of the U.K. windfall tax is that of a U.S. income tax. The tax is based on net income, and the fact that the Labour government chose to characterize it as a tax on the difference between two values is not dispositive under Treasury Regulation § 1.901(2). Therefore, the tax is creditable under § 901. The judgment of the Third Circuit is reversed.

TERRORISM

The unlawful use of force or violence against persons or property in order to coerce or intimate a *government or the civilian population in furtherance of political or social objectives.*

Boston Bomber To Be Tried in Civilian Court

One of the worst stories to come out of 2013 was that of the horrific bombing massacre of innocent participants and bystanders at the annual Boston Marathon in Massachusetts, traditionally held on "Patriots' Day" for many years, and in 2013 held on April 15. After two separate home-made bombs violently exploded among the unsuspecting and happy crowds near the finish line, three persons (including a child) were killed. Another 264 were wounded, many with critically disfiguring injuries and limb amputations. The emotional trauma for thousands of persons who witnessed the tragedy as it unfolded was unspeakable. Three days later, police officer Sean Collier, on duty at the Massachusetts Institute of Technology (MIT), was intentionally shot and killed during an unsuccessful attempt to carjack his service vehicle, but another vehicle was subsequently carjacked.

Within a matter of days, two suspects had been identified and accosted, on live 24-hour national television, no less. One was killed in a police shoot-out during attempted capture; the other, his younger brother, was wounded and taken into CUSTODY. Shortly thereafter, the suspects' ties to radical Islamic ideology were brought to light. After best determining the Muslim brothers' motive(s), U.S. FEDERAL BUREAU OF INVESTIGATION (FBI) officials classified the Boston Marathon bombings as an "act of terrorism." They also learned that attacks had been planned at least as early as February 6, when one of the brothers purchased 48 mortars containing explosive powder from a fireworks store in New Hampshire.

The fact that the remaining (living) suspect was in custody hardly ended the matter. He was later identified as 19-year-old Dzhokhar Tsarnaev, a naturalized U.S. citizen. This raised new legal questions for the Obama administration. Should he be charged with federal crimes and tried in a civilian court? Should he be labeled an "enemy combatant" and tried in a military **tribunal**? Should he, as an American citizen and resident of Cambridge, Massachusetts, be turned over to state authorities and tried under state law in state court? Each one of these

Emergency personnel on the scene of the Boston Marathon bombings, April 15, 2013.
DAVID L. RYAN/THE BOSTON GLOBE/GETTY IMAGES

choices had appurtenant legal consequences, both in terms of what rights were to be afforded the suspect, as well as what procedures officials could employ in holding and questioning him.

The term "enemy combatant," employed by the Bush administration, refers to a captured fighter in a war who is not entitled to prisoner of war status because he or she does not meet the definition of lawful combatant. Enemy combatants can be held indefinitely for questioning before being charged or released, and the term is primarily associated with prisoners being held at Guantanamo Bay. President Obama, upon taking office, told Americans that "enemy combatant" was a term that his administration would not employ, and that he would close Guantanamo Bay. But Republican Senators JOHN MCCAIN and Lindsey Graham insisted that Tsarnaev be considered an ENEMY COMBATANT for purposes of interrogation only to give interrogators more time to gain information from him.

After capture, Tsarnaev was transported to Boston's Beth Israel Deaconess Medical Center, where he lay in a quasi-comatose state for several days, listed in serious condition. Meanwhile, investigating officials had to quickly decide whether he should receive *Miranda*

warnings when he was medically and mentally competent to answer questions. (*Miranda v. Arizona,* 384 U.S. 436, 86 S. Ct. 1602, 16 L. Ed. 2d 694 (1966), giving persons in custody the right to remain silent and to obtain legal counsel when being questioned by police.)

In the alternative, since he had not acted alone, officials could employ the "public safety exception" to giving a person his or her *Miranda* warnings. The U.S. SUPREME COURT first acknowledged such an exception several decades earlier, in *New York v. Quarles,* 467 U.S. 649, 104 S. Ct. 2626, 81 L. Ed. 2d 550 (1984). The public safety exception (to giving someone *Miranda* warnings) recognizes the possibility of an immediate and imminent threat to the public at large, and permits exigent questions to a suspect, e.g., were there other attacks planned or imminent, either by him or others, who does he know, whom is he associated with, does he know of or communicate with terrorist organizations that are planning to attack, etc.

The problem here was that Tsarnaev, in his condition, was not fully (medically) competent to answer questions, and most legal experts advised a 48-hour limit to the public safety exception. Federal officials called in the High Value Detainee Interrogation Group (which includes investigators from the FBI and CIA who specialize in obtaining intelligence from TERRORISM suspects). They invoked the public safety exception and gleaned what they could from Tsarnaev as he came in and out of consciousness.

Within 48 hours of Tsarnaev's custodial arrest, White House Press Secretary Jay Carney announced on April 22 that he would not be treated as an enemy combatant. "We will prosecute this terrorist through a civilian system of justice," he said. "Under U.S. law, United States citizens cannot be tried in military commissions. It is important to remember since 9/11, we have used the federal court system to convict and incarcerate hundreds of terrorists." Tsarnaev had been given his *Miranda* warnings on April 21, 2013.

On June 27, 2013, a federal **grand jury** returned a 30-count INDICTMENT against Tsarnaev, who remained in a federal prison hospital. Seventeen of the charges carried up to life in prison or the death penalty. The more serious charges included: using WEAPONS OF MASS DESTRUCTION resulting in death and CONSPIRACY; bombing of a place of public use resulting in death and conspiracy; malicious destruction of property resulting in death and conspiracy; use of a firearm during and in relation to a crime of violence resulting in death; CARJACKING resulting in serious bodily injury; interference with commerce by threats of violence; and aiding and **abetting**.

Tsarnaev's ARRAIGNMENT was scheduled for July 10, 2013 in U.S. **District Court** in Boston. The case was assigned (by random assignment) to Judge George A. O'Toole, Jr. A Harvard Law School graduate, O'Toole was nominated to the district court by President BILL CLINTON in 1995.

Lawyer Lynne Stewart Resentenced to Ten Years Imprisonment for Aiding Convicted Terrorist

Lawyers are rarely convicted and imprisoned for activities related to representing their clients. Some lawyers are sanctioned for CONTEMPT during the course of a trial but as OFFICERS OF THE COURT, lawyers typically comply with ethical canons. However, in the case of lawyer Lynne Stewart, her violation of administrative measures relating to her conduct with incarcerated terrorist Sheikh Omar Ali Abdel Rahman, led to her conviction on several federal charges. In *U.S. v. Stewart*, 686 F.3d 156 (2012), the Second

Circuit Court of Appeals upheld the resentencing of Stewart to 10 years in prison. In doing so, the court used statements by Stewart after her initial sentencing to 28 months in prison against her.

Sheikh Abdel Rahman was convicted in New York federal **district court** in 1995 for a variety of crimes that included the soliciting the MURDER of Egyptian President Hosni Mubarek while he was visiting New York, attacking U.S. military installations, and conspiring to bomb the New York World Trade Center in 1993, an attempt which was successful. The Second Circuit upheld his conviction in 1999. Lynne Stewart served on Abdel Rahman's legal team during his trial and appeal, and continued to visit him at a federal prison in Rochester, Minnesota. She was required to sign, under penalty of PERJURY, an agreement to comply with "Special Administrative Measures" (SAMs) before she could visit Abdel Rahman. Under the terms of the SAMs, Stewart agreed not to use her meetings, correspondence or phone calls with Abdel Rahman "to pass messages between third parties (including, but not limited to, the media) and Abdel Rahman." Stewart ignored the SAMs and smuggled messages to and from Abdel Rahman, while supposedly serving in her capacity as a lawyer. Most of the messages dealt with the continuation of a ceasefire declared by an Egyptian militant group that sought to overthrow the Egyptian government by violent means. The group asked Abdel Rahman's advice on whether to continue the ceasefire.

Stewart visited Abdel Rahman twice in May 2000. He dictated several messages to Stewart's translator that dealt with the ceasefire issue. Stewart smuggled these messages out of the prison. In June 2000, Stewart spoke to a Cairo reporter and told him that Abdel Rahman was withdrawing his support for the ceasefire. Seven days later she faxed to the same reporter a statement that reaffirmed Abdel Rahman's position that the ceasefire should end. In 2002, Stewart was indicted for these actions and in 2005 a jury convicted her of conspiring to DEFRAUD the United States by violating SAMs, providing and concealing material support to a CONSPIRACY to kill and kidnap persons in a foreign country, conspiracy to provide and conceal such support, and making false statements. The district court sentenced Stewart to

28 months in prison. On appeal, the Second Circuit upheld the convictions but sent the case back for resentencing. The appeals court concluded that the court had failed to consider whether Stewart committed perjury during her trial, which could enhance her prison sentence for OBSTRUCTION OF JUSTICE. The Second Circuit also directed the court to clarify whether it had applied a TERRORISM enhancement contained in the federal sentencing guidelines. Finally, the appeals court directed the court to consider whether the sentence to be given was appropriate in light of the magnitude of the offense.

On remand, the district court imposed a much stiffer sentence. It explicitly applied the terrorism enhancement. It then concluded that Stewart had made a series of false statements at trial that were intended to deceive the jury. The court also considered two statements made by Stewart after her original sentencing. On the courthouse steps after her being sentenced to 28 months in prison, Stewart told reporters she had no regrets over her actions and that, while she did not look forward to going to jail, "as my clients have said to me, 'I can do that standing on my head.'" In a television interview three years later, Stewart was asked if she would do anything differently in 2000 if she knew what she knew today. Stewart replied that "I don't, I'd like to think I would not do anything differently. I would do it again. I might handle it a little differently, but I would do it again." The district court concluded that Stewart believed the sentence was a trivial sentence and that under federal law the court needed to impose a tougher sentence to reflect the seriousness of the offense, promote respect for the law, and provide just punishment. Upon resentencing, Stewart was ordered to prison for 10 years.

On appeal, Stewart argued that the district court violated her FIRST AMENDMENT rights by using her out-of-court statements against her in determining her sentence. She contended that the court's use of her statements would have a "chilling effect" on future public statements on matters of PUBLIC INTEREST by others. She believed her statements were ambiguous and that the Second Circuit should adopt a rule that would prohibit such statements from being used against a DEFENDANT when sentencing her.

A three-judge panel of the Second Circuit rejected Stewart's First Amendment claims. The court concluded that she was not punished for violating a government restriction on speech but for her crimes of conviction. The district court sought to assess Stewart's history and personal characteristics through her statements in and out of court. A court may consider such statements if they are relevant to the issues involved in a sentencing proceeding. However, the Second Circuit made clear that a defendant could not be sentenced more harshly based on that person's political beliefs. Stewart argued that she had been prosecuted and punished for her political beliefs, yet the court found nothing in the record to support the assertion that the district court did so. In addition, the court noted that there were other factors involved in sentencing her to a longer prison term, including the terrorism enhancement.

The Second Circuit also upheld the terrorism enhancement and the obstruction of justice enhancement.

Second Circuit Throws Out Freedom of Information Request for Terrorist Detainee Records

Opponents of the tactics used by the U.S. government to obtain information from terrorist detainees during the Bush administration have filed a number of civil actions against the government and government officials. Some of these cases involved detainees who sought damages for the way they were interrogated. In other cases, organizations sought government documents that dealt with interrogation methods and the persons who were, in the government's terms, subjected to these "enhanced interrogation techniques," or EITs. In *American Civil Liberties Union v. Department of Justice* 681 F.3d 61 (2012), the Second Circuit ruled that these organizations could not use the FREEDOM OF INFORMATION ACT (FOIA) to secure these records because of national security exceptions contained in FOIA.

In 2003, the American Civil Liberties Union (ACLU) and several other HUMAN RIGHTS groups submitted a FOIA request to the CENTRAL INTELLIGENCE AGENCY (CIA), the Department of Justice (DOJ), and other federal agencies, seeking the disclosure of records concerning the treatment of detainees, the deaths of detainees while in U.S. CUSTODY, and the rendition, since September 11, 2001, of detainees and other individuals to countries known to use torture or illegal interrogation methods.

In 2004, the organizations filed suit in federal court, seeking to compel the government to release any responsive documents it had withheld from disclosure. Since that time, the government has disclosed thousands of documents in response to these FOIA requests. Among these documents were four memoranda authored by the DOJ's Office of Legal Counsel (OLC) between August 2002 and May 2005, dealing with questions with respect to the application of EITs to detainees held in CIA custody. The government released unclassified versions of these memos with limited redactions.

Two of these memos, from May 2005, became the center of controversy in the federal lawsuit, with the ACLU challenging the redactions. The government claimed that under the FOIA, it was entitled to redact classified information. Exemptions 1 and 3 of the FOIA allow the government to withhold classified information contained in records that deal with "intelligence methods," "intelligence activities," and CIA "functions." The **district court** examined the unredacted OLC memoranda in private, without the parties being present. The court rejected the government's argument because it viewed the classified information as a "source of authority" for interrogation rather than as a "method of interrogation." As a compromise, the court offered to let the government replace references to classified information with alternative language meant to preserve the meaning of the text.

The ACLU also sought records relating to the use of EITs. In May 2009, the court ordered the government to compile a list of documents related to the contents of 92 destroyed videotapes of detainee interrogations that occurred in 2002. The CIA identified 580 documents and selected a sample of 65 documents for the district court to review for potential releases. One of these documents was a photograph of the terrorist Abu Zubaydah, dated October 11, 2002. The government withheld all of the records pursuant to FOIA exemptions 1 and 3. It defended its decision because the records consisted primarily of communications to CIA headquarters from a covert CIA facility where interrogations were being conducted, and included "sensitive intelligence and operational information concerning the interrogations of Abu Zubaydah." The ACLU argued that the EITs were not "intelligence methods" within

the meaning of the CIA's withholding authorities because President BARACK OBAMA in 2009 had repudiated the use of these EITs and had declared waterboarding unlawful. It also contended the CIA had failed to provide any explanation as to why the photograph of Abu Zubaydah should be withheld under either Exemptions 1 or 3. The district court reviewed the sample documents privately and made preliminary rulings upholding the government's nondisclosure of all but one document. The court agreed with the government that the photograph of Abu Zubaydah revealed "a lot more information" than the detainee's identity. It also rejected the ACLU's argument that the President's declaration was a sufficient basis for rejecting the government's position. Both sides filed an appeal with the Second Circuit.

A three-judge panel of the Second Circuit, in a unanimous decision, overturned the district court's ruling on the OLC memoranda but upheld the court's refusal to release the records on waterboarding and the photograph of Abu Zubaydah. Judge Richard Wesley, writing for the court, concluded that Exemption 1 resolved the OLC memoranda "easily." Exemption 1 permits the government to withhold information "specifically authorized under criteria established by an EXECUTIVE ORDER to be kept secret in the interest of national defense or foreign policy" if that information has been "properly classified pursuant to such Executive order." The government argued that the redacted information in the memoranda was properly classified under an executive order that authorizes the classification of information concerning "intelligence activities (including special activities), intelligence sources or methods, or cryptology." The government contended that the district court was wrong when it said the redacted information pertained to a "source of authority" rather than a "method of interrogation." Based on a private review of the unredacted memos and the government's classified declarations, the court agreed that the redacted information was properly classified because it pertains to intelligence activity. Disclosing the redacted portions "would reveal the existence and scope of a highly classified, active intelligence activity." Moreover, the district court erred when it offered the government the chance to change the memoranda by replacing classified text with new unclassified information. The FOIA does not permit the alteration of any document.

As to the records relating to waterboarding and the photograph of Abu Zubaydah in CIA custody, Judge Wesley agreed with the district court that Exemption 3 permits the withholding of the information. Exemption 3 permits the government to withhold information from public disclosure provided that the information is "specifically exempted from disclosure by statute" and that the exemption **statute** "requires that the matters be withheld from the public in such a manner as to leave no discretion on the issue" or "establishes particular criteria for withholding or refers to particular types of matters to be withheld." The government argued that the records and photograph pertain to an "intelligence method" under a section of the National Security Act of 1947 (NSA) and to CIA "function" under a section of the Central Intelligence Act of 1949. The ACLU did not dispute that these statutes qualified as exemption statutes under Exemption 3. The only question was whether the withheld material relates to an intelligence method or functions of the CIA. The court rejected the ACLU's claim that the President's declaration that the practice of waterboarding was illegal meant that waterboarding was no longer an "intelligence method." Judge Wesley concluded that the language of the NSA Act did not support this type of limitation. In addition, there were practical difficulties with the ACLU's approach. It would be difficult for an agency officer charged with FOIA requests to determine whether the government "has sufficiently demonstrated the legality of the method to justify withholding" the record. The same difficulty would apply to a court. As to the photograph of Abu Zubaydah, the court, after reviewing it in private, found that the photo related to an "intelligence source or method."

TOBACCO

D.C. Circuit Strikes Down Graphic Warnings on Cigarette Packaging as First Amendment Violations

With the enactment in 2009 of the Family Smoking Prevention and Tobacco Control Act, Pub. L. No. 111-31, 123 Stat. 1776 (2009), the FOOD AND DRUG ADMINISTRATION (FDA) was given wide-ranging authority to regulate the manufacture and sale of cigarettes and other tobacco products. Congress directed the FDA to issue regulations that would require color graphics on cigarette packaging that would depict the negative health consequences of smoking. Tobacco companies filed a federal lawsuit challenging the nine graphic images the FDA selected, arguing that these requirements violated their FIRST AMENDMENT rights. The District of Columbia **Circuit Court** of Appeals agreed in *R.J. Reynolds Tobacco Company v. Food and Drug Administration*, 696 F.3d 1205 (2012), striking down the use of the images and sending the issue back to the FDA for further consideration.

The act directed the DEPARTMENT OF HEALTH AND HUMAN SERVICES to issue regulations that required "color graphics depicting the negative health consequences of smoking." The act also required all cigarette packages to bear one of nine textual warnings (cigarettes are addictive; tobacco smoke harms your children; cigarettes cause cancer; cigarettes cause strokes and heart disease; smoking during pregnancy can harm your body; smoking can kill you; tobacco smoke causes fatal lung disease in nonsmokers; and quitting smoking now greatly reduces serious risks to your health). In addition, the act required these new textual warnings and graphic images to occupy the top 50% of the front and back panels of all cigarette packaging and the top 20% of all printed cigarette advertising. Congress gave the FDA 24 months to issue regulations implementing these provisions and mandated the new labeling take effect 15 months after the issuance of the rule.

The FDA submitted the proposed rule for public comment in November 2010. It included 36 graphic images that could be displayed with the new textual warnings. The FDA noted that as part of its preliminary benefit analysis the U.S. smoking rate would not decrease because of this new rule. The FDA issued its final rule in June 2011, reducing the number of graphic images from 36 to 9. The images included "color images of a man exhaling cigarette smoke through a tracheotomy hole in his throat; a plume of cigarette smoke enveloping an infant receiving a kiss from his or her mother; a pair of diseased lungs next to a pair of healthy lungs; a diseased mouth afflicted with what appears to be cancerous lesions; a man breathing into an oxygen mask; a bare-chested male cadaver lying on a table, and featuring what appears to be post-autopsy chest staples down the middle of his torso; a woman weeping uncontrollably; and a man wearing a t-shirt that features a 'no smoking' symbol and the words 'I QUIT.'" In addition to the textual warning and graphic image, each package would have to prominently display 1-800-QUIT-NOW, a number which smokers could call to inquire about smoking cessation programs.

The tobacco companies filed a lawsuit to prevent the use of the graphic images. They contended that the rule unconstitutionally compelled speech and that such speech did not fit within the "commercial speech" exception to the First Amendment. This exception permits certain government-mandated, informational disclosures to be evaluated under a less restrictive standard. The plaintiffs argued that the highest standard, the **strict scrutiny** of constitutional review, be applied to the rule. The **district court** agreed with the plaintiffs. The commercial speech exception allows the government to require disclosure only of "purely factual and uncontroversial information." Even if the government meets this burden, the information may still violate the First Amendment if the disclosures are "unjustified or unduly burdensome." The graphic images selected by the FDA did not meet the commercial speech exception because they were "crafted to evoke a strong emotional response calculated to provoke the viewer to quit or never start smoking." This objective was very different from disseminating purely factual and uncontroversial information.

Moreover, the court concluded that the graphic images were neither factual nor accurate. The images attempted to symbolize facts about smoking but they failed to "convey any factual information supported by evidence about the actual health consequences." The court was also troubled by the placement of the toll free number on the package. This did not "promote informed choice" but rather served to advocate to consumers that they should "QUIT NOW." Therefore, this was an "impermissible **expropriation** of a company's advertising space for Government advocacy." Applying STRICT SCRUTINY, the court ruled that the FDA's interest in advocating that the public not buy a legal product was not a compelling interest. In addition, the court found that the rule was not narrowly tailored to protect the plaintiffs' First Amendment rights.

The FDA appealed to the D.C. Circuit Court of Appeals. The court, in a 2-1 decision, upheld the lower court decision but used an "intermediate scrutiny" standard of review. Judge Janice Rogers Brown, writing for the majority, noted that restrictions on commercial speech usually employ the intermediate scrutiny standard. This standard requires the government to prove that its asserted interest is substantial, that the restriction directly and materially advances the interest, and that the restriction is narrowly tailored. The majority concluded that it was appropriate to use in this case.

As to the substantial interest at stake, Judge Brown found that the only explicitly asserted interest was an interest in reducing smoking rates. Turning to the second prong of the standard, she examined whether the graphic warning requirements directly advanced this interest. A restriction that provides "only ineffective or remote support for the government's purposes" is not sufficient. The judge concluded that the FDA had not provided a "shred of evidence" showing that the graphic warnings would "directly advance" its interest in reducing the number of Americans who smoke. The FDA had relied on graphic warning programs in other countries to justify the rule but the court found these studies were not authoritative or convincing as to the point that the warnings actually reduced smoking rates. This "questionable social science" doomed the rule under intermediate scrutiny. The court did not need to examine whether the warnings were narrowly tailored. It vacated the rule as a violation of the First Amendment and sent the matter back to the FDA, where it may consider alternatives or produce stronger evidence to justify such images.

D.C. Circuit Upholds Injunction Against Tobacco Companies

The U.S. government as well as state governments have prevailed in lawsuits against U.S. tobacco manufacturers that alleged the tobacco industry mislead generations of smokers about the health risks of smoking. In 2009, Congress took a major step in regulating the industry with the passage of the Family Smoking Prevention and Tobacco Control Act (Pub.L. 111-31). The law gave the FOOD AND DRUG ADMINISTRATION (FDA) the authority to lower the amount of nicotine in tobacco products and to bar candy-flavored products that appeal to young people. The law restricts the use of misleading labels such as "light" and "low tar" and it requires the tobacco companies to place even larger warning labels on their products. Based on this new law, tobacco manufacturers went back into federal court to ask that an INJUNCTION imposed upon them in 2009, months before the Tobacco Act became law, be lifted. The companies argued that the injunction was no longer needed because the new law would eliminate the possibility that they would commit future violations. The **Circuit Court** of Appeals for the District of Columbia, in *U.S. v. Philip Morris USA Inc.*, 566 F.3d 1095 (2012) upheld the continuance of the injunction.

In 1999, the federal government sued several cigarette manufacturers and related trade organizations for civil violations of the Racketeer Influenced and Corrupt Organizations Act (RICO). The government contended that the defendants had conspired to deceive consumers about the health effects and addictiveness of smoking. It sought injunctions that would end these practices. The federal **district court** conducted a nine-month **bench trial**, after which it made over 4000 findings of fact and imposed an extensive set of injunctions. The court found more than 100 RICO violations that spanned more than 50 years. The misstatements and acts of concealment "were made intentionally and deliberately . . . as part of a multi-faceted, sophisticated scheme to defraud." Based on this long history of misconduct, the court concluded that there was a reasonable likelihood that the defendants would continue to commit the same types of violations in the future. The court issued an injunction that prohibited the defendants from making false or deceptive statements about cigarettes, or "conveying any express or implied health message or health descriptor for any cigarette brand." It also ordered the defendants to issue "corrective statements" in various media outlets about the health effects of smoking. In 2009, the D.C. Circuit upheld all but four aspects of the injunction order and remanded the case to the district court for further proceedings on these narrow issues alone. The appeals court noted that the injunctions were broad but ruled that breadth was warranted to prevent future violations.

One month after the appeals court decision, the Tobacco Control Act was signed into law. Under the law, the FDA was given a large enforcement budget and the authority to impose monetary penalties on cigarette manufacturers who violated the law's provisions. Based on the provisions of the act, the defendants asked the district court to vacate its injunctions. The defendants contended that the act's restrictions on their conduct eliminated any reasonable likelihood that they would commit future RICO violations. They also asserted in the alternative that the court should vacate the injunctions out of deference to the FDA's new primary jurisdiction over cigarette sales and marketing. The district court rejected both arguments and left the injunctions in place. As to the first argument, which was jurisdictional, the court found that the defendants were still reasonably likely to commit future RICO violations because, based on their past conduct, they were likely not to comply with the Tobacco Control Act. In addition, the new law targeted different conduct than the injunctions did. The court also noted that the defendants had filed pending lawsuits challenging the new law that had resulted in the invalidation of some of its provisions, with the possibility of more provisions being struck down by the courts. As to the argument that the court defer to the FDA, the court chose to retain jurisdiction because of its expertise in RICO cases and the dissimilarities between the RICO **statute** and the Tobacco Control Act.

A three-judge panel of the D.C. Circuit upheld the lower court ruling. Judge Janice Rogers Brown, writing for the panel, noted that under RICO, a district court has jurisdiction to prevent and restrain RICO violations only if the court finds the DEFENDANT exhibited a reasonable likelihood of committing future RICO violations. The district court had found such a likelihood but the defendants argued that the court twice applied the wrong legal standard. First, the court failed to apply the intervening legislation doctrine. Under this doctrine, cases become moot where a new law is enacted while the case is on appeal and the law resolves the legal dispute. Judge Brown distinguished a line of intervening legislation cases from the Tobacco Control Act because in those cases the new laws made it "impossible for the court to grant any effectual relief whatever." By contrast, the Tobacco Control Act did not make it impossible for the defendants to commit future RICO violations. The act did not **repeal** RICO, exempt the defendants from RICO's application, or "legislate the defendants out of existence."

The defendants' second argument was that the district court had imposed a "formidable burden" of proof that required them to show under their voluntary compliance the "allegedly wrongful behavior could not reasonably be expected to recur." The defendants claimed that the court should not have imposed this BURDEN OF PROOF because their claimed future compliance with RICO was not "voluntary" since it was mandatory under the terms of the Tobacco Control Act. Judge Brown pointed out that the district court found that the Tobacco Control Act was not likely to produce compliance when RICO had not. The penalties under the new law were not as sweeping as under RICO. Therefore, it was reasonable to conclude that the injunction was required to produce compliance.

The appeals court also found unpersuasive the argument that the district court should defer its jurisdiction to the FDA. The district court had more expertise than the FDA as to whether the defendants would commit future RICO violations. The court had handled the case for 13 years and had a "unique insight into the defendants' tendency to circumvent or ignore the law." Such deference might be appropriate if it came near the beginning of the case, as it would promote judicial efficiency, but such was not the case here.

Second Circuit Strikes Down Anti-Tobacco Signs at Point of Sale

The 1965 Federal Cigarette Labeling and Advertising Act, 15 U.S.C. §§ 1331–1341, limits the content and format of warnings that must appear on cigarette packages and in cigarette advertisements. The Labeling Act includes a **preemption** provision that limits the extent to which states may regulate the labeling, advertising, and promotion of cigarettes. In 2009, the New York City Board of Health adopted a resolution requiring all tobacco retailers to display signs bearing graphic images showing certain adverse health effects of smoking. The board did so as part of its ongoing efforts to discourage cigarette use by educating New Yorkers about the dangers of smoking. Two cigarette retailers, two trade associations, and three of the largest cigarette manufacturers filed a federal lawsuit, alleging that the Labeling Act preempted the board's resolution. In *23-34 94th Street Grocery Corp. v. N.Y. City Board of Health*, 685 F.3d 174 (2d Cir. 2012), the Second **Circuit Court** of Appeals agreed, finding that the act

clearly prohibited the type of signs that the board required cigarette retailers to display.

The Board of Health on September 22, 2009, approved a resolution amending the New York City Health Code. The resolution applied to "[a]ny person in the business of selling tobacco products face-to-face to consumers in New York City." The resolution required those who engage in face-to-face sales to prominently display signs warning against the dangers of tobacco and promoting smoking cessation. The resolution contained several requirements. The resolution required retailers to display one small sign within three inches of a cash register or place where a person would make payment. This sign could not be obstructed and had to be easily read by customers. The resolution also required retailers to display a large sign that was at least four feet off the ground. The large sign could not be obstructed and must be placed where a customer could easily read it.

Under the resolution, a retailer would have a choice to display one of three approved signs. The first sign showed an X-ray image of a cancerous lung along with the warning reading "Smoking Causes Lung Cancer." A second sign showed a photograph of a decayed tooth with the warning reading "Smoking Causes Tooth Decay." The third sign showed an MRI of a brain with damaged tissue with a message reading "Smoking Causes Stroke." The resolution further required each sign to state "Quit Smoking Today" and a phone number for assistance in quitting smoking.

The city's purpose in passing the resolution was to "promote further reductions in smoking prevalence in New York City." The messages were designed to address the pervasive use of cigarettes and the general lack of awareness about the dangers of tobacco use. Supporters of the resolution noted how prominent tobacco advertisements were in retail areas. The city required the photos included on the messages because studies had shown that pictorial warnings were more effective than text-only messages, especially among youth.

Congress addressed cigarette ads when it passed the Federal Cigarette Labeling and Advertising Act. The Act's purpose was "to establish a comprehensive Federal program to deal with cigarette labeling and advertising." The Act requires cigarette manufacturers to inform the public about adverse health effects of cigarettes by including warnings on each package of cigarettes and in each advertisement of cigarettes. The Act also stated that "commerce and the national economy may be (A) protected to the maximum extent consistent with [the Act's declared policy] and (B) not impeded by diverse, non-uniform, and confusing cigarette labeling and advertising regulations with respect to any relationship between smoking and health."

The **statute** also contains a PREEMPTION provision that restricts the ability of states and local governments from regulating the advertising and labeling of cigarettes. The preemption provision prohibits a state from requiring a "statement relating to smoking and health" other than the statement required by the federal law. The preemption section also provides that "no requirement or PROHIBITION based on smoking and health shall be imposed under State law with respect to the advertising or promotion of any cigarettes." The statute allows a state or locality to impose specific bans "on the time, place, and manner, but not content, of the advertising or promotion of any cigarette."

A group of retailers along with the largest three tobacco manufacturers brought suit in the U.S. **District Court** for the Southern District of New York. The plaintiffs filed a motion for **summary judgment**, arguing that the Federal Labeling and Advertising Act preempted the New York regulation. The plaintiffs also argued that the regulation violated the plaintiffs' FIRST AMENDMENT rights and that the action exceeded the New York Board of Health's authority under the state constitution.

The district court focused its attention on the plaintiffs' preemption argument. The court concluded that regulation focused on the promotion of cigarettes, disagreeing with the city's characterization that the signs were something other than promotions. Accordingly, the district court declared that the New York City regulation was null and void. *23-34 94th Street Grocery Corp. v. N.Y. City Board of Health*, 757 F. Supp. 2d 407 (S.D.N.Y. 2010).

The defendants appealed the decision to the Second Circuit Court of Appeals. A three-judge panel of the court unanimously agreed with the lower court ruling. Judge Denny Chin, writing for the court, noted that to determine whether federal law preempts a state or local law, the court must look to Congress's intent. However,

the existence of an express preemption clause does not immediately resolve the case. The court must still review the substance and scope of Congress's displacement of state law. Therefore, the court examines the statute as a whole to determine the extent to which the federal law supplants state law. A federal statute does not supplant state law unless Congress "has made such an intention clear and manifest."

Turning to the Labeling Act, Judge Chin concluded that the labeling requirement and the preemption provision of the Act expressed Congress's intent that states may not require additional warnings to be displayed by the manufacturer. The Act expressly preempted state requirements "with respect to the advertising or promotion" of cigarettes. Though both sides agreed that the city's signage regulations were a "requirement or prohibition based on smoking and health," they did dispute whether the regulations were "with respect to the advertising or promotion of" cigarettes. The plaintiffs argued that the requirement was with respect to promotion, while the city contended that it was only a requirement with respect to the sale of cigarettes.

The court sided with the plaintiffs, finding that the city requirements went to the promotion of cigarettes. Judge Chin noted that the word "promotion" was not defined in the Labeling Act, but that in ordinary usage the word meant "the furtherance of the acceptance and sale of merchandise through advertising, publicity, or discounting." Tobacco promotion included the distribution of coupons and free samples, and the payment to retailers for placing tobacco products in desirable store locations. Therefore, "to the extent a product display furthers the sale of the merchandise, it is a type of promotion." The city's signage requirements, by its terms, affected the promotion of cigarettes. Placing a graphic warning adjacent to a tobacco product display necessarily affected the "content of the image projected and the message conveyed to the consumer by that display."

The city contended that the signage requirements only dealt with the sale of cigarettes. It was not regulating or restricting a manufacturer's ability to advertise or promote. Rather, it was only requiring any establishment that sold cigarettes to post warning signs, regardless of whether any advertising or promotion occurred at the particular retail establishment. Judge Chin rejected this argument, finding that the city ignored the practical effect the signage would have on the manufacturer's promotional activity at the retail location. Requiring a graphic warning sign in close proximity to a cigarette display had "practically the same effect as requiring a warning on the display itself, thereby directly affecting the content of the promotional message conveyed to consumers at the point of display." The display was clearly a form of promotion.

Judge Chin, while striking down the regulation, stressed that the court was not holding that every state or local regulation affecting promotion violated the Labeling Act. The Labeling Act permits laws regulating the time, place, or manner of promotional activity. For example, New York City's requirement that retailers display cigarettes only behind the counter or in a locked container was valid, as it only affected the place and manner of display. Only requirements "directly affecting the *content* of the manufacturer's promotional message to consumers are preempted." Finally, the court concluded that the preemption provision of the Labeling Act was supported by the overall **statutory** scheme.

Just weeks later, the U.S. Court of Appeals for the District of Columbia Circuit struck down different regulations issued by the Food and Drug Administration (FDA) requiring tobacco companies to print graphic warning signs on tobacco packages. The court in that case concluded that the agency had exceeded its statutory authority in enacting the regulation. *R.J. Reynolds Tobacco Co. v. FDA*, 696 F.3d 1205 (D.C. Cir. 2012). As a result of this ruling, the FDA delayed the implementation of new requirements through at least June 2013.

TRADEMARKS

Distinctive symbols of authenticity through which the products of particular manufacturers or the salable commodities of particular merchants can be distinguished from those of others.

Already, L.L.C. v. Nike, Inc.

Under the U.S. Constitution, **federal courts** only have jurisdiction to resolve cases and controversies. This means that the courts lack subject-matter jurisdiction when a dispute is "moot." In 2013, the U.S. Supreme Court resolved a trademark dispute between the large shoe manufacturer Nike, Inc., and a much smaller competitor, Already, L.L.C. The Court

concluded that Nike's unilateral agreement not to sue Already for trademark INFRINGEMENT rendered the case moot, thus depriving the federal courts of jurisdiction. *Already, L.L.C. v. Nike, Inc.*, 133 S. Ct. 721, 184 L. Ed. 2d 553 (2013).

Nike originally filed its trademark suit against Already (**doing business** as Yums) in the U.S. **District Court** for the Southern District of New York in July 2009. Nike based its suit on a number of claims under New York law as well as the federal trademark law contained in 15 U.S.C. §§ 1114 and 1125. Nike's suit focused on a shoe called the Air Force 1, which Nike designed in 1982. Nike has registered many TRADEMARKS with the U.S. Patent and Trademark Office, and Nike alleged that the Air Force 1 had several features protected by Nike's trademarks. Specifically, Nike argued that Already sold "footwear bearing a confusingly similar imitation" of Air Force 1.

Already filed a COUNTERCLAIM, asserting that Nike's registration was not in fact a trademark under federal law or New York state law. Already sought to cancel Nike's trademark under cancellation provisions in 15 U.S.C. § 1119. Moreover, Already argued that the parties had an "actual controversy" because the court needed to resolve whether Already had infringed on any rights that Nike allegedly had.

Nike unilaterally constructed a "Covenant Not to Sue," which Nike delivered to Already. The COVENANT obligated Nike

> to refrain from making any claim(s) or demand(s), or from commencing, causing, or permitting to be prosecuted any action in law or equity, against [Already] or any of its [successors or related entities and their customers], on account of any possible **cause of action** based on or involving trademark infringement, UNFAIR COMPETITION, or dilution, under state or federal law in the United Sates [sic] relating to the NIKE Mark based on the appearance of any of [Already]'s current and/ or previous footwear product designs, and any **colorable** imitations thereof, regardless of whether that footwear is produced, distributed, offered for sale, advertised, sold, or otherwise used in commerce before or after the Effective Date of this Covenant.

One month after Nike delivered the covenant, the district court held a hearing to determine whether the court still had subject-matter jurisdiction over the case. Already argued that the issues in the case were still ripe because of the appearance (according to Already) that Already had infringed upon Nike's trademark. Already stated that fear of future LITIGATION over the alleged trademark infringement injured the company's reputation and would deter investors from investing in the company.

The district court ruled that because of the covenant, the case had become moot. Already appealed the decision to the Second **Circuit Court** of Appeals, which affirmed the district court's decision. The courts noted that Nike and Already had not previously engaged in litigation, and the courts concluded that Already had failed to show that Nike was likely to continue the litigation given that Nike had delivered the covenant. The Second Circuit reviewed the totality of the circumstances, including "(1) the language of the covenant, (2) whether the covenant covers future, as well as past, activity and products, and (3) evidence of intention . . . on the part of the party asserting jurisdiction, to engage in new activity or to develop new potentially infringing products that arguably are not covered by the covenant." Based on its review of these factors, the Second Circuit concluded that Already had not shown that it suffered a continuing injury. *Nike, Inc. v. Already, L.L.C.*, 663 F.3d 89 (2d Cir. 2011).

Already appealed the decision to the U.S. Supreme Court, which agreed to review the case. In a unanimous decision, the Court affirmed the Second Circuit's decision. Chief Justice JOHN ROBERTS, JR., wrote the Court's opinion, with Justice ANTHONY KENNEDY writing a concurrence.

Roberts's opinion addressed the correct standard for the Court to apply. The Court concluded that the doctrine that applied to the case was the voluntary cessation doctrine. This doctrine applies when a DEFENDANT has voluntarily stopped the activity that led to the litigation. However, the Supreme Court has recognized that a defendant cannot render a case moot simply by ending its unlawful conduct once litigation has commenced. The Court has instead established that "a defendant claiming that its voluntary compliance moots a case bears the formidable burden of showing that it is absolutely clear the allegedly wrongful behavior could not reasonably be expected to recur." *Friends of the Earth, Inc. v. Laidlaw Environmental Services (TOC), Inc.*, 528 U.S. 167, 190, 120 S. Ct. 693, 145 L. Ed. 2d 610 (2000).

Like the lower courts, the Supreme Court focused its attention on the covenant, and the Court concluded that Nike could show that it was not likely to continue the trademark litigation in the future. Roberts wrote, "The breadth of this covenant suffices to meet the burden imposed by the voluntary cessation test. The covenant is unconditional and **irrevocable**. Beyond simply prohibiting Nike from filing suit, it prohibits Nike from making any claim or any demand. It reaches beyond Already to protect Already's distributors and customers. And it covers not just current or previous designs, but any colorable imitations."

Already pointed to evidence suggesting that potential investors had backed away from the company because of the threat that the litigation posed. Already also emphasized that a VICE PRESIDENT for Nike had suggested that retailers not carry Already's brands of shoes. Moreover, Already argued that the case was still ripe because the Court needed to address whether Nike's trademark was valid.

The Court nevertheless rejected Already's arguments. The Court concluded that Already had suffered only one legally cognizable injury, and that injury was based on Nike's efforts in court to enforce its trademark. Once Nike had agreed not to pursue the litigation in broad terms, Already could not reasonably expect the threat of litigation to recur. Therefore, the case was moot.

Justice Kennedy's concurrence was joined by Justices CLARENCE THOMAS, SAMUEL ALITO, and SONIA SOTOMAYOR. Kennedy agreed that the covenant was broad enough to ensure that Nike was not likely to sue again. However, Kennedy stressed that the party arguing that the case is moot should still have to meet a "formidable burden." Kennedy wrote,

> The formidable burden to show the case is moot ought to require the trademark holder, at the outset, to make a substantial showing that the business of the competitor and its supply network will not be disrupted or weakened by satellite litigation over mootness or by any threat latent in the terms of the covenant itself. It would be most unfair to allow the party who commences the suit to use its delivery of a covenant not to sue as an opportunity to force a competitor to expose its future business plans or to otherwise disadvantage the competitor and its business network, all in aid of deeming moot a suit the trademark holder itself chose to initiate.

VOTING RIGHTS ACT

An enactment by Congress in 1965 (42 U.S.C.A. § 1973 et seq.) that prohibits the states and their political subdivisions from imposing voting qualifications or prerequisites to voting, or standards, practices, or procedures that deny or curtail the right of a U.S. citizen to vote because of race, color, or membership in a language minority group.

Federal Court Rules a Texas Voting Map Discriminated Against Minorities

The U.S. **District Court** for the District of Columbia ruled that voting maps drafted by the Texas Legislature discriminated against minority voters on the basis of those voters' race. The court therefore ruled that Texas had violated the Voting Rights Act. The decision added to the confusion of the 2012 elections in the state, and because the court did not decide the case until August 2012, the state ended up using interim maps previously drawn by a federal district court in San Antonio.

The 2000 Census showed that Texas had a population of 20,851,280. Ten years later, the population in the state had increased by more than four million to a total of 25,145,741. A total of 89.2 percent of this growth was attributed to an increase in minority populations, especially with regard to the state's Hispanic population. As a result of the census, the number of representatives in the U.S. HOUSE OF REPRESENTATIVES increased from 32 to 36.

The state legislature's first legislative session occurred after the Census took place in 2011. In 2010, the Texas House Committee on Redistricting, the Texas House Judiciary Committee, and the Texas SENATE Select Committee on Redistricting held 19 field hearings throughout the state. These committees held the meetings to receive input from the public before formal redistricting occurred. However, a substantial number of citizens—especially from within minority communities—complained that the meetings were a "sham" or "just for show," because the committee did not have specific redistricting plans they could present to the citizens.

During the Texas Legislature's 2011 regular session, only informal discussions about redistricting took place. Some advocacy groups, such as the Mexican American Legal Defense and Educational Fund and the Mexican American Legislative Caucus, submitted proposed congressional maps. However, the Legislature took no action on redistricting during the regular session.

Instead, the Legislature addressed redistricting in a special session that began on May 31, 2011. The chairs of the House and Senate redistricting committees publicly released a proposed congressional redistricting map. Minority members of the Texas House of Representatives were not included in the preparation of the new map. The only two public hearings on the proposed map took place on June 2 and June 3. Experts on redistricting testified that the process followed to create the new maps was far less inclusive by comparison with redistricting efforts in the past.

The committees reviewed an alternative map, which also had not been subject to review by experts nor received input from minority members of the Texas House or Senate. Members of the Legislature had little time to propose other alternatives, and both committees approved the map. On July 18, 2011, Governor Rick Perry signed the bill containing the new congressional map.

Under the VOTING RIGHTS ACT OF 1965, 42 U.S.C. § 1973, several states and local areas must seek "preclearance" before changes to voting laws may take effect. States considered "covered jurisdictions" include those that have a history of discriminating against minorities. Texas is among the states that must seek preclearance. To do so, the state must seek approval from the attorney general of the United States or a three-judge panel of the U.S. District Court for the District of Columbia. Instead of submitting the redistricting plan for administrative review through the attorney general's office, the state instead asked the U.S. District Court in D.C. to issue a **declaratory judgment** that the redistricting plans complied with the Voting Rights Act. The state filed its action on July 19, 2011, which was one day after Perry signed the bill into law.

The LITIGATION became complicated. The Texas redistricting plans were also challenged in the U.S. District Court for the Western District of Texas in San Antonio. Because the state's primaries were scheduled for the early part of 2012, the state needed maps to use. The federal district court in San Antonio drafted a set of interim maps. However, the U.S. SUPREME COURT in *Perry v. Perez*, 132 S. Ct. 934, 181 L. Ed. 2d 900 (2012), struck these maps down and required the court to draft a new set of maps. The court in San Antonio drafted a new set of interim maps in an order filed on February 28, 2012.

In the preclearance case before the federal court in Washington, D.C., Texas had to prove that its redistricting plans had neither the effect nor the purpose of abridging minority voting rights. The Voting Rights Act prohibits states from approving retrogressive redistricting plans, which includes plans that increase the degree of DISCRIMINATION against minority

voters. To establish that the plan did not have the "effect" of abridging these rights, the state had "to insure that no voting-procedure changes would be made that would lead to a retrogression in the position of racial minorities with respect to their effective exercise of the electoral franchise." To determine whether racial minorities can effectively exercise their voting rights, courts consider the "ability of minority groups to participate in the political process" as well as the ability "to elect their choices to office."

In a lengthy opinion, the D.C. District Court concluded that the state's redistricting plan violated the Voting Rights Act. *Texas v. United States*, 887 F. Supp. 2d 133 (D.D.C. 2012). The court noted that the black and Hispanic communities made up 39.3 percent of the voting-age population. If the state allocated its congressional districts proportionately, the state would have had 14 minority districts out of the 36 districts under the redistricting plans. Instead, the new plans had only 10 minority districts, which was the same number that existed when the state had 32 congressional districts.

The court also found that the state had adopted the redistricting plans with a discriminatory purpose because state leaders had excluded minority representatives from participating in the mapping process. Moreover, some evidence showed that the new maps replaced one district's more active Hispanic voters and replaced them with voters who were less likely to vote. The effect of this change was to increase the voting power of the white voters in the district, according to the court's opinion.

Because the court did not decide the case until August 2012, lawmakers had little time to adopt a new map before the general election in November. The state used maps drafted by the federal district court in San Antonio during those general elections.

On June 25, 2013, the Supreme Court issued a ruling in *Shelby County v. Holder*, 133 S. Ct. 2612 (2013), that struck down key provisions of the Voting Rights Act. Because of the decision, Texas Attorney General Greg Abbott announced that Texas no longer had to seek preclearance from the U.S. District Court in Washington. However, a federal district court in San Antonio refused to dismiss a lawsuit that is challenging the redistricting plan adopted by the state in 2011.

Shelby County v. Holder

In the wake of the American Civil War, in 1870 the states ratified the FIFTEENTH AMENDMENT. Section 1 of the Amendment states: "The right of citizens of the United States to vote shall not be denied or abridged by the United States or by any State on account of race, color, or previous condition of servitude." The Amendment also contains a second section, which reads: "The Congress shall have power to enforce this article by appropriate legislation."

For nearly a century, Congress did little to enforce this Amendment. States found a variety of ways to prevent African Americans from exercising voting rights. A common method used in several southern states was to enact literacy tests that kept minorities from the voting booths. Although Congress attempted to outlaw the practices and to facilitate LITIGATION to end the discriminatory practices, the litigation was slow. Moreover, even where parties successfully challenged voting barriers, the affected states would find new ways to discriminate.

The first successful legislation to end these practices was the VOTING RIGHTS ACT OF 1965, Pub. L. No. 89-110, 79 Stat. 437. This Act made it illegal for a state to employ any "standard, practice, or procedure . . . imposed or applied . . . to deny or abridge the right of any citizen of the United

States to vote on account of race or color." The **statute** in general applies across the nation, but the Act also contains a provision that applies to states and local areas that have a history of DISCRIMINATION. These states and areas have had to "preclear" any voting changes with the federal government by following the procedures established in the Act.

In *Shelby County v. Holder*, 133 S. Ct. 2612 (2013), the SUPREME COURT reviewed whether key provisions of the Voting Rights Acts remain constitutional. Previous decisions had upheld the sections requiring some states to seek preclearance for their voting changes. However, in a 5–4 decision, the Court in *Shelby County* ruled that the formula used to determine which states and areas must seek preclearance was outdated. Although the Court did not strike down the entire Act, the decision weakened several key provisions and led many to criticize the Court for the decision.

When Congress enacted the Voting Rights Act, it established a formula in § 4 to determine which jurisdictions must seek preclearance. The formula focused on use of voting tests and low voter turnout. Covered jurisdictions included those that had "maintained a voting test or devices as of November 1, 1964, and had less than 50% voter registration or turnout in the

1964 presidential election." Jurisdictions originally covered included Alabama, Georgia, Louisiana, Mississippi, South Carolina, and Virginia. In subsequent years, the JUSTICE DEPARTMENT determined that the states of Alaska, Arizona, and Texas should also seek preclearance. Moreover, the Justice Department determined that certain counties in several states should have to seek preclearance. These counties are located in California, Florida, Michigan, New York, North Carolina, and South Dakota.

The Act established procedures that states and areas could use to remove themselves from the list of covered jurisdictions. This "bailout" procedure requires the state to obtain a **declaratory judgment** from a federal **district court** after proving that the jurisdiction had not used a test or device to abridge the right to vote on account of race or color. Although some local counties have used the bailout provision, no state ever successfully employed this provision.

States and areas that are covered jurisdictions must seek preclearance under § 5 of the Act. Preclearance requires these jurisdictions to seek approval for any voting change from the Justice Department or from the U.S. District Court for the District of Columbia. Congress reauthorized § 5 through legislation passed in 2006.

Several parties have challenged the constitutionality of the coverage formula established in § 4 as well as the preclearance requirements in § 5. In Supreme Court cases decided in 1966, 1973, 1980, and 1999, the Court upheld the constitutionality of the Act. The Act was again subject to review in the case of *Northwest Austin Municipal Utility District No. One v. Holder*, 557 U.S. 193, 129 S. Ct. 2504, 174 L. Ed. 2d 140 (2009). The Court decided the case on the basis of whether a local district within a covered state could apply for a bailout, and the Court declined to rule on whether the Act is constitutional. However, the Court made a number of statements in the decision questioning whether the Act's preclearance provisions remained justified.

Shelby County, Alabama, is part of a state that has had to seek preclearance under the Act. In 2010, the county brought suit against the U.S. attorney general (ERIC HOLDER) seeking a DECLARATORY JUDGMENT that §§ 4 and 5 are unconstitutional. The U.S. District Court for

the District of Columbia in 2011 upheld the Act, ruling that Congress had sufficient grounds to justify reauthorizing § 5 in 2006. The county then appealed the decision to the D.C. **Circuit Court** of Appeals, which affirmed. The **appellate court** reviewed evidence showing that covered jurisdictions remained areas with concentrated discrimination and found this evidence to be sufficient justification to uphold the formula established in § 4. *Shelby County v. Holder*, 679 F.3d 848 (D.C. Cir. 2012).

Shelby County then appealed the decision to the Supreme Court in what became one of the landmark cases of the Court's 2012 term. Chief Justice JOHN ROBERTS, JR., wrote for a 5–4 majority divided along ideological lines. Justice CLARENCE THOMAS concurred. Justice RUTH BADER GINSBURG wrote the DISSENT and was joined by the Court's three other liberal justices.

The majority noted that Congress had originally intended for the preclearance provisions to be temporary in nature. The Court reviewed its statements in *Northwest Austin*, where the Court stated that "the Act imposes current burdens and must be justified by current needs." Moreover, the Court added, "a departure from the fundamental principle of equal sovereignty requires a showing that a statute's disparate geographic coverage is sufficiently related to the problem that it targets."

Congress could justify the disparate geographic coverage in 1966 given the low voter turnout rates in the southern states to which preclearance has applied since Congress enacted the statute. However, as the Court stated, "things have changed dramatically" in the 50 years since Congress enacted the Voting Rights Act. As the Court noted in *Northwest Austin*, "[v]oter turnout and registration rates now approach parity. Blatantly discriminatory evasions of federal decrees are rare. And minority candidates hold office at unprecedented levels." The tests and devices addressed specifically in the Act have been forbidden across the nation for 40 years. Moreover, Congress acknowledged in 2006 that the percentage of minority voters had increased dramatically between 1965 and 2004.

The government presented evidence that purportedly showed the continued need for using the formula in § 4. This record suggested that discrimination in voting remains a general problem in the states that are covered jurisdictions. However, the Court stated, "a more fundamental problem remains: Congress did not use the record it compiled to shape a coverage formula grounded in current conditions. It instead reenacted a formula based on 40-year-old facts having no logical relation to the present day."

The Court noted that Congress could construct a new formula to determine whether jurisdictions need to seek preclearance based on current conditions. The Court stated: "Such a formula is an initial prerequisite to a determination that exceptional conditions still exist justifying such an 'extraordinary departure from the traditional course of relations between the States and the Federal Government.' Our country has changed, and while any racial discrimination in voting is too much, Congress must ensure that the legislation it passes to remedy that problem speaks to current conditions."

Ginsburg's dissent began by noting, "In the Court's view, the very success of § 5 of the Voting Rights Act demands its dormancy." However, Ginsburg noted, Congress determined that enough evidence showed the continued presence of discrimination in the area of voting that Congress reauthorized the Act. According to Ginsburg, "[t]hose assessments were well within Congress' province to make and should elicit this Court's unstinting approbation."

State of South Carolina v. United States

Under Section 5 of the VOTING RIGHTS ACT OF 1965, southern states that have a history of denying racial minorities the right to vote must submit changes in their election laws to the U.S. Attorney General for "preclearance." If the Attorney General refuses to approve these changes, a state may file a lawsuit in the U.S. **District Court** for the District of Columbia. A three-judge panel reviews the state law and makes a decision as to whether the law should be allowed to go into effect. The state of South Carolina followed this procedure in *State of South Carolina v. United States*, 898 F. Supp. 2d 30 (D.D.C. 2012). The court approved a new version of the state's voter ID law, finding that it did not have the effect of denying or abridging the right to vote on account of race or color.

In 1988, South Carolina enacted a voter ID law. Under the law, a voter must show a South Carolina driver's license, DMV photo ID card, or a non-photo voter registration card in order

A supporter of the Voting Rights Act at a rally at the South Carolina State House in Columbia, February 26, 2013.
RICHARD ELLIS/GETTY IMAGES

to vote. In May 2011, a new voter ID law was enacted which added three forms of qualifying photo ID to the original law. These photo IDs include a passport, a federal military photo ID, and a new free photo voter registration card. The new photo voter registration cards were to be obtained for free from county elections offices. Citizens had several options for obtaining the card. They could present their current non-photo voter registration card, or, if they were already registered to vote, they could verbally confirm their date of birth and the last four digits of their SOCIAL SECURITY number. Another option was presenting any photo ID, utility bill, bank statement, government check, paycheck, or other government document that showed the person's name and address. Another section of the new law authorized county DMV offices to issue DMV photo ID cards for free. They had previously cost $5. The voter was required to go to the local DMV office and present proof of South Carolina residency, U.S. citizenship, and Social Security number. Such proof usually required a voter to present either a birth certificate or a passport.

Another section of the law permitted citizens to use their non-photo voter registration cards to vote if the voter has "a reasonable impediment that prevents the elector from obtaining photographic identification." The voter was required to complete an AFFIDAVIT at the polling place attesting to his or her identity. The affidavit must list the voter's reason for not obtaining a photo ID. Together with the affidavit, the voter would be allowed to cast a provisional ballot, which the county board must find valid unless it had "grounds to believe the affidavit is false." Finally, the law required the South Carolina Election Commission to "establish an aggressive voter education program," and to disseminate information to poll managers and poll workers on election day.

A three-judge panel voted unanimously to approve the South Carolina law. Circuit Judge Brett Kavanaugh, writing for the court, noted that critics of the law had suggested that it was a very strict photo ID law. However, this criticism was based on a misunderstanding of how the law would work. The law, "as it has been authoritatively construed by South Carolina officials, does not have the effects that some expected and some feared." Initial fears about the law were based in part on how the "reasonable impediment" provision would be interpreted and enforced. If interpreted strictly, it could force voters, some of whom were poor and lacked transportation, to try to obtain new photo IDs. Judge Cavanaugh found that as the LITIGATION over the law unfolded, South Carolina officials told the court that they would err in favor of the voter who claimed a reasonable impediment and that any reason asserted by the voter on the affidavit had to be accepted, and the provisional ballot counted, unless the affidavit was false. In the court's view, the purpose of this provision was not to "second-guess the reasons that those voters have not yet obtained photo IDs." Therefore, voters who asserted that they lacked a birth certificate, have a disability, or did not have a car would be allowed to cast a provisional ballot. If the affidavit was challenged before the county board, the county board could not second-guess the reasonableness of the asserted reason, but only its truthfulness.

The DEPARTMENT OF JUSTICE contended that the affidavit requirement could "negate the efficacy of the reasonable impediment provision." The court disagreed. The affidavit needed to be notarized, but notaries were to be at polling places. Moreover, notaries could not charge the voter and could not require photo ID in order to notarize the affidavit. If a notary was not available, poll managers were authorized to witness affidavits and county election boards would be directed to count the accompanying provisional ballots.

Judge Kavanaugh next looked at whether the law as so interpreted satisfied Section 5 of the Voting Rights Act. South Carolina had the burden of showing the law did not have the purpose or effect of denying or abridging the right to vote on account of race and color. The new law could not "disproportionately and materially burden racial minorities as compared to the benchmark of the State's pre-existing law." The court found that as compared to the pre-existing law, the new law expanded the list of photo IDs that would qualify for voting. In addition, the new law made it "far easier" to obtain a photo ID than under the pre-existing law. Another strength of the new law was the accompanying outreach and educational measures to encourage and make it easier for voters without a photo ID to obtain one. Finally, the reasonable impediment provision eliminated "any disproportionate effect or material burden" that the law might cause. Therefore, the court did not find "any discriminatory retrogressive effect on racial minorities" under Section 5.

The court also found that South Carolina did not pass the law based on a discriminatory purpose. The legislature had asserted that the purpose of the new law was to deter voter **fraud** and enhance public confidence in the electoral system. The U.S. SUPREME COURT has recognized the legitimacy of this purpose and the three-judge panel concluded South Carolina's goals were legitimate and not pretextual "merely because of an absence of recorded incidents of in-person voter FRAUD in South Carolina."

Abortion

FIFTH CIRCUIT UPHOLDS TEXAS REGULATION THAT CUTS MEDICAID FUNDING TO ABORTION PROVIDERS

Excerpts from the Texas Women's Health Program law, enacted by the state legislature in 2012 as a replacment for the Medicaid Women's Health Program.

§ 39.31. Introduction.

(a) Governing rules. Notwithstanding any contrary provision in subchapter A of this chapter, this subchapter sets out rules governing the administration of the Texas Women's Health Program (TWHP) within the department's Primary Health Care Services program.

(b) Authority. This subchapter is authorized generally by Health and Safety Code § 12.001 and § 1001.071, and more specifically by Health and Safety Code § 31.002(a)(4)(C) and (H), § 31.003, and § 31.004, under which DSHS may establish a program providing primary health care services, including family planning services and health screenings, and to adopt rules governing the type of services to be provided, the eligibility of recipients, and administration of the program.

(c) Objectives. As reflected in several enactments of the Texas Legislature (including, but not limited to, § 32.024(c-1), Human Resources Code), the TWHP is established to achieve the following overarching objectives:

(1) To implement the state policy to favor childbirth and family planning services that do not include elective abortion or the promotion of elective abortion within the continuum of care or services;

(2) To ensure the efficient and effective use of state funds in support of these objectives and to avoid the direct or indirect use of state funds to promote or support elective abortion;

(3) To reduce the overall cost of publicly-funded health care (including federally-funded health care) by providing low-income Texans access to safe, effective services that are consistent with these objectives; and

(4) To the extent permitted by the Constitution of the United States and in addition to the restrictions imposed by this subchapter, to enforce § 32.024(c-1), Human Resources Code, and any other state law that regulates delivery of non-federally funded family planning services.

§ 39.32. Non-entitlement and Availability.

(a) No entitlement. This subchapter does not establish an entitlement to the services described in this subchapter.

(b) Fund availability. The services described in this subchapter are subject to the availability of appropriated funds. § 39.33. Definitions. The following terms, when used in this subchapter, have the following meanings unless the context clearly indicates otherwise. (1) Affiliate—(A) An individual or entity that has a legal relationship with another entity, which relationship is created or governed by at least one written instrument that demonstrates:

(i) common ownership, management, or control;

(ii) a franchise; or

(iii) the granting or extension of a license or other agreement that authorizes the affiliate to use the other entity's brand name, trademark, service mark, or other registered identification mark.

(B) The written instruments referenced in subparagraph (A) of this paragraph may include a certificate of formation, a franchise agreement, standards of affiliation, bylaws, or a license, but do not include agreements related to a physician's participation in a physician group practice, such as a hospital group agreement, staffing agreement, management agreement, or collaborative practice agreement.

(2) Applicant—A woman applying to receive services under TWHP, including a current recipient who is applying to renew.

(3) Budget group—Members of a household whose needs, income, resources, and expenses are considered in determining eligibility.

(4) Client—A woman who receives services through TWHP.

(5) Corporate entity—A foreign or domestic non-natural person, including a for-profit or nonprofit corporation, a partnership, and a sole proprietorship.

(6) Covered service—A medical procedure for which TWHP will reimburse an enrolled health-care provider, as listed in §39.39 of this title (relating to Covered Services).

(7) DSHS—The Department of State Health Services.

(8) Elective abortion—The intentional termination of a pregnancy by an attending physician who knows that the female is pregnant, using any means that is reasonably likely to cause the death of the fetus. The term does not include the use of any such means:

(A) to terminate a pregnancy that resulted from an act of rape or incest;

(B) in a case in which a woman suffers from a physical disorder, physical disability, or physical illness, including a life-endangering physical condition caused by or arising from the pregnancy, that would, as certified by a physician, place the woman in danger of death or risk of substantial impairment of a major bodily function unless an abortion is performed; or

(C) in a case in which a fetus has a severe fetal abnormality, meaning a life-threatening physical condition that, in reasonable medical judgment, regardless of the provision of life-saving treatment, is incompatible with life outside the womb.

(9) Family planning services—Educational or comprehensive medical activities that enable individuals to determine freely the number and spacing of their children and to select the means by which this may be achieved.

(10) Health-care provider—A physician, physician assistant, nurse practitioner, clinical nurse specialist, certified nurse midwife, federally qualified health center, family planning agency, health clinic, ambulatory surgical center, hospital ambulatory surgical center, laboratory, or rural health center.

(11) Health clinic—A corporate entity that provides comprehensive preventive and primary health care services to outpatient clients, which must include both family planning services and diagnosis and treatment of both acute and chronic illnesses and conditions in three or more organ systems. The term does not include a clinic specializing in family planning services.

(12) TWHP—Texas Women's Health Program.

(13) TWHP provider—A health-care provider that performs covered services.

§ 39.34. Client Eligibility.

(a) Criteria. A woman is eligible to receive services through TWHP if she:

(1) is 18 through 44 years of age, inclusive;

(2) is not pregnant;

(3) is not sterile, infertile, or unable to get pregnant because of medical reasons;

(4) has countable income (as calculated under § 39.36 of this title (relating to Financial Eligibility Requirements)) that does not exceed 185 percent of the Federal Poverty Level, as published annually in the Federal Register by the United States Department of Health and Human Services;

(5) is a United States citizen, a United States national, or an alien who qualifies under § 39.35(h) of this title (relating to Application Procedures);

(6) resides in Texas;

(7) does not currently receive benefits through a Medicaid program, Children's Health Insurance Program, or Medicare Part A or B;

(8) does not have creditable health coverage that covers the services TWHP provides, except as specified in subsection (d) of this section;

(9) is not a patient at a State mental hospital as defined in Health and Safety Code, § 571.003 (21); and

(10) is not incarcerated in any penal facility maintained under governmental authority. The term "incarcerated" means the involuntary physical restraint of a woman who has been arrested for or convicted of a crime.

(b) Age. For purposes of subsection (a)(1) of this section, an applicant is considered 18 years of age the month of her 18th birthday and 44 years of age through the month of her 45th birthday. A woman is ineligible for TWHP if her application is received the month before her 18th birthday or the month after she turns 45 years of age.

(c) Resources. DSHS or its designee does not request or verify resources for TWHP.

(d) Third-party resources. An applicant with creditable health coverage that would pay for all or part of the costs of covered services may be eligible to receive covered services if she affirms, in a manner satisfactory to DSHS or its designee, her belief that a liable third party may retaliate against her or cause physical or emotional harm if she assists DSHS or its designee (by providing information or by any other means) in pursuing claims against that third party. An applicant with such creditable health coverage who does not comply with this requirement is ineligible to receive TWHP benefits.

(e) Period of eligibility. A client is deemed eligible to receive covered services for 12 continuous months after her application is approved, unless:

(1) the client dies;

(2) the client voluntarily withdraws;

(3) the client no longer satisfies criteria set out in subsection (a) of this section;

(4) state law no longer allows the woman to be covered; or

(5) DSHS or its designee determines the client provided information affecting her eligibility that was false at the time of application.

(f) Transfer of eligibility. A woman who, when these rules becomes effective, receives services through the Medicaid Women's Health Program is automatically enrolled as a TWHP client and is eligible to receive covered services for as long as she would have been eligible for the Medicaid Women's Health Program.

§ 39.37. Denial, Suspension, or Termination of Services; Client appeals.

(a) Notice and opportunity for hearing. DSHS or its designee may deny, suspend, or terminate services to an applicant or client if it determines that the applicant or client is ineligible to participate.

(b) Notice and opportunity for a fair hearing. Before DSHS or its designee finalizes the denial, suspension, or termination under subsection (a) of this section, the applicant or client will be notified and provided an opportunity for a fair hearing.

(c) Appeal procedures. An applicant or client who is aggrieved by the denial, suspension, or termination of services under subsection (a) of this section may appeal the decision in accordance with Chapter 1, Subchapter C of this title (relating to Fair Hearing Procedures). An applicant or client may not appeal a decision to deny, suspend, or terminate services if the decision is the result of a decision by the State to reduce or stop funding the program.

§ 39.38. Health-Care Providers.

(a) Procedures. A TWHP provider must comply with the requirements set out in 1 TAC Chapter 354, Subchapter A, Division 1 (relating to Medicaid Procedures for Providers).

(b) Qualifications. A TWHP provider must ensure that:

(1) the provider does not perform or promote elective abortions outside the scope of the TWHP and is not an affiliate of an entity that performs or promotes elective abortions; and

(2) in offering or performing a TWHP service, the provider:

(A) does not promote elective abortion within the scope of the TWHP;

(B) maintains physical and financial separation between its TWHP activities and any elective abortion-performing or abortion-promoting activity, as evidenced by the following:

(i) physical separation of TWHP services from any elective abortion activities, no matter what entity is responsible for the activities;

(ii) a governing board or other body that controls the TWHP health care provider has no board members who are also members of the governing board of an entity that performs or promotes elective abortions;

(iii) accounting records that confirm that none of the funds used to pay for TWHP services directly or indirectly support the performance or promotion of elective abortions by an affiliate; and

(iv) display of signs and other media that identify TWHP and the absence of signs or materials promoting elective abortion in the provider's location or in the provider's public electronic communications; and

(C) does not use, display, or operate under a brand name, trademark, service mark, or registered identification mark of an organization that performs or promotes elective abortions.

(c) Defining "promote." For purposes of subsection (b) of this section, the term "promote" means advancing, furthering, advocating, or popularizing elective abortion by, for example:

(1) taking affirmative action to secure elective abortion services for a TWHP client (such as making an appointment, obtaining consent for the elective abortion, arranging for transportation, negotiating a reduction in an elective abortion provider fee, or arranging or scheduling an elective abortion procedure); however, the term does not include providing upon the patient's request neutral, factual information and nondirective counseling, including the name, address, telephone number, and other relevant information about a provider;

(2) furnishing or displaying to a TWHP client information that publicizes or advertises an elective abortion service or provider; or

(3) using, displaying, or operating under a brand name, trademark, service mark, or registered identification mark of an organization that performs or promotes elective abortions.

(d) Compliance information. Upon request, a TWHP provider must provide DSHS or its designee with all information DSHS or its designee requires to determine the provider's compliance with this section.

(e) Provider disqualification. If, after the effective date of this section, DSHS or its designee determines that a TWHP provider fails to comply with subsection (b) of this

section, DSHS or its designee will disqualify the provider from TWHP.

(f) Client assistance and recoupment. If a TWHP provider is disqualified, DSHS or its designee will take appropriate action to:

(1) assist a TWHP client to find an alternate provider; and

(2) recoup any funds paid to a disqualified provider for TWHP services performed during the period of disqualification.

(g) Certification. Upon initial application for enrollment in the TWHP, a provider must certify its compliance with subsection (b) of this section and any other requirement specified by DSHS or its designee. Each provider enrolled in TWHP must annually certify that the provider complies with subsection (b) of this section.

(h) Exemption from initial certification. The initial application requirement of subsection (g) of this section does not apply to a provider that certified and was determined to be in compliance with the requirements of the Women's Health Program administered by the Health and Human Services Commission pursuant to § 32.024(c-1), Human Resources Code.

§ 39.39. Covered Services.

A client may receive the following services through TWHP:

(1) annual family planning exam and Pap test;

(2) follow-up visits related to the chosen contraceptive method;

(3) counseling on specific methods and use of contraception (as part of evaluation and management services), including natural family planning and excluding emergency contraception;

(4) female sterilization;

(5) follow-up visits related to sterilization, including procedures to confirm sterilization;

(6) family-planning services as listed in the Texas Medicaid Provider Procedures Manual, including:

(A) pregnancy tests;

(B) sexually transmitted infection (STI) screenings;

(C) treatment of certain STIs;

(D) contraceptive methods; and

(7) lab services related to a service listed in paragraphs (1) - (6) of this section.

§ 39.40. Non-covered Services.

TWHP does not cover:

(1) counseling on and provision of abortion services;

(2) mammography and diagnostic services for breast cancer;

(3) treatment for any condition diagnosed during a TWHP visit, other than a sexually transmitted infection for which treatment is a covered service;

(4) a visit for a pregnancy test only;

(5) a visit for a sexually transmitted infection test only;

(6) a follow-up after an abnormal Pap test;

(7) counseling on and provision of emergency contraceptives; or

(8) other visits that cannot be appropriately billed with a permissible procedure code.

Gay and Lesbian Rights

UNITED STATES V. WINDSOR

Excerpts from the federal Defense of Marriage Act, passed by the United States Senate and House of Representatives on January 3, 1996.

Defense of Marriage Act

SECTION 1. SHORT TITLE.

This Act may be cited as the "Defense of Marriage Act".

SEC. 2. POWERS RESERVED TO THE STATES.

(a) IN GENERAL.—Chapter 115 of title 28, United States Code, is amended by adding after section 1738B the following:

§ 1738C. Certain acts, records, and proceedings and the effect thereof

"No State, territory, or possession of the United States, or Indian tribe, shall be required to give effect to any public act, record, or judicial proceeding of any other State, territory, possession, or tribe respecting a relationship between persons of the same sex that is treated as a marriage under the laws of such other State, territory, possession, or tribe, or a right or claim arising from such relationship."

SEC. 3. DEFINITION OF MARRIAGE.

(a) IN GENERAL.—Chapter 1 of title 1, United States Code, is amended by adding at the end the following:

§ 7. Definition of 'marriage' and 'spouse'

"In determining the meaning of any Act of Congress, or of any ruling, regulation, or interpretation of the various administrative bureaus and agencies of the United States, the word 'marriage' means only a legal union between one man and one woman as husband and wife, and the word 'spouse' refers only to a person of the opposite sex who is a husband or a wife."

Voting Rights Act

STATE OF SOUTH CAROLINA V. UNITED STATES

Section 5 of the Voting Rights Act of 1965 (Excerpted)

TITLE 42 — THE PUBLIC HEALTH AND WELFARE

CHAPTER 20 — ELECTIVE FRANCHISE

SUBCHAPTER I-A — ENFORCEMENT OF VOTING RIGHTS

§ 1973. Denial or abridgement of right to vote on account of race or color through voting qualifications or prerequisites; establishment of violation

(a) No voting qualification or prerequisite to voting or standard, practice, or procedure shall be imposed or applied by any State or political subdivision in a manner which results in a denial or abridgement of the right of any citizen of the United States to vote on account of race or color, or in contravention of the guarantees set forth in section 1973b(f)(2) of this title, as provided in subsection (b) of this section.

(b) A violation of subsection (a) of this section is established if, based on the totality of circumstances, it is shown that the political processes leading to nomination or election in the State or political subdivision are not equally open to participation by members of a class of citizens protected by subsection (a) of this section in that its members have less opportunity than other members of the electorate to participate in the political process and to elect representatives of their choice. The extent to which members of a protected class have been elected to office in the State or political subdivision is one circumstance which may be considered: Provided, That nothing in this section establishes a right to have members of a protected class elected in numbers equal to their proportion in the population.

§ 1973a. Proceeding to enforce the right to vote

(a) Authorization by court for appointment of Federal observers

Whenever the Attorney General or an aggrieved person institutes a proceeding under any statute to enforce the voting guarantees of the fourteenth or fifteenth amendment in any State or political subdivision the court shall authorize the appointment of Federal observers by the Director of the Office of Personnel Management in accordance with section 1973d of this title to serve for such period of time and for such political subdivisions as the court shall determine is appropriate to enforce the voting guarantees of the fourteenth or fifteenth amendment (1) as part of any interlocutory order if the court determines that the appointment of such observers is necessary to enforce such voting guarantees or (2) as part of any final judgment if the court finds that violations of the fourteenth or fifteenth amendment justifying equitable relief have occurred in such State or subdivision: *Provided*, That the court need not authorize the appointment of observers if any incidents of denial or abridgement of the right to vote on account of race or color, or in contravention of the voting guarantees set forth in section 1973b(f)(2) of this title (1) have been few in number and have been promptly and effectively corrected by State or local action, (2) the continuing effect of such incidents has been eliminated, and (3) there is no reasonable probability of their recurrence in the future.

(b) Suspension of use of tests and devices which deny or abridge the right to vote

If in a proceeding instituted by the Attorney General or an aggrieved person under any statute to enforce the voting guarantees of the fourteenth or fifteenth amendment in any State or political subdivision the court finds that a test or device has been used for the purpose or with the effect of denying or abridging the right of any citizen of the United States to vote on account of race or color, or in contravention of the voting guarantees set forth in section 1973b (f)(2) of this title, it shall suspend the use of tests and devices in such State or political subdivisions as the court shall determine is appropriate and for such period as it deems necessary.

(c) Retention of jurisdiction to prevent commencement of new devices to deny or abridge the right to vote

If in any proceeding instituted by the Attorney General or an aggrieved person under any statute to enforce the voting guarantees of the fourteenth or fifteenth amendment in any State or political subdivision the court finds that violations of the fourteenth or fifteenth amendment justifying equitable relief have occurred within the territory of such State or political subdivision, the court, in addition to such relief as it may grant, shall retain jurisdiction for such period as it may deem appropriate and during such period no voting qualification or prerequisite to voting or standard, practice, or procedure with respect to voting different from that in force or effect at the time the proceeding was commenced shall be enforced unless and until the court finds that such qualification, prerequisite, standard, practice, or procedure does not have the purpose and will not have the effect of denying or abridging the right to vote on account of race or color, or in contravention of the voting guarantees set forth in section 1973b(f)(2) of this title: *Provided*, That such qualification, prerequisite, standard, practice, or procedure may be enforced if the qualification, prerequisite, standard, practice, or procedure has been submitted by the chief legal officer or other appropriate official of such State or subdivision to the Attorney General and the Attorney General has not interposed an objection within sixty days after such submission, except that neither the court's finding nor the Attorney General's failure to object shall bar a subsequent action to enjoin enforcement of such qualification, prerequisite, standard, practice, or procedure.

§ 1973b. Suspension of the use of tests or devices in determining eligibility to vote

(a) Action by State or political subdivision for declaratory judgment of no denial or abridgement; three-judge district court; appeal to Supreme Court; retention of jurisdiction by three-judge court

(1) To assure that the right of citizens of the United States to vote is not denied or abridged on account of race or color, no citizen shall be denied the right to vote in any Federal, State, or local election because of his failure to comply with any test or device in any State with respect to which the determinations have been made

under the first two sentences of subsection (b) of this section or in any political subdivision of such State (as such subdivision existed on the date such determinations were made with respect to such State), though such determinations were not made with respect to such subdivision as a separate unit, or in any political subdivision with respect to which such determinations have been made as a separate unit, unless the United States District Court for the District of Columbia issues a declaratory judgment under this section. No citizen shall be denied the right to vote in any Federal, State, or local election because of his failure to comply with any test or device in any State with respect to which the determinations have been made under the third sentence of subsection (b) of this section or in any political subdivision of such State (as such subdivision existed on the date such determinations were made with respect to such State), though such determinations were not made with respect to such subdivision as a separate unit, or in any political subdivision with respect to which such determinations have been made as a separate unit, unless the United States District Court for the District of Columbia issues a declaratory judgment under this section. A declaratory judgment under this section shall issue only if such court determines that during the ten years preceding the filing of the action, and during the pendency of such action.

(A) no such test or device has been used within such State or political subdivision for the purpose or with the effect of denying or abridging the right to vote on account of race or color or (in the case of a State or subdivision seeking a declaratory judgment under the second sentence of this subsection) in contravention of the guarantees of subsection (f)(2) of this section;

(B) no final judgment of any court of the United States, other than the denial of declaratory judgment under this section, has determined that denials or abridgements of the right to vote on account of race or color have occurred anywhere in the territory of such State or political subdivision or (in the case of a State or subdivision seeking a declaratory judgment under the second sentence of this subsection) that denials or abridgements of the right to vote in contravention of the guarantees of subsection (f)(2) of this section have occurred anywhere in the territory of such State or subdivision and no consent decree, settlement, or agreement has been entered into resulting in any abandonment of a voting practice challenged on such grounds; and no declaratory judgment under this section shall be entered during the pendency of an action commenced before the filing of an action under this section and alleging such denials or abridgements of the right to vote;

. . .

(b) Required factual determinations necessary to allow suspension of compliance with tests and devices; publication in Federal Register

The provisions of subsection (a) of this section shall apply in any State or in any political subdivision of a State which (1) the Attorney General determines maintained on November 1, 1964, any test or device, and with respect to which (2) the Director of the Census determines that less than 50 per centum of the persons of voting age residing therein were registered on November 1, 1964, or that less than 50 per centum of such persons voted in the presidential election of November 1964. On and after August 6, 1970, in addition to any State or political subdivision of a State determined to be subject to subsection (a) of this section pursuant to the previous sentence, the provisions of subsection (a) of this section shall apply in any State or any political subdivision of a State which (i) the Attorney General determines maintained on November 1, 1968, any test or device, and with respect to which (ii) the Director of the Census determines that less than 50 per centum of the persons of voting age residing therein were registered on November 1, 1968, or that less than 50 per centum of such persons voted in the presidential election of November 1968. On and after August 6, 1975, in addition to any State or political subdivision of a State determined to be subject to subsection (a) of this section pursuant to the previous two sentences, the provisions of subsection (a) of this section shall apply in any State or any political subdivision of a State which (i) the Attorney General determines maintained on November 1, 1972, any test or device, and with respect to which (ii) the Director of the Census determines that less than 50 per centum of the citizens of voting age were registered on November 1, 1972, or that less than 50 per centum of such persons voted in the Presidential election of November 1972.

. . .

(c) "Test or device" defined

The phrase "test or device" shall mean any requirement that a person as a prerequisite for voting or registration for voting (1) demonstrate the ability to read, write, understand, or interpret any matter, (2) demonstrate any educational achievement or his knowledge of any particular subject, (3) possess good moral character, or (4) prove his qualifications by the voucher of registered voters or members of any other class.

(d) Required frequency, continuation and probable recurrence of incidents of denial or abridgement to constitute forbidden use of tests or devices

For purposes of this section no State or political subdivision shall be determined to have engaged in the use of tests or devices for the purpose or with the effect of denying or abridging the right to vote on account of race or color, or in contravention of the guarantees set forth in subsection (f)(2) of this section if (1) incidents of such use have been few in number and have been promptly and effectively corrected by State or local action, (2) the continuing effect of such incidents has been eliminated, and (3) there is no reasonable probability of their recurrence in the future.

(e) Completion of requisite grade level of education in American-flag schools in which the predominant classroom language was other than English

(1) Congress hereby declares that to secure the rights under the fourteenth amendment of persons educated in American-flag schools in which the predominant classroom language was other than English, it is necessary to prohibit the States from conditioning the right to vote of such persons on ability to read, write, understand, or interpret any matter in the English language.

(2) No person who demonstrates that he has successfully completed the sixth primary grade in a public school in, or a private school accredited by, any State or territory, the District of Columbia, or the Commonwealth of Puerto Rico in which the predominant classroom language was other than English, shall be denied the right to vote in any Federal, State, or local election because of his inability to read, write, understand, or interpret any matter in the English language, except that in States in which State law provides that a different level of education is presumptive of literacy, he shall demonstrate that he has successfully completed an equivalent level of education in a public school in, or a private school accredited by, any State or territory, the District of Columbia, or the Commonwealth of Puerto Rico in which the predominant classroom language was other than English.

(f) Congressional findings of voting discrimination against language minorities; prohibition of English-only elections; other remedial measures

(1) The Congress finds that voting discrimination against citizens of language minorities is pervasive and national in scope. Such minority citizens are from environments in which the dominant language is other than English. In addition they have been denied equal educational opportunities by State and local governments, resulting in severe disabilities and continuing illiteracy in the English language. The Congress further finds that, where State and local officials conduct elections only in English, language minority citizens are excluded from participating in the electoral process. In many areas of the country, this exclusion is aggravated by acts of physical, economic, and political intimidation. The Congress declares that, in order to enforce the guarantees of the fourteenth and fifteenth amendments to the United States Constitution, it is necessary to eliminate such discrimination by prohibiting English-only elections, and by prescribing other remedial devices.

(2) No voting qualification or prerequisite to voting, or standard, practice, or procedure shall be imposed or applied by any State or political subdivision to deny or abridge the right of any citizen of the United States to vote because he is a member of a language minority group.

(3) In addition to the meaning given the term under subsection (c) of this section, the term "test or device" shall also mean any practice or requirement by which any State or political subdivision provided any registration or voting notices, forms, instructions, assistance, or other materials or information relating to the electoral process, including ballots, only in the English language, where the Director of the Census determines that more than five per

centum of the citizens of voting age residing in such State or political subdivision are members of a single language minority. With respect to subsection (b) of this section, the term "test or device", as defined in this subsection, shall be employed only in making the determinations under the third sentence of that subsection.

(4) Whenever any State or political subdivision subject to the prohibitions of the second sentence of subsection (a) of this section provides any registration or voting notices, forms, instructions, assistance, or other materials or information relating to the electoral process, including ballots, it shall provide them in the language of the applicable language minority group as well as in the English language: Provided, That where the language of the applicable minority group is oral or unwritten or in the case of Alaskan Natives and American Indians, if the predominate language is historically unwritten, the State or political subdivision is only required to furnish oral instructions, assistance, or other information relating to registration and voting.

. . .

§ 1973c. Alteration of voting qualifications; procedure and appeal; purpose or effect of diminishing the ability of citizens to elect their preferred candidates

(a) Whenever a State or political subdivision with respect to which the prohibitions set forth in section 1973b(a) of this title based upon determinations made under the first sentence of section 1973b(b) of this title are in effect shall enact or seek to administer any voting qualification or prerequisite to voting, or standard, practice, or procedure with respect to voting different from that in force or effect on November 1, 1964, or whenever a State or political subdivision with respect to which the prohibitions set forth in section 1973b(a) of this title based upon determinations made under the second sentence of section 1973b(b) of this title are in effect shall enact or seek to administer any voting qualification or prerequisite to voting, or standard, practice, or procedure with respect to voting different from that in force or effect on November 1, 1968, or whenever a State or political subdivision with respect to which the prohibitions set forth in section 1973b(a) of this title based upon determinations made under the third sentence of section 1973b(b) of this title are in effect shall enact

or seek to administer any voting qualification or prerequisite to voting, or standard, practice, or procedure with respect to voting different from that in force or effect on November 1, 1972, such State or subdivision may institute an action in the United States District Court for the District of Columbia for a declaratory judgment that such qualification, prerequisite, standard, practice, or procedure neither has the purpose nor will have the effect of denying or abridging the right to vote on account of race or color, or in contravention of the guarantees set forth in section 1973b(f)(2) of this title, and unless and until the court enters such judgment no person shall be denied the right to vote for failure to comply with such qualification, prerequisite, standard, practice, or procedure: Provided, That such qualification, prerequisite, standard, practice, or procedure may be enforced without such proceeding if the qualification, prerequisite, standard, practice, or procedure has been submitted by the chief legal officer or other appropriate official of such State or subdivision to the Attorney General and the Attorney General has not interposed an objection within sixty days after such submission, or upon good cause shown, to facilitate an expedited approval within sixty days after such submission, the Attorney General has affirmatively indicated that such objection will not be made. Neither an affirmative indication by the Attorney General that no objection will be made, nor the Attorney General's failure to object, nor a declaratory judgment entered under this section shall bar a subsequent action to enjoin enforcement of such qualification, prerequisite, standard, practice, or procedure. In the event the Attorney General affirmatively indicates that no objection will be made within the sixty-day period following receipt of a submission, the Attorney General may reserve the right to reexamine the submission if additional information comes to his attention during the remainder of the sixty-day period which would otherwise require objection in accordance with this section. Any action under this section shall be heard and determined by a court of three judges in accordance with the provisions of section 2284 of title 28 and any appeal shall lie to the Supreme Court.

(b) Any voting qualification or prerequisite to voting, or standard, practice, or procedure with respect to voting that has the purpose of or will have the effect of diminishing the ability of any citizens of the United States on account of race or color, or in contravention of the guarantees set forth in section 1973b(f)(2) of this title, to elect their preferred candidates of choice denies or abridges the right to vote within the meaning of subsection (a) of this section.

(c) The term "purpose" in subsections (a) and (b) of this section shall include any discriminatory purpose.

(d) The purpose of subsection (b) of this section is to protect the ability of such citizens to elect their preferred candidates of choice.

§ 1973h. Poll taxes

(a) Congressional finding and declaration of policy against enforced payment of poll taxes as a device to impair voting rights

The Congress finds that the requirement of the payment of a poll tax as a precondition to voting (i) precludes persons of limited means from voting or imposes unreasonable financial hardship upon such persons as a precondition to their exercise of the franchise, (ii) does not bear a reasonable relationship to any legitimate State interest in the conduct of elections, and (iii) in some areas has the purpose or effect of denying persons the right to vote because of race or color. Upon the basis of these findings, Congress declares that the constitutional right of citizens to vote is denied or abridged in some areas by the requirement of the payment of a poll tax as a precondition to voting.

(b) Authority of Attorney General to institute actions for relief against enforcement of poll tax requirement

In the exercise of the powers of Congress under section 5 of the fourteenth amendment, section 2 of the fifteenth amendment and section 2 of the twenty-fourth amendment, the Attorney General is authorized and directed to institute forthwith in the name of the United States such actions, including actions against States or political subdivisions, for declaratory judgment or injunctive relief against the enforcement of any requirement of the payment of a poll tax as a precondition to voting, or substitute therefor enacted after November 1, 1964, as will be necessary to implement the declaration of subsection (a) of this section and the purposes of this section.

(c) Jurisdiction of three-judge district courts; appeal to Supreme Court

The district courts of the United States shall have jurisdiction of such actions which shall be heard and determined by a court of three judges in accordance with the provisions of section 2284 of title 28 and any appeal shall lie to the Supreme Court. It shall be the duty of the judges designated to hear the case to assign the case for hearing at the earliest practicable date, to participate in the hearing and determination thereof, and to cause the case to be in every way expedited.

. . .

§ 1973i. Prohibited acts

(a) Failure or refusal to permit casting or tabulation of vote

No person acting under color of law shall fail or refuse to permit any person to vote who is entitled to vote under any provision of subchapters A to C of this chapter or is otherwise qualified to vote, or willfully fail or refuse to tabulate, count, and report such person's vote.

(b) Intimidation, threats, or coercion

No person, whether acting under color of law or otherwise, shall intimidate, threaten, or coerce, or attempt to intimidate, threaten, or coerce any person for voting or attempting to vote, or intimidate, threaten, or coerce, or attempt to intimidate, threaten, or coerce any person for urging or aiding any person to vote or attempt to vote, or intimidate, threaten, or coerce any person for exercising any powers or duties under section 1973a(a), 1973d, 1973f, 1973g, 1973h, or 1973j(e) of this title.

(c) False information in registering or voting; penalties

Whoever knowingly or willfully gives false information as to his name, address or period of residence in the voting district for the purpose of establishing his eligibility to register or vote, or conspires with another individual for the purpose of encouraging his false registration to vote or illegal voting, or pays or offers to pay or accepts payment either for registration to vote or for voting shall be fined not more than $10,000 or imprisoned not more than five years, or both: *Provided, however,* That this provision shall be applicable only to general, special, or primary elections held solely or in part for the purpose of selecting or electing any candidate for the office of President, Vice President, presidential elector, Member of the United

States Senate, Member of the United States House of Representatives, Delegate from the District of Columbia, Guam, or the Virgin Islands, or Resident Commissioner of the Commonwealth of Puerto Rico.

(d) Falsification or concealment of material facts or giving of false statements in matters within jurisdiction of examiners or hearing officers; penalties

Whoever, in any matter within the jurisdiction of an examiner or hearing officer knowingly and willfully falsifies or conceals a material fact, or makes any false, fictitious, or fraudulent statements or representations, or makes or uses any false writing or document knowing the same to contain any false, fictitious, or fraudulent statement or entry, shall be fined not more than $10,000 or imprisoned not more than five years, or both.

(e) Voting more than once

(1) Whoever votes more than once in an election referred to in paragraph (2) shall be fined not more than $10,000 or imprisoned not more than five years, or both.

(2) The prohibition of this subsection applies with respect to any general, special, or primary election held solely or in part for the purpose of selecting or electing any candidate for the office of President, Vice President, presidential elector, Member of the United States Senate, Member of the United States House of Representatives, Delegate from the District of Columbia, Guam, or the Virgin Islands, or Resident Commissioner of the Commonwealth of Puerto Rico.

. . .

§ 1973j. Civil and criminal sanctions

(a) Depriving or attempting to deprive persons of secured rights

Whoever shall deprive or attempt to deprive any person of any right secured by section 1973, 1973a, 1973b, 1973c, or 1973h of this title or shall violate section 1973i(a) of this title, shall be fined not more than $5,000, or imprisoned not more than five years, or both.

(b) Destroying, defacing, mutilating, or altering ballots or official voting records

Whoever, within a year following an election in a political subdivision in which an observer has been assigned (1) destroys, defaces, mutilates, or otherwise alters the marking of a paper ballot which has been cast in such election, or (2) alters any official record of voting in such election tabulated from a voting machine or otherwise, shall be fined not more than $5,000, or imprisoned not more than five years, or both.

(c) Conspiring to violate or interfere with secured rights

Whoever conspires to violate the provisions of subsection (a) or (b) of this section, or interferes with any right secured by section 1973, 1973a, 1973b, 1973c, 1973h, or 1973i(a) of this title shall be fined not more than $5,000, or imprisoned not more than five years, or both.

(d) Civil action by Attorney General for preventive relief; injunctive and other relief

Whenever any person has engaged or there are reasonable grounds to believe that any person is about to engage in any act or practice prohibited by section 1973, 1973a, 1973b, 1973c, 1973e, 1973h, 1973i, or subsection (b) of this section, the Attorney General may institute for the United States, or in the name of the United States, an action for preventive relief, including an application for a temporary or permanent injunction, restraining order, or other order, and including an order directed to the State and State or local election officials to require them (1) to permit persons listed under subchapters A to C of this chapter to vote and (2) to count such votes.

(e) Proceeding by Attorney General to enforce the counting of ballots of registered and eligible persons who are prevented from voting

Whenever in any political subdivision in which there are observers appointed pursuant to subchapters A to C of this chapter any persons allege to such an observer within forty-eight hours after the closing of the polls that notwithstanding (1) their listing under subchapters A to C of this chapter or registration by an appropriate election official and (2) their eligibility to vote, they have not been permitted to vote in such election, the observer shall forthwith notify the Attorney General if such allegations in his opinion appear to be well founded. Upon receipt of such notification, the Attorney General may forthwith file with the district court an application for an order providing for the marking, casting, and counting of the ballots of such persons and requiring the inclusion of their votes in the total vote before the results of such election shall be deemed final and any force or effect given thereto. The district court shall hear and determine such matters immediately after the filing of such application. The remedy provided in this subsection shall not preclude any remedy available under State or Federal law.

(f) Jurisdiction of district courts; exhaustion of administrative or other remedies unnecessary

The district courts of the United States shall have jurisdiction of proceedings instituted pursuant to this section and shall exercise the same without regard to whether a person asserting rights under the provisions of subchapters A to C of this chapter shall have exhausted any administrative or other remedies that may be provided by law.

BIBLIOGRAPHY

ABORTION

FIFTH CIRCUIT UPHOLDS LOUISIANA ABORTION CLINICS LAW

Boonin, David. *A Defense of Abortion*, Cambridge University Press, 2002.

Kaczor, Christopher. *The Ethics of Abortion: Women's Rights, Human Life, and the Question of Justice*, Routledge, 2010.

FIFTH CIRCUIT UPHOLDS TEXAS REGULATIONS THAT CUTS MEDICAID FUNDING TO ABORTION PROVIDERS

Boonin, David. *A Defense of Abortion*, Cambridge University Press, 2002.

Kaczor, Christopher. *The Ethics of Abortion: Women's Rights, Human Life, and the Question of Justice*, Routledge, 2010.

NINTH CIRCUIT RULES ARIZONA ABORTION LAW UNCONSTITUTIONAL

Boonin, David. *A Defense of Abortion*, Cambridge University Press, 2002.

Kaczor, Christopher. *The Ethics of Abortion: Women's Rights, Human Life, and the Question of Justice*, Routledge, 2010.

NORTH CAROLINA JUDGE STRIKES DOWN ANTI-ABORTION LICENSE PLATE

Clark, Rebecca. "Choose Life: Officials Push Legislators to Approve Controversial License Plate." *Star* (Shelby, N.C.), October 10, 2009.

Jenkins, Colleen. "North Carolina Barred from Issuing 'Choose Life' License Plates." Reuters, December 10, 2012.

Winter, Michael. "U.S. Judge Bans N.C. 'Choose Life' License Plate." *USA Today*, December 10, 2012.

OKLAHOMA SUPREME COURT STRIKES DOWN ABORTION LAW

Boonin, David. *A Defense of Abortion*, Cambridge University Press, 2002.

Kaczor, Christopher. *The Ethics of Abortion: Women's Rights, Human Life, and the Question of Justice*, Routledge, 2010.

SEVENTH CIRCUIT STRIKES DOWN LAW BANNING STATE FUNDING TO ABORTION PROVIDERS

Boonin, David. *A Defense of Abortion*, Cambridge University Press, 2002.

Kaczor, Christopher. *The Ethics of Abortion: Women's Rights, Human Life, and the Question of Justice*, Routledge, 2010.

WILL STATES BE ABLE TO OUTLAW ABORTION?

Boonin, David. *A Defense of Abortion*, Cambridge University Press, 2002.

Kaczor, Christopher. *The Ethics of Abortion: Women's Rights, Human Life, and the Question of Justice*, Routledge, 2010.

ADMIRALTY AND MARITIME LAW

LOZMAN V. CITY OF RIVIERA BEACH, FLORIDA

Barnes, Robert. "Floating Home Is Not a Vessel, Supreme Court Says." *Washington Post,* January 15, 2013.

Green, Laura. "Supreme Court Weighs Whether Activist Lozman's Houseboat in Riviera Beach Was a Vessel." *Palm Beach Post,* October 2, 2012.

Stempel, Jonathan. "U.S. Supreme Court Sinks Florida City over Floating Home." Reuters, January 15, 2013.

AFFIRMATIVE ACTION

SIXTH CIRCUIT STRIKES DOWN MICHIGAN CONSTITUTIONAL AMENDMENT BANNING AFFIRMATIVE ACTION

Covington, Robert and Kurt Decker. *Employment Law in a Nutshell.* Saint Paul, MN: West Group, 2002. Second edition.

Lewis, Harold Jr., and Elizabeth Norman. *Civil Rights Law and Practice.* Saint Paul, MN: West Group, 2004.

Vieira, Norman. *Constitutional Civil Rights in a Nutshell.* Saint Paul, MN.: West Group, 1998.

AGRICULTURAL LAW

HORNE V. DEPARTMENT OF AGRICULTURE

Abcarian, Robin. "Another Wrinkle in Raisin Growers' Lawsuit." *Los Angeles Times,* June 18, 2013.

Doyle, Michael. "Supreme Court Chews over Case Pitting Raisin Farmers Against USDA." *Fort Worth Star-Telegram,* June 10, 2013.

Karst, Tom. "Supreme Court Backs Review of Raisin Challenge." *The Packer,* June 11, 2013.

AMERICANS WITH DISABILITIES ACT

SEVENTH CIRCUIT RULES EMPLOYERS DO NOT HAVE TO AUTOMATICALLY FILL VACANCIES WITH DISABLED EMPLOYEES

Goren, William. *Understanding the Americans with Disabilities Act, 2nd Edition.* American Bar Association, 2007.

Mezey, Susan. *Disabling Interpretations: The Americans With Disabilities Act In Federal Court.* University of Pittsburgh Press, 2005.

Tucker, Bonnie, and Adam Milani. *Federal Disability Law in a Nutshell, 3rd Edition.* West Publishing, 2004.

SIXTH CIRCUIT RULES ON STANDARD FOR DISABILITY CLAIM

Goren, William. *Understanding the Americans with Disabilities Act, 2nd Edition.* American Bar Association, 2007.

Mezey, Susan. *Disabling Interpretations: The Americans With Disabilities Act In Federal Court.* University of Pittsburgh Press, 2005.

Tucker, Bonnie, and Adam Milani. *Federal Disability Law in a Nutshell, 3rd Edition.* West Publishing, 2004.

ANTITRUST LAW

AMERICAN EXPRESS CO. V. ITALIAN COLORS RESTAURANT

Barnes, Robert. "Supreme Court Sides with American Express on Arbitration." *Washington Post,* June 20, 2013.

Hurley, Lawrence, and Andrew Longstreth. "Supreme Court Clamps Down on Class Actions in Merchants' Case." *Chicago Tribune,* June 20, 2013.

Kendall, Brent. "Supreme Court Stops Merchant Class-Action Suit vs. American Express." *Wall Street Journal,* June 20, 2013.

SUPREME COURT RULES THAT MUNICIPAL HOSPITAL ENTITY DOES NOT HAVE STATE-ACTION ANTITRUST IMMUNITY

Gellhorn, Ernest. *Antitrust Law And Economics In A Nutshell.* Saint Paul, MN.: West Group, 2004. Fifth edition.

American Bar Association. *Market Power Handbook: Competition Law and Economic Foundation,* 2006.

APPELLATE ADVOCACY

SUPREME COURT RULES MENTALLY INCOMPETENT INMATES CANNOT STAY THEIR APPEALS

Palmer, John. *Constitutional Rights of Prisoners.* New York: Anderson, 2006. Eighth edition.

Tomkovicz, James J. *The Right to the Assistance of Counsel: A Reference Guide to the United States Constitution.* Westport, Conn.: Greenwood, 2002.

ARBITRATION

OXFORD HEALTH PLANS V. SUTTER

Kralowec, Kimberly. "Another U.S. Supreme Court Decision Hinges on a Party Concession: *Oxford Health Plans v. Sutter.*" *UCL Practitioner,* June 17, 2013. http://www.uclpractitioner.com/2013/06/another-us-supreme-court-decision-hinges-on-a-party-concession-oxford-health-plans-llc-v-sutter.html

Oxford Health Plans v. Sutter, No. 12-135. www.supremecourt.gov/opinions/12pdf/12-135_e1p3.pdf

Oyez Project at Chicago-Kent College of Law. "*Oxford Health Plans v. Sutter.*" U.S. Supreme Court Media Report. http://www.oyez.org/cases/2010-2019/2012/2012_12_135

Parasharami, Archis. "Supreme Court: *Oxford Health Plans v. Sutter* Asks Whether Parties Agree to Class Arbitration by Failing to Mention It." February 28, 2013. http://www.insidecounsel.com/2013/02/28/supreme-court-emoxford-health-plans-v-sutter-em-as.

ASSASSINATION

GABRIELLE GIFFORDS

Baldrige, Peter D. *Gun Ownership and the Second Amendment.* New York: Nova Science Publishers, 2009.

Charles, Patrick J. *The Second Amendment: The Intent and Its Interpretation by the States and the Supreme Court.* Jefferson, N.C.: McFarland & Co., 2009.

ATTORNEY'S FEES

SEBELIUS V. CLOER

Hasen, Richard L. *Remedies: Examples and Explanations.* 3d ed. New York: Wolters Kluwer Law and Business, 2013.

Rossi, Robert L. *Attorneys' Fees.* 3d ed. Eagan, Minn.: West Group, 2001.

SUPREME COURT RULES PLAINTIFF ENTITLED TO ATTORNEYS' FEES BY OBTAINING INJUNCTION

Covington, Robert and Kurt Decker. *Employment Law in a Nutshell.* Saint Paul, MN: West Group. 2002. Second edition.

Lewis, Harold Jr., and Elizabeth Norman. *Civil Rights Law and Practice.* Saint Paul, MN: West Group, 2004.

Vieira, Norman. *Constitutional Civil Rights in a Nutshell.* Saint Paul, MN.: West Group, 1998.

AUTOMOBILES

NEW JERSEY SUPREME COURT UPHOLDS YOUNG DRIVER STICKER LAW

Curry, Allison, Melissa R. Pfeiffer, Russell Localio, and Dennis Durbin. "Gradauted Driver Licensing Decal Law: Effect on Young Probationary Drivers." *American Journal of Preventive Medicine,* January 2013.

Feeley, Jef. "New Jersey's Young-Driver Law Not Flawed, Court Concludes." Bloomberg, August 6, 2012. http://www.bloomberg.com/news/2012-08-06/new-jersey-s-young-driver-law-upheld-against-privacy-challenge.html

Hochman, Louis C. "Study: Decal Law Kept 1,600 Young Drivers Out of Crashes in First Year." NJ.com. October 24, 2012. http://www.nj.com/morris/index.ssf/2012/10/study_decal_law_kept_1600_youn.html

Spoto, MaryAnn. "N.J. Supreme Court Upholds Decal Law for Young Drivers." NJ.com, August 6, 2012. http://www.nj.com/news/index.ssf/2012/08/nj_supreme_court_not_an_invasi.html

SEVENTH CIRCUIT RULES PARKING TICKET VIOLATES FEDERAL PRIVACY LAW

Jellum, Linda D., and David Charles Hricik. *Modern Statutory Intepretation,* Carolina Academic Press, 2009.

Frickey, Phillip P., and Elizabeth Eskridge. *Legislation and Statutory Interpretation,* Foundation Press, 2006.

BANKRUPTCY

BULLOCK V. BANKCHAMPAIGN

"*Bullock v. BankChampaign.*" American Bankruptcy Institute. http://opinions.abi.org/0513-082-bullock-v-bankchampaign-na

Bullock v. BankChampaign, No. 11-1518. www.supremecourt.gov/opinions/12pdf/11-1518_97be.pdf

Oyez Project at Chicago-Kent College of Law. "*Bullock v. BankChampaign.*" http://www.oyez.org/cases/2010-2019/2012/2012_11_1518

Rosen, Zvi. "*Bullock v. BankChampaign*: Post-Decision SCOTUScast." Federalist Society, May 20, 2013. http://www.fed-soc.org/publications/detail/bullock-v-bankchampaign-post-decision-scotuscast

DEWEY & LEBOEUF LAW FIRM FILES FOR CHAPTER 11 BANKRUPTCY

Ax, Joseph, and Sakthi Prasad. "Dewey Files for Chapter 11 in Record Law Firm Collapse." Thomson Reuters, May 29, 2012. http://www.reuters.com

Byrne, Alanna. "Dewey Liquidation Plan Wins Court Approval." *Inside Counsel,* February 28, 2013.

Byrne, Alanna. "Steven Davis Agrees to Pay $511,145 to Resolve Claims Related to the Firm's Bankruptcy." *Inside Counsel,* April 23, 2013.

Harper, Steven J. "The Big Law Firm Story of the Year: Dewey & LeBoeuf." *American Law Daily,* January 4, 2013.

Randazzo, Sara, and Christine Simmons. "Dewey & LeBoeuf." *New York Law Journal,* July 16 and August 28, 2012.

Sullivan, Casey. "Dewey & LeBoeuf Ex-Chairman Agrees to Proposed $500,000 to Resolve Claims." *Insurance Journal,* April 24, 2013. http://www.insurancejournal.com/news/national/2013/04/24/289586.htm

Vorro, Alex. "Former Dewey Partner Sues Management, Claims They Were 'Running a Ponzi Scheme.'" *Inside Counsel,* June 14, 2012.

BIRTH CONTROL

MISSOURI BIRTH CONTROL LAW STRUCK BY FEDERAL COURT

Associated Press. "Missouri: Judge Strikes Down Birth Control Measure." *New York Times,* March 18, 2013.

Carlson-Thies, Stanley. "Which Religious Organizations Count as Religious? The Religious Employer Exemption of the Health Insurance Law's Contraceptives Mandate." Federalist Society, August 6, 2012. http://www.fed-soc.org/publications/detail/which-religious-organizations-count-as-religious

Guttmacher Institute. "State Policies in Brief: Insurance Coverage of Contraceptives." June 1, 2013. http://www.guttmacher.org/statecenter/spibs/spib_icc.pdf

Karmasek, Jessica M. "Koster: MO Won't Appeal Federal Court Ruling over Contraception Mandate." *Legal Newsline,* April 16, 2013. http://legalnewsline.com/news/240885-koster-mo-wont-appeal-federal-court-ruling-over-contraception-mandate

Sacriponte, Alison. "Federal Judge Blocks Missouri Birth Control Law." *JURIST,* Paperchase, March 18, 2013. http://jurist.org/paperchase/2013/18/03/federal-judge-blocks-birth-control-law.php

Tennant, Michael. "Federal Judge Overturns Missouri Law Nullifying Contraception Mandate." *New American,* March 19, 2013.

SIXTH CIRCUIT UPHOLDS OHIO LAW LIMITING ABORTION MEDICATION

Boonin, David. *A Defense of Abortion,* Cambridge University Press, 2002.

Kaczor, Christopher. *The Ethics of Abortion: Women's Rights, Human Life, and the Question of Justice,* Routledge, 2010.

CAPITAL PUNISHMENT

ARKANSAS SUPREME COURT STRIKES DOWN STATE EXECUTION LAW

Banner, Stuart. *The Death Penalty: An American History.* Cambridge, Mass.: Harvard UP, 2003.

Bedau, Hugo and Paul Cassell. *Debating the Death Penalty.* New York: Oxford UP, 2004.

Cohen, Stanley. *The Wrong Men: America's Epidemic of Wrongful Death Row Convictions.* New York: Carroll and Graf, 2003.

NINTH CIRCUIT ORDERS IDAHO TO PROVIDE FULL MEDIA ACCESS TO EXECUTIONS

Banner, Stuart. *The Death Penalty: An American History.* Cambridge, Mass.: Harvard UP, 2003.

Bedau, Hugo and Paul Cassell. *Debating the Death Penalty.* New York: Oxford UP, 2004.

Cohen, Stanley. *The Wrong Men: America's Epidemic of Wrongful Death Row Convictions.* New York: Carroll and Graf, 2003.

CHILD ABUSE

FALLOUT FROM JERRY SANDUSKY CHILD-ABUSE SCANDAL CONTINUES

Bello, Marisol. "Ex-Penn State President Spanier's Team Slams Sandusky Report." *USA Today,* August 22, 2012.

Eder, Steve. "Former Penn State President Is Charged in Sandusky Case." *New York Times,* November 1, 2012.

Gabriel, Trip. "Investigation to Focus on Governor's Handling of Penn State Abuse Case." *New York Times,* January 31, 2013.

CHILD CUSTODY

CHAFIN V. CHAFIN

"*Chafin v. Chafin.*" *New York Times,* December 11, 2012.

Stempel, Jonathan, and Terry Baynes. "Supreme Court to Hear International Child Custody Dispute." *Chicago Tribune,* August 13, 2012.

CIVIL RIGHTS

D.C. CIRCUIT THROWS OUT TORTURE LAWSUIT AGAINST RUMSFELD

Chemerinsky, Erwin. *Federal Jurisdiction.* Boston: Aspen, 2007. Fifth edition.

Little, Laura. *Federal Courts Examples & Explanations.*.Boston: Aspen, 2007.

Wright, Charles Alan. *Law of Federal Courts.* St. Paul, Minn.: West Group, 2002. Sixth edition.

CIVIL SERVICE

SUPREME COURT CLARIFIES PROCEDURES FOR FEDERAL CIVIL SERVICE APPEALS

Jellum, Linda D., and David Charles Hricik. *Modern Statutory Intepretation,* Carolina Academic Press, 2009.

Frickey, Phillip P., and Elizabeth Eskridge. *Legislation and Statutory Interpretation,* Foundation Press, 2006.

CLASS ACTION

COMCAST CORP. V. BEHREND

Dinkoff, Allan. "*Comcast v. Behrend*: Bigger Than We Thought at First Blush?" *New York Law Journal,* April 25, 2013.

Stempel, Jonathan. "Supreme Court Rules for Comcast in Class Action." Reuters, March 27, 2013.

Wyatt, Edward. "Court Rejects Antitrust Suit in Victory for Comcast." *New York Times,* March 27, 2013.

GENESIS HEALTHCARE V. SYMCZYK

Genesis HealthCare Corp. v. Symczyk, No. 11-1059. www.supremecourt.gov/opinions/12pdf/11-1059_5ifl.pdf

"*HealthCare Corp. v. Symczyk*: SCOTUS Allows Pick-Off of Named Plaintiff for $7500: Justice Kagan Is Not Impressed." *Impact Litigation Journal,* April 22, 2013.http://www.impactlitigation.com/2013/04/22/healthcare-corp-v-symczyk-scotus-allows-pick-off-of-named-plaintiff-for-7500-justice-kagan-is-not-impressed/

Liptak, Adam. "Supreme Court Rules in Favor of 1 Worker, but Not Another." *New York Times,* April 16, 2013.

Moller, Mark. "*Genesis HealthCare Corp. v. Symczyk*: Post-Decision SCOTUScast." Federalist Society, May 20, 2013. http://www.fed-soc.org/publications/detail/genesis-healthcare-corp-v-symczyk-post-decision-scotuscast

Oyez Project at Chicago-Kent College of Law. "*Genesis HealthCare Corp. v. Symczyk*." http://www.oyez.org/cases/2010-2019/2012/2012_11_1059

STANDARD FIRE INSURANCE COMPANY V. KNOWLES

Fitzpatrick, Brian. "*Standard Fire Insurance Company v. Knowles*: Post-Decision SCOTUScast." Federalist Society, February 27, 2013. http://www.fed-soc.org/publications/detail/standard-fire-insurance-co-v-knowles-post-decision-scotuscast

"*Standard Fire Insurance Company v. Knowles*." *Impact Litigation Journal,* March 25, 2013.

Standard Fire Insurance Company v. Knowles, No. 11-1450. www.supremecourt.gov/opinions/12pdf/11-1450_9olb.pdf

"Supreme Court Insurance Ruling a Setback for Class Action Claimants." *Insurance Journal,* March 20, 2013. http://www.insurancejournal.com/news/national/2013/03/20/285201.htm

CONGRESS OF THE UNITED STATES

STATE EMERGENCY MANAGEMENT LAWS UNDER THE 2013 SEQUESTER

Association of State and Territorial Health Officials. "Sequestration Fact Page." http://www.astho.org/Sequestration-Fact-Page

"Fact Sheet: Examples of How the Sequester Would Impact Middle Class Families, Jobs and Economic Security." White House Press Release, February 8, 2013. http://www.whitehouse.gov/the-press-office/2013/02/08/fact-sheet-examples-how-sequester

"Forest Service to States: Return $18 million, Blame Sequestration." CBSLocal, Washington, DC, May 3, 2013. http://www.washington.cbslocal.com/2013/05/03/forest-service-demands-states-return-18m

Ross, Brydon. "Sequestration Impact on Timber and Public Land Issues in States." Knowledge Center at The Council of State Governments, June 17, 2011. http://knowledgecenter.csg.org/drupal/content/sequestration-impact-timber-and-public-land-issues

Sequestration Report. White House Press Release, March 1, 2013. http://www.whitehouse.gov/sites/default/ . . ./fy13ombjcsequestrationreport.pdf

Spar, Karen, coordinator for Congressional Research Service. *Budget "Sequestration" and Selected Program Exemptions and Special Rules.* CRS Report for Congress, R42050, June 13, 2013

Vasilogambros, Matt. "Sequestration Hits Disaster Assistance, Weather Detection Spending." *Government Executive,* May 21, 2013.

CONSPIRACY

E-BOOK PUBLISHERS SETTLE PRICE-FIXING CASES

Albanesius, Chloe. "Report: Justice Department Sues Apple over E-Book Price Fixing." *PC Magazine,* April 11, 2012.

Bray, Chad, and Jeffrey A. Trachtenberg. "E-Books Pricing Settlement Approved." *Wall Street Journal,* September 6, 2012.

Chen, Brian X., and Julie Bosman. "Fallout From Apple's Loss on E-Books." *New York Times,* July 10, 2013.

Catan, Thomas, Jeffrey A. Trachtenberg, and Chad Bray. "U.S. Alleges E-Book Scheme." *Wall Street Journal,* April 11, 2012.

Elmer-DeWitt, Philip. "The Apple E-book Case Is Headed for the 2nd Circuit." *CNNMoney,* July 10, 2013.

COPYRIGHT

KIRTSAENG V. JOHN WILEY & SONS

American Bar Association. "*Kirtsaeng v. John Wiley & Sons, Inc.*: Docket 11-697." http://www.americanbar.org/publications/preview_home/11-697.html

Kirtsaeng v. John Wiley & Sons, Inc., No. 11-697. www.supremecourt.gov/opinions/11pdf/11-697_4g15.pdf

Oyez Project at Chicago-Kent College of Law. "*Kirsaeng v. John Wiley & Sons, Inc.*" http://www.oyez.org/cases/2010-2019/2012/2012_11_697

COUNTERFEITING

FIVE CHARGED WITH IMPORTING COUNTERFEIT TOYS FROM CHINA

Santora, Marc. "5 from Queens Charged in Toy-Smuggling Scheme." *New York Times,* February 6, 2013.

Sgueglia, Kristina. "5 Accused of Importing Counterfeit, Hazardous Toys." CNN.com, February 7, 2013.

Smythe, Christie. "Fake SpongeBobs, Dangerous Spider-Men Spur U.S. Charges." *Bloomberg*, February 6, 2013.

CRIMINAL LAW

BP Corporation Agrees to Plead Guilty to Criminal Charges in Gulf Oil Spill

Fowler, Tom. "BP Probed on Leak Estimates." *Wall Street Journal*, May 28, 2012.

Frieden, Terry. "First Criminal Charges Filed in BP Oil Spill." CNN News, April 24, 2012. http://www.cnn.com/2012/04/24/us/gulf-oil-spill

Krauss, Clifford, and John Schwartz. "BP Will Plead Guilty and Pay over $4 Billion." *New York Times*, November 15, 2012.

U.S. Department of Justice. "BP Exploration and Production Inc. Agrees to Plead Guilty to Felony Manslaughter, Environmental Crimes, and Obstruction of Congress Surrounding Deepwater Horizon Incident." DOJ Office of Public Affairs press release, November 12, 2012. http://www.justice.gov/opa/pr/2012/November/12-ag-1369.html

Smith v. United States

Dressler, Joshua. *Understanding Criminal Law*. 6th ed. New Providence, N.J.: LexisNexis, 2012.

Sheldon, Jonathan. *Federal Deception Law: FTC and CFPB Rules, RICO, False Claims Act, Telemarketing, Debt Relief, and Parallel State Statutes*. Boston, Mass.: National Consumer Law Center, 2012.

Singer, Richard G., and John Q. La Fond. *Criminal Law: Examples and Explanations*. 6th ed. New York: Wolters Kluwer Law and Business, 2013.

CRIMINAL PROCEDURE

Chaidez v. United States

Hurley, Lawrence, and Jonathan Stempel. "Supreme Court Won't Extend 2010 Immigration Ruling." Reuters, February 20, 2013.

Liptak, Adam. "Supreme Court Limits Reach of 2010 Ruling on Deportation Warning." *New York Times*, February 20, 2013.

Ovalle, David. "U.S. Supreme Court Ruling Affects Many Immigrant Convicts in South Florida." *Miami Herald*, February 20, 2013.

Florida v. Harris

Barnes, Robert. "Supreme Court Sides with Drug-Sniffing Dog; Supports Soldier's Child Custody Case." *Washington Post*, February 19, 2013.

Horowitz, Alexandra. "What the Dog Knows." *New Yorker*, February 23, 2013.

Liptak, Adam. "Question for Justices: Do Aldo and Franky's Noses Always Know?" *New York Times*, October 29, 2012.

Maryland v. King

LaFave, Wayne R. *Search and Seizure: A Treatise on the Fourth Amendment*. 5th ed. St. Paul, Minn.: West, 2012.

Liptak, Adam. "Justices Allow DNA Collection After an Arrest." *New York Times*, June 3, 2013.

Memmott, Mark. "Supreme Court Upholds Warrantless Collection of DNA." NPR, June 3, 2013.

United States v. Davila

Bonner, Mark. "*United States v. Davila*: Post-Argument SCOTUScast." Federalist Society, April 22, 2013. http://www.fed-soc.org/publications/detail/united-states-v-davila-post-argument-scotuscast

Oyez Project at Chicago-Kent College of Law. "*United States v. Davila*." http://www.oyez.org/cases/2010-2019/2012/2012_12_167

United States v. Davila, No. 12-167. www.supreme-court.gov/opinions/12pdf/12-167_d1oe.pdf

"*United States v. Davila*." *Texas Lawyer*, June 17, 2013. http://www.law.com/jsp/tx/LawDecisionTX.jsp?id=1371489809371

DEBTOR AND CREDITOR

Marx v. General Revenue Corporation

Herman, Paul A. "Supreme Court Sides with Debt Collector." *Palm Beach Post*, March 2, 2013.

Hobbs, Robert J., and Carolyn Carter. *Fair Debt Collection*. Boston, Mass.: National Consumer Law Center, 2011.

Taylor, Rebecca A. *Foreclosure Defense: A Practical Litigation Guide*. Chicago, Ill.: American Bar Association, 2011.

DEPARTMENT OF JUSTICE

Operation Fast and Furious "Gun-Walking" Scandal

Barrett, Paul M. "'Fast and Furious' Scandal Returns to Haunt Obama." *Bloomberg Businessweek*, May 21, 2013. http://www.businessweek.com/articles/2013-05-21/fast-and-furious-scandal-returns-to-haunt-obama

Flock, Elizabeth. "Dozens of FOIA Requests on Eric Holder Filed Before 'Fast and Furious' Became Public." *U.S. News and World Report*, March 11, 2013.

Reyes, Gerardo, and Santiago Wills. "Fast and Furious Scandal: New Details Emerge on How the U.S. Government Armed Mexican Drug Cartels."

ABC News, September 30, 2012. http://abcnews.go.com/ABC_Univision/News/fast-furious-scandal-details-emerge-us-government-armed/story?id=17352694

Wyler, Grace. "Here's What You Need to Know About the Gun Running Scandal That Could Destroy Obama's Attorney General." *Business Insider*, June 20, 2012. http://www.businessinsider.com/what-is-fast-and-furious-2012-6

DOUBLE JEOPARDY

EVANS V. MICHIGAN

Evans v. Michigan, No. 11-1327. www.supremecourt.gov/opinions/12pdf/11-1327_7648.pdf

Oyez Project at Chicago-Kent College of Law. "*Evans v. Michigan*." http://www.oyez.org/cases/2010-2019/2012/2012_11_1327

Sandburg, Michael. "*Lamar Evans v. Michigan*: Double Jeopardy & Acquittals Based on Error of Law." *Supreme Court Observer*, September 6, 2012. http://www.supremeobserver.com/2012/09/06/lamar-evans-v-michigan-double-jeopardy-acquittals-based-error-law/

Stempel, Jonathan. "Supreme Court Bars Defendant's Retrial After Judge Errs." Reuters, February 20, 2013. http://www.reuters.com/article/2013/02/20/us-usa-court-doublejeopardy-idUSBRE91J0UM20130220

DRUGS AND NARCOTICS

BIG PHARMACEUTICAL SETTLEMENTS IN 2012

Palmer, Eric. "10 Largest Settlements and Judgments." http://www.fiercepharma.com

Public Citizen's Health Research Group. "Pharmaceutical Industry Criminal and Civil Penalties: An Update." http://www.citizen.org/hrg2073

"Ranbaxy Pleads Guilty, to Pay $500 Million in U.S. Settlement." Reuters, May 13, 2013. http://www.reuters.com/article/2013/05/13/us-ranbaxy-settlement-idUSBRE94C0PT20130513

Szalavitz, Maia. "Pharma Behaving Badly." *Time*, September 17, 2012.

VOTERS IN COLORADO AND WASHINGTON LEGALIZE MARIJUANA

Gurmank, Sadie. "Coloradans Say Yes to Recreational Use of Marijuana." *Denver Post*, November 6, 2013.

Lauter, David. "Marijuana Legalization Wins Majority Support in Poll." *L.A. Times*, April 4, 2013.

Martin, Jonathan. "Voters Approve I-502 Legalizing Marijuana." *Seattle Times*, November 6, 2013.

EDUCATION LAW

FEDERAL GOVERNMENT STRUGGLES WITH STUDENT-LOAN INTEREST RATES

Elliott, Philip. "Student Loan Interest Doubles in July Due to Congressional Inaction." *Christian Science Monitor*, March 29, 2013.

Ensign, Rachel Louise. "A New Student-Loan Program Launches." *Wall Street Journal*, November 5, 2012.

Nawaguna, Elvina. "U.S. Congress Finally Votes to Cut Student Loan Interest Rates." Reuters, July 31, 2013.

Peters, Jeremy W., and Ashley Parker. "An Unusual Feat in Congress: Student Loan Bill Breezes On." *New York Times*, July 31, 2013.

ELECTION LAW

ARIZONA UPHOLDS ENGLISH PROFICIENCY REQUIREMENT FOR PUBLIC OFFICEHOLDERS

Jellum, Linda D., and David Charles Hricik. *Modern Statutory Intepretation*, Carolina Academic Press, 2009.

Frickey, Phillip P., and Elizabeth Eskridge. *Legislation and Statutory Interpretation*, Foundation Press, 2006.

LAVIN V. HUSTED

Cantor, Joseph E., and R. Sam Garrett. *Campaign Finance Legislation in Congress*. New York: Nova Science, 2008.

Griffith, Benjamin E., ed. *America Votes! A Guide to Modern Election Law and Voting Rights*. Chicago: American Bar Association, 2012.

U.S. House of Representatives, Committee on the Judiciary, Subcommittee on the Constitution, Civil Rights, and Civil Liberties. *First Amendment and Campaign Finance Reform After Citizens United: Hearing Before the Subcommittee on the Constitution, Civil Rights, and Civil Liberties of the Committee on the Judiciary, House of Representatives, One Hundred Eleventh Congress, Second Session, February 3, 2010*. Washington, D.C.: U.S. Government Printing Office, 2010.

ELECTRONIC SURVEILLANCE

CLAPPER V. AMNESTY INTERNATIONAL USA

Liptak, Adam. "Justices Turn Back Challenge to Broader U.S. Eavesdropping." *New York Times*, February 26, 2013.

Posner, Eric. "Why Amnesty Will Lose at the Supreme Court." Slate.com, October 26, 2012.

Samp, Rich. "Supreme Court Observations: *Clapper v. Amnesty International*." *Forbes*, March 1, 2013.

EMINENT DOMAIN

KOONTZ V. ST. JOHNS RIVER WATER MANAGEMENT DISTRICT

American Bar Association. "*Coy A. Koontz, Jr., v. St. Johns River Water Management District*: Docket No. 11-1447." http://www.americanbar. org/publications/preview_home/11-1447.html

Frank, Richard. "Supreme Court Rules for Property Owner in *Koontz v. St. Johns River Water Management District*." *Legal Planet* (UCLA Berkeley Law), June 25, 2013.

Koontz v. St. Johns River Water Management District, No. 11-1447. http://www.supremecourt.gov/ opinions/12pdf/11-1447_4e46.pdf

Oyez Project at Chicago-Kent College of Law. "*Koontz v. St. Johns River Water Management District*." http://www.oyez.org/cases/2010-2019/ 2012/2012_11_1447

EMPLOYMENT DISCRIMINATION

SUPREME COURT CLARIFIES WHO IS A SUPERVISOR UNDER TITLE VII

Covington, Robert and Kurt Decker. *Employment Law in a Nutshell*. Saint Paul, MN: West Group. 2002. Second edition.

Lewis, Harold Jr., and Elizabeth Norman. *Civil Rights Law and Practice.* Saint Paul, MN: West Group, 2004.

Vieira, Norman. *Constitutional Civil Rights in a Nutshell*. Saint Paul, MN.: West Group, 1998.

ENVIRONMENTAL LAW

AMERICAN TRUCKING ASSOCIATIONS, INC. V. CITY OF LOS ANGELES

Epstein, Richard, and Michael Greve, eds. *Federal Preemption: States' Powers, National Interests*. Washington, D.C.: AEI Press, 2007.

Savage, David G. "High Court to Hear Case on Port of L.A.'s Clean Truck Program." *Los Angeles Times*, January 11, 2013.

Stam, John Henry, and Carolyn Whetzel. "Supreme Court Says Federal Law Preempts Clean Truck Provisions for Los Angeles Port." *Environment Reporter*, June 14, 2013.

ARIZONA VOTERS VETO OWNERSHIP OF GRAND CANYON

"Arizona Defeats Ballot Measure Contesting Grand Canyon Ownership." Thomas Reuters Foundation, November 7, 2012.

Arizona Department of State, Office of the Secretary of State. "Proposition 120." http://www.azsos. gov/election/2012/info/PubPamphlet/english/ prop120.htm

Crawford, Amanda J. "Arizona Claims Grand Canyon as Fires Fuel Sovereignty Push." October 22, 2012. http://www.bloomberg. com/news/2012-10-22/wildfires-fuel-sovereignty- push

Fischer, Howard. "Under Prop. 120, Arizona Declares Sovereignty over Federal Land." *East Valley Tribune*, September 23, 2012.

Johanson, Mark. "Arizona: Grand Canyon Is Not National Treasure, It's Ours." *International Business Times*, October 23, 2012. http://www.ibtimes. com/arizona-grand-canyon-not-national- treasure-its-ours-852561

DECKER V. NORTHWEST ENVIRONMENTAL DEFENSE CENTER

Decker v. Northwest Environmental Defense Center, No. 11-338. www.supremecourt.gov/opinions/ 12pdf/11-338_kifl.pdf

Himebaugh, Daniel. "*Decker v. Northwest Environmental Defense Center*: Post-Decision SCOTUScast." Federalist Society, March 29, 2013. http://www.fed-soc.org/publications/detail/ decker-v-northwest-environmental-defense- center-post-decision-scotuscast

Himebaugh, Daniel. "Fighting Unnecessary Regulatory Restrictions on Forest Maintenance: *Decker v. Northwest Environmental Defense Center*." Pacific Legal Foundation News, March 29, 2013. http://www.pacificlegal.org/cases

Oyez Project at Chicago-Kent College of Law. "*Decker v. Northwest Environmental Defense Center*." Available at http://www.oyez.org/cases/ 2010-2019/2012/2012_11_338

EPA WINS MULTIPLE CHALLENGES TO SULFUR DIOXIDE RULES

Cremeans, Jamie. "Federal Appeals Court Upholds EPA Sulfur Dioxide Regulations." *Chicago Tribune*, July 21, 2012. http://jurist.org/paperchase/ 2012/07/federal-appeals-court-upholds-epa- sulfur-dioxide-regulations.php

National Environmental Development Association's Clean Air Project v. EPA. http://www.cadc. uscourts.gov/internet/opinions.nsf/5391ED 8F071268D185257A41004F5B2F/$file/10-1252- 1384735.pdf

Schoenberg, Tom. "EPA Sulfur Dioxide Rules Upheld by U.S. Court of Appeals." Bloomberg, July 9, 2011. http://www.bloomberg.com/news/ 2012-07-20/epa-sulfur-dioxide-rules-upheld-by- u-s-court-of-appeals.html

Stempel, Jonathan. "Supreme Court Won't Hear Challenge to EPA Rulemaking." *Chicago Tribune*, January 22, 2013.

Tracy, Tennile. "Court Upholds EPA's Sulfur Dioxide Rules." *Wall Street Journal*, Paperchase, July 20, 2012.

Los Angeles County Flood Control District v. Natural Resources Defense Council, Inc.

Ferrey, Steven. *Environmental Law: Examples and Explanations.* New York: Wolters Kluwer Law and Business, 2013.

Flournoy, Alyson C., and David M. Driesen. *Beyond Environmental Law: Policy Proposals for a Better Environmental Future.* New York: Cambridge University Press, 2010.

Salzman, James, and Barton H. Thompson, Jr. *Environmental Law and Policy.* 3d ed. New York: Foundation Press, 2010.

Tarrant Regional Water District v. Herrmann

American Bar Association. "11-889 Tarrant Regional Water District v. Herrmann Public Education." http://www.americanbar.org/publications/ preview_home/11-889.html

Oyez Project at Chicago-Kent College of Law. "*Tarrant Regional Water District v. Herrmann.*" http://www.oyez.org/cases/2010-2019/2012/ 2012_11_889

Tarrant Regional Water District v. Herrmann, No. 11-889. www.supremecourt.gov/opinions/12pdf/ 11-889_5ie6.pdf

Tarrant Regional Water District v. Herrmann. Environmental Law Reporter, vol. 43, issue 17 (2013). http://elr.info/litigation/43/20127/tarrant-regional-water-district-v-herrmann

ERISA

U.S. Airways v. McCutchen

Liptak, Adam. "Supreme Court Rules in Favor of 1 Worker, but Not Another." *New York Times,* April 16, 2013.

Oyez Project at Chicago-Kent College of Law. *US Airways v. McCutchen.* http://www.oyez.org/cases/ 2010-2019/2012/2012_11_1285

US Airways v. McCutchen, No. 11-1285. www. supremecourt.gov/opinions/12pdf/11-1285_i4dk. pdf

ESTABLISHMENT CLAUSE

Eighth Circuit Allows Ten Commandments Lawsuit to Proceed

Barron, Jerome and Thomas Dienes. *First Amendment Law in a Nutshell.* West, 2008. Fourth edition.

Farber, Daniel. *The First Amendment: Concepts and Insights.* Foundation Press, 2002.

Fourth Circuit Rules Upholds Public School Credits for Off-Campus Religious Classes

Barron, Jerome and Thomas Dienes. *First Amendment Law in a Nutshell.* West, 2008. Fourth edition.

Farber, Daniel. *The First Amendment: Concepts and Insights.* Foundation Press, 2002.

Second Circuit Strikes Down Town Board Led Prayer

Barron, Jerome and Thomas Dienes. *First Amendment Law in a Nutshell.* West, 2008. Fourth edition.

Farber, Daniel. *The First Amendment: Concepts and Insights.* Foundation Press, 2002.

ESTATE PLANNING

Hillman v. Maretta

Jacobs, Deborah L. "Supreme Court Favors Ex-Wife over Widow in Battle for Life Insurance Proceeds." *Forbes,* June 3, 2013.

Reese, Diana. "Will the Widow or the Ex-Wife Get the Money? Supreme Court to Decide." *Washington Post,* April 22, 2013.

EX POST FACTO LAWS

Supreme Court Rejects Criminal Sentence for violating the Ex Post Facto Clause

Branham, Lynn. *The Law of Sentencing and Corrections in a Nutshell.* West Group, 2005.

Stith, Kate. *Fear of Judging: Sentencing Guidelines in the Federal Courts.* U of Chicago P, 1998.

Tonry, Michael. *Sentencing Matters.* Oxford UP, 2004.

EXTORTION

Sekhar v. United States

American Bar Association. "*Sekhar v. United States*: Docket No. 12-357." http://www.americanbar. org/publications/preview_home/12-357.html

Bancroft PLLC. "Supreme Court Rules Unanimously for Bancroft in *Sekhar v. US.*" June 27, 2013. http://www.bancroftpllc.com/ supreme-court-rules-unanimously-for-bancroft-in-sekhar-v-us

Oyez Project at Chicago-Kent College of Law. "*Sekhar v. United States.*" http://www.oyez.org/ cases/2010-2019/2012/2012_12_357

Sekhar v. United States, No. 12-357. www. supremecourt.gov/opinions/12pdf/12-357_bq7c. pdf

FAMILY LAW

Adoptive Couple v. Baby Girl

Adoptive Couple v. Baby Girl, No. 10-1062. http:// www.supremecourt.gov/opinions/12pdf/12-399_q86b.pdf

Feldman, Noah. "The Momentous Supreme Court Ruling You Totally Missed." Bloomberg, June 27, 2013. http://www.bloomberg.com/news/2013-06-27/the-momentous-supreme-court-ruling-you-totally-missed.html

National Congress of American Indians. "U.S. Supreme Court Upholds Indian Child Welfare Act in *Adoptive Couple v. Baby Girl*." *Time*, June 23, 2011.

Oyez Project at Chicago-Kent College of Law. *Adoptive Couple v. Baby Girl*. http://www.oyez.org/cases/2010-2019/2012/2012_12_399

FEDERAL COMMUNICATIONS COMMISSION

CITY OF ARLINGTON V. FCC

Barbagallo, Paul. "Former Top FCC Officials Disagree on Impact of Latest Take on Chevron Deference Rules." Telecommunications Law Resource Center, June 4, 2013.

Hurley, Lawrence. "U.S. Justices Endorse FCC Authority in Cellphone Tower Case." Reuters, May 20, 2013.

Liptak, Adam. "Supreme Court Hears Argument on the F.C.C.'s Authority to Rule on Cellphone Towers." *New York Times*, January 16, 2013.

FEDERAL TORT CLAIMS ACT

LEVIN V. UNITED STATES

Associated Press. "Court: Can Guam Man Sue Gov't over Surgery?" September 25, 2012.

Bascetta, Cynthia A. *Federal Tort Claims Act: Information Related to Implications of Extending Coverage to Volunteers at HRSA-Funded Health Centers*. Washington, D.C.: U.S. Government Accountability Office, 2009.

Figley, Paul. *A Guide to the Federal Tort Claims Act*. Chicago: Section of Administrative Law and Regulatory Practice, American Bar Association, 2012.

SUPREME COURT CLARIFIES EXCEPTION TO THE FEDERAL TORT CLAIM ACT

Jellum, Linda D., and David Charles Hricik. *Modern Statutory Intepretation*, Carolina Academic Press, 2009.

Frickey, Phillip P., and Elizabeth Eskridge. *Legislation and Statutory Interpretation*, Foundation Press, 2006.

FIFTH AMENDMENT

SALINAS V. TEXAS

Oyez Project at Chicago-Kent College of Law. "*Salinas v. Texas*." http://www.oyez.org/cases/2010-2019/2012/2012_12_246

Salinas v. Texas, No. 12-246. www.supremecourt.gov/opinions/12pdf/12-246_7l48.pdf

Scheidegger, Kent S. "*Salinas v. Texas*: Post-Argument SCOTUScast." Federalist Society, April 22, 2013. http://www.fed-soc.org/publications/detail/salinas-v-texas-post-argument-scotuscast

FIRST AMENDMENT

AGENCY FOR INTERNATIONAL DEVELOPMENT V. ALLIANCE FOR OPEN SOCIETY INTERNATIONAL, INC.

Agency for International Development v. Alliance for Open Society International, Inc., No. 12-10. www.supremecourt.gov/opinions/12pdf/12-10_21p3.pdf

Jaffe, Erik. "*Agency for International Development v. Alliance for Open Society International*: Post-Decision SCOTUScast." Federalist Society, June 25, 2013. http://www.fed-soc.org/publications/detail/agency-for-international-development-v-alliance-for-open-society-international-post-decision-scotuscast

Oyez Project at Chicago-Kent College of Law. "*Agency for International Development v. Alliance for Open Society International*." http://www.oyez.org/cases/2010-2019/2012/2012_12_10

EIGHTH CIRCUIT UPHOLDS LAW BANNING PICKETING AT FUNERALS

Barron, Jerome, and Thomas Dienes. *First Amendment Law in a Nutshell*. West, 2008. Fourth edition.

Farber, Daniel. *The First Amendment: Concepts and Insights*. Foundation Press, 2002.

INDIANA FEDERAL COURT ALLOWS TALIBAN PRAYER IN PRISON

Associated Press. "'American Taliban' Seeks Group Prayer in Ind. Prison." August 27, 2012. http://www.firstamendmentcenter.org/american-taliban-seeks-group-prayer-in-ind-prison

Castillo, Mariano. "'American Taliban' Seeks Group Prayer in Ind. Prison." CNN News, January 14, 2013. http://www.cnn.com/2013/01/12/us/american-taliban-prison-prayer

Smith, Brandon. "ACLU Says Prison Still Not Accommodating Muslim Prayers." Indiana Public Media News, June 27, 2013. http://indianapublicmedia.org/news/aclu-federal-prison-allowing-muslim-prayer-51578/

Wilson, Charles. "Indiana Prison Warden: Muslims Can Pray in Pairs." ABC News, June 27, 2013. http://abcnews.go.com/m/story?id=19508244&sid=81

PRESIDENT SIGNS LAW RESTRICTING PROTESTS AT VETERANS' FUNERALS

Cohen, Tom. "Church Says Military Funeral Protests Will Continue Despite New Restrictions." CNN

News, August 3, 2012. http://www.cnn.com/2012/08/03/politics/military-funerals-protests

Compton, Matt. "President Obama Signs Honoring America's Veterans and Caring for Camp Lajeune Families Act of 2102." White House Blog, August 6, 2012. http://www.whitehouse.gov/blog/2012/08/06/president-obama-signs-honoring-americas-veterans-and-caring-camp-lejeune-families-ac

"H.R. 1627." U.S. Government Printing Office. http://www.gpo.gov/fdsys/pkg/BILLS-112hr1627enr/pdf/BILLS-112hr1627enr.pdf

Malik, Angela. "New Ban on Military Funeral Protests Sparks First Amendment Debate." *Daily Caller*, August 15, 2012. http://http://dailycaller.com/2012/08/15/new-ban-on-military-funeral-protests-sparks-first-amendment-debate/

SEVENTH CIRCUIT RULES ILLINOIS LAW BARRING AUDIO RECORDING OF POLICE OFFICERS VIOLATES FIRST AMENDMENT

Barron, Jerome, and Thomas Dienes. *First Amendment Law in a Nutshell.* West, 2008. Fourth edition.

Farber, Daniel. *The First Amendment: Concepts and Insights.* Foundation Press, 2002.

THIRD CIRCUIT RULES NEWS MEDIA HAS NO FIRST AMENDMENT RIGHT TO REPORT FROM POLLING PLACES

Barron, Jerome, and Thomas Dienes. *First Amendment Law in a Nutshell.* West, 2008. Fourth edition.

Farber, Daniel. *The First Amendment: Concepts and Insights.* Foundation Press, 2002.

FOURTH AMENDMENT

MASSACHUSETTS HIGH COURT UPHOLDS WARRANTLESS SEARCH OF CELLPHONE

Dash, Samuel. *The Intruders: Unreasonable Searches and Seizures from King John to John Ashcroft.* Rutgers University Press, 2004.

Cammack, Mark and Norman Garland. *Advanced Criminal Procedure in a Nutshell.* West Publishing Co., 2001.

Long, Carolyn. *Mapp v. Ohio: Guarding Against Unreasonable Searches And Seizures.* UP of Kansas, 2006.

SUPREME COURT LIMITS SEARCH WARRANT DETENTION BY POLICE

Dash, Samuel. *The Intruders: Unreasonable Searches and Seizures from King John to John Ashcroft.* Rutgers University Press, 2004.

Cammack, Mark and Norman Garland. *Advanced Criminal Procedure in a Nutshell.* West Publishing Co., 2001.

Long, Carolyn. *Mapp v. Ohio: Guarding Against Unreasonable Searches And Seizures.* UP of Kansas, 2006.

SUPREME COURT STRIKES DOWN DRUG-SNIFFING DOG SEARCH

Dash, Samuel. *The Intruders: Unreasonable Searches and Seizures from King John to John Ashcroft.* Rutgers University Press, 2004.

Cammack, Mark and Norman Garland. *Advanced Criminal Procedure in a Nutshell.* West Publishing Co., 2001.

Long, Carolyn. *Mapp v. Ohio: Guarding Against Unreasonable Searches And Seizures.* UP of Kansas, 2006.

SUPREME COURT WARRANTLESS BLOOD TEST UNCONSTITUTIONAL

Dash, Samuel. *The Intruders: Unreasonable Searches and Seizures from King John to John Ashcroft.* Rutgers University Press, 2004.

Cammack, Mark and Norman Garland. *Advanced Criminal Procedure in a Nutshell.* West Publishing Co., 2001.

Long, Carolyn. *Mapp v. Ohio: Guarding Against Unreasonable Searches And Seizures.* UP of Kansas, 2006.

FRAUD

AMGEN, INC. v. CONNECTICUT RETIREMENT PLANS AND TRUST FUNDS

Amgen, Inc. v. Connecticut Retirement Plans and Trust Funds, No. 11-1085. http://www.supremecourt.gov/opinions/12pdf/11-1085_9o6b.pdf

Oyez Project at Chicago-Kent College of Law. "*Amgen, Inc. v. Connecticut Retirement Plans and Trust Funds.*" http://www.oyez.org/cases/2010-2019/2012/2012_11_1085

Stempel, Jonathan, Lawrence Hurley, and David Ingram. "Amgen Loses as Top U.S. Court Backs Class Actions." Reuters, February 27, 2013. http://www.reuters.com/article/2013/02/27/us-usa-amgen-ruling-idUSBRE91Q0RL20130227

FREEDOM OF SPEECH

ARIZONA SUPREME COURT EXTENDS FIRST AMENDMENT PROTECTION TO TATTOO PARLORS

Favate, Sam. "Arizona Supreme Court Says Tattoos Are Free Speech." *Wall Street Journal*, September 10, 2012.

Gaynor, Tim. "Top Arizona Court Rules Tattooing Is Protected Speech." Reuters, September 7, 2012.

Nelson, Gary. "Arizona Supreme Court in Mesa Case: 1st Amendment Protects Tattoos." *The Republic*, September 7, 2012.

EIGHTH CIRCUIT STRIKES DOWN ST. LOUIS TRAFFIC ORDINANCE

Amar, Vikram David. *The First Amendment, Freedom of Speech: Its Constitutional History and the*

Contemporary Debate. Amherst, N.Y.: Prometheus Books, 2008.

Kersch, Ken I. *Freedom of Speech: Rights and Liberties Under the Law.* Santa Barbara, Calif.: ABC-CLIO, 2003.

GAY AND LESBIAN RIGHTS

CHATTERJEE V. KING

Pinello, Daniel. *Gay Rights and American Law.* Cambridge UP, 2003.

Alsenas, Linda. *Gay America: Struggle for Equality.* Amulet Press, 2008.

HOLLINGSWORTH V. PERRY

Badgett, M. V. Lee. *When Gay People Get Married: What Happens When Societies Legalize Same-Sex Marriage.* New York: NYU Press, 2010.

Liptak, Adam. "Justices Say Time May Be Wrong for Gay Marriage Case." *New York Times,* March 26, 2013.

Matthews, Dylan. "Everything You Need to Know About the Supreme Court's Same-Sex Marriage Cases." *Washington Post,* March 26, 2013.

Villeneuve, Marina. "Gay Marriage Rulings: Joy, Sadness Outside Supreme Court." *Los Angeles Times,* June 26, 2013.

UNITED STATES V. WINDSOR

Mears, Bill. "Supreme Court Strikes Down Federal Provision on Same-Sex Marriage Benefits." *CNN,* June 27, 2013. http://www.cnn.com

The Oyez Project. "United States v. Windsor" U.S. Supreme Court Media Report. http://www.oyez.org/cases/2010-2019/2012/2012_12_307

United States v. Windsor, No. 12-307. http://www.supremecourt.gov/opinions/12pdf/12-307_6j37.pdf

GUN CONTROL

FIFTH CIRCUIT UPHOLDS LAW BANNING COMMERCIAL HANDGUN SALES TO PERSONS UNDER 21

Baldrige, Peter D. *Gun Ownership and the Second Amendment.* New York: Nova Science Publishers, 2009.

Charles, Patrick J. *The Second Amendment: The Intent and Its Interpretation by the States and the Supreme Court.* Jefferson, N.C.: McFarland & Co., 2009.

THE FUTURE OF GUN CONTROL AFTER NEWTOWN

Baldrige, Peter D. *Gun Ownership and the Second Amendment.* New York: Nova Science Publishers, 2009.

Charles, Patrick J. *The Second Amendment: The Intent and Its Interpretation by the States and the*

Supreme Court. Jefferson, N.C.: McFarland & Co., 2009.

HABEAS CORPUS

JOHNSON V. WILLIAMS

Burnett, Katherine. "Johnson v. Williams-Post Decision." The Federalist Society publication, February 21, 2013. http://www.fed-soc.org/publications/detail/johnson-v-williams-post-decision

Johnson v. WIlliams, No. 11-465. http://www.supremecourt.gov/opinions/12pdf/11-465_g314.pdf

Liptak, Adam. "Supreme Court Limits Reach of 2010 Ruling on Deportation Warning." *New York Times,* February 20, 2013.

The Oyez Project at IIT Chicago-Kent College of Law. "Johnson v. Williams." U.S. Supreme Court Media Report. http://www.oyez.org/cases/2010-2019/2012/2012_11_465

McQUIGGIN V. PERKINS

Campbell, Ward. "McQuiggen v. Perkins-Post Decision." The Federalist Society publication, March 27, 2013. http://www.fed-soc.org/publications/detail/mcquiggen-v-perkins-post-decision

Liptak, Adam. "Case Asks When New Evidence Means a New Trial." *New York Times,* November 12, 2012.

McQuiggen v. Perkins, No. 12-126. http://www.supremecourt.gov/opinions/12pdf/12-126_lkgn.pdf

The Oyez Project at IIT Chicago-Kent College of Law. "McQuiggen v. Perkins." U.S. Supreme Court Media Report. http://www.oyez.org/cases/2010-2019/2012/2012_12-126

TREVINO V. THALER

Campbell, Ward. "Trevino v. Thaler-Post Decision." The Federalist Society publication, March 27, 2013. http://www.fed-soc.org/publications/detail/trevino-v-thaler-post-decision

The Oyez Project at IIT Chicago-Kent College of Law. "Trevino v. Thaler." U.S. Supreme Court Media Report, http://www.oyez.org/cases/2010-2019/2012/2011_11-10189

Trevino v. Thaler, No. 11-10189. http://www.supremecourt.gov/opinions/12pdf/11-10189_6k47.pdf

HATE CRIME

RUTGERS STUDENT CONVICTED FOR WEBCAM SPYING ON HOMOSEXUAL ROOMMATE

Allen, Jonathan. "Convicted of Hate Crime, Former Rutgers Student Gets Gay Support." Reuters, May 18, 2012. http://www.reuters.com

Koenigs, Michael, et al. "Rutgers Trial: Dharun Ravi Sentenced to 30 Days in Jail." ABC News report, May 21, 2012. http://abcnews.go.com/US/rutgers-trial

Zernike, Kate. "Jury Finds Spying in Rutgers Dorm Was a Hate Crime." *New York Times,* March 16, 2012.

IMMIGRATION

ARIZONA V. INTER TRIBAL COUNCIL OF ARIZONA, INC.

Arizona v. Inter Tribal Council of Ariz. Inc., No. 12-71. http://www.supremecourt.gov/opinions/12pdf/12-71_7l48.pdf

Caso, Anthony T. "Arizona v. Inter Tribal Council of Ariz. Inc.-Post Argument." The Federalist Society publication, March 29, 2013. http://www.fed-soc.org/publications/detail/arizona-v-inter-tribal-council-of-ariz-inc-post-argument

Liptak, Adam. "Justices to Review Voter Law in Arizona." *New York Times,* October 15, 2012.

The Oyez Project. "Arizona v. Inter Tribal Council of Ariz. Inc." U.S. Supreme Court Media Report. http://www.oyez.org/cases/2010-2019/2012/2012_12-71

Zebley, Julia. "Supreme Court to Consider Arizona Eligibility Law." *Jurist,* October 16, 2012. http://jurist.org/paperchase/2012/10/supreme-court-to-consider-arizona-eligibility-law.php

MONCRIEFFE V. HOLDER

Broyles, Scott. "Moncrieffe v. Holder-Post Decision." The Federalist Society publication. http://www.fed-soc.org/publications/detail/moncrieffe-v-holder-post-decision

Moncrieffe v. Holder, No. 11-702. http://www.supremecourt.gov/opinions/12pdf/11-702_9p6b.pdf

The Oyez Project. "Moncrieffe v. Holder." U.S. Supreme Court Media Report. http://www.oyez.org/cases/2010-2019/2012/2012_11_702

INTERNATIONAL LAW

KIOBEL V. ROYAL DUTCH PETROLEUM

Grannis, Frederic. "Kiobel Decision Closes the Door to Claims Under Alien Tort Statute Based on Overseas Conduct." JDSupra Law News, May 27, 2013. http://www..jdsupra.com/legalnews/kiobel-decision-closes-the-door-to-claim-50860/

Kiobel v. Royal Dutch Petroleum, No. 10-1491.http://www.supremecourt.gov/opinions/12pdf/10-1491_l6gn.pdf

Kontorovich, Eugene. "Kiobel v. Royal Dutch Petroleum." The Federalist Society publication, April 23, 2013. http://www.fed-soc.org/publications/detail/Kiobel-v-Royal-Dutch-Petroleum-post-decision

The Oyez Project at IIT Chicago-Kent College of Law. "Kiobel v. Royal Dutch Petroleum." U.S. Supreme Court Media Report. http://www.oyez.org/cases/2010-2019/2011/2011_10-1491

KIDNAPPING

NEW YORK COURT OF APPEALS RULES THAT CUSTODIAL PARENT CAN BE CONVICTED OF KIDNAPPING

Cammack, Mark and Norman Garland. *Advanced Criminal Procedure in a Nutshell.* St. Paul, MN: West Publishing Co., 2001.

Dripps, Donald. *About Guilt and Innocence: The Origins, Development, and Future of Constitutional Criminal Procedure.* Praeger, 2002.

Sprack, John. *A Practical Approach to Criminal Procedure.*Oxford University Press, 2006. Eleventh edition.

LABOR LAW

MICHIGAN PASSES RIGHT TO WORK LAW

Bennett, William J. "A Victory for Right-to-Work Laws." *CNN,* December 13, 2012.

Daum, Kristen M. "Judge: Right-to-Work Challenge Alleging OMA Violation Will Move Forward." The Lansing *State Journal,* June 27, 2013.

National Conference of State Legislatures. "Right to Work Resources." http://www.ncsl.org/issues-research/labor/

NLRB: FACEBOOK POSTINGS WERE PROTECTED ACTIVITIES

Greenhouse, Steven. "Even If It Enrages Your Boss, Social Net Speech Is Protected." *New York Times,* January 21, 2013.

Nicholas, Adele. "The Risks and Rewards of Social Media." *Inside Counsel,* May 2013.

Trottman, Melanie. "NLRB Faults Company for Firing Workers over Facebook Posts." *Wall Street Journal,* May 18, 2011.

LAWYERS

FLORIDA SUPREME COURT APPROVES NEW LAWYER ADVERTISING RULES

Kaczor, Bill. "Fla. Justices Loosen Lawyer Advertising Rules." *Bloomberg Businessweek,* February 1, 2013.

Koppel, Nathan. "Florida Court Strikes Down Limits on Lawyer Advertising." *Wall Street Journal,* October 4, 2011.

Koppel, Nathan. "Objection! Funny Legal Ads Draw Censure." *Wall Street Journal,* February 7, 2008.

New York Lawyer Disbarred for Stealing Client Money

Keshner, Andrew. "Ex-Crowell & Moring Lawyer Pleads Guilty to Client Theft." *AmLaw Daily*, October 2, 2012.

Slattery, Denis, and John Doyle. "Lawyer on the Lam." *New York Daily News*, January 21, 2012.

Strumpf, Dan. "BigLaw Lawyer Cops to Stealing $10 Million from Clients." *Wall Street Journal*, October 2, 2012.

LIMITATIONS

Sebelius v. Auburn Regional Medical Center

Lovitky, Jeffrey. "The Appellate Implications of Sebelius v. Auburn Regional Medical Center." *JURIST-Sidebar*, February 14, 2013. http://jurist.org/sidebar/2013/02/jeffrey-lovitky-sebelius-auburn.php

Sebelius v. Auburn Regional Medical Center, No. 11-1231. http://www.supremecourt.gov/opinions/12pdf/11-1231_32q3.pdf

The Oyez Project (IIT Chicago-Kent College of Law. "Sebelius v. Auburn Regional Medical Center." U.S. Supreme Court Media Report. http://www.oyez.org/cases/2010-2019/2012/2012_11_1231

Young, Evan A. "Sebelius v. Auburn Regional Medical Center-Post-Decision." The Federalist Society publication, March 27, 2013. http://www.fed-soc.org/publications/detail/sebelius-v-auburn-regional-medical-center-post-decision

MEDICAID

WOS v. E.M.A.

Semple, James. "WOS v. EMA- Medical Liens." *Delaware Insurance Law Report*, April 3, 2013. http://www.delawareinsurancelawreport.com>-cases

The Oyez Project at Chicago-Kent College of Law. "Wos v. E.M.A." U.S. Supreme Court Media Report. http://www.oyez.org/cases/2010-2019/2012/2012_12_98

Wos v. E.M.A., No. 12-98. http://www.supremecourt.gov/opinions/12pdf/12-98_9ol1.pdf

MILITARY LAW

Bradley Manning Acquitted of Aiding the Enemy, Found Guilty of Espionage Violations

Associated Press. "Army Pfc. Bradley Manning Admits in Court to Giving Secret Documents to WikiLeaks." *New York Daily News*, March 2, 2013.

Carter, Chelsea J., Ashley Fantz, and Larry Shaughnessy. "Bradley Manning Acquitted of Aiding the Enemy But Guilty of Espionage Violations." *CNN*, July 31, 2013.

Nakashima, Ellen. "Messages from Alleged Leaker Bradley Manning Portray Him as Despondent Soldier." *Washington Post*, June 10, 2010.

Poulsen, Kevin, and Kim Zetter. "U.S. Intelligence Analyst Arrested in WikiLeaks Video Probe." *Wired*, June 6, 2010.

Savage, Charlie. "Soldier Admits Providing Files to WikiLeaks." *New York Times*, February 28, 2013.

——. "Manning, Facing Prison for Leaks, Apologizes at Court-Martial Trial." *New York Times*, August 15, 2013.

Military Sexual Assaults Create Jurisdictional Debate

Dvorak, Petula. "Military Could Learn From Cops In Sexual Assault Cases." *The Washington Post Local*, May 9, 2013.

Shapira, Ian. "Jury Trial Set for Jeffrey Krusinski, Air Force Officer Accused of Sexual Battery." *The Washington Post*, May 9, 2013.

Steinhauer, Jennifer. "Complex Fight in Senate Over Curbing Military Assaults." *The New York Times*, June 14, 2013.

Steinhauer, Jennifer. "Sexual Assaults In Military Raise Alarm in Washington." *The New York Times*, May 7, 2013.

U.S. Department of Defense. "2012 Workplace and Gender relations Survey of Active Military Members." May 15, 2013. http://www.ncdsv.org/images/DO2_2012-workplace-and-gender-relations

U.S. Department of Defense, Sexual Assault Prevention and Response Unit. "Annual Report 2012." http://www.www.sapr.mil/index.php/annual-reports

MURDER

Connecticut Elementary School Shooting Kills 20 Children

Candiotti, Susan, Greg Botelho, and Tom Watkins. "Newtown Shooting Details Revealed in Newly Released Documents." CNN.com, March 29, 2013.

Lysiak, Matthew, and Bill Hutchinson. "Emails Show History of Illness in Adam Lanza's Family, Mother Had Worries About Gruesome Images." *New York Daily News*, April 7, 2013.

Mahony, Edmund H., and Dave Altimari. "A Methodical Massacre: Horror and Heroics." *Hartford Courant*, December 15, 2012.

Stanglin, Doug. "Adam Lanza's Mom Was Alarmed by His Gruesome Images." *USA Today,* April 8, 2013.

FORMER MURDER SUSPECT CASEY ANTHONY FACES NUMEROUS LEGAL CHALLENGES

Associated Press. "Trustee for Bankrupt, Unemployed Casey Anthony Wants to Sell Her Life Story to Pay Off Debts." *New York Daily News,* March 18, 2013.

Mello, Michael. "Casey Anthony Asks Bankruptcy Court to Block Sale of Life Story." *L.A. Times,* April 6, 2013.

Stapleton, AnneClaire, and Holly Yan. "Casey Anthony Files for Bankruptcy as She Vows to 'Keep Fighting' Legal Issues." CNN.com, January 28, 2013.

GEORGE ZIMMERMAN ACQUITTED IN THE DEATH OF TRAYVON MARTIN

Alcindor, Yamiche, and Steph Solis. "Zimmerman Trial Judge Is No-Nonsense." *USA Today,* July 4, 2013.

Alvarez, Lizette. "Zimmerman Forgoes Pretrial Hearing, Taking Issue of Immunity to a Jury." *New York Times,* April 30, 2013.

CNN Wire Staff. "New Judge Named in Trayvon Martin Case" CNN.com, August 31, 2012.

Gray, Melissa. "Fired Florida Officer Defends Use of 'Trayvon Martin' Targets." CNN.com, April 15, 2013. http://www.cnn.com/2013/04/14/us/florida-trayvon-martin-targets

JAMES HOLMES KILLS 12 AND INJURES 58 IN THEATER SHOOTING

Castillo, Mariano, and Chelsea J. Carter. "Background of Colorado Shooting Suspect Full of Contrasts." CNN.com, July 22, 2012.

Ingold, John. "James Holmes Seeks Not Guilty Insanity Plea in Aurora Theater Shooting." *Denver Post,* May 7, 2013.

Watkins, Tom, and Dana Ford. "Police: Evidence of 'Calculation,' 'Deliberation' in Colorado Shooting." CNN.com, July 21, 2012.

PATENTS

APPLE WINS $1 BILLION IN PATENT SUIT AGAINST SAMSUNG

Albanesius, Chloe. "Apple Wins Big in Patent Case Against Samsung." *PC Magazine,* August 24, 2012.

Poeter, Damon. "Apple's Huge Win Over Samsung: What They're Saying." *PC Magazine,* August 24, 2012.

Vascellaro, Jessica E. "Apple Wins Big in Patent Case." *The Wall Street Journal,* August 25, 2012.

Wingfield, Nick. "Jury Awards $1 Billion to Apple in Samsung Patent Case." *New York Times,* August 24, 2012.

ASSOCIATION FOR MOLECULAR PATHOLOGY V. MYRIAD GENETICS, INC.

American Bar Association. "12-398 Public Education: Association for Molecular Pathology v. Myriad Genetics, Inc. PPL Montana, LLC v. Montana." Undated. http://www.americanbar.org/publications/preview_home/12-398.html

Association for Molecular Pathology v. Myriad Genetics, Inc., No. 12-398. http://www.supremecourt.gov/opinions/12pdf/12_398_1b7d.pdf

The Oyez Project. "Association for Molecular Pathology v. Myriad Genetics, Inc." U.S. Supreme Court Media Report. http://www.oyez.org/cases/2010-2019/2012/2012_12_398

BOWMAN V. MONSANTO

Bowman v. Monsanto Company, No. 11-796. http://www.supremecourt.gov/opinions/12pdf/11-796_c07d.pdf

Liptak, Adam. "Supreme Court Supports Monsanto in in Seed-Replication Case." *New York Times,* May 13, 2013.

Murphy, Eamon. "Bowman v. Monsanto: The Price We All Pay for Roundup Ready Seeds." http://www.dailyfinance.com/on/monsanto-gmo-roundup-ready-seeds-patents-food-prices

The Oyez Project at IIT Chicago-Kent College of Law. "Bowman v. Monsanto." U.S. Supreme Court Media Report. http://www.oyez.org/cases/2010-2019/2012/2012_11_796

COURTS CONTINUALLY GRAPPLE WITH BIOTECHNOLOGY PATENT ISSUES

Bittman, Mark. "Why Do G.M.O.'s Need Protection?" *New York Times,* April 2, 2013.

Fisher, Daniel. "The Curious Case of Human Gene Patents." *Forbes,* May 22, 2013.

Ghose, Tim. "6 Ways Gene Patent Case Could Impact Biotechnology" *Live Science,* April 15, 2013.

Knowles, David. "Senator Seeks to Overturn So-Called Monsanto Protection Act." *New York Daily News,* May 22, 2013.

Liptak, Adam. "Supreme Court Supports Monsanto in Seed-Replication Case." *New York Times,* May 13, 2013.

Meldrum, Peter D. "Myriad Genetics: Patents Save Lives, Aid Innovation." *USA Today,* April 14, 2013.

Wright, Jacqueline D. "Implications of Recent Patent Law Changes on Biotechnology Research and Biotechnology Industry." *Virginia Journal of Law and Technology,* spring 1997.

FTC v. Actavis, Inc.

Actavis, Inc. "U.S. Supreme Court Reverses U.S. Court of Appeals Decision in FTC v. Actavis." Press release, June 17, 2013. http://ir.actavis.com/phoenix.zhtml?c=65778&p=irol-newsArticle&ID=1830404

Sagers, Christopher L. *Antitrust: Examples and Explanations.* New York: Wolters Kluwer Law & Business, 2011.

Sell, David. "Pharma Takes Some Comfort from 'Pay-to-Delay' Ruling." *Philadelphia Inquirer,* June 20, 2013.

Gunn v. Minton

Fields, Justin and Allison Cooper. "Gunn v. Minton: The End of Legal-Malpractice Actions in Federal Courts?" *Litigation,* http://www.americanbar.org/litigation/committees/professional/articles/spring2013-0513-gunn-v-minton

Gunn v. Minton, No. 11-1118. http://www.supremecourt.gov/opinions/11pdf/11-1118.pdf

The Oyez Project at IIT Chicago-Kent College of Law. "Gunn v. Minton." U.S. Supreme Court Media Report. http://www.oyez.org/cases/2010-2019/2012/2012_11_1118

PLAIN-ERROR RULE

Henderson v. United States

American Bar Association. "11-9307 Public Education: Henderson v. United States." http://www.americanbar.org/publications/preview_home/10-218.html

Drupal. "SCOTUS Blotter: Henderson v. United States." *American Criminal Law Review,* February 2013. http://www.amercancriminallawreview.com/Drupal/content/scotus-blotter-henderson-v-united-states

Henderson v. United States, No. 11-9307. http://www.supremecourt.gov/opinions/12pdf/11-9307_jhek.pdf

Reimer, Norman. "Henderson v. US and the Plain Error Rule: Metaphysics, Unicorns and Injustice." *Jurist,* December 11, 2012. http://jurist.org/hotline/2012/12/norman-reimer-henderson-us.php

PREEMPTION

Dan's City Used Cars v. Pelkey

Dan's City v. Pelkey, No. 12-52. http://www.supremecourt.gov/opinions/12pdf/12-52_1537.pdf

Savage, David. "Supreme Court Limits Towing Firms." *Los Angeles Times,* May 14, 2013.

The Oyez Project. "Dan's City v. Pelkey." U.S. Supreme Court Media Report. http://www.oyez.org/cases/2010-2019/2012/2012_12-52

PRESIDENTIAL POWERS

D.C. Circuit Strikes Down Obama Recess Appointments

Barron, Jerome, and C. Thomas Dienes. *Constitutional Law in a Nutshell.* West, 2005.

Graves, Scott, and Robert Howard. *Justice Takes a Recess: Judicial Recess Appointments from George Washington to George W. Bush,* Lexington Books, 2010.

PRIVACY

Maracich v. Spears

Hitchcock, Cornish F., ed. *Guidebook to the Freedom of Information and Privacy Acts.* Eagan, Minn.: West, 2012.

Hurley, Lawrence. "Supreme Court Bars Lawyers from Accessing Drivers' Database." Reuters, June 17, 2013.

Matthews, Dylan. "The Supreme Court Rules Lawyers Can't Use DMV Records to Find Clients." *Washington Post,* June 17, 2013.

PRIVILEGES AND IMMUNITIES

Supreme Court Upholds Virginia's Bar on Providing Public Information to Non-Virginians

Smith, Kelvin. *Freedom Of Information: A Practical Guide To Implementing The Act.* Library Association Publisher Ltd, 2004.

PRODUCT LIABILITY

Mutual Pharmaceutical Co. v. Bartlett

Mutual Pharmaceutical Co. v. Bartlett, No. 12-142. http://www.supremecourt.gov/opinions/12pdf/12-142_8njq.pdf

Noonan, Kevin. "Mutual Pharmaceutical Co. v. Bartlett." http://patentdocs.org/2013/06/mutual-pharmaceutical-v-bartlett-2013/html

The Oyez Project. "Mutual Pharmaceutical Company v. Bartlett" U.S. Supreme Court Media Report. http://www.oyez.org/cases/2010-2019/2012/2012_12_142

SEARCH AND SEIZURE

ACLU Requests FBI Memoranda About GPS Tracking

Hitchcock, Cornish F., ed. *Guidebook to the Freedom of Information and Privacy Acts.* Eagan, Minn.: West, 2012.

U.S. Department of Justice. *Guide to the Freedom of Information Act.* Washington, D.C.: U.S. Government Printing Office, 2009.

Zetter, Kim. "ACLU Sues FBI to Get GPS-Tracking Memos." *Wired,* August 15, 2012.

SECOND AMENDMENT

SECOND CIRCUIT UPHOLDS NEW YORK CONCEALED CARRY LAW

Baldrige, Peter D. *Gun ownership and the Second Amendment.* New York: Nova Science Publishers, 2009.

Charles, Patrick J. *The Second Amendment: The Intent and Its Interpretation by the States and the Supreme Court.* Jefferson, N.C.: McFarland & Co., 2009.

SEVENTH CIRCUIT PANEL STRIKES DOWN BAN ON CONCEALED WEAPONS

Associated Press. "Federal Court Strikes Down Illinois Ban on Carrying Concealed Weapons." FoxNews.com, December 11, 2012.

Long, Ray, Annie Sweeney, and Monique Garcia. "Concealed Carry: Court Strikes Down Illinois' Ban." *Chicago Tribune,* December 11, 2012.

"A Revealing Move on Concealed Carry." *Chicago Tribune,* April 17, 2013.

SECURITIES AND EXCHANGE COMMISSION

GABELLI V. SEC

El-Boghdady, Dina. "Supreme Court to Hear Gabelli Appeal of SEC Civil Fraud Penalties." *Washington Post,* January 1, 2013.

Fisher, Daniel. "Mario Gabelli Rescues Sam Wyly from SEC Fines." *Forbes,* June 6, 2013.

Lynch, Sarah N., and Jonathan Stempel. "Supreme Court Skeptical of SEC Power in Gabelli Case." Reuters, January 8, 2013.

SENTENCING

ALLEYNE V. UNITED STATES

Editorial Board. "Restoring Due Process." *New York Times,* January 12, 2013.

Feldman, Noah. "Clarence Thomas' Legal Time Machine Zooms to 1789." *Miami Herald,* June 19, 2013.

Hurley, Lawrence, and Jonathan Stempel. "Justices Say Juries, Not Judges, Must Decide Facts." Reuters, June 17, 2013.

DESCAMPS V. UNITED STATES

Descamps v. United States, No. 11-9540. http://www.supremecourt.gov/opinions/12pdf/11-95408m58.pdf

Federal Public Defender of Arizona. "U.S. Supreme Court News." http://www.fpdaz.org/News-usCrt.html

The Oyez Project. "Descamps v. United States." U.S. Supreme Court Media Report. Available at http://

www.oyez.org/cases/2010-2019/2012/2012_11_9540

SEX OFFENSES

SEVENTH CIRCUIT RULES INDIANA SEX OFFENDER REGISTRY VIOLATES DUE PROCESS

Lewis, Harold Jr., and Elizabeth Norman. *Civil Rights Law and Practice.* West Group, 2004.

Palmer, John. *Constitutional Rights of Prisoners.* Anderson Pub. Co., 2006. Eighth edition.

Vieira, Norman. *Constitutional Civil Rights in a Nutshell.* West Group, 1998.

SEVENTH CIRCUIT STRIKES DOWN SEX OFFENDER SOCIAL MEDIA BAN

Barron, Jerome, and Thomas Dienes. *First Amendment Law in a Nutshell.* West Group, 2004. Third edition.

Farber, Daniel. *The First Amendment: Concepts and Insights.* Foundation Press, 2002.

UNITED STATES V. KEBODEAUX

American Bar Association. "12-418 Public Education: United States v. Kebodeaux." http://www.americanbar.org/publications/preview_home/12-418.html

Barnett, Randy. "United States v. Kebodeaux-Post Argument." The Federalist Society publication, April 17, 2013. http://www.fed-soc.org/publications/detail/united-states-v.-kebodeaux-post-argument

The Oyez Project. "United States v. Kebodeaux." U.S. Supreme Court Media Report. http://www.oyez.org/cases/2010-2019/2012/2012_12-418

United States v. Kebodeaux No. 12-418. https://www.supremecourt.gov/opinions/11pdf/12-418_7k8b.pdf

SOVEREIGN IMMUNITY

UNITED STATES V. BORMES

The Oyez Project. "United States v. Bormes." U.S. Supreme Court Media Report. Available at http://www.oyez.org/cases/2010-2019/2012/2012_11_192

"Supreme Court Deals a Blow to Credit Card Privacy." *Chicago Tribune,* November 13, 2012.

United States v. Bormes, No. 11-192. http://www.supremecourt.gov/opinions/12pdf/11-192_p246.pdf

SPEEDY TRIAL

SUPREME COURT DISMISSES APPEAL ON RIGHT TO A SPEEDY TRIAL

Cammack, Mark. *Advanced Criminal Procedure in a Nutshell.* St. Paul, MN.: Thomson West, 2006. Second edition.

Garcia, Alfredo. *The Fifth Amendment: A Comprehensive Approach.* Westport, CT.: Greenwood Press, 2002.

Stuart, Gary L. *Miranda: The Story of America's Right to Remain Silent.* Tucson: U of Arizona P, 2008.

SPORTS LAW

CYCLIST LANCE ARMSTRONG ADMITS TO YEARS OF DOPING

Macur, Juliet. "Armstrong Admits Doping, and Says He Will Testify." *New York Times,* January 14, 2013.

Macur, Juliet. "Details of Doping Scheme Paint Armstrong as Leader." *New York Times,* October 10, 2012.

Palmer, Brian. "Lance Armstrong Case Prompts Question: Why Is There So Much Doping in Cycling?" *Washington Post,* January 21, 2013.

NATIONAL FOOTBALL LEAGUE SUSPENDS NEW ORLEANS SAINTS PLAYERS AND COACHES FOR BOUNTY SYSTEM

Associated Press. "Suspensions of 4 Players in New Orleans Saints Bounty Case Are Vacated." *Seattle Times,* December 11, 2012.

Battista, Judy. "Tagliabue Lifts Suspensions but Not Blame in Bounty Case." *New York Times,* December 11, 2012.

Triplett, Mike. "New Orleans Saints Bounty Case Has Some Closure Now—but No Winners." *Times-Picayune,* January 17, 2013.

SURROGATE MOTHERHOOD

NEW JERSEY SUPREME COURT UPHOLDS LAW PREVENTING INFERTILE WOMEN FROM BEING LEGAL PARENTS

Jellum, Linda D., and David Charles Hricik. *Modern Statutory Intepretation,* Carolina Academic Press, 2009.

Frickey, Phillip P., and Elizabeth Eskridge. *Legislation and Statutory Interpretation,* Foundation Press, 2006.

TAXATION

PPL CORP. V. COMMISSIONER OF INTERNAL REVENUE

Hurley, Lawrence. "U.S. Justices Rule for PPL Corp in Overseas Tax Case." Reuters News Release, May 20, 2013. http://www.reuters.com/article/2013/05/20/us-usa-court-ppl-tax-idUSBRE94JOGM20130520

PPL Corp. v. Commissioner of Internal Revenue, No. 12-43. http://www.supremecourt.gov/opinions/12pdf/12-43_g20h.pdf

Sandefur, Christine. "PPL Corp. v. Commissioner of Internal Revenue-Post Decision." The Federalist Society publication. http://www.fed-soc.org/publications/detail/ppl-corp-v-commissioner-of-internal-revenue-post-decision

The Oyez Project. "PPL Corp. v. Commissioner of Internal Revenue." U.S. Supreme Court Media Report. http://www.oyez.org/cases/2010-2019/2012/2012_12-43

TERRORISM

BOSTON BOMBER TO BE TRIED IN CIVILIAN COURT

Chappell, Bill. "Miranda Rights and Tsarnaev: Ex-U. S. Attorney General Weighs In." NPR, April 21, 2013. http://www.npr.org/ . . . /miranda-righs-and-tsarnaev-ashcroft-says-u-s-move-is-the-right-one

Killough, Ashley and Gregory Wallace. "Dzhokhar Tsarnaev, 'Enemy Combatant' for Interrogation Purposes Only, Says Sen. Lindsey Graham." WPTV News, April 21, 2013. http://www.wptv.com/dpp/news/national/dzhokhar-tsarnaev-enemy-combatant-for-interroga . . .

Milbank, Dana. "The Fiasco of Military Tribunals." *Orlando Sentinel,* April 24, 2013.

Sterling, Joe. "Indictment Returned Against Boston Bombing Suspect Dzhokhar." *CNN,* June 28, 2013. http://www.CNN.com

U.S. Dept. of Defense, Federal Bureau of Investigations. "Updates on Investigation Into Multiple Explosions in Boston." June 27, 2013. http://www.fbi.gov/news/updates-on-investigation-into-multiple-explosions-in-boston

"White House: Tsarnaev Won't Be Tried as Enemy Combatant." *USA Today,* April 22, 2013.

LAWYER LYNNE STEWART RESENTENCED TO TEN YEARS IMPRISONMENT FOR AIDING CONVICTED TERRORIST

Branham, Lynm. *The Law of Sentencing and Corrections in a Nutshell.* West Group, 2005.

Stith, Kate. *Fear of Judging: Sentencing Guidelines in the Federal Courts.* U of Chicago P, 1998.

Tonry, Michael. *Sentencing Matters.* Oxford UP, 2004.

SECOND CIRCUIT THROWS OUT FREEDOM OF INFORMATION REQUEST FOR TERRORIST DETAINEE RECORDS

Smith, Kelvin. *Freedom Of Information: A Practical Guide To Implementing The Act,* Library Association Publisher Ltd., 2004.

TOBACCO

D.C. CIRCUIT STRIKES DOWN GRAPHIC WARNINGS ON CIGARETTE PACKAGING AS FIRST AMENDMENT VIOLATIONS

Barron, Jerome and Thomas Dienes. *First Amendment Law in a Nutshell.* West Group, 2004. Third edition.

Farber, Daniel. *The First Amendment: Concepts and Insights.* Foundation Press, 2002.

D.C. Circuit Upholds Injunction Against Tobacco Companies

Epstein, Richard. *Federal Preemption.*AEI Press, 2007.

O'Reilly, James. *Federal Preemption of State and Local Law.*American Bar Association, 2006.

Zimmerman, Joseph. *Congressional Preemption.* State University of New York Press, 2006.

Second Circuit Strikes Down Anti-Tobacco Signs at Point of Sale

Derthick, Martha A. *Up in Smoke: From Legislation to Tobacco Politics.* 3d ed. Washington, D.C.: CQ Press, 2012.

Gifford, Donald G. *Suing the Tobacco and Lead Pigment Industries: Government Litigation as Public Health Prescription.* Ann Arbor: University of Michigan Press, 2010.

TRADEMARKS

Already, L.L.C. v. Nike, Inc.

Bason, Tamlin. "What Did We Learn from *Already v. Nike*?" Bloomberg BNA, January 17, 2013.

Fisher, Daniel. "Supreme Court Rejects Lawsuit over Nike Trademarks." *Forbes,* January 9, 2013.

Kane, Siegrun D. *Kane on Trademark Law: A Practitioner's Guide..* 5th ed. New York: Practising Law Institute, 2007.

VOTING RIGHTS ACT

Federal Court Rules a Texas Voting Map Discriminated Against Minorities

Dimino, Michael, Bradley Smith, and Michael Solimine. *Voting Rights and Election Law.* New Providence, N.J.: LexisNexis, 2010.

Fernandez, Manny. "Federal Court Finds Texas Voting Maps Discriminatory." *New York Times,* August 28, 2012.

Griffith, Benjamin E., ed. *America Votes! A Guide to Modern Election Law and Voting Rights.* 2d ed. Chicago: American Bar Association, 2012.

Shelby County v. Holder

Blum, Edward. *The Unintended Consequences of Section 5 of the Voting Rights Act.* Washington, D.C.: AEI Press, 2007.

Dimino, Michael, Bradley Smith, and Michael Solimine. *Voting Rights and Election Law.* New Providence, N.J.: LexisNexis, 2010.

Griffith, Benjamin, ed. *American Votes! A Guide to Modern Election Law and Voting Rights.* 2d ed. Chicago: American Bar Association, 2012.

Liptak, Adam. "Supreme Court Invalidates Key Part of Voting Rights Act." *New York Times,* June 25, 2013.

State of South Carolina v. United States

Currie, David. *Federal Jurisdiction in a Nutshell.* West Group, 1999.

Lewis, Harold Jr., and Elizabeth Norman. *Civil Rights Law and Practice.* West Group, 2004.

Vieira, Norman. *Constitutional Civil Rights in a Nutshell.* West Group, 1998.

Abet: To encourage or incite another to commit a crime. This word is usually applied to aiding in the commission of a crime. To abet another to commit a murder is to command, procure, counsel, encourage, induce, or assist. To facilitate the commission of a crime, promote its accomplishment, or help in advancing or bringing it about.

Administrative Law: The body of law that allows for the creation of public regulatory agencies and contais all of the statutes, judicial decisions, and regulations that govern them.

Administrative Procedure: The methods and processes before administrative agencies, as disitnguished from judicial procedure, which applies to courts.

Admiralty: A court whose jurisdiction covers maritime legal matters.

Affirmative Defense: A new fact or set of facts that operates to defeat a claim even if the facts supporting that claim are true.

Allocation: The apportionment or designation of an item for a specific purpose or to a particular place.

Ambit: A boundary line that indicates ownership of a parcel of land as opposed to other parcels; an exterior or enclosing line. The limits of a power or jurisdiction. The delineation of the scope of a particular subject matter.

Amount in Controversy: The value of the relief demanded or the amount of monetary damages claimed in a lawsuit.

Antitrust Law: Antitrust law refers to legislation enacted by the federal and various state governments to regulate trade and commerce by preventing unlawful restraints, price-fixing, and monopolies; to promote competition; and to encourage the production of quality goods and services at the lowest prices, with the primary goal of safeguarding public welfare by ensuring that consumer demands will be met by the manufacture and sale of goods at reasonable prices.

Appellate: Relating to appeals, which are reviews by superior courts of decisions made by inferior courts or administrative agencies.

Appellate Court: An appellate court has jurisdiction to review decisions of a trial-level or other lower court.

Assault: At common law, an intentional act by one person that creates an apprehension in another of an imminent harmful or offensive contact.

Attorney-Client Privilege: In the law of evidence, a client's privilege to refuse to disclose, and to prevent any other person from disclosing, confidential communications between the client and his or her attorney. Such privilege protects communications between attorney and client that are made for the purpose of furnishing or obtaining professional legal advice or assistance. That privilege that permits an attorney to refuse to testify as to communications from the client. It belongs to the client, not the attorney, and hence only the client may waive it. In federal courts, state law is applied with respect to such privilege.

Bad Faith: The fraudulent deception of another person; the intentional or malicious refusal to perform some duty or contractual obligation.

Battery: At common law, an intentional unpermitted act causing harmful or offensive contact with the "person" of another.

Belief: Mental reliance on or acceptance of a particular concept, which is arrived at by weighing external evidence, facts, and personal observation and experience.

Bench Trial: A trial conducted before a judge presiding without a jury.

Beyond A Reasonable Doubt: The standard that must be met by the prosecution's evidence in a criminal prosecution.

Bounds: The boundary lines of land, with their terminal points and angles. A way of describing land by listing the compass directions and distances of the boundaries. It is often used in connection with the Government Survey System.

Burglary: The criminal offense of breaking and entering a building illegally for the purpose of committing a crime.

Case Law: Legal principles enunciated and embodied in judicial decisions that are derived from the application of particular areas of law to the facts of individual cases.

Cause of Action: The fact or combination of facts that gives a person the right to seek judicial redress or relief against another. Also, the legal theory forming the basis of a lawsuit.

Certiorari: [*Latin, To be informed of.*] At COMMON LAW, an original writ or order issued by the Chancery or King's Bench, commanding officers of inferior courts to submit the record of a cause pending before them to give the party more certain and speedy justice.

Circuit Court: A specific tribunal that possesses the legal authority to hear cases within its own geographical territory.

Civil Action: A lawsuit brought to enforce, redress, or protect rights of private litigants—the plaintiffs and the defendants—not a criminal proceeding.

Civil Procedure: The methods, procedures, and practices used in civil cases.

Class Action: A class action is a lawsuit that allows a large number of people with a common interest in a matter to sue or be sued as a group.

Collateral: Related; indirect; not bearing immediately upon an issue. The property pledged or given as a security interest, or a guarantee for payment of a debt, that will be taken or kept by the creditor in case of a default on the original debt.

Collective Bargaining Agreement: The contractual agreement between an employer and a LABOR UNION that governs wages, hours, and working conditions for employees and which can be enforced against both the employer and the union for failure to comply with its terms. Such an agreement is ordinarily reached following the process of COLLECTIVE BARGAINING. A high profile example of such bargaining happens in the world of professional BASEBALL.

Common Law: The ancient law of England based upon societal customs and recognized and enforced by the judgments and decrees of the courts. The general body of statutes and case law that governed England and the American colonies prior to the American Revolution; the principles and rules of action, embodied in case law rather than legislative enactments, applicable to the government and protection of persons and property that derive their authority from the community customs and traditions that evolved over the centuries as interpreted by judicial tribunals; a designation used to denote the opposite of statutory, equitable, or civil, for example, a common-law action.

Confession: A statement by which an individual acknowledges his or her guilt in the commission of a crime.

Constitutional Law: Constitutional law is the written text of the state and federal constitutions. It includes the body of judicial precedent that has gradually developed through a process in which courts interpret, apply, and explain the meaning of particular constitutional provisions and principles during a legal proceeding. Executive, legislative, and judicial actions that conform to the norms prescribed by a constitutional provision are also included.

Consumer Protection: Consumer protection laws are federal and state statutes governing sales and credit practices involving consumer goods. Such statutes prohibit and regulate deceptive or unconscionable advertising and sales practices, product quality, credit financing and reporting, debt collection, leases, and other aspects of consumer transactions.

Corpus: *[Latin, Body, aggregate, or mass.]*

Court of Appeal: An intermediate federal judicial tribunal of review that is found in thirteen judicial districts, called circuits, in the United States; a state judicial tribunal that reviews a decision rendered by an inferior tribunal to determine whether it made errors that warrant the reversal of its judgment.

Criminal Law: Criminal law comprises a body of rules and statutes that define conduct prohibited by the government because it threatens and harms public safety and welfare and that establishes punishment to be imposed for the commission of such acts.

Criminal Procedure: The framework of laws and rules that govern the administration of justice in cases involving an individual who has been accused of a crime, beginning with the initial investigation of the crime and concluding either with the unconditional release of the accused by virtue of acquittal (a judgment of not guilty) or by the imposition of a term of punishment pursuant to a conviction for the crime.

Cruel And Unusual Punishment: Such punishment as would amount to torture or barbarity, any cruel and degrading punishment not known to the COMMON LAW, or any fine, penalty, confinement, or treatment that is so disproportionate to the offense as to shock the moral sense of the community.

Declaratory Judgment: Statutory remedy for the determination of a justiciable controversy where the plaintiff is in doubt as to his or her legal rights. A binding adjudication of the rights and status of litigants even though no consequential relief is awarded.

Defamation: Any intentional false communication, either written or spoken, that harms a person's reputation; decreases the respect, regard, or confidence in which a person is held; or induces disparaging, hostile, or disagreeable opinions or feelings against a person.

District Court: A designation of an inferior state court that exercises general jurisdiction that it has been granted by the constitution or statute which created it. A U.S. judicial tribunal with original jurisdiction to try cases or controversies that fall within its limited jurisdiction.

Entity: A real being; existence. An organization or being that possesses separate existence for tax purposes. Examples would be corporations, partnerships, estates, and trusts. The accounting entity for which accounting statements are prepared may not be the same as the entity defined by law.

Equal Protection: The constitutional guarantee that no person or class of persons shall be denied the same protection of the laws that is enjoyed by other persons or other classes in like circumstances, in their lives, liberty, property, and pursuit of happiness.

Escrow: Something of value, such as a deed, stock, money, or written instrument, that is put into the custody of a third person by its owner, a grantor, an obligor, or a promisor, to be retained until the occurrence of a contingency or performance of a condition.

Et seq.: An abbreviation for the Latin *et sequentes* or *et sequentia,* meaning "and the following."

Excise: A tax imposed on the performance of an act, the engaging in an occupation, or the enjoyment of a privilege. A tax on the manufacture, sale, or use of goods or on the carrying on of an occupation or activity, or a tax on the transfer of property. In current usage the term has been extended to include various license fees and practically every internal revenue tax except the income tax (e.g., federal alcohol and tobacco excise taxes).

Federal Courts: The federal courts are the U.S. judicial tribunals created by Article III of the Constitution, or by Congress, to hear and determine JUSTICIABLE controversies.

Felony: A serious crime, characterized under federal law and many state statutes as any offense punishable by death or imprisonment in excess of one year.

First Impression: The initial presentation to, or examination by, a court of a particular QUESTION OF LAW.

Fiscal: Relating to finance or financial matters, such as money, taxes, or public or private revenues.

Forfeiture: The involuntary relinquishment of money or property without compensation as a consequence of a breach or nonperformance of some legal obligation or the commission of a crime. The loss of a corporate charter or franchise as a result of illegality, malfeasance, or nonfeasance. The surrender by an owner of his or her entire interest in real property, mandated by law as a punishment for illegal conduct or negligence. Under old English law, the release of land by a tenant to the tenant's lord due to some breach of conduct, or the loss of goods or chattels (articles of PERSONAL PROPERTY) assessed as a penalty against the perpetrator of some crime or offense and as a recompense to the injured party.

Fraud: A false representation of a matter of fact—whether by words or by conduct, by false or misleading allegations, or by concealment of what should have been disclosed—that deceives and is intended to deceive another so that the individual will act upon it to her or his legal injury.

Fraudulent: The description of a willful act commenced with the SPECIFIC INTENT to deceive or cheat, in order to cause some financial detriment to another and to engender personal financial gain.

Freedom of Speech: Freedom of speech is the right, guaranteed by the FIRST AMENDMENT to the U.S. Constitution, to express beliefs and ideas without unwarranted government restriction.

Good Cause: Legally adequate or substantial grounds or reason to take a certain action.

Good Faith: Honesty; a sincere intention to deal fairly with others.

Grand jury: A panel of citizens that is convened by a court to decide whether it is appropriate for the government to indict (proceed with a prosecution against) someone suspected of a crime.

Habeas Corpus: *[Latin, You have the body.]* A writ (court order) that commands an individual or a government official who has restrained another to produce the prisoner at a designated time and place so that the court can determine the legality of custody and decide whether to order the prisoner's release.

Harmless Error: A trivial technical error of law determined by an appellate court not to require a reversal of a judgment or the setting aside of a verdict or a new trial.

Hate Crime: A crime motivated by racial, religious, gender, sexual orientation, or other prejudice.

Husband And Wife: A man and woman who are legally married to one another and are thereby given by law specific rights and duties resulting from that relati

Involuntary Manslaughter: The act of unlawfully killing another human being unintentionally.

Interlocutory: Provisional; interim; temporary; not final; that which intervenes between the beginning and the end of a lawsuit or proceeding to either decide a particular point or matter that is not the final issue of the entire controversy or prevent irreparable harm during the pendency of the lawsuit.

Irrevocable: Unable to cancel or recall; that which is unalterable or irreversible.

Judicial Review: A court's authority to examine an executive or legislative act and to invalidate that act if it is contrary to constitutional principles.

Jurisprudence: From the Latin term *juris prudentia,* which means "the study, knowledge, or science of law"; in the United States, more broadly associated with the philosophy of law.

Legal Proceedings: All actions that are authorized or sanctioned by law and instituted in a court or a tribunal for the acquisition of rights or the enforcement of remedies.

Libel And Slander: Two TORTS that involve the communication of false information about a person, a group, or an entity such as a corporation. Libel is any DEFAMATION that can be seen, such as a writing, printing, effigy, movie, or statue. Slander is any defamation that is spoken and heard.

Lien: A right given to another by the owner of property to secure a debt, or one created by law in favor of certain creditors.

Liquidate: To pay and settle the amount of a debt; to convert assets to cash; to aggregate the assets of an insolvent enterprise and calculate its liabilities in order to settle with the debtors and the creditors and apportion the remaining assets, if any, among the stockholders or owners of the corporation.

Magistrate: Any individual who has the power of a public civil officer or inferior judicial officer, such as a JUSTICE OF THE PEACE.

Manslaughter: The unjustifiable, inexcusable, and intentional killing of a human being without deliberation, premeditation, and malice. The unlawful killing of a human being without any deliberation, which may be involuntary, in the commission of a lawful act without due caution and circumspection.

Medicaid: Medicaid is a joint federal-state program that provides health care insurance to low-income persons.

Medicare: Medicare is a federally funded system of health and hospital insurance for persons aged 65 and older and for disabled persons.

Misdemeanor: Offenses lower than felonies and generally those punishable by fine, penalty, FORFEITURE, or imprisonment other than in a penitentiary. Under federal law, and most state laws, any offense other than a felony is classified as a misdemeanor. Certain states also have various classes of misdemeanors (e.g., Class A, B, etc.).

Mitigating Circumstances: Circumstances that may be considered by a court in determining culpability of a defendant or the extent of damages to be awarded to a plaintiff. Mitigating circumstances do not justify or excuse an offense but may reduce the severity of a charge. Similarly, a recognition of mitigating circumstances to reduce a damage award does not imply that the damages were not suffered but that they have been partially ameliorated.

Monopoly: An economic advantage held by one or more persons or companies deriving from the exclusive power to carry on a particular business or trade or to manufacture and sell a particular item, thereby suppressing competition and allowing such persons or companies to raise the price of a product or service substantially above the price that would be established by a free market.

Of Counsel: A term commonly applied in the PRACTICE OF LAW to an attorney who has been employed to aid in the preparation and management of a particular case but who is not the principal attorney in the action.

Ordinance: A law, statute, or regulation enacted by a municipal corporation.

Pension: A pension is a benefit, usually money, paid regularly to retired employees or their survivors by private businesses and federal, state, and local governments. Employers are not required to establish pension benefits but do so to attract qualified employees.

Prayer: The request contained in a bill in EQUITY or a civil COMPLAINT that the court grant the process, aid, or relief that the plaintiff or countersuing defendant seeks (such as the type of remedy, either money damages or an injunction, and the form or dollar amount). Following the pleading's description of the conflict and allegations, the prayer tends to begin with "Wherefore," followed by the specific action or award wanted.

Preemption: A doctrine based on the SUPREMACY CLAUSE of the U.S. Constitution that holds that certain matters are of such a national, as opposed to local, character that federal laws preempt or take precedence over state laws. As such, a state may not pass a law inconsistent with the federal law.

Preliminary Injunction: A temporary order made by a court at the request of one party that prevents the other party from pursuing a particular course of conduct until the conclusion of a trial on the merits.

Prevailing Party: The litigant who successfully brings or defends an action and, as a result, receives a favorable judgment or verdict.

Private International Law: A branch of jurisprudence arising from the diverse laws of various nations that applies when private citizens of different countries interact or transact business with one another.

Privilege against Self-Incrimination: The right to refuse to provide testimony in a trial or other legal proceeding that could subject one to criminal prosecution.

Privileges and Immunities: Concepts contained in the U.S. Constitution that place the citizens of each state on an equal basis with citizens of other states in respect to advantages resulting from citizenship in those states and citizenship in the United States.

Probable Cause: Probably cause refers to a level of reasonable belief which occurs when apparent facts discovered through logical inquiry lead a reasonably intelligent and prudent person to believe that an accused person has committed a crime, thereby warranting his or her prosecution, or that a cause of action has accrued, justifying a civil lawsuit.

Purchaser: One who buys property from another person by an agreement.

Putative: Alleged; supposed; reputed.

Rebuttable Presumption: A conclusion as to the existence or nonexistence of a fact that a judge or jury must draw when certain evidence has been introduced and admitted as true in a lawsuit but that can be contradicted by evidence to the contrary.

Redress: Compensation for injuries sustained; recovery or restitution for harm or injury; damages or equitable relief. Access to the courts to gain REPARATION for a wrong.

Repeal: The ANNULMENT or abrogation of a previously existing statute by the enactment of a later law that revokes the former law.

Robbery: The taking of money or goods in the possession of another, from his or her person or immediate presence, by force or intimidation.

Search: A hunt by law enforcement officials for property or communications believed to be evidence of a crime.

Seizure: Forcible possession; a grasping, snatching, or putting in possession.

Service of Process: Delivery of a writ, summons, or other legal papers to the person required to respond to them.

Settlement: The act of adjusting or determining the dealings or disputes between persons without pursuing the matter through a trial.

Solicitation: Urgent request, plea, or entreaty; enticing, asking. The criminal offense of urging someone to commit an unlawful act.

Sovereign Immunity: The legal protection that prevents a sovereign state or person from being sued without consent.

State Action: State action refers to a requirement for claims that arise under the due process clause of the Fourteenth Amendment and civil rights legislation, for which a private citizen seeks relief in the form of damages or redress based on an improper intrusion by the government into his or her private life.

State Interest: A broad term for any matter of public concern that is addressed by a government in law or policy.

Statute: A statue is an act of a legislature that declares, proscribes, or commands something; it is a specific law, expressed in writing.

Statute of Limitations: A statute of limitations is a type of federal or state law that restricts the time within which legal proceedings may be brought.

Statutory: Created, defined, or relating to a statute; required by statute; conforming to a statute.

Strict Scrutiny: A standard of JUDICIAL REVIEW for a challenged policy in which the court presumes the policy to be invalid unless the government can demonstrate a compelling interest to justify the policy.

Subject Matter Jurisdiction: The power of a court to hear and determine cases of the general class to which the proceedings in question belong.

Substantive Due Process: The substantive limitations placed on the content or subject matter of state and federal laws by the Due Process Clauses of the Fifth and Fourteenth Amendments to the U.S. Constitution.

Summary Judgment: A procedural device used during civil litigation to promptly and expeditiously dispose of a case without a trial. It is used when there is no dispute as to the material facts of the case and a party is entitled to judgment as a matter of law.

Third Party: A generic legal term for any individual who does not have a direct connection with a legal transaction but who might be affected by it.

Time, Place, And Manner Restrictions: Limits that government can impose on the occasion, location, and type of individual expression in some circumstances.

Trustee: An individual or corporation named by an individual who sets aside property to be used for the benefit of another person, to manage the property as provided by the terms of the document that created the arrangement.

U.S. Code: A multivolume publication of the text of statutes enacted by Congress.

Writ: An order issued by a court requiring that something be done or giving authority to do a specified act.

Writ of Certiorari: A writ that a superior appellate court issues in its discretion to an inferior court, ordering it to produce a certified record of a particular case it has tried, in order to determine whether any irregularities or errors occurred that justify review of the case; a device by which the SUPREME COURT OF THE UNITED STATES exercises its discretion in selecting the cases it will review.

Zoning: The separation or division of a municipality into districts, the regulation of buildings and structures in such districts in accordance with their construction and the nature and extent of their use, and the dedication of such districts to particular uses designed to serve the GENERAL WELFARE.

A.	Atlantic Reporter	ACS	Agricultural Cooperative Service
A. 2d	Atlantic Reporter, Second Series	ACT	American College Test
AA	Alcoholics Anonymous	Act'g Legal Adv.	Acting Legal Advisor
AAA	American Arbitration Association; Agricultural Adjustment Act of 1933	ACUS	Administrative Conference of the United States
AALS	Association of American Law Schools	ACYF	Administration on Children, Youth, and Families
AAPRP	All African People's Revolutionary Party	A.D. 2d	Appellate Division, Second Series, N.Y.
AARP	American Association of Retired Persons	ADA	Americans with Disabilities Act of 1990
AAS	American Anti-Slavery Society	ADAMHA	Alcohol, Drug Abuse, and Mental Health Administration
ABA	American Bar Association; Architectural Barriers Act of 1968; American Bankers Association	ADC	Aid to Dependent Children
		ADD	Administration on Developmental Disabilities
ABC	American Broadcasting Companies, Inc. (formerly American Broadcasting Corporation)	ADEA	Age Discrimination in Employment Act of 1967
		ADL	Anti-Defamation League
		ADR	Alternative dispute resolution
		AEC	Atomic Energy Commission
ABM	Antiballistic missile	AECB	Arms Export Control Board
ABM Treaty	Anti-Ballistic Missile Treaty of 1972	AEDPA	Antiterrorism and Effective Death Penalty Act
ABVP	Anti-Biased Violence Project	A.E.R.	All England Law Reports
A/C	Account	AFA	American Family Association; Alabama Freethought Association
A.C.	Appeal cases		
ACAA	Air Carrier Access Act		
ACCA	Armed Career Criminal Act of 1984	AFB	American Farm Bureau
		AFBF	American Farm Bureau Federation
ACF	Administration for Children and Families	AFDC	Aid to Families with Dependent Children
ACLU	American Civil Liberties Union	aff'd per cur.	Affirmed by the court
ACRS	Accelerated Cost Recovery System	AFIS	Automated fingerprint identification system

AFL	American Federation of Labor	Ann. Dig.	Annual Digest of Public International Law Cases
AFL-CIO	American Federation of Labor and Congress of Industrial Organizations	ANRA	American Newspaper Publishers Association
AFRes	Air Force Reserve	ANSCA	Alaska Native Claims Act
AFSC	American Friends Service Committee	ANZUS	Australia-New Zealand-United States Security Treaty Organization
AFSCME	American Federation of State, County, and Municipal Employees	AOA	Administration on Aging
		AOE	Arizonans for Official English
AGRICOLA	Agricultural Online Access	AOL	America Online
AIA	Association of Insurance Attorneys	AP	Associated Press
		APA	Administrative Procedure Act of 1946
AIB	American Institute for Banking	APHIS	Animal and Plant Health Inspection Service
AID	Artificial insemination using a third-party donor's sperm; Agency for International Development	App. Div.	Appellate Division Reports, N.Y. Supreme Court
		Arb. Trib., U.S.-British	Arbitration Tribunal, Claim Convention of 1853, United States and Great Britain Convention of 1853
AIDS	Acquired immune deficiency syndrome		
AIH	Artificial insemination using the husband's sperm	Ardcor	American Roller Die Corporation
AIM	American Indian Movement		
AIPAC	American Israel Public Affairs Committee	ARPA	Advanced Research Projects Agency
AIUSA	Amnesty International, U.S.A. Affiliate	ARPANET	Advanced Research Projects Agency Network
AJS	American Judicature Society	ARS	Advanced Record System
ALA	American Library Association	Art.	Article
Alcoa	Aluminum Company of America	ARU	American Railway Union
		ASCME	American Federation of State, County, and Municipal Employees
ALEC	American Legislative Exchange Council		
ALF	Animal Liberation Front	ASCS	Agriculture Stabilization and Conservation Service
ALI	American Law Institute		
ALJ	Administrative law judge	ASM	Available Seatmile
All E.R.	All England Law Reports	ASPCA	American Society for the Prevention of Cruelty to Animals
ALO	Agency Liaison		
A.L.R.	American Law Reports		
ALY	*American Law Yearbook*	Asst. Att. Gen.	Assistant Attorney General
AMA	American Medical Association	AT&T	American Telephone and Telegraph
AMAA	Agricultural Marketing Agreement Act	ATFD	Alcohol, Tobacco and Firearms Division
Am. Dec.	American Decisions	ATLA	Association of Trial Lawyers of America
amdt.	Amendment		
Amer. St. Papers, For. Rels.	American State Papers, Legislative and Executive Documents of the Congress of the U.S., Class I, Foreign Relations, 1832–1859	ATO	Alpha Tau Omega
		ATTD	Alcohol and Tobacco Tax Division
		ATU	Alcohol Tax Unit
		AUAM	American Union against Militarism
AMS	Agricultural Marketing Service	AUM	Animal Unit Month
AMVETS	American Veterans (of World War II)	AZT	Azidothymidine
		BAC	Blood alcohol concentration
ANA	Administration for Native Americans	BALSA	Black-American Law Student Association

BATF	Bureau of Alcohol, Tobacco and Firearms	CAFE	Corporate average fuel economy
BBS	Bulletin Board System	Cal. 2d	California Reports, Second Series
BCCI	Bank of Credit and Commerce International	Cal. 3d	California Reports, Third Series
BEA	Bureau of Economic Analysis		
Bell's Cr. C.	Bell's English Crown Cases	CALR	Computer-assisted legal research
Bevans	United States Treaties, etc. *Treaties and Other International Agreements of the United States of America, 1776–1949* (compiled under the direction of Charles I. Bevans, 1968–76)	Cal. Rptr.	California Reporter
		CAP	Common Agricultural Policy
		CARA	Classification and Ratings Administration
		CATV	Community antenna television
		CBO	Congressional Budget Office
BFOQ	Bona fide occupational qualification	CBS	Columbia Broadcasting System
BI	Bureau of Investigation	CBOEC	Chicago Board of Election Commissioners
BIA	Bureau of Indian Affairs; Board of Immigration Appeals	CCC	Commodity Credit Corporation
BID	Business improvement district	CCDBG	Child Care and Development Block Grant of 1990
BJS	Bureau of Justice Statistics	C.C.D. Pa.	Circuit Court Decisions, Pennsylvania
Black.	Black's United States Supreme Court Reports	C.C.D. Va.	Circuit Court Decisions, Virginia
Blatchf.	Blatchford's United States Circuit Court Reports	CCEA	Cabinet Council on Economic Affairs
BLM	Bureau of Land Management		
BLS	Bureau of Labor Statistics	CCP	Chinese Communist Party
BMD	Ballistic missile defense	CCR	Center for Constitutional Rights
BNA	Bureau of National Affairs		
BOCA	Building Officials and Code Administrators International	C.C.R.I.	Circuit Court, Rhode Island
		CD	Certificate of deposit; compact disc
BOP	Bureau of Prisons	CDA	Communications Decency Act
BPP	Black Panther Party for Self-defense	CDBG	Community Development Block Grant Program
Brit. and For.	British and Foreign State Papers	CDC	Centers for Disease Control and Prevention; Community Development Corporation
BSA	Boy Scouts of America		
BTP	Beta Theta Pi		
Burr.	James Burrows, *Report of Cases Argued and Determined in the Court of King's Bench during the Time of Lord Mansfield* (1766–1780)	CDF	Children's Defense Fund
		CDL	Citizens for Decency through Law
		CD-ROM	Compact disc read-only memory
BVA	Board of Veterans Appeals	CDS	Community Dispute Services
c.	Chapter	CDW	Collision damage waiver
C³I	Command, Control, Communications, and Intelligence	CENTO	Central Treaty Organization
		CEO	Chief executive officer
		CEQ	Council on Environmental Quality
C.A.	Court of Appeals		
CAA	Clean Air Act	CERCLA	Comprehensive Environmental Response, Compensation, and Liability Act of 1980
CAB	Civil Aeronautics Board; Corporation for American Banking		

cert.	*Certiorari*	CLEO	Council on Legal Education Opportunity; Chief Law Enforcement Officer
CETA	Comprehensive Employment and Training Act		
C & F	Cost and freight	CLP	Communist Labor Party of America
CFC	Chlorofluorocarbon		
CFE Treaty	Conventional Forces in Europe Treaty of 1990	CLS	Christian Legal Society; critical legal studies (movement); Critical Legal Studies (membership organization)
C.F. & I.	Cost, freight, and insurance		
C.F.R	Code of Federal Regulations		
CFNP	Community Food and Nutrition Program	C.M.A.	Court of Military Appeals
CFTA	Canadian Free Trade Agreement	CMEA	Council for Mutual Economic Assistance
CFTC	Commodity Futures Trading Commission	CMHS	Center for Mental Health Services
Ch.	Chancery Division, English Law Reports	C.M.R.	Court of Military Review
		CNN	Cable News Network
CHAMPVA	Civilian Health and Medical Program at the Veterans Administration	CNO	Chief of Naval Operations
		CNOL	Consolidated net operating loss
CHEP	Cuban/Haitian Entrant Program	CNR	Chicago and Northwestern Railway
CHINS	Children in need of supervision	CO	Conscientious Objector
CHIPS	Child in need of protective services	C.O.D.	Cash on delivery
		COGP	Commission on Government Procurement
Ch.N.Y.	Chancery Reports, New York		
Chr. Rob.	Christopher Robinson, *Reports of Cases Argued and Determined in the High Court of Admiralty* (1801–1808)	COINTELPRO	Counterintelligence Program
		Coke Rep.	Coke's English King's Bench Reports
		COLA	Cost-of-living adjustment
CIA	Central Intelligence Agency	COMCEN	Federal Communications Center
CID	Commercial Item Descriptions		
		Comp.	Compilation
C.I.F.	Cost, insurance, and freight	Conn.	Connecticut Reports
CINCNORAD	Commander in Chief, North American Air Defense Command	CONTU	National Commission on New Technological Uses of Copyrighted Works
C.I.O.	Congress of Industrial Organizations	Conv.	Convention
		COPA	Child Online Protection Act (1998)
CIPE	Center for International Private Enterprise	COPS	Community Oriented Policing Services
C.J.	Chief justice		
CJIS	Criminal Justice Information Services	Corbin	Arthur L. Corbin, *Corbin on Contracts: A Comprehensive Treatise on the Rules of Contract Law* (1950)
C.J.S.	Corpus Juris Secundum		
Claims Arb. under Spec. Conv., Nielsen's Rept.	Frederick Kenelm Nielsen, *American and British Claims Arbitration under the Special Agreement Concluded between the United States and Great Britain, August 18, 1910* (1926)	CORE	Congress on Racial Equality
		Cox's Crim. Cases	Cox's Criminal Cases (England)
		COYOTE	Call Off Your Old Tired Ethics
		CPA	Certified public accountant
CLASP	Center for Law and Social Policy	CPB	Corporation for Public Broadcasting, the
CLE	Center for Law and Education; Continuing Legal Education	CPI	Consumer Price Index
		CPPA	Child Pornography Prevention Act

CPSC	Consumer Product Safety Commission	DARPA	Defense Advanced Research Projects Agency
Cranch	Cranch's United States Supreme Court Reports	DAVA	Defense Audiovisual Agency
CRF	Constitutional Rights Foundation	D.C.	United States District Court; District of Columbia
CRR	Center for Constitutional Rights	D.C. Del.	United States District Court, Delaware
CRS	Congressional Research Service; Community Relations Service	D.C. Mass.	United States District Court, Massachusetts
CRT	Critical race theory	D.C. Md.	United States District Court, Maryland
CSA	Community Services Administration	D.C.N.D.Cal.	United States District Court, Northern District, California
CSAP	Center for Substance Abuse Prevention	D.C.N.Y.	United States District Court, New York
CSAT	Center for Substance Abuse Treatment	D.C.Pa.	United States District Court, Pennsylvania
CSC	Civil Service Commission		
CSCE	Conference on Security and Cooperation in Europe	DCS	Deputy Chiefs of Staff
		DCZ	District of the Canal Zone
CSG	Council of State Governments	DDT	Dichlorodipheny-ltricloroethane
CSO	Community Service Organization	DEA	Drug Enforcement Administration
CSP	Center for the Study of the Presidency	Decl. Lond.	Declaration of London, February 26, 1909
C-SPAN	Cable-Satellite Public Affairs Network	Dev. & B.	Devereux & Battle's North Carolina Reports
CSRS	Cooperative State Research Service	DFL	Minnesota Democratic-Farmer-Labor
CSWPL	Center on Social Welfare Policy and Law	DFTA	Department for the Aging
		Dig. U.S. Practice in Intl. Law	Digest of U.S. Practice in International Law
CTA	*Cum testamento annexo* (with the will attached)	Dist. Ct.	D.C. United States District Court, District of Columbia
Ct. Ap. D.C.	Court of Appeals, District of Columbia		
Ct. App. No. Ireland	Court of Appeals, Northern Ireland	D.L.R.	Dominion Law Reports (Canada)
Ct. Cl.	Court of Claims, United States	DMCA	Digital Millennium Copyright Act
Ct. Crim. Apps.	Court of Criminal Appeals (England)	DNA	Deoxyribonucleic acid
		Dnase	Deoxyribonuclease
Ct. of Sess., Scot.	Court of Sessions, Scotland	DNC	Democratic National Committee
CTI	Consolidated taxable income		
CU	Credit union	DOC	Department of Commerce
CUNY	City University of New York	DOD	Department of Defense
Cush.	Cushing's Massachusetts Reports	DODEA	Department of Defense Education Activity
CWA	Civil Works Administration; Clean Water Act	Dodson	Dodson's Reports, English Admiralty Courts
DACORB	Department of the Army Conscientious Objector Review Board	DOE	Department of Energy
		DOER	Department of Employee Relations
Dall.	Dallas's Pennsylvania and United States Reports	DOJ	Department of Justice
		DOL	Department of Labor
DAR	Daughters of the American Revolution	DOMA	Defense of Marriage Act of 1996

DOS	Disk operating system	ERTA	Economic Recovery Tax Act of 1981
DOT	Department of Transportation	ESA	Endangered Species Act of 1973
DPT	Diphtheria, pertussis, and tetanus	ESF	Emergency support function; Economic Support Fund
DRI	Defense Research Institute		
DSAA	Defense Security Assistance Agency	ESRD	End-Stage Renal Disease Program
DUI	Driving under the influence; driving under intoxication	ETA	Employment and Training Administration
DVD	Digital versatile disc	ETS	Environmental tobacco smoke
DWI	Driving while intoxicated		
EAHCA	Education for All Handicapped Children Act of 1975	et seq.	*Et sequentes* or *et sequentia* ("and the following")
		EU	European Union
EBT	Examination before trial	Euratom	European Atomic Energy Community
E.coli	Escherichia coli		
ECPA	Electronic Communications Privacy Act of 1986	Eur. Ct. H.R.	European Court of Human Rights
ECSC	Treaty of the European Coal and Steel Community	Ex.	English Exchequer Reports, Welsby, Hurlstone & Gordon
EDA	Economic Development Administration	Exch.	Exchequer Reports (Welsby, Hurlstone & Gordon)
EDF	Environmental Defense Fund		
E.D.N.Y.	Eastern District, New York	Ex Com	Executive Committee of the National Security Council
EDP	Electronic data processing		
E.D. Pa.	Eastern-District, Pennsylvania	Eximbank	Export-Import Bank of the United States
EDSC	Eastern District, South Carolina	F.	Federal Reporter
		F. 2d	Federal Reporter, Second Series
EDT	Eastern daylight time		
E.D. Va.	Eastern District, Virginia	FAA	Federal Aviation Administration; Federal Arbitration Act
EEC	European Economic Community; European Economic Community Treaty		
		FAAA	Federal Alcohol Administration Act
EEOC	Equal Employment Opportunity Commission	FACE	Freedom of Access to Clinic Entrances Act of 1994
EFF	Electronic Frontier Foundation	FACT	Feminist Anti-Censorship Task Force
EFT	Electronic funds transfer	FAIRA	Federal Agriculture Improvement and Reform Act of 1996
Eliz.	Queen Elizabeth (Great Britain)		
Em. App.	Temporary Emergency Court of Appeals	FAMLA	Family and Medical Leave Act of 1993
ENE	Early neutral evaluation	Fannie Mae	Federal National Mortgage Association
Eng. Rep.	English Reports		
EOP	Executive Office of the President	FAO	Food and Agriculture Organization of the United Nations
EPA	Environmental Protection Agency; Equal Pay Act of 1963	FAR	Federal Acquisition Regulations
ERA	Equal Rights Amendment	FAS	Foreign Agricultural Service
ERDC	Energy Research and Development Commission	FBA	Federal Bar Association
		FBI	Federal Bureau of Investigation
ERISA	Employee Retirement Income Security Act of 1974		
		FCA	Farm Credit Administration
ERS	Economic Research Service	F. Cas.	Federal Cases

FCC	Federal Communications Commission	FJC	Federal Judicial Center
FCIA	Foreign Credit Insurance Association	FLSA	Fair Labor Standards Act
		FMC	Federal Maritime Commission
FCIC	Federal Crop Insurance Corporation	FMCS	Federal Mediation and Conciliation Service
FCLAA	Federal Cigarette Labeling and Advertising Act	FmHA	Farmers Home Administration
FCRA	Fair Credit Reporting Act	FMLA	Family and Medical Leave Act of 1993
FCU	Federal credit unions		
FCUA	Federal Credit Union Act	FNMA	Federal National Mortgage Association, "Fannie Mae"
FCZ	Fishery Conservation Zone		
FDA	Food and Drug Administration	F.O.B.	Free on board
		FOIA	Freedom of Information Act
FDIC	Federal Deposit Insurance Corporation	FOMC	Federal Open Market Committee
FDPC	Federal Data Processing Center	FPA	Federal Power Act of 1935
FEC	Federal Election Commission	FPC	Federal Power Commission
FECA	Federal Election Campaign Act of 1971	FPMR	Federal Property Management Regulations
Fed. Cas.	Federal Cases	FPRS	Federal Property Resources Service
FEHA	Fair Employment and Housing Act	FR	Federal Register
FEHBA	Federal Employees Health Benefit Act	FRA	Federal Railroad Administration
FEMA	Federal Emergency Management Agency	FRB	Federal Reserve Board
		FRC	Federal Radio Commission
FERC	Federal Energy Regulatory Commission	F.R.D.	Federal Rules Decisions
		FSA	Family Support Act
FFB	Federal Financing Bank	FSB	Federal'naya Sluzhba Bezopasnosti (the Federal Security Service of Russia)
FFDC	Federal Food, Drug, and Cosmetics Act		
FGIS	Federal Grain Inspection Service	FSLIC	Federal Savings and Loan Insurance Corporation
FHA	Federal Housing Administration	FSQS	Food Safety and Quality Service
FHAA	Fair Housing Amendments Act of 1998	FSS	Federal Supply Service
		F. Supp.	Federal Supplement
FHWA	Federal Highway Administration	FTA	U.S.-Canada Free Trade Agreement of 1988
FIA	Federal Insurance Administration	FTC	Federal Trade Commission
		FTCA	Federal Tort Claims Act
FIC	Federal Information Centers; Federation of Insurance Counsel	FTS	Federal Telecommunications System
		FTS2000	Federal Telecommunications System 2000
FICA	Federal Insurance Contributions Act	FUCA	Federal Unemployment Compensation Act of 1988
FIFRA	Federal Insecticide, Fungicide, and Rodenticide Act		
FIP	Forestry Incentives Program	FUTA	Federal Unemployment Tax Act
FIRREA	Financial Institutions Reform, Recovery, and Enforcement Act of 1989	FWPCA	Federal Water Pollution Control Act of 1948
FISA	Foreign Intelligence Surveillance Act of 1978	FWS	Fish and Wildlife Service
		GAL	Guardian ad litem
FISC	Foreign Intelligence Surveillance Court of Review	GAO	General Accounting Office; Governmental Affairs Office

GAOR	General Assembly Official Records, United Nations	HFCA	Health Care Financing Administration
GAAP	Generally accepted accounting principles	HGI	Handgun Control, Incorporated
GA Res.	General Assembly Resolution (United Nations)	HHS	Department of Health and Human Services
GATT	General Agreement on Tariffs and Trade	Hill	Hill's New York Reports
GCA	Gun Control Act	HIRE	Help through Industry Retraining and Employment
Gen. Cls. Comm.	General Claims Commission, United States and Panama; General Claims United States and Mexico	HIV	Human immunodeficiency virus
Geo. II	King George II (Great Britain)	H.L.	House of Lords Cases (England)
Geo. III	King George III (Great Britain)	H. Lords	House of Lords (England)
GHB	Gamma-hydroxybutrate	HMO	Health Maintenance Organization
GI	Government Issue	HNIS	Human Nutrition Information Service
GID	General Intelligence Division	Hong Kong L.R.	Hong Kong Law Reports
GM	General Motors	How.	Howard's United States Supreme Court Reports
GNMA	Government National Mortgage Association, "Ginnie Mae"	How. St. Trials	Howell's English State Trials
GNP	Gross national product	HUAC	House Un-American Activities Committee
GOP	Grand Old Party (Republican Party)	HUD	Department of Housing and Urban Development
GOPAC	Grand Old Party Action Committee	Hudson, Internatl. Legis.	Manley Ottmer Hudson, ed., *International Legislation: A Collection of the Texts of Multipartite International Instruments of General Interest Beginning with the Covenant of the League of Nations* (1931)
GPA	Office of Governmental and Public Affairs		
GPO	Government Printing Office		
GRAS	Generally recognized as safe		
Gr. Br., Crim. Ct. App.	Great Britain, Court of Criminal Appeals		
GRNL	Gay Rights-National Lobby	Hudson, World Court Reps.	Manley Ottmer Hudson, ea., *World Court Reports* (1934–)
GSA	General Services Administration		
Hackworth	Green Haywood Hackworth, *Digest of International Law* (1940–1944)	Hun	Hun's New York Supreme Court Reports
Hay and Marriott	Great Britain. High Court of Admiralty, *Decisions in the High Court of Admiralty during the Time of Sir George Hay and of Sir James Marriott, Late Judges of That Court* (1801)	Hunt's Rept.	Bert L. Hunt, *Report of the American and Panamanian General Claims Arbitration* (1934)
		IAEA	International Atomic Energy Agency
		IALL	International Association of Law Libraries
HBO	Home Box Office	IBA	International Bar Association
HCFA	Health Care Financing Administration	IBM	International Business Machines
H.Ct.	High Court	ICA	Interstate Commerce Act
HDS	Office of Human Development Services	ICBM	Intercontinental ballistic missile
Hen. & M.	Hening & Munford's Virginia Reports	ICC	Interstate Commerce Commission; International Criminal Court
HEW	Department of Health, Education, and Welfare		

ICJ	International Court of Justice	ITA	International Trade Administration
ICM	Institute for Court Management	ITI	Information Technology Integration
IDEA	Individuals with Disabilities Education Act of 1975	ITO	International Trade Organization
IDOP	International Dolphin Conservation Program	ITS	Information Technology Service
IEP	Individualized educational program	ITT	International Telephone and Telegraph Corporation
IFC	International Finance Corporation	ITU	International Telecommunication Union
IGRA	Indian Gaming Regulatory Act of 1988	IUD	Intrauterine device
IJA	Institute of Judicial Administration	IWC	International Whaling Commission
IJC	International Joint Commission	IWW	Industrial Workers of the World
ILC	International Law Commission	JAGC	Judge Advocate General's Corps
ILD	International Labor Defense	JCS	Joint Chiefs of Staff
Ill. Dec.	Illinois Decisions	JDL	Jewish Defense League
ILO	International Labor Organization	JNOV	Judgment *non obstante vere-dicto* ("judgment nothing
IMF	International Monetary Fund		to recommend it" or
INA	Immigration and Nationality Act		"judgment notwithstand-ing the verdict")
IND	Investigational new drug	JOBS	Jobs Opportunity and Basic
INF Treaty	Intermediate-Range Nuclear Forces Treaty of 1987		Skills
		John. Ch.	Johnson's New York Chancery Reports
INS	Immigration and Naturalization Service	Johns.	Johnson's Reports (New York)
INTELSAT	International Telecommunications Satellite Organization	JP	Justice of the peace
		K.B.	King's Bench Reports (England)
Interpol	International Criminal Police Organization	KFC	Kentucky Fried Chicken
Int'l. Law Reps.	International Law Reports	KGB	Komitet Gosudarstvennoi
Intl. Legal Mats.	International Legal Materials		Bezopasnosti (the State
IOC	International Olympic Committee		Security Committee for countries in the former
IPDC	International Program for the Development of		Soviet Union)
	Communication	KKK	Ku Klux Klan
		KMT	Kuomintang (Chinese,
IPO	Intellectual Property Owners		"national people's party")
IPP	Independent power producer	LAD	Law Against Discrimination
IQ	Intelligence quotient	LAPD	Los Angeles Police
I.R.	Irish Reports		Department
IRA	Individual retirement account; Irish Republican Army	LC	Library of Congress
		LCHA	Longshoremen's and Harbor Workers Compensation Act of 1927
IRC	Internal Revenue Code		
IRCA	Immigration Reform and Control Act of 1986	LD50	Lethal dose 50
		LDEF	Legal Defense and Education Fund (NOW)
IRS	Internal Revenue Service		
ISO	Independent service organization	LDF	Legal Defense Fund, Legal Defense and Educational Fund of the NAACP
ISP	Internet service provider		
ISSN	International Standard Serial Numbers	LEAA	Law Enforcement Assistance Administration

L.Ed.	Lawyers' Edition Supreme Court Reports	Mercy	Movement Ensuring the Right to Choose for Yourself
LI	Letter of interpretation		
LLC	Limited Liability Company	Metc.	Metcalf's Massachusetts Reports
LLP	Limited Liability Partnership		
LMSA	Labor-Management Services Administration	MFDP	Mississippi Freedom Democratic party
LNTS	League of Nations Treaty Series	MGT	Management
		MHSS	Military Health Services System
Lofft's Rep.	Lofft's English King's Bench Reports	Miller	David Hunter Miller, ea., *Treaties and Other International Acts of the United States of America* (1931–1948)
L.R.	Law Reports (English)		
LSAC	Law School Admission Council		
LSAS	Law School Admission Service	Minn.	Minnesota Reports
LSAT	Law School Aptitude Test	MINS	Minors in need of supervision
LSC	Legal Services Corporation; Legal Services for Children	MIRV	Multiple independently targetable reentry vehicle
LSD	Lysergic acid diethylamide		
LSDAS	Law School Data Assembly Service	MIRVed ICBM	Multiple independently targetable reentry vehicled intercontinental ballistic missile
LTBT	Limited Test Ban Treaty		
LTC	Long Term Care		
MAD	Mutual assured destruction	Misc.	Miscellaneous Reports, New York
MADD	Mothers against Drunk Driving	Mixed Claims Comm.,Report of Decs	Mixed Claims Commission, United States and Germany, Report of Decisions
MALDEF	Mexican American Legal Defense and Educational Fund		
Malloy	William M. Malloy, ed., *Treaties, Conventions International Acts, Protocols, and Agreements between the United States of America and Other Powers* (1910–1938)	M.J.	Military Justice Reporter
		MLAP	Migrant Legal Action Program
		MLB	Major League Baseball
		MLDP	Mississippi Loyalist Democratic Party
		MMI	Moslem Mosque, Incorporated
Martens	Georg Friedrich von Martens, ea., *Noveau recueil général de traités et autres actes relatifs aux rapports de droit international* (Series I, 20 vols. [1843–1875]; Series II, 35 vols. [1876–1908]; Series III [1909–])	MMPA	Marine Mammal Protection Act of 1972
		Mo.	Missouri Reports
		MOD	Masters of Deception
		Mod.	Modern Reports, English King's Bench, etc.
Mass.	Massachusetts Reports	Moore, Dig. Intl. Law	John Bassett Moore, *A Digest of International Law*, 8 vols. (1906)
MCC	Metropolitan Correctional Center		
MCCA	Medicare Catastrophic Coverage Act of 1988	Moore, Intl. Arbs.	John Bassett Moore, *History and Digest of the International Arbitrations to Which United States Has Been a Party*, 6 vols. (1898)
MCH	Maternal and Child Health Bureau		
MCRA	Medical Care Recovery Act of 1962		
MDA	Medical Devices Amendments of 1976	Morison	William Maxwell Morison, *The Scots Revised Report: Morison's Dictionary of Decisions* (1908–09)
Md. App.	Maryland, Appeal Cases		
M.D. Ga.	Middle District, Georgia		

M.P.	Member of Parliament	NAVINFO	Navy Information Offices
MP3	MPEG Audio Layer 3	NAWSA	National American Woman's
MPAA	Motion Picture Association of		Suffrage Association
	America	NBA	National Bar Association;
MPAS	Michigan Protection and		National Basketball
	Advocacy Service		Association
MPEG	Motion Picture Experts	NBC	National Broadcasting
	Group		Company
mpg	Miles per gallon	NBLSA	National Black Law Student
MPPDA	Motion Picture Producers		Association
	and Distributors of	NBS	National Bureau of Standards
	America	NCA	Noise Control Act; National
MPRSA	Marine Protection, Research,		Command Authorities
	and Sanctuaries Act of	NCAA	National Collegiate Athletic
	1972		Association
M.R.	Master of the Rolls	NCAC	National Coalition against
MS-DOS	Microsoft Disk Operating		Censorship
	System	NCCB	National Consumer
MSHA	Mine Safety and Health		Cooperative Bank
	Administration	NCE	Northwest Community
MSPB	Merit Systems Protection		Exchange
	Board	NCF	National Chamber
MSSA	Military Selective Service Act		Foundation
N/A	Not Available	NCIP	National Crime Insurance
NAACP	National Association for the		Program
	Advancement of Colored	NCJA	National Criminal Justice
	People		Association
NAAQS	National Ambient Air Quality	NCLB	National Civil Liberties
	Standards		Bureau
NAB	National Association of	NCP	National contingency plan
	Broadcasters	NCSC	National Center for State
NABSW	National Association of Black		Courts
	Social Workers	NCUA	National Credit Union
NACDL	National Association of		Administration
	Criminal Defense Lawyers	NDA	New drug application
NAFTA	North American Free Trade	N.D. Ill.	Northern District, Illinois
	Agreement of 1993	NDU	National Defense University
NAGHSR	National Association of	N.D. Wash.	Northern District,
	Governors' Highway Safety		Washington
	Representatives	N.E.	North Eastern Reporter
NALA	National Association of Legal	N.E. 2d	North Eastern Reporter,
	Assistants		Second Series
NAM	National Association of	NEA	National Endowment for the
	Manufacturers		Arts; National Education
NAR	National Association of		Association
	Realtors	NEH	National Endowment for the
NARAL	National Abortion and		Humanities
	Reproductive Rights	NEPA	National Environmental
	Action League		Protection Act; National
NARF	Native American Rights Fund		Endowment Policy Act
NARS	National Archives and Record	NET Act	No Electronic Theft Act
	Service	NFIB	National Federation of
NASA	National Aeronautics and		Independent Businesses
	Space Administration	NFIP	National Flood Insurance
NASD	National Association of		Program
	Securities Dealers	NFL	National Football League
NATO	North Atlantic Treaty	NFPA	National Federation of
	Organization		Paralegal Associations

NGLTF	National Gay and Lesbian Task Force	NPL	National priorities list
NHL	National Hockey League	NPR	National Public Radio
NHRA	Nursing Home Reform Act of 1987	NPT	Nuclear Non-Proliferation Treaty of 1970
NHTSA	National Highway Traffic Safety Administration	NRA	National Rifle Association; National Recovery Act
Nielsen's Rept.	Frederick Kenelm Nielsen, *American and British Claims Arbitration under the Special Agreement Concluded between the United States and Great Britain, August 18, 1910* (1926)	NRC	Nuclear Regulatory Commission
		NRLC	National Right to Life Committee
		NRTA	National Retired Teachers Association
		NSA	National Security Agency
		NSC	National Security Council
NIEO	New International Economic Order	NSCLC	National Senior Citizens Law Center
NIGC	National Indian Gaming Commission	NSF	National Science Foundation
		NSFNET	National Science Foundation Network
NIH	National Institutes of Health		
NIJ	National Institute of Justice	NSI	Network Solutions, Inc.
NIRA	National Industrial Recovery Act of 1933; National Industrial Recovery Administration	NTIA	National Telecommunications and Information Administration
NIST	National Institute of Standards and Technology	NTID	National Technical Institute for the Deaf
NITA	National Telecommunications and Information Administration	NTIS	National Technical Information Service
		NTS	Naval Telecommunications System
N.J.	New Jersey Reports	NTSB	National Transportation Safety Board
N.J. Super.	New Jersey Superior Court Reports	NVRA	National Voter Registration Act
NLEA	Nutrition Labeling and Education Act of 1990	N.W.	North Western Reporter
NLRA	National Labor Relations Act	N.W. 2d	North Western Reporter, Second Series
NLRB	National Labor Relations Board	NWSA	National Woman Suffrage Association
NMFS	National Marine Fisheries Service	N.Y.	New York Court of Appeals Reports
No.	Number		
NOAA	National Oceanic and Atmospheric Administration	N.Y. 2d	New York Court of Appeals Reports, Second Series
		N.Y.S.	New York Supplement Reporter
NOC	National Olympic Committee		
NOI	Nation of Islam	N.Y.S. 2d	New York Supplement Reporter, Second Series
NOL	Net operating loss		
NORML	National Organization for the Reform of Marijuana Laws	NYSE	New York Stock Exchange
		NYSLA	New York State Liquor Authority
NOW	National Organization for Women	N.Y. Sup.	New York Supreme Court Reports
NOW LDEF	National Organization for Women Legal Defense and Education Fund	NYU	New York University
		OAAU	Organization of Afro American Unity
NOW/PAC	National Organization for Women Political Action Committee	OAP	Office of Administrative Procedure
NPDES	National Pollutant Discharge Elimination System	OAS	Organization of American States

OASDI	Old-age, Survivors, and Disability Insurance Benefits
OASHDS	Office of the Assistant Secretary for Human Development Services
OCC	Office of Comptroller of the Currency
OCED	Office of Comprehensive Employment Development
OCHAMPUS	Office of Civilian Health and Medical Program of the Uniformed Services
OCSE	Office of Child Support Enforcement
OEA	Organización de los Estados Americanos
OEM	Original Equipment Manufacturer
OFCCP	Office of Federal Contract Compliance Programs
OFPP	Office of Federal Procurement Policy
OIC	Office of the Independent Counsel
OICD	Office of International Cooperation and Development
OIG	Office of the Inspector General
OJARS	Office of Justice Assistance, Research, and Statistics
OMB	Office of Management and Budget
OMPC	Office of Management, Planning, and Communications
ONP	Office of National Programs
OPD	Office of Policy Development
OPEC	Organization of Petroleum Exporting Countries
OPIC	Overseas Private Investment Corporation
Ops. Atts. Gen.	Opinions of the Attorneys-General of the United States
Ops. Comms.	Opinions of the Commissioners
OPSP	Office of Product Standards Policy
O.R.	Ontario Reports
OR	Official Records
OSHA	Occupational Safety and Health Act
OSHRC	Occupational Safety and Health Review Commission
OSM	Office of Surface Mining
OSS	Office of Strategic Services

OST	Office of the Secretary
OT	Office of Transportation
OTA	Office of Technology Assessment
OTC	Over-the-counter
OTS	Office of Thrift Supervisors
OUI	Operating under the influence
OVCI	Offshore Voluntary Compliance Initiative
OWBPA	Older Workers Benefit Protection Act
OWRT	Office of Water Research and Technology
P.	Pacific Reporter
P. 2d	Pacific Reporter, Second Series
PAC	Political action committee
Pa. Oyer and Terminer	Pennsylvania Oyer and Terminer Reports
PATCO	Professional Air Traffic Controllers Organization
PBGC	Pension Benefit Guaranty Corporation
PBS	Public Broadcasting Service; Public Buildings Service
P.C.	Privy Council (English Law Reports)
PC	Personal computer; politically correct
PCBs	Polychlorinated biphenyls
PCIJ	Permanent Court of International Justice Series A-Judgments and Orders (1922–30) Series B-Advisory Opinions (1922–30) Series A/B-Judgments, Orders, and Advisory Opinions (1931–40) Series C-Pleadings, Oral Statements, and Documents relating to Judgments and Advisory Opinions (1923–42) Series D-Acts and Documents concerning the Organization of the World Court (1922 –47) Series E-Annual Reports (1925–45)
PCP	Phencyclidine
P.D.	Probate Division, English Law Reports (1876–1890)
PDA	Pregnancy Discrimination Act of 1978
PD & R	Policy Development and Research

Pepco	Potomac Electric Power Company	PURPA	Public Utilities Regulatory Policies Act
Perm. Ct. of Arb.	Permanent Court of Arbitration	PUSH	People United to Serve Humanity
PES	Post-Enumeration Survey	PUSH-Excel	PUSH for Excellence
Pet.	Peters' United States Supreme Court Reports	PWA	Public Works Administration
PETA	People for the Ethical Treatment of Animals	PWSA	Ports and Waterways Safety Act of 1972
PGA	Professional Golfers Association	Q.B.	Queen's Bench (England)
PGM	Program	QTIP	Qualified Terminable Interest Property
PHA	Public Housing Agency	Ralston's Rept.	Jackson Harvey Ralston, ed.,
Phila. Ct. of Oyer and Terminer	Philadelphia Court of Oyer and Terminer		*Venezuelan Arbitrations of 1903* (1904)
PhRMA	Pharmaceutical Research and Manufacturers of America	RC	Regional Commissioner
		RCRA	Resource Conservation and Recovery Act
PHS	Public Health Service		
PIC	Private Industry Council	RCWP	Rural Clean Water Program
PICJ	Permanent International Court of Justice	RDA	Rural Development Administration
Pick.	Pickering's Massachusetts Reports	REA	Rural Electrification Administration
PIK	Payment in Kind	Rec. des Decs.	G. Gidel, ed., *Recueil des*
PINS	Persons in need of supervision	des Trib. Arb. Mixtes	*décisions des tribunaux arbitraux mixtes, institués par les traités de paix* (1922–30)
PIRG	Public Interest Research Group		
P.L.	Public Laws	Redmond	Vol. 3 of Charles I. Bevans,
PLAN	Pro-Life Action Network		*Treaties and Other*
PLC	Plaintiffs' Legal Committee		*International Agreements*
PLE	Product liability expenses		*of the United States of*
PLI	Practicing Law Institute		*America, 1776–1949*
PLL	Product liability loss		(compiled by C. F.
PLLP	Professional Limited Liability Partnership		Redmond) (1969)
		RESPA	Real Estate Settlement Procedure Act of 1974
PLO	Palestine Liberation Organization	RFC	Reconstruction Finance Corporation
PLRA	Prison Litigation Reform Act of 1995	RFRA	Religious Freedom Restoration Act of 1993
PNET	Peaceful Nuclear Explosions Treaty	RIAA	Recording Industry Association of America
PONY	Prostitutes of New York		
POW-MIA	Prisoner of war-missing in action	RICO	Racketeer Influenced and Corrupt Organizations
Pratt	Frederic Thomas Pratt, *Law of Contraband of War, with a Selection of Cases from Papers of the Right Honourable Sir George Lee* (1856)	RLUIPA	Religious Land Use and Institutionalized Persons Act
		RNC	Republican National Committee
		Roscoe	Edward Stanley Roscoe, ed.,
PRIDE	Prostitution to Independence, Dignity, and Equality		*Reports of Prize Cases Determined in the High Court Admiralty before the*
Proc.	Proceedings		*Lords Commissioners of*
PRP	Potentially responsible party		*Appeals in Prize Causes and*
PSRO	Professional Standards Review Organization		*before the judicial Committee of the Privy Council from*
PTO	Patents and Trademark Office		*1745 to 1859* (1905)

ROTC	Reserve Officers' Training Corps
RPP	Representative Payee Program
R.S.	Revised Statutes
RTC	Resolution Trust Corp.
RUDs	Reservations, understandings, and declarations
Ryan White CARE Act	Ryan White Comprehensive AIDS Research Emergency Act of 1990
SAC	Strategic Air Command
SACB	Subversive Activities Control Board
SADD	Students against Drunk Driving
SAF	Student Activities Fund
SAIF	Savings Association Insurance Fund
SALT	Strategic Arms Limitation Talks
SALT I	Strategic Arms Limitation Talks of 1969–72
SAMHSA	Substance Abuse and Mental Health Services Administration
Sandf.	Sandford's New York Superior Court Reports
S and L	Savings and loan
SARA	Superfund Amendment and Reauthorization Act
SAT	Scholastic Aptitude Test
Sawy.	Sawyer's United States Circuit Court Reports
SBA	Small Business Administration
SBI	Small Business Institute
SCCC	South Central Correctional Center
SCLC	Southern Christian Leadership Conference
Scott's Repts.	James Brown Scott, ed., *The Hague Court Reports*, 2 vols. (1916–32)
SCS	Soil Conservation Service; Social Conservative Service
SCSEP	Senior Community Service Employment Program
S.Ct.	Supreme Court Reporter
S.D. Cal.	Southern District, California
S.D. Fla.	Southern District, Florida
S.D. Ga.	Southern District, Georgia
SDI	Strategic Defense Initiative
S.D. Me.	Southern District, Maine
S.D.N.Y.	Southern District, New York
SDS	Students for a Democratic Society
S.E.	South Eastern Reporter

S.E. 2d	South Eastern Reporter, Second Series
SEA	Science and Education Administration
SEATO	Southeast Asia Treaty Organization
SEC	Securities and Exchange Commission
Sec.	Section
SEEK	Search for Elevation, Education and Knowledge
SEOO	State Economic Opportunity Office
SEP	Simplified employee pension plan
Ser.	Series
Sess.	Session
SGLI	Servicemen's Group Life Insurance
SIP	State implementation plan
SLA	Symbionese Liberation Army
SLAPPs	Strategic Lawsuits Against Public Participation
SLBM	Submarine-launched ballistic missile
SNCC	Student Nonviolent Coordinating Committee
So.	Southern Reporter
So. 2d	Southern Reporter, Second Series
SPA	Software Publisher's Association
Spec. Sess.	Special Session
SPLC	Southern Poverty Law Center
SRA	Sentencing Reform Act of 1984
SS	*Schutzstaffel* (German, "Protection Echelon")
SSA	Social Security Administration
SSI	Supplemental Security Income
START I	Strategic Arms Reduction Treaty of 1991
START II	Strategic Arms Reduction Treaty of 1993
Stat.	United States Statutes at Large
STS	Space Transportation Systems
St. Tr.	State Trials, English
STURAA	Surface Transportation and Uniform Relocation Assistance Act of 1987
Sup. Ct. of Justice, Mexico	Supreme Court of Justice, Mexico
Supp.	Supplement
S.W.	South Western Reporter

S.W. 2d	South Western Reporter, Second Series	UDC	United Daughters of the Confederacy
SWAPO	South-West Africa People's Organization	UFW	United Farm Workers
		UHF	Ultrahigh frequency
SWAT	Special Weapons and Tactics	UIFSA	Uniform Interstate Family Support Act
SWP	Socialist Workers Party		
TDP	Trade and Development Program	UIS	Unemployment Insurance Service
Tex. Sup.	Texas Supreme Court Reports	UMDA	Uniform Marriage and Divorce Act
THAAD	Theater High-Altitude Area Defense System	UMTA	Urban Mass Transportation Administration
THC	Tetrahydrocannabinol	U.N.	United Nations
TI	Tobacco Institute	UNCITRAL	United Nations Commission on International Trade Law
TIA	Trust Indenture Act of 1939		
TIAS	Treaties and Other International Acts Series (United States)	UNCTAD	United Nations Conference on Trade and Development
TNT	Trinitrotoluene		
TOP	Targeted Outreach Program	UN Doc.	United Nations Documents
TPUS	Transportation and Public Utilities Service	UNDP	United Nations Development Program
TQM	Total Quality Management	UNEF	United Nations Emergency Force
Tripartite Claims Comm., Decs. and Ops.	Tripartite Claims Commission (United States, Austria, and Hungary), Decisions and Opinions	UNESCO	United Nations Educational, Scientific, and Cultural Organization
		UNICEF	United Nations Children's Fund (formerly United Nations International Children's Emergency Fund)
TRI-TAC	Joint Tactical Communications		
TRO	Temporary restraining order		
TS	Treaty Series, United States	UNIDO	United Nations Industrial and Development Organization
TSCA	Toxic Substance Control Act		
TSDs	Transporters, storers, and disposers	Unif. L. Ann.	Uniform Laws Annotated
		UN Repts. Intl. Arb. Awards	United Nations Reports of International Arbitral Awards
TSU	Texas Southern University		
TTBT	Threshold Test Ban Treaty		
TV	Television	UNTS	United Nations Treaty Series
TVA	Tennessee Valley Authority	UPI	United Press International
TWA	Trans World Airlines	URESA	Uniform Reciprocal Enforcement of Support Act
UAW	United Auto Workers; United Automobile, Aerospace, and Agricultural Implements Workers of America		
		U.S.	United States Reports
		U.S.A.	United States of America
		USAF	United States Air Force
U.C.C.	Uniform Commercial Code; Universal Copyright Convention	USA PATRIOT Act	Uniting and Strengthening America by Providing Appropriate Tools Required to Intercept and Obstruct Terrorism Act
U.C.C.C.	Uniform Consumer Credit Code		
UCCJA	Uniform Child Custody Jurisdiction Act	USF	U.S. Forestry Service
		U.S. App. D.C.	United States Court of Appeals for the District of Columbia
UCMJ	Uniform Code of Military Justice		
UCPP	Urban Crime Prevention Program	U.S.C.	United States Code; University of Southern California
UCS	United Counseling Service		

U.S.C.A.	United States Code Annotated	Wall.	Wallace's United States Supreme Court Reports
U.S.C.C.A.N.	United States Code Congressional and Administrative News	Wash. 2d	Washington Reports, Second Series
USCMA	United States Court of Military Appeals	WAVES	Women Accepted for Volunteer Service
USDA	U.S. Department of Agriculture	WCTU	Women's Christian Temperance Union
USES	United States Employment Service	W.D. Wash.	Western District, Washington
		W.D. Wis.	Western District, Wisconsin
USFA	United States Fire Administration	WEAL	West's Encyclopedia of American Law; Women's Equity Action League
USGA	United States Golf Association	Wend.	Wendell's New York Reports
USICA	International Communication Agency, United States	WFSE	Washington Federation of State Employees
		Wheat.	Wheaton's United States Supreme Court Reports
USMS	U.S. Marshals Service	Wheel. Cr. Cases	Wheeler's New York Criminal Cases
USOC	U.S. Olympic Committee		
USSC	U.S. Sentencing Commission	WHISPER	Women Hurt in Systems of Prostitution Engaged in Revolt
USSG	United States Sentencing Guidelines		
U.S.S.R.	Union of Soviet Socialist Republics	Whiteman	Marjorie Millace Whiteman, Digest of International Law, 15 vols. (1963–73)
UST	United States Treaties		
USTS	United States Travel Service	WHO	World Health Organization
v.	Versus	WIC	Women, Infants, and Children program
VA	Veterans Administration		
VAR	Veterans Affairs and Rehabilitation Commission	Will. and Mar.	King William and Queen Mary (Great Britain)
		WIN	WESTLAW Is Natural; Whip Inflation Now; Work Incentive Program
VAWA	Violence against Women Act		
VFW	Veterans of Foreign Wars		
VGLI	Veterans Group Life Insurance	WIPO	World Intellectual Property Organization
Vict.	Queen Victoria (Great Britain)	WIU	Workers' Industrial Union
		W.L.R.	Weekly Law Reports, England
VIN	Vehicle identification number	WPA	Works Progress Administration
VISTA	Volunteers in Service to America	WPPDA	Welfare and Pension Plans Disclosure Act
VJRA	Veterans Judicial Review Act of 1988	WTO	World Trade Organization
V.L.A.	Volunteer Lawyers for the Arts	WWI	World War I
		WWII	World War II
VMI	Virginia Military Institute	Yates Sel. Cas.	Yates's New York Select Cases
VMLI	Veterans Mortgage Life Insurance	YMCA	Young Men's Christian Association
VOCAL	Victims of Child Abuse Laws		
VRA	Voting Rights Act	YWCA	Young Women's Christian Association
WAC	Women's Army Corps		

TABLE OF
CASES CITED

A

ACLU of North Carolina v. Conti, 5
Adoptive Couple v. Baby Girl, 105
Agency for International Development v. Alliance for Open Society International, Inc., 112
Alleyne v. United States, 201
Already, L.L.C. v. Nike, Inc., 228
American Express Co. v. Italian Colors Restaurant, 19–20
American Trucking Associations, Inc. v. City of Los Angeles, 86–87
Amgen, Inc. v. Connecticut Retirement Plans and Trust Funds, 126
Amnesty International USA v. Clapper, 82
Amnesty International USA v. McConnell, 82
Anderson v. City of Hermosa Beach, 128
Anthony v. State, 170
Apprendi v. New Jersey, 201
Arizona v. Rumsey, 71
Asarco LLC v. U.S. Environmental Protection Agency, 90
Association for Molecular Pathology v. United States Patent and Trademark Office, 181
Association of Molecular Pathology v. Myriad Genetics, Inc., 181

B

Basic, Inc. v. Levinson, 126
Behrend v. Comcast Corp., 49
Bowman v. Monsanto Co., 178
Bullock v. BankChampaign, 33

C

Castle v. Hayes Freight Lines, Inc., 87
Center for Constitutional Rights v. United States, 166
Chafin v. Chafin, 43
Chaidez v. United States, 61–62
Chevron U.S.A., Inc. v. Natural Resources Defense Council, Inc., 107
Citizens United v. Federal Election Commission, 81
City of Arlington v. FCC, 106–107

City of Riviera Beach v. That Certain Unnamed Gray, Two-Story Vessel Approximately Fifty-Seven Feet in Length, 12
Clapper v. Amnesty International USA, 81, 83
Cloer v. Secretary of Health & Human Services, 27
Coleman v. City of Mesa, 128
Comcast Corp. v. Behrend, 48
Costco Wholesale Corporation v. Omega, 55

D

Decker v. Northwest Environmental Defense Center, 88
District of Columbia v. Heller, 137, 196, 198
Dolan v. City of Tigard, 84

E

Enterprise Wheel, 25
Evans v. Michigan, 70

F

Florida v. Harris, 62–63
Fong Foo v. United States, 70
Friends of the Earth, Inc. v. Laidlaw Environmental Services (TOC), Inc., 229
FTC v. Actavis, Inc., 180, 182
FTC v. Watson Pharmaceuticals, Inc., 182

G

Gabelli v. SEC, 199–200
Genesis HealthCare Corp. v. Symczyk, 49
Georgia-Pacific West v. Northwest Environmental Defense Center, 88

H

Harrell v. Fla. Bar, 158
Harris v. United States, 201
Hillman v. Maretta, 100
Hispanics United of Buffalo, 156–157
Hollingsworth v. Perry, 132–133
Horne v. Department of Agriculture, 15–16
Horne v. U.S. Department of Agriculture, 16

I

In re Amendments to the Rules Regulating the Florida BarSubchapter 4–7, Lawyer Advertising Rules, 158–159
In re American Express Merchants' Litigation, 20
In re Electronic Books Antitrust Litigation, 55
In re: Oil Spill by the Oil Rig "Deepwater Horizon," 58

J

Johanns v. Livestock Marketing Ass'n, 6

K

King v. State, 64
Kirtsaeng v. John Wiley & Sons, Inc., 55
Koontz v. St. Johns River Water Management District, 83

L

Lavin v. Husted, 80–81
Lawrence v. Texas, 133
Levin v. United States, 108–109
Lewis v. Continental Bank Corp., 50
Los Angeles County Flood Control District v. Natural Resources Defense Council, Inc., 91
Lozman v. City of Riviera Beach, Florida, 11-12

M

Maracich v. Spears, 188–189
Maretta v. Hillman, 101
Marx v. General Revenue Corporation, 67–68
Maryland v. King, 63
Massachusetts v. EPA, 90
McDonald v. Chicago, 198
McMillan v. Pennsylvania, 201
Minnesota v. Murphy, 111
Moore v. Madigan, 198–199
Mullaney v. Wilbur, 59
Myers Industries, 157

N

National Environmental Development Association's Clean Air Project v. EPA, 90
Natural Resources Defense Council, Inc. v. County of Los Angeles, 92
Neal v. Clark, 34
Neder v. United States, 104
Nike, Inc. v. Already, L.L.C., 229
Nollan v. California Coastal Commission, 84
Northwest Austin Municipal Utility District No. One v. Holder, 234

O

Oxford Health Plans v. Sutter, 24

P

Padilla v. Kentucky, 61
Perry v. Brown, 134
Perry v. Perez, 232

Q

Quality King Distributors v. L'anza Research International, 56

R

R.J. Reynolds Tobacco Co. v. FDA, 228
Romer v. Evans, 133–134
Rumsfeld v. Forum for Academic and Institutional Rights, Inc., 113

S

Salinas v. Texas, 110
Sebelius v. Cloer, 26–27
SEC v. Gabelli, 200
Sekhar v. United States, 103
Shelby County v. Holder, 232–234
Shepard v. Madigan, 198
Smith v. United States, 59
Snyder v. Phelps, 116
South Florida Water Management District v. Miccosukee Tribe, 92
Stahl v. City of St. Louis, Mo., 129–130
Standard Fire Insurance Company v. Knowles, 51
Stolt-Nielsen v. AnimalFeeds International Corp., 24
Strickland v. Washington, 61

T

Tarrant Regional Water District v. Herrmann, 92
Teague v. Lane, 61–62
Texas v. United States, 232
Trautmann v. Christie, 30
23-34 94th Street Grocery Corp. v. N.Y. City Board of Health, 226-227

U

U.S. Airways v. McCutchen, 94
United States v. Alleyne, 202
United States v. Apple, Inc., 55
United States v. Davila, 65
United States v. Jones, 195
United States v. Mix, 58
United States v. Moore, 60
United States v. Windsor, 135

NOTE: *Page numbers appearing in boldface indicate major treatment of entries. Italicized page numbers refer to photos.*

A

Abbott, Greg, 232
Abbott Industries, 72
ABC News, 69–70
Abduction
    defined, 153–154
    international statutes, 43, 44
    kidnapping, by custodial
        parents, 153–154
Abortion, **1–11**
    government speech, 5–7
    procedures regulation, 1–2, 8, 9
    protests, 28–29, 114
    related drugs/medical abortion,
        7, 8, 10, 36–38
    states' laws and cases, 4–5,
        7–11, 36–38
    viability of fetus, 4–5, 8, 9, 10
Abortion clinics, 1–2, 8, 10,
    36–37, 114
Abortion funding, 2–4, 8–9,
    10–11
Abortion-inducing drugs, 7, 8, 10,
    36–38, *37*
Abortion-Inducing Drugs Safety
    Act (Oklahoma, 2011), 7
Academic credit, 97–98
Access tests, 119–120
Acquittals
    defined, 70
    midtrial, 70, 71
Act 490 (Louisiana, 2010), 1
Actavis, Inc., 182–183
"Actual innocence" claims,
    143–144

Adjudication, 142
Admiralty and Maritime Law,
    11–13
Adopt-a-Highway programs, 130
Adoption
    family law, 105–106
    gay and lesbian families,
        131–132
Adoptive Couple v. Baby Girl
    (2013), 105–106
Advertising
    cigarettes, 226–228
    lawyers, rules, 158–159, 188,
        189
Affiliation, legal determination,
    3–4
Affirmative Action, **13–15**
Affirmative defenses, 59, 60, 85
AFL-CIO, 155–156
African American voting
    disenfranchisement, 233–235
Age discrimination, 19, 47–48
Age Discrimination in
    Employment Act (1967), 19
Age rules, gun sales, 137, 140
Agencies
    budgets, 52, 53
    First Amendment, 112
    statute construction and
        interpretation, 107–108
*Agency for International
    Development v. Alliance for
    Open Society International, Inc.*
    (2013), 112–113
Aggravated Unlawful Use of a
    Weapon statute (Illinois), 198
Agri-Tech, Inc., 102
Agricultural Law, **15–17**
    See also Seeds and seed patents
Agricultural Marketing Agree-
    ment Act (1937), 15–17

Agriculture Marketing Service, 16
Aichele, Carol, 119–120
Aiding the enemy, 164, 166
AIDS organizations, 112–113
Air pollution
    environmental law, 86–87, 88,
        90–91
    sulfur dioxide rules, 90–91
Airlines
    employees with disabilities,
        17–18
    ERISA, 94–95
al Qaeda, 82
Alabama, voting rights, 234–236
Albin, Barry, 215
Alcohol, blood concentrations,
    124–125
Alexander, Travis, 171
Alien Tort Statute (1789), 150–151
Alito, Samuel
    antitrust law cases, 49
    arbitration cases, 25
    class action cases, 49
    copyright cases, 56
    criminal procedure cases, 65, 66
    double jeopardy cases, 71
    electronic surveillance cases, 81,
        82, 83
    eminent domain cases, 84
    employment discrimination
        cases, 85
    environmental law cases, 92
    estate planning cases, 101
    family law cases, 106
    FCC cases, 107
    Fifth Amendment cases, 111
    gay and lesbian rights cases,
        134, 137
    habeas corpus cases, 142, 144,
        145
    immigration cases, 150

international law cases, 151
plain-error rule, 185
privacy cases, 189
privileges and immunities cases, 190, 191
product liability cases, 192
search and seizure cases, 195
sentencing cases, 202, 204
sex offender cases, 207
speedy trial cases, 209–210
trademark cases, 229
voter qualification cases, 149
Alleyne, Allen Ryan, 201–202
Alleyne v. United States (2013), 201–202
Alliance for Open Society International, 112–113
Alpert, Bruce, 200
Already, L.L.C. v. Nike, Inc. (2013), 228–229
Alvarez, Anita, 118–119
Amazon.com, 54–55
Amchan, Arthur, 157
Amendment 64 (Colorado, 2012), 73–74
American Civil Liberties Union (ACLU)
abortion, 5, 6, 7
First Amendment cases, 118–119
human rights, 221–222
labor law, 155–156
prisoners' rights, 115, 116, 221–222
search and seizure, 195–196
surveillance, 82, 83
American Congress of Obstetricians and Gynecologists, 10
American Express, 20, 21
American Express Co. v. Italian Colors Restaurant (2013), 20
"American Rule," litigation costs, 26–27
American Trucking Associations, Inc. v. City of Los Angeles (2013), 86–87
Americans for Responsible Solutions, 26, 138
Americans with Disabilities Act (1990), **17–19**
Amgen Inc., 72–73, 126–127
Amgen Inc. v. Connecticut Retirement Plans and Trust Funds (2013), 72–73, 126–127
Amnesty International, 82–83
Anthony, Casey, 169–171
Anthony, Caylee, 169–171
Anthony, George, 170
Anti-gay hate crimes, 145–146
Anti-gay protests, funerals, 113, 116–117

Anticompetitive actions, governments, 21–22
Antidepressant drugs, 72
Antipsychotic drugs, 72
Antiterrorism and Effective Death Penalty Act (1996), 141, 142, 143, 144
Antitrust Law, **19–22**, 49
class action suits, 20, 48–49
publishing pricing and conspiracy, 54–55
reverse settlement agreements/ patents, 182–183
suits against NCAA, 43
Appellate Advocacy, **22–24**
Apple Inc., *176*
conspiracy and pricing, e-books, 54–55
iPhone patent suit, 175–176
Appointments, political, 186–188
Apprendi v. New Jersey (2000), 201, 202
Arabic language, use, 115
Aranesp (medication), 72–73
Arbitration, 19–21, **24–25**
Arias, Jodi, 171
Aristone Realty Capital, 159, 160
Arizona
abortion law, 4–5, 9
assassination attempts, 25–26
election law, 78–80, 147–149
environmental law, 87–88
freedom of speech, 127–129
habeas corpus cases, 144, 145
immigration policy, 88, 147–149
Arizona League of Conservation Voters, 88
Arizona v. Inter Tribal Council of Arizona (2013), 147–149, *148*
Arizona v. Rumsey (1984), 71
Arkansas
abortion laws, 9
capital punishment, 39–40
class action cases, 51
marijuana laws, 74
water resources, 93
Arkansas Dept. of Health and Human Servs. v. Ahlborn (2006), 163
Arlington, Texas, 106–107
Armed Career Criminal Act (1984), 202–203, 204
Armstrong, Lance, 210–212, *211*
Arnquist, Steve, 88
Arntsen, Douglas, 159–160
Arson, 70–71
Artificial insemination, 214
Artistic expression, 128

Asarco LLC, 91
Assange, Julian, 165
Assassination, **25–26**
Assault and battery claims and immunity, 107, 108, 110
Assault weapons, 26, 138, 168–169, 173–174
Association for Molecular Pathology v. Myriad Genetics, Inc. (2013), 176–178, 181
Association of State and Territorial Health Officials, 53
Attorneys. *See* Attorney's Fees; Lawyers
Attorney's Fees, **26–29**
civil procedure, 67, 68
cost sharing, 94, 95
offers of judgment, 50
redressability, 97
Auburn Regional Medical Center, 161
Auction sales, 186
Audio recording
evidence, 172
First Amendment rights, 117–119
Aurora, Colorado, movie theater shootings (2012), 138, 169, 173–174
"Australian system" of voting, 120
Automatic and assault weapons, 26, 138, 168–169, 173–174
Automobiles, **29–32**
dealerships, 188, 189
drunk driving, 124–125
preemption cases, 185–186
search and seizure laws, 30, 62–63, 195
Avandia (medication), 72

B

Background checks, gun purchases, 26, 138, 139, 169
Bad faith, 34, 47, 67, 68
Baez, Jose, 170
Bailey, Chunon, 122–123
Bailey v. United States (2013), 121–122
Balanced Budget and Emergency Deficit Control Act (1985), 52
Baldwin, Cynthia, 42, 43
Bales, Scott, 128
Ball State University, 84–86
Ballester, Pierre, 211
Ballistics, 111, 112
Ballots, voting, 120
Bank fraud, 102
Bankruptcy, **33–35**
Casey Anthony, 169, 170–171
debtor and creditor, 67

Bar boards and associations, 158, 159

Barnett. Paul M., 69

Bartlett, Karen, 191–193

Basic, Inc. v. Levinson (1988), 126

Battery claims, 108–109, 109–110, 166

BCN (real estate firm), 159, 160

Bender, Paul, 88

Beneficiaries, life insurance, 100–101

Benefits, employee. *See* Federal benefits; Health insurance; Pension funds; Retirement plans

Benson, Tom, 213

Berman, Glenn, 146

Berzon, Marsha, 5

Bhagwati, Anu, *167*

Bias, juries, 142

Bias intimidation, 145–146

Bible schools, 97–98

"Big Pharma." *See* Pharmaceutical industry

Biotechnology industry, 180

Biotechnology patents, 176–181

Bipartisan Campaign Reform Act (2002), 81

Bipartisan Legal Advisory Group, House of Representatives, 136

Birth certificates, 214

Birth Control, 8, **35–38**

Birth-related injuries, settlements, 163–164

Bivens actions, 46

Bivens v. Six Unknown Agents of the Federal Bureau of Investigation (1971), 46

Block, Sharon, 187

Blood tests, and search and seizure, 65, 124–125

Bloomberg, Michael, 138

Board of Immigration Appeals, 149

Bolick, Clint, 128–129

Booking procedures, 65, 121

Bootleg goods, copyright and trademark violations, 56, 57

Bormes, James, 208

Boston Marathon bombings, 2013, 218–220, *219*

Botsford, Margot, 121

"Bounty system," NFL, 212–214, *213*

Bowman, Vernon, 178–179, 180–181

Bowman v. Monsanto Company (2013), 178–179, 181

Boyer, Jonathan, 209–210

Boyer v. Louisiana (2013), 209–210

BP Exploration and Production, Inc., 58–59

BRCA1 and BRCA2 genes, 177, 178, 181

Breast cancer genes, 177, 178, 181

Breathelyzer tests, 124

Breuer, Lanny, 57, 58

Brewer, Jan, 4, 88

Breyer, Stephen
  admiralty and maritime law cases, 12–13
  antitrust law cases, 182
  bankruptcy cases, 34
  child custody cases, 45
  class action cases, 49, 50, 51
  copyright cases, 56
  criminal procedure cases, 65, 66
  electronic surveillance cases, 83
  employment discrimination cases, 85–86
  ERISA cases, 95
  FCC cases, 107, 108
  Fifth Amendment cases, 112
  gay and lesbian rights cases, 134, 136
  habeas corpus cases, 144, 145
  immigration cases, 150
  international law cases, 151
  patent cases, 182
  plain-error rule, 185
  privacy cases, 189
  product liability cases, 192
  sentencing cases, 202
  sex offender cases, 207
  speedy trial cases, 210

Bribery
  extortion, 103
  pharmaceutical and medical industries, 72
  state government officials and contractors, 80

British taxation, 217–218

Broadcasting industry
  class action suits, 48–49
  government regulation, 106–108

Brook, Chris, 7

Brown, Janice Rogers, 224, 225, 226

Brutinel, Robert, 79

Buckles, Frederick R., 129–130

Budget Control Act (2011), 52

Bullock, Randy Curtis, 33–34

Bullock v. BankChampaign (2013), 33–34

Bullying, 145–146, 157, 165, 169

Bunsow, Henry, 35

Burdens of proof
  defenses, 59–60

searches and seizures, 64

tobacco industry, 226

Burglary, 153, 203–204

Burns, Larry, 26

Bush, George W., 45–46, 69, 82, 187, 221

Byra, Michelle, 156

C

Cable service providers, 48–49

Cabrera, Alejandrina, 78–80

Calabresi, Guido, 99–100

California
  agricultural commodities, 15–16
  environmental law, 86–87, 91–92
  habeas corpus cases, 141–142
  marriage law, 132–134, *133*
  Penal Code, 142, 203, 204

"Call of Duty" (video game), 169

Camp Lejeune (North Carolina), 116

Campaign contributions, 80–81

Campaign finance reform
  history, 80
  laws, 81

Campos, William, 57

Canada, 135

Cancer genes, 177, 178, 181

Canning, Noel, 187–188

Capital Punishment, **39–42**
  inmates, appellate advocacy, 22–23
  methods, 39–40
  press access, 40–42
  sentencing, 144

"Career criminals," 202–204

Carney, Jay, 220

Carolina Pregnancy Care Fellowship, 6

Cars. *See* Automobiles

Carter, Sean, 23, 24

Case within a case, 183

Castle v. Hayes Freight Lines, Inc. (1954), 87

Cause of action, 46, 84, 109, 150, 156, 184, 192, 199, 200, 201

cDNA, 176, 177, 181

Cellphones
  patents, 175–176, *176*
  searches and seizures, 120–121

Cemeteries, protests in, 113–114, 116–117

Censorship, 112–113

Census data, 231

Center for Medicare & Medicaid Services, 160–161

Centers for Disease Control and Prevention (CDC), studies, 139

Central Intelligence Act (1949), 223

Central Intelligence Agency (CIA), 219–220, 221–223

Chafin, Jeffrey Lee, 43–45

Chafin v. Chafin (2013), 43–44

Chaidez, Roselva, 61–62

Chaidez v. United States (2013), 61–62

Chapter 11 bankruptcy, 34–35

Chatterjee, Bani, 131–132

Chatterjee v. King (2012), 131–132

Chavez, Edward, 132

Check fraud, 102

Chemical injection, capital punishment, 39–40

Cherokee Nation, 105–106

Chevron U.S.A., Inc. v. Natural Resources Defense Council (1984), 107, 108

Child Abuse, **42–43**

Child Custody, **43–45**
  family law and adoption, 105, 131–132
  gay and lesbian families, 131–132
  kidnapping, 153–154

Child support
  family law, 105
  out-of-state petitions, 190

Children's health
  drug usage and safety, 72, 73
  hazardous materials, toys, 56–57

Chin, Denny, 227–228

Chinese exports, 56–57

Choice Incorporated of Texas v. Greenstein, 1

Choose Life (organization), 6

Christie, Chris, 215

Cigarettes, 223–226

Citizens United v. Federal Election Commission (2010), 81

Citizenship
  American terrorists, 218–220
  child custody cases, 44
  drug offenses and, 149–150
  state, privileges, 190–191
  voter registration, 147–149, 235

City of Arlington v. FCC (2013), 107–108

Civil action
  environmental law, 92
  maritime law, 11
  rules against, 24
  terrorism cases, 221
  See also Class Action

Civil Procedure, Federal Rules of, 21, 48, 49, 67, 68

Civil Rights, 28, **45–46**
  See also Gay and Lesbian Rights

Civil Rights Act (1964), 18, 19, 84–86

Civil Rights Attorney's Fees Awards Act (1976), 28, 29

Civil Service, **46–48**

Civil Service Reform Act (1978), 46–48

Claiborne, Dennis, 120–121

Clapper, James R., Jr., 82–83

Clapper v. Amnesty International USA (2013), 82–83

Class Action, **48–51**
  antitrust and arbitration suits, 20, 24, 48–49
  privacy suits, 189
  securities fraud suits, 126–127

Class Action Fairness Act (2005), 51

Class arbitration, 20, 24–25

Class certification, 48, 49, 51, 126–127

Classified information
  freedom of information requests, 195, 221–223
  leaks, 164–166

Clay, Eric, 19

Clean Air Act (1972), 88, 90

Clean Water Act (1972), 58, 59, 89, 91–92

Cleland, John, 42

Clementi, Tyler, 145–146

Climate change-related regulation, 91

Clinoril (medication), 191

Clinton, Bill, 187, 220

Cloer, Melissa, 27–28

Closely held corporations, 56–57

Co-workers, 84, 85
  See also Work environment

Coercion, 103–104, 111

Cole, R. Guy, Jr., 13–15

Cole-Rivera, Marianna, 156–157

Coleman, Ryan and Laetitia, 128–129

Coleman v. Thompson (1991), 144

Collective actions vs. class actions, 50

Collective bargaining
  Fair Labor Standards Act, 50
  rights, 157
  sports, 213
  state ballot measures, 155

Colleges and universities
  admissions committees, 14
  affirmative action, 13–15
  child abuse, 42–43

hate crimes, 145–146

Collette, William, 156

Collier, Sean, 218

Colorado
  marijuana laws, 73–75
  marriage law, 133

Columbia Christians for Life, 28

Comcast Corp., 48–49

Comcast Corp. v. Behrend (2013), 48–49

Commercial speech, 224

Common-fund doctrine, 94, 95

Common-law rule, 59, 104

Communications regulation, 106–108

Competency
  forced medication, trials, 25, 26
  mentally incompetent defendants, 22–24, 26, 174
  right to counsel, 23

Computer hackers, 165

Concealed weapons, 196–199, *199*

Conception, human, 9

Concerted activity, 157

Concussion injuries, 212

Confessions, murder, 143, 209

Congress of the United States, **51–53**
  agencies and legislative authority, 106–107
  agriculture oversight, 15
  block grant funds, 11
  campaign finance investigations, 80
  Defense of Marriage Act, 136
  estate planning systems, 100, 101
  gun control, 138, 139, 169
  military oversight, 167, *167*
  NGO appropriations, 112, 113
  obstruction, 58
  partisanship, 116
  patent legislation, 181, 184
  population and representatives, 231
  recess appointments, 187–188
  Senate Armed Services Committee, 167, *167*
  student loan interest rates, 77–78
  See also specific legislation

Congressional redistricting, 231–232

Connecticut Retirement, 72, 126–127

"Conscience claims," 35–36

Consent
  evidence gathering, 121
  medical procedures, 108–109
  recording and eavesdropping, 117–118

Consolidated and Further
   Continuing Appropriations Act
   (2013), 181
Conspiracy, **53–55**
   guilty pleas, 65–66
   terrorism, 220
   withdrawal, 59–60
Consumer Finance Protection
   Bureau, 78
Consumer Product Safety Act
   (1972), 57
Consumer Product Safety
   Improvement Act (2008), 57
Consumer protection
   counterfeit goods, 56–57
   drugs and medications, 72–73
   laws, 57, 186
   product liability cases,
      191–193
Contador, Alberto, 211
Content-based restrictions
   balance and fairness, 6
   content neutrality, 118, 119, 129
   protest signs, 28–29, 114, 129
Contraception. *See* Birth Control
Contracts
   arbitration, 20, 24, 25
   ERISA plans, 95
Controlled Substances Act (1970),
   149–150
Copyright, **55–56**
Copyright Act (1976), 55, 56, 57
Copyright exhaustion, 55
Coram nobis, 61
Corbett, Tom, 43
Cordray, Richard, 80
Corporate liability
   Alien Tort Statute, 150–151
   criminal acts, 58–59
Corporate power
   antitrust cases, 21, 22
   elections, 81
Cost-sharing
   benefit plans, 94, 95
   health insurance birth control,
      36
*Costco Wholesale Corporation v.
   Omega* (2013), 55, 56
Cote, Denise, 54, 55
Cotton seeds, 180
Counseling, birth control, 2, 36
Counterfeiting, **56–57**
Court-martials, 167
Courtroom behavior, 146
Covenants not to sue, 228
Cox, Fred B., 129
Crandell, Chester, 87–88
Crawford, Amanda J., 88
Credit card companies and
   agreements, 20, 21

Credit card processing, 208
Crime rates and gun availability,
   139, 140
Crimes of conviction, 220–221
Criminal Law, **57–60**
   ex post facto laws, 101–103
   state law examples, 70–71
Criminal Procedure, **60–66**
   drugs arrests, 62–63, 120–123,
      123–124, 195
   Federal Rule of, 65, 185
   plain error, 185
   state law examples, 71, 121
Crowell & Moring (Law firm),
   159–160
Cruel and unusual punishment,
   39–40
Cruickshank, Gordon, 53
Crump, Catherine, 196
Cruz-Moore, Lydia, 156–157
Cudahy, Richard, 17–18
Cuello, Sonia, 79
Curley, Tim, 42, 43
Curtilage, homes, 123, 124
Custody
   adoption, 105–106, 131–132
   gay and lesbian couples,
      131–132
   kidnapping, 153–154
Cyberbullying, 145–146, 157
Cyclists, 210–212, *211*

D

Daiichi Sankyo, 73
Dan's City Used Cars v. Pelkey
   (2013), 185–186
The Dark Knight Rises (2012),
   173–174
Davila, Anthony, 65–66
D'Avino, Rachel, 138, 168
Davis, Saundra, 85
Davis, Steven, 35
D.C. Circuit Court of Appeals
   civil rights cases, 45–46
   civil service cases, 47
   criminal cases, 60
   environmental law cases, 90, 91
   limitations cases, 161
   presidential powers, 186–188
   tobacco cases, 223–226, 228
   voting rights cases, 234
DEA. *See* U.S. Drug Enforcement
   Administration (DEA)
Deadly force, 172
Death penalty. *See* Capital
   Punishment
Debt, student loans, 77–78
Debt collectors, 67–68
Debtor and Creditor, **67–68**

*Decker v. Northwest Environmental
   Defense Center* (2013), 88–90
Deepwater Horizon BP oil spill
   (2010), 58–59
Defalcation (bankruptcy law),
   33–34
Defamation suits, 170, 172, 213
Defense of Marriage Act (1996),
   135–137
Delays, trials, 209–210
Demonstrations and protests.
   See Public protests
Dennis, James, 2
Depakote (medication), 72
Department of Justice, **68–70**
   conspiracy and price-fixing
      cases, 54–55
   counterfeiting cases, 56–57
   criminal cases, 58
   Defense of Marriage Act,
      135–136
   environmental cases, weigh-in,
      91
   environmental crimes, 58
   hate crime cases, 173
   investigations, 68–70, *69*, 73
   terrorism detainee information
      requests, 221–222
   voting rights, 234, 235, 236
Departments of Motor Vehicles
   (DMV), 6, 31, 188–189, 235
Deportation
   defendants' risks and
      understanding, 61–62
   drug offenses, 149
   hate crimes perpetrators, 146
Descamps, Matthew, 203–204
Descamps v. United States (2013),
   203–204
Design-defect product liability
   laws, 192
Destruction of evidence, 122, 124,
   125
Detainee Treatment Act (2005),
   45–46
Detainees, military, 45–46, 83,
   219, 221–223
Detention, search procedures,
   121–123
Development and construction
   projects, 12, 53, 83, 84
Dewey & LeBoeuf law firm, 34–35
DiCarmine, Stephen, 35
Dicta, 5
Dictionary Act, 135
Diplomatic cables, 165, 166
Directed verdict, 70, 71
Disabled persons
   Americans with Disabilities Act,
      17–19

birth-related injuries,
settlements, 163–164
Disaster relief funding, 53
Disbarment, 159–160
Discovery rule, 199, 200–201
Discretionary relief, 149
Dishonorable discharge, 167, 207
Disparate treatment, 133, 134
District of Columbia v. Heller
(2008), 137, 196, 197–198, 198
Disturbing the peace, 28
Divorce
child custody, 44
estate planning, 100–101
same-sex couples, 131
Dixon, Jay, 35–36
DNA, 176–177, *177*
collection and evidence, 63–65,
64
and gene patenting, 176–178
"Doe, John" cases
civil rights, 45–46
sex offenders, 205–206
Dolan v. City of Tigard (1994), 84
Doping scandals, 210–212, *211*
Double Jeopardy, **70–71**
Drain, Steve, 117
Drivers, getaway cars, 141–142,
201–202
Drivers' licenses and rights, 29–31,
188–189
Driver's Privacy Protection Act
(1994), 31–32, 188, 189
Driving while intoxicated, 124–125
Drug cartels, 69–70
Drug Price Competition and
Patent Term Restoration Act
(1984), 181–182, 183
Drug rehabilitation, in sentencing,
185
Drug-sniffing dogs, 62–63,
123–124
Drugs and Narcotics, **71–75**
criminal law cases, 59–60
criminal procedure cases,
62–63, 120–123
defendants' immigration
statuses, 61
immigration and trafficking,
149–150
legalization, 73–75, *74*
medication labeling and use, 7,
8, 36–38, 72–73, 191–193
medication safety and efficacy,
126, 127
medication safety and liability,
73, 191–193
overcharging, 72
patents, 181–183
side effects, 191

taxation, 75
trade and related violence,
69–70, 121
Due process rights and violations
abortion, 2
criminal law, 59
Defense of Marriage Act, 136
employment, 46
freedom of speech, 128,
129–130
right to counsel, 23
sex offenses, 204–205
See also Fourteenth
Amendment

E

E-books, 54–55
Eavesdropping laws, 117–119
Economic recessions, 34–35
EdFund, 67
Education
employees and unions, 155–156
funding, 53
Education Law, **77–78**
Effective-vindication rule
(arbitration), 21
Egyptian politics, 220
Eighth Amendment, civil rights
claims, 46
Eighth Circuit Court of Appeals
Americans with Disabilities Act,
17
civil service cases, 47–48
class action cases, 51
Establishment Clause cases,
95–97
First Amendment cases, 113–114
freedom of speech cases, 129
Election, 2012
education topics, 78
gun control, 138
poll access, 119
state ballot measures, 87
Texas redistricting, 231, 232
Election Assistance Commission
(EAC), 147, 148–149
Election Law, **78–81**
redistricting, 231–232
voter registration, 147–149
Election officials, 81, 119, 236
Elections, history, 120
Elections Clause, U.S.
Constitution, 147, 148
Electrocution, 39
Electronic Communications
Privacy Act (1986), 195
Electronic Surveillance, **81–83**
GPS use, 195–196

webcam use, 145–146
Eleventh Circuit Court of Appeals
admiralty and maritime law
cases, 12, 13
antitrust law cases, 22, 182, 183
bankruptcy cases, 34
child custody cases, 43–45
criminal procedure cases, 66
Embezzlement, 33, 34
Emergency management laws,
51–53
Eminent Domain, **83–84**
Emissions standards and rules,
90–91
Employee benefits. *See* Health
insurance; Pension funds;
Retirement plans
Employee communication,
156–157
Employee Retirement Income
Security Act (1974), **94–95**
Employer liability
bankruptcy, 35
discrimination, 18, 19, 84–85
Employment Discrimination,
84–86
affirmative action programs,
13, 15
age, 19, 47–48
Civil Rights Act, 18, 19, 84–86
civil service, 46–48
disability, 18–19
racial, 85
seniority programs, 17, 18
Employment law
Americans with Disabilities Act,
17–19
civil service, 46–48
See also Employment
Discrimination; Labor Law
Endangered species, 53
Enemy combatants, 46, 219, 220
English language proficiency, and
election law, 78–80
"English Rule," litigation costs, 27
"Enhanced interrogation
techniques," 221–223
Enhanced sentencing, 202–204
Environmental cleanup projects,
58–59
Environmental groups, 88, 90
Environmental Law, **86–94**
BP oil spill, criminal acts,
58–59
fines, 58, 59
international, 150–151
lands, and eminent domain,
83–84
Environmental Protection Agency
(EPA), 90

rules challenges cases, 90–91
rules interpretations cases, 88–90
Equal Employment Opportunity Commission (EEOC)
Americans with Disabilities Act, 17–18
civil service discrimination cases, 46–48
employment discrimination cases, 85–86
Equal protection
abortion clinics, 2, 3, 4
affirmative action, 13, 14
parenthood, 214
See also Fourteenth Amendment
Equal Protection Clause, US Constitution
automobile laws, 30
gay and lesbian rights cases, 133–134, 135
physical access rights, 119
Equitable tolling, 160, 161
ERISA (Employee Retirement Income Security Act (1974)), **94–95**
Erythropoietin, 211
Escamilla, Juan Carlos, 79
Escrow funds, 159–160
Espionage, 164–166
Espionage Act (1917), 164, 166
Establishment Clause, **95–100**
See also First Amendment
Estate Planning, **100–101**
Estate taxes, 100, 135, 136
Evans, Lamar, 70–71
Evans v. Michigan (2013), 70
Evictions, 12
Evidence
concealing/destroying, 122, 124, 125
gathering methods, and Fourth Amendment, 62–65, 121, 123–124, 195–196
new, and "actual innocence," 143–144
tampering, 145, 146, 222
George Zimmerman case, 171, 172
Ex Post Facto Laws, **101–103**
Executions. *See* Capital Punishment
Executive orders, 222
Executive privilege, 68–70
Experience and logic test, 120
Experimental-use patents, 183–184
Expert testimony
language proficiency and election law, 79

medical malpractice, 163
murder cases, 172
Exports, counterfeit goods, 56–57
Extortion, **103–104**

F

FA Technology Ventures, 103–104
Facebook
support pages, 166
usage, and labor law, 156–157
Failure-to-warn claims, 192–193
Fair Credit Reporting Act (2012), 208
Fair Debt Collection Practices Act (1977), 67–68
Fair Labor Standards Act (FLSA) (1938), 49, 50
Fair notice, 129–130
Falk, Ken, 116
False Claims Act (1863), 210, 212
False pretenses, 189
Family Law, **105–106**
gay and lesbian families, 131–132
surrogacy, 214–215
Family planning services and funding, 2–3, 8–9, 10–11
Family Smoking Prevention and Tobacco Control Act (2009), 223, 224–225, 226
Fargo, North Dakota, 95–97
Father-child relationships, 105, 106, 131–132, 214
FDA. *See* U.S. Food and Drug Administration (FDA)
Federal Arbitration Act (1925), 19–21, 24, 25
Federal Aviation Administration Authorization Act (1994), 86–87, 185–186
Federal Bankruptcy Code, 33
Federal benefits, 135–137
Federal budget, 52
Federal Bureau of Investigation (FBI)
Boston Marathon bombing investigation, 218, 219–220
budget/staffing, 53
"Operation Fast and Furious," 69
search and seizure cases, 195–196
Federal Cigarette Labeling and Advertising Act (1965), 226–228
Federal Communications Commission, **106–108**
Federal courts
admiralty and maritime law, 12
claims, 16, 27

conspiracy cases, 54–55, 60
criminal procedure, 61, 62
See also specific appeals courts
Federal Drivers Privacy Protection Act (1994), 30
Federal Emergency Management Agency (FEMA), 53
Federal employees
benefits and estate planning, 100–101
civil service, 46–48
tort liability, 109–110
Federal Employees' Group Life Insurance Act (1954), 100–101
Federal firearms licensees, 137, 140
Federal Forms, voter registration, 147–149
Federal Hazardous Substances Act (1960), 57
Federal lands
funding and cuts, 52–53
sovereignty and jurisdiction, 87–88
Federal Maritime Lien Act (1910), 11
Federal Rule of Criminal Procedure, 65, 185
See also Criminal Procedure
Federal Rules of Civil Procedure, 21, 48, 49, 67, 68
Federal Sentencing Guidelines, 65, 101, 102
Federal Tort Claims Act, **108–110**
Federal Trade Commission Act (1914), 182
Federal Trade Commission v. Phoebe Putney Health System, Inc. (2013), 21–22
Fertilization stage, conception, 9
Fetal viability, 4–5, 8, 9, 10
Feudale, Barry, 43
Fiduciary duty, 33–34
Fifteenth Amendment, 233
Fifth Amendment, **110–112**
agricultural law, 15, 16, 17
double jeopardy, 70–71
Due Process Clause, 23, 201
eminent domain, 83, 84
equal liberty, 136
right to counsel, 23
Fifth Circuit Court of Appeals
abortion cases, 1–4, 8–9
FCC cases, 107, 108
gun control cases, 137
habeas corpus cases, 145
immigration cases, 149
plain-error rule, 185
sex offender cases, 206–207

Financial investigations, 35
Firearm use, sentencing, 201–202
Firearms industry, 138
Firefighter funerals, 117
Firings, 156–157, 166
First Amendment, **112–120**
   abortion access cases, 2–3
   advertising, 158
   audio recordings, 117–119
   campaign contributions/
      election law, 80–81
   government and hybrid speech,
      5–7
   press access, 40–42, 119–120
   public protests, 28–29,
      113–115, 116–117
   Second Amendment
      applications, 197
   social media usage rights, 205,
      206
   tattoo parlors protection,
      127–129
   tobacco industry, 223, 224, 227
   See also Establishment Clause
First sale doctrine (copyright),
   55–56
Flaum, Joel, 206
Fleissig, Audrey, 35–36
Florida
   admiralty and maritime law,
      12–13
   criminal procedure, 62–63
   environmental law, 92
   Fourth Amendment cases,
      123–124
   land/water management, and
      eminent domain, 83–84
   lawyer advertising rules,
      158–159
   murder cases, 169–173
   sentencing guidelines, 102–103
Florida v. Harris (2013), 62–63
Florida v. Jardines (2013), 123–124
Flynn, Terence, 187
Fong Foo v. United States (1962),
   70, 71
Food, Drug, and Cosmetic Act
   (1938), 191–192
Food safety, 53
Football programs
   child abuse, 42–43
   scandals and sports law,
      212–214, *213*
Forced medication, 25, 26
Foreclosure, 12
Foreign intelligence collection,
   81–82
Foreign Intelligence Surveillance
   Act (FISA) (1978), 81–82
Foreign Intelligence Surveillance

Court, 82
Forensic sciences, 63–64, *64*
Foreseeability concept, 22
Forests, resources, 53, 87–88,
   89–90
Fossil fuel emissions, 90–91
Fourteenth Amendment
   abortion and, 2, 4, 38
   defense methods, 59
   Due Process Clause, 38, 59,
      129–130, 198, 201, 204, 205
   searches, cellphones, 121
Fourth Amendment, **120–125**
   civil rights cases, 46
   core values, 123–124
   evidence collection, 63–64, 65
   Foreign Intelligence
      Surveillance Act and, 81–82
   search and seizures, 30, 46, 62,
      64, 82, 120–121, 195
Fourth Circuit Court of Appeals
   attorney's fees cases, 29
   Establishment Clause cases,
      97–98
   privacy cases, 189
   sentencing cases, 202
   speech types consideration, 6–7
Fox, James, 5
Franklin, Craig A., 167
Fraternal Order of Eagles, 96
Fraud, **125–127**
   bankruptcy law, 33, 34
   ex post facto laws and, 102–103
   guilty pleas, criminal
      procedure, 61–62, 65–66
   by lawyers, 159–160
   Medicaid funds, 80, 81
   securities, 59, 72, 126–127,
      200–201
   voting, risks, 119, 120,
      235–236
Fraud-on-the-market, 126
"Free-tonnage" goods, 15–16
Freedom of Information Act
   (1966), 196, 221–223
Freedom of Information Act
   (Virginia), 190–191
Freedom of information laws,
   188–189, 190–191, 196
Freedom of information requests,
   189, 195, 221–223
Freedom of Speech, **127–130**
   lawyers, advertising, 158
   non-governmental
      organizations, 112–113
   organizational, 3, 4
   tattoo parlors, 127–129
   See also First Amendment;
      Time, place, and manner
      regulations

Freedom of the press, 40–42
Freeh, Louis, 42–43
Freeport-McMoRan Copper &
   Gold, Inc., 91
*Friends of the Earth, Inc. v. Laidlaw
   Environmental Services (TOC),
   Inc.* (2000), 229
FTC. *See* U.S. Federal Trade
   Commission (FTC)
FTC v. Actavis, Inc. (2013),
   182–183
Fujita, Scott, 213, 214
Fulton, Sybrina, 172
Funerals, picketing, 113–115,
   116–117

G

Gabelli, Marc, 200
Gabelli Funds, L.L.C., 200–201
Gabelli v. SEC (2013), 199–201
Galloway, Susan, 99
Gavin, Thomas, 43
Gay and Lesbian Rights, **131–137,**
   133
   child custody, 131–132
   history, 133
   marriage, 132–135, *133*
Gene mutation, 176–177, 178, 181
General Revenue Corporation,
   67–68
Generic drugs, 73, 181–182,
   191–193
Genesis HealthCare, 50
*Genesis HealthCare Corp. v.
   Symczyk* (2013), 49–50
Genetically patented seeds,
   178–179, 180–181
Genetics, human, 176–178, 181
Georgia
   hospital authorities, 21–22
   immigration and drug laws,
      149–150
Georgia-Pacific, 89–90
*Georgia-Pacific West v. Northwest
   Environmental Defense Center*
   (2013), 88–90
Gestational age, 4–5, 8, 9, 37
Giffords, Gabrielle, 25–26, 138
Gillibrand, Kirsten E., 167
Ginsburg, Ruth Bader
   antitrust law cases, 49
   child custody cases, 44, 45
   class action cases, 49, 50
   copyright cases, 56
   criminal procedure cases, 62,
      65, 66
   employment discrimination
      cases, 85–86
   ERISA cases, 95

Federal Tort Claims Act cases, 109
Fifth Amendment cases, 112
fraud cases, 127
gay and lesbian rights cases, 134, 136
habeas corpus cases, 144, 145
immigration cases, 150
international law cases, 151
limitations cases, 161
plain-error rule, 185
preemption cases, 186
privacy cases, 189
product liability cases, 192
sentencing cases, 202
sex offender cases, 207
speedy trial cases, 210
voting rights cases, 234, 235
GlaxoSmithKline, 71, 72
Glenn, Martin, 35
Global Fund to Fight AIDS, Tuberculosis and Malaria, 112
Global positioning system (GPS), 195–196
Goldman, Ronald, 171
Gonzales, Ernest, 22–24
Gonzalez, Zenaida, 170–171
Gonzalez Act, 109
Goodell, Roger, 212–214
Google Android OS, 176
Gossip, 156–157
Gottschall, Joan B., 61–62
Government Data Collection and Dissemination Practices Act (Virginia), 190, 191
Government employees. *See* Federal employees
Government speech, 6–7
Government websites, 208
GPS devices, 195–196
Grable & Sons Metal Products v. Darue Engineering (2005), 184
Graduated drivers license laws, 29–31
Graham, Lindsey, 219
Grainery, Inc., 102
Gramm-Rudman-Hollings Act (1985), 52
Grand Canyon National Park, 87–88, *88*
Grant, Larry, 128
Graphic messages
cigarette packaging, 223–224, 228
cigarette point-of-sale purchasing, 226–227
protest signs, 28–29
Gratz v. Bollinger (2003), 13
Greece, New York, 98–99
Greenaway, Joseph, 119–120

Greenhouse gas emissions rules, 90
Griffin, Richard, 187
Group prayer, 115–116
Guantanamo Bay, Cuba, detention facility, 82, 219
Guilty pleas
classified information leaks, 164, 166
criminal procedure, 61–62, 65–66
encouragement, 65, 66
plain-error rule, 185
Gulf of Mexico BP oil spill (2010), 58–59
Gun Control, **137–140,** 169
groups, 25, 26, 138–139
illegal firearms trafficking, 69–70
protests supporting, *139*
Gun economy and lobby, U.S., 138–139
Gun ownership, 139
"Gun walking," 68–70
Gunn, Jerry, 183–184
Gunn v. Minton (2013), 183–184
Gunter, Jim, 39–40
Guttmacher Institute, 8, 36
Guy, John, 172

H

Habeas Corpus
cases, **141–145**
competency, defendants, 22, 23
Habitual offenders laws, 202–204
Hachette, 54
Hagel, Chuck, 167
Hague Convention on the Civil Aspects of International Child Abduction, 43, 44
Hales, Lynne, 43–45
Hamilton, Tyler, 211
Hammond, Natalie, 138, 168
Handgun sales, 137, 140
Harassment
debt collection, 67, 68
sexual, 167–168
workplace, 84–86, 156–157, 167–168
Hardship, demonstrating
abortion clinics, 1, 2, 9
employees with disabilities cases, 17–18
Hargrove, Anthony, 213
Harlan, John, 34
Harmless error rule, 66
HarperCollins, 54
Harrell, Jr., William, 158
Harris, Clayton, 62–63
Harris v. United States (2002), 201, 202

Hatch-Waxman Act (1984), 181–182, 183
Hate Crimes, **145–146**
murder as, 173
petitions, group designations, 117
Havrilla, Rebekah, *167*
Hayes, James T., 57
Hazardous products, 56–57
Headstart Advisers, Ltd., 200
Health care provider choice, 9, 10–11
Health departments
funding, 53
licensing power, 1–2, 9
Health insurance
birth control coverage, 35–36
doctor billing, 72
Employee Retirement Income Security Act (1974), 94–95
payment reimbursements, 94–95, 160–161, 163–164
Health warnings, tobacco, 223–225, 226–228
"Heat of passion," 59
Hedge funds, 200
Heightened scrutiny, 118, 197–198
Helms, Susan J., 166–167
Henderson, Amarcion, 185
Henderson, Rodney, 143
Henderson v. United States (2013), 185
Hepatitis vaccinations, 27
Herbert, Gary, 88
Herbicide-resistant seeds, 178–179, 180–181
Hickenlooper, John, 73–74
High-risk prison populations, 115–116
Hillman, Jacqueline, 100–101
Hillman, Warren, 100–101
Hillman v. Maretta (2013), 100–101
Hispanics United of Buffalo, Inc., 156–157
HIV/AIDS organizations, 112–113
Hobbs, Ray, 39–40
Hobbs Act (1946), 103, 104
Hochsprung, Dawn, 138, 168
Hoens, Helen, 215
Holder, Eric, 58, 69, 82, 234
Hollingsworth v. Perry (2013), 133
Hollowell, Steven, 101–103
Holmes, James, 138, 169, *173,* 173–174
Homicide
cases, 110–111
gun risks, 139
See also Murder

Homosexual marriage. *See* Same-sex marriage

Homosexual rights. *See* Gay and Lesbian Rights

Homosexuality, public protests against, 113, 116–117

Honoring America's Veterans and Caring for Camp Lejeune Families Act (2012), 116

Horne, Marvin and Laura, 16

Horne v. Department of Agriculture (2013), 16

Horowitz, Michael, 69

Hospitals

antitrust cases, 21–22

reimbursement compensation, 160–161

Houseboats, 12–13

Howard, Marcia Morales, 158

Hulbert, Roger, 190–191

Human chains (protest method), 117

Human genetics, patenting, 176–178, 181

Human rights inquiries, 221–223

Humboldt Acquisition Corporation, 18–19

Hunter v. Erickson (1969), 14, 15

Hurricane Sandy (2012), 53

Husted, Jon, 80–81

"Hybrid" speech, 6, 7

Hyde Amendment (1977), 10

I

Idaho, 40–42

Identifying marks, 4

Identity theft, 188

Iglesias, Lourdes, 156–157

Illegal firearms trafficking, 68–70

Illinois

concealed weapons, 198–199, *199*

First Amendment cases, 117–119

Immigration, **147–150**

defendants' statuses, 61–62

states' policies, 88

Immigration and Naturalization Act (1952), 149

Immunities and privileges, 190–191

Immunity from litigation

bankruptcy cases, 35

government employees and officials, 46, 108, 109, 110, 208

Immunization programs, 27, 53

Imports, counterfeit goods, 56–57

In-camera hearings, 65, 66

In vitro fertilization, 214

Incest, 170

Incompetency, mental, 22–24, 25, 26, 174

Indian Child Welfare Act (1978), 105–106

Indiana

abortion funding, 9, 10–11

labor laws, 155

sex offender laws, 204–206

Individualized suspicion, 64

Industrial Stormwater Rule (EPA), 89–90

Ineffective counsel, 143–144, 145–146

Infertility, and surrogacy, 214–215

Infrastructure projects

funding, 53

land rights and eminent domain, 83

Infringement, patents, 175–176, 177, 178, 179, 180–182, 183, 184

Infringement, trademarks, 228–229

Initiative 502 (Washington, 2012), 74

Injury, purposeful, in NFL, 212–214, *213*

Insanity defense, 174

Intellectual property. *See* Counterfeiting; Patents; Trademarks

Intelligence statutes, 223

Interest rates, student loans, 77–78

Interference with a criminal investigation, 170

Interlocutory appeals, 71, 127, 151

Intermediate scrutiny review standard, 114, 115, 140, 224

Internal Revenue Code, 217

Internal Revenue Service (IRS)

estate taxes, 135

filing, 217

owings, bankruptcies, 170

International AIDS Vaccine Initiative, 112

International Brotherhood of Teamsters, 187

International Law, **150–151**

child abduction, 43, 44

copyright, 55–56

search and seizure, 195

taxation, 217–218

Interrogation

processes, 45, 46, 170

silence responses, 110–112

terrorists, 219–220, 221–223

Interstate commerce

environmental law, 87

medications, 191–192

water access, 92, 93, 94

Interstate compacts, 93–94

Invega (medication), 72

Inventions, 180, 181

See also Patents

Investment Advisers Act (1940), 200

Involuntary manslaughter, 58

iPhone, 175–176

Iraq War (2003-2011), 45, 46, 164–166

Issa, Darrell, 69

J

Jaffer, Jameel, 83

Jardines, Joelis, 123–124

Jeantel, Rachel, 172

Jepsen, George, 55

Job opportunities, Americans with Disabilities Act, 17–19

Johanns v. Livestock Marketing Ass'n (2005), 6–7

John Wiley & Sons, Inc., 55–56

Johnson & Johnson, 72

Johnson v. United States (1997), 185

Johnson v. Williams (2013), 141–142

"The Joker" (character), 173

Jolly, E. Grady, 3–4

Jones, Antoine, 195–196

Jones, Damarr, 143

Jones, Jack Harold, 39–40

Jones, Theodore T., 154

Judicial review

abortion cases, 2

arbitration cases, 25

Foreign Intelligence Surveillance Act, 83

limitations cases, 161

seeking, mixed cases, 47, 48

voter registration cases, 148–149

Judiciary Act (1789), 150

Juries

class action suits, 51

convictions, 143

criminal law cases, 60

high-profile acquittals, 170, 171–172

juror dismissal, 142

right to unanimous, 142

sentencing, 201–202, *202*

verdicts dismissed, military crime cases, 167

Jurisdiction

admiralty and maritime law, 11–13

agricultural law, 15, 16–17

gay and lesbian rights cases, 136–137
mixed cases, 47–48
patent cases, 183, 184
subject matter, 50, 51, 184, 208, 228–229
Just compensation, 15, 83, 84

K

Kagan, Elena
antitrust law cases, 20, 21, 49
arbitration cases, 25
civil service cases, 47, 48
class action cases, 49, 50
copyright cases, 56
criminal procedure cases, 62, 63, 65, 66
debtor and creditor cases, 68
eminent domain cases, 84
employment discrimination cases, 85–86
environmental law cases, 87
ERISA cases, 95
Fifth Amendment cases, 112
First Amendment cases, 113
gay and lesbian rights cases, 134, 136
habeas corpus cases, 144, 145
immigration cases, 150
international law cases, 151
patents cases, 178, 181
plain-error rule, 185
product liability cases, 192
sentencing cases, 202, 204
sex offender cases, 207
speedy trial cases, 210
Kaluza, Robert, 58
Kansas, 9
Kavanaugh, Brett, 236
Kebodeaux, Anthony, 207
Kedeshian, Claire, 57
Kelly, Linda, 42
Kelly, Mark, 25, 26, 138
Kennedy, Anthony
admiralty and maritime law cases, 12
antitrust law cases, 49, 182
class action cases, 49, 50
copyright cases, 56
criminal procedure cases, 65, 66
electronic surveillance cases, 83
environmental law cases, 90
ERISA cases, 95
FCC cases, 107
Fifth Amendment cases, 111
Fourth Amendment cases, 122–123
fraud cases, 127

gay and lesbian rights cases, 134, 136
habeas corpus cases, 144, 145
immigration cases, 150
international law cases, 151
Medicaid cases, 164
patent cases, 182
plain-error rule, 185
privacy cases, 189
sex offender cases, 207
trademark cases, 229
voter qualification cases, 149
Kessler, Jeffrey, 35
Kethledge, Raymond, 81
Kickbacks
lawyers, 159
state government officials and contractors, 80
Kidnapping, 43, 44, **153–154**
Kindle (e-reader device), 54–55
King, Alonzo Jay, 63–64
King, Daniel, *173*
King, Taya, 131–132
Kiobel, Esther, 150–151
Kiobel v. Royal Dutch Petroleum (2013), 150
Kirtsaeng, Supap, 55–56
Kirtsaeng v. John Wiley & Sons, Inc. (2013), 55–56
Kloeckner, Carolyn, 47
Kloeckner v. Solis (2012), 47–48
Knock-off products, 57
Knowles, Greg, 51
Koontz, Coy A., Sr., 83–84
Koontz v. St. Johns River Water Management District (2013), 83–84
Koster, Chris, 36
Kronk, Roy, 171
Krusinski, Jeffrey, 166–167

L

L.A. Confidential: Les Secrets de Lance Armstrong (Walsh and Ballester), 211
Labeling
cigarettes, 223–225, 226–228
drugs, 7, 8, 36–38, 191–193
generic drugs, 191, 192–193
Labor Law, **155–157**
protected speech and activities, 156–157
Right to Work laws, 155–156
Labor-Management Reporting and Disclosure Act (1959), 156
Labor unions, 155, 156, 187
Labour Party (UK), 217, 218
Lamictal (medication), 72
Lamo, Adrian, 165

Land-use permits, 83–84
Landis, Floyd, 211
Lanza, Adam, 138, 168–169
Lanza, Nancy, 138, 168–169
Larceny
bankruptcy law, 33
by lawyers, 159–160
Late term abortion, 8
Law enforcement
automobile-related, 31–32
citizen recording rights, 117–119
criminal procedure cases, 62–64, 65, 121
search warrant detention, 121–123
searches and seizures, 31–32, 62–65, 123–124, 195–196
tort claims, 110
Law firms
criminal lawyers, 159–160
lawyer advertising, 158–159
mergers and bankruptcy, 34–35
Law of nations, 150, 151
Lawrence v. Texas (2003), 133
Lawyers, **157–160**
advertising and solicitation rules, 158–159, 188–189
advice, and immigration status, 61–62
aiding terrorists, 220–221
appellate advocacy, 22, 23
attorney's fees, 26–29
civil rights cases, 28
complications, speedy trial, 209–210
court-appointed, and criminal procedure, 65, 66
crimes and disbarment, 159–160
ineffective counsel claims, 143–144, 145–146
legal malpractice, 183–184
Leaks, classified information, 164–166
Leases
antitrust issues, 21–22
patent development and, 183–184
Leavitt, Richard, 41–42
Lefemine, Steven, 28–29
Lefemine v. Wideman (2012), 28
Legalization of marijuana, 73–74, *74*
LeMond, Greg, 210
Leonard, Leo, 153–154
Lester, Kenneth R., Jr., 172
Lethal injection, 39–41
Levin, Carl, 167
Levin, Steven, 108–109

Levin v. United States (2013),
   108–109
Lewis, Alan, 160
Lewis, Brian, *167*
Lewis, Susan, 18–19
Lewis v. Continental Bank Corp.
   (1990), 50
Liability
   corporate, 58–59, 150–151
   employer, 18, 19, 35, 84–85
   medical malpractice, 109
   product, 191–193
   vicarious, 85
License plates, 5–6
Licensed characters, trademarks,
   57
Life insurance, 100–101
Life sentences without parole, 26,
   64, 143, 144
Limitations, **160–161**
Lincoln Law (1863), 210, 212
Lind, Denise, 164
Lindh, John Walker, 115–116
Liquidation, bankruptcy, 34–35
Literacy, English language
   election law, 78–80
   literacy tests, 233
Little Tucker Act (1887), 208
Livestrong (foundation), 210, 212
Location tracking, 195–196
Logging, 53, 87–88
Loomis, Mickey, 213, 214
Lopez v. Gonzales (2006), 149
Lorenzi, Thomas, 209
Lorillard Tobacco Co. v. Reilly
   (2001), 186
*Los Angeles County Flood Control
   District v. Natural Resources
   Defense Council, Inc.* (2013),
   91–92
Los Angeles Times, 166
Loughner, Jared Lee, 25–26
Louisiana
   abortion clinics laws, 1–2, 9
   BP oil spill, 2010, 58–59
   water resources, 93
Louisiana Capital Assistance
   Center, 209
Lozman, Fane, 12–13
*Lozman v. City of Riviera Beach,
   Florida* (2013), 12–13

M

Macmillan, 54, 55
Madigan, Lisa, 199
Magistrate judges, 65–66, 124
Mail fraud, 61
Mail voter registration, 147–148
Malfeasance, 159

Malpractice
   legal, 183–184
   medical, 108, 109, 163
Management and Storage of
   Surface Water (MSSW)
   permits, 83–84
Mandatory minimum sentencing,
   201–202
Manning, Bradley, 164–166, *165*
Manslaughter, in pollution cases,
   58
Maracich v. Spears (2013),
   188–189
Maretta, Judy, 100–101
Marijuana
   convictions, offense levels,
      149–150
   legalization, 73–75, *74*
   searches, 123
Marinas, 12
Maritime jurisdiction, federal,
   11–13
Market share
   monopoly tactics, 48
   smartphones, 176
Market timing, 200
Marketing
   agricultural commodities,
      15–16
   cigarettes, 227–228
   pharmaceuticals, 72–73
Marriage, defining, 133, 135, 137
Marsh v. Chambers (1983), 99
Martin, Trayvon, 171–173
Martinez v. Ryan (2012), 144, 145
Marx, Olivea, 67–68
*Marx v. General Revenue
   Corporation* (2013), 67–68
Maryland, public safety and
   criminal procedure, 63–65
Maryland v. King (2013), 63–64
Massachusetts, Fourth
   Amendment cases, 120–121
Massachusetts v. EPA (2007), 90
Material misrepresentation, fraud,
   126
Materiality, 126, 127
Maternity, 131–132, 214–215
Matsch, Richard P., 68
*Mayo Collaborative Services v.
   Prometheus Laboratories* (2010),
   178
Mayors Against Illegal Guns, 138,
   139
McBurney, Mark, 190–191
McBurney v. Young (2013),
   190–191
McCain, John, 219
McCaskill, Claire, 167
McCoy, BriGette, *167*

McCutchen, James, 94–95
McDonald v. Chicago (2010), 198
McKeague, David, 38
McMillan v. Pennsylvania (1986),
   201
McNeely, Tyler, 124–125
McQueary, Mike, 42, 43
McQuiggin v. Perkins (2013),
   142–144
Media access
   capital punishment, 40–42
   pharmaceutical industry, 71–72
   polling places, 119–120
   terrorism events, 218
Medicaid, 11, **163–164**
   abortion funding, 2–4, 8, 10–11
   cases, 163–164
   pharmaceutical pricing, 72
   providers, campaign
      contributions, 80–81
   reimbursement compensation,
      160–161, 163–164
   state funding totals, examples, 11
Medicaid Act, 9, 10, 11
Medical abortion, 7, 8, 10, 36–38
Medical malpractice, 108, 109,
   163
Medical marijuana, 74
Medicare
   pharmaceutical pricing, 72
   reimbursement compensation,
      160–161
Medication of prisoners, 25, 26
Meininger, Stephen, 171
Meldrum, Peter D., 181
Melloy, Joseph, 129–130
Merit Systems Protection Board
   (MSPB), 46–48
Mesa, Arizona, 128–129
Metatags, websites, 159
Methamphetamine, 62–63
Method of Execution Act
   (Arkansas, 2008), 39–40
Mexican drug cartels and
   violence, 69–70
Michigan
   affirmative action cases, 13–15
   civil procedure, 156
   double jeopardy, 70–71
   Right to Work Law, 155–156
Michigan State University,
   13–15
Michigan v. Summers (1981), 121,
   122–123
Middleton, Bryant, 122
Mifepristone (drug), 7, 8, 10, 37,
   38
Migratory Bird Treaty Act (1918),
   58
Military funerals, *117*

Military funerals, picketing, 113, 116–117
Military Law, **164–168**
  classified information, 164–166
  sexual assaults, 166–168, *167*
  torture and civil rights cases, 45–46
Military prosecutors, 166–167
Millbrook, Kim, 110
Millbrook v. United States (2013), 109–110
Minnesota v. Murphy (1984), 111
Minority voters, 231–232, 234–236
Minton, Vernon, 183–184
Miranda v. Arizona (1966), 219
Miranda warnings, 110, 111, 170, 219, 220
Miscarriages of justice exceptions, 143, 144
Misdemeanors, 149–150, 166, 205
Misoprostol (drug), 7, 37
Misrepresentation, business dealings, 35
Missouri
  birth control laws, 35–36
  First Amendment cases, 113–115, 129–130
  Fourth Amendment cases, 124–125
  funerals picketing, 113–115
Missouri v. McNeely (2013), 124–125
Mistrials, 111
Mitigating circumstances, 144–145
Mix, Kurt, 58
Mixed cases, 46–48
Moncrieffe, Adrian, 149–150
Moncrieffe v. Holder (2013), 149–150
Monopolies, 181
  broadcasting industry, 48
  credit card industry, 20, 21
  hospitals, 21–22
  pharmaceutical industry, 182
  publishing industry, 54
  seed patents, 179, 180–181
Monsanto, 178–179, *179,* 180–181
Monuments, religious, 95–97
Moore, Karen Nelson, 37–38
Moore, Michael, *199*
Mootness, 49–50, 228–229
Mortgage debt and defaults, 77, 78
Moss, Robert, 97–98
Mother-child relationships, 131–132, 214–215
Motor vehicle accidents, 29, 31
Moving Ahead for Progress in the 21st Century Act (2012), 77

Mubarek, Hosni, 220
Mueller, Robert, 196
Mullaney v. Wilbur (1975), 59
Multiple sclerosis (MS), 27
Municipal separate storm-sewer systems, 92
Murder, **168–174**
  assassinations, 25–26
  confessions, 143, 209
  convicts, appellate advocacy, 22–23
  defenses, 59
  felony-murder rule, 141, 142
  former suspects, 169–171
  habeas corpus cases, 141–142, 143–144
  mass shootings, 26, 70, 138, 168–169, *169,* 173–174
  media spectacles, 169–173
  threats, 153, 154
  See also Homicide
Murphy, Anna Marie, 138, 168
Murphy, Dianna, 114, 115
Muslim prayer, 115–116
Mutual funds, 200
Mutual Pharmaceutical, 192–193
Mutual Pharmaceutical Company v. Bartlett (2013), 191–193
Myerscough, Sue E., 198
Myriad Genetics, 177, 178, 181

N

NAACP, *233*
Narcotics. *See* Drugs and Narcotics
NASDAQ, 183
National Abortion Federation, 10
National Association of Securities Dealers, Inc., 183
National Center for Injury Control and Prevention, 139
National Childhood Vaccine Injury Act (1986), 27, 28
National Collegiate Athletic Association (NCAA), 42, 43
National Environmental Development Association, 90–91
National Football League, 212–214, *213*
National Institutes of Health, 139
National Labor Relations Act (1935), 156, 157
National Labor Relations Board (NLRB), 156, 187, 188
National parks, 87–88, *88*
National Pollutant Discharge Elimination System (NPDES) permits, 89

National Rifle Association (NRA), 137, 138–139, 169
National Right to Life, 8
National security
  domestic terrorism, 218–220
  international terrorism, 221–223
  leaks of classified information, 164–166
National Security Act (1947), 223
National Security Agency (NSA), 82
National Voter Registration Act (1993), 147–149
Native American assistance programs, 53
Native Americans, family law cases, 105–106
Natural disasters
  emergency management laws, 52, 53
  relief programs, 53
  trial delays, 209
Natural Resource Defense Council (NRDC), 91, 92
Natural resources
  purpose, debate, 88
  revenue generation and use, 53, 87–88
  scarce, use, 92–93
Navigable waters, 89, 92
Navy Criminal Investigative Service (NCIS), 45
NBC, 172
Neal v. Clark (1878), 34
Necessary and Proper Clause, U.S. Constitution, 207
Neder v. United States (1999), 103–104
Negligence
  BP oil spill, 2010, 58
  legal malpractice, 183, 184
  medical, 108, 109
  sports, 212
  tort claims, 108, 109, 110
  work environments, 84, 85, 110
Nelson, Debra, 172
New Hampshire, 186, 192–193
New Jersey
  automobile laws, 29–31
  surrogate motherhood, 214–215
New Mexico, 131–132
New Orleans Saints, 212–214, *213*
New York
  disbarment, 159–160
  Establishment Clause cases, 98–99
  gay and lesbian rights, 135, 136
  gun laws, 196–198
  kidnapping, 153–154
  tobacco, health warnings, 226–228

New York City Board of Health, 226

New York v. Quarles (1984), 219

Newspapers
    access rights, and First Amendment, 119–120
    leaked information policy, 165, 166
    military members' crimes reporting, 166–167

Newtown, Connecticut, school shootings (2012), 26, 138, 139, 168–169, *169*

Niemeyer, Paul, 98

Nigeria, petroleum extraction and exploitation, 150–151

Nike, Inc., 228–229

911 calls, 172

Ninth Circuit Court of Appeals
    abortion cases, 4–5, 9
    agricultural law, 15–17
    appellate advocacy cases, 23
    assassination cases, 26
    capital punishment cases, 40–42
    citizenship and election law, 147, 148
    environmental law cases, 87, 89, 91, 92
    Federal Tort Claims Act cases, 109, 110
    fraud cases, 126, 127
    freedom of speech cases, 128
    habeas corpus cases, 142
    immigration, 147, 148
    sentencing cases, 203

Noel Canning v. National Labor Relations Board (2013), 187–188

Nollan v. California Coastal Commission (1987), 84

Non-steroidal anti-inflammatory drugs, 191–193

Norquist, Grover, 139

North Carolina
    license plates, and government speech, 5–7
    Medicaid, 163–164

North Dakota, 9

Northwest Austin Municipal Utility District No. One v. Holder (2009), 234

Nucleotides, 176, 178

Nugent, Donald C., 80–81

O

Obama, Barack
    Defense of Marriage Act, 135–136
    executive privilege, 68–70
    gun control, 138, 139
    health care policy, 36
    on Trayvon Martin murder, 172–173
    military law, 167
    presidential powers, 186–188
    sequestration, budget, 52
    student loan policy, 77, *78*
    terrorism policy, 218, 219–220, 222, 223
    veterans policy, 116

Obstruction of justice
    BP oil spill, 2010, 58–59
    child abuse cases, 42
    terrorism cases, 221

Occupational Safety and Health Administration (OSHA), 53

O'Connor, Sandra Day, 148

"Off-label" medication use
    medical abortion, 7, 8, 36–38
    medications, pharmaceutical marketing, 72

Ohio
    abortion laws, 36–38, *37*
    campaign finance law, 80–81

Oil spills, 58–59

Oklahoma
    abortion laws, 7, 8, 9, 10
    water resources and environmental laws, 92–94

Oliver, John, 116

Olympic sports and athletes, 210, 212

O'Mara, Mark, 172

Omnibus Crime Control and Safe Streets Act (1968), 137, 140

Open Meetings Act (Michigan, 1976), 155

"Open shop" free labor, 155

Operating systems (OS), 175, 176

"Operation Castaway" (Florida), 70

"Operation Fast and Furious" (Department of Justice), 68–70, *69*

"Operation Wide Receiver" (Department of Justice), 69

Oregon
    marijuana laws, 74, 75
    timber, 89–90

O'Toole, George A., Jr., 220

Outpatient abortion facilities, 1–2, 9

Outpatient Abortion Facility Licensing Law (Louisiana, 2001), 1–2, 9

Overbuilder theory, 48, 49

Owen, Priscilla, 2

Oxford Health Plans, 24, 25

Oxford Health Plans v. Sutter (2013), 24

P

Packaging, cigarettes, 223–225

Paddock Laboratories, 182

Padilla v. Kentucky (2010), 61–62

Pain, fetal, 4, 9

Paper balloting, 120

Parentage Act (New Jersey), 214, 215

Parental rights
    adoption, 105–106
    kidnapping charges, 153–154
    surrogacy, 214–215

Parking tickets, 31–32

Parks, national, 87–88, *88*

Parole, life sentences without, 26, 64, 143, 144

Partisanship, U.S. politics, 116, 155–156

Patent Act (1790), 177

Patent exhaustion, 178, 179, 181

Patents, **175–184**
    antitrust law and, 182–183
    biotech, 176–181
    invalidation, 183
    legal malpractice, 183–184
    software, 175–176

Paternal rights, 105–106, 131–132

Paterno, Joe, 42, 43

Pathfinder International, 112–113

Patient Protection and Affordable Care Act (2010), 36

Paxil (medication), 72

Pay.gov, 208

Payton, Sean, 213, 214

Pedraja, William, 123

Pelkey, Robert, 186

Penguin, 54, 55

Pennsylvania
    child abuse cases, 42–43
    First Amendment cases, 119–120

Pennsylvania State University, 42–43

Pension funds
    bankrupted firms, 35
    fund decisions, 103
    unions, 187
    See also Retirement plans

Performance-enhancing drugs, 210–212, *211*

Perjury
    child abuse cases, 42
    terrorism cases, 220, 221
    voter registration, 147, 148
    George Zimmerman case, 172

Perkins, Floyd, 143–144

Perry, Kris, *133*

Perry, Rick, 232

Perry v. Perez (2012), 232

Peterson, Laci, 171
Peterson, Scott, 171
Petroleum industry
    BP Gulf of Mexico oil spill
        (2010), 58–59
    international law, 150–151
Peugh, Marvin, 101–103
Peugh v. United States (2013),
    101–103
PG Publishing Company, 119–120
Pharmaceutical industry
    patents, 181–183
    product liability, 191–193
    suits and settlements, 71–73,
        126, 127
Phelps, Fred, 117
Phelps-Roper, Shirley and Megan,
    114
Phifer, Demetrius, 120–121
Phoebe Putney Health Systems,
    Inc., 21
Photo ID, 235–236
Photography
    9/11 evidence, 129
    rights, public spaces, 118
    terrorist detainee evidence,
        222–223
    See also Video recording
Phthalates, 57
Picketing
    abortion clinics, 28–29, 114
    funerals, 113–115, 116–117
Pinsky, Drew, 72
Piracy (copyright), 56
Piracy (sea terrorism), 151
Pittsburgh Post-Gazette, 119–120
Plain-Error Rule, **184–185**
Planned Parenthood, 8
    identifying mark, 4
    Indiana, 9, 10–11
    medical abortion, 36–38
    Ohio, 36–38
    Texas, 2, 3, *3,* 4, 8–9
Planned Parenthood v. Casey
    (1992), 5, 7, 9, 10
Plater, Zygmunt, 91
PLIVA, Inc. v. Messing (2011),
    192–193
Point-of-sale advertising, 226–228
Police forces. *See* Law
    enforcement
Police power, eminent domain, 84
Political action committees
    election law, 81
    gun control, 25, 138
Polling places, 119–120, 236
Ponzi schemes, 35
Population growth, 231
Port of Los Angeles, 86, 87

Posner, Richard, 199
*PPL Corp. v. Commissioner of
    Internal Revenue* (2013),
    217–218
Prado, Edward, 137, 140
Prayer
    prisoners' rights, 115–116
    public buildings and meetings,
        98–100
Preclearance, voting laws, 232,
    233, 234–235
Preemption, **185–186,** 192
    estate planning, 100
    Supremacy Clause, 86, 148, 149
    tobacco laws, 227
    water statutes, 92, 93
Preliminary injunctions
    abortion access cases, 2–3, 9,
        10–11
    capital punishment cases, 39,
        41–42
    election law cases, 80
    First Amendment cases,
        112–113, 119
    patent cases, 176
Premises searches, 121–122
Presidential elections. *See*
    Election, 2012
Presidential Powers, **186–188**
*Presumed Guilty—Casey Anthony:
    The Inside Story* (Baez), 170
Price-fixing cases, 54–55
Pricing
    agricultural commodities,
        15–16
    e-books, 54
    hospital services, 21
    pharmaceutical drugs, 181–182,
        183
    stocks, 126
Prior-restraint law, 197
Prisoners' rights
    appellate advocacy, 22–23
    correction of registry errors,
        204–205
    forced medication, 25, 26
    habeas corpus, 141, 142–145
    religious, 115–116
    tort claims, 109–110
Privacy, **188–189**
    conversational, 119
    DNA collection, 64, 65
    drivers and automobiles, 30,
        31–32, 188–189
    electronic surveillance, 82, 83,
        195–196
    First Amendment rights and,
        114–115, 117, 119
    invasion, and hate crimes,
        145–146

    medical patient information, 161
    searches and seizures, 30, 64,
        65, 196
    voting, 120
Private communications, 118–119
Private/governmental speech, 6
Privileges and Immunities, **190–191**
Pro bono legal services, 34
Pro-choice messages, 6, 7
Pro-life messages, 5–7, 28–29, 114
Probable cause
    intelligence collection, 82
    searches and seizures, 62–63,
        64, 65, 121, 122, 123–124,
        125, 196
Product Liability, **191–193**
Professionalism, employee com-
    munication, 156–157
Promotion, legal determinations,
    3–4
Promotions, marketing, 227
Proper cause requirements, 196,
    197, 198
Property rights
    agricultural law, 15, 16
    eminent domain, 83–84
    extortion, 103–104
    preemption, 185–186
Proposal 2 (Michigan, 2006),
    13–14, 15
Proposal 2 (Michigan, 2012), 155
Proposition 8 (California),
    132–134, *133*
Proposition 120 (Arizona), 87–88
Proposition 200 (Arizona), 148
Prostitution, 112–113
Protests and demonstrations. *See*
    Public protests
Provider Reimbursement Review
    Board, 161
Providing false information, 169,
    170
Provisional ballots, 236
Pseudoephedrine, 62–63
Psychiatric evaluations, 23, 26
Public access
    polling places, 119–120
    redistricting meetings,
        231–232
    stage government buildings,
        155–156
Public Citizen, 71–72
Public displays, religious content,
    95–97
Public health issues
    gun violence, 139
    sexually transmitted disease,
        11
    tobacco, 223–228
Public information, 190–191

Public interest
    communications infrastructure, 107
    media access, 40–42, 119–120
Public lands
    funding and cuts, 52–53
    sovereignty and jurisdiction, 87–88
Public protests
    funerals, picketing, 113–115, 116–117
    gun control support, *139*
    labor law, 155–156
    9/11 questions, 129–130
    policing, and recording of, 118
    pro-gun control, *139*
    pro-life demonstrations, 28–29, 114
Public schools, 97–98
Public speech
    First Amendment protections, 117–119, 130
    government-sponsored, 5–7
Publishing industry
    access rights, and First Amendment, 119–120
    price-fixing cases, 54–55
Punch, William, 159
Purchase-and-lease transactions, 21–22
Purdue, Bev, 6

Q

Qaeda, al-, 82
Quality King Distributors v. L'anza Research International (1998), 56
Quid pro quo theory, 180
Quitting smoking, 223, 224, 226
Quotas, affirmative action, 13
Quran, 115, 116

R

R. M. Stark & Co., 183, 184
Racial discrimination
    congressional redistricting, 231–232
    employment discrimination cases, 85–86
    voting, 233–235
Racial profiling, 172–173
Racially-motivated murder, 171, 172–173
Racketeer Influence and Corrupt Organizations Act (RICO) (1970), 59, 60, 225–226
Rahman, Abdel, 220–221
Rainey, David I., 58
Raisins, 15–16
Rambler, Terry, *148*

Ranbaxy Laboratories, Ltd., 73
Random House, 54
Rape, evidence, 64
Rational-basis standing, 30
Ravi, Dharun, 145–146
Real estate tax records, 190, 191
"Reasonable accommodation," employees with disabilities, 17–18
Rebuttable presumption
    fraud cases, 126
    habeas corpus cases, 141, 142
Recess appointments, 186–188
Recessions, economic, 34–35
Recording rights, 117–119
Red River and Red River Compact, 92–94
Red River Freethinkers, 96–97
Redistricting, 231–232
Redressability, 97
Regal Real Estate, 159, 160
Registries, sex offender, 204–205, 206–207
Rehabilitation Act (1973), 18, 19
Rehabilitative sentencing, 185
Reimbursement, medical expenses, 94–95, 160–161, 163–164
Reinhardt, Stephen, 41–42
Released Time Credit Act (South Carolina, 2007), 97
Religious content
    public displays, 95–97
    town meetings, 98–100
Religious education, 97–98
Religious employers, birth control, 36
Religious Freedom Restoration Act (1993), 115
Religious liberty
    prisoners' prayer rights, 115–116
    state bills, 35–36
Repayment plans, debt, 78
Reporting, sexual, 166, 167–168
Reporting rights
    capital punishment, 40–42
    polling places, 119–120
Reselling, copyright law, 55–56
Resentencing, 101–102, 221
"Reserve-tonnage" goods, 15–16
Resident aliens, 149–150
Restrainment, 153–154
Retaliation, 167
Retirement plans
    Employee Retirement Income Security Act (1974), 94–95
    estate planning, 100–101
    fraud cases, 72–73, 126–127
    fund decisions, 103

Retrials
    after mistrial, 111
    double jeopardy considerations, 70, 71
Retroactive application, rules, 61–62, 101–103
Reverse settlement agreements, 182, 183
Rhoades, Paul, 41
Right to counsel
    advice and consequences, 61, 62
    competence issues, 23
Right to speedy trial, 208–210
"Right to Work" laws, 155–156
Ripple, Kenneth, 31–32
Risperdal (medication), 72
R.J. Reynolds Tobacco Company, 223, 228
Robbery
    convicts, appellate advocacy, 22–23
    extortion, 103
    sentencing, 141–142, 201–202
Roberts, John
    antitrust law cases, 49, 182, 183
    child custody cases, 44, 45
    class action cases, 49, 50
    copyright cases, 56
    criminal procedure cases, 65, 66
    electronic surveillance cases, 83
    ERISA cases, 95
    FCC cases, 107, 108
    Fifth Amendment cases, 111
    First Amendment cases, 113
    gay and lesbian rights cases, 134, 136
    habeas corpus cases, 144, 145
    immigration cases, 150
    international law cases, 151
    Medicaid cases, 164
    patents cases, 182, 183, 184
    plain-error rule, 185
    privacy cases, 189
    Securities and Exchange Commission cases, 200, 201
    sentencing cases, 202
    sex offender cases, 207
    trademark cases, 229
    voting rights cases, 234
Roe v. Wade (1973), 5, 8–9
Rohrabacher, Dana, 75
Roll, John, 26
Romer v. Evans (1996), 133, 134
Rosenberg, Mark, 139
Roundup Ready seeds, 178–179, 180–181
Rousseau, Lauren, 138, 168
Royal Dutch Petroleum, 150–151

RU-486 (drug), 7, 8, 10, 36–38
Rules, criminal procedure, 61
Rumsfeld, Donald, 45–46
Rumsfeld v. Forum for Academic and Institutional Rights, Inc. (2006), 113
Rural education funding, 53
Rutgers University, 145–146
Ryan v. Gonzales (2013), 22–24

S

"Safe harbor" accommodations, 36
Safety laws
    federal and state authority, 86, 87
    motor vehicles, 29–31
    tattoo parlors, 127
Safety rules, sports, 212–214
Salinas, Genovevo, 111–112
Salinas v. Texas (2013), 110–111
Same-sex marriage, 131, 132–135, *133*
Samour, Carlos, Jr., 174
Samsung, 175–176, *176*
Sanctity of Eternal Rest for Veterans Act (2011), 116
Sanders, Joel, 35
Sandusky, Jerry, 42–43
Sandy Hook Elementary school shootings (2012), 26, 138, 139, 168–169, *169*
Scalia, Antonin
    antitrust law cases, 20, 49
    attorney's fees cases, 28
    child custody cases, 45
    class action cases, 49, 50
    copyright cases, 56
    criminal law cases, 60
    criminal procedure cases, 65, 66
    electronic surveillance cases, 83
    environmental law cases, 90
    ERISA cases, 95
    extortion cases, 103–104
    FCC cases, 107, 108
    Federal Tort Claims Act cases, 109
    First Amendment cases, 113
    Fourth Amendment cases, 123–124
    fraud cases, 127
    gay and lesbian rights cases, 134, 135, 136–137
    habeas corpus cases, 142, 144, 145
    immigration cases, 150
    international law cases, 151
    Medicaid cases, 164
    patents cases, 178

plain-error rule, 185
search and seizure cases, 195
sex offender cases, 207
sovereign immunity cases, 208
speedy trial cases, 209
voter qualification cases, 149
Schepers, David, 204–205
Schieffer, Bob, 211
Schizophrenia, 25, 26
Schmerber v. California (1966), 125
School release programs, 97–98
School shootings, 26, 138, 139, 168–169, *169*
Schultz, Gary, 42, 43
Search and Seizure, **195–196**
    automobiles, 30, 62–63, 125, 195
    cellphones, warrantless searches, 120–121
    civil rights, 46
    criminal procedure, 62–63, 64, 65, 121, 122, 123–124, 125, 195
    Fourth Amendment, 62–63, 64, 65, 121, 122, 195
    Supreme Court rule exceptions, 121
    tort environment, 110
    tracking technology, 195–196
Search warrant detention, 121–123
Sebelius, Kathleen, 161
Sebelius v. Auburn Regional Medical Center (2013), 160–161
Sebelius v. Cloer (2013), 27–28
Second Amendment, **196–199**
    central rights, 137, 199
    concealed carry, 196–199
    gun rights and gun control, 26, 137, 138–139, 140, 198
Second Circuit Court of Appeals
    antitrust law, 20
    electronic surveillance cases, 82
    Establishment Clause cases, 98–100
    extortion cases, 103–104
    First Amendment cases, 113
    Fourth Amendment cases, 122
    gay and lesbian rights cases, 135
    international law cases, 150, 151
    Second Amendment cases, 196–198, *197*
    Securities and Exchange Commission cases, 200, 201
    terrorism cases, 220–223
    tobacco cases, 226–228
    trademark cases, 229
Second-degree kidnapping, 154

Second-degree murder, 171–172, 209
Second Mile (charity organization), 42
Secretaries of State, state-level, 80–81, 119
Secure Rural Schools program, 53
Secure Schools and Community Self-Determination Act (2000), 53
Securities and Exchange Commission, **199–201**
    rules, 126, 200
    securities fraud cases, 59, 126, 200–201
Securities Exchange Act (1934), 126
Securities fraud, 59, 72, 126–127, 200–201
Seeds and seed patents, 178–179, *179*, 180–181
Seizures, imported goods, 56–57
Sekhar, Giridhar, 103–104
Sekhar v. United States (2013), 103–104
Self-defense
    as affirmative defense, 59
    gun laws, 137, 196–198, 198–199
    George Zimmerman murder of Trayvon Martin, 171, 172
Self-incrimination, 110–112
    See also Fifth Amendment
Self-regulation, military crimes, 166–167
Senate Armed Services Committee, 167, *167*
Senne, Jason, 31–32
Sentelle, David, 46, 91, 187–188
Sentencing, **201–204**
    assassinations, 26
    combination crimes, 141–142, 201–202, 202–204
    errors, 185
    ex post facto laws, 101–103
    federal guidelines, 65, 101, 102, 185
    mandatory minimum, cases, 201–202
    manipulation attempts, 65–66
    resentencing, 101–102, 221
    sexual assault, 167, 204
Separation of powers, 188
    capital punishment laws, 39–40
    judicial/legislative powers, 144
    military matters, 46
September 11, 2011 terrorist attacks
    anti-terrorism since, 220
    questioning groups, 129–130

Sequestration, Congress, 51–53, *52*

Seventh Circuit Court of Appeals
abortion cases, 9, 10–11
Americans with Disabilities Act, 17–18
automobiles cases, 31–32
criminal procedure cases, 61–62
employment discrimination cases, 85
First Amendment cases, 117–119
Second Amendment cases, 198–199
sex offenses cases, 204–205, 205–206

Sex discrimination cases, 47–48

Sex industry, and disease, 112–113

Sex Offender Registration and Notification Act (2006), 206–207

Sex offenders
regestries, 204–205, 206–207
social media use, 205–206

Sex Offenses, 42–43, **204–207**

Sexual assault
DNA evidence, 64
incest, 170
military cases and scope, 166–168, *167*
prevention programs, 166, 167
tort claims, 110

Sexual harassment, 167–168

Sexual reporting and statistics, 166, 167–168

Sexually transmitted diseases, monitoring, 11

Sham meetings and committees, 231

Shelby County v. Holder (2013), 232–235

Shell Petroleum Development Company, 150–151

Shepard v. United States (2005), 203–204

Sheppard, Christal, 176

Sherlach, Mary, 138, 168

Sherman Antitrust Act (1890), 48, 55

Shuette, Bill, 156

Sierra Club, 88

Signs
anti-tobacco, 226–228
protest tools, 28–29, 113, 116, 129, *139*

Silence, at questioning, 110–112

Silvicultural Rule (EPA), 89–90

Simon & Schuster, 54

Simpson, Nicole, 171

Simpson, O.J., 171

Sixth Amendment, 201
mandatory sentencing guidelines, 102
right to counsel, 23, 61, 62
right to speedy trial, 208–210
right to unanimous jury, 142

Sixth Circuit Court of Appeals
abortion cases, 37–38
affirmative action cases, 13–15
Americans with Disabilities Act, 18–19
appellate advocacy cases, 23
election law cases, 80–81
habeas corpus cases, 143–144

Slogans, 158

Smartphones, 120, 121, 175–176, *176*
design and functionality, 175–176
market share, 176

Smith, Calvin, 59–60

Smith, Robert S., 153–154

Smith, Scott, 128

Smith, Will, 213, 214

Smith v. United States (2013), 59–60

Smoking. *See* Marijuana; Tobacco

Snoop Lion, *74*

Snowe, Olympia, 116

Snyder, Matthew, 116

Snyder v. Phelps (2011), 116

Social media, 156
labor law, 156–157
lawyers, advertising, 159
privacy invasion and hate crimes, 145–146
protest groups' use, 117, 166
sex offenders, 205–206
WikiLeaks, 164–166

Social norms, 124

Social Security Administration data, 161

Social Security income, 160, 161

Sodomy laws, 133

Software patents, 175–176

Solicitation of children, sex offenders, 206

Solicitation of clients, lawyers, 188–189

Solvay Pharmaceuticals, 182

Sosa v. Alvarez-Machain (2004), 150

Soto, Victoria Leigh, 138, 168

Sotomayor, Sonia
admiralty and maritime law cases, 12, 13
antitrust law cases, 20, 22, 49
attorney's fees cases, 28
class action cases, 49, 50
copyright cases, 56

criminal procedure cases, 62, 65, 66
debtor and creditor cases, 68
double jeopardy cases, 71
employment discrimination cases, 85–86
environmental law cases, 93
ERISA cases, 95
estate planning cases, 101
ex post facto cases, 102–103
Fifth Amendment cases, 112
Fourth Amendment cases, 125
gay and lesbian rights cases, 134, 136
habeas corpus cases, 144, 145
immigration cases, 149
international law cases, 151
limitations cases, 161
plain-error rule, 185
product liability cases, 192–193
search and seizure cases, 195
sentencing cases, 202
sex offender cases, 207
speedy trial cases, 209, 210
trademark cases, 229

South Carolina
adoption cases, 105–106
privacy cases, 188–189
religious and public education, 97–98
Voting Rights Act, *235*, 235–236

South Florida Water Management District v. Miccosukee Tribe (2004), 92

Sovereign Immunity, 108–109, 109–110, **208**

Soybeans, 178–179, 180–181

Spanier, Graham, 42, 43

Spartanburg Bible Education in School Time, 97–98

"Special Administrative Measures," 220

Specialty license plates, 5–7

Speedy Trial, **208–210**

Sports injuries, 212–214, *213*

Sports Law, 43, **210–214**

Sports programs, child abuse, 42–43

Spyer, Thea Clara, 135

St. Louis, Missouri, 129–130

Stafford Loans, 77

Stahl, Donald E., 129–130

Stalking, 32, 146, 188

Stamos, Theo, 166

"Stand your ground" laws, 172

Standard Fire Insurance Company v. Knowles (2013), 51

Standing, 134
custody cases, 131–132

electronic surveillance cases, 81, 82

elements/proving, 96–97

First Amendment cases, 118

gay and lesbian rights cases, 131–132, 133, 134, 136

stare decisis, 17

State abortion restrictions, 4–5, 7–11, 36–38

State-action antitrust immunity, 21–22

State attorneys general
  case review, 199
  elections, 80–81

State budgets
  federal sources, and emergency management, 52–53
  natural resource sales and management, 52–53, 87–88

State constitutions
  election law, 79, 80
  environmental law, 87
  labor law, 155, 156
  marriage law, 132–134

State departments of corrections, 204–205

State departments of health
  abortion, 1–2, 9
  surrogate motherhood, 214

State Departments of Motor Vehicles (DMV), 5–6, 31, 188–189, 235

State emergency management laws, 51–53

State environmental standards, 88

State law. See Preemption; Supremacy Clause, U.S. Constitution; specific states

State Penal Codes, 142

State Supreme Courts. See specific states

State voting laws, 233, 234, 235–236

Statutes, 107–108

Statutes of limitations
  attorney's fee compensation, 27
  criminal defenses, 59–60
  exceptions, 199

Statutory limitations periods, 161

Stephens, Linda, 99

Stevens, John Paul, 61

Stevens-Johnson Syndrome, 191

Stewart, Lynne, 220–221

Stiehl, William D., 198

Stier, Sandy, 133

Stinson, Jane Magnus, 115

Stolt-Nielsen v. AnimalFeeds International Corp. (2010), 24–25

Storage, 186

Storm damage, 51

Stormwater runoff, 89–90, 91–92

Strickland v. Washington (1984), 61, 62

Strict scrutiny test, 114, 224

Student loan debt and payment, 77–78

Substantive due process rights and violations
  abortion cases, 4, 38
  civil rights cases, 46

Suicide
  hate crimes, 145–146
  murderers, 138, 168

Sulfur dioxide, 90–91

Sulindac (medication), 191–193

Sullivan Law (New York, 1911), 197

Supervisors, workplace environments, 84–86

Supremacy Clause, U.S. Constitution, 86
  abortion cases, 10
  election laws, 147, 148
  estate planning cases, 101
  immigration cases, 147
  religious liberty laws, 36

Supreme Court. See U.S. Supreme Court; specific cases and justices

Surrogate Motherhood, 214–215

Surveillance, electronic. See Electronic Surveillance

Sutter, John, 24, 25

Sutton, Jeffrey, 18–19

Sykes, Diane, 11, 118–119

Symczyk, Laura, 50

Szalavitz, Maia, 71

T

Tablet products
  conspiracy and price-fixing, 54–55
  patents, 175–176, *176*

Tagliabue, Paul, 212, 214

Takings Clause, Fifth Amendment
  agricultural law, 15, 16, 17
  eminent domain, 83, 84

Taliban, 115–116

Tapia v. United States (2011), 185

Tariffs, environmental, 86, 87

Tarrant Regional Water District v. Herrmann (2013), 92–93

Tattoo parlors, 127–129

Tax fraud cases, 65–66

Tax records, nature of information, 190, 191

Taxation, **217–218**
  estates, 100, 135
  marijuana, 75

Taylor v. United States (1990), 203

Teague v. Lane (1989), 61, 62

Teen drivers, 29–31

Telecommunications Act (1996), 107

Telephone records, 120, 121

Ten Commandments, displays, 95–97

Tenth Circuit Court of Appeals
  Americans with Disabilities Act, 17
  debtor and creditor cases, 68
  environmental law cases, 93

Territoriality, 151

Terrorism, **218–223**
  aiding, 220–221
  Antiterrorism and Effective Death Penalty Act (1996), 141, 142, 143, 144
  Boston Marathon bombings, 2013, 218–220, *219*
  detainee records, 221–223
  9/11 questioning groups, 129–130

Terrorists and terrorist groups
  domestic, 218–220, *219*
  intelligence gathering attempts, 82, 221–223
  piracy, 151
  prayer in prison, 115–116
  torture and civil rights cases, 45–46, 221–223

Terry, Brian, 69

Testimonials, 158

Texas, 231
  abortion funding, 2–4, 8–9
  gun laws cases, 137
  murder cases and habeas corpus, 144–145
  patent/legal malpractice cases, 183–184
  redistricting, 231–232
  water resources, 93–94

Texas Computer Exchange Network (TEXCEN), 183–184

Texas EquuSearch, 171

Texas Health and Human Services Commission, 3

Thefts, by lawyers, 159–160

Third Circuit Court of Appeals
  arbitration cases, 24–25
  class action cases, 49–50
  ERISA cases, 95
  Federal Tort Claims Act cases, 110
  First Amendment cases, 119–120
  taxation, 217

Third-party tort settlements, 163

Thomas, Clarence
  agricultural law cases, 16
  antitrust law cases, 49
  appellate advocacy cases, 23
  arbitration cases, 25
  attorney's fees cases, 28
  class action cases, 49, 50
  copyright cases, 56
  criminal procedure cases, 62, 65, 66
  debtor and creditor cases, 68
  electronic surveillance cases, 83
  environmental law cases, 87
  ERISA cases, 95
  estate planning cases, 101
  Federal Tort Claims Act cases, 110
  Fifth Amendment cases, 111–112
  First Amendment cases, 113
  fraud cases, 127
  gay and lesbian rights cases, 134, 137
  habeas corpus cases, 144, 145
  immigration cases, 150
  international law cases, 151
  Medicaid cases, 164
  patents cases, 178, 181
  plain-error rule, 185
  privacy cases, 189
  sentencing cases, 202
  speedy trial cases, 209
  taxation, 217–218
  voter qualification cases, 149
  voting rights cases, 234
Threats
  child endangerment, 153, 154
  debt collection, 67–68
Tidwell, Thomas, 53
Tillett, Ellen, 97–98
Timber harvesting and sales, 53, 87–88, 89–90
Time, place, and manner regulations
  elections, 148
  pickets and protests, 113–115, 117
  promotions, 228
  tattoo parlors' freedom of speech, 128
Time-of-appeal standard, 185
Timmer, Ann Scott, 128
Tobacco, **223–228**
Tobacco industry, 223, 224–226, 227, 228
Tort claims
  Alien Tort Statute (1789), 150
  legislation and cases, 108–110
  third-party settlements, 163
  timeframes, 199

Tort reform, 27
Torture
  civil rights cases, 45–46
  terrorism interrogation questions, 221–223
Tour de France, 210, 211, *211*
Tourism, 75
Towing, vehicles, 185–186
Town board meetings, 98–100
Toxic epidermal necrolysis, 191–193
Toys, trade, 56–57
Tracking devices, 195–196
Trademark Counterfeiting Act (1984), 57
Trademarks, 56–57, **228–229**
Traffic ordinances, 129–130
Trevino v. Thaler (2013), 144–145
Trucking, 86–87
Trusts, 33–34
Tsarnaev, Dzhokhar, 218–220
Tucker, Barry, 64
Tucker Act (1887), 16–17
Tygart, Travis, 212

U

Uhlmann, David, 91
Unanimity, juries, 142
Unfair labor practices, 157
Uniform Code of Military Justice, 165
Uniform Parentage Act (New Mexico, 1986), 131, 132
Unions, labor, 155, 156, 187
United Airlines, 17
United Kingdom, taxation, 217–218
United Nations, medical agencies, 112
United States Court of Federal Claims, 208
United States Panel of Multidistrict Litigation, 54–55
United States v. Davila (2013), 65–66
United States v. Jones (2012), 195–196
United States v. Kebodeaux (2013), 206–207
United States v. Windsor (2013), 133, 135–137
United States v. Wood (1936), 142
Universities. *See* Colleges and universities; specific universities
University of Michigan, 13–15
Unjust enrichment, 94, 95
Unlawful Use of Weapons statute (Illinois), 198

Unreasonable search and seizure. *See* Search and Seizure
Unsolved cases, DNA evidence, 64
U.S. Agency for International Development (USAID), 112–113
U.S. Air Force, 166–167
U.S. Airways, 17–18, 94–95
U.S. Anti-Doping Agency, 210, 212
U.S. Army Court of Criminal Appeals, 166
U.S. Bureau of Alcohol, Tobacco, and Firearms (ATF), 69–70
U.S. Chamber of Commerce, 21
U.S. Code, 199–200
U.S. Customs and Border Protection
  anti-firearms programs, 69–70
  counterfeit goods seizures, 56–57
U.S. Department of Agriculture, 15–16
U.S. Department of Defense, 45, 166, *167*, 167–168
U.S. Department of Education, 77, 78
U.S. Department of Health and Human Services (HHS)
  birth control, 36
  First Amendment cases, 112–113
  grant statutes, 10–11
  heath care reimbursement policy, 161
  tobacco, 223
  vaccine program, 27
U.S. Department of Homeland Security, 149
U.S. Department of Housing and Urban Development (HUD), 53
U.S. Department of Justice. *See* Department of Justice
U.S. Department of Labor, 47–48
U.S. Department of the Treasury, 208
U.S. Drug Enforcement Administration (DEA), 123
U.S. Federal Trade Commission (FTC)
  antitrust cases, 21–22, 182, 183
  patents cases, 182, 183
U.S. Food and Drug Administration (FDA)
  abortion-inducing drugs, 7, 8, 36–38
  drug approvals, 126, 191–192
  drugs naming, 182
  drugs standards, 73

tobacco cases, 223–224, 228
tobacco regulation, 223–224,
    225, 228
U.S. Forest Service, 53
U.S. Leadership Against HIV/
    AIDS, Tuberculosis, and
    Malaria Act (2003), 112
U.S. Marine Corps, 45
U.S. Navy, 108
U.S. Patent and Trademark Office,
    57, 176, 177, 183, 228
U.S. Postal Service Cycling Team,
    210–212
U.S. Supreme Court
    abortion, 4, 5, 7, 8–9, 38
    admiralty and maritime law, 12
    advertising, 158
    affirmative action, 13, 14
    agricultural law, 16–17
    antitrust, 20–21, 22, 48–49,
        182–183
    appellate advocacy, 22–24
    arbitration, 24–25
    attorney's fees, 27–28, 29
    automobile laws, 30
    child custody, 43–45
    civil rights, 19, 46
    civil service, 46–48
    class action, 48–51
    congressional redistricting, 232
    criminal law, 59–60, 149
    criminal procedure, 61–66
    debtor and creditor, 67–68
    double jeopardy, 70–71
    education, 97
    electronic surveillance, 81–82
    employees with disabilities,
        17–18
    employment discrimination,
        84–86
    environmental law, 86–87,
        88–90, 91–93
    ERISA, 94–95
    estate planning, 100–101
    ex post facto laws, 101–103
    extortion, 103–104
    family law, 105–106
    Federal Communications
        Commission, 107–108
    federal power, 87
    Federal Tort Claims Act,
        108–110
    Fifth Amendment, 110–112
    First Amendment, 112–113,
        114, 116, 117, 119
    Fourth Amendment, 121–125
    fraud, 72, 126–127
    gay and lesbian rights, 133, 133,
        134–135

gun control, 137
habeas corpus, 141–142, 143,
    144, 145
immigration, 147–150
international law, 150–151
jurisdiction, 183, 184
legislative prayer, 99
limitations cases, 160–161
Medicaid, 163–164
patents, 176–181, 182–183
plain-error rule, 185
preemption, 185–186
privacy, 188–189
privileges and immunities,
    190–191
product liability, 191–193
rule exceptions, 121, 124, 125
rule introductions, 61
search and seizure, 195
Second Amendment, 196,
    197–198, 199
Securities and Exchange
    Commission, 200–201
sentencing, 201–202, 203–204
sex offender laws, 206–207
sovereign immunity, 208
speedy trial, 208–210
taxation, 217–218
trademarks, 228–229
types of speech, 6–7
Voting Rights Act, 232, 233,
    233–235, 236
U.S. Tax Code, 217
US Airways, 17–18
US Airways, Inc. v. Barnett (2002),
    17–18
US Airways v. McCutchen (2013),
    94–95
Utah, 88

V

Vacatur, 65, 66
Vaccine programs, 27, 53
Vance, Cyrus, 160
Vance, Maetta, 85
Vance v. Ball State University
    (2013), 84–86
Variable interest rates, 77
Vessels, marine, 11–13
Veterans' funerals, 116–117, *117*
Video games, 169
Video recording
    First Amendment rights, 118
    hate crimes, 145–146
    terrorist interrogation, 222
Vidrine, Donald J., 58
Vilma, Jonathan, 213, *213,* 214
Vilsack, Tom, 53

Virginia
    family law and estate planning,
        100–101
    public information policy,
        190–191
Virginia Polytechnic Institute and
    State University shootings
    (2007), 138, 168
Visitation rights, gay and lesbian
    families, 131–132
Vitt, Joe, 213, 214
Voice votes, 120
Voter disenfranchisement, 233
    intimidation, 119, 120, 233–234
    redistricting, 231–232
Voter laws
    identification, 119, 148,
        235–236
    registration, 147–149
Voter turnout, 233–234
Voting
    fraud, prevention, 148, 235–236
    methodology history, 120
    polling places, media access,
        119–120
    rights history, 233–234
Voting Rights Act, **231–236,** *233,*
    235
    provisions struck, 232, 233–236
    Section 5, *235,* 235–236
    violations rulings, 231–232

W

Waivers of immunity, 108, 109
Walsh, David, 211
War on terrorism, and civil rights,
    45–46
Warrantless searches
    blood, 124–125
    cellphones, 120–121
    exceptions, 121, 124, 125
    GPS, 195
    home surroundings, 123–124
Warren S. Henderson Wetlands
    Protection Act (Florida, 1984),
    83
Washington, 73, 74–75
Washington Post, 165, 166–167
Washington v. Seattle Sch. Dist.
    No. 1 (1982), 14, 15
Water pollution
    disasters, 58–59
    environmental law and cases,
        88, 89–90, 91–92
Water Resources Act (Florida,
    1972), 83
Water resources and rights, 83,
    92–93
Waterboarding, 222, 223

Watercraft, in admiralty and maritime law, 11–13
Watergate scandal (1974), 80
Watson Pharmaceuticals, 182
Wayne State University, 13–15
Web search optimization, 159
Webcam surveillance, 145–146
Websites
  government, 208
  lawyers', 158–159
Weissmann, Andrew, 195–196
Wellbutrin (medication), 72
Wesley, Richard, 197, 222, 223
West, Don, 172
Westboro Baptist Church, 113, 114, 115, 116, 117
Wetlands, 83–84
Wetlands Resource Management (WRM) permits, 83–84
Wetterling Act (1994), 207
Wheeler, David, 169
Wheetley, William, 62–63
Whistleblowers
  military, 164–166
  pharmaceutical industry transgressions, 72
White, Charles, *233*
Whitlock, Craig, 166–167

Wideman, Dan, 28
WikiLeaks, 164–166
Wildfires, 88, 117
Williams, Ann Claire, 199
Williams, Evan, 57
Williams, Gregg, 212, 213, 214
Williams, Tara, 141–142
Winders, Amanda, *3*
Windfall taxes, 217
Windsor, Edith, *135,* 135–137
Winfrey, Oprah, 212
Wireless telecommunications infrastructure, 107
Withdrawal from conspiracy, 59–60
Withholding of documents, 58
Wollman, Roger, 96, 97
Women's Health Program (WHP) (Texas), 2–4, 8
Wood, Diane, 205
Woods, James, 35
Work environment
  employee communication, 156–157
  hostile, discrimination cases, 47–48, 84–86
  sexual harassment and assault, 167–168

  supervisors, defined, 84–86
Workplace safety, 53
World Health Organization, 112
Wos v. EMA (2013), 163–164
Writ of coram nobis, 61
Writ of habeas corpus, 141, 142–143
  See also Habeas Corpus
Wrongful termination, 43

X

XL Specialty Insurance Co., 35
Xun Energy, Inc., 160

Y

Young drivers, 29–31

Z

Zimmerman, George, *171,* 171–173
Zimmerman, Shellie, 172
Zoning
  business types and applications, 128
  telecommunications equipment, 107
Zubaydah, Abu, 222–223